# DEPARTMENT OF FINANCE AND PERSONNEL FOR NORTHERN IRELAND

The Final Report of the
Land Law Working Group

# VOLUME 3

# DRAFT LEGISLATION

THE GROUND RENTS ORDER

THE COMMONHOLD ORDER

THE LANDLORD AND TENANT ORDER

THE SUCCESSION ORDER

THE PROPERTY (CONSEQUENTIAL PROVISIONS) ORDER

THE ENDURING POWERS OF ATTORNEY (NORTHERN
IRELAND CONSEQUENTIAL AMENDMENT) ORDER

TABLES

BELFAST: HMSO
1990

ISBN 0 337 23527 9

# TABLE OF CONTENTS

RECOMMENDED DRAFT ORDER IN COUNCIL UNDER
PARAGRAPH 1 OF SCHEDULE 1 TO THE NORTHERN
IRELAND ACT 1974

---

DRAFT STATUTORY INSTRUMENTS

---

**1989 No.     (N.I.    )**

**NORTHERN IRELAND**

**Ground Rents (Northern Ireland) Order 1989**

*To be laid before Parliament in draft*

*Made*

*Coming into operation in accordance with Article 1(2)*

ARRANGEMENT OF ORDER

Article

*Introductory*

SCHEDULES:

At the Court at        , the        day of        1989

Present,

The Queen's Most Excellent Majesty in Council

Whereas a draft of this order has been approved by a resolution of each House of Parliament:

Now, therefore, Her Majesty, in exercise of the powers conferred by paragraph1 of Schedule 1 to the Northern Ireland Act 1974 and of all other powers enabling Her in that behalf, is pleased, by and with the advice of Her Privy Council, to order, and it is hereby ordered, as follows:–

Introductory

**Title and commencement**

1.—(1) This Order may be cited as the Ground Rents (Northern Ireland) Order 1989.

(2)   This Order comes into operation as follows –

(a)   the provisions of the Order other than Articles 5 (with Schedule 1), 29, 30 and 31 on such day or days as the Head of the Department of Finance and Personnel may by order appoint ("the first appointed day");

(b)   Articles 5 (with Schedule 1), 29, 30 and 31 on such day or days subsequent to any day appointed under sub-paragraph (a) as the Head of that Department may by order appoint ("the second appointed day").

# EXPLANATORY NOTE

## ARTICLE 1

This Article deals with the title of the Order and its commencement.

*Paragraph (1)* gives the title.

*Paragraph (2)* provides for the commencement. A commencement which depends upon an appointed day occurs immediately on the expiration of the day before that day (Interpretation Act, section 14(2)).

*sub-paragraph (a)* The provisions of the Order, except Articles 5 (compulsory redemption of ground rents) and 29 to 31 (prohibition of creation of certain periodic payments which are or are equivalent to ground rents), come into operation on a day or days to be appointed by an order made by the Head of the Department of Finance and Personnel (during direct rule, made by the Department). This is referred to in the Order as "the first appointed day".

*sub-paragraph (b)* Articles 5 (with Schedule 1), 29, 30 and 31 come into operation on such later day as may be so appointed. Different days may be appointed for different Articles. The day appointed under this sub-paragraph for any Article is referred to in this Order in relation to that Article as "the second appointed day" (Article 2(2)). Section 17(5) of the Interpretation Act also allows different days to be appointed for different purposes of the same Article.

### General interpretation

**2.**—(1) The Interpretation Act (Northern Ireland) 1954 applies to Article 1 and the following provisions of this Order as it applies to a Measure of the Northern Ireland Assembly.

(2) In this Order –

"the Act of 1971" means the Leasehold (Enlargement and Extension) Act (Northern Ireland) 1971;

"building scheme" means a scheme (express or implied) under which land (whether freehold or leasehold) is divided into two or more parcels subject to obligations which are reciprocally enforceable between owners of the parcels;

"certificate of redemption" is to be construed in accordance with Article 15(5);

"counter-notice" has the meaning given by Article 8(2);

"covenant" (except where that expression last occurs in Article 24(5)) includes a promise in writing which is not a deed, an agreement to make a covenant, a proviso, a declaration and a condition and, so far as it makes a provision that could have been framed as a covenant, a limitation;

"dwelling-house" means land used, or intended to be used, wholly for the purposes of a private dwelling;

"equity-sharing lease" means a lease of land, the general effect of which is to provide –

(a) that, in consideration for the granting of the lease, the lessee shall pay a capital sum, representing a part payment in respect of the cost of acquisition of the premises demised, and a rent; and

(b) that the lessee may make additional part payments towards the said cost of acquisition and may exercise an option to purchase the whole or part of the lessor's reversion in the premises demised;

"fee farm grant" means a grant of a fee simple reserving or charging a perpetual rent (whether or not the relation of landlord and tenant subsists between the person entitled to receive the rent and the person liable to pay it) and includes a sub-fee farm grant;

"fee farm rent" means the rent payable under a fee farm grant;

"the first appointed day" means a day appointed under Article 1(2)(a); and if different days are appointed for different provisions or for different purposes of the same provision, any reference in such a provision to the first appointed day is a reference to the day appointed for the coming into operation of that provision or its coming into operation for the purpose in question;

"the land" in relation to a ground rent or a superior rent means the land subject to the ground rent or superior rent, and in connection with a redeemed ground rent or superior rent means the land formerly subject to it;

"the Land Registration Act" means the Land Registration Act (Northern Ireland) 1970;

"lease" means the writing which creates a leasehold estate, and includes a sub-lease;

"lessor" and "lessee" include the successors in title to, respectively, the original lessor and the original lessee;

"mortgage" includes a charge, and "mortgagor" and "mortgagee" include respectively the person who is entitled to land which is subject to a charge and the person in whose favour a charge is created, and the successors in title to, respectively, the original mortgagor and the original mortagee;

"notice" means notice in writing;

"possession" includes the receipt of, or the right to receive, rents and profits, if any (but not the right to receive a ground rent or a superior rent);

"prescribed" (but not in Article 18(2) and not "prescribe" in Article 38(3)) means prescribed by rules;

"the redemption date", subject to Article 13(4), has the meaning given by Article 7(1) and, in relation to any redemption notice, means the redemption date specified in that notice;

"redemption money" is to be construed in accordance with Article 14;

"redemption notice" means a notice served under Article 7(1);

"the Registrar" means the Registrar of Titles;

"rent" includes both a rentcharge and a rent service;

"rentcharge", except in Article 3(2), means any annual or periodic sum charged on or issuing out of land, except –

(a) a fee farm rent;

(b) rent reserved by a lease (including an oral lease or an implied lease);

(c) interest;

"rent-owner" means the person to whom a ground rent is, or before redemption of the ground rent was, payable by virtue of his being entitled to the next superior estate to the rent-payer's in the land, or, where the ground rent is or was a fee farm rent the person who is or was entitled to receive it from the rent-payer;

"rent-payer" means a person entitled to an estate in land carrying a vested right to possession of the land by virtue of which he is liable to pay a ground rent, and "the rent-payer", in relation to any ground rent or any land, means the person who is, or before redemption of the ground rent was, liable to pay that ground rent or a ground rent to which that land is or was subject;

"rules" means Land Registry Rules made in pursuance of Article 38;

"the second appointed day" means a day appointed under Article1(2)(b); and if different days are appointed for different provisions there mentioned, or for different purposes of the same provision, any reference in such a provision to the second appointed day is a reference to the day appointed for the coming into operation of that provision or its coming into operation for the purpose in question;

"statutory provision" has the meaning given by section 1(f) of the interpretation Act (Northern Ireland) 1954;

"superior rent" means a rent which is, or before redemption of a ground rent was, payable to a person entitled to an estate or interest in land superior to a rent-owner's;

"superior owner" means a person who is, or before redemption of a ground rent was, entitled to a superior rent.

(3)  In this Order any reference to the giving of security includes the finding of satisfactory sureties.

(4)  For the purposes of this Order land is not to be treated as used otherwise than wholly for the purposes of a private dwelling by reason of one or more than one of the following circumstances –

(a)  that one or more than one room on the land suitable for being used for letting singly for residential purposes is so let, whether by way of a tenancy or of a licence and whether with or without board or other services or facilities (so long as all, or substantially all, such rooms are not so let);

(b)  that the land includes a garage, outhouse, garden, yard, court, forecourt or other appurtenance which is not used, or not used wholly, for the purposes of a private dwelling;

(c)  that part of the land, not being a garage, outhouse, garden, yard, court, forecourt or other appurtenance, is used partly for the purposes of a private dwelling and partly for other purposes, unless that part was constructed, or has been adapted, for those other purposes;

(d)  that a person who resides on the land, or part of it, is required or permitted to reside there in consequence of his employment or of holding an office.

(5)  For the purposes of this Order land is intended to be used for the purposes of a private dwelling –

(a)  if it comprises or contains all or part of a building constructed or adapted for use for those purposes, or

(b)  if it is contemplated for the purposes of any relevant agreement or instrument to be the site of, or of part of, such a building (and it is so contemplated if that contemplation appears from the agreement or instrument or if, at the time when the agreement or instrument was made, planning permission had been applied for or was in force for the erection on the land of, or of part of, such a building or for the conversion of an existing building situated wholly or partly on the land into such a building); and the construction on the land, subsequent to any agreement or instrument made or executed on or after the first appointed day, of, or of part of, such a building, or the conversion subsequent thereto of an existing building into such a building or part of such a building, if (in either case) begun before the expiration of five years from the date of such making or execution, is conclusive evidence that the construction or conversion was contemplated at the time when the agreement was made or the instrument executed;

and, for the purposes of sub-paragraph (b) an agreement is relevant if it is an agreement for the conveyance of the land and an instrument is relevant if it is a conveyance of the land ("conveyance" for this purpose including a transfer of registered land and the grant or an assignment of a lease).

(6)   In paragraph (5)(b) "planning permission" has the same meaning as in the Planning (Northern Ireland) Order 1972.

(7)   For the purposess of this Order, except Article 28 and Schedule 4, a lease which is, by virtue of that Article and that Schedule, to be construed as a lease for a term of any period is deemed to have been originally granted for a term of that period and the fact (if it is the case) that the lease is determinable after any event is to be ignored.

# EXPLANATORY NOTE

## ARTICLE 2

This Article provides for the interpretation of expressions used in the Order.

*Paragraph (1)* attracts the Interpretation Act (Northern Ireland) 1954 (referred to in these notes as the "Interpretation Act").

*Paragraph (2)* defines expressions which appear in the Order as follows –

| *Expression* | *Article* |
|---|---|
| "the Act of 1971" | 6(2)(b), (4); 32(4); 41 |
| "building scheme" | 24(2)(g); 25 |
| "certificate of redemption" | 12; 15; 16; 18; 19; 23; 24(1)(a); Sch. 1 para. 1(e) |
| "counter-notice" | 8; 9; 10; 11; 13; 15 |
| "covenant" | 3(3); 12(1)(a); 15(1); 19(3); 23(2); 24; 25; 27(8); 29(2); Sch. 3 |
| "dwelling-house" | 5; 32(1) |
| "equity-sharing lease" | 6(2)(c); 31(5)(d) |
| "fee farm grant" | 2(2) ("fee farm rent") and passim |
| "fee farm rent" | 2(2) ("rentcharge"); 3(1)(a) and passim |
| "the first appointed day" | 2(5)(b); 27; 28; 32(2); 33; 41; Sch. 3 |
| "the land" | passim |
| "the Land Registration Act" | 9; 16(3); 19(6); 21; 38 |
| "lease" | passim |
| "lessor" and "lessee" | 31(3); 35(1); Sch. 3 paras. 5, 7; Sch. 4 para. 2 |
| "mortgage", "mortgagor", "mortgagee" | 5(7); 8(2); 15(3); 17(3); 19(10); 23; 25(6); 31(3), (5)(c); 35(3); Sch. 3 para. 2(2) |
| "notice" | 7(1); 10; 11; Sch. 3 paras. 5(b), 7(2)(b); Sch.4 para. 2 (see also "counter-notice" and "redemption notice") |
| "possession" | 2(2) ("rent-payer") |
| "prescribed" | 8(1)(ii); 13(2); 21; 38 |
| "the redemption date" | 7; 8(1); 10(1)(b); 11; 13; 17; 23(2); Sch. 2 |

| Expression | Article |
|---|---|
| "redemption money" | 3(1); 4; 8; 9; 10; 11; 13; 14; 15; 18; 20; 21; 34; 37; 39(2)(b); Sch. 2 |
| "redemption notice" | 2(2) ("the redemption date"); 6(3); 7; 8; 11; 12; 13 |
| "the Registrar" | 5(11); 9; 11; 13; 15; 18; 19; 20; 21; 23(2); 38 |
| "rent" | 2(2) ("rentcharge"; "superior rent"); 3; 28(1) |
| "rentcharge" | 2(2) ("rent"); 26; 30 |
| "rent-owner" | passim |
| "rent-payer" | passim |
| "rules" | 2(2) ("prescribed"); 15(2); 20; 38 |
| "the second appointed day" | 5(5); 29; 30; 31; 33; Sch. 1 para. 4 |
| "statutory provision" | 6(6); 26(1)(d); 30(3)(e) |
| "superior rent" | 2(2) ("superior owner"); 3(1); 8(2); 12; 17; 39(2)(a); Sch. 1 |
| "superior owner" | 8(2); 12: 17; 19; 33(2) |

*Paragraph (3)* defines references to the giving of security as including the finding of satisfactory sureties. "Security" is mentioned in Articles 8(1)(ii), 9(1)(b), 13(2)(c).

*Paragraph (4)* relieves the strictness of the definition of "dwelling-house" in paragraph (2) as meaning land used, or intended to be used, *wholly* for the purposes of a private dwelling. Land is not prevented from being wholly so used merely because –

(a) lodgers are taken in (so long as all, or substantially all, the available accommodation is not devoted to them);

(b) an outbuilding, garden, yard, etc., is used for other purposes (e.g. commercial stock is stored in an outbuilding, garden produce is sold, or a yard is used for parking lorries);

(c) a part of the land, not falling within (b), is used partly for non-domestic purposes (e.g. working from home), so long as it has not been constructed or adapted for those purposes;

(d) the land is used for the residence of an office-holder or an employee.

*Paragraph (5)* explains what is meant by references in the Order to land "intended to be used" for the purposes of a private dwelling (Articles 2(2) ("dwelling-house"), 6(6) ("flat")). It is so intended if it is or contains a building constructed or adapted for those purposes or is intended as the site of such a building (e.g. if it is the subject of a covenant restricting its

1066

use to those purposes, or it is the subject of, or of an application for, planning permission for its use for those purposes). Where, within five years after a sale of land, a dwelling-house is erected (or is the result of an adaptation), the erection (or adaptation) is conclusive evidence that the land was, at the time of the sale, intended to be used for the purposes of a private dwelling. Five years is the period within which planning permission must normally be acted upon (Planning (Northern Ireland) Order 1972 Article 25(1)(a)).

*Paragraph (6)* defines "planning permission" for the purpose of paragraph (5)(b).

*Paragraph (7)* applies to leases for lives which are converted by Article 28 and Schedule 4 into e.g., leases for 90 years determinable after the falling of a life. Such leases are deemed to have been granted for the converted term and any provision for their premature termination is to be ignored.

**Interpretation: "ground rent"**

**3.**—(1) In this Order "ground rent" means –

(a)  a fee farm rent; or

(b)  the rent payable under a lease originally granted for a term of more than 50 years,

but does not include a superior rent; and "the ground rent", in relation to any land or any rent-owner or rent-payer or redemption money, means the ground rent to which the land is, or before redemption of the ground rent was, subject or which the rent-owner or rent-payer is or was, respectively, entitled to be paid or liable to pay, or in respect of which the redemption money was paid under Article 8(1)(i) or lodged with the Registrar under Article 13.

(2)  For the purposes of paragraph (1)(a) it is immaterial whether a rent is a rentcharge or a rent service.

(3)  Where the amount of a ground rent is subject to alteration in consequence of a breach of covenant (whether it is to be increased from a lower amount to a higher amount in the event of a breach or is subject to reduction from a higher amount to a lower amount so long as there is no breach), for the purposes of this Order the amount of the ground rent is the lower amount.

# EXPLANATORY NOTE

## ARTICLE 3

This Article defines the expression "ground rent".

*Paragraph (1)* defines "ground rent" as –

*sub-paragraph (a)* a fee farm rent;

*sub-paragraph (b)* the rent payable under a lease originally granted for more than 50 years.

See also the restriction in Article 6(2)(a) which prevents the redemption provisions of the Order from applying where fewer than 50 years of the term of any lease are left to run. A ground rent is the rent payable by a fee farm grantee or tenant in possession – it does not include a superior rent (defined in Article 2(2)).

Where, in connection with any land, the Order refers to "the ground rent", it means the ground rent on that land.

*Paragraph (2)* makes it clear that it is immaterial whether a rent is a rentcharge or a rent service. Some fee farm rents are rentcharges and some are rents service: all rents under leases are rents service.

*Paragraph (3)* provides for the case where the fee farm grant or lease makes provision for an increase in the amount of ground rent to be payable in the event of the grantee or lessee committing a breach of covenant. The provision may be either for the imposition of a penal rent (£x to be increased to £(x+y) in the event of a breach) or for the reduction of a rent higher than that intended to be paid in the ordinary run of things (£(x+y) reduced to £x so long as there is no breach of covenant). In either case, for the purposes of the Order the ground rent is the lower figure (that is, £x).

Schedule 2, paragraphs 3 and 4, provide for ground rents which are variable in other circumstances.

*The redemption of ground rents*

**Power of rent-payer to redeem ground rent**

**4.** Subject to Article 6, a rent-payer may redeem the ground rent to which his land is subject by paying the redemption money appropriate to the ground rent in accordance with the provisions of this Order and otherwise complying with the requirements of this Order.

# EXPLANATORY NOTE

## ARTICLE 4

This Article establishes the basic right of a rent-payer to redeem his ground rent by paying the redemption money appropriate to the rent. But this right is in some cases qualified and in others excluded by Article 6. The expression "the redemption money" is explained by Article 14 and Schedule 2. The relevant requirements of this Order are mainly those contained in Articles 7 to 14, although certain other provisions import requirements (e.g. Article 38(3) – fees).

## Compulsory redemption in case of dwelling-house

**5.**—(1) Subject to Article 6 and paragraphs (3) and (5), a conveyance of a dwelling-house to be held for a legal estate subject to a ground rent is ineffective to pass such an estate.

(2) Paragraph (1) does not affect any right arising in equity.

(3) Where a conveyance to which paragraph (1) applies is a purported conveyance of a fee simple, it has effect as an agreement binding the purported grantor to redeem the ground rent at no expense to the purported grantee; and upon the redemption of the ground rent the conveyance has effect, and is deemed always to have had effect, in accordance with its terms but subject to the provisions of this Order, as if paragraph (1) had not been applicable.

(4) Where a conveyance to which paragraph (1) applies is a purported assignment of a lease, the conveyance has effect as an agreement binding the purported assignor –

(a) to acquire a fee simple absolute in possession in the dwelling-house, free from any ground rent, at no expense to the purported assignee, and

(b) to convey that fee to the purported assignee at no expense to the purported assignee and without any consideration (save the consideration specified in the purported assignment).

(5) Paragraph (1) does not apply to a conveyance made before the second appointed day or to a conveyance made on or after that day in pursuance of a contract made before that day.

(6) An agreement made on or after the second appointed day –

(a) where it is an agreement to convey a fee simple subject to a ground rent, has effect as an agreement to redeem the ground rent, at no expense to the person to whom the conveyance is to be made, and to convey the fee simple free from the ground rent;

(b) where it is an agreement to assign a lease subject to a ground rent, has effect as an agreement such as is mentioned in paragraph (4)(a) and (b) (references to the purported assignee and the consideration specified in the purported assignment being read as references to the intended assignee and the consideration intended to be specified in the intended assignment).

(7) Where part of land held for a legal estate subject to a ground rent is conveyed, the ground rent is deemed for the purposes of this Order to be charged exclusively on the part of the land which is being conveyed ("the land conveyed") unless the parties to the conveyance have agreed with the rent-owner and all mortgagees (if any) of the land or the ground rent that the ground rent be either –

(a) charged exclusively on the part of the land which is being retained ("the land retained") or other land; or

(b) apportioned between the land conveyed and the land retained.

(8)  Schedule 1 has effect for the purposes of paragraph (7) and in relation to the indemnity agreements mentioned in that Schedule.

(9)  An agreement to which paragraph (7)(a) or (b) applies is a conveyance for the purposes of the Registration of Deeds Acts or, where it relates to registered land, shall have its effect registered in the appropriate register on an application made by either party to the agreement.

(10)  In this Article "conveyance" means a conveyance or other assurance of land for value in money or money's worth and includes a transfer of registered land and an assignment of a lease but not a grant of a lease or a mortgage (and, accordingly, references to a conveyance or assignment are to be read, where appropriate, as references to a transfer).

(11)  Where a conveyance such as is mentioned in paragraph (1) is a transfer of registered land, the Registrar shall refuse to accept the transfer unless he is satisfied either that the conveyance is one to which paragraph (1) does not apply or that it falls within paragraph (3) and the ground rent has been redeemed.

# EXPLANATORY NOTE

## ARTICLE 5

This Article comes into operation on a second appointed day (i.e. a day subsequent to that fixed for Article 4). It applies where a dwelling-house held subject to a ground rent is to be conveyed for money or money's worth (this would include a nominal sum). The ground rent must be redeemed before the conveyance is made. If it is not, the conveyance is ineffective to pass a legal estate.

*Paragraph (1)* renders a purported conveyance (defined in paragraph (10)) ineffective to pass a legal estate, if the ground rent is not redeemed before the conveyance is made. The legal estate may be a freehold estate or a leasehold estate, depending upon whether the ground rent is a fee farm rent or the rent under a lease.

*Paragraph (2)* is a saving for the equitable interest which vests in the purchaser when a contract for sale is made. This entitles the purchaser to call for a valid conveyance.

*Paragraph (3)* applies where the ground rent which ought to have been redeemed, but has not been redeemed, is a fee farm rent. The person making the conveyance has an obligation to redeem the rent at his own expense. Once this is done, the fee simple, being now free from rent, vests in the purchaser with retrospective effect.

*Paragraph (4)* applies where the ground rent is payable under a lease. The purported conveyance (in this case, assignment of the lease – see paragraph (10)) cannot have effect as such; but it does have effect as an agreement by the purported assignor –

*sub-paragraph (a)* to redeem the ground rent and acquire a fee simple, and

*sub-paragraph (b)* to convey the fee simple to the purported assignee;

and to do both these things at no expense to the assignee.

*Paragraph (5)* prevents the Article applying to a conveyance made before the second appointed day or where a conveyance is made on or after the second appointed day in fulfilment of a contract made before then. The latter part of this prevents the Article having an adverse effect on a transaction which is on the point of completion when the second appointed day arrives.

*Paragraph (6)* applies to an agreement to convey a house subject to a ground rent where the agreement is made on or after the second appointed day. The agreement has the same effect as a purported conveyance (or, in the case of a lease, assignment) has under paragraph (3) or (4).

*Paragraph (7)* applies where part only of a holding of land subject to a ground rent is conveyed. The ground rent is treated as being payable out of the land conveyed and therefore it must be redeemed, leaving not only the land conveyed, but also the land retained, free of ground rent for the future. But where the parties, including any mortgagee, agree that the ground rent should be charged wholly on the land retained or other land or that it should be apportioned between the land conveyed and the land retained, effect is given to their agreement. (Schedule 1, paragraphs 1 to 3). Where the opening provision of the paragraph has effect, Article 19(4) is relevant.

*Paragraph (8)* attracts Schedule 1 for the purposes of paragraph (7). Schedule 1 also contains provisions about indemnities against claims for the payment of more than the agreed proportion of ground rent following an apportionment (paragraph 4).

*Paragraph (9)* makes an agreement under paragraph (7)(a) or (b) registrable in the registry of deeds or the Land Registry.

*Paragraph (10)* defines "conveyance". It includes a transfer (of registered land) and the assignment of an existing lease. It also includes any other assurance of a legal estate, provided it is for value in money or money's worth. But it does not include a new lease, including a sub-lease (see Articles 2(2) and 31) or a mortgage (although mortgages by conveyance are abolished by Article 114 of the Property Order, this exception leaves open the possibility that Article 5 of this Order will come into operation before Article 114).

*Paragraph (11)* is a reminder for the Registrar of Titles not to accept a transfer of registered land made subject to a ground rent, where the circumstances are such that paragraph (1) applies (unless the transfer is one of freehold land and it has been retrospectively validated by the redemption of the ground rent).

**Exceptions to, or restrictions on, Articles 4 and 5**

**6.**—(1) Articles 4 and 5 do not apply where the ground rent is a nominal ground rent (that is, a ground rent of a yearly sum of less than £1 or a peppercorn or other rent having no money value).

(2) Article 4 does not apply where the rent-payer holds the land under a lease, and –

(a) the unexpired residue of the term of the lease (whether as originally granted or as subsequently extended) is less than 50 years on the date of making a conveyance to which Article 5(1) would apply were it not for this provision, or will be less than 50 years on the redemption date (where Article 5(1) would not so apply); or

(b) the term of the lease has been extended under the Act of 1971; or

(c) the lease is an equity-sharing lease; or

(d) the lease is a mining lease (including any lease in connection with the working of a mine or quarry or the treatment, preparation for sale, storage, removal or disposal of the produce or refuse of a mine or quarry); or

(e) the lease is of agricultural land (including farm houses and farm buildings); or

(f) the rent-owner or a superior owner is the National Trust for Places of Historic Interest or Natural Beauty and the Trust's estate in the land is vested in it inalienably under section 21 of the National Trust Act 1907;

nor does Article 5 apply in a case mentioned in sub-paragraph (a), (b), (c) or (f).

(3) Articles 4 and 5 do not apply where the rent-payer holds the land under a lease and –

(a) before the service of a redemption notice, a notice to terminate the lease has been served on the rent-payer in accordance with the terms of the lease; or

(b) proceedings, otherwise than by the rent-payer, in any court for recovery of possession of the land, or proceedings under Article 57, 59 or 68 of the Landlord and Tenant (Northern Ireland) Order 1989, begun (in any case) before the service of a redemption notice, are pending.

(4) Article 4 does not apply where the ground rent is payable under a lease which has been the subject of a notice to acquire the fee simple or obtain an extension under section 2 of the Act of 1971, unless the notice has been withdrawn under section 7 of that Act.

(5) Where a flat or house forms part of a development of flats or of houses or of both flats and houses together with (in any case) common parts, –

(a) Article 4 does not empower a rent-payer to redeem the ground rent to which his flat or house is subject, unless the requirements of sub-paragraph (b) are satisfied; and Article 5 does not apply to such a flat or house;

(b) the requirements mentioned in sub-paragraph (a) are that –

   (i) the ground rents in respect of all the flats or houses, or all the flats and all the houses, in the development are redeemed together; and

   (ii) all the rent-payers, and (except where Article 19(7) will apply) the owner of the common parts, agree to make a development scheme under Part IX of the Property (Northern Ireland) Order 1989 or promote a commonhold under the Commonhold (Northern Ireland) Order 1989 for the future management of the development.

(6)   In paragraph (5) –

"common parts" means any parts of the development or facilities therein not included in a lease or grant of a flat or house which, in consideration of a periodic payment which is not merely nominal, are provided or used for the accommodation (direct or indirect) of the rent-payers or their tenants or licensees or any of them or members of their households or staffs or their visitors, and includes (where relevant, having regard to the terms of the lease or grant) boundary walls or fences, gardens, roads, paths, parking or drying areas, areas for waste storage or disposal, play areas, rooms or areas reserved for the use of the manager of the development or his staff, sewers, drains, watercourses, water tanks, pipes, gutters, cables, wires, ducts, utility rooms, forecourt, steps, staircases, passages, lifts and the structure and exterior of buildings (but does not include any sewer, drain, watercourse, pipe, cable, wire, duct or installation which is vested in a government department or a body established under a statutory provision);

"development" means land comprising flats or houses, or flats and houses, together (in either case) with common parts;

"flat" means a unit of occupation in a building which contains two or more such units, whether the divisions between the units are horizontal or vertical or at an angle between horizontal and vertical or all or any two of those and whether the unit is used or intended to be used wholly for the purposes of a private dwelling, or partly for those purposes and partly for other purposes or wholly for other purposes;

"house" means a unit of occupation that is not a flat;

"unit of occupation" means a building or part of a building which is leased or granted to a rent-payer subject to a ground rent;

and paragraph (5) applies to a distinct part of a development as it applies to the whole of a development.

# EXPLANATORY NOTE

## ARTICLE 6

This Article contains exceptions to the provisions for voluntary redemption of ground rents (Article 4) or compulsory redemption (Article 5).

*Paragraph (1)* sets out an exception which applies to both freehold and leasehold rents, i.e., nominal ground rents, namely, ground rents of less than £1 or non-monetary ground rents. In the case of a nominal leasehold ground rent, the leasehold estate may be enlarged into a fee simple under Article 56 of the Landlord and Tenant Order. A nominal rent charged on a freehold may become statute-barred under the Limitation Order, depending on the circumstances (if the rent is one penny "if demanded", the rent-payer will not become in adverse possession of the rent until a demand is made).

*Paragraph (2)* sets out exceptions for leasehold rents –

   (*a*)   leases with less than 50 years left to run;

   (*b*)   leases extended under the Leasehold (Enlargement and Extension) Act (Northern Ireland) 1971;

   (*c*)   equity-sharing leases (see Article 2(2));

   (*d*)   mining leases;

   (*e*)   agricultural leases;

   (*f*)   leases where the National Trust is the rent-owner or a superior owner (cf. 1907 c. cxxxvi s. 21).

Sub-paragraph (e) (agricultural leases) would apply to a lease of a farm originally granted for more than 125 years which was excluded from vesting in the Northern Ireland Land Commission by section 20 of the Northern Ireland Land Act 1925 as having 60 or more years of the term unexpired. There is no exception for fee farm rents payable in respect of farms. These are redeemable under Article 4 (but not compulsorily redeemable under Article 5, which applies only to dwelling-houses – similarly Article 5 is inapplicable in case (d) (mining leases)).

*Paragraph (3)* prevents Articles 4 and 5 from applying where the rent-payer's lease is in course of being terminated by notice, or where court proceedings by the landlord for possession of the land are pending. Cf. Article 12 which prevents re-entry or ejectment while redemption of a ground rent is pending.

*Paragraph (4)* prevents Article 4 from applying where the rent-payer has, before the first appointed day (see Article 41), initiated the procedure for enlarging his leasehold estate into a fee simple under the Act of 1971 or where he has, before, on or after that day, initiated the procedure for obtaining an extension of the term of his lease. Article 5 does apply, so if the rent-payer wishes to sell his dwelling-house he must either complete the enlargement or extension under the Act of 1971 or he must terminate the proposed enlargement or extension under the Act of 1971 by serving a notice of withdrawal under section 7 of that Act, thus leaving it open for himself to take advantage of Article 4.

*Paragraph (5)* restricts the application of Article 4 to certain developments (or distinct parts of developments – see paragraph (6)) which consist of flats or houses, or flats and houses, together with common parts in respect of which periodic payments are made. One rent-payer cannot redeem his ground rent unless all the other rent-payers join with him in doing so and agree to make a formal development scheme under Part IX of the Property Order or a commonhold declaration. And Article 5 is excluded so that, on the sale of a flat (or house) there is no restriction on a legal estate passing even though the ground rent continues.

*Paragraph (6)* contains definitions –

"common parts" means parts of the development not included in a lease or grant to a rent-payer but provided for the benefit of the rent-payers in consideration of periodic payments. The expression includes fences, gardens, roads or paths, parking areas, areas for drying clothes or disposing of rubbish, stairs, passages and so on. It also includes common facilities as where a single television aerial is installed to serve all the flats in a building.

"development" means the land comprising flats (with or without houses) or houses and common parts. If the landlord has reserved part of the land for his sole benefit (and not, e.g. for his use as manager of the flats) that part is not part of the development.

"flat" means a unit of occupation in a building containing two or more such units. The units may be divided horizontally (as in the case of flats properly so called) or vertically (as for terrace or semi-detached houses: but the only such houses to be caught by the definition would be those with common parts e.g. "town-houses" with shared facilities such as private roads) or partly horizontally and partly vertically (as for masionettes) or at an angle (as where a boundary follows the line of a staircase). The expression is not confined to dwellings but also includes offices and shops (which may be held by a landlord at a ground rent and leased by him on periodic or short-term tenancies – in this case the landlord is the rent-payer).

"house" means a unit of occupation which is not a flat. In effect, in view of the definition of "flat" this means a detached house.

"unit of occupation" means the premises which are the subject of a lease or grant to a rent-payer at a ground rent (and not let at a commercial rent).

These definitions are also applied by Article 31(6) for the purposes of Article 31(5)(e).

Where a development falls into distinct parts (e.g. where there are two or more separate blocks of flats within the over-all development area) paragraph (5) applies to each distinct part (i.e. each separate block, with its adjoining common parts). This means that all the rent-payers of a block can unite to redeem their ground rents, even though the rent-payers of another block do not do so. The question whether separate blocks constitute "distinct parts" will be a question of fact in each case – e.g. this may not be so where common parts overlap, as where car parking facilities or approach roads are shared.

## Initiation of redemption procedure

**7.**—(1) A rent-payer who wishes to redeem his ground rent shall serve on the rent-owner a notice ("a redemption notice") of his intention to redeem the ground rent on, or as soon as reasonably practicable after, a date specified in the notice ("the redemption date").

(2) The redemption date must not be less than six weeks, and not more than eight weeks, after the date of service of the redemption notice.

(3) A redemption notice served by a rent-payer enures for his benefit and the benefit of his successors in title, whether or not there is any change in the rent-owner.

(4) Where two or more lands held under different titles subject to ground rents payable to the same rent-owner are contiguous (or, in the case of more than two, every one is contiguous to some other) and are occupied by the same rent-payer, they may, for the purposes of this Order, be treated as one land and the aggregate of the ground rents may be treated as one ground rent.

(5) Where land comprised of two or more parcels, legal estates in all or any of which are vested in separate persons, is subject to a single ground rent, all those persons may combine to redeem the ground rent.

# EXPLANATORY NOTE

## ARTICLE 7

This Article provides for the initiation by the rent-payer of the procedure for the redemption of a ground rent.

*Paragraph (1)* provides for the service on the rent-owner of a notice of the rent-owner's intention to redeem the ground rent on a specified date. The length of the period of notice is provided for in paragraph (2). Provisions about the service of notices are contained in Article 35 and section 24 of the Interpretation Act. The form of notice will be prescribed by rules under Article 38.

*Paragraph (2)* requires the period of notice to be six to eight weeks. The upper limit of eight weeks prevents the rent-payer from specifying an excessively lengthy period during which some of the rent-owner's remedies would be suspended by Article 12. The lower limit gives the rent-owner time to contact superior owners or mortgagees of rents in order to obtain their consent to the payment of the redemption money in a convenient way that will safeguard their interests (but that consent must be conveyed to the rent-payer at least one week before the redemption date – Article 8(1)).

*Paragraph (3)* makes it clear that when a rent-payer has served a notice of intention to redeem, the notice enures for the benefit of his successors in title. Thus, a notice served by a prospective vendor of land allows the redemption procedure to be continued and completed by his successor, in the event of his death. And where there is a change in the rent-owner (or his agent – Article 35(1)(b)) the continuance and completion of the procedure are not prejudiced.

*Paragraph (4)* allows ground rents to be consolidated for purposes of redemption where, for example, plot A has been leased to a rent-payer and the adjoining plot B is subsequently the subject of a supplementary lease.

*Paragraph (5)* deals with the converse case where a number of parcels of land are subject to a single ground rent. This can happen in a case such as is mentioned in paragraph 1.8 of the Interim Report, where, although land is held in separate ownerships, the landlord, for his own convenience has granted a single lease subject to a single ground rent; or in the case mentioned in paragraph 14 of the Law Commission's Report on Rentcharges (Law Com. No. 68) where a developer sells the last plot in his development subject to the whole of the burden of a rentcharge on the whole development (but with benefit of second rentcharges on the other plots) – although this last case would be unusual in Northern Ireland. The paragraph allows the holders of the plots to combine in order to redeem the ground rent. Where they do not combine, Article 18 applies.

Article 38(7) allows rules to modify the Order in order to give effect to paragraph (4) or (5) of this Article. For example, under paragraph (5) there will only be a single notice of intention to redeem and a single counter-notice under Article 8; but each plot-holder will need to have a certificate of redemption, so rules may allow copies of counter-notices and receipts (suitably certified) to be treated as certificates.

### Procedure where all other interests concur: the counter-notice

**8.**—(1) Where, during the period beginning with the service of a redemption notice and ending one week before the redemption date, there is served on the rent-payer a counter-notice –

(a) requiring payment to a specified person of a specified sum as, or (where paragraph 3 of Schedule 2 applies) as a first instalment of, the redemption money; and

(b) certifying that, upon such payment, the ground rent will be redeemed and, if the estate of the rent-payer in the land is a leasehold estate, that estate will be enlarged into an estate in fee simple,

the rent-payer obtains a full and final discharge of the land from the ground rent-

(i) by paying the redemption money in accordance with the counter-notice, or

(ii) where the redemption money is payable by instalments under paragraph 3(4) of Schedule 2, by paying the first instalment in accordance with the counter-notice and giving a prescribed security to secure the payment of the remaining instalments,

and also (in either case) by paying, in accordance with the counter-notice, any specified amount in respect of arrears of ground rent which will be due and recoverable at the redemption date and any specified apportionment of ground rent for the period from the last day for payment of ground rent before the redemption date to the redemption date.

(2) For the purposes of this Order, a counter-notice is a notice –

(a) purporting to be signed by or on behalf of the rent-owner; and

(b) stating –

(i) that the land is subject to no superior rent, or

(ii) that every superior owner has agreed to the terms of the counter-notice; and

(c) stating –

(i) that there is no mortgage of the rent-owner's estate or interest or of any superior owner's estate or interest, or

(ii) that every mortgagee of any such estate or interest has agreed to the terms of the counter-notice,

as well as containing the requirement and certificate referred to in paragraph(1)(a) and (b).

(3) Failure of a counter-notice to specify any arrears of ground rent or any apportionment of ground rent does not prejudice the right of the rent-owner to recover them, and, if not specified, they are recoverable by him as debts in any court of competent jurisdiction, but not otherwise.

(4) In this Article "specified" means specified in the counter-notice.

# EXPLANATORY NOTE

## ARTICLE 8

After service of a redemption notice under Article 7, either the rent-owner may respond in order to facilitate the redemption procedure, or he may fail to respond. Or it may not be possible to serve on him a notice under Article 7 because his name or address is unknown. This Article deals with the first of these situations and Article 13 with the other two.

*Paragraph (1)* Where the rent-payer has served on his rent-owner a notice of intention to redeem his ground rent, a counter-notice (defined in paragraph (2)) may be served on him. The counter-notice must specify the person to whom the redemption money is to be paid and certify that, on payment of that money, the ground rent will be redeemed and, if the rent-payer's estate in the land is leasehold, that estate will be enlarged into a fee simple. The counter-notice may also specify any arrears of ground rent that are outstanding and any apportionment of ground rent for a broken period from the last day for payment of rent to the redemption date. If the rent-payer pays the redemption money to the specified recipient and pays the specified arrears and apportioned amount of ground rent, he obtains a full and final discharge from the ground rent. In certain exceptional cases, i.e. those involving a building lease where the amount of ground rent to be paid by the developer increases with the progress of development (paragraph(1)(ii) and Schedule 2 paragraph 3) the redemption money may be payable by instalments. In these cases it is sufficient for the rent-payer to pay the first instalment and provide a security (which may include sureties – Article 2(3)), in accordance with rules, to secure the remaining instalments.

*Paragraph (2)* defines a counter-notice as a notice –

*sub-paragraph (a),* purporting to be signed by the rent-owner or on his behalf (e.g. by his solicitor or other agent). The rent-payer is not concerned to see that the signature is genuine – he may accept the counter-notice at its face value.

*sub-paragraph (b)* stating either that the land is subject to no superior rent or that every superior rent-owner concurs in the counter-notice.

*sub-paragraph (c)* stating either that there is no incumbrance of the ground rent or any superior rent or that every incumbrancer concurs in the counter-notice.

In addition to these matters the counter-notice must contain the requirement mentioned in paragraph (1)(a) for the payment of the redemption money to a specified person and a provisional certificate of redemption which will become operative on the payment of the specified sum. The counter-notice may also (but is not bound to) demand payment of any arrears or apportionment of ground rent (see paragraph (1)). If it does, the payment of such arrears and apportionment is a condition of redemption being completed: if it does not, the arrears and appor-tionment must be pursued by the rent-owner and recovered separately (paragraph (3)).

If there is a dispute as to whether the amount of the redemption money, or the amount of any arrears or apportionment, is correctly specified, the dispute may be resolved under Article 9. In practice, there is unlikely to be much room for a dispute about the redemption money or an apportionment, because these are the subject of simple arithmetical calculations; but there could be a dispute about arrears if they have been allowed to mount up for a number of years and the parties' memories have grown hazy.

The form of counter-notice will be prescribed by rules under Article 38. It is envisaged that it and the originating notice under Article 7 will be printed together, perhaps with one as a tear-off part of the other.

Penalties for incorrect statements in a counter-notice are provided for in Article 36 (offences) and Article 37 (civil remedy in damages).

*Paragraph (3)* allows any arrears or apportionment of ground rent *not* specified in a counter-notice to be recovered as a debt (and in no other way) – cf. Article 13(3)(b). Once the redemption money is paid, these cease to be a charge of any kind on the land, and other remedies such as entry or forfeiture are overreached. The fact that agreed arrears and apportionments can conveniently be collected with the redemption money should encourage rent-owners to co-operate in using the counter-notice procedure. The recovery of arrears or apportionments of superior rents is dealt with in Article 17(4).

*Paragraph (4)* defines "specified" when used in the Article. It means specified in the counter-notice.

**Correction of counter-notice following dispute about money payable or security**

**9.**—(1) Any question arising –

(a) as to the correctness of any sum specified in a counter-notice as –

    (i) the redemption money (or a first instalment of it);

    (ii) arrears of ground rent;

    (iii) apportioned ground rent; or

(b) as to the adequacy of any security for future instalments of the redemption money;

may be referred to and determined by the Registrar.

(2) Section 2 of the Land Registration Act (power of Registrar to summon witnesses) applies for the purposes of this Order as if the reference in subsection (1) of that section to any matter relating to registration under that Act included any question such as is mentioned in paragraph (1).

(3) Sections 6 and 7 of the Land Registration Act (appeal and reference to the High Court: appeal from High Court) apply for the purposes of this Order as if the reference in subsection (2) of section 6 to a question arising in the course of registration under that Act included any question such as is mentioned in paragraph (1), as if any reference in that section to the High Court included a reference to the county court, and as if, in relation to the decision of a county court, section 7 provided for an appeal to lie on a question of law to the Court of Appeal and in any other case to the High Court with the leave of the High Court.

(4) On determining a question such as is mentioned in paragraph (1), the Registrar, or, on appeal, the county court, the High Court or the Court of Appeal (as the case may be), may direct the counter-notice to be corrected by attaching a copy of the Registrar's order or the court's order, as the case may be, or otherwise as may be directed by the Registrar or the court.

(5) The Registrar may make such order about the costs of a reference to him under this Article and the person by whom they are to be borne as he in his discretion thinks fit; and section 8 of the Land Registration Act (enforcement by High Court of order of Registrar) applies to such an order as if the reference in that section to that Act included this Order.

# EXPLANATORY NOTE

## ARTICLE 9

This Article enables disputes about the correctness of sums required by a counter-notice to be paid, or the adequacy of security proposed to be given, to be resolved.

*Paragraph (1)* enables disputes to be referred to the Registrar. These are disputes about the amount of redemption money (or a first instalment of it), arrears of ground rent, or apportionment of ground rent, or the adequacy of security offered for future instalments of redemption money.

*Paragraph (2)* attracts section 2 of the Land Registration Act empowering the Registrar to summon witnesses.

*Paragraph (3)* attracts sections 6 and 7 of the Land Registration Act under which, where the Registrar adjudicates on a reference to him, there is a right of appeal to the High Court, or, where he declines to adjudicate, he may refer the dispute to the High Court. The paragraph gives the county court concurrent jurisdiction with the High Court (the particular county court having jurisdiction is identified by section 42(2) of the Interpretation Act). There is a right of appeal from the county court to the Court of Appeal on a question of law and to the High Court (with the leave of that Court) on a question of fact.

*Paragraph (4)* empowers the Registrar or court, upon adjudicating, to direct the counter-notice to be corrected.

*Paragraph (5)* gives the Registrar power to award costs. The award of costs is at his discretion.

**Correction of counter-notice where money cannot be paid in accordance with it**

10.—(1) Where –

(a) the redemption money cannot, or cannot conveniently, be paid in accordance with the counter-notice by reason of the absence, incapacity or death of a person named in the counter-notice as the person to whom the redemption money is to be paid or for any other sufficient reason; and

(b) a notice purporting to be signed by or on behalf of the rent-owner stating that reason and giving other directions for the payment of the redemption money is served on the rent-payer before the redemption date,

the notice mentioned in sub-paragraph (b) is, for the purposes of this Order, deemed to form part of the counter-notice.

(2)   In paragraph (1) "death" includes, in relation to a body corporate or unincorporate, dissolution.

# EXPLANATORY NOTE

## ARTICLE 10

This Article allows a counter-notice to be corrected where payment of the redemption money cannot be made to a person named in it because he is absent, has become incapable of accepting the money or has died, or where it cannot conveniently be made to him for some sufficient reason.

*Paragraph (1)* provides for the service on the rent-payer of a further notice amending the counter-notice by substituting some other person as the authorised recipient of the redemption money. The notice must be served before the redemption date. The notice is deemed to be part of the counter-notice (see, e.g. Article13(1)(c)).

*Paragraph (2)* applies the Article to the dissolution of a company or partnership in the same way as it applies to the death of a natural person.

## Termination of redemption procedure

**11.**—(1) Where a rent-payer –

(a)  has served a redemption notice on a rent-owner; and

(b)  has not, in response, been served with a counter-notice;

he may withdraw the redemption notice by a notice served on the rent-owner.

(2)  Where –

(a)  a rent-owner has been served with a redemption notice and, in response, has served a counter-notice; and

(b)  the rent-payer has not, before the expiration of one week from the redemption date, paid-

    (i)  the redemption money (or, where it is payable by instalments, the first instalment of it), together with

    (ii)  any amounts specified in the counter-notice as arrears and apportionment of ground rent; and

(c)  no question such as is mentioned in Article 9 is pending before the Registrar or on appeal from or reference by him; and

(d)  the redemption money (or the first instalment of it) and the documents and particulars mentioned in paragraph (2) of Article 13 have not been lodged with the Registrar in consequence of circumstances such are mentioned in paragraph (1)(c) of that Article;

the rent-owner may serve on the rent-payer a notice requiring him to pay the money referred to in sub-paragraph (b)(i) together with any amounts such as are mentioned in sub-paragraph (b)(ii), in accordance with the counter-notice, within the period of two weeks from the date of service of the notice and stating that, in the event of such payment not being made, the redemption notice and the counter-notice shall cease to have effect; and, where such payment is not made within that period, those notices cease to have effect on the expiration of that period.

(3)  Where –

(a)  a rent owner has been served with a redemption notice but has not, in response, served a counter-notice, and

(b)  the redemption date has passed and the rent-payer has not lodged with the Registrar the redemption money (or the first instalment of it) and the documents and particulars mentioned in paragraph (2) of Article 13, and

(c)  the rent-owner considers that the delay in lodging that money and those documents and particulars is unreasonable,

the rent-owner may apply to the county court for a declaration that the documents and particulars have not been lodged as soon as reasonably practicable after the redemption date as required by paragraph (1) of Article 13, and on the making of such a declaration the redemption notice ceases to have effect.

1091

# EXPLANATORY NOTE

## ARTICLE 11

This Article permits a rent-payer or a rent-owner to terminate proceedings for the redemption of a ground rent in certain circumstances.

*Paragraph (1)* applies to a rent-payer. If he has served a redemption notice but has not been served with a counter-notice, he may serve a notice (in writing – Article 2(2)) on the rent-owner withdrawing the redemption notice.

*Paragraph (2)* applies to a rent-owner. If a rent-payer has served a redemption notice and in response the rent-owner has served a counter-notice, but the rent-payer has not complied with the counter-notice, the rent-owner may allow the rent-payer two weeks in which to pay the money due under the counter-notice, and, if payment is not made, both the redemption notice and the counter-notice cease to have effect. However, this right is suspended while any reference or appeal on the terms of the counter-notice is pending, and it does not apply where the rent-payer has been unable to make payment in accordance with the counter-notice and has, instead, lodged the redemption money (and the other documents and particulars mentioned in Article 13) with the Registrar.

*Paragraph (3)* applies to a rent-owner who has not served a counter-notice (e.g. because he has been unable to obtain the concurrence of superior owners under Article 8(2)(b)(ii)). In such a case the rent-payer is empowered by Article 13(1) to lodge the redemption money (together with prescribed documents and particulars) with the Registrar of Titles, but he must do this "on or as soon as reasonably practicable after the redemption date". If he delays unreasonably, not only is he holding up the redemption, but he is depriving the rent-owner of any right he may have of re-possessing the land for non-payment of ground rent, because of the suspension of that right by Article 12. This paragraph empowers an aggrieved rent-owner to apply to the county court for a declaration that the documents and particulars have not been lodged as soon as reasonably practicable. Such a declaration terminates the redemption proceedings.

## Exclusion of re-possession of land while redemption is pending

**12.**—(1) Without prejudice to any other civil remedy of the rent-owner's or a superior owner's, while the redemption of a ground rent is pending –

(a) any covenant giving the rent-owner or a superior owner a right to enter or re-enter the land when ground rent or a superior rent is in arrear, or in the event of any other breach of covenant, is not enforceable;

(b) section 52 of the Landlord and Tenant Law Amendment Act (Ireland)1860 (proceedings for ejectment when year's rent in arrear) does not apply to the land;

(c) no application may be made under Article 57 of the Landlord and Tenant (Northern Ireland) Order 1989.

(2) For the purposes of this Article redemption of a ground rent is pending between the service of a redemption notice and either –

(a) the completion or sealing of a certificate of redemption, or

(b) either –

    (i) where the rent-payer withdraws the redemption notice by a notice served under Article 11(1), the service of the last-mentioned notice, or

    (ii) where the rent-owner has served a notice under Article 11(2) which has not been complied with, the expiration of the period mentioned in the notice, or

    (iii) where the county court makes a declaration under Article 11(3), the date of the declaration,

whichever first occurs.

(3) Where the county court has made a declaration under Article 11(3) in relation to a ground rent, paragraph (1) does not apply while the redemption of the ground rent is pending in consequence of the service of a redemption notice in relation to that ground rent at any time after the date of the declaration.

# EXPLANATORY NOTE

## ARTICLE 12

This Article prevents a rent-owner or a superior owner from taking advantage of a right of entry (e.g. to intercept rents) or re-entry (i.e. to re-possess the land permanently) or of his existing statutory right to have a tenant ejected for non-payment of ground rent while the redemption of the ground rent is pending.

*Paragraph (1)* lists three sanctions which are not available to a rent-owner while redemption of a ground rent is pending. These are –

*sub-paragraph (a)* a right of entry or re-entry conferred by the grant or lease which created the rent (the reference to a covenant giving a right of entry or re-entry includes a proviso – Article 2(2)), and

*sub-paragraph (b)* the right to apply to the court for an order of ejectment under section 52 of the Landlord and Tenant Law Amendment Act (Ireland) 1860 (Deasy's Act) when a year's rent is in arrear. (Because it is possible that this Order may take effect before the repeal of that section, the reference is to the existing law.)

*sub-paragraph (c)* an application under Article 57 of the Landlord and Tenant Order for a termination order or a remedial order.

The paragraph also affects any such sanction which would otherwise be available to a superior owner when a superior rent is in arrear. The paragraph does not affect a covenanted right of entry (e.g. to view the state of repair) as distinct from a right to enter in consequence of a breach of covenant.

*Paragraph (2)* defines the period within which the redemption of a ground rent is pending. It is the period beginning with the service of a redemption notice and ending with the completion or sealing of a certificate of redemption (see Article 15(6)) (when the ground rent and superior rents – Article 17 – cease to exist and the sanctions in question become irrelevant) or the aborting by the rent-payer of the redemption proceedings under Article 11(1) or the termination of these proceedings by the rent-owner under Article 11(2) or by virtue of a declaration made by the county court under Article 11(3).

*Paragraph (3)* prevents a rent-payer from harassing his rent-owner by serving repeated redemption notices and not following them up.

**Procedure where a redemption notice cannot be served, all other interests do not concur or payment cannot be made in accordance with counter-notice**

13.—(1)  Where –

(a)  the rent-payer cannot serve a redemption notice because he does not know the name and address of the rent-owner or his agent or a notice sought to be served by post has been returned by the Post Office; or

(b)  the rent-payer has served such a notice but a counter-notice has not been served on him during the period mentioned in Article 8(1); or

(c)  a counter-notice has been so served but the rent-payer is unable to make payment to the person specified in the counter-notice in accordance with the counter-notice,

the rent-payer, on or as soon as reasonably practicable after the redemption date, may lodge with the Registrar the redemption money, or where that money is payable by instalments under paragraph 3 of Schedule 2, the first instalment of it, together with the documents and particulars mentioned in paragraph(2).

(2)  Those documents and particulars are –

(a)  where paragraph (1)(b) applies, a copy of the redemption notice together with evidence of its service;

(b)  where paragraph (1)(c) applies, copies of the redemption notice and the counter-notice together with particulars of the reasons why payment cannot be made;

(c)  where the redemption money is payable by instalments under paragraph 3 of Schedule 2, a prescribed security for the payment of the second instalment and any subsequent instalments;

(d)  in every case, such documents or particulars as may be prescribed.

(3)  Where a sum is lodged with the Registrar under paragraph (1) in respect of the whole or a first instalment of the redemption money and the documents and particulars required by paragraph (2) are also lodged, –

(a)  the lodgment operates as a full and final discharge of the land from the ground rent; but

(b)  sub-paragraph (a) does not prejudice the liability of the rent-payer to pay any arrears of the ground rent due and recoverable at the redemption date and any apportionment of the ground rent for the period from the last day for payment of ground rent before the redemption date to the redemption date, and any such arrears and apportionment are recoverable by the rent-owner as a debt in any court of competent jurisdiction, but not otherwise.

(4)  Where the rent-payer cannot serve a redemption notice because he does not know the name and address of the rent-owner or his agent, for the purposes of this Order the redemption date is such date as the rent-payer may fix.

# EXPLANATORY NOTE

## ARTICLE 13

This Article confers a jurisdiction on the Registrar of Titles where a redemption notice cannot be served, where all rent-owners, superior owners and their incumbrancers (if any) do not concur in empowering the rent-payer to discharge his obligations in respect of ground rent by making payment to an agreed person, or where payment to such an agreed person cannot be made.

*Paragraph (1)* sets out three cases in which Article applies.

*sub-paragraph (a):* where the rent-payer does not know his immediate superior's name and address and so cannot serve a redemption notice (i.e. a notice of his intention to redeem the ground rent under Article 7) or where an attempted service by post has been unsuccessful.

*sub-paragraph (b):* where the rent-payer has served a redemption notice, but has not received a counter-notice within five to seven weeks (i.e. a week before the date for redemption specified in the redemption notice – see Articles 7(2) and 8(1)).

*sub-paragraph (c):* where the rent-payer has served a redemption notice and has been served with a counter-notice, but redemption cannot proceed in accordance with the counter-notice for some reason e.g. because the person specified as payee either in the counter-notice or in a notice served under Article 10(1)(b) (which is deemed to be part of the counter-notice) has died.

In any of those cases the rent-payer may redeem his ground rent by paying to the Registrar the redemption money (or, in the case of certain building land, a first instalment of the redemption money) together with the documents and particulars mentioned in paragraph (2).

*Paragraph (2)* If the rent-payer had served a redemption notice but had not received a counter-notice, he must lodge a copy of the redemption notice. If he had received a counter-notice but is unable to comply with it, he must lodge a copy of the counter-notice as well as a copy of his redemption notice. Where redemption money in respect of building land is payable by instalments, the money lodged will relate only to the first instalment, so the rent-payer must give a prescribed security for the payment of future instalments. Acceptable securities will be those prescribed by rules (Article 38), and for this purpose "security" may include the finding of sureties (Article 2(3)). The rent-payer must also lodge any documents or particulars prescribed by rules (e.g. particulars of any mortgage of the land which is subject to the ground rent – Article 15(3)(a)).

*Paragraph (3)* states the consequences of lodging the requisite money, documents and particulars with the Registrar –

*sub-paragraph (a):* The land is discharged from the ground rent. This is so even where only a first instalment of the redemption money is paid. In that case, the security for the payment of future instalments given in accordance with rules takes the place of the land.

*sub-paragraph (b):* Any obligation of the rent-payer in respect of arrears or apportionment of ground rent is not affected. Any amount remaining due for those is recoverable as a debt, but not otherwise (i.e. any right of entry or forfeiture which the rent-owner formerly had has disappeared – cf. Articles 8(3) and 17(4)). Where redemption money is lodged with the Registrar, no lodgment can be accepted in respect of arrears or apportionment of ground rent. Those are recoverable only under this sub-paragraph. The Registrar is concerned only with safeguarding the capital value of the ground rent; it is for the rent-owner to enforce the payment of income.

*Paragraph (4)* Normally "The redemption date" is the date specified as such in a redemption notice (Article 7(1)). Where the rent-payer cannot serve a redemption notice because he does not know the name and address of the rent-owner or his agent, the redemption date is such date as the rent-payer may fix. In effect this means that he can make a lodgement with the Registrar whenever he chooses to do so.

## The redemption money

**14.** The amount of the redemption money appropriate to any ground rent is to be determined in accordance with Schedule 2, and the other provisions of that Schedule have effect.

# EXPLANATORY NOTE

## ARTICLE 14

This Article provides the basis for determining the amount of the redemption money.

The Article attracts Schedule 2 which (paragraphs 1 and 2) lays down the rule that the amount of the redemption money is to be ascertained by multiplying the annual amount of the ground rent by a number of years purchase fixed by the Department of Finance and Personnel. Where a ground rent is subject to increase during the progression of the development of the land or is subject to periodic review, paragraphs 3 and 4 respectively indicate how the annual amount of the rent is to be determined for the purpose of this multiplication.

The "other provisions" of Schedule 2 referred to in the Article are those permitting redemption money to be paid by instalments in certain cases.

## Certificate of redemption

**15.**—(1) When a rent-payer pays a sum in respect of redemption money (or a first instalment of redemption money) to a person specified in a counter-notice, that person is under an obligation to give the rent-payer a receipt for the sum, and that obligation is deemed to be a covenant of the instrument which created the ground rent.

(2) The receipt mentioned in paragraph (1) shall be entered on the counter-notice; but rules may make provision about the circumstances in which a receipt not so entered is deemed to be so entered, in which other evidence of payment is deemed to be a receipt, and in which a copy of a counter-notice is deemed to be the counter-notice.

(3) Where redemption money (or a first instalment of it) is lodged with the Registrar in accordance with Article 13, the Registrar shall prepare in duplicate and seal with the seal of the central office of the Land Registry a certificate that the ground rent has been redeemed and send one of the certificates-

(a) where particulars lodged under Article 13(2)(d) disclose the existence of a mortgage of the rent-payer's estate and the fact (if it is the case) that the mortgagee is entitled to possession of the documents relating to the mortgagor's title to the land, to that mortgagee;

(b) in any other case, to the rent-payer.

(4) Where the Registrar sends a certificate to a mortgagee under paragraph (3)(a), the Registrar shall inform the rent-payer of the fact.

(5) A counter-notice in relation to which paragraph (2) has been or is deemed to have been complied with or a certificate which has been sealed under paragraph (3) is, for the purposes of this Order, a certificate of redemption.

(6) In this Order a certificate of redemption is said to be completed when a receipt is entered on or deemed to be entered on a counter-notice as mentioned in paragraph (2), and is said to be sealed when it is sealed by the Registrar under paragraph (3) with the seal of the central office.

# EXPLANATORY NOTE

ARTICLE 15

This Article defines a certificate of redemption of a ground rent.

*Paragraph (1)* requires the "specified person" (Article 8(1)(a)) to whom redemption money is paid to give a receipt for it.

*Paragraph (2)* Article 8(1)(b) has already required a counter-notice to be in the form of a conditional certificate of the redemption of the ground rent and, in the case of a ground rent created by a lease, the enlargement of the rent-payer's leasehold estate into a fee simple. This paragraph requires the receipt for the redemption money to be entered on the counter-notice, thus completing the certificate of redemption. But the original counter-notice may have been lost or destroyed (e.g. in a fire) or a rent-owner or his agent may neglect to return the counter-notice with the receipt completed. In this case rules may allow the receipt to be attached to a copy of the counter-notice, or if no receipt is forthcoming may allow the rent-payer to attach such other evidence as the rules permit. This might be a statutory declaration averring payment, possibly supported by a paid cheque or a facsimile of a paid cheque. If this is done, the rules may deem the requirements of the paragraph to be complied with. (A paid cheque in favour of a creditor for an amount equal to his debt is not, by itself, evidence of payment of the debt, but rules could make it so if supported by a declaration -especially a contemporaneous declaration).

*Paragraph (3)* Where redemption money is lodged with the Registrar, he will prepare a certificate of redemption in duplicate under his seal. One of the duplicates will be retained by him for the record and for the purpose of his preparing a certified copy if he is required to do so. Where the Registrar has been notified of a mortgage on the land, he will send the other certificate to the mortgagee, if the mortgagee is entitled to hold the title deeds: in any other case he will send it to the rent-payer. Where the land is registered land, the Registrar, before sending the certificate out, may make such change in the register as the case requires (Article19(6)), if the necessary fee has been paid.

*Paragraph (4)* Where the Registrar sends a certificate to a mortgagee, the Registrar must inform the rent-payer.

*Paragraph (5)* formally gives the title "certificate of redemption" to a counter-notice bearing a receipt for redemption money (or, in accordance with rules, supported by evidence of payment), or a certificate sealed under paragraph (3).

*Paragraph (6)* defines, for other provisions of the Order (Articles 12(2)(a), 19(1),(2), 24(1), Schedule 1 paragraphs 1(e), 2(1)(d)) when a certificate of redemption is "completed" (under paragraph (2)) or "sealed" (under paragraph (3)).

*Consequences of redemption*

## Effect of certificate of redemption

**16.**—(1) Subject to paragraph (2), a certificate of redemption is conclusive evidence –

(a) of the redemption of the ground rent to which it relates; and

(b) of the operation in relation to the land, and any other parcel or parcels of land affected, of Articles 17, 18, 19, 22, 23, 24 and 25.

(2) Where the court is satisfied that a certificate of redemption has been obtained by fraud and that the certificate can be cancelled without hardship to a purchaser of the land in good faith for value, the court may order the certificate to be cancelled and, where the certificate relates to registered land, may order the register to be rectified accordingly.

(3) In paragraph (2) "the court" has the meaning given by section 4 of the Land Registration Act (references in that section to that Act being read as including references to this Order).

# EXPLANATORY NOTE

## ARTICLE 16

This Article states the effect of a certificate of redemption.

*Paragraph (1)* makes a certificate of redemption conclusive evidence of the redemption of the ground rent to which it relates. The certificate is the essential link in the chain of title founding the rent-payer's new estate. But there is one case in which a court may go behind the certificate. This is dealt with in paragraph (2). The certificate is also conclusive evidence of the operation of the Order in relation to the land (i.e. the land formerly subject to the ground rent – Article 2(2)); e.g. the certificate, by virtue of Article 19, vests a freehold estate in a former leaseholder. As to the operation of the certificate in relation to other parcels of land, see Articles 18, 19(5) and 24(6).

*Paragraph (2)* empowers the court to direct that a certificate of redemption be cancelled if the court is satisfied –

(*a*)  that the certificate had been obtained by fraud, and

(*b*)  that the certificate can be cancelled without hardship to a purchaser of the land in good faith for value (including marriage but not including natural love and affection which is only "good" consideration).

A certificate might be obtained by fraud where, e.g., the rent-owner has falsely stated that all superior owners have agreed to payment of the redemption money to a particular person, when he knows that they have not done so.

*Paragraph (3)* attracts the definition of "the court" in section 4 of the Land Registration Act (i.e. the High Court or, in relation to matters coming within the jurisdiction of a county court, the county court). The particular county court having jurisdiction is defined by section 42(2) of the Interpretation Act (Northern Ireland) 1954, i.e. the court prescribed by county court rules or, if no court is so prescribed, the county court having jurisdiction over the whole or any part of the division in which ... the premises are situated.

### Superior rents

**17.**—(1) When a ground rent is redeemed, all superior rents (if any) to which the land is subject are also redeemed or, where they are charged on other land as well as the land, are redeemed to the extent that they are apportionable to the land (and, for the purpose of this Article, a superior rent which, apart from this Article, would not be apportionable to parts of land which is subject to it is hereby made so apportionable).

(2) Any apportionment under paragraph (1) shall be made by reference to the respective areas of the lands concerned.

(3) The extent to which a superior rent is redeemed by virtue of paragraph(1) may be increased by an agreement to which any mortgagee of the superior rent is a party; but it may not be reduced except to the extent necessary to permit an apportionment to be made on a reasonable approximation of areas.

(4) Any arrears of a superior rent which are due and recoverable at the redemption date, and any apportionment of such a rent for the period from the last day for the payment of the rent before the redemption date to the redemption date, are recoverable by the superior owner from the person primarily liable to pay the rent (that is to say, the rent-owner or, where there are intermediate superior owners, the most superior of them) as debts in any court of competent jurisdiction, and not otherwise.

(5) This Article does not prejudice Article 5(7) and (8) and Schedule 1.

# EXPLANATORY NOTE

## ARTICLE 17

This Article is concerned with the effect on superior rents of the redemption of a ground rent. The Article is not concerned with the marshalling of rents prior to redemption (that is dealt with, in certain cases, by Schedule 1) but rather with the effect of redemption which follows any marshalling.

*Paragraph (1)* provides that, on the redemption of a ground rent, all superior rents out of the same land are also redeemed. If a superior rent is payable out of a larger area of land than the land which had been subject to the redeemed ground rent, the superior rent is to be apportioned, and is redeemed, to the extent that it is apportionable to the ground rent's land (see paragraph (2)). ("The land" is defined in Article 2(2)).

*Paragraph (2)* requires any apportionment under paragraph (1) to be made by reference to the respective areas (and not values) of the lands concerned (ground rent being, or originally having been, a measurement of site value). Any question arising may be referred to the Lands Tribunal (Article 39(2)(a)).

*Paragraph (3)* allows the parties to agree that a superior rent is to be redeemed to a greater (but not, save as mentioned below, a lesser) extent than would be the case upon a strict apportionment under paragraph (1). This could happen where the rent-payer holds two or more parcels subject to different ground rents but the same superior rent. The purpose of this provision is to encourage the early redemption of head rents, especially where a strict apportionment would produce a very small amount or be unduly troublesome. Where the superior rent is mortgaged, the mortgagee must be a party to the agreement (so that he may make sure of getting part repayment or that his security is still adequate). There is one case in which a superior rent may be redeemed to a lesser extent than is required by a strict apportionment. That is where it is convenient and reasonable to calculate the apportionment on an approximate basis. E.g. if a superior rent is payable out of land that has been divided into a number of plots leased at ground rents, the plots may be treated as equal for purposes of the apportionment, even though they may vary slightly in size (so that marginally too much superior rent is attributed to some plots and marginally too little to others).

*Paragraph (4)* allows any arrears or apportionment in time of a superior rent to be recovered as a debt and not otherwise – i.e. following redemption, any right of entry or forfeiture disappears cf. Articles 8(3) and 13(3)(b).

*Paragraph (5)* is a saving for Article 5(7) and (8) and Schedule 1 (see below).

The effect of this Article, Article 5(7) and (8) and Schedule 1 on superior rents can be summarized as follows –

1.   A ground rent which is to be redeemed must be redeemed with respect to the whole parcel of land which is subject to it. If a superior rent is limited to that parcel, the whole of the superior rent is redeemed; but if a superior rent applies to the parcel together with other land, the superior rent is apportioned and only the portion attributable to the parcel is redeemed (unless the rent-owner, the superior owner and any mortgagee of the superior rent agree that the superior rent be redeemed to a greater extent).

2.   Where a ground rent is to be redeemed because of a sale of only part of the parcel of land containing a dwelling-house which is subject to it, then –

(*a*)  in the absence of an agreement such as is referred to in sub-paragraph (b) or (c), a superior rent which affects more of the parcel than the part sold is deemed (as is also the ground rent) to be charged exclusively on the part sold to the exclusion of the unsold part, unless the superior rent also affects other land, in which case the superior rent is apportioned between the parcel and the other land and the amount of it apportioned to the parcel is treated as charged only on the part sold;

(*b*)  the rent-owner and the rent-payer may agree, with the concurrence of any mortgagee of the ground rent, that the ground rent is to be loaded onto the land retained. In this event any superior rent is also loaded onto the land retained, and the land conveyed, being free of ground rent, is not subject to Article 5(1). Where the vendor's estate is leasehold, the purchaser will take an assignment of the lease free from all rent, subject to the covenants which would have continued to affect the land conveyed if it had been enfranchised under the Order, but free from all other covenants in the lease and superior instruments;

(*c*)  the rent-owner and the rent-payer may agree that the ground rent is to be apportioned between the land conveyed and the land retained. Where there is a mortgage of the land or the ground rent, the mortgagee must join in the agreement. In this event, the land conveyed is subject only to the part of the ground rent apportioned to it, and that part must be redeemed – the redemption will extend to so much of a superior rent as is apportioned to the part (this apportionment being under Article 17).

## Lands in separate occupation subject to single ground rent

**18.**—(1) Where land comprised of two or more parcels, legal estates in all or any of which are vested in separate persons, is subject to a single ground rent and the rent-payers do not combine under Article 7(5) to redeem the ground rent, the payment of the redemption money by a rent-payer entitled to any parcel or parcels frees all the parcels from the ground rent, and at the request of the person entitled to any other parcel or parcels the rent-payer or, as the case may be, the Registrar on being satisfied of the facts shall deliver to that person a copy of the certificate of redemption.

(2) Where the rent-payer delivers a copy of the certificate of redemption under paragraph (1), he may, as a condition of delivering it, require the person making the request to pay not more than the appropriate sum to cover the cost of preparing and, where necessary, posting the copy; and for this purpose the appropriate sum is a sum equivalent to that prescribed under Article 38(3) as the fee payable to the Registrar for a similar service.

(3) A rent-payer entitled to any parcel or parcels who pays redemption money may require reimbursement of all or an appropriate part (as the case may be) of that money and his reasonable costs properly incurred for the purposes of the redemption-

(a) where he has been indemnified against payment of the ground rent or any part of it, from the indemnifior; or

(b) where he has not been so indemnified, from the person entitled to any other parcel, unless he himself has indemnified that person against any demand for ground rent.

# EXPLANATORY NOTE

ARTICLE 18

This Article deals with the case where lands occupied by two or more different persons are, together, subject to a single ground rent. The circumstances in which this can occur are mentioned in the Explanatory Note on Article 7(5).

*Paragraph (1)* applies where land subject to a ground rent is divided into parcels some or all of which are owned by separate persons. Article 7(5) allows those persons to combine for the purpose of redeeming the ground rent. If they do not combine and redemption is compulsory under Article 5 because a parcel containing a dwelling-house is to be conveyed and there is no agreement about the charging or apportionment of the ground rent (Article 5(7)(a) and (b)), the vendor of the house must redeem the whole ground rent (Article 5(7)). This paragraph makes it clear that the redemption of the whole ground rent by one parcel owner enures for the benefit of all the other parcel owners, each of whom is entitled to a copy of the certificate of redemption. The certificate of redemption will identify only the parcel conveyed, but it could be combined with other evidence (e.g. a statutory declaration) to establish the redemptive effect on other parcels. That redemptive effect is stated in paragraph (4) of Article 19, in combination with paragraph (1) or (2) of that Article.

*Paragraph (2)* allows a rent-payer who supplies a copy of a certificate of redemption to charge a sum for the cost of preparing it. He may also charge the cost of postage, if the copy is sent through the Post Office. Where the Registrar supplies a copy he will charge a fee prescribed under Article 38(3). The charge made by a rent-payer must be not more than that fee. The paragraph does not permit the rent-payer to withhold the copy until any sum due to him under paragraph (3)(b) has been paid, because this could place another parcel-owner at the mercy of an unreasonable demand made by the rent-payer.

*Paragraph (3)* is concerned with the position of a rent-payer who is compelled to redeem the ground rent charged on all the parcels of land in order that his own parcel may be freed.

*sub-paragraph (a)* Where he has been indemnified against payment of all the ground rent, he may require reimbursement by the indemnifior; where he has been indemnified against having to pay part of the ground rent, he may require reimbursement as to that part.

*sub-paragraph (b)* Where he has not the benefit of an indemnity (and he himself is not an indemnifior) he can claim proportionate reimbursement from the owners of the other plots.

In a case of partial reimbursement, any dispute about the appropriate part of the redemption money to be paid by an indemnifior or parcel-holder can be referred to the Lands Tribunal (Article 39). Reimbursement extends to costs of a reasonable amount properly incurred as well as to the redemption money.

1108

**Effect of redemption on titles**

**19.**—(1) Subject to paragraph (3), where, immediately before the completion or sealing of a certificate of redemption, the land was held by the rent-payer for a freehold estate, the certificate of redemption operates by virtue of this provision (subject only to registration in the Land Registry where the rent-payer's estate is registered land) to discharge that estate absolutely from all estates or interests of the rent-owner and any superior owners and any person claiming under or through him or them or a predecessor in title of his or theirs.

(2) Subject to paragraph (3), where, immediately before the completion or sealing of a certificate of redemption, the land was held by the rent-payer for a leasehold estate, the certificate operates by virtue of this provision (subject only to registration in the Land Registry where the rent-payer's estate is registered land) to convert the rent-payer's estate into an estate in fee simple and, accordingly, the title of the rent-owner or any superior owner to the fee simple is extinguished and all other estates or interests in the land of the rent-owner or any superior owners or any person claiming under or through him or them or a predecessor in title of his or theirs are extinguished (but without prejudice to Article 25(4) and (5)(a)).

(3) Paragraphs (1) and (2) do not prejudice Article 20 nor do they affect the power of the rent-owner or a superior owner to enforce a covenant enforceable by him which is continued by paragraph (2) of Article 24 or his liability to have a covenant to which that paragraph applies enforced against him.

(4) Where, under Article 5(7), a ground rent is deemed to be charged exclusively on the land conveyed, references in paragraphs (1) and (2) to the land include both the land conveyed and the land retained (and, accordingly, references to the rent-payer include the person who would have been the rent-payer in relation to the land retained had the deeming provision not taken effect.

(5) Where the circumstances are such that Article 18 applies, references in paragraphs (1) and (2) to the land and the rent-payer include references to the other parcel or parcels and the person, or the respective persons, in whom that other parcel or those other parcels are vested; and references in paragraph (6) shall be construed similarly.

(6) In the case of registered land, a certificate of redemption (including one sealed by the Registrar) is sufficient authority for the Registrar –

(a) where the rent-payer's estate in the land is registered in the register of freeholders, to discharge any burden such as is mentioned in paragraph 2 of Part I of Schedule 6 to the Land Registration Act and make such alteration in the class of title with which the land is registered as appears to him appropriate;

(b) where the rent-payer's estate in the land is registered in the register of leaseholders and an application is made under subsection (1) of section 27 of the Land Registration Act, to cancel the entry relating to the title to that estate in that register and register the estate in fee simple vested in the rent-payer by virtue of paragraph (2) in accordance with that section;

and to make such consequential entries, changes or cancellations as appear to him appropriate.

(7)   Where all the rent-payers in a development to which Article 6(5) applies have agreed to promote a commonhold under the Commonhold (Northern Ireland) Order 1989 and the owner of the common parts is not a body corporate of which all the rent-payers (and no other) are members or all the rent-payers do not own the common parts in undivided shares, their combined certificates of redemption operate to vest an estate in fee simple in the common parts of the development in the rent-payers as tenants in common at law (notwithstanding any restriction on the creation of legal tenancies in common or on the number of persons who may be trustees for equitable tenants in common) pending the coming into existence of a commonhold association, the interest of each rent-payer in those parts being appurtenant to this flat or house, devolving or passing therewith and being incapable of alienation apart therefrom; and, where the development is registered land, those certificates are sufficient authority for the Registrar to register the effect of the operation of this paragraph in the appropriate register.

(8)   A certificate of redemption is a conveyance for the purposes of the Registration of Deeds Acts.

(9)   Section 6 of the Conveyancing Act 1881 or Article 95 of the Property (Northern Ireland) Order 1989 (conveyance carries easements, etc., appertaining to land conveyed) applies to the vesting effected by virtue of this Article as if the certificate of redemption were a conveyance within the meaning of that Act or Order.

(10)   A mortgagee to whom a certificate of redemption is sent under Article 15(3)(a) or Article 23(2) is under an obligation to submit the certificate for registration in the Registry of Deeds or, as the case requires, the Land Registry, if it has not already been registered there (and may charge to the mortgagor his reasonable costs properly incurred in doing so); and such an obligation is deemed to be included in the instrument or agreement containing the terms of the mortgage.

# EXPLANATORY NOTE

## ARTICLE 19

This Article sets out the effect of the redemption of a ground rent on the titles of the rent-payer, the rent-owner and any superior owners.

*Paragraph (1)* applies where the rent-payer's estate is a freehold one (i.e. where he holds under a fee farm grant). The certificate of redemption operates to discharge the estate from all interests of the rent-owner and superiors and any derivative interests. Where the estate is registerd in the Land Registry, this takes effect only when the necessary change is made in the register (cf. paragraph (6) and Article 24(1)(b)).

*Paragraph (2)* makes a certificate of redemption operate, where the rent-payer's estate before redemption was a leasehold estate, to vest a fee simple estate in him. This happens at once in the case of unregistered land, but, where the rent-payer's title is registered, only when an entry is made in the appropriate register in the Land Registry (see paragraph (6)). There is a saving for Article 25(4) and (5)(a) under which certain covenants for the protection of amenities continue to be enforceable by or against a former rent-owner by a redeeming rent-payer, so long as the former remains rent-owner in respect of other parcels of land in the same development.

*Paragraph (3)* contains a cross-reference to Article 20 under which, when redemption money lodged with the Registrar is paid into the Exchequer, the persons entitled to the money (including both the rent-owner and superior owners) can recover it, (in other words, the rights of those persons take a different form), and to Article 24(2) which continues the effect of certain covenants.

*Paragraph (4)* applies paragraphs (1) and (2) in a case where, on a sale of part of land subject to a ground rent, the whole ground rent is deemed to be charged on the land conveyed (Article 5(7); Sch. 1 para. 1). Those paragraphs operate in relation to both the land conveyed and the land retained.

*Paragraph (5)* applies paragraphs (1) and (2) to cases where a rent-payer holding one parcel of land has redeemed the whole of a ground rent payable out of that and one or more other parcels. Article 18 frees the other parcels (as well as that held by the rent-payer) from the ground rent; this paragraph applies paragraph (1) or (2) so as to leave the other parcel-holders with unencumbered freehold estates or (as the case requires) vest freehold estates in them.

*Paragraph (6)* is concerned with registered land. A certificate of registration is sufficient to authorise the Registrar –

*sub-paragraph (a):* where the ground rent was a fee farm rent, to cancel the entry of the burden of the rent and change the registration with (typically) a good fee farm grant title into registration of a freehold estate with an absolute title;

1111

*sub-paragraph (b):* where the rent-payer's estate was leasehold and was registered in the register of leaseholders, to cancel the entry in the register of leaseholders and register the rent-payer with such title as appears to him appropriate – e.g. in the register of freeholders with an absolute title or a possessory title as the circumstances require. Section 27 of the Land Registration Act and rule 36 of Land Registry Rules will apply. Normally where the rent-payer's title is registered in the register of leaseholders the rent-owner's (or a superior owner's) title will be registered in the register of freeholders. But this may not be the case, e.g. where the leaseholder's title was registered under section 15 of the Small Dwellings Acquisition Act 1899 (c. 44).

The Registrar will act under section 36(1)(f) of the Land Registration Act. The paragraph gives the Registrar power to make any consequential alterations in a register which he thinks proper. Thus, where under sub-paragraph (b) a rent-payer's title in the register of leaseholders is superseded by registration in the register of freeholders, if the rent-owner's title is registered (either in the register of freeholders or the register of leaseholders) the Registrar will cancel that entry (and similarly with superior titles).

The paragraph does not deal with the case where the rent-owner's (or a superior owner's) title was registered in the register of freeholders but the rent-payer's leasehold title is not registered in the register of leaseholders (but is simply registered as a burden under the Land Registration Act, Schedule 6, Part I, paragraph 6). As to this, see paragraph 1.3.20 of the report.

*Paragraph (7)* applies where the rent-payers of flats (or other developments) have combined to redeem their ground rents with a view to promoting a commonhold declaration. As well as the various certificates of redemption vesting fees simple in the rent-payers in respect of their respective units, the certificates have the combined effect of vesting a fee simple in the common parts in all the rent-payers. Articles 19 and 21 of the Property Order (which prevent the creation of legal tenancies in common and restrict to four the number of joint owners who can be trustees for tenants in common) do not apply. This vesting will not take place where the common parts are already vested in the rent-payers as tenants in common or in a company of which they (and only they) are members; but it will apply where those parts are vested in the developer, provided he agrees – cf. Article 6(5)(b)(ii). This paragraph does not apply where the making of a development scheme is envisaged, because where the developer was the owner of common parts before redemption there is no reason why they should not remain vested in him. A development scheme would in no way worsen his situation.

*Paragraph (8)* makes a certificate of redemption, in the case of unregistered land, a conveyance for the purposes of the Registration of Deeds Act and so subject to registration if the rent-payer's new estate is to have proper priority over interests subsequently created. The expression "the Registration of Deeds Acts" is defined in section 46(2) of the Interpretation Act (as substituted by section 21(2) of the Registration of Deeds Act (Northern Ireland) 1970).

*Paragraph (9)* applies section 6 of the Conveyancing Act 1881 in order to give the fee simple estate which has replaced a former leasehold estate all the ". . .privileges, easements, rights and advantages whatsoever appertaining or reputed to appertain to the land . . . or enjoyed with . . . the land" – i.e. an easement or profit created in favour of the rent-owner or a superior owner will continue so as to benefit the fee simple in the hands of the former rent-payer, if and so far as it is capable of doing so. After the coming into operation of Article 95 of the Property Order (which is in similar terms), that Article will apply instead of section 6.

*Paragraph (10)* requires a mortgagee to whom a certificate of redemption has been sent by the Registrar under Article 15(3)(a) or by the mortgagor under Article 23(2) to have it registered in the Registry of Deeds or the Land Registry (as the case requires) if it has not already been registered there. The Registrar may have sealed a certificate in respect of either unregistered land or registered land. He will not be concerned with registering the former in the Registry of Deeds – that is a matter for the parties. He may register the latter in the appropriate Land Registry register immediately after sealing the certificate if the proper fee has been paid in advance. If the fee has not already been paid, he will have to send the certificate to the rent-payer or his mortgagee with a request that it be submitted for registration accompanied by the fee.

### Disposal of redemption money lodged with the Registrar: claims thereto

**20.**—(1) Redemption money lodged with the Registrar under Article 13 shall be transferred to the Exchequer.

(2) When the Registrar is satisfied in accordance with rules that any person is entitled to payment of money so lodged, he shall certify accordingly: a person aggrieved by a refusal of the Registrar so to certify may appeal to the Lands Tribunal, and, if the Tribunal is satisfied that the appellant is entitled to payment of such money, it may order accordingly.

(3) Rules made for the purposes of paragraph (2) may define circumstances in which the Registrar may be satisfied as mentioned in that paragraph.

(4) On receipt of a certificate of the Registrar, or an order of the Lands Tribunal, under paragraph (2), the Department of Finance and Personnel ("the Department") shall issue out of the Consolidated Fund such sums as are necessary to provide for the payment so certified or ordered, and shall make such payment.

(5) Where the Department pays any moneys to any person in pursuance of a certificate or order under paragraph (2), the Department shall pay to him interest upon those moneys from the date of their transfer to the Exchequer under paragraph(1) until the time of the payment of the moneys and interest to the person entitled thereto and shall issue out of the Consolidated Fund such sums as are necessary to provide for that interest.

(6) The rate of interest payable under paragraph (5) shall be such rate as may be determined by the Department.

# EXPLANATORY NOTE

## ARTICLE 20

This Article is concerned with the handling of redemption money lodged with the Registrar under Article 13 and the payments to be made to persons claiming an interest in that money. As to paragraphs (4) to (6), see section 43 of the Mineral Development Act (Northern Ireland) 1969 (c. 35).

*Paragraph (1)* requires redemption money lodged with the Registrar to be paid into the Exchequer of Northern Ireland (Interpretation Act, s. 43(2)).

*Paragraph (2)* empowers the Registrar to give a certificate if he is satisfied that a claim to money so lodged is valid: if he refuses a certificate, the claimant may appeal to the Lands Tribunal, which may make an order to the effect that the claim is valid.

*Paragraph (3)* empowers Land Registry Rules to define circumstances in which the Registrar may be satisfied about a claim (e.g. if time has been given for other possible claimants to the same money – say, superior owners or mortgagees – to come in, and they have not done so, rules may allow them to be ignored). The general power to make rules (in Article 38(4)) is also relevant and would allow, e.g., the form and manner of making claims to be prescribed.

*Paragraph (4)* On the Registrar's certificate, or the Lands Tribunal's order, the amount payable to the claimant is to be issued out of the Consolidated Fund of Northern Ireland.

*Paragraph (5)* provides for interest on money issued under paragraph (4).

*Paragraph (6)* allows the rate of interest to be fixed.

## Register of redemption moneys

**21.**—(1) The Registrar shall keep in the prescribed form –

(a) a register of redemption moneys which have been lodged with him under Article 13, and

(b) such indexes to the register as may be prescribed.

(2)   Section 81 of the Land Registration Act (searches) applies for the purposes of this Order as if –

(a) "register" included the register kept under paragraph (1) and "the land" included the land in relation to which redemption money has been lodged with the Registrar and that money;

(b) subsections (3) and (4) were omitted.

# EXPLANATORY NOTE

## ARTICLE 21

This Article requires the Registrar to keep a register of redemption moneys lodged with him, and an index or indexes.

*Paragraph (1)* requires the register and indexes to be kept in the form prescribed by Land Registry Rules. Indexing might first be done under the names of rent-payers who make lodgments. If such rent-payers are required to state the names of their rent-owners, any superior owners and any incumbrancers (so far as known to them – see Article 13(2)(d)), there could be further index entries and where a number of rents form a pyramid, the shape of the pyramid could gradually emerge and facilitate other claims. Indexing by reference to addresses would also obviously be helpful in the future.

*Paragraph (2)* provides for searches in the register.

## Continuance of rights and equities affecting leasehold estate

**22.**—(1)  The fee simple estate which by virtue of Article 19(2) vests in a rent-payer who previously had held a leasehold estate is for all purposes (except as provided in Article 24(1)) a graft on the leasehold estate and is subject to any rights or equities arising from its being such a graft.

(2)  Any provision of a will in respect of such a leasehold estate operates instead on the fee simple.

# EXPLANATORY NOTE

## ARTICLE 22

This Article applies where the redemption of the ground rent to which a leasehold estate was subject has enlarged that estate into a fee simple.

*Paragraph (1)* ensures that all rights and equities that affected the former leasehold estate are preserved against the new fee simple estate. The paragraph follows the precedents of section 14(3) of the Land Law (Ireland) Act 1887 and section 3(2) of the Leasehold (Enlargement and Extension) Act (Northern Ireland) 1971. The paragraph operates by making the new fee simple estate a graft upon the former leasehold estate. The effect of this is that a right or equity is as clearly established as if the rent-payer by deed had declared that he held the land under the same trusts and to and for the same purposes as the previous leasehold estate had been held for: cf. *per* O'Connor MR, *Re White and Hague's Contract* [1921] 1 IR 138 at 143. By virtue of Article 19(5), the paragraph applies not only to the land primarily subject to the redemption procedure but also to any other parcel or parcels of land which are concurrently freed from ground rent.

*Paragraph (2)* makes testamentary dispositions of the estate created by the lease operate on the fee simple.

For corresponding provisions in connection with the conversion of perpetually renewable leases, see paragraphs 2(1) and 3(1) of Schedule 3.

**Mortgages and leases**

**23.**—(1) Where by virtue of Article 19 a certificate of redemption operates to vest an estate in fee simple in land in a rent-payer who previously had held a leasehold estate in the land, –

(a) any mortgage of the leasehold estate continues to have effect as if it were, and had originally been created as, a mortgage of the fee simple, and, in particular, –

    (i) where the instrument creating the mortgage was an assignment of the leasehold estate, it has effect (so far as permitted by law) as if it were a conveyance of the fee simple;

    (ii) where the instrument creating the mortgage was a sub-lease, it has effect (so far as permitted by law) as if it were a lease for a term equivalent to the term of the sub-lease;

(b) any sub-lease of the land (which did not create a ground rent) has effect as if it were a lease for a term equivalent to the term of the sub-lease, and any mortgage of the estate created by such a sub-lease has effect as if it were a mortgage of the estate created by such a lease.

(2) Where the land is subject to a mortgage by the terms of which the mortgagee is entitled to possession of the documents relating to the mortgagor's title to the land, there is deemed to be included in the instrument or agreement containing the terms of the mortgage a covenant binding the mortgagor to deliver the certificate of redemption to the mortgagee as soon as reasonably practicable after the redemption date, if the certificate has not been sent to the mortgagee by the Registrar under Article 15(3)(a).

(3) This Article does not prejudice the generality of Article 22.

# EXPLANATORY NOTE

## ARTICLE 23

This Article expands on Article 22 in relation to mortgages (defined by Article 2(2) as including charges) and leases (defined by Article 2(2) as including sub-leases). Article 22 continues a mortgage or sub-lease of the leasehold estate against the new fee simple: this Article explains how that happens.

*Paragraph (1)* provides that where, on the redemption of a ground rent, a leasehold estate is enlarged into a fee simple, –

*sub-paragraph (a)* any mortgage of the leasehold estate continues as a mortgage of the fee simple and –

*head (i):* a mortgage by assignment of the leasehold estate is to be treated as a mortgage by conveyance of the fee simple, and

*head (ii):* a mortgage by sub-lease is to be treated as one by lease for a term equal to that of the sub-lease. As "lease" is defined by Article 2(2) as including a sub-lease, a mortgage by sub-sub-lease (if such occurs) will be converted into a mortgage by sub-lease. A corresponding provision in relation to perpetually renewable leases is contained in paragraph 2(2) of Schedule 3. See also Article 31(3). The words "(so far as permitted by law)" refer to Article 114 of the Property Order, which abolishes mortgages by assignment or demise. This may or may not come into operation with this Article.

*sub-paragraph (b)* any sub-lease granted out of the rent-payer's leasehold estate is elevated into a lease carved out of his newly-acquired fee simple. (The sub-paragraph does not need to operate on sub-sub-leases, because they continue to be leasehold estates carved out of superior leasehold estates). A sub-lease to which this provision applies will be one not granted at a ground rent. If it had been so granted, the sub-lessee would be the rent-payer for the purposes of the Order.

*Paragraph (2)* imports into the mortgage deed or other agreement (e.g. in the case of an equitable mortgage by deposit of title deeds, the oral agreement or memorandum of deposit) a term requiring the mortgagor to deliver the certificate of redemption to the mortgagee. This applies only where the mortgagee is entitled to possession of the title deeds and not, e.g., to a second mortgage (where the mortgagee will normally not be so entitled).

*Paragraph (3)* is a saving for Article 22.

**Covenants**

**24.**—(1) Except as provided by this Article –

(a) upon the completion or sealing of a certificate of redemption, where the land is unregistered land, or

(b) upon the making of any relevant alteration, cancellation or entry in a register (in accordance with Article 19(6)), where the land is registered land,

all covenants concerning the land by virtue of the rent-payer's fee farm grant or lease, or any superior fee farm grant or lease, or any collateral instrument, cease to have effect.

(2) Covenants of the following kinds continue to benefit or, as the case may be, burden the land, that is to say, –

(a) covenants for title, including –

(i) a covenant that a former vendor had a good right to convey, or lease, the whole property and interest he had agreed to sell,

(ii) covenants for quiet enjoyment, freedom from incumbrances and further assurance,

(iii) covenants by a former assignor of a lease that the lease was valid and in full force and that the rent had been paid and the covenants in the lease duly performed;

(b) the covenant to give a receipt which is imported by Article 15(1);

(c) subject to paragraph 4 of Schedule 1, covenants for indemnities;

(d) a covenant categorizing boundary fences as party fences;

(e) the following covenants in connection with works, namely, –

(i) a covenant to do works on, or to permit works to be done on, access to be had to, or any activity to be pursued on, the land for the benefit of other land,

(ii) a covenant to pay for, or contribute towards the cost of, works done on other land where the works benefit the land;

(f) covenants for the protection of amenities, including –

(i) a covenant (however expressed) not to use any building on the land otherwise than for the purposes of a private dwelling (but not, without prejudice to any other head of this sub-paragraph, any other covenant restricting the user of such a building),

(ii) covenants against causing nuisance, annoyance, damage or inconvenience to neighbours,

(iii) covenants against interfering with facilities which benefit neighbours,

(iv) a covenant against building works on land intended by the fee farm grant or lease to be used solely as amenity land;

(g) any covenants which were reciprocally enforceable between the rent-payer and his neighbours immediately before the redemption of the ground rent by virtue of a building scheme.

(3)   After the event mentioned in sub-paragraph (a) or (b) (whichever is applicable) of paragraph (1) (whether that event occurs in relation to both parties or only one party), a covenant to which paragraph (2)(d) applies has effect as a covenant by each party to contribute one-half of the cost of repairing or renewing a fence categorized as a party fence.

(4)   Where an agreement to make a development scheme or to promote a commonhold is entered into as mentioned in Article 6(5)(b)(ii), paragraph (2)(g) has effect subject to the terms of the development scheme or commonhold declaration.

(5)   Where a covenant to which paragraph (2) applies is framed in terms of a condition or limitation, it has effect following the redemption of the ground rent as though it were framed as a covenant (in the strict sense).

(6)  Where the circumstances are such that Article 18 applies, references in this Article to the land and the rent-payer include references to the other parcel or parcels and the person, or the respective persons, in whom that other parcel is or those other parcels are vested.

# EXPLANATORY NOTE

## ARTICLE 24

This Article identifies the covenants that survive the redemption of a ground rent; all covenants concerning the land, except those so identified, cease to have effect. "Covenant" is defined in Article 2(2) as including a promise in writing which is not a deed, an agreement to make a covenant, a proviso, a declaration, a condition and, in some cases, a limitation.

*Paragraph (1)* lays down the basic rule that redemption results in the disappearance of all the covenants in the fee farm grant or lease which concern the land. This rule is subject to the exceptions in paragraph (2).

*Paragraph (2)* lists covenants which enure.

*sub-paragraph (a):* Covenants for title. These include covenants by a person who made a conveyance of a fee simple (in the case of a fee farm rent) or granted a lease that he had a right to do so; covenants for quiet enjoyment; and a covenant by the assignor of a lease that the lease was in force, the rent paid and the covenants observed. Although covenants for title given on a conveyance of a fee simple have the status of personal covenants so far as the covenantor is concerned, this is not so with corresponding covenants in a lease. The effect of the Article and Article 25 is that covenants for title expressed or implied on the grant of a lease are put in much the same position as covenants on a conveyance of a fee simple, i.e., they are enforceable by the covenantee and his successors in title but only against the covenantor or the person who was successor to the covenantor immediately before the rent-payer became vested with a fee simple (Article 25(1)).

*sub-paragraph (b):* The covenant to give a receipt for the redemption money (or the first instalment of it) which is imported into the lease or fee farm grant by Article 15(1).

*sub-paragraph (c):* Indemnities, e.g. against being charged with the cost of street or other works.

*sub-paragraph (d):* A covenant (in practice, a declaration – but see the definition of "covenant" in Article 2(2)) designating a fence as a party fence. Paragraph (3) explains the future effect of such a covenant.

*sub-paragraph (e):* Covenants about works. These may be to do works, or allow them to be done, on the land for the benefit of other land, or to pay for works on other land which benefit the land (e.g. road or sewerage works or repairs to a sea wall). Where these are contained in a lease or a fee farm grant under Deasy's Act, they burden or benefit (in accordance with their nature) successive landlords and tenants: in the case of a fee farm grant not under Deasy's Act, the benefit of the covenants runs with the title to the dominant land but their burden does not run with the title to the servient land, although a covenant to pay for, or contribute to the cost of works may be enforceable under the rule in *Halsall v. Brizell* [1957] Ch. 169, not as a covenant, but on the ground that a person cannot

1124

take the benefit of a deed without undertaking its obligations. The Article and Article 25 continue this position.

*sub-paragraph (f):* Covenants for the protection of amenities. The main examples are –

(*i*) A covenant to use a house only as a private dwelling. Other restrictions on user are not preserved under this head, but may come under some other head (e.g. breach of a covenant not to use the land to keep animals may equally be a breach of the covenant against causing a nuisance).

(*ii*) Covenants against causing nuisance, annoyance, damage or inconvenience to neighbours.

(*iii*) Covenants against interfering with facilities which benefit a neighbour. Where B's water pipes, sewers or electricity cables run under A's land, B will normally have an easement which is protected by Article 22. If A has expressly covenanted not to interfere with those facilities, the covenant will be continued by this provision.

(*iv*) A covenant against building on land shown by the terms of the deed to be intended to be kept undeveloped, e.g., land granted by a supplementary lease as an extension to a garden.

*sub-paragraph (g):* Covenants which were formerly mutually enforceable between the rent-payer and his neighbours by reason of forming part of a building scheme (defined in Article 2(2) as a scheme under which land is divided into two or more parcels subject to obligations which are reciprocally enforceable between both or all the owners of the parcels). Most of these will already have been covered in the preceding provisions: this sub-paragraph preserves the former position in exceptional cases. This sub-paragraph can apply only to building schemes involving no common parts. Where there are common parts (as in the case of blocks of flats or private streets) Article 6(5) requires a new-style development scheme to be made, or a commonhold to be promoted, if ground rents are to be redeemed. Any existing building scheme is likely to be one implied by equity because of the reciprocity of obligations. It might relate to freehold or leasehold land (a "letting scheme"); but so far as leaseholds are concerned the law is obscure and a letting scheme is most likely to be found only in relation to flats.

*Paragraph (3)* states the future effect of party fence declarations (which are within the definition of "covenant" in Article 2(2)), where the ground rent payable by either one or both of the neighbours is redeemed. They are converted into positive covenants by each party to pay half the cost of repairing or replacing the fence. These covenants bind successors in title by virtue of Article 25(3).

*Paragraph (4)* is concerned with the future effect of the building scheme covenants preserved by paragraph (2)(g): these are subject to any formal development scheme or commonhold declaration made by all the former rent-payers conjointly. Where the land encompassed by a building scheme includes common parts, no participant in the scheme can redeem his ground rent unless all the other participants joint with him in doing so (Article 6(5)): where there are no common parts, ground rents can be redeemed piecemeal and the existing building scheme covenants will apply indefinitely.

*Paragraph (5)* makes certain covenants (in the sense defined in Article 2(2)) which were framed as conditions or limitations have effect for the future as if they were covenants in the ordinary sense. The concept of a condition or a limitation as such will no longer be relevant to the relation between the former rent-owner and the former rent-payer.

*Paragraph (6)* modifies the Article to meet the situation where a number of parcels of land are subject to a single ground rent and the redemption of the rent by one parcel-owner has the effect, under Article 18, of freeing all the parcels from it (cf. Article 19(5)).

By the Consequential Provisions Order, covenants burdening the land which are continued by this Article are added to the list of burdens affecting registered land without registration which is contained in Schedule 5 to the Land Registration Act. That list already contains (as item 6) "In the case of a registered leasehold estate, all express and implied covenants, conditions and liabilities incident to the lease under which the estate is held".

Provisions of this Article are applied with modifications by paragraphs 1(e) and 2(d) of Schedule 1 where land subject to a ground rent is divided on sale.

**Enforcement of covenants**

**25.**—(1)  A covenant to which Article 24(2)(a) or (b) applies is enforceable by the covenantee and his successors in title but only against the person against whom the covenant was enforceable immediately before the event mentioned in sub-paragraph (a) or (b) of Article 24(1).

(2)  A covenant to which Article 24(2)(c) applies is enforceable by the covenantee and his successors in title against the covenantor and his successors in title.

(3)  A covenant to which Article 24(2)(d) and (3) apply is enforceable by each party and his successors in title against the other party and his successors in title.

(4)  Subject to paragraph (5), a covenant to which Article 24(2)(e) or (f) applies is enforceable by or against the same person as it would have been enforceable by or against had the ground rent not been redeemed (and for this purpose a person taking a conveyance of the estate in fee simple which is vested in a rent-payer following redemption of the ground rent payable under a lease is in the same position as an assignee of the lease would have been in had there been no redemption).

(5)  For the purposes of the enforcement of the covenants for the protection of amenities to which Article 24(2)(f) applies, after the first operation of Article 24 in respect of a parcel of any land there is to be taken to subsist (if it does not subsist apart from this provision) a building scheme in respect of the land in which all the occupiers holding parcels under dispositions in substantially similar terms from the same rent-owner are participants, and accordingly –

(a)  not only do those covenants continue to be enforceable by and against the rent-owner and his successors so long as he or they continue as such in relation to any participant, but

(b)  the covenants are also enforceable by and against each of the various participants among themselves, whether or not their ground rents have been redeemed.

(6)  For the purposes of paragraph (5) –

(a)  a rent-owner and his predecessors and successors in title are to be taken to be the same rent-owner;

(b)  a mortgagee in possession of land which is or is taken to be subject to a building scheme is to be taken to be a participant in the building scheme.

(7)  A covenant to which Article 24(2)(g) applies continues to be enforceable by each participant in the building scheme against every other participant and by and against their respective successors in title.

# EXPLANATORY NOTE

## ARTICLE 25

This Article indicates by or against whom the covenants continued by paragraph (2) of Article 24 may be enforced.

*Paragraph (1)* applies to the covenants for title preserved by Article 24(2)(a) and the covenant to give a receipt for the redemption money preserved by Article 24(2)(b). These are enforceable by the covenantee and his successors in title but only against the covenantor personally.

*Paragraph (2)* is concerned with covenants for indemnities (e.g. indemnifying someone from having to pay road-making expenses or a ground rent). These are enforceable both by and against successors in title.

*Paragraph (3)* is concerned with the covenant by each party to pay one-half of the cost of repairing or replacing a party fence which is substituted by Article 24(3) for a party fence declaration. It, too, is enforceable both by and against the parties' successors.

*Paragraph (4)* makes positive covenants and amenity covenants enforceable by or against the same persons as if the ground rent had not been redeemed. This is subject to paragraph (5), which in one direction extends and in another limits the class of persons who may enforce, or against whom may be enforced, covenants for the protection of amenities. The paragraph explains what is meant by the "same person" as a covenant would have been enforceable by or against if there had been no redemption. If there had been no redemption, an alienee of a lessee rent-payer's estate would have been an assignee of the lease; following redemption, an alienee will be a transferee of the fee simple. For the purposes of the paragraph these are the same person.

*Paragraph (5)* deems a building scheme (defined in Article 2(2)) to exist (if one does not already exist) for the purpose of enabling amenity covenants to be enforced between neighbours. Amenity covenants include (Article 24(2)(f)) restrictions on the use of houses otherwise than as private dwellings, promises not to cause nuisance, annoyance, damage or inconvenience to neighbours, and restrictions on building on amenity land. Neighbours are those holding their land from the same rent-owner on substantially similar terms. The paragraph does not expressly require the premises to be adjacent or adjoining, because in practice the covenants usually would be irrelevant unless this were so. The covenants also continue to be enforceable by or against the rent-owner and his successors so long as he or they continue as such. This is concerned only with those cases in which the rent-owner remains rent-owner (in the strict sense) of some other parcel because the ground rent on that parcel has not yet been redeemed. In practice few amenity covenants would, because of their nature, be enforceable against the rent-owner: but he may have covenanted to keep land in his own possession undeveloped as amenity land. In relation to participants in the deemed building scheme, enforcement *inter se* is irrespective of whether or not any particular ground rent has been redeemed. So a rent-payer may enforce, say, a covenant against

1128

nuisance, not only against a participant who has also redeemed his ground rent but also against one who has not.

*Paragraph (6)* qualifies paragraph (5) in two ways –

*sub-paragraph (a)* occupiers hold under the same rent-owner if they hold under any of a series of rent-owners with the same title (as where a development begun by A is continued by B and completed by C);

*sub-paragraph (b)* a mortgagee in possession is, for the purposes of enforcing a covenant, a participant in a deemed building scheme.

*Paragraph (7)* is concerned with covenants reciprocally enforceable by neighbours under a building scheme (but not a building scheme involving "common parts" as with flats or private streets). If any such scheme exists, the covenants will continue to be enforceable between the participants in the scheme (for the time being) among themselves. Where a building scheme involves common parts (as defined by Article 6(6)) there can be no redemption of ground rents unless they are all redeemed together and a development scheme or commonhold is formed (Article 6(5)).

*The redemption of certain other periodic payments*

**Application of certain provisions of Order to certain other periodic payments**

26.—(1) In this Article "periodic payment" means –

(a) any annual or periodic sum payable to the Department of Agriculture on account of the Church Temporalities Fund;

(b) a quit rent;

(c) a tithe rentcharge;

(d) any other rentcharge except a rentcharge created by or under a settlement, by way of indemnity, under a statutory provision or by, or in accordance with the requirements of, any order of a court.

(2)   The following provisions of this Order (and no others) apply to a periodic payment so far as they are applicable, namely Articles 2, 4, 7 to 16, 19, 20, 21, 23(2), 33 to 38 and 40 and paragraphs 1 and 2 of Schedule 2, as if the periodic payment were a ground rent and with any necessary consequential modifications.

# EXPLANATORY NOTE

## ARTICLE 26

This Article applies the Order to periodic payments which are not ground rents.

*Paragraph (1)* defines the periodic payments to which the Article applies. They are –

    (*a*) payments to the Church Temporalities Fund;

    (*b*) quit rents;

    (*c*) tithe rentcharges;

    (*d*) other rentcharges, except settlement rentcharges or those created by way of indemnity or under a statutory provision or court order (c.f. Article 30(3)(b), (d), (e), (f): an annuity to be enjoyed with an exclusive right of residence in or on the whole of any land (Article 30(3)(c)), if it is charged on the land, is, in effect, a settlement rentcharge because the right must be made the subject of a settlement (Property Order, Article 33(1))).

"Rentcharge" is defined in Article 2(2).

*Paragraph (2)* lists the provisions of the Order which apply to periodic payments. They are –

Article  2 – Definitions
Article  4 – Voluntary redemption
Article  7 – Initiation of redemption procedure
Article  8 – Procedure where all other interests concur: the counter-notice
Article  9 – Correction of counter-notice following dispute about money payable or security
Article 10 – Correction of counter-notice where money cannot be paid in accordance with it
Article 11 – Termination of redemption procedure
Article 12 – Exclusion of re-possession of land while redemption is pending
Article 13 – Procedure where a redemption notice cannot be served, all other interests do not concur or payment cannot be made in accordance with counter-notice
Article 14 – The redemption money
Article 15 – Certificate of redemption
Article 16 – Effect of certificate of redemption
Article 19 – Effect of redemption on titles
Article 20 – Disposal of redemption money lodged with the Registrar: claims thereto
Article 21 – Register of redemption moneys
Article 23(2) – Delivery of certificate of redemption to mortgagee
Article 33 – Avoidance of certain agreements and powers
Article 34 – Settled land
Article 35 – Service of documents

*Prohibition of transactions giving rise to ground rents, etc., and conversion of certain existing leases*

## Perpetually renewable leases

**27.**—(1) This Article applies to –

(a) a lease for a life or lives renewable for ever;

(b) a lease for a life or lives with any concurrent or reversionary term of years, renewable for ever;

(c) a lease for a term of years renewable for ever.

(2) On and after the first appointed day, a lease to which this Article applies is incapable of being created at law or in equity.

(3) Any instrument made on or after the first appointed day which contains a purported grant of a lease to which this Article applies of any land is void; any agreement made on or after that day to make such an instrument is also void; and any agreement to assign, or any purported assignment, of such a lease made on or after that day has effect as an agreement to convey, or a conveyance of, a fee simple.

(4) Subject to paragraph (5), where immediately before the first appointed day any lease to which this Article applies was subsisting and would have continued to subsist apart from the provisions of this Article and Schedule 3, the estate created by the lease is, on that day, converted by virtue of this paragraph into an estate in fee simple subject to a fee farm rent.

(5) Where a lease coming within paragraph (4) was subject to one or more than one sub-lease (other than a sub-lease by way of mortgage) which also (by virtue of the definition of "lease" in Article 2(2)) comes within that paragraph, the reference in that paragraph to the estate created by the lease is, to the extent of the land which is the subject of the sub-lease, to be construed as a reference to the estate created by the sub-lease (or the more or most subordinate sub-lease, if more than one).

(6) For the purposes of paragraphs (4) and (5), Schedule 3 contains provisions subject to which the estate in fee simple is held and provides for the amount of the fee farm rent; and the other provisions of that Schedule also have effect.

(7) Where immediately before the first appointed day an agreement to grant a lease to which this Article applies was subsisting, the agreement continues to have the effect provided for in section 37 of the Renewable Leasehold Conversion Act 1849 (that is to say, it is deemed to be an agreement for a conveyance of the land concerned at a fee farm rent).

(8) A mere covenant for renewal on the same terms in any lease is not to be taken to require the inclusion of another covenant for renewal in the renewed lease, unless the contrary intention is expressed or implied in the original lease.

(9) For the purposes of this Article a lease is subsisting so long as the rent provided for by it is being paid, notwithstanding that the lease has

fallen due for renewal but has not been renewed or that a fine payable on renewal has not been paid; and for this purpose rent is being paid if no rent is in arrear.

# EXPLANATORY NOTE

ARTICLE 27

This Article provides for the conversion into fee farm grants of leases for lives renewable for ever (whether or not with any concurrent or reversionary term of years) or leases for years renewable for ever.

*Paragraph (1)* defines the leases to which the Article applies. They are leases for lives, for terms of years or for a combination of lives and terms of years which (in any case) are renewable for ever.

*Paragraph (2)* re-affirms the principle that a lease to which the Article applies is incapable of being created either at law or in equity. In fact, it has not been possible to create such leases since the coming into force of the Renewable Leasehold Conversion Act 1849 (save for leases granted under pre-Act agreements), but the paragraph forms a foundation for paragraph (3).

*Paragraph (3)* renders any future attempt to create such a lease void. It overrides the Act of 1849 which would have converted purported leases into fee farm grants. Any future attempt to assign an existing lease is to be treated as an agreement to convey or a conveyance (as the case requires) of the fee simple into which the tenant's estate is converted by paragraph (4).

*Paragraph (4)* converts existing leases to which the Article applies into fee farm grants: the tenant's estate, in consequence, becomes a fee simple. "Fee farm rent" is defined in Article 2(2).

*Paragraph (5)* Where there is a lease, and one or more sub-leases, to which the Article applies, the conversion provided for in paragraph (4) operates on the sub-lease (or the most junior sub-lease) and the sub-lessee becomes a fee simple owner. Superior sub-leases (if any) and the head lease become, in effect, superior fee farm grants giving rise to fee farm rents (Schedule 3, paragraph 1(3)). Sub-leases which are not perpetually renewable are dealt with in Schedule 3, paragraph 4.

*Paragraph (6)* activates Schedule 3 for the purpose of settling the provisions of the fee farm grant into which the lease is converted.

*Paragraph (7)* operates upon an existing agreement to grant a lease to which the Article applies. If the agreement was made before the first appointed day it is enforceable as an agreement to make a fee farm grant. Any provision of the agreement for the payment of fines or fees on renewal will be void -the effect of section 37 of the Renewable Leasehold Conversion Act 1849 is continued. If such an agreement is made on or after the first appointed day it is rendered void by paragraph (3). In practice, no such agreement should have been made since 1849, but the paragraph provides for the extremely remote possibility.

*Paragraph (8)* answers the question: Does a covenant for renewal on the same terms contained in a lease make the lease a perpetually renewable one on the ground that the renewed lease will also contain a covenant for renewal, and so *ad infinitum*? – The answer is "No". At common law, when a covenant by a lessor conferred a right to renewal of the lease, the new grant to contain the same or the like covenants and provisos as were contained in the lease, the courts refused to give literal effect to that language; the reference to the same covenants was construed as not including the option covenant itself. This limited the tenant's right to one renewal. The option to renew was to be contained in the second and subsequent leases only if there were clear words showing that this was intended: e.g. "(including this covenant)": *Caerphilly Concrete Products Ltd.* v. *Owen* [1972] 1 WLR 372. The paragraph gives statutory effect to this rule.

*Paragraph (9)* applies to leases which are subsisting in the sense that rent is being paid under them, even though the leases have, strictly, terminated because the need to renew them on a past renewal date has been overlooked (and so no renewal fine has been paid). As such leases are regarded by both parties as still subsisting (even though through a mistake of fact or law), they are treated as subsisting leases for the purposes of this Article.

**Leases for lives, etc.**

**28.**—(1)  This Article applies to a lease at a rent or in consideration of a fine –

(a)  for a life or lives; or

(b)  for a life or lives with a concurrent term of any period; or

(c)  for a life or lives with a reversionary term of any period; or

(d)  for a term of any period determinable with a life or lives or on the marriage of a specified person (including the lessee) or on the happening of any other event.

(2)  On and after the first appointed day, a lease to which this Article applies is incapable of being created at law or in equity.

(3)  Any agreement made on or after the first appointed day to grant a lease to which this Article applies is void; any instrument made on or after that day which purports to grant such a lease, is void; and any agreement to assign, or any purported assignment, of such a lease made on or after that day has effect as an agreement to assign, or an assignment, of the lease into which the lease which is the subject of the agreement or purported assignment was converted by paragraph (4) and Schedule 4.

(4)  Where immediately before the first appointed day any lease to which this Article applies, or any agreement to grant such a lease, was subsisting and would have continued to subsist apart from the provisions of this Article and Schedule 4, the lease or agreement has effect on and after that day in accordance with the provisions of Schedule 4.

# EXPLANATORY NOTE

## ARTICLE 28

This Article prohibits, for the future, leases which are limited to expire on a death or some other contingency and converts existing leases into terms of fixed periods subject to special provisions for their earlier determination by notice.

*Paragraph (1)* sets out the kinds of lease to which the Article applies. These are –

(*a*) a lease for a life or lives, which may be those of the tenant or tenants or of some third parties;

(*b*) a lease for a life or lives with a concurrent term of a stated period – the lease will last at least for that period and, if a relevant life survives that period, until that life (or the last survivor, if more than one) falls;

(*c*) a lease for a life or lives with a reversionary term – the lease will last for the life, or the longer or longest of the lives, plus the stated term;

(*d*) a lease for a stated term determinable with a life or lives or on a specified marriage or on the happening of some other event – the lease will terminate on the happening of the contemplated event during its term, but will otherwise run its full course and then expire. Where the event contemplated is marriage, it must be marriage to a particular person: a limitation which could become operative on marriage to anyone at all would be void as contrary to public policy.

The paragraph applies to a lease only if it is at a rent or subject to payment of a fine. A gratuitous lease (taking effect under a settlement) is not affected.

*Paragraph (2)* declares a lease to which the Article applies to be incapable of being created at law or in equity.

*Paragraph (3)* renders void future agreements for the creation of such leases or future purported grants of such leases (i.e. agreements or purported grants made on or after the first appointed day), and makes future assignments of such leases operate on the leases substituted by paragraph (4) and Schedule 4.

*Paragraph (4)* applies to existing leases or agreements for leases (i.e. those in force immediately before the first appointed day). Leases are converted in accordance with Schedule 4, and an agreement for a lease has effect in accordance with that Schedule. The general effect of the Schedule is to substitute for the uncertain period provided for in the lease or agreement a fixed period, with the lease (or a lease entered into in consequence of the agreement) made terminable by notice on the occurrence of an event which would otherwise have terminated the lease *ipso facto*.

**Fee farm grants**

**29.**—(1) Subject to paragraph (3), on and after the second appointed ⸱ day a fee farm grant is incapable of being made at law or in equity.

(2) In relation to any land, any agreement made on or after the second appointed day to make a fee farm grant, or any instrument made on or after that day which purports to make a fee farm grant the making of which is prohibited by this Article, operates as, respectively, an agreement to convey or a conveyance of a fee simple in the land subject to any fine specified in the agreement or instrument but free from the fee farm rent so specified and any covenants or other provisions which (directly or indirectly) relate to the rent or are for the benefit of the intended rent-owner as such.

(3) This Article does not prohibit the making of a fee farm grant in pursuance of an agreement made before the second appointed day, nor does it prejudice Article 27.

# EXPLANATORY NOTE

## ARTICLE 29

This Article and the two following come into operation on the second appointed day.

The Article prohibits the future creation of fee farm rents by prohibiting (subject to a transitional exception) future fee farm grants.

*Paragraph (1)* prevents a fee farm grant from being made at law or in equity.

*Paragraph (2)* operates upon future agreements to make fee farm grants or future purported fee farm grants. For an agreement there is substituted an agreement to convey a fee simple in the land. A purported fee farm grant has effect as a simple conveyance of a fee simple. Any fine agreed upon must be paid, but any provision for a fee farm rent or for the protection of such a rent is ignored.

*Paragraph (3)* allows a fee farm grant to be made on or after the second appointed day in pursuance of an agreement made before that day. Paragraph (2) does not affect such an agreement because it applies only to "a fee farm grant the making of which is prohibited by this Article". Paragraph (3) also contains a saving for Article 27, paragraph (7) of which allows a fee farm grant to be made after the first appointed day in substituted performance of an agreement made before that day to grant a perpetually renewable lease. If implementation of the agreement were delayed, it is possible that the fee farm grant would not come to be made until the second appointed day or after.

**Rentcharges**

**30.**—(1) Subject to paragraph (3), on and after the second appointed day a rentcharge is incapable of being created at law or in equity.

(2) Any agreement made on or after the second appointed day, and any instrument made on or after that day, is void to the extent that it provides for the creation of, or purports to create, a rentcharge the creation of which is prohibited by this Article.

(3) This Article does not prohibit the creation of a rentcharge –

(a) in pursuance of an agreement made before the second appointed day;

(b) as an annuity under a settlement;

(c) as an annuity to be enjoyed with an exclusive right of residence in or on the whole of any land;

(d) which is payable under an agreement of indemnity to the owner of a legal estate in land contingently upon his being made to pay the whole or part of a rent in respect of all or part of that land or in respect of a larger area of land of which that land forms or formed part;

(e) under any statutory provision;

(f) by, or in accordance with the requirements of, any order of a court.

# EXPLANATORY NOTE

## ARTICLE 30

This Article prohibits the future creation of rentcharges, subject to certain exceptions. "Rentcharge" is defined in Article 2(2).

*Paragraph (1)* prohibits the creation of rentcharges, either at law or in equity.

*Paragraph (2)* severs any instrument made after the second appointed day which purports to create a prohibited rentcharge: the principal disposition (if any) made by the instrument is valid, but the rentcharge is void. The paragraph similarly operates upon future agreements to create rentcharges.

*Paragraph (3)* allows the future creation of –

*sub-paragraph (a)* rentcharges already agreed to be created

*sub-paragraphs (b) and (c)* rentcharges under settlements or joined with exclusive rights of residence in the whole of any land

*sub-paragraph (d)* indemnity rentcharges

*sub-paragraph (e)* statutory rentcharges – e.g. under the Public Health (Ireland) Act 1878 ss. 244, 245

*sub-paragraph (f)* rentcharges created by court order – e.g. a court order formalising a family arrangement – or in accordance with a court order – e.g. by an instrument settled by conveyancing counsel to the court on the court's instructions.

## Long leases

**31.**—(1) Without prejudice to Article 27(1)(c) and (2) or Article 28(4), and subject to paragraph (5), on and after the second appointed day a lease for a term of more than 50 years ("a long lease") is incapable of being created at law or in equity.

(2)  In relation to any land, any agreement made on or after the second appointed day to grant a long lease the creation of which is prohibited by this Article, and any instrument made on or after that day which purports to grant such a lease, has effect (in either case) as an agreement binding the prospective or purported lessor –

(a)  to acquire a fee simple absolute in possession in the land (if he does not already own such a fee) at no expense to the intended lessee (that is to say, the person designated in the agreement or instrument as the prospective or purported lessee), and

(b)  to convey that fee to the intended lessee at no expense to the intended lessee and without any consideration (save any fine specified in the agreement or instrument).

(3)  Where the leasehold estate purported to be created by an instrument such as is mentioned in paragraph (2) is subject to a mortgage, the mortgage binds the fee simple, when conveyed, as if it had been created in relation to the fee simple, and, in particular, –

(a)  where the instrument creating the mortgage purported to be an assignment of the leasehold estate, it has effect (so far as permitted by law) as if it were a conveyance of the fee simple;

(b)  where the instrument creating the mortgage purported to be a sub-lease, it has effect (so far as permitted by law) as if it were a lease by way of mortgage for a term equivalent to the term of the sub-lease;

and the purported lessor's duty to acquire and convey the fee simple is enforceable by the mortgagee, whether he is in possession or not, as though the mortgagee were a party to the agreement second-mentioned in paragraph (2) (and, accordingly, that paragraph applies as if references in it to the intended lessee, except the first reference in sub-paragraph (b), included the mortgagee).

(4)  For the purposes of this Article a lease is for a term exceeding a given period if (although expressed to be for a term of or less than that period) it is, by virtue of any provision of the lease or of a collateral agreement, capable of being extended or renewed for any period or periods which, taken with the original term, in the aggregate exceed the given period (ignoring any part of the term falling before the date of the grant of the lease).

(5)  This Article does not prohibit –

(a)  the grant of a long lease in pursuance of an agreement made before the second appointed day;

(b)  the grant of a concurrent lease;

1143

(c) the grant of a long lease by way of mortgage (so far as permitted by law);

(d) the grant of an equity-sharing lease;

(e) the grant of a long lease of a flat or house contained in a development where other flats or houses in the same development are the subject of –

(i) long leases granted before the second appointed day, or

(ii) agreements to which sub-paragraph (a) applies, or

(iii) long leases to which this paragraph applies, or

(iv) other tenancies (except a tenancy granted by the rent-payer of a unit of occupation);

(f) the grant of a long lease following the exercise of an option to have such a lease, where the option was contained in a lease granted before the second appointed day.

(6) In paragraphs (2) and (3) references to the prospective lessor or the purported lessor and to the intended lessee include their respective successors in title; and in paragraph (5)(e) "development", "flat", "house" and "unit of occupation" have the same meanings as in Article 6(6).

# EXPLANATORY NOTE

## ARTICLE 31

This Article prohibits the future creation of long leases. A "long lease" is a lease for more than 50 years.

*Paragraph (1)* provides that no long lease may be created either at law (by a written lease) or in equity (e.g. by entry following an agreement for a lease) after the Article comes into force. This prohibition is subject to the exceptions in paragraph(5). The prohibition does not need to extend to perpetually renewable leases, because they are already provided for by Article 27. There is also an exception where there was a pre-first appointed day agreement for a lease to which Article 28 applies.

*Paragraph (2)* states the effect of a long lease purported to be made despite the prohibition in paragraph (1). The purported lease is to operate as a contract binding the purported lessor to acquire the fee simple (if he has not already got it) and convey it to the intended lessee or (if he has died) his personal representatives or (if he has disposed of his interest in the land) his assignee (paragraph (6)). The acquisition of the fee simple must be effected without expense to the intended lessee, and the conveyance of the fee simple must also be without such expense and without payment of any consideration by the intended lessee save the amount of any fine specified in the invalid lease. The expenses in question will not necessarily all be borne by the purported lessor – if the lease is a sub-lease, the lessor may have recourse under the paragraph against the head landlord (as to the cost of acquiring the fee simple). An agreement for a prohibited lease has a similar effect.

*Paragraph (3)* applies where a lease granted in contravention of the prohibition in paragraph (1) has been mortgaged. When the fee simple has been conveyed to the purported lessee, the mortgage will automatically have effect as a mortgage of the fee simple. In the meantime, the duty of the purported lessor to acquire (if necessary) and convey the fee simple will be enforceable by the mortgagee as well as by the lessee. If the mortgage was created before the commencement of Article 114 of the Property Order, it will have effect as assignment or lease by way of mortgage. If created thereafter it will have effect as a charge of the fee simple by way of legal mortgage.

*Paragraph (4)* makes it clear that a lease is to be treated as one for a term of more than 50 years if, although expressed to be for a shorter period it is subject to a provision for renewal which would bring it beyond the specified figure. But where a lease is granted with retrospective effect any part of the term falling before the date of the lease is to be ignored for this purpose.

*Paragraph (5)* sets out exceptions to the prohibition on future long leases. These are –

    (a) a lease granted under an agreement made before the second appointed day;

(*b*) a concurrent lease (i.e. a lease of the reversion on another lease);

(*c*) a mortgage granted in the form of a long lease before the commencement of Article 114 of the Property Order;

(*d*) an equity-sharing lease – this is a lease under which the lessee must make a part payment and pay rent, and may make further part payments and exercise an option to purchase: such a lease may be granted by the Northern Ireland Housing Executive under Article 31 of the Housing (Northern Ireland) Order 1981 (N.I. 3) or (to a secure tenant claiming to exercise the right to buy) under Article 29 of the Housing (Northern Ireland) Order 1986 (N.I. 13), or it may be granted by a housing association;

(*e*) the grant of a long lease of a flat or house in an existing leasehold development consisting of flats or houses together with (in either case) common parts (cf. Article 6(5), (6)). The Housing Executive may have granted previous long leases of flats for a term of 125 years or more (Housing (N.I.) Order 1983, Article 17(1)(b)) and may continue to grant such leases in the same block in the future; or it may grant a first long lease in a block where the other tenants continue to have periodic tenancies ("other tenancies"). Where the first periodic tenant to exercise his right to buy did so on or after the second appointed day and all the other tenants similarly exercised their rights from time to time, the last tenant to do so would come under head (iii), the other long leases in the block not coming under any of heads (i), (ii) or (iv). The exception also applies to private developments which were begun on a leasehold basis before the second appointed day: any development begun on or after that day would have to be on a freehold basis by means of a development scheme under the Property Order or a commonhold;

(*f*) the grant of a reversionary long lease (i.e. a lease immediately following on an expiring existing lease) so long as the grant follows the exercise by the lessee of an option in the expiring lease (but not an option for perpetual renewal, which is caught by Article 27).

The Article does not affect the extension of a lease under the Leasehold (Enlargement and Extension) Act (Northern Ireland) 1971, because such an extension can be made on one occasion only for a term of not more than 50 years and is made under a statutory provision (and not a provision of a lease or a collateral agreement such as is mentioned in paragraph (4)).

*Paragraph (6)* defines "prospective lessor", "purported lessor" and "intended lessee" for the purposes of paragraphs (2) and (3) as including their successors in title (see the note on paragraph (2)); and the paragraph also attracts the definitions in Article 6(6) of "flat", "house", "development" and "unit of occupation" for the purposes of paragraph(5)(e).

*Miscellaneous*

## Avoidance of certain rent review provisions

**32.**—(1) Subject to paragraphs (4) and (5), this Article applies to any of the following instruments executed after 1 August 1983, that is to say, –

(a) a fee farm grant;

(b) a lease of a dwelling-house originally granted for a term of more than 50 years;

(c) a lease of land, other than a dwelling-house, originally granted for a term of more than 125 years;

(d) an agreement collateral to any instrument mentioned in sub-paragraph (a), (b) or (c).

(2) Subject to paragraphs (4) and (5), this Article also applies to an instrument which is –

(a) a lease of land, other than a dwelling-house, originally granted on or after the first appointed day for a term of more than 50 years;

(b) an agreement collateral to such a lease.

(3) Any provision of an instrument to which this Article applies for the review of a ground rent on one or more than one occasion is of no effect.

(4) Nothing in this Article affects section 18(3) of the Act of 1971, which allows the rent fixed on the extension of a lease under that Act to be made subject to revision.

(5) This Article does not apply to a building lease or to a fee farm grant for purposes corresponding to those of a building lease merely because provision is made for increases in the ground rent which are related to periods or events in the progress of building or related activities.

# EXPLANATORY NOTE

## ARTICLE 32

This Article renders ineffective certain provisions for the increase of ground rents contained in instruments executed after 1 August 1983 (the date of publication of the Land Law Working Group's Interim Report on Ground Rents and other Periodic Payments). Paragraph (1) implements the recommendations in paragraphs 4.19 and 4.22(8) of the Interim Report. Paragraph (2) brings the Article into accord with paragraph 1.5.24 of the final Report, which recommends that the maximum term of a non-residential lease (as well as of a residential lease) should be 50 years. Because of the effect of Articles 29 and 31 this Article applies to (1) instruments falling within paragraph (1) which were executed between 1 August 1985 and the first appointed day, and (2) instruments falling within paragraph (1) or (2) which (i) were executed on or after the first appointed day and before the second appointed day or (ii) were executed on or after the second appointed day in pursuance of Article 29(3) or 31(5).

*Paragraph (1)* lists the instruments to which the Article applies. They are any of the following executed after 1 August 1983, namely, –

    (*a*)  a fee farm grant (including a sub-grant: Article 2(2));

    (*b*)  a lease (including a sub-lease: Article 2(2)) of a dwelling-house for a term exceeding 50 years;

    (*c*)  a lease of land, other than a dwelling-house, for a term exceeding 125 years;

    (*d*)  an agreement collateral to any instrument mentioned under (a) to (c).

*Paragraph (2)* extends the list in paragraph (1) to include a lease of land, other than a dwelling-house, granted on or after the first appointed day for a term exceeding 50 years.

*Paragraph (3)* contains the substantive provision of the Article – any provision for ground rent review in an instrument to which the Article applies is of no effect.

*Paragraph (4)* is a saving for section 18(3) of the Leasehold (Enlargement and Extension) Act (Northern Ireland) 1971 which allows the rent fixed on an extension of a lease under that Act to be made subject to revision on the expiration of 25 years after the date on which the old lease would have expired (i.e. on one occasion only, because the maximum extension of the old lease is 50 years).

*Paragraph (5)* makes an exception for rents under building leases and corresponding fee farm rents where the ground rent is geared to increase as development of the land progresses.

**Avoidance of certain agreements and powers**

**33.**—(1) So much of any agreement as provides that any provision of this Order shall not apply in relation to a person or that the application of any such provision shall be varied, modified or restricted in any way in relation to a person is void.

(2) So much of any agreement as requires a rent-payer to bear in any way (whether by reimbursement or otherwise) costs incurred or liable to be incurred by a rent-owner or superior owner in connection with the operation of this Order is void.

(3) Where immediately before the first appointed day a power to create a lease to which Article 27 or 28 applies was in existence, that power ceases to have effect on that day save to the extent necessary to give effect to an agreement in accordance with Article 27(7) or Article 28(4).

(4) Where immediately before the second appointed day a power either to make a fee farm grant the making of which is prohibited by Article 29 or to create a rentcharge or a long lease the creation of which is prohibited by Article 30 or 31 was in existence, that power ceases to have effect on that day save to the extent necessary to give effect to an agreement in accordance with Article 29(3), Article 30(3) or Article 31(5), as the case may be.

(5) Any power is void to the extent that –

(a) where it is purported to be conferred on or after the first appointed day, it purports to empower the creation of a lease to which Article 27 or 28 applies; or

(b) where it is purported to be conferred on or after the second appointed day, it purports to empower the making of a fee farm grant the making of which is prohibited by Article 29 or to empower the creation of a rentcharge or a long lease the creation of which is prohibited by Article 30 or 31 respectively.

# EXPLANATORY NOTE

## ARTICLE 33

This Article makes void certain agreements which would deprive a rent-payer of the full benefit of the Order. It also restricts or makes void powers conferred by settlements to enter into transactions restricted or prohibited by the Order.

*Paragraph (1)* prevents the parties to a lease or fee farm grant from contracting out of the Order. The paragraph applies to "any agreement", (whether contained in a lease or a fee farm grant or contained in a collateral agreement or made in any other way).

*Paragraph (2)* prevents a rent-owner from requiring a rent-payer to bear any costs incurred by the rent-owner in connection with or in consequence of the redemption of a ground rent. The word "costs" is defined in section 46(2) of the Interpretation Act as including fees, charges, disbursements, expenses or remuneration.

*Paragraph (3)* restricts an existing power to create a perpetually renewable lease or a lease for lives so as to limit the exercise of the power to the creation of such a lease on or after the first appointed day in pursuance of an agreement made before that day.

*Paragraph (4)* restricts an existing power to make a fee farm grant or create a rentcharge or long lease so as to limit the power to transactions not prohibited by Article 29, 30 or 31 respectively.

*Paragraph (5)* renders void the future conferring of a power to enter into a transaction prohibited by Articles 27 to 31.

**Settled land**

**34.**—(1) Capital money of a settlement, and any personal estate held on the same trusts as the settled land, may be applied in payment of redemption money or of any costs incurred under this Order.

(2) Redemption money receivable is capital money for the purposes of a settlement.

(3) The payment of redemption money is included among the purposes for which a tenant for life or the trustees of a settlement may raise money.

# EXPLANATORY NOTE

## ARTICLE 34

This Article contains provisions about settled land, that is, where a rent-payer's interest, or the rent-owner's (or a superior owner's) interest, is held on the trusts of a settlement.

*Paragraph (1)* enables capital money to be applied in payment of redemption money or costs.

*Paragraph (2)* treats redemption money receivable as capital money.

*Paragraph (3)* empowers a tenant for life or trustees to raise money by mortgage of the settled land in order to pay redemption money.

Other provisions about settled land, in connection with the conversion of perpetually renewable leases, are contained in Schedule 3, paragraph 9.

**Service of documents**

35.—(1) Any document permitted or required by this Order to be served on a rent-owner or lessor is duly served on him if it is served –

(a) on any person who acts as agent for the rent-owner or lessor in respect of the land in question; or

(b) on the person who last demanded or received ground rent or rent for the land.

(2) Any document permitted or required by this Order to be served on a rent-owner may, where joint tenants or tenants in common are the rent-owners of any ground rent, be served on any one of them in respect of that rent, and such service is deemed to be service on both or all of them.

(3) Where the estate of a rent-owner is subject to a mortgage and either the mortgagee is in possession or a receiver is in receipt of the rents and profits, any document required or permitted by this Order to be served on the rent-owner may, instead, be served on the mortgagee or the receiver, as the case may be.

# EXPLANATORY NOTE

## ARTICLE 35

This Article contains provisions about the service of documents.

*Paragraph (1)* permits a document which is to be served on a rent-owner (Article 7) or a lessor (Schedule 3, paragraph 7(2)(b); Schedule 4, paragraph 2) to be served on

*sub-paragraph (a)* his agent in respect of the land, or

*sub-paragraph (b)* the person who last demanded or received ground rent, or rent, for the land.

*Paragraph (2)* applies where co-owners (whether joint tenants or tenants in common) are the rent-owners of a ground rent. Any document permitted or required by the Order to be served on the rent-owner may be served on any one of them. For example, where trustees are the legal owners of a ground rent, a notice is sufficiently served if it is served on any one trustee.

*Paragraph (3)* allows a document required or permitted (Articles 7(1), 11(1)) to be served on a rent-owner to be served, instead, on a mortgagee in possession of the rent-owner's interest or a receiver appointed by a mortgagee.

General provisions about the service of documents are contained in section 24 of the Interpretation Act.

**Offences**

**36.**—(1) A person who, in any document served or lodged under this Order –

(a) makes a statement which he knows to be false; or

(b) recklessly makes a statement which is false,

is guilty of an offence and is liable on summary conviction to a fine not exceeding level 4 on the standard scale.

(2) For the purposes of paragraph (1) a statement is made recklessly if it is made regardless of whether it is true or false, whether or not the person making it had reasons for believing that it might be false; and in that paragraph and this paragraph "false" means false to a material degree.

# EXPLANATORY NOTE

## ARTICLE 36

This Article penalises false statements, e.g., in a counter-notice under Article 8 or in documents or particulars lodged with the Registrar under Article 13 or in a claim made to the Registrar for payment of a sum representing redemption money (Article 20(2)).

*Paragraph (1)* makes it an offence for a person, in a document, to make a statement he knows to be false or recklessly to make a statement which is false. The maximum fine on summary conviction is that fixed for level 4 on the standard scale of fines in Article 5 of the Fines and Penalties (Northern Ireland) Order 1984 (at present £1,000 – Criminal Penalties etc. (Increase) Order (Northern Ireland) 1984, SR1984 No. 253). The expression "standard scale" is defined in section 42(4) of the Interpretation Act (as amended by paragraph 2 of Schedule 6 to the Order of 1984). A redemption notice or counter-notice is "served" (Articles 7, 8); documents under Article 13 are "lodged".

*Paragraph (2)* explains what is meant by "recklessly". Under the civil law of fraud a statement is made recklessly if it is made "careless of whether it be true or false" *(Derry v. Peek* (1889) 14 App. Cas. 337). There is some conflict of authority as to whether the same definition applies in criminal law, or whether carelessness alone is insufficient and there must be an element of dishonesty. The paragraph makes it clear that the word "recklessly" is to be given its ordinary meaning. The paragraph follows section 14(2)(b) of the Trade Descriptions Act 1968. The paragraph also makes it clear that a false statement is relevant only if it is material.

The Article does not make it an offence for a person to issue a purported copy of a counter-notice (Article 13(2)(b) or a certificate of redemption (Article 18(1)) which is not a true copy. It is expected that rules will require a person issuing such a copy to certify it as a true copy. Any inaccuracy in the copy will then fall within Article 10 of the Perjury (Northern Ireland) Order 1977 (NI 19) which makes it an indictable offence for a person knowingly and wilfully to make a statement false in a material particular . . . (b) in [a] . . . certificate . . . or other document which he is authorised or required to make, attest or verify by any enactment.

## Civil remedy for misstatement

**37.** Where in consequence of any misstatement made in any document served or lodged under this Order a person has suffered loss, the person who made the misstatement is liable to damages in respect of the misstatement notwithstanding that the misstatement was not made fraudulently, unless he proves that he had reasonable ground to believe and did believe up to the time of payment of the redemption money or other sum in question that the facts represented were true.

# EXPLANATORY NOTE

## ARTICLE 37

This Article provides a civil remedy in damages for a person who suffers loss because of a misstatement in a document. For example, a counter-notice may have incorrectly stated that there was no person superior to the rent-owner who was entitled to a rent out of the land, and, in consequence, the protection which would have been provided for a superior owner by the lodgment of redemption money with the Registrar of Titles may have been lost. It is not necessary for the misstatement to have been made fraudulently, but it is a defence for the defendant to show that, up to the time when the redemption money or other sum (e.g. a sum paid by the Department of Finance and Personnel in discharge of a claim to redemption money) was paid, he had reasonable ground to believe, and did believe, that the facts represented were true. This means that, where the person signing a counter-notice discovers, after the notice has been served, that the notice contains a misstatement, he must tell the rent-payer at once. A redemption notice or a counter-notice is "served" (Articles 7, 8); documents under Article 13 are "lodged".

The Article is based on section 2(1) of the Misrepresentation Act (Northern Ireland) 1967 (c. 14).

A prosecution under Article 36 does not prejudice proceedings for damages under this Article (Interpretation Act, section 20(4)).

## Application of provisions of the Land Registration Act

**38.**—(1) Section 3 of the Land Registration Act (indemnity of Registrar, officers or persons acting in good faith pursuant to any authority conferred by or under that Act) applies for the purposes of this Order as if references in it to that Act included references to this Order.

(2) Sections 70 and 71 of, and Schedule 9 to, the Land Registration Act (the Insurance Fund; claims for compensation) apply for the purposes of this Order as if-

(a) the references in section 70(1), (2) and (4) to that Act included references to this Order, and

(b) the reasons for loss listed in paragraph 1(1) of Schedule 9 included an error in a sealed certificate of redemption or in a copy of such a certificate delivered by the Registrar and the payment of a sum on a certificate given by the Registrar otherwise than in accordance with rules made under Article 20(3).

(3) An order under subsection (1) of section 84 of the Land Registration Act may prescribe the fees to be taken in the Land Registry for the purposes of this Order as well as for the purposes of that Act, and accordingly any reference in that section to that Act includes a reference to this Order.

(4) Land Registry Rules under subsection (3) of section 85 of the Land Registration Act may be made for giving effect to this Order as well as for giving effect to that Act, and accordingly in the introductory words of that subsection, and in paragraphs (a), (k) and (n) of that subsection, references to that Act include references to this Order.

(5) Any express provision of this Order relating to rules does not prejudice the generality of paragraph (4) and the said section 85(3).

(6) For the purposes of this Order, the reference in section 85(3)(k) of the Land Registration Act to documents to be given includes documents to be served or lodged.

(7) Rules may make such provisions (including modifications of this Order) as are necessary or expedient to give effect to the purposes of this Order in cases falling within Article 7(4) or (5); and any rules making such modifications of this Order are subject to affirmative resolution (and not to negative resolution as provided by subsection (4) of section 85 of the Land Registration Act for rules made under subsection (3)).

(8) Rules may require the authentication in a prescribed manner of a copy of a document, where the copy is permitted or required by this Order to be lodged or delivered.

# EXPLANATORY NOTE

## ARTICLE 38

This Article applies and modifies provisions of the Land Registration Act for the purposes of the Order (see also Article 16(3)).

*Paragraph (1)* gives to the Registrar and officials of the Land Registry acting in good faith for the purposes of the Order the same indemnity from personal liability as he and they have when acting for purposes of the Land Registration Act.

*Paragraph (2)* attracts the provisions of that Act relating to the Insurance Fund. A claim can be made against that Fund for loss suffered because of an error in a certificate of redemption sealed by the Registrar or in a copy of such a certificate delivered by the Registrar, or because of a wrongful transfer of a sum representing ground rent which has been made on a certificate given by the Registrar (not being a certificate given in reliance of rules which, e.g., allow a possible claimant to be ignored if he does not come in after notice).

*Paragraph (3)* makes provision for the fees to be taken in the Land Registry in connection with any function performed by the Registrar for the purposes of this Order – in particular, for the preparation and delivery of a certificate of redemption under Article 15(3) or of a copy of a certificate (cf. Article 18), and in connection with the preparation, under Article 20, of a certificate of entitlement to money lodged with the Registrar under Article 13. The Article attracts and adapts section 84(1) of the Land Registration Act which (as modified by the Departments (Northern Ireland) Order 1982 (NI 6) Arts. 5(b) & 9 and Sch. 1 Pt. II & Sch. 2) empowers the Department of the Environment by an order made after consultation with the Land Registry Rules Committee, with the approval of the Department of Finance and Personnel and subject to affirmative resolution of the Assembly (negative resolution of either House of Parliament during direct rule) to prescribe the fees to be taken in the Land Registry. The fees must be fixed at such amounts as to cover all expenses payable under, and incidental to, the working of the Order.

*Paragraph (4)* extends the power, conferred by section 85 of the Land Registration Act, to make rules regulating proceedings in the Land Registry to include proceedings under the Order. Subsection (3) of section 85 (as modified by the Northern Ireland Constitution Act 1973 Sch. 5 para. 7(1) and, during direct rule, by the Northern Ireland Act 1974 Sch. 1 para. 2(1)(b), and as further modified by the Departments (Northern Ireland) Order 1982 Art. 5(b) and Sch. 1 Pt. II) empowers the Department of the Environment, with the advice and assistance of the Land Registry Rules Committee, to make rules providing for the practice and procedure to be followed in the Land Registry and generally for giving effect to the Act of 1970. The paragraph adapts references in section 85(3) to the Act of 1970 so as to include references to the Order. In particular, rules may prescribe anything which, under the Order (e.g. Article 13(2)(d)) is to be prescribed (section 85(3)(a)), may fix the form and contents of documents required or authorised to be used or given under or for the purposes of the Order (section 85(3)(k)) and may require security for the costs of any appeal under the Order (e.g. under Article 9(3)) (section 85(3)(n)).

*Paragraph (5)* makes it clear that any express provision in the Order about rules (e.g. Article 20(2) or (3) or paragraph (7) or (8) of this Article) does not (by seeming to suggest an inference that subsection (3) of section 85 may have a narrow scope) prejudice the generality of that subsection as adapted by paragraph (4).

*Paragraph (6)* reconciles the language of the Order about the service or lodging of documents with the language of section 85(3).

*Paragraph (7)* makes subject to affirmative resolution (negative resolution at Westminster during direct rule) any rules which make modifications in the Order for the purposes of paragraph (4) or (5) of Article 7 (various ground rents payable to a single rent-owner or various lands subject to a single ground rent). See the note on Article 7(5).

*Paragraph (8)* enables rules to prescribe how copies of documents are to be authenticated (e.g. for the purposes of Articles 13(2)(a) or (b) and 18(1)).

**Jurisdiction of Lands Tribunal**

**39.**—(1) Any question arising as to the matters mentioned in paragraph (2) may be referred to and determined by the Lands Tribunal.

(2)   The matters referred to in paragraph (1) are –

(a)   the apportionment of a superior rent under Article 17;

(b)   what part of redemption money or costs is appropriate for the purposes of Article 18(3) and whether any costs were reasonable and properly incurred;

(c)   what abatement is appropriate for the purposes of sub-paragraph (3) of paragraph 3 of Schedule 2 and what instalments and intervals are appropriate for the purposes of sub-paragraph (4) of that paragraph;

(d)   the date on which a fine is to be taken to be payable (as mentioned in paragraph 7(2)(c) of Schedule 3);

(e)   the amount of, and any other matter affecting, the additional rent payable under paragraph 7 of Schedule 3.

(3)   In determining any dispute affecting the additional rent payable under paragraph 7 of Schedule 3, the Lands Tribunal may depart from the provisions of heads (a) to (g) of paragraph 7(2) to such extent as appears to it expedient in the circumstances of the case for the purpose of resolving the issue in a fair and convenient manner.

(4)   In determining any dispute as to the amount of the instalments of such additional rent, the Lands Tribunal may take into account the loss of any right to refuse renewal of a lease which the former lessor (within the meaning of Schedule 3) would have had if this Order had not been made.

# EXPLANATORY NOTE

## ARTICLE 39

This Article lists provisions of the Order for the purposes of which the Lands Tribunal has jurisdiction to determine disputes. In addition, the Tribunal has an appellate jurisdiction under Article 20(2).

*Paragraph (1)* provides that any question arising as mentioned in paragraph (2) may be referred to, and determined by, the Lands Tribunal.

*Paragraph (2)* sets out the heads of jurisdiction. They are –

*sub-paragraph (a)* The apportionment of a superior rent under Article 17(1) and (2) where the land formerly subject to a redeemed ground rent is only part of the land subject to a superior rent.

*sub-paragraph (b)* The determination of what part of redemption money and costs paid by a rent-payer is to be paid to him by an indemnifior or another plot-holder.

*sub-paragraph (c)* The determination of what abatement is to be made in the redemption money for a ground rent payable by a developer to take account of an agreement for a reduction of ground rent before or during the period of development (Schedule 2 paragraph 3(3)); or, where the redemption money is payable by instalments, the amounts or frequency of instalments (Schedule 2, paragraph 3(3)(4)).

*sub-paragraph (d)* Where an adjustment of rent under a perpetually renewable lease is to be made to take account of future fines of uncertain date, the fixing of the date on which a fine is to be taken to be payable (Schedule 3, paragraph 7(2)(c)).

*sub-paragraph (e)* The fixing of the additional rent payable under paragraph 7 of Schedule 3.

*Paragraph (3)* empowers the Lands Tribunal to depart from the detailed rules in paragraph 7(2)(a) to (g) of Schedule 3 if the Tribunal thinks that, on the facts of the particular case, some other approach would give a fair result which can be applied more conveniently.

*Paragraph (4)* provides that, in fixing additional rent under paragraph 7 of Schedule 3, the Tribunal may take account of the former lessor's loss of any right he may have had to refuse renewal of the lease. This is broader than paragraph 7(2)(g) (increase of additional rent as compensation for loss of right to forfeit the lease should the lessee not renew in time). The expression "the former lessor" is defined in Schedule 3, paragraph 10.

## Application to the Crown

**40.**   This Order binds the Crown.

# EXPLANATORY NOTE

## ARTICLE 40

This Article provides for the application of the Order to the Crown. Northern Ireland legislation does not bind the Crown unless it is named (Interpretation Act, section 7). The Crown may be involved as rent-owner or rent-payer, or as the owner of a quit rent (Article 26(1)(b)). See also Article 26(1)(a).

**Cesser of Act of 1971 as to enlargement of leases to which this Order applies**

**41.**  On or after the first appointed day no notice of intention to acquire a fee simple shall be served under section 2 of the Act of 1971 in respect of any land subject to a ground rent to which Article 4 applies.

...LANATORY NOTE

...he initiation of the enlargement procedure
...rgement and Extension) Act (Northern Ire-
...st appointed day (see Article 1(2)) in any case
...cf. Article 6). On or after that day, new
... the ground rent payable out of a leasehold
...ate into a fee simple must be begun under the
...ars or more of its term left to run. If there are
...n, the lessee may still enlarge his lease under
...hat he comes within section 1(2)(a) and (3) of
...eady started under the Act of 1971 are not
...lder withdraws the notice that initiated those
...otice of discontinuance under section 7 of the
Act of 1971 (see Article 6(4) of the Order), he may begin proceedings
afresh under the Order, if he is not debarred by Article 6 from doing so.

The Article does not affect the initiation or continuance of proceedings
under the Act of 1971 for the extension of a lease. Nor does the Article
affect the power of a lessor and lessee to come to a voluntary agreement
for the redemption of a ground rent, if they prefer to proceed in that
manner rather than under the Order.

## Repeal

**42.** Without prejudice to Article 27(7) (saving for section 37), the Renewable Leasehold Conversion Act 1849 is hereby repealed.

# EXPLANATORY NOTE

ARTICLE 42

The Renewable Leasehold Conversion Act 1849 empowered the owner of a lease of land in perpetuity to require the owner of the reversion to grant the land to him in fee simple subject to a perpetual yearly fee farm rent. A number of grants under the Act (fee farm conversion grants) have been made. But the Act was permissive and did not affect the continuance of perpetually renewable leases where the lessees did not call for the execution of grants. Any such leases which have survived to the present day are, in effect, converted into fee farm grants by Article 27, with effect from the first appointed day. On and after that day no fee farm conversion grant can be made, so the provisions of the Act of 1849 – save one – can have no effect. The excepted provision is section 37, which is kept in force to a limited extent by Article 27(7). Section 37 provided that purported perpetually renewable leases made after 31 July 1849 were to have effect as fee farm grants, and contracts for such leases were to have effect as contracts for fee farm grants. Article 27(7) continues this so far as it relates to a contract made before the first appointed day for the grant of a perpetually renewable lease. On and after that day the contract is continued to be treated as one for the making of a fee farm grant. A contract made on or after the first appointed day is void (Article 27(3)).

# SCHEDULES

## SCHEDULE 1

Articles 5
17(5),
24(2)(c).

### EFFECT OF CHARGING OR APPORTIONMENT OF GROUND RENT ON CONVEYANCE OF PART OF LAND

*Ground rent deemed to be charged exclusively on land conveyed*

1. Where, under Article 5(7), on a conveyance of part of land any ground rent to which the land was theretofore subject is deemed to be charged exclusively on the land conveyed, –

  (a) the ground rent is extinguished with respect to the land retained;

  (b) any superior rent to which (with or without other land) the land, or any part of the land greater than, and including, the land conveyed, was theretofore subject is deemed to be charged on the land conveyed to the extent mentioned in sub-paragraph (c) and is extinguished with respect to the land retained;

  (c) the extent to which a superior rent is deemed to be charged on the land conveyed is –

    (i) where the superior rent was charged only on all or part of the land conveyed and the land retained (taken together), the whole of it is deemed to be charged on the land conveyed;

    (ii) where the superior rent was charged on all or part of the land conveyed and the land retained (taken together) together with other land, it is apportionable (by reference to the respective areas of the lands concerned) between the land conveyed and the land retained (taken together) on the one hand and the other land on the other hand, and the part apportioned to the land conveyed and the land retained is deemed to be charged on the land conveyed;

  (d) accordingly, the land retained is discharged from the ground rent and any superior rent and, subject to sub-paragraph (e), from all covenants contained (expressly or by reference) in the instrument which created the ground rent or any superior rent, or any collateral instrument;

  (e) paragraphs (2), (3) and (5) of Article 24 (continuance of certain covenants) apply to the land retained as if the ground rent extinguished with respect to that land had been redeemed (and a certificate of redemption completed or sealed) under this Order and those covenants are enforceable in accordance with Article 25;

  (f) the conveyance and the ground rent are subject to Article 5(1) to (6) and (9) to (11).

*Ground rent agreed to be charged exclusively on land retained or other land*

2. Where, under Article 5(7)(a), there is an agreement that a ground rent be charged exclusively on the land retained or other land, then, subject to the terms of the agreement, –

(a) the ground rent is extinguished with respect to the land conveyed;

(b) any superior rent is charged exclusively on the land retained or the other land (or on the land retained or the other land together with any additional land which is already subject to it) and is extinguished with respect to the land conveyed;

(c) accordingly, the land conveyed is discharged from the ground rent and any superior rent and, subject to sub-paragraph (d), it is also discharged from all covenants contained (expressly or by reference) in the instrument which created the ground rent or any superior rent or any collateral instrument;

(d) paragraphs (2), (3) and (5) of Article 24 (continuance of certain covenants) apply to the land conveyed as if the ground rent extinguished with respect to that land had been redeemed (and a certificate of redemption completed or sealed) under this Order and those covenants are enforceable in accordance with Article 25;

(e) the ground rent is charged exclusively on the land retained or the other land, and consequently the conveyance and the ground rent are not subject to Article 5(1) to (6) and (9) to (11).

*Ground rent agreed to be apportioned between land conveyed and land retained*

3. Where, under Article 5(7)(b), there is an agreement that a ground rent be apportioned between the land conveyed and the land retained, the apportionment has effect and –

(a) the land retained is subject only to payment of the portion of the ground rent apportioned in respect of it by the agreement and payment of the portion of any superior rent apportioned in respect of it under Article 17, and to the performance and observance of the covenants contained (expressly or by reference) in the instrument which created the ground rent and the superior rent respectively or any collateral instrument so far as those covenants are applicable to that portion;

(b) the conveyance and the portion of the ground rent apportioned in respect of the land conveyed are subject to Article 5(1) to (6) and (9) to (11), and the portion of any superior rent apportioned in respect of that land is subject to Article 17(1).

*Indemnity agreements*

4. Where, immediately before the second appointed day, the owner of part only of land subject to a ground rent was entitled to the benefit of an agreement of indemnity for payment of the whole or part of the ground rent, whereby that whole or part was charged on land retained by the person liable for payment under the indemnity or on other land, then, on a conveyance on or after that day of all or part of that part of the land, –

(a) in the case of an indemnity for payment of the whole of the ground rent, the ground rent is deemed to be charged exclusively on the land retained by that person or the other land, and paragraph 2 applies as if an agreement to charge under Article 5(7)(a) had been made;

(b)   in the case of an indemnity for payment of part of the ground rent, paragraph 3 applies to the portions of the ground rent fixed by the indemnity agreement as if it were an agreement made under Article 5(7)(b);

but this paragraph does not prevent the persons mentioned in Article 5(7) from making a new agreement under Article 5(7)(a) or (b) to replace the indemnity agreement.

# EXPLANATORY NOTE

This Schedule applies where there is a division of land. It explains the effect of a ground rent's being deemed to be charged exclusively on the land conveyed (Article 5(7)), or of an agreement to charge the ground rent exclusively on the land retained or other land or to apportion it. The Schedule also contains provisions about indemnity agreements.

*Paragraph 1* sets out the consequences of the deeming provision in Article 5(7) which (in the absence of agreement to the contrary) treats the whole of the ground rent charged on land which becomes divided on a sale as payable out of the part of the land that is sold

*sub-paragraph (a)* The ground rent is extinguished as to the land retained.

*sub-paragraph (b), (c)(i)* Superior rents are treated in the same way as the ground rent, i.e. they are deemed to be charged on the land conveyed and are extinguished as to the land retained.

*sub-paragraph (c)(ii)* Where a superior rent is charged on other land together with the land divided on sale, it will be apportioned between the two and the part apportioned to the latter will be deemed to be charged on the land conveyed and extinguished as to the land retained.

*sub-paragraph (d)* The consequence of the preceding provisions is that the land retained is discharged from the ground rent and any superior rent; it is also discharged from all covenants (except those continued by sub-paragraph (e)) which were contained in the instrument which created the ground rent or a superior rent or in any collateral instrument. Cf. Article 19(4).

*sub-paragraph (e)* applies Article 24(2) to the land retained, so that (as an exception to sub-paragraph (d)) covenants for title, works, indemnities or amenities, and building scheme covenants, continue to apply to the land retained and are enforceable under Article 25.

*sub-paragraph (f)* The whole of the ground rent being now loaded on the land conveyed, the land is now subject to Article 5(1) as regards that whole, i.e. the ground rent must be redeemed before the conveyance is completed.

The deeming provision which this paragraph amplifies will have effect where, in the absence of an effective counter-notice, the redemption money is lodged with the Registrar under Article 13. Where there is an effective counter-notice, the rent-owner and superior owners will have joined in agreeing how the redemption money is to be paid, and this would give an opportunity for agreeing, say, an apportionment of ground rent or superior rents, were that desired.

*Paragraph 2* states the consequences of an agreement that the ground rent be charged on the land retained or other land. Such an agreement may be convenient where the area of the land conveyed is small in proportion to the area of the entire land (as where a narrow strip of land is sold for the widening of a driveway).

1173

*sub-paragraph (a)* The ground rent is extinguished as to the land conveyed.

*sub-paragraph (b)* Superior rents (except where they are the subject of special agreements with the superior owners) are treated as charged on the land retained or the other land (or where a particular superior rent was charged on a wider area of land, as charged on the land retained or the other land together with, in either case, so much of that wider area as is left after subtraction of the land conveyed).

*sub-paragraph (c)* The land conveyed is thereupon discharged from the ground rent, the superior rents and all associated covenants (except those continued by sub-paragraph (d)).

*sub-paragraph (d)* applies Article 24(2) to the land conveyed. Covenants for title, works, indemnities or amenities, and building scheme covenants, continue to apply to the land conveyed and are enforceable as provided in Article 25. This provision is for the protection of a superior owner who is not a party to the agreement. (If an agreement is made to which all superior owners and their incumbrancers are parties, the agreement will be outside Article 5(7)(a), and Article 24(2) – and the other provisions of this paragraph – will not apply.)

*sub-paragraph (e)* The whole of the ground rent is payable out of the land retained or the other land.

*Paragraph 3* applies where there is an agreement to apportion the ground rent. An apportionment may be convenient where the ground rent is of a large amount.

*sub-paragraph (a)* The land retained is subject only to the amounts of ground rent and superior rent apportioned to it, and to any relevant covenants. The agreement referred to in the opening words of the paragraph refers only to ground rent, so any apportionment of a superior rent will be under Article 17.

*sub-paragraph (b)* Article 5(1) applies to the land conveyed and its apportioned ground rent. Article 17(1) applies to any apportioned superior rent.

*Paragraph 4* is concerned with indemnities. It takes substantive effect on the second appointed day because it is on that day that there substantially ceases to be any possibility of a further indemnity being given in a new sub-fee farm grant (Article 29) or a new long lease (Article 31) (although it is just possible that such a grant or lease may be made in performance of a pre-existing agreement). In effect, the paragraph makes indemnities which formerly were only equitable take effect at law.

*sub-paragraph (a)* applies to an indemnity against having to pay the whole of a ground rent: the whole ground rent is charged on the land retained by the indemnifior.

*sub-paragraph (b)* applies to a partial indemnity: this is treated as an apportionment to which paragraph 3 applies.

# SCHEDULE 2

## THE REDEMPTION MONEY

Article 8(1)(ii), 13(2)(e), 14, 39(2)(c).

1. The redemption money appropriate to a ground rent is the sum produced by multiplying the yearly amount of the ground rent by the figure fixed by an order under paragraph 2 as the number of years purchase applicable for a period which includes the date which is the redemption date in relation to that ground rent.

2.—(1) The Department of Finance and Personnel may by order made subject to negative resolution fix a figure as being the number of years purchase applicable to ground rents in relation to which the redemption date falls within a period specified in the order.

(2)  The figure fixed under sub-paragraph (1) for any period is to be reckoned by –

(a) estimating as a percentage the yield of such security or securities as may be specified in the order on such basis as may be so specified, and

(b) dividing 100 by the figure so obtained, and

(c) rounding up the quotient to the nearest whole number (if it is not a whole number).

3.—(1) Where land held under a building lease or under a fee farm grant for purposes corresponding to those of a building lease is subject to a ground rent in relation to which there is an agreement providing for one or more than one increase (whether periodic or dependent on a contingency) in the amount of the ground rent related to periods or events in the progress of building or related activities, the provisions of sub-paragraphs (2) to (5) have effect for the purposes of this Schedule.

(2)  Subject to sub-paragraph (3), the yearly amount of the ground rent is to be taken to be the greatest annual amount that can become payable in accordance with the agreement (assuming, where an increase is dependent on a contingency, that the contingency will happen).

(3)  The amount arrived at under sub-paragraph (2) is subject to such abatement as is appropriate to take account of the period or periods during which ground rent would be payable, or likely to be payable, at a reduced rate in accordance with the agreement if the ground rent were not redeemed.

(4)  The redemption money is payable by such instalments at such intervals of time as are appropriate in all the circumstances, except that, where any instalment after the first is due and unpaid for seven days the whole unpaid balance of the redemption money becomes immediately payable.

(5)  In this paragraph "contingency" does not include a breach of covenant such as is mentioned in Article 3(3).

4.(1) This paragraph applies for the purpose of determining, for the purposes of paragraph 1, the yearly amount of a ground rent which is subject to periodic review (not being an increase to which paragraph 3 applies).

(2)   If the redemption notice is served within one year after the date of —

(a)   the creation of the ground rent, or

(b)   a review of the ground rent,

the yearly amount of the ground rent is to be taken to be its amount as created or, as the case may be, its amount immediately following the review (or the most recent review).

(3)   If the redemption notice is served more than one year after the date of the creation of the ground rent or its review (or most recent review), the yearly amount of the ground rent is to be taken to be that which it would have been if the ground rent had been reviewed on the anniversary of the date of its creation last preceding the date of service of the redemption notice in accordance with all the provisions for review except any provision about the dates of, or the length of periods between, reviews.

(4)   For the purposes of this paragraph, a single review the occasion for which has not yet arisen or arrived is a periodic review.

# EXPLANATORY NOTE

SCHEDULE 2

This Schedule explains how the amount of the redemption money is calculated.

*Paragraph 1* contains the basic rule: the amount of the redemption money is the figure produced by multiplying the annual amount of the ground rent by the appropriate number of years purchase. The appropriate number of years purchase is that fixed under paragraph 2 for a period which includes the redemption date (i.e. the date specified in the rent-payer's notice of intention to redeem as the target date for redemption: Article 7(1)).

*Paragraph 2* empowers the Department of Finance and Personnel to make an order fixing the number of years purchase applicable for redemptions within a specified period, where the redemption date (within the meaning of Article 7(1)) falls within that period.

*sub-paragraph (1)* confers that power. The figure must be fixed for a period specified in the order – i.e. the period must have a specified beginning (say, 1 January) and a specified end (say, 31 March or 30 June or 31 December). If movements in the stock market during the running of a period render it desirable to fix a new figure, that can be done under section 17(2) of the Interpretation Act by revoking the order and making a new one.

*sub-paragraph (2)* says how the number of years purchase is to be arrived at. The yield of a specified security (for example, 3½% War Stock taken at its middle market price at the end of the week preceding the making of the order) is to be taken as a percentage, divided into 100, and the result rounded up to the nearest whole figure.

*Paragraph 3* is concerned with building leases and corresponding fee farm grants ground rent on which is subject to increases during, or on the expiration of, the period of development.

*sub-paragraph (1)* attracts the following sub-paragraphs in this situation.

*sub-paragraph (2)* treats as the ground rent the greatest annual amount which can become payable. E.g., if the ground is £x for the first year, £y for the second and £z thereafter, the amount of the ground rent for the purposes of the Order is £z. But this is subject to adjustment under sub-paragraph (3).

*sub-paragraph (3)* provides for such adjustment of the amount of ground rent ascertained under sub-paragraph (2) as is appropriate to take account of periods during which a reduced ground rent is payable (or would be payable if the ground rent were not redeemed).

*sub-paragraph (4)* makes the redemption money payable by such instalments at such intervals as are appropriate. This is to take account of the fact that the developer cannot be expected to be able to find all the redemption money until the whole, or a substantial part, of his development has been completed. Payment of the first instalment triggers off the redemption (Articles 8(1)(ii) and 13(1) and (3)(a)); if the second or any subsequent instalment is overdue for 7 days, the unpaid balance of the redemption money is immediately payable.

Article 39(2)(c) empowers the Lands Tribunal to determine any dispute about what adjustment of the amount of ground rent is appropriate or what instalments are appropriate.

*sub-paragraph (5)* excludes from the meaning of "contingency" a breach of covenant which causes the amount of ground rent actually payable to be increased. (See Article 3(3)).

*Paragraph (4)* applies where the amount of a ground rent is subject to periodic review.

*sub-paragraph (1)* attracts the following sub-paragraphs in this situation.

*sub-paragraph (2)* applies where the redemption notice is served within one year of either the creation of the ground rent or a review: the yearly amount of the ground rent is its amount as created or its amount following the review (as the case may be) – the words "or the most recent review" take account of the not very likely possibility that a ground rent may be reviewed twice in one year.

*sub-paragraph (3)* applies where the redemption notice is served more than a year after the creation or review of the ground rent. The ground rent is to be reviewed as at the last-preceding anniversary of its creation, and the amount resulting from that review is its yearly amount for redemption purposes.

*sub-paragraph (4)* applies where a ground rent is subject to a review on one occasion only (e.g. where a lease has been granted for 60 years with a review after 30). That review is to be accelerated for the purposes of sub-paragraph (3) as if it were a periodic review.

# SCHEDULE 3

## CONSEQUENCES OF CONVERSION OF PERPETUALLY RENEWABLE LEASES

### *Continuance of certain provisions of lease or sublease*

1.—(1) The estate in fee simple which comes into existence under paragraph (4), or paragraphs (4) and (5), of Article 27 ("the fee simple") takes effect in substitution for the estate created by the lease or sub-lease to which that paragraph, or those paragraphs, applied ("the lease"), and, subject to the necessary consequences of that substitution (and, in particular, to sub-paragraph (2)), the provisions of the lease then subsisting are the provisions subject to which the fee simple is held.

(2) The following provisions of the lease do not apply –

(a) provisions about the falling of lives or the renewal of the lease or, subject to paragraph 7, the payment of fines, fees or costs upon, for or in respect of renewal;

(b) provisions prohibiting or restricting assignment, sub-demise or parting with possession;

(c) any other provisions that are repugnant to a fee simple;

but, subject thereto, the fee simple is (without prejudice to paragraphs 5 to 8 and 10) subject to a perpetual fee farm rent payable in the same amounts, at the same times and recoverable in the same manner as the rent under the lease and is subject to the same conditions, covenants, exceptions and reservations as in the lease.

(3) Where the lease is a sub-lease such as is mentioned in Article 27(5), the fee simple is also subject to a fee farm rent equal to the rent payable under the superior lease, or, as the case requires, to fee farm rents equal to the rents payable under the respective superior sub-lease or sub-leases and the superior lease, but subject to any agreement for indemnity relating to those rents.

### *Rights and equities*

2.—(1) Subject to the provisions of this Schedule (and, in particular to paragraph 1(2)), the fee simple is for all purposes a graft on the estate created by the lease and is subject to any rights or equities arising from its being such a graft.

(2) Without prejudice to the generality of sub-paragraph (1), any mortgage of the estate created by the lease continues to have effect as if it were, and had been created as, a mortgage of the fee simple, and, in particular, –

(a) where the instrument creating the mortgage was an assignment of the estate created by the lease, it has effect (so far as permitted by law) as if it were a conveyance of the fee simple;

(b) where that instrument was a sub-lease, it has effect (so far as permitted by law) as if it were a lease for a term equivalent to the term of the sub-lease.

## Testamentary dispositions

3.—(1) Any provision of a will in respect of the estate created by the lease operates instead on the fee simple.

(2) Any such provision in respect of the estate created by a superior lease or sub-lease such as is mentioned in paragraph 1(3) operates instead on the fee farm rent.

## Sub-leases not perpetually renewable

4. Sub-leases not coming within Article 27(5) continue to have effect, and, in the case of a sole sub-lease or, where there are two or more sub-leases, in the case of the more or most superior of them, does so as though created out of the fee simple.

## Implied covenants

5. The fee simple is subject to –

(a) an implied covenant by the owner thereof to notify in writing the former lessor, his solicitor or agent of every conveyance or devolution of the fee simple (including all probates or letters of administration), and the covenant so implied is in substitution for any express covenant to notify the former lessor, his solicitor or agent of assignments or devolutions and to pay fees and costs in respect of such notification;

(b) a covenant by the former lessor that, if the owner of the fee simple produces, within one year from the first appointed day, the lease or sufficient evidence of it (including an assignment of part of the land comprised in the lease), with any particulars required to show that the lease was subsisting for the purposes of Article 27 immediately before that day, to the former lessor or his solicitor or agent, the former lessor, his solicitor or agent will, subject to the payment of his reasonable costs properly incurred, if the fact that the lease was subsisting for those purposes is admitted or proved, endorse notice of that fact on the lease, assignment or copy thereof, at the expense of the owner of the fee simple; and such endorsement, signed by or on behalf of the former lessor, is, in favour of a purchaser, conclusive evidence that the lease was subsisting as aforesaid, either in respect of the whole or part of the land, as the case may be.

## Liability of original owner of the fee simple

6.—(1) The person who becomes the owner of the fee simple on the first appointed day is, notwithstanding any stipulation to the contrary, liable for fee farm rent accruing and for breaches of covenants and conditions committed only during the period he remains such owner.

(2) Sub-paragraph (1) does not affect the liability of any person in respect of rent accruing, or the breach of any covenant or condition occurring, before the first appointed day.

1180

*Adjustment of rent to compensate for loss of fines*

7.—(1) Where, under the lease, any fine was payable by the lessee on renewal, then an amount to be ascertained as hereinafter provided, unless commuted, is payable to the person entitled to the fee farm rent as additional rent; but no sums payable for the costs of examination of the lessee's title or of granting a new lease or any other work which is rendered unnecessary by this Order is to be taken into account in ascertaining the additional rent.

(2) In default of agreement and subject to the exercise by the Lands Tribunal of the powers conferred on it by Article 39, the following provisions have effect for the purpose of ascertaining the instalments of additional rent –

(a) the additional rent is to be ascertained on the basis of the fine which would have been payable on the occasion of the first renewal after the first appointed day, if this Order had not been made;

(b) where the lessee had a right to renew at different times, the occasion of the first renewal is such date as he may, by notice served on the lessor within one year after the first appointed day, select from among the dates at which he would have been entitled to renew his lease, had it remained renewable, or, in default of such notice, the last day on which he would have been entitled to renew;

(c) where the time at or within which the fine must be paid is not definitely fixed by or ascertainable from the lease, the fine is to be taken to be payable on such date as may be determined by the Lands Tribunal in accordance with Article 39(2)(d) on a reference made by either the owner of the fee simple or the person entitled to the fee farm rent;

(d) the yearly amount of the additional rent is to be ascertained by dividing the amount of the fine payable by the lessee on renewal by the number of years which represents the interval or average interval occurring between the dates of renewal;

(e) the additional rent is payable by, as nearly as may be, equal instalments at the times at which the fee farm rent is payable, the first instalment falling due on the day for payment of fee farm rent which occurs on or nearest to the first anniversary of the first appointed day;

(f) the additional rent is deemed to be part of the fee farm rent for all purposes, including any covenant for payment of rent or for entry or re-entry contained in the lease;

(g) if the lessee was liable to forfeit his right of renewal if he made default in payment of a fine or in doing any other act or thing within a time ascertained by the dropping of a life, but not otherwise, then five per cent. of the existing rent of the land (that is to say, the rent payable under the terms of the lease immediately before the first appointed day), or such other percentage of that rent as may be agreed under paragraph 8(1)(a)(iv), is to be treated as added to the fine payable by the lessee on renewal for the purpose of ascertaining the amount of the instalments of additional rent and as compensation to the lessor for loss of his right of re-entry (present or future) which would have accrued, if this Order had not been made, by reason of any such liability to forfeit the right of renewal;

(h) notwithstanding that, under the lease, any unpaid fine on a renewal carries interest, no instalment of additional rent payable in lieu thereof carries interest.

(3)   Where by virtue of paragraph 1(3) more than one fee farm rent is payable, this paragraph applies to each of those rents in accordance with the terms of their respective leases.

8.—(1)   Where –

(a) the owner of the fee simple and the person entitled to the fee farm rent agree upon –

   (i) the commutation or discharge of any claims in respect of additional rent, or any part of it;

   (ii) the interval or average interval between dates of renewal;

   (iii) the amount of instalments of additional rent;

   (iv) the percentage of the existing rent which is to be treated as added to a fine under paragraph 7(2)(g);

   (v) the amount of the fee farm rent (including the instalments of additional rent) which is to be apportioned in respect of any part of the land comprised in the lease; and

(b) a statement in writing of the agreement is endorsed on or attached to the lease (or a counterpart of it or an assignment of the benefit of it) and is signed by the owner and that person;

the statement is conclusive evidence of the matters stated in it, and where the agreement involves an apportionment such as is mentioned in head (a)(v), the former lessee's covenants are to be apportioned in regard to the land to which the apportionment relates.

(2)   The reasonable costs properly incurred of and incidental to the agreement and any negotiations therefor are to be borne by the owner of the fee simple.

### Powers of trustees

9.—(1)   A power authorising a trustee or other person to apply or direct the application of or raise any money for or in discharge of fines, fees or costs payable on the renewal of the lease is hereby deemed to authorise the payment, application or raising of money for the commutation of any additional rent made payable by this Order.

(2)   If the former lessor's estate is held under, or on the trusts of, a settlement or on trust for sale, any commutation money is to be treated as

capital money or proceeds arising from the sale of the land (as the case requires).

(3)   If the estate of the owner of the fee simple is held under, or upon the trusts of, a settlement or on trust for sale, the commutation money may be paid out of capital money or other property (not being land) held together with, or on the same trusts as, the land.

## Interpretation

10.   In this Schedule references to the former lessor are to the person who, immediately before the first appointed day, was successor in title to the grantor of the lease; and, where the context permits, references to the former lessor include a successor in title of his.

# EXPLANATORY NOTE

## SCHEDULE 3

This Schedule complements Article 27 by making detailed provision for the conversion of perpetually renewable leases into fee farm grants.

*Paragraph 1* describes the concomitants of the lessee's new fee simple estate (substituted by Article 27(4) for his former lesser freehold estate). It carries the provisions of the original lease into that fee simple estate, save for those about the effect of the falling of the specified life or lives or the renewal of the lease, restrictions on assignment, sub-demise or parting with possession and any other provisions repugnant to a fee simple. Where there are perpetually renewable sub-leases, the fee simple goes to the most junior sub-lessee (Article 27(5)) and the head lessor and the sub-lessors have fee farm rents.

*Paragraph 2* makes the substituted lease subject to all the same equities and incumbrances as the original one. The paragraph makes it clear that the statutory conversion does not invest the lessee with any kind of exceptional statutory title. His title to the fee simple is no better than his title to the original lease. Sub-paragraph (2) contains consequential provisions in respect of mortgages.

*Paragraph 3* makes testamentary dispositions of the estate created by the lease operate on the fee simple, and of the reversion on the lease operate on the fee farm rent.

*Paragraph 4* preserves any existing sub-lease which was granted for a term of years and not subject to perpetual renewal.

*Paragraph 5* implies two covenants governing the substituted fee simple –

(a) its owner must notify the former lessor or his agent of every change in title to the fee simple (including a grant of representation to a deceased owner) – any provision of the original lease for the payment of fees or costs on such notification is rendered void;

(b) if the owner produces to the former lessor or his agent, within a year of the first appointed day, evidence that the original lease is one to which Article 27 applies, the former lessor must endorse that fact on the lease (or any assignment or copy, if that is produced instead of the original lease); such endorsement is conclusive evidence that there existed a right of renewal bringing the lease under Article 27.

*Paragraph 6* excludes any provision of the original lease which makes a lessee answerable for defaults in paying rent or observing the covenants or conditions of the lease which occurred before he became the lessee or which may occur after he ceases to be the lessee. In future, a lessee (now become a fee simple owner) will be liable only for defaults occurring while he is the owner. But this paragraph does not affect his liability (if any) for defaults which occurred before the first appointed day.

*Paragraph 7* is concerned with increasing the fee farm rent payable out of the substituted fee simple (which would otherwise, by virtue of paragraph

1, be the same as the rent payable under the lease immediately before the first appointed day) so as to take account of the lessor's loss of fines on renewal of the original lease.

*sub-paragraph (1)* provides that fines may either be commuted or may be averaged out into instalments in the form of an increase of rent. The instalments form a permanent addition to the fee farm rent. Where costs would have been payable to the landlord on a renewal they are to be disregarded, because the work contemplated will no longer be necessary.

*sub-paragraph (2)* sets out a number of rules for determining the amounts of the instalments. The lessor and lessee may vary these rules by agreement or, if a dispute about the instalments is referred to the Lands Tribunal, the Tribunal may depart from any rule (except that in head (h) prohibiting interest) if it thinks it expedient to do so in order to achieve a fair result (Article 39(3)). "Expedient", in this context, means "advantageous for furthering the purposes of the legislation". The rules are –

(*a*) The additional rent is based on the fine that would have been payable on the first renewal of the lease after the Order came into force if Article 27 had not changed the nature of the lease.

(*b*) Where the lessee had an option in choosing the particular date on which the lease was renewable (and the fine, therefore, payable), the renewal date is to be selected by him within a year of the first appointed day. If he does not make a selection within the year, the relevant date is that of the last day on which he could have elected to renew the lease.

(*c*) Where the date of renewal is uncertain and unascertainable and the parties do not agree upon a date, the Lands Tribunal may choose a date, if asked to do so by either party.

(*d*) In order to ascertain the yearly amount of the additional rent, the amount of the fine is divided by the number of years in the interval between the renewal dates (or in the average interval, where this had proved variable in the past).

(*e*) The yearly amount of the additional rent is further sub-divided into instalments corresponding in number to the rent payments made during the year – where rent is payable half-yearly there will be two instalments; where it is payable quarterly, four; and so on. The first instalment is payable on the first anniversary of the first appointed day (or as near thereto as a day for paying rent occurs).

(*f*) For all purposes, an instalment of additional rent is treated as part of the fee farm rent. So, failure to pay an instalment with the rent is a breach of the lessee's covenant to pay the rent and allows the lessor to exercise any right he may have of making a temporary or permanent entry on the land ("covenant" is defined in Article 2(2) as including a proviso).

(*g*) Where the lessee was liable to forfeit his right of renewal if he did not exercise it within a stipulated period after the dropping of a life specified in the lease, the conversion of the estate created by the lease into a fee simple deprives the lessor of the possibility that he might be able to oust the lessee should the lessee fail to exercise his right within that period. To compensate the lessor, the instalments of additional rent are increased. This is to be done by adding to the amount of the fine a sum equal to 5% of the rent which was payable under the lease immediately before the first appointed day or such other percentage as the parties may agree (paragraph 8(1)(a)(iv).

(*h*) Even though the lease provides that fines not paid promptly are to carry interest, no interest is payable on instalments of additional rent in arrear.

*Paragraph 8* gives effect to agreements between lessors and lessees on matters affecting the additional rent which is payable under paragraph 7.

*sub-paragraph (1)* makes a memorandum endorsed on or attached to the title deeds (and signed by both parties) of the amount of the instalments of additional rent, their apportionment (where part of the land is sold separately) or certain matters affecting their calculation, conclusive evidence of the matters recorded in the memorandum. (Cf. paragraph 5(b) which makes an endorsement confirming that the lease was subsisting conclusive in favour of a purchaser). Where the instalments are apportioned between various parts of the land, any sanctions for non-payment of rent are similarly apportioned.

*sub-paragraph (2)* renders the lessee responsible for paying any expense incurred by the lessor in relation to the agreement (including agents' fees incurred in preliminary negotiations).

*Paragraph 9* contains a number of consequential provisions which are relevant where there is a trust or settlement.

*sub-paragraph (1)* A power to raise money in order to pay fines or other sums on renewal includes power to raise money for the purpose of commuting the additional rent which would otherwise replace those fines.

*sub-paragraph (2)* Where there is a settlement of the lessor's estate, any commutation money received is to be treated as capital.

*sub-paragraph (3)* Where there is a settlement of the lessee's estate, commutation money may be paid out of capital.

*Paragraph 10* defines "the former lessor" as the successor in title, immediately before the first appointed day, to the person who originally granted the lease. Where the context permits (e.g. in paragraph 5(a)) a reference to the former lessor includes a successor in title of his.

## SCHEDULE 4

## CONVERSION OF LEASES FOR LIVES, ETC., AND OF CERTAIN AGREEMENTS FOR SUCH LEASES

1.   Where the lease, or the lease provided for in the agreement, is of a kind mentioned in an entry in the first column of the following Table, the lease has effect, or the agreement is to be construed as providing for it to have effect, as a lease of the kind mentioned in the corresponding entry in the second column.

### TABLE

| *Lease created or provided for* | *Lease to be construed as* |
|---|---|
| A lease for a life or lives. | A lease for a term of 90 years determinable after the dropping of the only or last life. |
| A lease for a life or lives with a concurrent term of any period. | A lease for – <br>(a) where the period of the concurrent term exceeds 90 years, that concurrent term absolutely (calculated from the date of the grant), <br>(b) where the period of the concurrent term is 90 years or less, a term of 90 years determinable after the dropping of the only or last life or after the termination of the concurrent term, or, if the life or lives have already dropped, after the termination of the concurrent term. |
| A lease for a life or lives with a reversionary term of any period. | A lease for a term of 90 years plus the period of the reversionary term, this combination of terms being determinable after the determination of the reversionary term (calculated from the dropping of the only or last life). |
| A lease for a term of any period determinable with a life or lives or on the marriage of a specified person (including the lessee) or on the happening of any other event. | A lease for a term of that period determinable after the dropping of the only or last life or the marriage of the specified person or the happening of the other event. |

2.   Where, in any entry in the second column of the Table, a lease is stated to be determinable, this is a reference to its being determinable by at least one month's notice served either by the lessor on the lessee or by the lessee on the lessor determining the lease on one of the quarter days specially applicable to the tenancy or, if there are no quarter days so applicable, on one of the usual quarter days.

# EXPLANATORY NOTE

## SCHEDULE 4

This Schedule complements Article 28(4) by making detailed provision for the conversion of leases determinable by a death, marriage with a particular person, or some other event into leases for fixed terms of years (subject to determination by notice after the happening of the death or other event in question).

*Paragraph 1* operates upon existing leases or agreements for leases and provides for the conversion of the leases in accordance with the Table in the paragraph; an agreement to grant a lease for lives or determining on some contingency is to be construed as an agreement to grant the corresponding lease shown in the Table.

The Table shows details of the conversion:

*entry 1* A lease for a life or lives (e.g. a lease to A for his life, for the life of B, or for the lives of B and C and the survivor of them) becomes a lease for 90 years determinable on the falling of the life or the survivor of the lives.

*entry 2* A lease for a life or lives with a concurrent term (e.g. to A for 10 years and until the death of B should B survive that period) becomes –

 (*a*) where the concurrent term is more than 90 years, a lease for that concurrent term alone; or

 (*b*) where the concurrent term is 90 years or less, a lease for –

 (i) where the lives have not all dropped, 90 years determinable after the dropping of the life or lives or the termination of the concurrent term (whichever last occurs), or

 (ii) where the lives have all dropped, 90 years determinable after the termination of the concurrent term.

*entry 3* A lease for a life or lives with a reversionary term (e.g. to A for the life of B and 10 years thereafter) becomes a lease for a term of 90 years plus the reversionary term, this combined term being determinable after the termination of the reversionary term (calculated from the dropping of the life or last life).

*entry 4* A lease for a term of years –

 (*a*) determinable with a life or lives (e.g. to A for 10 years should he live so long), or

 (*b*) determinable on the marriage of a specified person (including the lessee) e.g. to A for 10 years should she not marry B), or

 (*c*) determinable on the happening of some other event (e.g. Black-acre to A for 10 years should he not acquire Whiteacre within that period),

becomes a lease for that term of years determinable after the death, marriage or other event.

*Paragraph 2* provides that when a lease is stated in the Table to be determinable, this means that it is determinable by a notice in writing (see

1188

Article 2(2)) given by either party to the other to take effect on one of the quarter days specially applicable to the tenancy or, if none are specially applied, one of the usual quarter days – Lady Day (25 March), Midsummer Day (24 June), Michaelmas (29 September) or Christmas Day. The advantage of this notice procedure is that the termination of the tenancy is formalised and made clear to both parties. Otherwise, the tenancy would end, e.g. upon the death of the specified life (or the survivor of the specified lives), possibly without either party being aware of it. The terms of the lease would then cease to be applicable and rent, as such, would not be payable, although a sum equivalent to the rent would become recoverable by the lessor as a payment for use and occupation. This only serves to complicate the matter: it is better if the lease can be formally kept in existence until it is brought to an end with due notice on both sides.

RECOMMENDED DRAFT ORDER IN COUNCIL UNDER
PARAGRAPH 1 OF SCHEDULE 1 TO THE NORTHERN
IRELAND ACT 1974

---

## DRAFT STATUTORY INSTRUMENTS

---

**1989 No.     (N.I.     )**

**NORTHERN IRELAND**

**Commonhold (Northern Ireland) Order 1989**

*To be laid before Parliament in draft*

*Made*

*Coming into operation in accordance with Article 1(2)*

## ARRANGEMENT OF ORDER

Article

## SCHEDULES:

At the Court at　　　　　, the　　　　　day of　　　　　1989

Present,

The Queen's Most Excellent Majesty in Council

Whereas a draft of this Order has been approved by a resolution of each House of Parliament:

Now, therefore, Her Majesty, in exercise of the powers conferred by paragraph 1 of Schedule 1 to the Northern Ireland Act 1974 and of all other powers enabling Her in that behalf, is pleased, by and with the advice of Her Privy Council, to order, and it is hereby ordered, as follows:
–

**Title and commencement**

1.—(1) This Order may be cited as the Commonhold (Northern Ireland) Order 1989.

(2) This Order comes into operation on such day as the Head of the Department of Finance and Personnel may by order appoint.

1192

# EXPLANATORY NOTE

## ARTICLE 1

This Article gives the title of the Order and provides for its substantive provisions to come into operation on a day to be appointed by the Head (i.e. the political head) of the Department of Finance and Personnel – during the period of direct rule this power is exercisable by the Department subject to the direction and control of the Secretary of State (Northern Ireland Act 1974 c. 28 Sch. 1 para.2(1)(b), (2)). The provisions take effect immediately on the expiration of the day before the appointed day (Interpretation Act (Northern Ireland) 1954 s. 14(2)).

## Interpretation: general

**2.**—(1) The Interpretation Act (Northern Ireland) 1954 applies to Article 1 and the following provisions of this Order as it applies to a Measure of the Northern Ireland Assembly.

(2)   In this Order –

"administration" includes control and management and "administer" is to be construed accordingly;

"class 1 resolution" has the meaning given by Article 3, and in relation to a commonhold association means a class 1 resolution of that association;

"common expenses" means the costs of administration of a commonhold and any other costs of the commonhold association and includes any costs declared by this Order to be common expenses;

"commonhold" means freehold registered land which is divided into separate units all of which, together with any common parts, are managed as a whole, and in respect of which a commonhold is created by the registration of the effect of a commonhold declaration;

"commonhold association" means the association which comes into existence under Article 7 upon the registration of the effect of a commonhold declaration, and "the commonhold association", in relation to any commonhold, means the association which exists for that commonhold;

"the Commonhold Association Constitution Rules" means the Rules set out in Schedule 3;

"commonhold bye-laws" means bye-laws made under Article 7(3)(c), and "the commonhold bye-laws", in relation to any commonhold, means the bye-laws made for that commonhold;

"commonhold declaration" means a declaration made under Article 6 and "the commonhold declaration", in relation to any commonhold, means the declaration the registration of the effect of which created the commonhold;

"common parts", subject to paragraph (2) of Article 5 for the purposes of that Article, means all the parts of a commonhold not included in some unit and parts within a unit which benefit other units, and, in particular, means parts provided, or to be provided, or used for the convenience (direct or indirect) of the owners, tenants or licensees of units, or any of them, members of their households or staffs or their visitors, and includes boundary walls or fences, gardens, roads, paths, parking or drying areas, areas for waste storage or disposal, play areas, rooms or areas reserved for the use of staff of the commonhold association, sewers, drains, water tanks, watercourses, pipes, gutters, cables, wires, ducts, utility rooms, forecourt, steps, staircases, passages, lifts and the structure of buildings, and their exterior so far as not forming part of a unit (but does not include any sewer, drain, watercourse, pipe, cable, wire, duct or installation which is vested in a government department or a body established under a statutory provision as defined by section 2(f) of the Interpretation Act (Northern Ireland) 1954);

"common property" means the common parts and any apparatus, equipment, facility or thing provided for use in, or in connection with, them;

"contribution" means a contribution towards common expenses assessed and levied on a unit owner;

"equity-sharing lease" means a lease which has the general effect described in Article 31(6) of the Housing (Northern Ireland) Order 1981;

"facilities" includes lighting, heating, hot water, attendance and services;

"the Land Registration Act" means the Land Registration Act (Northern Ireland) 1970;

"Land Registry Rules" means rules made under section 85(3) of the Land Registration Act;

"member" means a member of a commonhold association, and in relation to any commonhold association means a member of that association;

"modifications" means additions, omissions, amendments, adaptations, applications, extensions, restrictions and substitutions;

"mortgage" includes a charge, and "mortgagee" is to be construed accordingly;

"newly built", in relation to a unit, includes a unit formed by the substantial reconstruction (including internal reconstruction), or the adaptation, of a building;

"notice" means a notice in writing;

"occupier" includes a person in receipt of rent or payments equivalent to rent and "occupation" is to be construed accordingly;

"office copy", in relation to an order of the court, means a copy purporting to be sealed with the seal of the court;

"ordinary resolution" means a resolution passed by a majority vote of members present and voting in person or by proxy at a general meeting of a commonhold association;

"prescribed", except in Article 24(4), means prescribed by Land Registry Rules;

"the promoter", in relation to a commonhold, means the person who signs the commonhold declaration;

"provisional member" means a person who is entered in the register of members as a member pending production to the commonhold association of proof of the registration of his title in the Land Registry;

"registered", except in relation to registration in the register of members, means registered by the Registrar in the register of freeholders in the Land Registry, and "register" and "registration" are to be construed accordingly;

"register of members" means the register of members of a commonhold association kept under rule 3 of the Commonhold Association Constitution Rules;

"the Registrar" means the Registrar of Titles;

"services" includes the taking out and keeping up of a policy of insurance;

"staff" includes employees or agents acting as such;

"unit" means, except in Articles 5 and 26, a part of a commonhold which is owned freehold, or leasehold under an equity-sharing lease granted by a freeholder, by a person other than the commonhold association; or, in relation to a commonhold proposed to be promoted, a parcel of freehold land which, upon or after the creation of the commonhold, will become a unit;

"unit entitlement" has the meaning given by Schedule 1, Part I, paragraph 8;

"unit owner" means a person who is registered in the register of members as the owner of a unit or as a person who is entitled to exercise the powers of an owner and includes a person who remains so registered after the vesting of his unit in the commonhold association under Article 20(9), but does not include a mortgagee who, under rule 7(1)(j) of the Commonhold Association Constitution Rules, is entitled to cast votes allocated to a unit; and references to the owner of a unit are to be construed accordingly;

"working days" means days on which the Land Registry is open for public business.

# EXPLANATORY NOTE

## ARTICLE 2

This Article provides for the interpretation of the Order.

*Paragraph (1)* attracts the Interpretation Act (Northern Ireland) 1954. As the Order, although of the nature of primary legislation in character, is subordinate in form, in the absence of this provision it might be thought that it should be governed only by the Interpretation Act 1978 c. 30 (s. 23(1)). The Act of 1954 applies to Northern Ireland legislation generally, so its attraction by the Order enables the Order to be construed in the same way as other such legislation.

*Paragraph (2)* defines certain expressions which appear in the Order as follows –

| *Expression* | *Article* |
|---|---|
| "administration", "administer" | 2(2) ("common expenses"); 7(3)(a); Sch. 3 rule 12(1); Sch. 4 paras. 2(d), 3(1)(a)(i), (2)(b) |
| "class 1 resolution" | 3; 4; 7(8); 16(7), (8); 17; 18(1), (5); 19; 20; 21; 22; Sch. 3 rules 4(5), (7), (9), 5(8), 7(1)(b), (e), (j), 12(1); Sch. 4 para. 3(2); Sch. 5 Pt. II |
| "common expenses" | 2(2) ("contribution"); 4(2); 9(1); 18(3); 19(4); Sch. 1 Pt. I para. 8(b); Sch. 4 para. 8(3) |
| "commonhold" | passim |
| "commonhold association" | passim |
| "the Commonhold Association Constitution Rules" | 2(2) ("register of members", "unit owner"); 7(2)(e), (9); 8; 18(4); 20(12); 25; Sch. 3 |
| "commonhold bye-laws" | Sch. 2 paras. 2, 3(n), (o); Sch. 4 para. 1(1)(h); Sch. 5 Pt. I para. 5, Pt. II para. 12 |
| "commonhold declaration" | 6; 7; 10; 13; 14; 17(1), (2)(a); 19(5), (9)(b); 21; 22; Sch. 1 Pt. I; Sch. 2 para. 1, 3(f); Sch. 3 rules 1, 2(1), 4(1), 7(1)(i); Sch. 4 para. 9(3)(4); Sch. 5 |
| "common parts" | 2(2) ("commonhold", "common property"), 5(2); 7(5), (6); 9(2); 14; 16(1), (8), (11); 20(9); 22(2); Sch. 1 Pt. I para. 4, Pt II paras. 2, 3; Sch. 2 paras. 1, 3; Sch. 3 rule 12(2)(a); Sch. 4 para. 1; Sch. 5 |
| "common property" | 10(2)(d)(e); 11(1)(b); Sch. 1 Pt. I para. 7(b); Sch. 2 paras. 1(k), 3; Sch. 4 paras. 1(1)(a), 2(a)(g), 3(1)(a)(ii), 8(4); Sch. 5 Pt. II para. 8 |

| *Expression* | *Article* |
|---|---|
| "contribution" | 9(1); 20(6)(d); Sch. 1 Pt I para. 8(b); Sch. 4; Sch. 5 |
| "equity-sharing lease" | 2(2) ("unit"); 12(6), (7); 20(8), (9), (13), (15); Sch. 3 rules 2(1), (3), 3(7), (8); Sch. 4 para. 1(1)(i), 12 |
| "facilities" | 2(2) ("common property"); 7(2)(f); Sch. 4 para. 2(e)(f) |
| "the Land Registration Act" | 2(2) ("Land Registry Rules"); 24; Sch. 4 para. 12(3) |
| "Land Registry Rules" | 2(2) ("prescribed"); 8(c); 20(7), (8); 21(6); 24 |
| "member" | 4(3); 7(11); 9; 20(9); Sch. 3 passim |
| "modifications" | 6(4), (6); 7(5), (9), (10); 17(2)(3); 19(9)(b); 20(7); 21(6); 23 |
| "mortgage", "mortgagee" | 6(8); 11; 12; 16; 19(5); 20(1)(a), (2)(a), (9)(b); 21; 22; Sch. 1 Pt. I para. 9; Sch. 3 rules 3(7), 7(1)(j), 15(4); Sch. 4 para. 1(1)(i) |
| "newly built" | 10(1); 17(1); Sch. 3 rule 4(1) |
| "notice" | 16; Sch. 3 rules 3(2), (5), 4, 15; Sch. 4 paras. 10, 12 |
| "occupier" | 6(6); 13; Sch. 2 para. 3(c) |
| "office copy" | 4(3); 6(8)(a); 12(4); 18(6); 20(2)(a)(b), (4)(a) |
| "ordinary resolution" | 7(3)(c), (9)-(11); 16(7), (12); 18(1); 23; Sch. 3 rules 7(1)(a)(c), 8(5)(g), 12; Sch. 4 para. 9(4), (5); Sch. 5 Pt. II para. 13 |
| "prescribed" | 6(3); 10(1); 11(1); 12(6); 17(1); 19(6); 20(2)(a), (8); 24(8); Sch. 1 Pt. I para. 10; Sch. 3 rule 16; Sch. 4 para. 1(1)(f) |
| "the promoter" | 6; 7; 10; 11; 12; 22(2); Sch. 5 |
| "provisional member" | 16(11); Sch. 3 rule 3 |
| "registered", "register", "registration" | 4(3); 6(1); 7(5), (11); 11(1); 16(7), (8), (11), (12); 17(1); 20; 24(3); Sch. 2 para. 3(a); Sch. 3 rules 2(3), 3(2), 4(1); Sch. 4 para. 11 |
| "the Registrar" | 4(3); 6; 7; 8; 10(4); 16(8)(b), (12); 18(6); 19(9)(b); 20; 24; Sch.1, Pt. I para. 6; Sch. 4 para. 9(5) |
| "services" | 2(2) ("facilities"); 10; Sch. 2 para. 1(b); Sch. 4 para. 1(2) |
| "staff" | 7(2)(f), (3)(c); 14(5)(e); Sch. 2 paras. 3(l), (m), (o); Sch. 4 para. 1(1)(f), 2(a), (f) |

| *Expression* | *Article* |
|---|---|
| "unit" | passim |
| "unit entitlement" | 9(1); 16(7), (8)(a), (9); 17(2); 20(9)(b), (15); Sch. 1 Pt. I para. 8; Sch. 3 rules 4(8), 7(1)(j); Sch. 4 para. 7 |
| "unit owner", "owner of a unit" | passim |
| "working days" | 20(1)(a) |

**Interpretation: class 1 resolutions**

**3.** For the purposes of this Order a class 1 resolution is a resolution of which at least 30 days' prior notice has been given and which –

(a) is passed at a duly convened general meeting of a commonhold association by the concurrence of all the votes capable of being cast in respect of all the units in the commonhold, or

(b) is passed at such a meeting by the concurrence of at least 80 per cent., but not all, of those votes and approved by the court under Article 4(1),

the votes being cast by persons entitled to exercise the power of voting who are present in person or by proxy at the time of its passing.

# EXPLANATORY NOTE

## ARTICLE 3

This Article defines the expression "class 1 resolution".

A class 1 resolution is a resolution of which at least 30 days' notice has been given and which –

(a) has been passed unanimously by all those entitled to vote (a mortgagee is entitled to vote under Schedule 3 rule 7(1)(j), and his vote supersedes any cast by his mortgagor or a lower-ranking mortgagee); or

(b) has been passed by at least 80% of the votes and approved by the court under Article 4(1).

All the persons voting must be present in person or by proxy at the meeting at which the resolution is passed. A class 1 resolution, unlike an ordinary resolution (Schedule 3, rule 5(8)), cannot be approved by a memorandum signed by those entitled to vote.

The power to seek court approval of a resolution passed by a 80% (or larger) majority prevents a small minority from unreasonably preventing a step being taken which is in the interests of the commonhold (see the references under "class 1 resolution" in the explanatory note on Article 2(2)), or gets around the difficulty which can be caused when a unit owner cannot be traced (so long as at least 80% can be traced, attend and support the resolution).

Where a class 1 resolution is to be moved for termination of the commonhold, at least 30 working days' (i.e. days on which the Land Registry is open for public business) notice of intention to move it must be registered in the register of commonhold associations in the Land Registry (see Article 8).

The Article does not require the concurrence of a lessor of an equity-sharing lease to a class 1 resolution: but the lease may bind the lessee not to vote in favour of, or against, the resolution without the lessor's consent.

**Class 1 resolutions: further provisions**

**4.**—(1) Where a resolution proposed as a class 1 resolution has been passed by the concurrence of at least 80 per cent., but not all, of the votes capable of being cast, the persons who voted in favour of the resolution may make application to the court for approval of the resolution, and the court may make an order approving the resolution if it considers that it is reasonable in all the circumstances for the resolution to be passed.

(2)   Where the court makes an order under paragraph (1) –

(a)   the costs of the applicants are common expenses unless, and to the extent that, the court otherwise directs;

(b)   the costs of the respondents are common expenses only if, and to the extent that, the court so directs.

(3)   A commonhold association has a duty to lodge a copy of every class 1 resolution, and an office copy of every order under paragraph (1), in the Land Registry (and the Registrar shall register the effect of every resolution of which a copy is so lodged and file the resolution, and, until the effect is registered, the resolution has no operation); and a commonhold association has a duty to send a copy of every class1 resolution, and every order under paragraph (1), to every member within seven days of the date of their lodgment in the Land Registry.

(4)   References in paragraph (3) to a class 1 resolution or a court order include any scheme approved by the resolution or settled in connection with the order.

# EXPLANATORY NOTE

## ARTICLE 4

This Article contains provisions ancillary to Article 3. Those provisions cannot be included in that Article, because they do not deal only with interpretation.

*Paragraph (1)* permits a majority of at least 80% voting in favour of a class 1 resolution to ask the court, by approving the resolution, to dispense with the concurrence of the minority. The court may make an approving order if it considers it reasonable for the resolution to be passed. By virtue of Article 24(1), "the court" has the meaning given by section 4 of the Land Registration Act.

*Paragraph (2)* makes the costs of the application common expenses unless the court otherwise orders. The costs of the respondents are not common expenses, but the court may order all or part of them to be so treated, if it considers it right to do so.

*Paragraph (3)* makes a class 1 resolution ineffective until a copy of it (and an office copy of any approving court order) is registered in the Land Registry. The paragraph also requires the commonhold association to send a copy (which, in the case of the order, need not be an office copy) to each member of the association. An office copy is one purporting to be sealed with the seal of the court (Article 2(2)). For the High Court, "purporting" is not strictly necessary, because documents bearing its seal are judicially noticed (Judicature (Northern Ireland) Act 1978, s. 115(4)); but documents bearing the seal of a county court are ordinarily to be received in evidence only if "duly sealed" (County Courts (N.I.) Order 1980 Art. 59(2)).

*Paragraph (4)* requires a scheme approved by a class 1 resolution or settled by the court in connection with such a resolution to be registered and circulated to members together with the resolution.

**Prohibition of conveyance of freehold flats otherwise than as units in a commonhold**

5.—(1) Any purported conveyance of a flat for an estate in fee simple absolute in possession, and any agreement for such a conveyance, has no effect at law or in equity unless the flat is, or, in the case of an agreement, is or is to be, a unit in a commonhold.

(2)  In paragraph (1) –

"conveyance" includes a transfer of registered land;

"flat" means a parcel consisting of a unit of accommodation constructed or adapted for use solely for the purposes of a private dwelling in a building containing four or more such units (whether or not the building also contains other units which are not so constructed or adapted), where –

(a)  each such unit is dependent to a substantial degree on one or more than one other such unit for support or shelter, and

(b)  the boundary, or part of the boundary, between at least two such units is horizontal, and

(c)  the owners or occupiers of such units, or any of them, share or may share in the enjoyment of common parts;

"common parts" has the meaning given by Article 2(2) with the substitution for the reference to a commonhold of a reference to the building mentioned in the definition of "flat" and any adjacent land.

(3)  The fact (if it is the case) that a building contains other units as well as flats does not affect the requirement of Article 6(1) that a commonhold must be constituted for the whole of the land to which it relates with all buildings erected or to be erected on it.

# EXPLANATORY NOTE

## ARTICLE 5

This Article prevents the conveyance of freehold flats which are not part of a commonhold. The Article does not affect the conveyance of a flat held under a long lease; but, if the Ground Rents Order is made, long leases will not be capable of being created in the future (except in certain transitional cases).

*Paragraph (1)* nullifies any purported conveyance of a flat for an estate in fee simple, and any agreement for such a conveyance, unless the flat is (or, if not yet constructed, is to be) a unit in a commonhold.

*Paragraph (2)* contains definitions. It is put beyond any possible doubt that a conveyance includes a transfer of registered land; and "flat" is defined as a unit which is (or is to be) used solely for the purposes of a private dwelling. Thus units which are (say) solely shops or offices are outside the Article, although if a building contains two or more stories of flats as well as shops or offices (or shops and offices) the fact that the flats must be in a commonhold requires the other units also to be in a commonhold (cf. para. (3) and Article 6(1)). This does not apply where there is only one storey of flats above, say, shops, because in that case there is no horizontal boundary between flats. The use of commonhold is compulsory only when there are at least 4 flats in the building.

*Paragraph (3)* provides a link with Article 6(1), emphasising that part of a building (in the present case, the flats) cannot form a commonhold on its own: the commonhold must extend to the whole of the building (i.e. both flats and other units, if any).

## Creation of commonhold

**6.**—(1) A commonhold is created in respect of land by the registration in the register of freeholders in the Land Registry of the effect of a declaration ("the commonhold declaration") signed by the promoter, that is to say, –

    (a)  the registered owner of a freehold estate with absolute title in the land, or

    (b)  the owner of an estate in fee simple absolute in possession in the land who concurrently applies for registration as owner of a freehold estate with absolute title,

that the whole of the land described in the declaration with all buildings erected or to be erected on it constitutes a commonhold.

(2)   Where the commonhold declaration is made by a promoter such as is mentioned in paragraph (1)(b), its effect shall not be registered before registration of his absolute freehold title to the land.

(3)   The commonhold declaration must be in the prescribed form and contain, or have annexed to it in the prescribed manner, the particulars listed in Part I of Schedule 1; and when the Registrar has registered the effect of the declaration in accordance with paragraph (1) he shall file the declaration.

(4)   Where the name proposed by the promoter for the commonhold is the same as the name of an existing commonhold or so similar as, in the opinion of the Registrar, to be liable to give rise to confusion, the Registrar, after consulting the promoter, may make such modifications in the proposed name as he thinks fit and alter the commonhold declaration accordingly.

(5)   The provisions of Part II of Schedule 1 apply to define the boundaries of units, except to the extent that an inconsistent definition is contained in the commonhold declaration.

(6)   The commonhold declaration attracts the rights and obligations attaching to units which are set out in Schedule 2 (and must record that it does so), and those rights and obligations attach permanently to each unit and, except where expressly limited to unit owners, benefit or bind (as the case may be) any person in occupation of a unit as well as the unit owner, in accordance with Article 13; the provisions of that Schedule may be modified for the purposes of the declaration by express textual modifications set out in the declaration, but not otherwise.

(7)   The commonhold declaration or any bye-laws made under Article 7(3)(c) must not contain a provision which, directly or indirectly, restricts the right of a unit owner to convey his unit; but this provision does not prejudice paragraph 3(f) or (g) of Schedule 2 (restrictions on use of unit; prohibition of sub-division).

(8)   Where the promoters of a commonhold are existing owners of separately owned units acting together –

(a) the commonhold declaration must be accompanied by the consent to the creation of a commonhold of the mortgagees referred to in Article 22(1)(a) and (2) or the consent of at least 80 per cent. (by number and not by value) of those mortgagees together with an office copy of a court order under Article 22(3) dispensing with the consent of the remainder;

(b) the commonhold declaration may contain such transitional provisions as the promoters consider necessary or expedient (including provisions for the transfer of funds, the duty of the commonhold association to discharge debts already incurred, and the assessment, levying and recovery of contributions in respect of such debts).

# EXPLANATORY NOTE

## ARTICLE 6

This Article deals with the creation of a commonhold.

*Paragraph (1)* sets out the basic requirements. A declaration (called a "commonhold declaration") must be lodged in the Land Registry by the promoter of the commonhold, stating that all the land described in the declaration (with all buildings which are already erected on the land or which may be erected there in the future) forms a commonhold. This begins to operate as soon as its effect is registered in the register of freeholders. The promoter may be a builder who is also a developer, a developer who is not a builder and who employs a builder to adapt existing buildings or erect new buildings, or all the owners of existing flats, acting together, who wish to form their flats and common parts into a commonhold. The developer must be the registered owner of a freehold estate with absolute title in the land; or, if he is the freehold owner of unregistered land, he may apply concurrently for registration of his absolute title and the creation of a commonhold.

*Paragraph (2)* makes it clear that where an owner of unregistered land applies for registration of his title and creation of a commonhold, the registration of title must take effect first.

*Paragraph (3)* requires the commonhold declaration to be in the prescribed form (see Article 2(2) ("prescribed") and Article 24) and to include the particulars listed in Schedule 1, Part I. The Registrar is to file the declaration and it may be inspected by members of the public and copies requisitioned (Article 24(3)).

*Paragraph (4)* provides for the case where the promoter has chosen a name for his commonhold which is likely to cause confusion with some other commonhold already in existence. The Registrar of Titles may modify the proposed name (see Article 2(2) ("modifications")), after telling the promoter of the change he intends to make and considering any representations the promoter makes. E.g., if the title Bellevue Commonhold is proposed and there is already a commonhold of that name, the Registrar might suggest the interposition of some distinguishing word such as one showing the locality of the new commonhold.

*Paragraph (5)* attracts Schedule 1 Part II which contains rules defining the boundaries of units. Those rules may be qualified or superseded by other rules set out in the commonhold declaration. E.g., paragraph 2 excludes structural walls from being parts of units; but, in a mixed development where some units are flats and others are detached houses, the operation of the paragraph would need to be confined to the flats, the definition of the units which consist of houses being extended to the whole of the houses. The definitions of boundaries may subsequently be modified by a class 1 resolution: this would be a very rare event, but would be possible where, e.g., a roof void originally treated as part of a top-floor flat was later thought better to be treated as a common part (or the reverse).

*Paragraph (6)* attracts to a commonhold the rights and obligations set out in Schedule 2. Some of these affect only the owners of units; but, save where this is expressly stated, both owners and occupiers of units are bound. E.g., only owners are liable to pay a service charge (referred to as a "contribution") (paragraph 3(i)), but occupiers, as well as owners, must refrain from damaging the common parts and must observe the commonhold bye-laws (paragraph 3(l), (n)). (Exceptionally, paragraph 3(c) of Schedule 2 expressly refers to the owner or occupier of a unit, but this is necessary to give meaning to the word "he" which follows in the phrase "any defect of which he is aware".) Those rights and obligations attach permanently to each unit: any prospective purchaser of a unit will know of them because either they apply without qualification (and can be seen from the legislation) or they have been expressly modified by the commonhold declaration and the effect of the modifications can be seen by a search in the Land Registry -consequently there is no other provision dealing with the running of obligations. The machinery by which obligations bind owners and occupiers, and are enforceable, is contained in Article 13. Any modification of Schedule 1 which is made by the commonhold declaration (or, later, by a class 1 resolution – Article 17(2)) must be by express textual modifications so that the purchaser of a unit may see clearly precisely in what way the provisions intended for his protection are being altered. The paragraph recognises that modifications may be necessary in some circumstances: e.g., where a unit in an office building consists of an entire floor, the unit owner may wish to sub-divide it into smaller freehold offices and paragraph 3(g) would be inappropriate (a sub-division of the unit entitlement would also have to be provided for). Paragraph (6), like Article 13, applies to the circumstances as they occur (Interpretation Act, section 31(1)), so any reference to an owner or occupier is to the owner or occupier for the time being.

*Paragraph (7)* prevents restrictions being imposed on a unit owner which prevent him from freely alienating his unit. But this does not allow him to transfer his unit so as to allow the purchaser to use it in a way contrary to the purpose of the commonhold – e.g., if the commonhold consists of domestic flats, a unit owner cannot purport to allow the purchaser to use it for commercial purposes; or if the units are clearly intended to provide sheltered accommodation for, say, elderly or incapacitated persons, any transfer must be in accordance with that intent. Nor can a unit owner alienate his unit or part of it by sub-division (unless the commonhold declaration or a class 1 resolution permits him to do so).

*Paragraph (8)* applies where the promoters of a commonhold are the owners of existing flats acting together (an existing development – say, a block of formerly leasehold flats in respect of which all the ground rents have been redeemed – cannot be converted into commonhold unless all the unit owners agree).

*sub-paragraph (a)* all the mortgagees of the units must concur (or at least 80% of them if the court dispenses with the consent of the remainder) – "the court" has the same meaning as in the Land Registration Act (Article 24(1));

*sub-paragraph (b)* the commonhold declaration will need to include transitional provisions – e.g. funds will need to be transferred from any existing flat-owner's management company to the new commonhold association, and the new association will need to be able to levy contributions on its members in respect of pre-existing debts. The transitional provisions may be such as the promoters think necessary or expedient: in this context "expedient" means advantageous for furthering the purposes of the transaction.

## The commonhold association

**7.**—(1) Upon the registration of the effect of the commonhold declaration there comes into existence for the purposes of the commonhold thereby created (and only for those purposes) a body corporate ("the commonhold association") by the corporate name contained in the commonhold declaration.

(2)  The commonhold association –

(a)  may sue or be sued in its corporate name;

(b)  has power to enter into contracts in its corporate name, and to do so that, as regards third parties, the association is deemed to have the same power to make contracts as an individual has;

(c)  has power to hold land vested in it by virtue of this Order and to acquire personal property for the purposes of the association and dispose of it at pleasure; but has no power to acquire additional land or to dispose of or charge, or create easements, obligations, rights or privileges in favour of third persons in, any land vested in it otherwise than as permitted by sub-paragraph (d) or paragraph (8) (and an inhibition to this effect shall be entered in the register of freeholders without any application or consent);

(d)  has power to acquire easements, obligations, rights or privileges over land adjacent to the commonhold for the benefit of unit owners and to incur obligations in connection with any such easement, right or privilege;

(e)  subject to the Commonhold Association Constitution Rules, has the right to regulate its own procedure and business;

(f)  has the right to employ such staff as may be found necessary for the performance of its functions and to provide them with such accommodation, facilities and equipment as is necessary.

(3)  The general functions of the commonhold association are –

(a)  the duty to administer the commonhold for the benefit of all the unit owners and to give effect to the rights attaching to units so far as they relate to the commonhold association or the common parts;

(b)  the duty to comply with the obligations referred to in paragraph (10) and the right to exercise the powers there mentioned;

(c)  the power to regulate the use of the commonhold by the owners or occupiers of units, members of their households or staffs, and their visitors, and to make bye-laws for that purpose by ordinary resolution;

(d)  any other functions provided for in the commonhold declaration.

(4)  The commonhold association is a non-profit making body, and the other functions mentioned in paragraph (3)(d) and the other activities mentioned in paragraph 2(h) of Schedule 4 may not include the carrying on of any activity for profit, and any charge for amenities or services under paragraph 2(e) of Schedule 4 must not give a profit.

1211

(5)    Where the commonhold is promoted otherwise than by existing owners of separately owned units acting together, upon the registration of the first transfer of a unit to a purchaser any common parts vest in the commonhold association and the Registrar shall register the association's title (and modify the promoter's title accordingly) and issue a land certificate to that effect; or where units in the commonhold are completed in phases, upon the registration of the first transfer of a unit in any phase any common parts included in that phase so vest (and the Registrar shall act accordingly).

(6)    Where the promoters are existing owners of separately owned units acting together, the common parts vest in the commonhold association upon the registration of the effect of the commonhold declaration.

(7)    The vesting mentioned in paragraphs (5) and (6) takes effect by virtue of the commonhold declaration and those respective paragraphs and without the need for any other instrument.

(8)    Without prejudice to paragraph (2)(d), the commonhold association, with the authority of a class 1 resolution, may acquire land additional to that vested in it under paragraph (5) or (6), or may dispose of or charge, or create easements obligations, rights or privileges in favour of third persons in, any land vested in it.

(9)    The commonhold association is to operate in accordance with the Commonhold Association Constitution Rules: those Rules cannot be modified by the commonhold declaration or otherwise, except that where Schedule 3 is modified by an order of the Department of Finance and Personnel under Article 23, the commonhold association may, by an ordinary resolution, make a corresponding modification in the Rules as they apply to it.

(10)    The commonhold association is to comply with the obligations, and has the powers, set out in Schedule 4, and the other provisions of that Schedule apply to the association; paragraph 2 of that Schedule (miscellaneous powers) may be modified in relation to a commonhold by the commonhold declaration and other provisions of that Schedule may be so modified in consequence (and only in consequence) of the modification by the commonhold declaration of any provision of Schedule 2, but only (in either case) by express textual modifications, and not otherwise, except that where any provision of Schedule 4 is modified by an order such as is mentioned in paragraph (9), the commonhold association may, by an ordinary resolution, make a corresponding modification in the provision so modified as it applies to the association.

(11)    A commonhold association has a duty to lodge a copy of every ordinary resolution under paragraph (9) or (10) in the Land Registry (and the Registrar shall register the effect of every resolution of which a copy is so lodged and file the resolution, and, until the effect is registered, the resolution has no operation); and a commonhold association has a duty to send a copy of every such resolution to every member within seven days of the date of its lodgment in the Land Registry.

1212

# EXPLANATORY NOTE

## ARTICLE 7

This Article contains provisions about the commonhold association which automatically comes into existence, for the purposes of administering the commonhold, immediately upon the creation of a commonhold.

*Paragraph (1)* provides for the commonhold association's coming into existence as a body corporate. The name of the association is that set out in the commonhold declaration (which must be the name of the commonhold – which always ends with the word "Commonhold" – followed by the word "Association") – Schedule 1, Part I, paragraphs 1, 2.

*Paragraph (2)* sets out the attributes of the commonhold association as a body corporate. These largely follow section 19(1)(a) and (b) of the Interpretation Act.

*sub-paragraph (a)* it may sue or be sued in its corporate name;

*sub-paragraph (b)* it may enter into contracts and, so far as third parties are concerned, the *ultra vires* rule does not apply to it;

*sub-paragraph (c)* it has power to hold land, to acquire personal property and to dispose of that personal property; the commonhold land vests in it automatically (paragraphs (5), (6)) but it is limited in its power to acquire additional land, to dispose of land, to charge land, or to create easements, obligations rights or privileges in favour of third persons over the commonhold land (see paragraph (8));

*sub-paragraph (d)* it may acquire easements or other rights over adjacent land for the benefit of unit owners (e.g. it may acquire a right of way over a private road and enter into an obligation to contribute to the cost of repairing it);

*sub-paragraph (e)* it may regulate its own procedure (but subject to compliance with the Commonhold Association Constitution Rules set out in Schedule 3);

*sub-paragraph (f)* it may employ staff and provide them with accommodation, facilities (see Article 2(2)) and equipment (e.g. a resident porter may have living quarters, lighting, heating, hot water, etc.).

*Paragraph (3)* sets out the basic functions of a commonhold association. These are amplified or added to elsewhere in the Order (especially in Schedule 4).

*sub-paragraph (a)* the duty to administer the commonhold for the benefit of all (this includes control and management – Article 2(2)): the association must also give effect to unit owners' rights (e.g. under Article 12(3), Schedule 2 para. 1, Schedule 3 rule 14 or Schedule 4 para. 4(3), 8(2));

*sub-paragraph (b)* the duty to comply with the obligations, and the right to exercise the powers, set out in Schedule 4;

*sub-paragraph (c)* the power to regulate the use of the commonhold by the owners or occupiers of units, their families or (where units are offices or shops) their staffs and by their visitors – this power may be exercised through commonhold bye-laws (which can be made by ordinary resolution (see Article 2(2)) of the association: the bye-laws are statutory instruments and can be amended, altered, rescinded or revoked – Interpretation Act ss. 1(c), (d); 17(2)). Owners and occupiers of units must use their best endeavours to ensure that the bye-laws are observed by tenants, members of their (or their tenants') households or staffs or their visitors (Schedule 2 paragraph 3(o)). The subjects of bye-laws might include the keeping of animals, disposal of rubbish, loud music, the display of posters or signs, hanging clothes on balconies, traffic regulation (parking, one-way roads, pedestrian ways, service roads for delivery vehicles), security (entry phones, locking-up, porterage) or restrictions on the use of facilities (no unaccompanied child in lift; no ball-games in the car park);

*sub-paragraph (d)* the commonhold declaration may confer other functions.

*Paragraph (4)* makes it clear that a commonhold association is a non-profit making body: it may neither carry on any activity for profit nor be purported to be empowered to do so. E.g., if the association provides extra facilities for some unit owners – say, garages – it may make a charge sufficient to defray outgoings, overheads or depreciation, but it must not make a profit.

*Paragraph (5)* provides for the vesting of the common parts of a commonhold in the commonhold association, in the case of a new development. Where all the development is completed in a single phase, the common parts vest in the association upon the first registration in the Land Registry of a transfer of a unit to a purchaser; where the development is carried out in two or more phases (the commonhold declaration must provide for this – Schedule 1, Part I, paragraph 7) the common parts included in any phase vest in the commonhold association upon the first registration of a transfer of a unit included in that phase. The vesting is automatic – the registration by the Registrar of the title of the first purchaser (or of the first purchaser in the relevant phase) is the signal for him to register the commonhold association's title (in lieu of the title of the promoter).

*Paragraph (6)* applies a different rule where the promoters are all the owners of existing flats acting together: the common parts vest in the commonhold association immediately upon the commonhold's coming into existence. Where the promoters were formerly the long lessees of flats, but had combined to redeem their ground rents, the effect of the redemption will have been that, not only does the freehold of each owner's flat vest in him, but also the freehold of the common parts vests in all the owners as tenants in common. If the title to the land is already registered, the Registrar of Titles will substitute the commonhold association as owner at the same time as he registers the effect of the commonhold declaration; if the title is not already registered, the promoters will need to apply for registration before or at the same time as they lodge the commonhold declaration (Article 6(1)(b)).

*Paragraph (7)* makes it clear that the vesting of the common parts in the commonhold association has automatic effect – no instrument of transfer is necessary.

*Paragraph (8)* states the limited circumstances in which a commonhold association may, exceptionally (see paragraph (2)(c)), acquire additional land, dispose of land, charge land or create easements, obligations, rights or privileges in favour of third persons over land. It may do so only with the authority of a class 1 resolution. But this does not affect its power under paragraph (2)(d) to acquire easements or other rights for the benefit of unit owners.

*Paragraph (9)* requires a commonhold association to operate in accordance with the Commonhold Association Constitution Rules set out in Schedule 3. Those Rules are immutable, except in one situation – where the Department of Finance and Personnel modifies the Rules for commonholds to be created in the future (Article 23), an existing commonhold may apply the modification to itself by an ordinary resolution (see Article 2(2)). This enables an existing association to have the benefit of modifications which are intended to overcome some difficulty found to occur in the application of the Rules.

*Paragraph (10)* applies Schedule 4 to a commonhold association. Like Schedule 3, Schedule 4 is immutable, save in two respects. First, paragraph 2, which gives the association a number of discretionary powers may be modified (e.g. added to or restricted) by the commonhold declaration or a class 1 resolution; and secondly, where the commonhold declaration (or such a resolution) makes modifications in Schedule 2 it may make consequential modifications in Schedule 4 (e.g. if the commonhold has no common parts and references to such parts are, therefore, omitted from Schedule 2, in consequence of those omissions references to common parts may also be omitted from Schedule 4). But there is the same power as is conferred by paragraph (9) in the case of Schedule 3 to modify Schedule 4 by ordinary resolution so as to adopt the effect of a modification made for future commonholds by an order of the Department.

*Paragraph (11)* requires a commonhold association to lodge every ordinary resolution under paragraph (9) or paragraph (10) in the Land Registry and send a copy to each of its members. No such resolution is operative before its effect is registered in the Land Registry. (Cf. Article 16(12) and Schedule 4 paragraph 9(5)).

**Register of commonhold associations**

**8.** The Registrar shall keep a register of commonhold associations and enter in the register, in respect of each such association –

(a) its corporate name;

(b) its address for the service of documents and any change in that address notified by a return delivered to the Registrar under rule 16 of the Commonhold Association Constitution Rules;

(c) the effect of any document lodged in the Land Registry to which Land Registry Rules apply this Article.

# EXPLANATORY NOTE

## ARTICLE 8

This Article requires the Registrar of Titles to keep a register of commonhold associations. The register is to show –

*paragraph (a)* the name of every commonhold association;

*paragraph (b)* its address for service of documents (and any change in that address);

*paragraph (c)* the effect of any document lodged in the Land Registry to which Land Registry Rules apply the Article. E.g., rules may require the appointment of an administrator (Article 18) to be noted in the register.

A class 1 resolution to terminate a commonhold cannot be moved unless at least 30 working days' notice of the intention to move it has been registered in the register of commonhold associations (Article 20(1)(a)).

**Money obligations of commonhold association**

**9.**—(1) The members of a commonhold association are personally liable (in the case of trustees or representatives in their fiduciary or representative capacity and, if more than one, jointly) for any debt or other money obligation of the association to the extent of their respective liabilities to contribute to common expenses in accordance with their unit entitlements, and no further.

(2) Where an application has been made to the Enforcement of Judgments Office for the enforcement of a money judgment against a commonhold association, the Office has no power to make an order imposing a charge on any common part of the commonhold for securing the payment of the amount recoverable on foot of the judgment or any part of it, and Article 46 of the Judgments Enforcement (Northern Ireland) Order 1981 has effect accordingly.

(3) Where it appears to the Enforcement of Judgments Office that a money judgment against a commonhold association for the enforcement of which an application has been made under the Judgments Enforcement (Northern Ireland) Order 1981 cannot be enforced against the association within a reasonable time, the judgment may, with the leave of the court, be enforced against the members of the association in accordance with paragraph (1) as if the judgment had been given against them personally.

(4) In paragraph (3) "the court" means the court by which the judgment was given or, where that court was a county court or a court of summary jurisdiction, any similar court sitting for the same county court division or petty sessions district.

# EXPLANATORY NOTE

## ARTICLE 9

This Article is concerned with the extent of the liability of members of a commonhold association for the association's debts (in the event of the association proving insolvent), and with the enforcement of unsatisfied judgments against the association.

*Paragraph (1)* restricts the liability of a member of a commonhold association for the association's debts to the proportion of those debts which his unit entitlement with respect to contributions bears to the total unit entitlements of all members (see Schedule 1, Part I, paragraph 8(b)).

*Paragraph (2)* prevents a money judgment against a commonhold association from being enforced by a charge on the common parts.

*Paragraph (3)* allows a money judgment against a commonhold association to be enforced against the members personally, if it cannot be enforced against the association within a reasonable time. The consent of the court which gave the judgment (or a court of like standing) is necessary. Cf. the Judgments Enforcement (Northern Ireland) Order 1981, Article 17(4), (5) as to enforcement of judgments granted against a firm or against a person in a name other than his own (e.g., a business name).

*Paragraph (4)* deals with the problem that (for the purposes of leave for enforcement against individuals under paragraph (3)), whereas the High Court is a continuing court (Judicature (Northern Ireland) Act 1978, section 57(1)), county courts and courts of summary jurisdiction are not. In relation to those courts, the reference in paragraph (3) to the court (i.e. the court by which the judgment was given) is treated as a reference to a county court or, as the case may be, a court of summary jurisdiction sitting for the same division or district. Cf. Judgments Enforcement (Northern Ireland) Order 1981, Article 17(6).

## The built rule and phasing of development

**10.**—(1) Before the execution of the instrument of transfer to a first purchaser of a unit in a commonhold consisting of a development of newly built units, the whole development or, where the development is being conducted in phases (in accordance with the commonhold declaration), the whole of the phase which includes that unit, must be structurally complete and all services installed, and a certificate to that effect and stating that the commonhold declaration has been complied with, in the prescribed form and signed by a person with the prescribed qualifications, ("a certificate of compliance") must be lodged in the Land Registry and (in consequence of that certificate) the inhibition mentioned in paragraph (4) must have been removed.

(2) Where the development is being conducted in phases –

(a) the whole of a building must be included in a single phase and a phase must comprise all buildings on the land to which the phase relates;

(b) there must be no more than four phases;

(c) the first phase must contain at least 25 per cent. of all the units of the commonhold;

(d) common property serving any units must be included in the same phase as those units or the next-following phase;

(e) any phase which includes common property serving units in a previous phase must itself include at least 25 per cent. of the units.

(3) If paragraph (1) or any provision of paragraph (2) is not complied with in respect of any development or phase, any contract for the purchase of a unit in the development or phase and any transfer executed in pursuance of such a contract is voidable by the purchaser and any money paid by the purchaser under that contract or for an option in respect of a unit is recoverable by him as on a total failure of consideration.

(4) The Registrar, without any application or consent, may enter on the register of freeholds such inhibitions on the registration of transfers of title of any part of the promoter's land as he considers necessary to enforce compliance with paragraphs (1) and (2), and may remove any such inhibition upon receipt of a relevant certificate of compliance (which is, for the Registrar, sufficient evidence of compliance with those paragraphs, or, where the development is being conducted in phases, sufficient evidence of compliance in relation to the phase to which the certificate relates).

(5) In paragraph (1) the reference to the installation of services is to –

(a) the installation of such pipes, cables, wires or sockets as are necessary and sufficient for the supply of water and electricity and for the disposal of waste water and sewage (but not fixtures, fittings or appliances for making use of the supply of water or electricity or taps, basins, sinks, baths or sanitary conveniences); and

(b)  the taking out and keeping up of a policy of insurance;

and in paragraph (3) the reference to an option in respect of a unit includes a right of pre-emption, registration of an interest to have a contract and any similar right.

# EXPLANATORY NOTE

## ARTICLE 10

This Article lays down the built rule (that, except where a development is phased, the whole development must be structurally complete before the first transfer of a unit to a purchaser) and rules about the phasing of development where units in a newly-built or adapted building are not released on the market all at once. Where the development is being conducted in phases, Schedule 1, Part I, paragraph 7 requires the commonhold declaration to show the number of phases proposed, the land, units and common property to be comprised in each phase, the dates of commencement and completion of each phase and any rights reserved to the promoter until completion of the development (e.g. rights of way or of storing materials).

*Paragraph (1)* applies where units are being developed in a new or adapted building. If the development is not phased, the whole development must be structurally complete and all services installed before the execution of the first transfer of a unit to a purchaser; if it is being phased, the whole of each phase must be structurally complete and all services installed before the first transfer of a unit in that phase. In either case, a certificate of compliance with the requirement must be lodged in the Land Registry (and the inhibition mentioned in paragraph (4) removed by the Registrar) before the transfer is made.

*Paragraph (2)* lays down rules for phases. An intent to comply with these will be reflected in the particulars included in, or annexed to, the commonhold declaration.

*sub-paragraph (a)* A building cannot be included partly in one phase and partly in another: the whole building must be in a single phase. All the buildings intended to be erected on the area of land designated for a particular phase must be completed in that phase.

*sub-paragraph (b)* The number of phases may not exceed four.

*sub-paragraph (c)* The first phase must contain at least a quarter of all the units in the commonhold.

*sub-paragraph (d)* The common property serving any units must be included in the same phase as those units (e.g. entrances, stairs, passageways) or in the next phase (e.g. making up of estate roads).

*sub-paragraph (e)* Where a phase includes common property serving units in a previous phase, it must include at least 25% of the units (i.e. the completion of common property serving units currently on offer cannot be held over as forming part of a formal or illusory phase).

*Paragraph (3)* contains a sanction for non-compliance with paragraph (1) or (2). A purchaser may treat the sale as void and recover any payment he has made (including option money – for the extended meaning of this term, see paragraph(5)).

*Paragraph (4)* provides for the entry in the Land Registry of inhibitions against the registration of transfers of units before a certificate of compliance is lodged: such a certificate enables the Registrar of Titles to discharge the relevant inhibition (he need make no further inquiries).

*Paragraph (5)* explains the reference in paragraph (1) to services being installed and adapts it to suit the taking out and keeping up of a policy of insurance (see the definition of "services" in Article 2(2). The paragraph also extends the reference in paragraph (3) to money paid for an option to include money paid for a right of pre-emption or money paid to have a person recorded as a prospective purchaser.

**Mortgages of commonhold**

11.—(1) Subject to paragraph (2), where a commonhold is created in respect of land which is subject to a mortgage at the time of creation, or where a mortgage of land within a commonhold is created by the promoter after the creation of the commonhold, no transfer of any unit is valid or effective, nor shall it be registered, unless –

(a) the mortgage is discharged before the instrument of transfer is executed; or

(b) the mortgagee joins in the transfer so as to release the unit, and any common property serving it, from the mortgage;

and a certificate to that effect, in the prescribed form and signed by the prescribed person, is lodged in the Land Registry.

(2) Paragraph (1) does not apply where the promoters are existing owners of separately owned units acting together and the only mortgages are of separate units.

# EXPLANATORY NOTE

ARTICLE 11

This Article is concerned to see that units in a commonhold which are sold to purchasers are not subject to any prior mortgages (which includes charges – Article 2(2)). Schedule 1, Part I, paragraph 9 requires disclosure in the commonhold declaration of all estates and interests (including mortgages) affecting the commonhold land and, in the case of a mortgage, of the debt secured.

*Paragraph (1)* applies where either the land is already subject to a mortgage at the time when the commonhold is created or a mortgage is created by the promoter after the commonhold has come into existence (e.g. to finance construction). A purported transfer of a unit has no effect unless either the mortgage is discharged before execution of the transfer or the mortgagee joins in the transfer to release the unit, and the common property serving it, from the mortgage.

*Paragraph (2)* prevents paragraph (1) from applying where the only prior mortgages are of pre-existing units all the owners of which have joined together to create a commonhold. Where such owners have already created mortgages of their units (e.g. to building societies or banks), the mortgagees will have agreed to the creation of a commonhold or had their agreement dispensed with by the court (Article 6(8)(a)), and the mortgages will continue to bind the units (the unit owners being freeholders before the commonhold was created and continuing to be freeholders thereafter).

**Information to be given to purchasers of units, to unit owners or their mortgagees and to lessees**

**12.**—(1) A person proposing to purchase the freehold of a unit ("the purchaser") is entitled to be supplied –

(a) by the promoter, with the documents and information mentioned in Part I of Schedule 5, where the purchase is from the promoter;

(b) by the vendor, with the documents and information mentioned in Part II of that Schedule, where the purchase is from a unit owner other than the promoter or from such a unit owner's mortgagee.

(2) Where the promoters of a commonhold were existing owners of separately owned units acting together, the purchase of the freehold of a unit from such an owner or his mortgagee is deemed to be a purchase from a unit owner other than the promoter or, as the case may be, the mortgagee of such a unit owner, and, accordingly, sub-paragraph (b) (and not sub-paragraph (a)) of paragraph (1) applies.

(3) A unit owner or his mortgagee, on serving a written request on the commonhold association, is entitled to be supplied by the association, without charge, with so much of the information mentioned in Part II of Schedule 5 as is not already in the possession of the unit owner.

(4) Any reference in Part I or Part II of Schedule 5 to an office copy includes –

(a) a copy of an office copy which is a reproduction made with a photographic or other device for reproducing documents in facsimile, where the copy contains a certificate signed by the promoter (where Part I applies) or the secretary or chairman of the commonhold association (where Part II applies) to the effect that the copy is a true and complete copy of the office copy; and

(b) a copy of a copy which complies with sub-paragraph (a), where the further copy complies with that sub-paragraph, taking references in it to an office copy as references to the copy from which the further copy is made.

(5) Where the documents and information mentioned in Part I or, as the case may be, Part II of Schedule 5 are not supplied to the purchaser before the formation of a contract for the purchase of a unit, the purchaser is entitled to rescind the contract.

(6) A person proposing to become the lessee of a unit otherwise than under an equity-sharing lease is entitled to be supplied by the lessor with a notice in the prescribed form setting out consequences of the unit's being contained in a commonhold; failure to supply the notice does not affect the validity of the lease, but where in consequence of such failure the lessee suffers loss he is entitled to recover compensation from the lessor by action in the court.

(7) The lessor of an equity-sharing lease is not a vendor to his lessee for the purposes of paragraph (1)(b); but where such a lessor has been supplied with the documents and information referred to in paragraph

(1)(a) or paragraph (1)(b) in connection with his purchase of the freehold of a unit, it is his duty to give the originals or copies of those documents and that information to the lessee.

# EXPLANATORY NOTE

## ARTICLE 12

This Article with Schedule 5 requires certain information to be given to the prospective purchaser of a unit. The exact information depends upon whether the purchase is to be from the promoter of the commonhold or a previous purchaser of the unit. Existing unit owners may also require information already given to them to be up-dated; and prospective lessees must be notified of the possible consequences to them of a leased unit being in a commonhold.

*Paragraph (1)* distinguishes between the purchase of a unit from the promoter and its purchase from an ordinary unit owner. The promoter must supply the documents and information listed in Part I of Schedule 5; the "ordinary" vendor must supply those listed in Part II. The main differences between the two Parts are that an "ordinary" vendor need not disclose the promoter's title but must give particulars of the recent or current operation of the commonhold association (accounts, reserves, contributions, bye-laws) and of anything affecting the future of the association (unusual debts or obligations, litigation, disputes, proposals for termination).

*Paragraph (2)* modifies paragraph (1) where the promoters of the commonhold were existing owners of separately owned units acting together – these are in the position of "ordinary" vendors.

*Paragraph (3)* enables unit owners (or their mortgagees) to obtain so much of the information mentioned in Schedule 5, Part II, as is not already in their possession. This is to enable existing owners to keep up to date with developments as well as to supply the information to prospective purchasers.

*Paragraph (4)* allows facsimile copies of office copies to be supplied, instead of office copies, subject to safeguards. Cf. the Powers of Attorney Act 1971 (c. 27) s.3.

*Paragraph (5)* allows the purchaser to rescind the contract for purchase if he is not given the documents and information required by paragraph (1) and Schedule 5.

*Paragraph (6)* requires a unit owner who proposes to lease his unit to supply the prospective lessee with a notice setting out the consequences of the unit's being contained in a commonhold (cf. Article 20(10), (11), (12); Schedule 3 rule 3(7); Schedule 4 paras. 1(1)(i), 10). This only applies between the original lessor and the original lessee ("lessor" and "lessee" are not defined to include their successors in title). If the notice is not served the lease is not, on that account, rendered invalid; but if, in consequence, the lessee suffers loss he may sue for compensation.

*Paragraph (7)* prevents the lessor of an equity-sharing lease (see Report para. 3.2.15) from being treated as a vendor to his lessee for the purposes

1228

of paragraph (1)(b). But such a lessor who has obtained the documents and information mentioned in paragraph (1) on his acquisition of the fee simple in the unit must give them (or copies) to the lessee.

**Nature of obligations of commonhold association, unit owners, etc.,**

**13.**—(1) The provisions of the commonhold declaration and of Part II of Schedule 1 and Schedules 2, 3 and 4, bind the commonhold association, the unit owners and (so far as they are not expressly limited to unit owners) the occupiers of units to the same extent as if those provisions were contained in a deed executed by the commonhold association and each unit owner or occupier and the deed contained covenants on the part of the commonhold association with each unit owner or occupier and on the part of every unit owner or occupier with every other unit owner or occupier and with the commonhold association to observe all those provisions.

(2)   References in this Article to Part II of Schedule 1 and to Schedules 2 and 4 are to that Part and those Schedules as they are applicable having regard to any modification made by the commonhold declaration or a class 1 resolution; and references to Schedule 3 or 4 are to that Schedule as it is applicable having regard to any modification made by an ordinary resolution under Article 7(9) or (10).

# EXPLANATORY NOTE

## ARTICLE 13

This Article provides the basis on which provisions scheduled to the Order bind the commonhold association and the owners or occupiers of units, and it also specifies a particular method of enforcement.

*Paragraph (1)* makes the commonhold declaration and Schedule 1 Part II (so far as not superseded by the declaration), Schedule 2, Schedule 3 and Schedule 4 bind the commonhold association, owners of units and, except where limited to owners, occupiers (which includes a tenant in receipt of rent from a sub-tenant – Article 2(2) ("occupier")) as if contained in a deed which included covenants to observe all those provisions. Cf. Companies (Northern Ireland) Order 1986, Article 25(1). References to the owners or occupiers of units are to the owners or occupiers for the time being (Interpretation Act, section 31(1)). The provision in the Companies (Northern Ireland) Order 1986, Article 25(2) to the effect that money due under the deemed covenants is a debt is not reproduced here – see, instead, Article15(1)(b) and Schedule 4, paragraph 9(1).

*Paragraph (2)* restricts references in the Article to Schedule 1, Part II, Schedule 2 and Schedule 4 to those provisions so far as they are applicable. Schedule 1, Part II, Schedule 2, Schedule 3 and Schedule 4 (as to paragraph 2, and otherwise consequentially) may be modified by the commonhold declaration or a class 1 resolution (Article 17(2)); and Schedule 3 or 4 may be modified under Article 7(9) or (10) by an ordinary resolution in order to apply to an existing commonhold modifications made under Article 23 for future commonholds.

**Extent of enforceability of obligations**

**14.**—(1) An obligation under this Order, other than a restrictive or access obligation, is enforceable in respect of any contravention of the obligation against every person bound by the obligation at the time of the contravention.

(2) A restrictive or access obligation is enforceable against any person in respect of (but only in respect of) conduct of that person while bound by the obligation which consists or, as the case may be, will consist –

(a) in the doing of an act prohibited by the obligation; or

(b) in allowing the doing of such an act by another person whether or not the other person is bound by the obligation.

(3) For the purposes of this Order, a contravention of an obligation is to be treated (if it would not otherwise be treated as a continuing contravention) as continuing so long as either –

(a) the obligation remains capable of being complied with apart from any requirement as to time; or

(b) the contravention continues adversely to affect the enjoyment of the whole or any part of any unit or the common parts.

(4) Nothing in paragraph (3) entitles any person to a remedy in respect of a contravention of an obligation if, by virtue of the statute of limitation, he would not, apart from that paragraph, have been entitled to that remedy.

(5) For the purposes of this Article –

(a) "obligation" includes a duty to give effect to a right, and an obligation imposed by a commonhold declaration is an obligation under this Order;

(b) a restrictive obligation is an obligation under paragraph 3(d), (e), (f), (g), (h), (l), (n) or (o) of Schedule 2, or any corresponding provision applicable to the commonhold;

(c) an access obligation is an obligation under paragraph 3(j) of Schedule 2, or under paragraph 3(k) of that Schedule so far as relating to paragraph 1(i) or (j), or under any corresponding provision applicable to the commonhold;

(d) the references in paragraph (2) to an act prohibited by an access obligation are to be construed as references to any conduct restricting or denying the access which the obligation requires to be afforded;

(e) references in that paragraph and in sub-paragraph (d) to conduct include references to acts and omissions and, in relation to any person, include references to the acts and omissions of members of that person's household or of his staff;

and, for the purposes of paragraph (2)(b), a person allows the doing of anything which he has the right to prevent if he does not take reasonable steps to enforce that right.

# EXPLANATORY NOTE

## ARTICLE 14

This Article identifies the persons who, being bound by an obligation under the Order (see paragraph (5)(a)), are liable for a particular contravention of it.

*Paragraph (1)* lays down the basic rule that an obligation of a positive nature can be enforced against everyone bound by it at the time of its contravention. Restrictive obligations and access obligations are excluded because, in their case, any contravention will be a positive act and action can be taken against the persons doing that act (and need not be taken against those not doing it). But in the case of a positive obligation contravention consists in inaction, and there can be no ground for signalling out one inactive person from another. Although an access obligation is positive in form it will normally be contravened by a definite action, rather than by inaction (see paragraph (5)(d)).

*Paragraph (2)* deals with the contravention of a restrictive or access obligation (defined in paragraph (5)(b), (c)). A person bound by the obligation is answerable if he does the prohibited act himself or allows another to do it (see final words of paragraph (5)).

*Paragraph (3)* deems a contravention to continue so long as –

*sub-paragraph (a)* the obligation is capable of being complied with (ignoring any requirement that it should be performed within a certain time); or

*sub-paragraph (b)* the adverse consequences of the contravention continue.

An obligation can be framed in such a way that any contravention will recur so long as the wrongful state of affairs continues: in this case a person buying a unit is liable for the contravention to the extent that it continues after he becomes owner. This paragraph deals with a case where the obligation is not so framed. A new owner will be answerable for it so long as the adverse consequences continue after he assumes ownership and the obligation remains capable of being performed. An obligation is not incapable of being performed only because a time laid down for doing a thing has expired without its being done.

*Paragraph (4)* makes deemed continuing contraventions under paragraph (3) subject to the rules governing the limitation of actions. In this they differ from true continuing contraventions which do not become subject to those rules until the contravention ceases. The expression "statute of limitation" is defined in section 46(2) of the Interpretation Act.

*Paragraph (5)* is explanatory of the previous paragraphs.

*sub-paragraph (a)* defines "obligation" as including a duty to give effect to a right: some duties are expressly referred to in the Order as obligations (e.g. Schedule 2, para. 3; Schedule 4, para. 1), while others are not expressly so referred to, although the existence of an obligation is clear. E.g. as unit owners have certain rights over the common parts (Schedule 2 para. 1(c) to (g)), the commonhold association has a duty to give effect to those rights (subject to bye-laws) (Article 7(3)(a)). The sub-paragraph also makes it clear that "obligation under this Order" includes an obligation imposed by the commonhold declaration rather than by the Order itself.

*sub-paragraph (b)* defines "restrictive obligation" by reference to Schedule 2, paragraph 3. Sub-paragraphs (d), (e), (f), (g) and (l) of that paragraph are framed in negative terms. Sub-paragraphs (h), (n) and (o) are, or are partly, in positive terms, but their effect is inherently restrictive – the duty to comply with the conditions of a policy of insurance is, in substance, a duty not to contravene them; and similarly with bye-laws, which are likely to impose restrictions rather than demand positive action.

*sub-paragraph (c)* defines "access obligation" by reference to Schedule 2 paragraphs 3(j) and (k).

*sub-paragraph (d)* clears up any doubts which might arise through access obligations being treated by paragraph (2) in the same way as restrictive obligations. It treats conduct restricting or denying access as the doing of a prohibited act.

*sub-paragraph (e)* defines "conduct" as including acts and omissions; and the acts or omissions of a person's servants or agents are attributed to him.

The final words of the paragraph make it clear that the reference in paragraph (2)(b) to allowing the doing of an act is not restricted to express permission. A person allows something to be done if he has the right to prevent it and does not exercise that right to a reasonable degree. (Cf. Schedule 2, para. 4).

**Remedies for enforcement**

**15.**—(1) Without prejudice to paragraphs 10 and 12 of Schedule 4, the following remedies, namely –

(a) proceedings for an injunction (including a mandatory injunction) or other equitable relief,

(b) an action for sums due under the obligation,

(c) an action for damages (whether in respect of pecuniary or non-pecuniary kinds of damage),

are available in the event of a contravention or, in the case of proceedings for an injunction, a threatened contravention of an obligation under this Order.

(2)  Where there has been a contravention of a restrictive or access obligation, a person against whom the obligation is enforceable in accordance with Article 14 is not liable, except by virtue of section 92 of the Judicature (Northern Ireland) Act 1978 or Article 34 of the County Courts (Northern Ireland) Order 1980 (damages in lieu of injunction, etc.), for damages in respect of the contravention unless at the time of the conduct by virtue of which the obligation is so enforceable against him he was bound by the obligation by virtue of his being a unit owner.

(3)  For the purposes of the Law Reform (Miscellaneous Provisions) Act (Northern Ireland) 1948 and the Fatal Accidents (Northern Ireland) Order 1977 a contravention of an obligation is to be treated as the fault of the persons against whom the obligation is enforceable; and in this paragraph "fault", in relation to that Act of 1948, means fault within the meaning of that Act.

(4)  In this Article "obligation" means an obligation under this Order as defined by Article 14 and "restrictive obligation", "access obligation" and "conduct" have the same meaning as in that Article.

# EXPLANATORY NOTE

## ARTICLE 15

This Article deals with the remedies available in the event of a contravention of an obligation under the Order (see paragraph (4)).

*Paragraph (1)* sets out the remedies for contravention of an obligation. They are –

*sub-paragraph (a)* an injunction (including a mandatory injunction) or other equitable relief. An injunction would be a convenient way of enforcing a restrictive or access obligation; and a mandatory injunction would be appropriate for some kinds of positive obligation. Similarly, "other equitable relief" could include an order for specific performance; in *Posner* v. *Scott-Lewis* [1986] 3WLR 531 specific performance of a covenant to employ a resident porter for flats was ordered, the employment of a non-resident porter being insufficient.

*sub-paragraph (b)* action for sums due under the obligation, where the obligation is one to pay money.

*sub-paragraph (c)* action for damages, e.g. where failure to repair has led to personal injury or economic loss.

The paragraph does not affect Schedule 4 paragraph 10 or 12 which respectively allow contributions in arrear to be recovered from a tenant (to the extent of his rent) or provide for a lien.

*Paragraph (2)* provides that a person can be liable for common law damages (as distinct from damages in lieu of equitable relief) in the event of a contravention of a restrictive or access obligation only if his interest is that of a unit owner (i.e. an occupier is not liable for such damages).

*Paragraph (3)* applies the Law Reform (Miscellaneous Provisions) Act (Northern Ireland) 1948 and the Fatal Accidents (Northern Ireland) Order 1977 to a case where, in consequence of a failure to fulfil an obligation (e.g. to light or repair a staircase) a person suffers damage. If the damage is partly due to the injured person's own fault, the damages payable to him may be reduced accordingly. In the Act of 1948 "fault" is defined as meaning negligence, breach of statutory duty or other act or omission which gives rise to a liability in tort or would, but for that Act, give rise to the defence of contributory negligence.

*Paragraph (4)* gives expressions defined in Article 14 the same meanings for the purposes of this Article.

## Adverse possession

**16.**—(1) The owner of a unit cannot acquire by adverse possession any other unit or part of a unit, or any common part of the commonhold.

(2) The commonhold association cannot acquire by adverse possession any unit or part of a unit.

(3) Article 21(1) of the Limitation (Northern Ireland) Order 1989 (limitation to 12 years of period within which action may be brought for the recovery of land) does not apply to an action between one unit owner and another or between the commonhold association and a unit owner for recovery of any part of the commonhold (and, accordingly, Article 26 of that Order (extinction of title) does not apply).

(4) Where a person other than a unit owner is in occupation of a unit and has not been recorded by the commonhold association as a mortgagee or tenant of the unit, the commonhold association may serve on him a notice requiring him to serve on the association a notice stating whether he claims to have acquired, or to be in the course of acquiring, any rights in respect of the unit by adverse possession.

(5) Where a person serves a notice on the commonhold association (under paragraph (4) or otherwise) claiming to have acquired a right in respect of a unit by adverse possession, the commonhold association or any person interested in the commonhold may serve on him a notice requiring him to apply for registration of his possessory title.

(6) Where a person ("the squatter") claims to have acquired by adverse possession any part of the commonhold, he shall not be registered in the Land Registry as owner of that part with a possessory title unless he has served notice of his claim on the commonhold association (under paragraph (4) or otherwise) and a copy of the notice showing the date of service is attached to his application for registration.

(7) Where the squatter claims rights in part only of a unit, the commonhold association, before registering him in the register of members, must determine the unit entitlements of both that part of the unit and the remainder of the unit, making those respective parts separate units: where the aggregate of those unit entitlements is equal to the former unit entitlement of the whole unit, that determination may be made by ordinary resolution, but otherwise it must be made by a class 1 resolution.

(8) Where the squatter claims rights in any part of the common parts

(a) the commonhold association may by a class 1 resolution declare that part to be a unit and assign a unit entitlement to it; or

(b) if, on an application made by the squatter for registration of a possessory title to that part, the Registrar is satisfied that the interests of other unit owners will not be prejudiced, the Registrar may direct that the part in question is to cease to be part of the commonhold.

(9) If the squatter is aggrieved by a unit entitlement determined under paragraph (7) or assigned under paragraph (8)(a) he may appeal to the court, which may make such order as it considers appropriate.

(10) If a person on whom a notice is served under paragraph (4) does not serve the notice required under that paragraph or the squatter on whom a notice has been served under paragraph (5) does not apply for registration of his title within (in either case) the period of 28 days of the service of the commonhold association's (or other person's) notice, upon the expiration of that period he ceases to be entitled to any rights he may have acquired, or have been in course of acquiring, by adverse possession.

(11) Where a person serves on the commonhold association a notice that he claims to have acquired, or to be in course of acquiring, rights by adverse possession in a unit or part of a unit, or in a common part in respect of which a resolution is passed under paragraph (8)(a), the association may register him as a provisional member; and where a person is registered as the owner of a unit or part of a unit with possessory title he is to serve on the commonhold association notice of the date of registration.

(12) A commonhold association has a duty to lodge a copy of every ordinary resolution under paragraph (7) in the Land Registry (and the Registrar shall register the effect of every resolution of which a copy is so lodged and file the resolution, and, until the effect is registered, the resolution has no operation); and a commonhold association has a duty to send a copy of every such resolution to every member within seven days of the date of its lodgment in the Land Registry.

# EXPLANATORY NOTE

## ARTICLE 16

This Article modifies the law of adverse possession in relation to a commonhold. Generally, a person taking possession of land to the exclusion of the true owner can rely on that possession to defeat a claim to the land made by any person other than the dispossessed owner; and on the expiration of the limitation period under the Limitation (Northern Ireland) Order 1989 (basically 12 years, but subject to extension in certain circumstances) the dispossessed owner, too, can be defeated. References in the Article to the service of notices attract section 24(2) of the Interpretation Act.

*Paragraph (1)* prevents a unit owner from acquiring a possessory title to any other unit (or part of a unit) or a common part.

*Paragraph (2)* prevents the commonhold association from acquiring a possessory title to a unit (or part of a unit).

*Paragraph (3)* is consequential on paragraphs (1) and (2) and excludes the normal application of the Limitation Order where either of those paragraphs applies.

*Paragraph (4)* applies where a person other than a unit owner is in occupation of a unit and has not been recorded by the commonhold association as a mortgagee or tenant under Schedule 4 paragraph 1(1)(i). (A mortgagee or tenant is not bound to notify the association of his interest, but it is to his advantage to do so.) The association may be aware of facts which rule out the likelihood of the occupier's being in adverse possession – e.g. where a unit owner gives his mother occupation of his unit or where a corporate owner gives occupation to an employee or director. If it does not know of such facts or has reason to suspect that the occupier's occupation is adverse to the owner, it may require him to serve a notice stating whether he claims rights accruing or accrued by adverse possession.

*Paragraph (5)* Where an occupier claims to have acquired a possessory title to a unit, the commonhold association may require him to apply for registration of that title in the Land Registry.

*Paragraph (6)* deals with the opposite situation to paragraph (5) – where the occupier might wish to apply for registration of his possessory title without the commonhold association's being aware of it. He must serve notice of his claim on the association before he makes his application to the Land Registry (and he must attach a copy of the notice, showing the date of service, to his application).

*Paragraph (7)* applies to a case where a squatter claims rights over only part of a unit. This situation is unlikely to apply to private flats (although it could do so where, e.g., a roof void is designated as part of one particular top-floor flat): it could arise where a large unit consisting of, say, a whole floor of a building or a row of shops is divided into separate offices or shops intended to be leased. Before the commonhold association registers such a squatter as a member of the association, it must sub-divide the unit by giving separate unit entitlements to the part of the unit which is adversely occupied and the remainder of the unit. Normally this will consist of a division of the existing unit entitlement of the original unit; if the total of the new unit entitlements exceeds the original unit entitlement, other unit owners will be affected (because the denominator of the fraction mentioned in Schedule 1, Part I, paragraph 8(a) will be altered) and a class 1 resolution under Article 17(2)(c) will be needed.

*Paragraph (8)* applies where the squatter (who must be an outsider – not a unit owner (paragraph (1)) claims a possessory title to a common part. There are two possibilities, either –

*sub-paragraph (a)* the commonhold association may declare that part to be a unit and assign a unit entitlement to it. (Because the introduction of a new unit will affect existing unit owners, a class 1 resolution is required for this purpose.)

*sub-paragraph (b)* the squatter may apply for registration of his possessory title and ask the Registrar to have the part in question excluded from the commonhold, and the Registrar may accede if he thinks the other unit owners' interests will not be prejudiced. (The Registrar may come to this view if the part is on the fringe of the commonhold, bearing in mind that proof of an adverse possession involves proof of exclusion of the unit owners and the commonhold association for 12 years – as where the squatter has fenced off the land from the rest of the commonhold and enjoyed it with contiguous property of his own.)

*Paragraph (9)* applies where the commonhold association ascribes a unit entitlement to the part of the commonhold possessed by the squatter (paragraph (7) or (8)(a)). If the squatter is aggrieved by that unit entitlement, he may appeal to the court.

*Paragraph (10)* applies where, under paragraph (4), the commonhold association requires a person in occupation of a unit to state whether he has acquired, or is in course of acquiring, a possessory title, or where, under paragraph (5) a person has told the association that he claims to have acquired such a title and the association has required him to apply for registration of it. If, in either case, the person concerned does not comply with the requirement he loses any rights he may have acquired, or have been in course of acquiring, by adverse possession. This means, if he continues in possession (which he seems unlikely to be allowed to do now that the commonhold association and any unit owner affected is aware of the situation), he must begin to count his years of adverse possession anew.

*Paragraph (11)* permits a person in adverse possession who notifies the commonhold association of his status to be registered as a provisional member of the associaton. This enables contributions to be levied on him: otherwise, if the limitation period is not yet fully run and the dispossessed owner cannot be traced, the association could not recover contributions in respect of a unit without exercising its lien (which it may be unwilling to do, in case the missing owner should turn up again before the limitation period has expired). When the squatter becomes registered in the Land Registry as a possessory owner, he must serve on the association notice of the date of registration. The association will then show him in the register of members as a full member.

*Paragraph (12)* requires an ordinary resolution under paragraph (7) to be lodged in the Land Registry (cf. Article 7(11) and Schedule 4 paragraph 9(5)).

**Revocation of commonhold declaration or modification of certain provisions**

17.—(1) At any time before the making of the first contract for the sale of a newly built unit in a commonhold consisting of a development of such units, the promoter may lodge in the Land Registry a declaration in the prescribed form that the commonhold declaration is cancelled, and, upon the registration of the effect of a declaration under this paragraph, the commonhold declaration ceases to have effect.

(2) Without prejudice to Article 7(10) (modification, in certain circumstances, by ordinary resolution) a commonhold association may, by a class 1 resolution, –

(a) modify the commonhold declaration;

(b) without prejudice to the generality of sub-paragraph (a), modify the definitions of the boundaries of units;

(c) without prejudice to the generality of sub-paragraph (a) or Article 16(7), vary the unit entitlement of any unit or units with respect to any purpose;

(d) modify Schedule 2 (as that Schedule applies to the association);

(e) modify paragraph 2 of Schedule 4 (as that paragraph applies to the association) and make consequential modifications of other provisions of Schedule 4.

(3) Any modification or variation made under paragraph (2) must be by express textual modifications and not otherwise.

# EXPLANATORY NOTE

## ARTICLE 17

This Article allows a commonhold declaration relating to a new development to be cancelled at any time before the first sale of a unit. It also allows variations in certain provisions which might have been made by the commonhold declaration to be made subsequently by a class 1 resolution.

*Paragraph (1)* applies to a new commonhold development. If the promoter lodges in the Land Registry a declaration cancelling the commonhold declaration, as soon as the effect of the cancelling declaration is registered the commonhold declaration ceases to have effect. This must be done before the first sale of a unit.

*Paragraph (2)* allows to be made, by a class 1 resolution, modifications of certain provisions which could have been made by the commonhold declaration (see Articles 6(5), (6) and 7(10)) and of the commonhold declaration itself. The provisions concerned are the definitions of boundaries in Schedule 1, Part II (or alternative definitions contained in the commonhold declaration), Schedule 2 (rights and obligations attaching to units) and paragraph 2 of Schedule 4 (miscellaneous powers of the commonhold association).

*Paragraph (3)* The modifications must be made by express textual amendments, so that the extent to which they derogate from the scheduled provisions, or (where definitions of boundaries were contained in the commonhold declaration to the exclusion of Schedule 1, Part II) the original provision, is quite clear.

**Appointment of administrator**

**18.**—(1) On the application of the commonhold association or any person interested in the commonhold, the court may appoint an individual or a body corporate as an administrator ("the administrator") to exercise in the name and on behalf of the association the functions with respect to administration of the association or of its executive committee or both, or such of those functions as the court may direct (including functions exercisable by an ordinary resolution of the association, but not functions exercisable by a class 1 resolution).

(2)  The court may appoint the administrator for an indefinite period or a fixed period on such terms and conditions as to remuneration or otherwise as it thinks fit, and, on the application of the administrator or any person referred to in paragraph (1) the court (or, in the case of a county court, a court sitting for the same division) may remove or replace him as it thinks appropriate.

(3)  The costs of the administrator are common expenses.

(4)  The administrator shall not delegate any of the functions vested in him under this Article without the approval of the court; but where he is empowered to exercise functions of the executive committee he may (unless the court otherwise directs) without that approval exercise the power of appointing agents conferred on the executive committee by rule 12(2)(a) of the Commonhold Association Constitution Rules.

(5)  The administrator shall convene annual general meetings of the commonhold association and may convene extraordinary general meetings (including a meeting to consider a resolution to be proposed as a class 1 resolution), and meetings of the executive committee, if and when he thinks fit.

(6)  The administrator, or, where he is replaced, his replacement, shall lodge in the Land Registry an office copy of the court order appointing him, and, where the court removes the administrator without replacement, it shall direct such person as it considers appropriate to lodge in the Land Registry an office copy of the relevant order; and the Registrar is to register the effect of any such order.

(7)  For the purposes of this Article the persons interested in a commonhold include any creditor (whether present, contingent or prospective) of the commonhold association.

(8)  In this Article "executive committee" in relation to a commonhold association means the committee appointed for that association under Rule 8 of the Commonhold Association Constitution Rules.

# EXPLANATORY NOTE

## ARTICLE 18

This Article empowers the court to appoint an administrator for a commonhold (e.g. where the commonhold association is not functioning or is paralysed by lack of consensus).

*Paragraph (1)* enables the commonhold association or any person interested in the commonhold (say, a unit owner, a mortgagee (who may be a unit owner's mortgagee or, exceptionally, the association's mortgagee – see Article 7(8)) or a creditor of the association's) to ask the court to appoint an administrator for the commonhold. Any appointment is at the court's unfettered discretion, and may extend to all the functions of the association and its executive committee or any lesser number of those functions, except that an administrator may not be empowered to exercise any function which is exercisable by a class 1 resolution. By virtue of Article 24(1), "the court" has the meaning given by section 4 of the Land Registration Act.

*Paragraph (2)* The period of the administrator's term of office and, except as provided in paragraph (3) as to costs, the terms and conditions of his appointment are in the discretion of the court. If the administrator, or any person who could make an application under paragraph (1), asks it to do so, the court may remove the administrator without replacing him, or may remove him and appoint another in his place.

*Paragraph (3)* declares the administrator's costs to be common expenses (see Article 2(2)). The expression "costs" is defined in section 46(2) of the Interpretation Act as including fees, charges, disbursements, expenses or remuneration.

*Paragraph (4)* prevents an administrator from sub-delegating his powers or duties (Interpretation Act, s. 46(2) ("functions")), except with the court's approval; but where he exercises functions of the executive committee he may exercise that committee's normal power of acting through agents unless the court directs him not to do so.

*Paragraph (5)* empowers the administrator to call meetings. He must call annual general meetings (e.g. to lay accounts and inform members of the progress of his administration) and may call extraordinary general meetings (including meetings to consider class1 resolutions); and where the members have carried out their duty to appoint an executive committee he may call meetings of the committee (e.g. to take their views on matters arising).

*Paragraph (6)* requires an administrator, when appointed, to lodge in the Land Registry an office copy of the court order appointing him. The appointment is not conditional upon the order being lodged or its effect registered, because the proceedings of the court are in the public domain. Similarly a court order terminating an administration must be lodged. The

Registrar of Titles is under a duty to register the effect of an apponting order or a terminating order.

*Paragraph (7)* makes it clear that a creditor may apply for the appointment of an administrator.

*Paragraph (8)* defines "executive committee".

**Repair, reconstruction or protection of buildings**

**19.**—(1) Where –

(a) a building which comprises or forms part of a commonhold has sustained damage, or

(b) the commonhold association, on competent advice, is satisfied that such a building is likely to sustain damage unless preventive or remedial works are executed,

the commonhold association has a duty promptly to repair or reconstruct the building or execute those works unless, by a class 1 resolution, it resolves that the commonhold be terminated and Article 20 is complied with.

(2) Where damage such as is mentioned in paragraph (1) has been caused, or is apprehended as likely to be caused, by or in consequence of some wrongful act or omission of a third person, proceedings in respect of the damage may be taken by the commonhold association against that person on its own account and on behalf of the owners of, and any other persons interested in, the respective units (who may be described sufficiently in any process as "the unit owners", without further particulars).

(3) Without prejudice to the consequences of any proceedings such as are mentioned in paragraph (2) and subject to any order made by the court under paragraph (9)(a), the proceeds of insurance (if any) shall be used to repair or reconstruct a building, or execute works, under this Article.

(4) Any deficiency in the costs of repair, reconstruction or works which remains after applying any sum recovered in proceedings or any insurance money is part of the common expenses.

(5) When it becomes the duty of a commonhold association to reconstruct a building (other than an ancillary building), or to execute works, under paragraph (1), the association shall, as soon as is reasonably practicable, draw up a scheme for the purpose and, if the scheme (in either its original or an amended form) is adopted by a class 1 resolution, it thereupon becomes binding on the association and all the owners and occupiers of units in the same way as the commonhold declaration is binding on them, and also becomes binding on all mortgagees and tenants of any part of the commonhold.

(6) For the purposes of paragraph (5), a certificate of a person with prescribed qualifications that the work necessary to reinstate a building amounts to reconstruction is conclusive of that fact.

(7) Where, in the absence of the concurrence of some of the votes capable of being cast on a class 1 resolution adopting a scheme under paragraph (5), application is made to the court for approval of the resolution, the court may, after hearing any representations on behalf of any unit owners or the mortgagees of any part of the commonhold, settle a scheme which, having regard to the rights and interests of the unit owners generally, appears just and equitable for the reconstruction of the building or the execution of the works, and such a scheme is binding in the same way as one adopted under paragraph (5).

(8)    A scheme under paragraph (5) may include such provisions as the meeting approving the scheme considers expedient, including provisions –

(a)  for the reconstruction of the building to a design different from that of the original or from materials different from those of the original, or both;

(b)  for the reconstruction of part only of the building;

(c)  for the payment of compensation to unit owners whose units are not to be reconstructed;

(d)  consequential provisions;

and, where the court settles a scheme under paragraph (7), it may make an order requiring any unit owner whose unit has been damaged and who does not agree to participate in the scheme to transfer his unit to the other unit owners concerned in such shares and on payment of such compensation as the court thinks just.

(9)    In the exercise of its powers under paragraphs (7) and (8), the court may make such orders as it considers appropriate for giving effect to the scheme, including orders –

(a)  directing how insurance money received in respect of damage should be applied;

(b)  directing such consequential modifications to be made by the Registrar to the commonhold declaration or in the register of freeholders as the court thinks necessary;

(c)  imposing such terms and conditions as it thinks fit.

(10)  The requirement in paragraph (5) that a scheme for the reconstruction of a building or the execution of preventive or remedial works be approved by a class 1 resolution does not preclude the commonhold association from carrying out, without such approval and as part of its administrative functions, such works as, on competent advice, it is satisfied are necessary to meet an emergency.

ARTICLE 19

This Article sets out the duties of a commonhold association where a building in the commonhold has sustained damage (e.g. by fire) or where damage has not yet been sustained but is anticipated (e.g. because of some flaw in the design or construction of a building or of some occurrence such as subsidence, upheaval, slippage or an excavation which threatens to affect the site).

*Paragraph (1)* sets out two situations –

*sub-paragraph (a)* where a building which comprises or forms part of a commonhold has sustained damage;

*sub-paragraph (b)* where the commonhold association, on competent advice, is satisfied that such a building is likely to sustain damage unless preventive or remedial works are executed.

In either of these situations, the commonhold association has a duty to repair or reconstruct the building, or execute the works, promptly, unless it passes a class 1 resolution that the commonhold be terminated (as it is empowered to do by Article 20).

*Paragraph (2)* applies where the damage has been caused, or is apprehended, from some wrongful act of a person (e.g. an excavation which results, or is likely to result, in loss of support). Proceedings in respect of that act (e.g. for damages or an injunction) may be taken by the commonhold association on behalf of itself and the unit owners.

*Paragraph (3)* requires any insurance money received in respect of the damage to be applied towards the cost of repair, reconstruction or works. If sufficient compensation çan be obtained under paragraph (2), there may be no insurance money; and the court is empowered by paragraph (9)(a) to give contrary directions as to the application of insurance money (e.g. where the whole building is not to be reinstated). By virtue of Article 24(1), "the court" has the meaning given by section 4 of the Land Registration Act.

*Paragraph (4)* causes any deficiency in the costs of repair, reinstatement or works which is not covered by compensation or insurance to be defrayed as a common expense.

*Paragraph (5)* requires the commonhold association to prepare a scheme for the reconstruction (but not the mere repair) of a building or for the carrying out of preventive works. The scheme must be approved by a class 1 resolution, and, when approved binds all occupiers, mortgagees and tenants of units (as well as all unit owners and the commonhold association). A scheme is not required for the reconstruction of a building which is merely ancillary – e.g. a block of garages or a gardener's shed.

*Paragraph (6)* enables it to be determined whether work needed to restore damage is repair or reconstruction. Repair consists of a replacement of worn or damaged parts; reconstruction is more fundamental and involves substantial re-building, possibly to a different design. The certificate of a person who has qualifications prescribed by Land Registry Rules (he might be, say, an architect) is conclusive.

*Paragraph (7)* deals with the case where, because all persons entitled to vote on a class1 resolution do not support it, but at least 80% of them do, the court is asked to approve the resolution (Article 4(1)). The court may settle a scheme (which may be the scheme proposed by the commonhold association, or such variation of that scheme as the court thinks just and equitable, or a completely new scheme) – the court has a wide discretion to do what is best in the interests of the unit owners.

*Paragraph (8)* empowers a scheme –

*sub-paragraph (a)* to provide for the reconstruction of the building to a new design (the reconstructed building need not be an exact replica of the original);

*sub-paragraph (b)* to provide for the reconstruction of only part of the building;

*sub-paragraph (c)* to provide for compensating owners whose units are not to be reinstated;

*sub-paragraph (d)* to include consequential provisions.
Where a minority of unit owners object to the proposed scheme and the matter goes to the court, the court may order the assenting owners to buy out the dissenting owners, and fix terms.

*Paragraph (9)* gives the court such ancillary powers as it considers appropriate for giving effect to the scheme settled by it. These include –

*sub-paragraph (a)* application of insurance money;

*sub-paragraph (b)* consequential amendments of the commonhold declaration or the register of freeholders kept in the Land Registry;

*sub-paragraph (c)* the imposition of terms and conditions.

*Paragraph (10)* makes it clear that the duty to propose a scheme to a meeting convened to consider a class 1 resolution (of which at least 30 days' notice must be given – Article 3) does not prevent the execution of emergency works. The decision to execute such works is an administrative function, and so exercisable by the executive committee in the name of the commonhold association, unless the association by ordinary resolution otherwise directs.

**Termination of commonhold**

**20.**—(1) A commonhold is terminated –

(a) where, not less than 30 working days after the registration in the register of commonhold associations kept under Article 8 of notice of intention to move such a resolution, the commonhold association passes a class 1 resolution that the commonhold be terminated and the mortgagees referred to in Article 22(1)(b) and (2) concur; or

(b) where, in the absence of such a resolution, the court on the application of any person interested in the commonhold orders the commonhold to be terminated because, in its opinion, circumstances have arisen which, having regard to the rights and interests of all persons interested in the commonhold as a whole, make it just and equitable that the commonhold be terminated;

and the other requirements of this Article are complied with.

(2) It is the duty of the commonhold association to lodge in the Land Registry –

(a) a certificate in the prescribed form of the concurrence of the mortgagees referred to as mentioned in paragraph (1)(a) together with an office copy of any court order under Article 22(3) dispensing with the concurrence of any mortgagees;

(b) an office copy of any court order under paragraph (1)(b).

(3) Without prejudice to Article 4(3), a class 1 resolution in relation to which such concurrence is given (or dispensed with) has no operation until the effect of the concurrence (or dispensation) is registered; but a court order under paragraph (1)(b) comes into operation in accordance with its terms (irrespective of registration, unless the order provides otherwise).

(4) Together with a resolution under paragraph (1)(a) or a court order under paragraph (1)(b) there must be lodged in the Land Registry –

(a) a copy of a resolution or an office copy of a court order under paragraph (5) appointing a liquidator (and the Registrar shall register the effect of the resolution or order);

(b) all the land certificates and certificates of charge outstanding in relation to land comprised in the commonhold (and it is the duty of the person holding such a certificate to deliver it to the commonhold association for the purpose of lodgment).

(5) A person who is qualified to act as an insolvency practitioner (within the meaning of the Insolvency (Northern Ireland) Order 1989) must be appointed liquidator of the commonhold association –

(a) by the meeting which passes the class 1 resolution to terminate the commonhold, or

(b) by the court which makes an order for termination of the commonhold.

1252

(6) Without prejudice to paragraphs (7) and (8), the general functions of the liquidator are –

(a) to exercise the functions of the commonhold association and its executive committee so far as is necessary or expedient for the proper winding up of the association;

(b) to realize such of its assets as are not already money (or readily realizable into money) under the control of the liquidator;

(c) to pay its debts;

(d) to assess and levy contributions on and recover them from members, so far as is necessary for the payment of debts and costs;

(e) to pay any balance remaining under the control of the liquidator to the persons entitled to it.

(7) Land Registry Rules may apply provisions of the Insolvency (Northern Ireland) Order 1989 or of company insolvency rules for the purposes of the liquidation and dissolution of a commonhold, with such modifications as the rules specify, and may make other provision for those purposes.

(8) Land Registry Rules shall require the liquidator to open and maintain with a financial institution of a prescribed kind an account ("the commonhold liquidation account") into which all money realised from the assets of the commonhold association is to be paid; and rules shall contain provisions to ensure that, where a member's share of the balance mentioned in paragraph (6)(e) is subject to the estate of the lessor of an equity-sharing lease or the interest of a mortgagee who has recorded his interest with the commonhold association, the liquidator may make no payment to the member out of the commonhold liquidation account in respect of that share without the consent of the lessor or mortgagee.

(9) Upon the registration of the effect of a resolution or court order for the termination of a commonhold all the land comprised in the commonhold becomes vested in the commonhold association by virtue of this paragraph and without the need for any other instrument, and the Registrar shall cancel the entries in the register of freeholders of the titles of the commonhold association to the common parts and of the respective unit owners to their units (or, where there is an equity-sharing lease of a unit, the entry in the register of freeholders of the lessor's estate and the entry in the register of leaseholders of the lessee's estate) and register the commonhold association in the register of freeholders as the owner of all that land free from any charge except one imposed under Article 7(8), but subject to an inhibition (which may be entered without any application or consent) that all money payable in respect of a transfer of the land or any part of it must be paid to the credit of the commonhold liquidation account; and thereafter –

(a) the interest of a member in the commonhold is his net share (or, pending the liquidation of all the commonhold association's assets, his prospective net share) of the balance of the commonhold liquidation account;

(b) the interest of a mortgagee of a member's former unit (where the mortgagee has recorded his interest with the commonhold association) is the right to have his debt discharged out of the member's share of the balance of the commonhold liquidation account on the basis of his unit entitlement with respect to the division of assets in accordance with its priority before any payment is made to the member.

(10) Upon the registration of the effect of a resolution or court order for the termination of a commonhold, all tenancies (of any degree) of, and all easements, obligations, rights and privileges over or other interests in, any part of the commonhold belonging to any person other than the commonhold association terminate, with the exception of –

(a) any charge imposed under Article 7(8);

(b) any easement, obligation, right or privilege which affected any part of the land comprised in the commonhold before the commonhold was created and which continued up to the date of registration of the resolution or order;

(c) any easement, obligation, right or privilege created after the creation of the commonhold which was created by, or with the consent of, the commonhold association and in the case of which any consideration payable was paid to the association.

(11) Where a tenancy or other interest affecting a unit terminates by virtue of paragraph (10), the unit owner's net share of the balance of the commonhold liquidation account is divisible between him and the person entitled to the tenancy or interest on the basis that the unit owner is entitled to the proportion of the net share which the value of the unit subject to the tenancy or interest immediately before the passing of the resolution, or the making of the court order, for termination bears to the value which the unit would have had at that time if free from the tenancy or interest; and the person entitled to the tenancy or interest is entitled to the remainder of the share.

(12) Where a person entitled to a tenancy to which paragraph (11) applies has had his name and address recorded by the commonhold association in the register of members in accordance with rule 3(7) of the Commonhold Association Constitution Rules and paragraph 1(1)(i) of Schedule 4, the division of the unit owner's share under paragraph (11) is to be made by the liquidator; otherwise it is to be made by the unit owner.

(13) Where a unit is subject to an equity-sharing lease, the unit owner's net share of the balance of the commonhold liquidation account is divisible between him and the lessor in proportion to their respective shares in the equity, and the division is to be made by the liquidator.

(14) For the purposes of this Article the persons interested in a commonhold include any creditor (whether present, contingent or prospective) of the commonhold association.

(15) In this Article any reference to a member's (or unit owner's) net share of the balance of the commonhold liquidation account is a reference

1254

to his share of that balance on the basis of his unit entitlement with respect to the division of assets less any mortgage debt, outstanding contributions, costs or other proper deductions, and any reference to the executive committee of a commonhold association is to the committee appointed for the association under rule 8 of the Commonhold Association Constitution Rules; and in paragraph (10) the reference to tenancies does not include equity-sharing leases.

# EXPLANATORY NOTE

ARTICLE 20

This Article sets out the procedure for terminating a commonhold.

*Paragraph (1)* sets out two ways in which termination procedure may be initiated –

*sub-paragraph (a)* by the commonhold association passing a class 1 resolution for termination, with the concurrence of the mortgagees of units and any mortgagee of the common parts (Article 22(1)(b) and (2)) (as to the concurrence of the lessor of an equity-sharing lease, see the Explanatory Note on Article 3);

*sub-paragraph (b)* by the court ordering termination because it is just and equitable to do so (cf. Companies (Northern Ireland) Order 1986, Article 479(g)): an application for such an order may be made by the common-hold association or any person interested in the commonhold (this includes unit owners, mortgagees and creditors as well as anyone else who can show an interest). By virtue of Article 24(1), "the court" has the meaning given by section 4 of the Land Registration Act.

*Paragraph (2)* places on the commonhold association the duty of lodging in the Land Registry –

*sub-paragraph (a)* a certificate (in the form prescribed by Land Registry Rules) of the concurrence of mortgagees in the class 1 resolution to terminate and also, where at least 80% but not all of the mortgagees have concurred, an office copy of the court order dispensing with the consent of the dissenters (Article 22(3)); or

*sub-paragraph (b)* an office copy of a court order to terminate the commonhold.

*Paragraph (3)* distinguishes between the time of taking effect of a class 1 resolution for termination and a court order for termination. A class 1 resolution does not, in any event, operate until its effect has been registered in the Land Registry (Article 4(3)); a class 1 resolution for termination does not operate until, in addition, the mortgagees' concur-rence (or the concurrence of at least 80% and a court order dispensing with the concurrence of the remainder) has been registered. But an order of the court for termination of the commonhold on the ground that termination is just and equitable comes into operation in accordance with the terms of the order (e.g. the court may order that termination proceedings begin at once, or on service of a copy of the order in a stipulated way, or upon registration of the effect of the order in the Land Registry).

*Paragraph (4)* requires other documents to be lodged in the Land Registry (as well as those mentioned in paragraph (2)). These are –

*sub-paragraph (a)* a copy of a resolution or (as the case requires) a court order appointing a liquidator;

*sub-paragraph (b)* all land certificates and certificates of charge relating to the commonhold. This would include the land certificate for the freehold held by an equity-sharing lessor and that for the leasehold held by the lessee. The duty to pass those to the commonhold association for lodgment could be enforced by mandatory injuction.

*Paragraph (5)* is concerned with the appointment of a liquidator (who must be qualified to act as an insolvency practitioner). The appointment must be made by the meeting which passes a class 1 resolution for termination or by the court which orders termination. Where the appointment is made by a meeting of the commonhold association it is not essential that it be made by a class 1 resolution (except where a class 1 resolution is stipulated, a meeting will normally act by an ordinary resolution); but it would be convenient for the resolution for termination and the resolution appointing a liquidator to be run together.

*Paragraph (6)* sets out the basic functions of a liquidator. They are –

*sub-paragraph (a)* to exercise the functions of the commonhold association so as to ensure an orderly winding-up. Normally, except where the association is required to act by a resolution, the functions of a commonhold association are discharged by its executive committee (Schedule 3, rule 12(1)); the appointment of a liquidator supersedes the exercise of administrative functions by the executive committee. The power to appoint agents is conferred on the executive committee by Schedule 3, rule 12(2)(a) – this power will be exercisable by the liquidator so long as he finds it necessary or expedient (i.e. advantageous for the purposes of the winding-up) to do so;

*sub-paragraph (b)* to liquidate the assets of the association;

*sub-paragraph (c)* to pay the association's debts;

*sub-paragraph (d)* to require members to pay contributions (Schedule 4, paras. 7-12) in order to discharge debts and costs (defined in section 46(2) of the Interpretation Act as including fees, charges, disbursements, expenses or remuneration).

*sub-paragraph (e)* to pay any surplus to the persons entitled (cf. paras. (11)–(13)).

*Paragraph (7)* empowers Land Registry Rules to apply (and modify) provisions of the Insolvency Order or company insolvency rules.

*Paragraph (8)* requires Land Registry Rules to oblige the liquidator to open a commonhold liquidation account with a financial institution of a kind prescribed by the rules (e.g. a bank or a building society). All money realised in the liquidation must be paid into this account; where a unit owner's mortgagee has recorded his interest with the commonhold association, no payment is to be made to the owner out of the account without the consent of the mortgagee, and similarly with the lessor of an equity-sharing lease (whose interest will have been recorded without any application by him – Schedule 3 rule 3(7), Schedule 4 para. 1(1)(i)).

*Paragraph (9)* causes the freehold title to all the land in the commonhold to vest in the commonhold association. This vesting takes effect immediately upon the registration in the register of freeholders of the effect of the class 1 resolution or court order for termination, and supersedes the titles of the unit owners to their units and of the common-hold association to the common parts. The registration of the new title is to be subject to an inhibition requiring the proceeds of any sale of the land to be paid into the commonhold liquidation account. After this conver-gence of titles in the commonhold association –

*sub-paragraph (a)* the interest of a member of the commonhold associ-ation in the commonhold is confined to his share in the balance of the commonhold liquidation account (that share is determined in accordance with his unit entitlement – Schedule 1, Part I, para.8(c));

*sub-paragraph (b)* the interest of a mortgagee of a unit is his right to have the mortgage debt discharged out of the member's share before any payment is made to the member. Where there are two or more mortgages they will be discharged in accordance with their respective priorities. However, this right to prior payment arises only where the mortgagee has recorded his interest with the commonhold association (Schedule 4, para. 1(1)(i)). (The liquidator cannot take account of a mortgagee (or tenant) of whose existence he is unaware.)

*Paragraph (10)* When the commonhold association is registered as owner of the whole commonhold under paragraph (9), all subsidiary interests in the commonhold cease except –

*sub-paragraph (a)* any charge imposed by the commonhold association on the common parts by authority of a class 1 resolution under Article 7(8);

*sub-paragraph (b)* easements, obligations, rights and privileges which preceded the creation of the commonhold and continued throughout its existence;

*sub-paragraph (c)* any easement, obligation, right or privilege which was created during the existence of the commonhold, if the following condi-tions were observed – the interest must have been created by the commonhold association or with its consent, and any payment for the interest must have been made to the association.

*Paragraph (11)* applies where a unit is subject to a tenancy. The tenancy terminates under paragraph (10), but the tenant is entitled to compen-sation for his loss, to be paid out of his landlord's share of the common-hold liquidation account. It is necessary to ascertain the value of the unit immediately before the termination proceedings began (a) subject to the tenancy and (b) as if free from any tenancy: the proportion $\frac{(a)}{(b)}$ gives the landlord's share of the net share of the commonhold liquidation account attributable to the unit, and the balance of that net share is the tenant's compensation. The paragraph also applies to other interests of value in a unit, but no attempt is made to define those interests. Whether the holder of an interest is entitled to compensation, depends upon whether the interest is capable of valuation – if it is a bare licence it probably will not be so capable, but if it is a licence coupled with an interest it may be.

*Paragraph (12)* makes it the duty of the liquidator to pay the compen-sation which is due to a tenant under paragraph (11), where the tenant has recorded his interest with the commonhold association. If the tenant has not recorded his interest, the liquidator will disregard him and pay the full amount of the unit owner's share to him: it will then be for the tenant to recover his compensation from the unit owner. (This paragraph applies only to tenants, and not to persons with "other interests", because only tenants and mortgagees can record their interests with the association- Schedule 4, para. 1(1)(i).)

*Paragraph (13)* provides for the division of a unit owner's share (in the case of an equity-sharing lease) between the lessor and lessee in proportion to their entitlements to the equity. The division will be made by the liquidator, because the lessor's interest will have been recorded by the commonhold association without the need of any application by him.

*Paragraph (14)* makes it clear that a creditor is a person interested in the commonhold. This includes a contingent or prospective creditor – cf. Article 18(7) and Companies (Northern Ireland) Order 1986 Art. 481(1).

*Paragraph (15)* defines the expressions "net share of the balance of the commonhold liquidation account" and "executive committee" and modifies the reference to tenancies in paragraph (10) so as to exclude equity-sharing tenancies (which are dealt with in paragraphs (9) and (13)).

## Reconstitution of commonhold, or constitution of development scheme

**21.**—(1) A scheme may be made under this Article where, having regard to all the circumstances, it appears expedient –

(a) to a commonhold association which passes a class 1 resolution that the commonhold be terminated, or

(b) to the court which approves such a resolution passed by the concurrence of at least 80 per cent., but not all, of the votes capable of being cast or which, under Article 22(3), dispenses with the concurrence of any of the mortgagees mentioned in paragraph (2), or

(c) to the court which orders a commonhold to be terminated,

that all or part of the commonhold should be made subject to a new commonhold declaration or to a development scheme under Part IX of the Property (Northern Ireland) Order 1989.

(2) The commonhold association may, by a class 1 resolution passed with the concurrence of the mortgagees referred to in Article 22(1)(b), adopt a scheme under this Article.

(3) The court may, after hearing any representations on behalf of any unit owners or the mortgagees of any part of the commonhold, settle a scheme under this Article containing such terms and conditions as appear just and equitable.

(4) A scheme under this Article –

(a) shall set out the provisions of the proposed commonhold declaration or development scheme;

(b) shall make provision for ensuring the fair division of the assets and liabilities of the commonhold association;

(c) may make provision for the payment of compensation, by any unit owners to any other unit owners;

(d) may contain such other provisions (including transitional provisions) as the commonhold association or, as the case may be, the court considers necessary or expedient.

(5) A scheme under this Article is binding on the commonhold association and all the owners and occupiers of units in the same way as the commonhold declaration is binding on them and is also binding on all mortgagees and tenants of any part of the commonhold.

(6) Land Registry Rules may make modifications in Article 20 for the purposes of this Article.

# EXPLANATORY NOTE

## ARTICLE 21

This Article permits all or part of a commonhold to be excluded from termination proceedings (e.g. where a commonhold consists of two or more blocks of flats or a block of flats and a number of detached houses, and one block (or the block) of flats is destroyed by fire, the commonhold might be terminated as to that block and reconstituted as to the remainder; or where all the buildings in a commonhold are destroyed a new commonhold may be constituted for the same area).

*Paragraph (1)* sets out the scope of the Article, which applies where a commonhold is to be terminated but circumstances render it expedient (i.e. in accord with the objects of the commonhold) that all or part of the commonhold should be reconstituted as a new commonhold or should be made the subject of a development scheme under the Property Order. A new commonhold declaration would be appropriate where the part of the commonhold to be preserved consists of or includes flats; a development scheme may be sufficient where the preserved part includes only houses. The Article is activated by a scheme made under paragraph (2) or paragraph (3).

*Paragraph (2)* empowers the commonhold association to adopt a scheme by class 1 resolution: the resolution must have the concurrence of all the mortgagees of any part of the commonhold whose names and addresses have been recorded by the commonhold association and whose concurrence has not been dispensed with by the court under Article 22(3).

*Paragraph (3)* empowers the court to settle a scheme. The court may exercise this power when it makes an order under Article 20(1)(b) for the termination of the commonhold or when it approves a class 1 resolution adopting a scheme or dispenses with the concurrence of any mortgagees in such a resolution (paragraph (1)(b), (c)).

*Paragraph (4)* lists certain provisions which a scheme must or may contain.

*sub-paragraph (a)* it must set out the proposed commonhold declaration or development scheme;

*sub-paragraph (b)* it must provide for the fair division of the assets and liabilities of the commonhold association ("assets" is defined in section 46(2) of the Interpretation Act as including property or rights of any kind);

*sub-paragraph (c)* it may require some unit owners to pay compensation to others;

*sub-paragraph (d)* it may contain other provisions (including some of a transitional nature) which are necessary or expedient (i.e. advantageous to further the purposes of the scheme).

*Paragraph (5)* makes the scheme binding on the commonhold association and owners, occupiers, mortgagees and tenants. The association and owners and occupiers are bound in accordance with Article 13.

*Paragraph (6)* empowers Land Registry Rules to modify Article 20 (termination procedure) for the purposes of this Article.

## Consent or concurrence of mortgagees

**22.**—(1) This Article applies to –

(a) the consent of mortgagees to the creation of a commonhold which must accompany a commonhold declaration under Article 6(8) where the promoters of the commonhold are the existing owners of separately owned units acting together;

(b) the concurrence of mortgagees in a class 1 resolution, as mentioned in Article 20(1)(a), for the termination of a commonhold or in a class 1 resolution under Article 21(2) for the reconstitution of a commonhold or the constitution of a development scheme.

(2) Subject to paragraph (3), the mortgagees referred to in sub-paragraph (a) of paragraph (1) are all the mortgagees of the units mentioned in that sub-paragraph or any common parts serving those units whose names and addresses are brought to the notice of the promoters as the result of reasonable enquiries made by them or otherwise and whose consent is not dispensed with under paragraph (3); and the mortgagees referred to in sub-paragraph (b) are all the mortgagees of units whose names and addresses have been recorded by the commonhold association, and any mortgagees of common parts, whose concurrence (in either case) is not dispensed with under paragraph (3).

(3) Where at least 80 per cent. (by number and not by value), but not all, of the mortgagees consent or concur, the promoters or, as the case may be, the commonhold association may apply to the court for an order dispensing with the consent or concurrence of the remaining mortgagees, and on an application under this paragraph the court may make such an order if it considers that it is reasonable in all the circumstances for it to do so.

# EXPLANATORY NOTE

## ARTICLE 22

This Article is concerned with the procedure for obtaining, or dispensing with, the consent or concurrence of mortgagees to certain developments.

*Paragraph (1)* sets out the developments to which the Article applies. These are –

*sub-paragraph (a)* the consent of mortgagees to the creation of a commonhold which is required by Article 6(8) where the promoters of the commonhold are the existing owners of separately owned units acting together (e.g. where the owners of flats which were formerly leasehold, having redeemed their ground rents, decide to form a commonhold);

*sub-paragraph (b)* the concurrence of mortgagees in a class 1 resolution to terminate a commonhold or, an existing commonhold having been made subject to the termination machinery, to reconstitute it or part of it as a new commonhold or under a development scheme.

*Paragraph (2)* identifies the mortgagees to whom the Article applies. These are, as to paragraph (1)(a) all the mortgagees of units or common parts whose names and addresses come to the notice of the promoters (who must make reasonable enquiries) and whose consent is not dispensed with by the court; and as to paragraph (1)(b) all the mortgagees of units whose names and addresses have been recorded by the commonhold association, and any mortgagees of common parts (who will be known to the commonhold association in any event), whose concurrence is not dispensed with by the court.

*Paragraph (3)* applies where at least 80%, but not all, of the mortgagees consent or concur: the court, on an application by the promoters or the commonhold association, may dispense with the consent or concurrence of the remainder if that seems a reasonable thing to do.

**Power to modify Schedules**

23.—(1) The Department of Finance and Personnel may by order make modifications in any of the Schedules to this Order; but no such order shall affect a Schedule in its application to a commonhold created before the commencement of the order, except where the order modifies Schedule 3 or Schedule 4 and the commonhold association decides by ordinary resolution in pursuance of Article 7(9) or (10) that the modification should apply to it.

(2)  No order is to be made under this Article unless a draft of it has been laid before, and approved by a resolution of, the Assembly.

# EXPLANATORY NOTE

ARTICLE 23

This Article gives the Department of Finance and Personnel power to make orders making modifications in any of the Schedules to the Order. "Modifications" is defined in Article 2(2) as additions, omissions, amendments, adaptations, applications, extensions, restrictions and substitutions. Any order made under this Article is subject to approval by the Assembly in draft: during the period of direct rule this means that the order is subject to annulment in pursuance of a resolution of either House of Parliament (Northern Ireland Act 1974 c. 28 Sch. 1 para. 3(3)).

An order modifying one of the Schedules does not affect any commonhold existing at the time when the order takes effect ("commencement" is defined in section 46(1) of the Interpretation Act). But where an order modifies the Commonhold Association Constitution Rules in Schedule 3, or any provision of Schedule 4 (which is concerned with regulating the administrative operation of a commonhold association), an existing commonhold association may apply the modifications to itself by passing an ordinary resolution (Article 7(9), (10)).

**Application of provisions of the Land Registration Act**

**24.**—(1) Section 2 of the Land Registration Act (summoning of witnesses), section 3 (indemnity of Registrar, officers or persons acting in good faith pursuant to any authority conferred by or under that Act) and Part II (jurisdiction of courts) apply for the purposes of this Order as if references in them to that Act included references to this Order.

(2) Sections 70 and 71 of, and Schedule 9 to, the Land Registration Act (the Insurance Fund; claims for compensation) apply for the purposes of this Order as if the references in section 70(1), (2) and (4) to that Act included references to this Order.

(3) Section 81(1) and (2) of the Land Registration Act (searches) apply to the register of commonhold associations as they apply to other registers, and section 81(1) applies to documents filed by the Registrar under this Order as it applies to a register (any reference to searching a register being construed as including inspecting such a document).

(4) An order under subsection (1) of section 84 of the Land Registration Act may prescribe the fees to be taken in the Land Registry for the purposes of this Order as well as for the purposes of that Act, and accordingly any reference in that section to that Act includes a reference to this Order.

(5) Land Registry Rules may be made for giving effect to this Order as well as for giving effect to that Act, and accordingly in the introductory words of subsection (3) of section 85 of the Land Registration Act, and in paragraphs (a), (k) and (n) of that subsection, references to that Act include references to this Order.

(6) Any express provision of this Order relating to Land Registry Rules does not prejudice the generality of paragraph (5) and the said section 85(3).

(7) For the purposes of this Order, the reference in section 85(3)(k) of the Land Registration Act to documents to be given includes documents to be served or lodged.

(8) Land Registry Rules may require the authentication in a prescribed manner of a copy of a document, where the copy is permitted or required by this Order to be lodged or delivered.

# EXPLANATORY NOTE

## ARTICLE 24

This Article applies certain provisions of the Land Registration Act for the purposes of the Order.

*Paragraph (1)* attracts section 2 (witnesses), section 3 (indemnities) and Part II (courts) of the Land Registration Act.

*Paragraph (2)* attracts provisions about the Insurance Fund.

*Paragraph (3)* attracts provisions about searches. It also allows documents filed by the Registrar (e.g. commonhold declarations, class 1 resolutions, certain ordinary resolutions) to be inspected and copies requisitioned.

*Paragraph (4)* enables fees to be prescribed by the Department of the Environment after consultation with the Land Registry Rules Committee.

*Paragraph (5)* allows Land Registry Rules to be made (by the Head of the Department of the Environment acting with the advice and assistance of the Land Registry Rules (Committee) for the purposes of the Order.

*Paragraph (6)* puts it beyond any possible doubt that the general power conferred by paragraph (5) is not narrowed in any way by any specific power to make rules for particular purposes which is conferred by the Order (e.g. Article 20(7), (8) (conduct of liquidation of commonhold), Article 21(6) (modifications of termination procedure where liquidation is not to extend to all of commonhold)).

*Paragraph (7)* modifies the language of section 85(3)(k) of the Land Registration Act (rules with respect to form and contents of documents required or authorised to be used or given under or for the purposes of the Act) to reconcile it with the language of the Order. References to serving documents occur in, e.g., Schedule 2 paragraph 3(a), Schedule 3 rule 15.

*Paragraph (8)* allows rules to provide for the manner of authentication of copies of documents (e.g. diagrams annexed to a commonhold declaration under Schedule 1, Part I, para. 6; copies of resolutions).

**Offences by commonhold association**

**25.**—(1) If a commonhold association –

(a) contravenes rule 15(3) of the Commonholds Association Constitution Rules (which requires a commonhold association which has no office in a building forming part of the commonhold to provide a receptacle suitable for the purpose of receiving articles by post); or

(b) contravenes rule 16 of those Rules (which requires a commonhold association to lodge in the Land Registry a return containing particulars of any alteration in its registered office),

the association is guilty of an offence and is liable on summary conviction to a fine not exceeding level 3 on the standard scale.

(2) Where a commonhold association is guilty of an offence under sub-paragraph(a) or (b) of paragraph (1), every member of the executive committee of the association who consented to, or connived at, the offence, or did not exercise all such reasonable diligence as he ought in the circumstances to have exercised to prevent the offence, is also guilty of an offence and is liable on summary conviction to the same fine.

(3) In paragraph (2) "the executive committee" of a commonhold association means the committee appointed for that association under rule 8 of the Commonhold Association Constitution Rules.

# EXPLANATORY NOTE

## ARTICLE 25

This Article provides for offences by the commonhold association.

*Paragraph (1)* causes two kinds of contraventions of the Order to involve summary offences ("contravention" is defined in section 46(1) of the Interpretation Act as including, in relation to any statutory provision, a failure to comply with that provision). Those contraventions are –

*sub-paragraph (a)* a failure to provide a post-box in accordance with rule 15(3) of the Commonhold Association Constitution Rules set out in Schedule 3. Such a box must be provided where the commonhold association does not have an office in a building forming part of the commonhold.

*sub-paragraph (b)* a failure to make a return to the Land Registry of a change in the address of the commonhold association's registered office (defined in rule 1 of those Rules as the address for service of documents – cf. Sch. 1 Pt. I para. 2).

The penalty for an offence is a fine not exceeding level 3 on the standard scale. The expression "standard scale" is defined in section 42(4) of the Interpretation Act (definition inserted by the Fines and Penalties (Northern Ireland) Order 1984 (NI 3) Sch. 6 para. 2 as the standard scale provided by Article 5 of that Order – i.e. the scale set out in Article 5(2) of that Order or as fixed by an order under Article 17 of that Order to take account of changes in the value of money).

*Paragraph (2)* causes a member of the executive committee who consents to or connives at the commonhold association's offence, or who does not exercise all such reasonable diligence as he ought, in the circumstances, to exercise to prevent an offence, to be guilty of a similar offence and subject to the same fine (cf. section 20(2) of the Interpretation Act).

*Paragraph (3)* defines the expression "the executive committee".

**Penalty for improper use of "commonhold" or "commonhold association"**

**26.** If any person offers a unit in a building for sale under a name of which the word "commonhold" is the last word, or carries on a business under a name of which the words "commonhold association" are the last words (ignoring the word "limited", if used, then, unless the building is or forms part of a commonhold or the business is the business of a commonhold association, that person is guilty of an offence and is liable on summary conviction to a fine not exceeding level 3 on the standard scale.

# EXPLANATORY NOTE

ARTICLE 26

This Article makes it an offence to use the word "commonhold" as the last word in the name of a development which is not a duly-constituted commonhold under the Order, or to use the words "commonhold association" as the last words in the name of a business organisation which is not a duly-constituted commonhold association.

# SCHEDULES

## SCHEDULE 1

Articles 6, 23.

## THE COMMONHOLD

### PART I

### PARTICULARS TO BE INCLUDED IN, OR ANNEXED TO, A COMMONHOLD DECLARATION

1.   The name of the commonhold (of which the last word must be "Commonhold").

2.   The corporate name (which must be the name of the commonhold followed by the word "Association"), and the address for service of documents, of the commonhold association.

3.   A description of every unit by reference to its number, location, floor area and (unless Part II is left to apply) boundaries and any other particulars necessary for its proper identification.

4.   A description by reference to a plan of any common parts included or to be included in the commonhold, by reference to their location, area, boundaries and purposes.

5.   A description of any building on, or being or to be constructed on, land within the commonhold including its location on the land, the number of storeys, basements, cellars and units and the principal materials of which it is, or is to be, constructed.

6.   Diagrams of any building on, or being or to be constructed on, the land, together with, where the construction of any building has been completed within the period of one year immediately preceding the lodgment of the commonhold declaration, or where the building is in course of construction, a certificate in the prescribed form and signed by a person with the prescribed qualifications stating that the building has been or is being constructed in accordance with the diagrams.

"Diagrams", in this paragraph, means plans, elevations and, so far as they are necessary to illustrate the lay-out of the building, sections and any other drawings which, in the opinion of the Registrar, the circumstances require.

7.   Where the development of the commonhold is to be conducted in phases –

(a)   the number of phases proposed;

(b)   the area of land, units and common property to be comprised in each phase;

(c)   the dates of commencement and completion of each phase;

(d)   any rights reserved to the promoter until completion of the development.

8.   The unit entitlement of each unit, that is to say, the proportion, expressed as a vulgar fraction, which determines –

1273

(a) the number of votes (being the numerator of the fraction, the denominator being the total number of votes capable of being cast) exercisable in respect of the unit at a meeting of the common-hold association;

(b) the part of the common expenses which is payable as a contribution in respect of the unit;

(c) the rights of the members of the commonhold association in a division of assets on the termination of the commonhold.

The proportion may be the same for all the units or may be different for different units. The same proportion may be fixed for all the purposes of sub-paragraphs (a), (b) and (c), or different proportions may be fixed for different purposes; but in any case the total of all the fractions, or all the fractions fixed for a particular purpose, must equal the number one. Where different proportions are fixed for different purposes, references to unit entitlement with respect to any purpose are to the proportion fixed for that purpose.

9.—(1) Subject to sub-paragraph (2), a statement of all legal estates, legal interests and equitable interests affecting land to be included in the commonhold, and, where such a legal or equitable interest is a mortgage, of the debt which is or may become outstanding under any such mortgage; or a statement that there is no such legal estate, legal interest or equitable interest.

(2)   Sub-paragraph (1) does not apply to –

(a)  the legal estate of the promoter;

(b)  where the promoters are existing owners of separately owned units acting together, any mortgages of the respective units which had been created by the owners or tenants of those units or their predecessors in title.

10.   Any other particulars which are prescribed.

## PART II

### BOUNDARIES OF UNITS

1.   The boundaries of a unit follow the walls, floors and ceilings of the unit in accordance with the following paragraphs.

2.   Where walls, floors or ceilings are of a structural nature, the boundary runs immediately below decorative level, that is to say, the level nearest the wall, floor or ceiling of any plaster, tiles or facing material (the remainder of the wall, floor or ceiling being a common part), except that the interior of any door and door frame, and of any window frame and all window or door glass in such a wall, and the surface of any balcony (but not its structure and wall or railings), form part of the unit.

3.   Where walls, floors or ceilings are not of a structural nature –

(a)  if they are wholly within the unit, they (but, in the case of floors or ceilings, not the beams supporting them) form part of the unit;

(b)  if they are not wholly within the unit (that is to say, if they divide the unit from another unit or a common part) –

   (i)  in the case of a wall the boundary is a line drawn vertically through the centre of the wall;

   (ii)  in the case of a floor or ceiling the boundary is a limit which includes in the unit both the floor and the ceiling, but not the beams supporting the floor or ceiling or the ceiling of the unit below or the floor of the unit above, and also not including –

   (A)  in the case of a ground-floor unit, any sub-floor, foundations or footings or damp-proof course or membrane, or any floor beams, or

   (B)  in the case of a top-floor unit, the roof and roof beams (including the beams in the roof void, if any, and any insulating material).

4.   In paragraph 3 "beams" includes joists, purlins, rafters, ribs and trusses and any other structural supports.

# EXPLANATORY NOTE

## SCHEDULE 1

This Schedule is concerned with matters incidental to the creation of a commonhold.

## PART I

This Part lists partculars which must be included in, or annexed to, a commonhold declaration.

*Paragraph 1* requires the name of the commonhold to be stated. The last word in the name must be "Commonhold".

*Paragraph 2* requires the corporate name of the commonhold association to be stated. This must be the name of the commonhold followed by the words "Association" (so the last two words of the name of the commonhold association will be "Commonhold Association"). The address of the commonhold association for service of documents must also be stated (any change in that address must be notified to the Land Registry in a return under rule 16 of the Commonhold Association Constitution Rules).

*Paragraph 3* requires a description of every unit to be given. A unit may be a residential flat, a shop or an office or several of these (depending upon the nature of the commonhold). The number of the unit, its location and its floor area must be stated (units will be transferred by reference to their respective numbers). The boundaries of units must also be defined, unless the promoters are content to leave Part II of the Schedule to apply (cf. Article 6(5)).

*Paragraph 4* requires the common parts to be described. Not only will plans of buildings show entrance halls, stairways, passages and lifts, but a plan of the surrounding land should show such features as roads, parking areas, drying areas and waste disposal areas.

*Paragraph 5* requires a description of the building to be given. This need not be a full specification but at least it should give such particulars of construction as would be of interest to an insurer or purchaser.

*Paragraph 6* requires plans, elevations, sections and other drawings (where relevant) of the building or any projected building to be given. Where the building has been completed within the previous year, or where it is in course of construction, a certificate by a qualified person (say, an architect or surveyor) must be attached stating that the building has been or is being constructed in accordance with the drawings. Where such a certificate is lodged for a building in course of construction, a further certificate (under Article 10(1)) will be needed when construction is complete and before any unit is transferred to its first purchaser.

*Paragraph 7* applies to a commonhold which is to be developed in phases (cf. Article 10). The following must be stated –

*sub-paragraph (a)* the number of phases;

*sub-paragraph (b)* what is comprised in each phase – units and common parts;

*sub-paragraph (c)* the dates of commencing and completing each phase;

*sub-paragraph (d)* any rights reserved to the promoter until the development is completed (e.g. a right to maintain a sign-board offering units for sale; the right to use roads for construction traffic; the right to deposit materials).

*Paragraph 8* requires the unit entitlement of each unit to be stated as a vulgar fraction. This evidences –

*sub-paragraph (a)* the number of votes which may be cast by the owner of each unit at a meeting of the commonhold association, as compared to the total number capable of being cast in respect of all units;

*sub-paragraph (b)* the proportion of the common expenses which is payable as a contribution in respect of each unit;

*sub-paragraph (c)* the proportion of the net assets of the commonhold to which each unit owner will be entitled on a winding up.

In the case of domestic flats, the same proportion will normally apply for each of these three purposes; but special features of a particular development may require different proportions to apply for different purposes – e.g. where a block of flats is topped by a luxurious penthouse, the penthouse may share the same proportion as other units for the purposes mentioned in sub-paragraph (a) or (b), but may be entitled to a different proportion for the purposes of sub-paragraph (c); and where a commonhold consists of flats and houses, or flats and shops, or shops and offices, differentiation may be necessary for any of the three purposes.

*Paragraph 9* requires a statement to be given of all legal estates (except the promoter's freehold estate), legal interests and equitable interests affecting the land (with certain exceptions); or a statement that there is no such estate or interest.

*sub-paragraph (1)* also requires, where a relevant interest is a mortgage, a statement of the amount, or maximum amount (e.g. where an overdraft is secured) of the mortgage debt. (Cf. Article 11 as to such debts.)

*sub-paragraph (2)* contains exceptions. There is no need to refer under this paragraph to the promoter's freehold estate (which will already have been described under Article 6(1)); and where existing flats are formed into a commonhold and individual flats are subject to separate mortgages, there is no need to list those mortgages. The mortgagees will already have consented to the creation of a commonhold, or have had their consent dispensed with by the court (Article 6(8)). (But the mortgagees would be wise to record their interests with the commonhold association as soon as it comes into existence – Schedule 4, para. 1(1)(i)).

*Paragraph 10* allows Land Registry Rules to prescribe other particulars to be included in, or annexed to, a commonhold declaration. (Article 2(2) ("prescribed").)

## PART II

This Part contains definitions of the boundaries of units which apply to the extent that inconsistent definitions are not contained in the common-hold declaration (Article 6(5)).

*Paragraph 1* causes the boundaries to follow the walls, floors and ceilings of units. This assumes that any appendage of a unit (e.g. a garage) will be a common part which the owner or occupier of the unit will be entitled to enjoy under an agreement with the commonhold association and for which a charge may be made (Schedule 4, para.2(e)): a space for keeping dust-bins will be similarly assigned (although a charge for this is unlikely). If some other definition is thought necessary, this paragraph will need to be superseded (e.g. if a detached house is part of a commonhold, the entire house and its garden, forecourt, etc., will form a unit).

*Paragraph 2* contains a special rule for a case where the boundaries follow walls, floors or ceilings of a structural nature. The boundary runs immediately below decorative level (e.g. the level of any plaster or other facing material), the bricks, blocks or concrete casting which forms, say, a wall being common parts: but the interior of doors, door frames and window frames, and all window or door glass form part of the unit. This means that the repainting or repair of the exterior of a door, door frame or window frame is a matter for the commonhold association, and of the interior for the unit owner who must also replace any broken glass. The surface of a balcony is part of the unit, but its structure and protective wall or railings are common parts and repairable by the commonhold association.

*Paragraph 3* contains rules which apply where boundaries follow walls, floors and ceilings not of a structural nature.

*sub-paragraph (a)* Walls, floors and ceilings wholly within a unit form part of the unit e.g. walls dividing rooms; floors and ceilings dividing part of a unit in one storey from a part in another storey – as where a top-floor flat carries the roof void (which may be used for domestic storage purposes), or where a freehold unit in an office building consists of a number of storeys (which may be divided into separate offices to be let on short-term tenancies).

*sub-paragraph (b)* Walls, floors and ceilings which divide one unit from another, or a unit from a common part, are owned as follows –

    (i) walls are divided down the centre (there will be implied cross-easements of support);

    (ii) in the case of floors and ceilings, the actual board, plasterboard or other substance constituting the floor or ceiling is part of the unit, but beams, sub-floors or other supports are common parts.

*Paragraph 4* defines "beam" as including a joist, purlin (i.e. a member supporting joists or rafters), rafter, rib, truss or other structural support.

## RIGHTS AND OBLIGATIONS ATTACHING TO UNITS

*Rights*

1.   The following rights attach to every unit –

(a)   the right to subjacent and lateral support and to shelter and protection from the other parts of the building containing the unit and from the site thereof and other parts of the commonhold;

(b)   the right to free and uninterrupted passage and running of sewage, water, gas and electricity and all services (including telephone, radio, television, heating and cooling services) from and to the unit or the common parts through the sewers, drains and watercourses, pipes, cables, wires and ducts in, under or passing through the commonhold;

(c)   the right for the unit owner and all persons authorised by him (in common with all other persons entitled to the like right) at all times by day or by night and for all purposes in connection with the use and enjoyment of the unit or the common parts to go, pass or repass over and along the roads, paths and forecourt shown on the plan contained in or annexed to the commonhold declaration and through and along the main entrances of the building and the passages, landings and staircases leading to the unit and to use the lifts provided (if any), and, as to roads, to do so with or without motor cars or other vehicles;

(d)   the right for the unit owner and all persons authorised by him (in common with all other persons entitled to the like right) to use any recreation area or garden shown as such on the plan contained in or annexed to the commonhold declaration for the purpose of recreation, and to use any areas so shown as provided for the purpose of parking for the parking of private motor-cars and motor-cycles only;

(e)   the right for the unit owner and all persons authorised by him (in common with all other persons entitled to the like right) to use for the purpose of drying clothes any part of the commonhold shown on the said plan as provided for that purpose;

(f)   the right for the unit owner and all persons authorised by him (in common with all other persons entitled to the like right) to use the part of the commonhold shown on the said plan as provided for the keeping of refuse for keeping refuse in not more than two closed receptacles (to be provided by the unit owner);

(g)   where a communal supply of water is made available for the washing of vehicles, the right for the unit owner and all persons authorised by him (in common with all other persons entitled to the like right) to use for that purpose water so supplied;

(h)   where the commonhold association has acquired any easement, right or privilege over land adjacent to the commonhold for the benefit of unit owners, to take advantage of that easement, right or privilege;

(i)   the right for the unit owner with servants or agents at all reasonable times on notice (except in the case of emergency) to enter into and upon other parts of the commonhold for the purpose of –

     (i)   repairing, cleansing, maintaining or renewing any such sewers, drains and watercourses, pipes, cables, wires and ducts as are mentioned in sub-paragraph (b);

    (ii)   laying down any new sewers, drains or watercourses, pipes, cables, wires or ducts in place thereof;

   (iii)   repairing, replacing or making safe any apparatus, equipment, facility or thing; or

   (iv)   replacing, renewing or restoring any shelter to which he is entitled;

   where that is necessary for the full enjoyment of his rights, causing as little disturbance as possible and making good or paying compensation for any damage caused;

(j)   the right for the unit owner with servants or agents at all reasonable times on notice (except in the case of emergency) to enter into and upon other parts of the commonhold for the purpose of repairing, maintaining, renewing, altering or rebuilding the unit or any part of the building or its site giving subjacent or lateral support, shelter or protection to the unit, so however that, except in case of emergency, no works affecting the common parts shall be executed otherwise than with the consent of the commonhold association;

(k)   the right to connect a television set in the unit with an aerial erected by or on behalf of the promoter or the commonhold association, where such an aerial is provided as a common property;

(l)   all ancillary rights reasonably necessary to make the foregoing rights effective.

2.   The rights set out in sub-paragraphs (c) to (h) of paragraph 1 are subject to any commonhold bye-laws.

### Obligations

3.   The following obligations attach to every unit, that is to say, obligations –

(a)   for the unit owner to serve notice on the commonhold association of the registration of his title to the unit and of the completion by him of any transfer or lease of his unit;

(b)   for the unit owner to keep his unit and all appurtenances in repair and properly maintained, and to make good any defect, decay or want of repair within a reasonable period specified in a notice served by the commonhold association;

(c)   for the owner or occupier of a unit to serve on the commonhold association notice of any defect of which hc is aware either in the unit or in the common parts;

(d) not to do anything, or allow anything to be done, which would prejudice the structure of the building, not to withdraw or lessen the support, shelter and protection given by the unit to any other unit, and (save with the consent of the commonhold association or in case of emergency) not to make, or allow to be made, any alteration or addition to the unit which would affect a common part;

(e) not to use the unit or allow it to be used –

    (i) for any dangerous or offensive purpose;

    (ii) in such a manner or for such a purpose as to cause any annoyance or inconvenience to the occupier of any other unit;

    (iii) for any purpose which is unlawful or which may be injurious to the reputation of the commonhold;

(f) where the purpose for which a unit is intended to be used is stated expressly by, or appears by necessary implication from, the terms of the commonhold declaration, not to use the unit, or allow it to be used, for any other purpose;

(g) not to sub-divide the unit;

(h) to comply with the conditions of any policy of insurance effected by the commonhold association, and not to do or allow to be done anything which may render such a policy void or voidable or which may cause an increased premium to be payable in respect of it;

(i) for the unit owner to pay the contributions levied on him by the commonhold association;

(j) to permit the commonhold association to enter the unit by its officers, servants or agents, at reasonable times and upon reasonable notice being given (except in case of emergency) for the purpose of –

    (i) inspecting the state of repair or carrying out any necessary repairs to, or preventing or limiting any damage to, the unit, any other unit or the common parts (the cost of any repairs to the unit being recoverable by the commonhold association from the unit owner as a debt);

    (ii) inspecting, maintaining, repairing or renewing any sewers, drains and watercourses, pipes, cables, wires and ducts existing in the unit and capable of being used in connection with the enjoyment of any other unit or the common parts;

    (iii) ascertaining whether the obligations attaching to the unit are being observed;

(k) to permit the exercise, in relation to the unit, of the rights attached by sub-paragraphs (a), (b), (i), (j) and (l) of paragraph 1 to other units;

(l) not to damage the common property or allow it to be damaged; and not to use the common property or allow it to be used in such a manner as unreasonably to interfere with the use and enjoyment

1281

of that property or of any unit by the owners or occupiers of units or members of their households or staffs, or their visitors;

(m) for the unit owner to compensate the commonhold association for any damage caused to the common property, either negligently or deliberately, by himself or the occupier of his unit or by members of their households or staffs or their visitors;

(n) to observe the commonhold bye-laws;

(o) for the owner and the occupier of a unit to use his best endeavours to ensure that his tenant, members of his or his tenant's household or staff and his or his tenant's visitors do not do anything which, if done by the owner, would be a breach of his obligations and that they observe the commonhold bye-laws.

4. For the purposes of paragraph 3, a person allows to be done anything which he has the right to prevent if he does not take reasonable steps to enforce that right.

# EXPLANATORY NOTE

## SCHEDULE 2

This Schedule sets out the rights and obligations which attach to units by virtue of Article 6(6). In its application to a particular commonhold, the Schedule may be modified by the commonhold declaration (Article 6(6)) or, subsequently, by a class 1 resolution (Article 17(2)), but only by express textual modifications.

### Rights

*Paragraph 1* lists the rights which attach to every unit. They are concerned mainly with support and shelter for the unit, the passage of services and the use of common parts. A unit owner may safeguard his unit by carrying out repairs or maintenance operations, or making any apparatus safe, in another unit or the common parts; but he must give prior notice to the other unit owner or, as the case may be, the commonhold association (so that he or it, being now aware of the need for the work, may undertake it) except in case of emergency (as where a tank is overflowing or there is a smell of gas).

*Paragraph 2* makes it clear that a unit owner's right to use the common parts must be exercised in accordance with any bye-laws made under Article 7(3)(c).

### Obligations

*Paragraph 4* lists the obligations which attach to units. A unit owner must keep the commonhold association informed of changes in title, keep his unit in good order, notify the association of any defect he notices in his unit or a common part, cause no damage to the building, not do anything in the unit which is dangerous, offensive, annoying or unlawful, use the unit only for the purpose it is meant to be used for (e.g. as a single private dwelling or as an office or as sheltered accommodation), not sub-divide the unit, comply with the conditions of the commonhold association's insurance policy, pay his contributions to common expenses, allow the commonhold association to enter and inspect his unit and do any necessary work there, allow other unit owners to exercise rights over his unit reciprocal to the rights he may exercise over their units, not abuse the common property or allow anyone else (e.g. his children, staff or visitors) to do so, and to comply with the commonhold bye-laws and do his best to see that his family, staff and visitors do so too.

*Paragraph 5* makes it clear that references in paragraph 4 (sub-paragraphs (d), (e), (f), (h) and (l)) to allowing anything to be done are not restricted to express permission. A person allows something to be done if he has the right to prevent it and does not exercise that right to a reasonable degree. (cf. Article 14(5)).

# SCHEDULE 3

## THE COMMONHOLD ASSOCIATION CONSTITUTION RULES

### *Interpretation*

1.  In this Part –

"the association" means the commonhold association;

"class 1 resolution" has the meaning given by Article 3;

"the chairman" (except in a reference to the chairman of a general meeting or the chairman of meeting of the executive committee, when it has the meaning given by rule 5(5) or rule 9(5), (6) respectively) means the chairman of the association;

"the commonhold declaration" means that declaration as varied by any modification or variation the effect of which is registered in the Land Registry;

"the executive committee" means the committee appointed under rule 8;

"general meeting" means a general meeting of the association;

"member" means a member of the association;

"ordinary resolution" means a resolution passed by a majority vote of members present and voting in person or by proxy at a general meeting;

"registered office" means the address for service of documents on the association included in the commonhold declaration or contained in a return lodged in the Land Registry under rule 16;

"secretary" means the secretary of the association.

### *Members*

2.—(1)  The first members are the owners of freeholds, or leaseholds under equity-sharing leases, in the respective units on the date of the registration of the commonhold declaration.

(2)   Where none of the units have been constructed by that date the person who is then registered as the owner of a freehold in the commonhold with an absolute title is the first member, and as the units become structurally complete that person becomes a member in right of each separate unit.

(3)   Every person who becomes registered in the Land Registry as the owner of a freehold, or a leasehold under an equity-sharing lease, in a unit thereupon becomes a member in right of that unit and every person who ceases to be so registered thereupon ceases to be a member (or, where he was the owner of more than one unit, ceases to be a member in right of that unit).

(4)   A person who is a member in right of two or more units is to be treated as a separate member in respect of each of those units except for the purpose of counting a quorum or voting on a show of hands, when he is to be treated as a single member.

(5)  Where a unit is owned by more than one person, each is a member, but, where a number or percentage of members is to be counted, those persons are to be treated as a single member (including where a member is counted for the purpose of counting a quorum or voting on a show of hands).

(6)  Where –

(a)  a person entitled to a unit by reason of the death or bankruptcy of a member or by reason of an order for the administration in bankruptcy of the estate of a deceased insolvent, or

(b)  a controller appointed for a member under Article 101 of the Mental Health (Northern Ireland) Order 1986,

supplies satisfactory evidence of his title or appointment to the chairman, he is to be treated as a member for the purpose of these rules in respect of the member's unit and to the exclusion of the member.

### Register of members

3.—(1)  The association is to keep a register of members.

(2)  When an instrument of transfer of a unit is executed, the transferor is to serve on the association notice of the date of execution; and, when the effect of the instrument is registered in the Land Registry, the transferee is to serve on the association notice of the date of registration.

(3)  Between the dates of service on the association of the notices served under paragraph (2), the transferee is a provisional member of the association (and is to be entered in the register of members as such).

(4)  Subject to paragraph 11 of Schedule 4 (contributions), a provisional member is entitled to all the benefits and is subject to all the duties of membership to the exclusion of his transferor.

(5)  Where the notice of registration of the transfer shows the name of the transferee as different from the name entered in the register of members as a provisional member, the association is to rectify the register.

(6)  Where a person is to be treated as a member under rule 2(6), that fact is to be noted in the register of members.

(7)  The record of the names and addresses of lessors of equity-sharing leases, mortgagees and tenants under paragraph 1(1)(i) of Schedule 4 is to be kept in the register of members.

(8)  Where an equity-sharing lease terminates otherwise than on transfer of a unit or by merger of the lessee's estate in the reversion on the acquisition of the reversion by him, the lessor's name is to be substituted for the lessee's in the register of members.

### General meetings

4.—(1)  A general meeting is to be held within three months after the registration of the commonhold declaration, or within three months after the execution of the instrument of transfer to the first purchaser of a unit in a commonhold consisting of a development of newly built units, whichever is the later.

(2) Subsequent general meetings ("annual general meetings") are to be held once in each calendar year, but so that no more than 15 months elapse between the date of the first general meeting and that of the first annual general meeting or between the date of one annual general meeting and that of the next.

(3) All general meetings after the first, other than annual general meetings, are extraordinary general meetings.

(4) All members are entitled to attend and (subject to rule 7) to vote at general meetings.

(5) If a class 1 resolution is proposed at a general meeting, all mortgagees of units whose names and addresses have been recorded by the association are entitled to receive notice of, to attend and (in accordance with rule 7(1)(j)) to vote at that general meeting.

(6) A general meeting is called by the secretary (or, if the office of secretary is vacant or the secretary is unable or unwilling to act, by those requiring the meeting) giving at least 14 days' notice to all those entitled to attend; but a general meeting may be called on less than 14 days' notice with the written consent of all those entitled to attend.

(7) Paragraph (6) does not prejudice Article 3, which requires at least 30 days' notice to be given where a resolution is to be proposed as a class 1 resolution.

(8) A general meeting (annual or extraordinary) is to be called at the request of the chairman or the executive committee; and an extraordinary general meeting is to be called upon a requisition in writing made by at least two members entitled to at least 10 per cent. of the total unit entitlement in respect of voting of all the units.

(9) Notice of a general meeting is to state –

(a) the time, date and place of the meeting;

(b) the nature of the meeting (annual or extraordinary);

(c) the general nature of the business to be transacted;

(d) the text of any class 1 resolution to be proposed;

(e) the right of a member to appoint a proxy to attend and vote at the meeting on his behalf;

and notice of an annual general meeting must be accompanied by a copy of the accounts and report required by rule 6 to be laid before the meeting.

(10) The proceedings at a general meeting are not invalidated by the fact that notice was accidentally not given to, or was not received by, anyone entitled to receive notice.

## Proceedings at general meetings

5.—(1) No business is to be transacted at any general meeting unless a quorum of persons entitled to vote is present at the time when the meeting proceeds to business.

(2) Ten per cent. of the persons entitled to vote (but not less than two of them) present in person or by proxy constitute a quorum.

(3) If within 15 minutes from the time appointed for a general meeting a quorum is not present, the meeting stands adjourned to the same day in the next week at the same place and time and, if at the adjourned meeting a quorum is not present within 15 minutes from the time appointed for the meeting, the persons entitled to vote who are present (if two or more) constitute a quorum; if two or more such persons are not then present, the meeting is to be abandoned.

(4) No business may be transacted at a general meeting unless it was specified in the notice of the meeting or it is of a trivial nature or a matter of immediate urgency which could not have been raised previously and the chairman of the meeting agrees.

(5) A general meeting is to be chaired by –

(a) the chairman of the executive committee, if he is present, or

(b) in his absence, a member of the executive committee selected by the members present; or

(c) if there is none, a member selected by the members present.

(6) The chairman of a general meeting may, with the consent of the meeting, adjourn it from time to time and from place to place: if any adjournment is for longer than 14 days, at least seven days' notice of the time and place at which the meeting is to be resumed must be given to all those then entitled to notice of the meeting.

(7) The secretary, or in his absence a person appointed by the chairman of the meeting for the purpose, is to take minutes of every general meeting and record them in a minute book.

(8) A resolution, other than a class 1 resolution, in writing signed by all those whose votes in favour of it at a general meeting at which they were present would have carried it unanimously, and recorded in the minute book, takes effect as if it had been passed at a general meeting.

## Laying of accounts

6. The executive committee shall lay before each annual general meeting the account and balance sheet prepared under paragraph 5 of Schedule 4 for the accounting year last preceding the date of the meeting and the auditor's report on them.

## Voting at general meetings

7.—(1) At a general meeting –

(a) an ordinary resolution is to be decided on a show of hands by the persons present and entitled to vote unless a poll is demanded by such a person;

(b) a class 1 resolution is to be decided on a poll;

(c) in the case of an ordinary resolution, a declaration by the chairman of the meeting that the resolution has on the show of hands been carried is conclusive evidence of the fact without proof of the number or proportion of votes recorded in favour of or against the resolution;

(d) a demand for a poll may be withdrawn;

(e) a poll shall be taken in such manner, in such place and at such time as the chairman thinks fit and the result of the poll is deemed to be the resolution of the meeting at which the poll was demanded or, in the case of a class 1 resolution, fell to be taken;

(f) pending the taking of a poll, the meeting may proceed to transact other business;

(g) in the case of equality in the votes whether on a show of hands or on a poll, the chairman of the meeting is not entitled to a casting vote in addition to any other vote he may have;

(h) on a show of hands, each member has one vote;

(i) on a poll each member has the number of votes allocated to his unit by the commonhold declaration, and all are to be cast together;

(j) on a class 1 resolution, a mortgagee of a unit whose name and address have been recorded by the association may cast the votes allocated to that unit by its unit entitlement, and votes so cast invalidate votes cast by or on behalf of the person who is a member in right of that unit or any mortgagee whose mortgage ranks lower in priority;

(k) where two or more persons are members in right of a unit, their vote is the vote of the first of them on the registrar to the exclusion of the other or others or, if he is not present and has not appointed a proxy, of the second (and so on) and the member entitled to vote is the member entitled to demand a poll.

(2) A person entitled to vote at a general meeting may appoint a proxy, who need not be a member, to attend a particular general meeting, or general meetings generally, to speak and vote on his behalf; where a proxy is appointed for a particular general meeting the appointment operates at all adjournments of the meeting unless the contrary is expressed.

(3) The appointment of a proxy must be in writing signed by the appointor or his solicitor, and may contain a direction for the proxy to vote either for or against a specified resolution: where it contains no such direction, the proxy may vote at his own discretion.

(4) Any dispute as to the qualification of a person tendering a vote at a general meeting is to be settled by the chairman of the meeting, whose decision is final and conclusive: any vote cast and not disallowed at the meeting is valid.

## The executive committee

8.—(1) At the first general meeting and at each annual general meeting an executive committee is to be appointed to hold office until the termination of the annual general meeting in the next-following year; but no formal appointment is necessary when sub-paragraph (3) applies.

(2) The executive committee is to consist of not less than two nor more than nine members.

(3) Where there are not more than nine members, the executive committee consists of all the members.

(4) An up-to-date list of members of the executive committee is, where possible, to be placed in a prominent position in the premises of the commonhold.

(5) A person ceases to be a member of the executive committee if –

(a) he ceases to be a member of the association;

(b) a disqualification order is made against him under Article 303 of the Companies (Northern Ireland) Order 1986;

(c) he becomes bankrupt or is a person by, for or in respect of whose affairs there has been made a deed of arrangement to which Chapter I of Part VIII of the Insolvency (Northern Ireland) Order 1989 applies;

(d) he is detained for treatment or is received into guardianship under the Mental Health (Northern Ireland) Order 1986;

(e) an enduring power of attorney granted by him is registered;

(f) he resigns his office by notice served on the association;

(g) except where the executive committee consists of all the members of the association, he is removed from office by an ordinary resolution of the association;

and a person is disqualified for becoming a member of the executive committee if, were he already a member, he would cease to be a member by virtue of sub-paragraph (b), (c), (d) or (e).

(6) Any casual vacancy on the executive committee may be filled by the remaining member or members of the committee; and where the association removes a member of the committee from office under paragraph (5)(g) it may appoint another member of the association in his place to hold office until the termination of the next annual general meeting.

(7) The executive committee is to appoint one of the members of the committee as its chairman: the appointment is to continue until the committee ceases to hold office or the chairman ceases to be a member of the committee.

(8) Where the association has only two members and they cannot agree who is to be chairman, the member whose surname stands first in alphabetical order is deemed to be appointed chairman, and, upon his

1289

appointment terminating, the other member is (subject to any agreement to the contrary) deemed to be appointed chairman in his place (and so on in rotation).

## Proceedings of the executive committee

9.—(1) Subject to paragraph (2), the quorum of the executive committee is such number as the committee may fix, being not less than one-half of the number of its members.

(2) Where the number of members of the executive committee is two or three, the quorum is two.

(3) A member of the executive committee is not entitled to appoint an alternate or proxy to act as a member of the committee on his behalf.

(4) A meeting of the executive committee is to be called by the secretary (or, if the office of secretary is vacant or the secretary is unable or unwilling to act, by those requiring the meeting) in accordance with any previous directions of the committee or by giving at least seven days' notice to all the members of the committee; the chairman or any two members of the committee may require a meeting to be called.

(5) A meeting of the executive committee is to be chaired by –

(a) the chairman of the committee, if he is present, or

(b) in his absence, a member of the committee selected by the members present.

(6) If the chairman of a meeting of the executive committee vacates the chair during the meeting, the members present may select another member to act as chairman.

(7) At meetings of the executive committee all matters are to be determined by simple majority vote and the chairman of the meeting has, in addition to an original vote, a casting vote in any case where the voting is equal.

(8) The secretary, or in his absence a person appointed by the chairman of the meeting for the purpose, is to take minutes of a meeting of the committee and record them in a minute book.

(9) A resolution in writing, signed by all the members of the executive committee and recorded in the minute book, takes effect as if it had been passed at a meeting of the committee.

(10) Subject to these Rules, the executive committee has power to regulate its own procedure.

(11) The validity of the proceedings of the executive committee is not affected by any vacancy amongst its members or by any defect in the appointment of a member.

(12) The association may pay members of the exccutive committee all reasonable expenses properly incurred in carrying out their duties.

(13)   The executive committee may, on behalf of the association and on whatever terms the committee thinks fit, employ any member of the committee to do work or provide services outside the scope of the ordinary duties of a member of the committee.

### Disclosure of interests

10.   A member of the executive committee who has a material interest in a matter considered by the committee must declare that interest, unless it is unreasonable to expect him to know of it: a general declaration by a member of the committee of a specified interest in any transaction or arrangement with a specified person or persons satisfies his obligation in respect of that interest.

11.   If a member of the executive committee has disclosed a material interest in a matter considered by the committee he may not vote on it, but if the committee resolves that the association should enter into or have an interest in any related transaction, –

(a)   he may be a party to it or have an interest in it, and

(b)   he is not accountable for any profit or benefit he derives from it, and

(c)   the transaction is not liable to be made void on that ground.

### Functions of the executive committee and responsibility of its members

12.—(1) The executive committee is to exercise the functions of the association with respect to administration save for those functions which are required by this Order to be exercised by an ordinary resolution or a class 1 resolution.

(2)   The executive committee may –

(a)   employ for and on behalf of the association such agents as it thinks fit in connection with the administration of the common parts of the commonhold and the exercise and performance of the functions of the association;

(b)   delegate to one or more than one of its members such of its functions as it thinks fit, and at any time revoke such delegation.

(3)   Paragraphs (1) and (2) have effect subject to any restriction imposed, or direction given, by an ordinary resolution.

(4)   Members of the executive committee must exercise, in the affairs of the committee, the degree of care and skill which would reasonably be expected of the owner of a freehold house, who had received no special instruction or training, when conducting his own affairs in relation to that house.

### Indemnity

13.—(1) A member of the executive committee is entitled to be indemnified out of the assets of the association in respect of costs incurred by him in defending any proceedings, whether civil or criminal, in which judgment is given in his favour or in which he is acquitted or in connection with any application in which relief is granted to him by the court from liability for negligence, default, breach of duty or breach of trust in relation to the affairs of the association.

(2)   The indemnity in paragraph (1) is without prejudice to any other indemnity to which a member of the executive committee may be entitled.

### Minutes

14.—(1) A member is entitled to inspect the minutes of general meetings and of meetings of the executive committee.

(2)   Reasonable facilities must be afforded to a member seeking to exercise this right, and no charge may be made.

### Service of documents

15.—(1) Any notice or other document which is to be served on the association is sufficiently served if sent by ordinary post, or delivered, to the association's registered office.

(2)   If at any time, for any reason, a document cannot be served in accordance with paragraph (1), it may be served on the association by leaving it at, or sending it by post to, the association at its office in a building forming part of the commonhold or, if there is no such office, by depositing it in the receptacle provided under paragraph (3).

(3)   If the association has no office such as is mentioned in paragraph (2) it shall cause to be provided and fixed at or near the front of a building forming part of the commonhold a receptacle suitable for the purpose of receiving articles by post, and on such a receptacle the name of the association shall be clearly stated.

(4)   Except where the person in question resides permanently in a building forming part of the commonhold, every member, mortgagee, tenant or other person having an interest in the commonhold shall notify the association of his address for service of documents upon him, and –

(a)   any documents sent to him by the association by ordinary post at that address, or left for him at that address, are sufficiently served on him; and

(b)   failure to notify such an address, or to give notice of a change in the address notified, excuses the association from any duty to serve a document on him otherwise than by leaving the document at the relevant unit or, as the case may be, sending it (as mentioned in sub-paragraph (a)) to the address last notified.

### Change of registered office

16.   Within 14 days after any alteration is made in the address which is the registered office of the association, the association shall lodge in the Land Registry a return in the prescribed form containing particulars of the alteration.

## The common seal

17. The executive committee shall provide for the safe custody of the common seal which shall only be used by the authority of the executive committee; and every instrument to which the seal is affixed shall be signed by at least two members of the committee.

## Voidability of certain contracts

18.—(1) Where a contract has been entered into by the association at a time when the majority of the votes which may be cast on a poll at a general meeting are not exercisable by or on behalf of purchasers of units, the contract is voidable by an ordinary resolution passed at any time within the period of six months immediately following the date when the majority of such votes became so exercisable.

(2) In paragraph (1) "purchaser" means a purchaser who has bought at any time (before, as well as after, the making of the commonhold declaration), but does not include a purchaser of two or more units who buys for the purpose of re-sale.

## The secretary

19.—(1) The association is to appoint a secretary, who need not be a member.

(2) The secretary has the functions conferred on him by these Rules, and such other functions as the association may assign.

## The chairman

20. The chairman of the executive committee is the chairman of the association.

# EXPLANATORY NOTE

## SCHEDULE 3

This Schedule sets out the Commonhold Association Constitution Rules which deal with the internal organization of a commonhold association. The rules cannot be varied by the commonhold declaration nor can they subsequently be varied by a resolution of the commonhold association (except for conformity with modifications made by the Department by order under Article 23, when the variation can be made by ordinary resolution).

### Rule 1

This rule contains definitions. Some definitions already contained in Article 2(2) are repeated here for the convenience of the association (e.g. "member"; "ordinary resolution").

### Rule 2

This rule defines who is a member of the association.

*Paragraphs (1), (2)* The owners of units at the time when the commonhold declaration is registered are the first members – these may be the owners of existing units who have agreed to form a commonhold, or, where new units have been built but not yet sold, the developer who is the owner of those units. Where no units have yet been built, the owner of the land (i.e. the promoter of the commonhold) is the first member, and as units become structurally complete (but services not necessarily installed as required by Article 10) he becomes a member in respect of the units or unit yet unsold). Where there is an equity-sharing lease the lessee is the owner, and will be registered as a member.

*Paragraph (3)* The second (and subsequent) member in respect of a unit is the person registered in the Land Registry as the owner of the unit: he becomes a member when his title is registered, and ceases to be a member in respect of a unit when a transfer by him of the unit is registered. (Of course, if he still owns another unit, he will continue to be a member in respect of that other unit.) But if he executes an instrument of transfer of his unit and notifies the association of it, his purchaser becomes a provisional member and, although the vendor continues to be a member until registration of the transfer, for most purposes the benefits and duties of membership shift to the purchaser – rule 3(4).

*Paragraph (4)* The owner of two or more units is treated as a separate member in respect of each of the units, but not for counting a quorum or voting on a show of hands.

*Paragraph (5)* Joint owners of a unit are both (or all) members; but for the purpose of reckoning a number or percentage of members (e.g. the number forming a quorum – rule 5(2)) they are to be treated as a single member.

1294

*Paragraph (6)* treats certain persons as standing in the place of a member, provided they satisfy the chairman of the association about their standing. They are executors, administrators, a trustee in bankruptcy and a controller appointed for a patient under the Mental Health Order.

## Rule 3

This rule provides for the keeping of a register of members.

*Paragraph (1)* imposes the duty to keep a register of members.

*Paragraph (2)* imposes duties on the transferor and the transferee of a unit. The transferor must notify the association of the date of execution of the transfer, and the transferee must notify it of the date of registration of his title.

*Paragraph (3)* Between the date when the association receives notice of the execution of the transfer and the date when it receives notice of the registration of the transfer in the Land Registry, the transferee is a provisional member of the association (and is to be entered in the register of members as a provisional member).

*Paragraph (4)* puts a transferee who is a provisional member in the place of his transferor for all purposes of membership, except that, until the association receives notice of the date of registration of the transfer in the Land Registry, the transferee and the transferor are jointly and individually liable for all unpaid contributions due to the association in respect of the unit (Schedule 4, para. 11).

*Paragraph (5)* requires the register of members to be corrected where the notice of registration of the transfer shows the transferee's name as being different from the name given in the notice of execution of the transfer.

*Paragraph (6)* applies where, under rule 2(6) a personal representative (or other representative) is treated as a member. The fact that he is to be so treated is to be noted in the register of members.

*Paragraph (7)* requires the record of the names and addresses of mortgagees and tenants under Schedule 4, paragraph 1(1)(i), to be kept in the register of members. This could conveniently be done if separate pages in the register book were allocated to separate units, so that the history of ownership, etc., of each unit could be found on a single page.

*Paragraph (8)* applies where the lessee drops out of an equity-sharing lease leaving the lessor in possession of a unit. The lessor is to be registered as owner of the unit.

## Rule 4

This rule contains provisions about general meetings of the association.

*Paragraph (1)* requires the first general meeting to be held within 3 months after the registration of the commonhold declaration or the first transfer of a newly built unit (whichever happens later).

*Paragraph (2)* Annual general meetings are to be held once in each calendar year, with not less than 15 months between one meeting and the next.

*Paragraph (3)* Other general meetings are extraordinary general meetings.

*Paragraph (4)* All members may attend and vote, except that where two or more are co-owners of a unit only one of them may vote (rule 2(5)) and they are entitled to cast the vote in the order in which their names appear in the register of members (rule 7(1)(k)).

*Paragraph (5)* Mortgagees of units whose names have been recorded with the association (rule 3(7)) are entitled to recieve notice of a meeting at which a resolution is to be proposed as a class 1 resolution and to attend and vote on the resolution. The vote of a mortgagee overrides the vote of the unit owner (or that of a mortgagee of lower priority) (rule 7(1)(j)).

*Paragraph (6)* Subject to paragraph (7), 14 days notice must be given of a general meeting, but a lesser period suffices if all entitled to attend agree. The meeting is to be called by the secretary (see rule 129) or, failing him, the members requiring the meeting.

*Paragraph (7)* makes it clear that the 30 days' notice required by Article 3 for a meeting to consider a class 1 resolution cannot be reduced.

*Paragraph (8)* says who may requisition a general meeting. The chairman (see rule 20) may require either an annual or an extraordinary general meeting to be called; at least two members having between them at least 10% of the voting rights may require an extraordinary meeting.

*Paragraph (9)* sets out various matters to be stated in the notice calling a general meeting. The right to appoint a proxy must be expressly stated.

*Paragraph (10)* contains a standard provision preventing a meeting's being invalidated through some-one's accidental failure to receive notice of a meeting (cf. e.g., Local Government Act (Northern Ireland) 1972 c. 9 Sch. 2 para. 2(4)).

## Rule 5

This rule deals with the conduct of general meetings.

*Paragraph (1)* requires the presence of a quorum at the time when the meeting proceeds to business.

*Paragraph (2)* defines a quorum – there must be at least 2 persons and they must be at least 10% of all those entitled to vote.

*Paragraph (3)* If no quorum appears within 15 minutes, the meeting stands adjourned for a week. If at least 2 persons entitled to vote attend the adjourned meeting, they form a quorum (even though they are not also 10% of all such persons); if at least 2 do not attend, the meeting is abandoned.

*Paragraph (4)* states what business may be transacted at a general meeting. It must be business stated in the notice of the meeting; but the chairman may allow business of a trivial nature or something urgent which could not have been raised before.

*Paragraph (5)* A general meeting is to be chaired by (in order of precedence) the chairman of the association (rule 20), a member of the executive committee selected by the members present, or a member selected by the members present.

*Paragraph (6)* The chairman has power to adjourn the meeting; if the adjournment is for more than 14 days, at least 7 days' notice of the adjourned meeting must be given.

*Paragraph (7)* requires minutes of general meetings to be kept. This is to be done by the secretary or, failing him, some-one appointed by the chairman of the meeting.

*Paragraph (8)* allows a resolution to be adopted by the written agreement of all those who would be entitled to vote on it if it were proposed at a general meeting; but this does not apply to a class 1 resolution.

## Rule 6

This rule requires the association's audited account and balance sheet to be laid before an annual general meeting. (Copies of them must be circulated with the notice calling the meeting – rule 4(9)).

## Rule 7

This rule says how voting is to be conducted at a general meeting.

*Paragraph (1)* sets out detailed rules about voting on a show of hands and the taking of a poll. Only an ordinary resolution can be passed on a show of hands (when each member has one vote, regardless of the unit entitlement of his unit); a poll is always necessary for a class 1 resolution and may be demanded for an ordinary resolution. The chairman has no casting vote. On a class 1 resolution a mortgagee of a unit who has recorded his interest with the association may cast the votes allocated to that unit by its unit entitlement (see Schedule 1, Part I, para. 8(a)).

*Paragraph (2)* allows a person who is entitled to vote at a general meeting to appoint a proxy for a particular meeting or for all general meetings. A proxy for all meetings might be appropriate where the member is a company. A corporate lender wishing to be represented at a meeting called to consider a class 1 resolution should appoint a proxy.

*Paragraph (3)* allows the appointor or his solicitor to sign the proxy form. The way in which the proxy is to vote may be specified, or it may be left open to him to vote as he thinks best.

*Paragraph (4)* requires any objection to the casting of a vote to be taken at the meeting. The chairman is to rule on any such objection, and his decision is final.

## Rule 8

This rule requires the association to have an executive committee through which the association will normally act in its day to day business (rule 12(1)).

*Paragraph (1)* requires an executive committee to be appointed each year.

*Paragraphs (2) and (3)* limit the maximum number of members of the committee to 9 and the minimum to 2. If there are only 9 members of the association (or fewer) they are all members of the committee (but this must be read subject to paragraph (5)).

*Paragraph (4)* requires a list of committee members to be displayed "where possible". It will be possible to display the list where there is a common entrance hall (as in a block of flats): it may not be possible in a commonhold (probably commercial) where there are no common parts.

*Paragraph (5)* sets out the circumstances in which a person ceases to be a member of the committee. The reference in sub-paragraph (c) to the Insolvency Order picks up Article 209 of that Order which relates to an arrangement for the benefit of creditors generally or, if the debtor is insolvent, for the benefit of 3 or more creditors. Sub-paragraph (e) refers to the registration (i.e. in the High Court) of an enduring power of attorney: this is a power granted in anticipation of the donor's becoming mentally incapable – it can be registered only when that event occurs.

*Paragraph (6)* deals with the filling of vacancies in the committee.

*Paragraph (7)* deals with the appointment of the chairman of the committee. He is also the chairman of the association (rule 20) and, if present, will be the chairman of a general meeting of the association (rule 5(5)).

*Paragraph (8)* covers the case where there are only 2 members and they cannot agree who is to be chairman. The one whose name comes first in alphabetical order takes the chair, which subsequently rotates between them.

## Rule 9

This rule regulates the proceedings of the executive committee.

*Paragraphs (1) and (2)* fix the quorum.

*Paragraph (3)* prevents a member of the committee from acting through a nominee.

*Paragraphs (4) to (11)* deal with procedure. Unlike the chairman of a general meeting, the chairman of a meeting of the executive committee has a casting vote (paragraph (7)).

*Paragraph (12)* allows the association to pay members of the executive committee reasonable expenses.

*Paragraph (13)* allows the executive committee to employ one of their number to do work for the association (he may not vote on this – rule 11).

## Rule 10

This rule requires a member of the executive committee to disclose his interest in any matter considered by the committee, unless it would be unreasonable to expect him to know of it (e.g. he may be a beneficiary of a trust which owns shares in a company). A general declaration that he has an interest in all business transacted with a particular firm is sufficient.

## Rule 11

This rule precludes a member of the committee from voting on a matter in which he has declared an interest.

## Rule 12

This rule sets out the functions of the executive committee.

*Paragraph (1)* enables the committee to exercise all the powers and requires it to fulfil the duties of the association with respect to administration – cf. Schedule 4 ("functions" includes powers and duties: Interpretation Act s. 46(2)). This does not extend to anything which is required to be done by ordinary resolution or a class1 resolution, and may be further restricted under paragraph (3).

*Paragraph (2)* empowers the committee to appoint agents (e.g. an estate agent who will organize cleaning or gardening services) and to appoint sub-committees (including a sub-committee of one).

*Paragraph (3)* allows the association to pass an ordinary resolution restricting or regulating the ways in which the committee may act under the preceding paragraphs.

*Paragraph (4)* defines the standard of care expected from members of the committee. It is the standard an ordinary householder would adhere to in looking after his own house.

## Rule 13

This rule allows members of the executive committee to be indemnified as to costs in cases where it is established that they did not act improperly. "Costs" includes expenses: Interpretation Act, s. 46(2).

## Rule 14

This rule empowers any member of the association to inspect (without charge) the minutes of meetings of the association or the executive committee. (A right to inspect other documents is conferred by Schedule 4, para. 4(3). See also Article 12(3) and Schedule 4 paras. 1(1)(f)(ii), 8(2)).

## Rule 15

This rule deals with the service of documents. If the association has no office in the commonhold to which notices may be sent, it must provide a post-box (failure to do so is an offence under Article 25).

## Rule 16

This rule requires any change in the association's registered office to be notified to the Land Registry (failure to make the necessary return is an offence under Article 25). The registered office may be at the common-hold, but it might, instead, be the office of an estate agent or solicitor.

## Rule 17

This rule deals with the use of the association's seal: its imprint must be attested by two committee members.

## Rule 18

This rule deals with contracts which may have been entered into in the early stages of a commonhold, when votes are exercisable by a builder or other developer, in terms which might be detrimental to purchasers of units who subsequently come along. E.g., the developer may have (in the name of the association) entered into an agreement with a firm in which he has an interest for the maintenance of the commonhold on terms which were unduly favourable to the firm and unduly detrimental to persons who subsequently became members of the commonhold association. The rule makes such a contract voidable by an ordinary resolution of the association within six months after the majority of the votes became capable of being cast by purchasers.

## Rule 19

This rule provides for the appointment and functions of the secretary.

## Rule 20

This rule declares the chairman of the executive committee to be also the chairman of the association.

## ADMINISTRATIVE FUNCTIONS OF COMMONHOLD ASSOCIATION

*Management obligations*

1.—(1) The commonhold association has obligations –

(a) to hold the common property and to keep it in a state of good and serviceable repair (including decorative repair), fair wear and tear excepted;

(b) to keep the roads, entrances, passages, landings, staircases, lifts and other common parts used as means of access to the units clean and reasonably lit;

(c) to put and keep any gardens included in the common parts in a proper state of cultivation;

(d) to paint the exterior parts of the building usually painted with two coats at least of good paint once every four years, or such other period as the association may decide by ordinary resolution, in such colour as the association may so decide or, failing such a decision, in the colour in which they were last previously painted;

(e) to ensure that boilers or lifts included in the common parts are regularly and competently inspected and serviced;

(f) to insure and keep insured against loss or damage by fire, flood, storm or tempest and against injury to third persons or damage to their property (whether within or without the commonhold), and any other perils which may be prescribed, the commonhold and any buildings, effects or property of an insurable nature, whether affixed to the commonhold or not, which are in or on the land (other than moveable property of, or in the custody of, the owners or occupiers of units, members of their households or staffs or their visitors) in their full replacement value (together with an appropriate sum in respect of architects' and surveyors' fees); and the association shall –

   (i) give written notice of any such insurance effected by it and of any change therein or termination thereof to each unit owner;

   (ii) on the written request of any unit owner, his mortgagee or any other person having an interest in the building to which the insurance relates, produce, without charge, for inspection by the person making the request, or any person authorised by him in writing, the policy or policies of insurance and the receipt or receipts for, or other documents providing evidence of the payment of, the last premium or premiums paid in respect thereof, and permit copies to be taken;

(g) to claim and receive the proceeds of any insurance taken out by it;

(h)  to enforce the obligations attaching to units and the commonhold bye-laws;

(i)  to keep a record of the names and addresses of lessors of equity-sharing leases, and of mortgagees or tenants of units who serve notice of their interests on the association, and to supply to each such lessor, mortgagee or tenant, at his request, a copy of the record;

(j)  to comply with notices or orders issued by any competent public authority requiring repairs to or work to be done in respect of the commonhold.

(2)  In sub-paragraph (1)(a), in relation to attendance and services "a state of good and serviceable repair" includes proper provision; and in sub-paragraph (1)(d) "paint" includes (with the necessary modifications) other protective treatment.

(3)  For the purposes of sub-paragraph (1)(f) the commonhold association is deemed to have an insurable interest in the commonhold land and the buildings, effects and property there mentioned, including the units and any effects and property contained in a unit (other than the moveable property excepted from that provision).

(4)  Any policy of insurance taken out under head (f) of sub-paragraph (1) is not liable to be brought into contribution with any other policy of insurance, save another policy taken out under that head in respect of the same land, building, effects or property.

### Miscellaneous powers of the commonhold association

2.  The commonhold association has power to –

(a)  purchase, hire or otherwise acquire personal property for use by unit owners or members of their households or staffs or their visitors in connection with their enjoyment of the common property;

(b)  borrow by overdraft or otherwise money required by it in the exercise of its functions;

(c)  secure the repayment of money borrowed by it, and the payment of interest thereon, by negotiable instrument, or (subject to Article 7(2)(c) and (8)) by charging any property vested in it, or by a combination of those means;

(d)  invest as it may determine any money standing to the credit of the fund for the administration of the commonhold or a reserve fund (where the money is not immediately required) and hold, sell or otherwise deal with any investments;

(e)  make an agreement with the owner or occupier of any unit for the provision of amenities or facilities by it to him, with or without charge;

(f)  provide, renew or improve recreation facilities for the benefit of unit owners, members of their households or staffs and their visitors;

1302

(g) do all other things necessary for, or reasonably incidental to, the administration of the common property or its extension or improvement;

(h) carry on any other activity which seems to the association to be conducive to the efficient performance of the duties of the association or the exercise of its powers and to further the aims of the commonhold.

*Funds*

3.—(1) The commonhold association has obligations to –

(a) establish and maintain funds which it reasonably considers adequate for the purposes of –

    (i) the administration of the commonhold (including the payment of outgoings as they fall due);

    (ii) the provision and maintenance of reserves for capital improvements or renewals of the common property or for other purposes for which provision ought reasonably to be made;

    (iii) the discharge of any other of its obligations;

(b) ensure that, subject to a reasonable degree of liquidity, funds are invested so as to produce a reasonable income;

(c) expend reserves for the purposes for which they were provided and maintained, when the occasion arises, but (subject to sub-paragraph (2)) for no other purpose;

(d) determine when and in what amounts money is to be raised for the purposes of head (a);

(e) raise the amounts so determined by assessing and levying contributions on, and recovering them from, the unit owners.

(2) The commonhold association may, by the authority of a class 1 resolution, –

(a) change the purpose for which a reserve fund is held;

(b) transfer all or part of a reserve fund to another reserve fund or to the fund for the administration of the commonhold, where the association considers that, in the foreseeable circumstances, the reserve fund is unnecessary or too great.

*Accounting records*

4.—(1) The commonhold association has obligations to –

(a) cause to be kept proper accounting records showing its transactions and its assets and liabilities, and

(b) establish and maintain a satisfactory system of control of its accounting records, its cash holdings and all its receipts and remittances.

1303

(2)   The accounting records must be such as to enable a true and fair view to be given of the state of affairs of the association and to explain its transactions.

(3)   The commonhold association has an obligation to keep its accounting records available for inspection at all reasonable times by any unit owner or any person authorised by him in writing and permit copies to be taken, and every unit owner has the right, either in person or by any person authorised by him in writing, to inspect the accounting records and take copies.

(4)   If the accounting records are kept in other than written form, readable copies must be made available for inspection on request.

(5)   Reasonable facilities must be afforded to a unit owner seeking to exercise the rights conferred by sub-paragraphs (3) and (4), and no charge may be made.

### Accounts and balance sheets

5.—(1) The commonhold association has an obligation to specify a period of 12 months as its accounting year.

(2)   The commonhold association has an obligation, in respect of each accounting year, to prepare –

(a)  a revenue account giving a true and fair view of the association's income and expenditure in the year, and

(b)  a balance sheet giving a true and fair view as at the end of the year of the association's affairs.

(3)   The first account and balance sheet prepared under sub-paragraph (2) may be in respect of the period between the first vesting of common parts in the association and the end of its first accounting year, whether that period is more or less than a year, so long as it is not more than 18 months.

(4)   The revenue account and balance sheet must be signed by at least two members of the executive committee.

### Audit

6.—(1) The commonhold association has an obligation to appoint an auditor, at each annual general meeting, to hold office until the termination of the next-following annual general meeting.

(2)   The auditor –

(a)  must be a person qualified for appointment as auditor of a company under Article 397 of the Companies (Northern Ireland) Order 1986;

(b)  must not be a member, employee or agent of the commonhold association or a partner, employer or employee of a member, employee or agent.

(3)   The auditor shall make a report to the association on the accounts audited by him, and the report must state whether in his opinion –

(a)   the revenue account gives a true and fair view of the state of the association's income and expenditure, and

(b)   the balance sheet gives a true and fair view of the state of affairs of the association as at the end of the accounting year; and

(c)   proper provision for purposes mentioned in paragraph 3(1)(a)(ii) or (iii) has been made, or any reserve or other fund is insufficient or excessive.

(4)   The auditor in preparing his report shall carry out such investigations as will enable him to form an opinion as to the following matters –

(a)   whether the association has kept proper accounting records in compliance with paragraph 4(1)(a);

(b)   whether the association has established and maintained a satisfactory system of control in compliance with paragraph 4(1)(b);

(c)   whether the accounts are in agreement with the association's accounting records;

and if he is of opinion that the association has failed in any respect to comply with paragraph 4, or if the accounts are not in agreement with the accounting records, he shall state that fact in his report.

(5)   The auditor –

(a)   has a right of access at all times to all the books, records, accounts, correspondence and documents of the association, and

(b)   is entitled to require from the members of the executive committee, officers, employees and agents of the association such information and explanation as he thinks necessary for the performance of his duties;

and if he fails to obtain all the information and explanations which, to the best of his knowledge or belief, are necessarry for the purposes of his audit, he shall state that fact in his report.

### Assessment of contributions

7.   Contributions are to be assessed on the owner of each unit in accordance with his unit entitlement with respect to contributions for that unit.

### Levying of contributions

8.—(1)  A contribution is levied by the commonhold association on a unit owner by service on him of a demand note stating –

(a)   the number of the unit in respect of which the contribution is payable;

(b)   the amount of the contribution; and

(c)   the period for which the contribution is payable.

(2) Upon the written request of any unit owner, the commonhold association shall, in relation to any contribution levied on him, furnish him, without charge, with –

(a) full particulars of the costs incurred by the association to meet all or part of which the contribution has been levied;

(b) full particulars of contributions levied on the other unit owners in respect of the same costs and of the apportionment of contributions between all the unit owners;

(c) such information or evidence (whether by furnishing copies of receipts, accounts, contracts or otherwise) as is sufficient to support those particulars.

(3) Where, in legal proceedings between the commonhold association and a unit owner, the court orders (as it is hereby empowered to do) that the unit owner should not be liable to contribute to the association's costs, and contributions are levied in respect of common expenses which include those costs, the contribution levied on that unit owner is to be reduced so as to give effect to the order and the contributions levied on the other unit owners are to be increased accordingly.

(4) A unit owner is not excused from his liability to pay all or any part of contributions levied by the commonhold association by his failure or inability to use, or by waiver of the enjoyment of, any common property or by abandonment of his unit.

(5) Subject to paragraph (4), any dispute as to the fairness of contributions or their apportionment between the unit owners may be referred to and determined by the court and, in its determination, the court may order a variation in or reapportionment of the contributions or make such other order relating to them as it considers fair in all the circumstances of the case (but may not vary the unit entitlement with respect to contributions).

### Payment of contributions, and interest

9.—(1) Any contribution assessed by the commonhold association on a unit owner becomes a debt due and payable upon the service of the demand note under paragraph 8 levying the contribution.

(2) Where a unit is owned by two or more persons, the debt mentioned in sub-paragraph (1) is due from them jointly and severally.

(3) Where any contribution or part of a contribution due from a unit owner to the commonhold association remains unpaid for more than 28 days after demand, interest is payable on it from the date when it became due and payable until the date of its payment at such rate (if any) as is specified in the commonhold declaration or under sub-paragraph (4), or, if no rate is so specified, at the rate prescribed by rules of court for the purposes of Article 127 of the Judgments Enforcement (Northern Ireland) Order 1981; and for the purposes of paragraphs 10, 11 and 12 interest on a contribution is part of the contribution.

(4)   Where the commonhold declaration does not specify a rate of interest for the purposes of sub-paragraph (2) the commonhold association may do so by ordinary resolution; and any rate of interest specified in the commonhold declaration or a resolution may be varied by an ordinary resolution.

(5)   The commonhold association has a duty to lodge a copy of every ordinary resolution under sub-paragraph (4) in the Land Registry (and the Registrar shall register the effect of every resolution of which a copy is so lodged and file the resolution, and, until the effect is registered, the resolution has no operation); and the commonhold association has a duty to send a copy of every such resolution to every member within seven days of the date of its lodgment in the Land Registry.

### Liability of tenant or licensee for unpaid contributions

10.—(1) Where the owner of a unit which is let to a tenant at a rent ("the owner") fails to pay to the commonhold association ("the association") a contribution which is due and payable in respect of the unit –

(a)   the association, after the contribution has remained unpaid for 28 days, may serve a notice on the tenant requiring him to pay to the association so much of the rent payable by the tenant to his landlord as is sufficient to discharge the contribution unpaid by the owner; and thereupon the tenant is under an obligation to pay to the association all rent payable under the lease, to be applied by the association in discharge of any contribution payable by the owner which has accrued before service of the notice, until such time as the association serves on the tenant a notice to cease such payment, and the association has all the rights and remedies of the landlord for enforcing payment of the tenant's rent;

(b)   the tenant may, before any action for breach of his obligation to pay rent is brought by the landlord against the tenant, pay to the association so much of the rent payable by the tenant to the landlord as is sufficient to discharge the contributions remaining unpaid by the owner.

(2)   The receipt of the association or its agent is a full discharge to the tenant as against the landlord in respect of all contributions paid under paragraph (1).

(3)   The receipt of the landlord for rent paid to him by the tenant before service of a notice under paragraph (1)(a) is a full discharge to the tenant as against the association in respect of all rent issuing out of and theretofore due from the premises, except so much rent (if any) as remains due from the tenant.

(4)   In this paragraph "rent" includes service charges and any other payments which the tenant has agreed to make to the landlord under his lease.

(5)   This paragraph applies to a licensee as it applies to a tenant, as if any periodic sums payable by the licensee were rent.

1307

(6)   This paragraph does not prejudice the rights and remedies of the association with respect to contributions, or the balance of contributions, as against the owner.

### Liability for unpaid contributions on transfer of unit

11.   Where a unit is transferred, the transferor and the transferee are jointly and severally liable for all unpaid contributions due to the commonhold association in respect of the unit up to the date when notice of the date of registration of the transfer is served on the commonhold association, but without prejudice to any right of either party to recover from the other all or any part of the amounts paid by him.

### Lien on unit for unpaid contributions

12.—(1)   The commonhold association has a first and paramount lien on every unit for all money due and payable by the unit owner in respect of contributions, and that lien has priority over any mortgage or the estate of the lessor of an equity-sharing lease.

(2)   For the purposes of section 11(2) of the Building Societies Act 1986 (class 1 advances), the lien is not an "other mortgage" of the unit.

(3)   The lien is not a registrable charge under any provision of the Land Registration Act (nor need any registered charge be created in respect of it under section 44 of that Act) or under Part XIII of the Companies (Northern Ireland) Order1986, but it is enforceable as if it were a registered charge on the land and the commonhold association were the registered owner of that charge); but the commonhold association shall not take steps to enforce the lien until it has served notice that the contribution is in arrear upon –

  (a)   the unit owner, and also, where the unit owner is a lessee under an equity-sharing lease, on the lessor, and

  (b)   where notice has been served on the association of a mortgage of the unit, the mortgagee,

and three months have elapsed since the date of service.

(4)   Where a unit is leased by the unit owner or a person deriving title under him and notice of the lease had been served on the commonhold association before a contribution became due and payable, enforcement of the association's lien under sub-paragraph (3) in respect of that contribution is subject to the continuance of the tenancy created by the lease, if the tenancy cannot be terminated by notice or otherwise.

# EXPLANATORY NOTE

## SCHEDULE 4

This Schedule sets out obligations and powers of a commonhold association. The only provision of the Schedule which can be varied by the commonhold declaration or a subsequent resolution is paragraph 2 (and any variation must be made by express textual modification); but if the Department modifies any provision of the Schedule by an order under Article 23, the commonhold association may apply the modification to itself by ordinary resolution.

### Paragraph 1

This paragraph sets out the management obligations of a commonhold association.

*sub-paragraph (1)* The primary duties of the association are to keep the common property (i.e. the common parts of land and buildings and any equipment provided for common use) in good order. The association must also insure that property and keep unit owners informed about the insurance. It must enforce the obligations attaching to units and the commonhold bye-laws, and it must keep a record of the names and addresses of mortgagees or tenants of units who serve notice of their interests on the association (cf. Schedule 3, rule 3(7)). The association must also keep a record of lessors of units under equity-sharing leases: there is no need for such lessors to notify the association of their interests, because their freehold estates will be registered in the Land Registry and therefore a matter of public record.

*sub-paragraph (2)* operates on sub-paragraph (1)(a), which requires the association to keep the common property in a state of good and serviceable repair. The expression "common property" is defined in Article 2(2) as including any facility, and "facility" is defined as including lighting, heating, hot water, attendance and services; "services" is defined as including the taking out and keeping up of a policy of insurance. In relation to attendance and services, this sub-paragraph adapts sub-paragraph (1)(a) so as to make it refer to the proper provision of these things.

*sub-paragraphs (3) and (4)* contain further provisions about the duty to insure. Although the commonhold association owns only the common property it is intended to insure both that property and all the units and their fixtures. For this purpose it is deemed to have an insurable interest in the whole. The policy taken out by the association has primacy over any policy which may be taken out by an individual unit owner. If the unit is destroyed, compensation will be payable under only one of the policies, and that will be the association's.

### Paragraph 2

This paragraph sets out subsidiary powers of the commonhold association. It may acquire personal property for use in connection with common property (e.g. garden seats; sports equipment in a games room), borrow money (but not by charging the common property, except with the authority of a class 1 resolution – Article 7(8)), and provide amenities with or without charge (e.g. separate solid fuel stores, or garages – but any charge should not give a profit – Article 7(4)).

The paragraph ends with general provisions to prevent doubts being raised about the ambit of the association's powers in incidental matters (but, in any event, the ultra vires rule does not apply so as to prejudice third parties – Article 7(2)(b)).

### Paragraph 3

This paragraph is concerned with the keeping and management of funds.

The commonhold association must keep funds reasonably sufficient for day-to-day administration of the commonhold, the provision of reserves for repairs or other heavy expenditure which is foreseeable and the discharge of any other obligations which may involve unusual expenditure. The association must form an opinion about the adequacy of its funds (and in this it may be helped by its auditor, who must report whether, in his opinion, proper provision of reserves has been made or whether any reserve fund is insufficient or excessive – paragraph 6(3)(c)). Reserves are to be applied for the purposes for which they were built up, and for no other purpose; but the association may, by a class 1 resolution, vary the purposes of any reserve fund or transfer money from one fund to another.

The association must estimate what money needs to be raised for its purposes and raise that money by assessing and levying contributions on the unit owners (paragraphs 7 and 8), and, if the contributions are not paid promptly, taking steps to recover them (paragraphs 9 to 12).

### Paragraph 4

This paragraph requires the commonhold association to keep proper accounting records and have a satisfactory system of financial control. Unit owners have a right to inspect the records and take copies.

### Paragraph 5

This paragraph requires the commonhold association to fix an accounting year and prepare a revenue account for each year and a balance sheet showing the state of the association's affairs at the end of each year.

### Paragraph 6

This paragraph deals with audit. The auditor must be independent of the association and any of its members, and must be a person who is qualified to be a company's auditor (most usually a chartered accountant or a certified accountant, but other persons may qualify under Article 397 of the Companies Order). The auditor has wide powers of investigation for the purpose of his forming an opinion whether the association has kept proper accounting records and has a proper system of financial control, and whether the accounts give a true and fair view of the association's financial situation.

## Paragraph 7

This paragraph requires contributions to be assessed on unit owners in accordance with their unit entitlements (cf. Schedule 1, Part I, para. 8(b)).

## Paragraph 8

This paragraph deals with the levying of contributions. A demand note must be served on each unit owner (see Schedule 3, Rule 15 as to service of notices) stating the number of the unit (see Schedule 1, Part I, para. 3), the amount of the contribution and the period for which the contribution is payable. If the unit owner wishes to have more information, he may request the association in writing to give him full particulars of the costs which the contributions are to cover and of the contributions levied on other owners and how the contributions have been assessed. (The association, if it wishes, may anticipate any such request by including the information in the demand note in the first instance, but it is not bound to do so.) Contributions may have to be adjusted so as not to follow unit entitlement strictly in a case where part of the expenditure the contributions are designed to finance was incurred in proceedings between the association and a unit owner and the court has directed that the unit owner is not liable to contribute to the association's costs. ("Costs" is defined in section 46(2) of the Interpretation Act as including fees, charges, disbursements, expenses or remuneration.)

*sub-paragraph (4)* makes it clear that a unit owner cannot claim to be excused paying his contribution, or cannot claim to have his contribution reduced, on the ground that he has abandoned his unit or that he does not or cannot use some particular facility (e.g. a ground floor owner is not allowed to have the cost of upkeep of a lift left out of the reckoning of his contribution). This does not affect an owner whose unit entitlement with respect to contributions has been fixed having regard to his inability to use some particular facility – it only prevents some-one whose contribution has been correctly computed looking for a rebate.

*sub-paragraph (5)* allows an appeal to the court against any contribution which is thought to be unfair.

## Paragraph 9

This paragraph deals with the payment of contributions. A contribution is recoverable by action from the unit owner by the association (Article 15(1)(b)): sub-paragraph (1) says when the sum falls due. Where a unit has two or more owners, the debt is due by them all collectively and also by each of them separately. Contributions left unpaid for 29 days or more carry interest at the rate fixed by the commonhold declaration or an ordinary resolution or, if none is so fixed, the rate applicable to judgment debts. Interest runs from the date when the contribution first became due.

## Paragraph 10

This paragraph applies where a contribution is overdue in respect of a unit which has been leased to a tenant. The tenant's rent can be intercepted and applied by the association in or towards satisfaction of the contribution.

## Paragraph 11

This paragraph applies where a unit is transferred after a contribution has been levied but before it is paid, or where a unit is transferred and a contribution is levied on the transferor before notice of registration of the transfer in the Land Registry is served on the commonhold association by the transferee. The transferor and the transferee are liable for the contribution (jointly and individually), but while this is the position as between them and the association it does not affect their rights *inter se*. In practice it is likely that the transferee will indemnify the transferor for any liability he may incur in respect of contributions for a period falling after the date of execution of the instrument of transfer (it is for the transferor to serve on the association notice of that date – Schedule 3, rule 3(2)).

## Paragraph 12

This paragraph gives the commonhold association a lien on each unit for outstanding contributions due in respect of the unit. The lien is enforceable as if it were a registered charge (provisions of Part I of Schedule 7 to the Land Registration Act apply giving the association all the rights and powers of a mortgagee by deed, including power to sell the unit); but before taking steps to enforce the lien the association must serve a notice on the unit owner and, where a mortgagee of the unit has recorded his interest with the association, the mortgagee, allowing three months for the payment of the contribution (with interest). Where, in enforcing its lien, the association sells a unit which is leased and the tenant's interest had been recorded with the association before the contribution was levied, the sale is subject to the tenancy.

## DOCUMENTS AND INFORMATION TO BE SUPPLIED TO PURCHASER OF FREEHOLD OF UNIT

### PART I

### PURCHASE OF FREEHOLD FROM PROMOTER

1.   Office copies of –

(a)  the promoter's title;

(b)  the commonhold declaration (including all particulars annexed to it);

(c)  the common parts title (except where the purchaser is the first purchaser from the promoter or a purchaser whose transfer is completed before the registration of the commonhold association's title under Article 7(5));

(d)  the entries in the register of commonhold associations relating to the commonhold association.

2.   Where the purchase occurs after a reserve or other fund under Schedule 4, paragraph 3(1)(a)(ii) or (iii) has been established, a statement of the amount of the fund, how it is built up and replaced, and on what it is to be spent.

3.   Particulars of the insurance of the commonhold.

4.   An estimate of the likely amount of contributions to be levied on the unit and a statement of how the amount is calculated.

5.   Copies of Schedules 1 to 4 and any commonhold bye-laws.

### PART II

### PURCHASE OF FREEHOLD FROM UNIT OWNER OTHER THAN PROMOTER, OR FROM MORTGAGEE

1.   Office copies of –

(a)  the commonhold declaration (including all particulars annexed to it);

(b)  the unit owner's title;

(c)  the common parts title;

(d)  the entries in the register of commonhold associations relating to the commonhold association.

2.   A copy of the latest accounts of the commonhold association and the auditor's report on those accounts.

3.   Up-to-date details of any reserve funds.

4.   The amount of the current contribution payable in respect of the unit.

5.   The amounts of any arrears of contribution due and payable in respect of the unit and in respect of any other unit.

6.   Particulars of any debts or other obligations of the commonhold association which are unusual in either their nature or their amount and which have actually been defrayed but have not yet been charged to unit owners, or which have been incurred, but not yet defrayed, or which have not yet been incurred (but are planned to be incurred).

7.   Particulars of any current or threatened litigation affecting the commonhold or of any claims which may give rise to litigation.

8.   Particulars of any disputes about the use of the common property.

9.   Particulars of the insurance of the commonhold.

10.   Particulars of any administrator appointed by the court.

11.   Particulars of any proposal to terminate the commonhold.

12.   Copies of Schedules 1 to 4 and any commonhold bye-laws.

13.   Office copies of all class 1 resolutions and of all ordinary resolutions under Article 7(9) or (10) or Article 16(7) or Schedule 4 paragraph 9(4) the effect of which has been registered in the Land Registry; and copies of all such resolutions which have been passed but the effect of which has not yet been registered.

# EXPLANATORY NOTE

## SCHEDULE 5

This Schedule sets out the documents and information which must be supplied to the purchaser of the freehold of a unit. Article 12(3) also entitles a unit owner, on written request, to be supplied with so much of the information (but not the documents) mentioned in Part II as is not already in his possession (so far as the documents are concerned, he will either have received them on the purchase of his unit or have been supplied with them as they became available during the currency of his ownership).

## PART I

This Part lists the documents and information to be supplied to a person buying a unit from the promoter of the commonhold (except a promoter who was an existing unit owner – Article 12(2)). Article 12(4) applies to the office copies mentioned in paragraph 1 so as to allow copies of office copies (properly certified) to suffice.

## PART II

This Part lists the documents and information to be supplied by a unit owner (other than a promoter of the commonhold) to his purchaser. Where any information listed is not already in the possession of the vendor, he is entitled to obtain it from the commonhold association under Article 12(3): he can also obtain particulars of the association's accounting records under Schedule 4, para. 4(3).

RECOMMENDED DRAFT ORDER IN COUNCIL UNDER
PARAGRAPH 1 OF SCHEDULE 1 TO THE NORTHERN
IRELAND ACT 1974

---

## DRAFT STATUTORY INSTRUMENTS

---

**1989 No.      (N.I.    )**

### NORTHERN IRELAND

**Landlord and Tenant (Northern Ireland) Order 1989**

*To be laid before Parliament in draft*

*Made*

*Coming into operation in accordance with Article 1(2)*

### ARRANGEMENT OF ORDER

Article

## PART I

### INTRODUCTORY

## PART II

### CREATION, ETC., OF TENANCY

## PART III

### OBLIGATIONS

*Preliminary*

1317

1318

## PART IV

## THE RUNNING AND EFFECT OF BENEFITS AND OBLIGATIONS

### Running of benefits and obligations

### Modification of obligations

### Enforcement of obligations

## PART V

## TERMINATION, ETC., OF TENANCY

### Methods of termination

SCHEDULES:

Schedule 1 – Licences to alienate, change user or make improvements.

Schedule 2 – Transitional provisions and savings.

Schedule 3 – Provisions applying where the relation of landlord and tenant already exists.

At the Court at                    , the              day of              1989

Present,

The Queen's Most Excellent Majesty in Council

Whereas a draft of this Order has been approved by a resolution of each House of Parliament:

Now, therefore, Her Majesty, in exercise of the powers conferred by paragraph 1 of Schedule 1 to the Northern Ireland Act 1974 and of all other powers enabling Her in that behalf, is pleased, by and with the advice of Her Privy Council, to order, and it is hereby ordered, as follows: –

## PART I

## INTRODUCTORY

**Title and commencement**

**1.**—(1) This Order may be cited as the Landlord and Tenant (Northern Ireland) Order 1989.

(2) This Order comes into operation on such day or days as the Head of the Department of Finance and Personnel may by order appoint.

(3) If different days are appointed for the coming into operation of different provisions of this Order, any reference in a provision to the commencement of the Order is a reference to the commencement of that provision.

# EXPLANATORY NOTE

ARTICLE 1

*Paragraph (1)* gives the title of the Order.

*Paragraph (2)* provides for the making of a commencement order or commencement orders, bringing the provisions of the Order into operation on an appointed day, or bringing different provisions into operation on appointed days.

*Paragraph (3)* applies where a provision of the Order refers to the commencement of the Order. If different days are appointed for the coming into operation of different provisions, any such reference in a provision is to the time of coming into operation of that provision. The expression "commencement" is defined in section 46(1) of the Interpretation Act.

## Interpretation

**2.**—(1) The Interpretation Act (Northern Ireland) 1954 applies to Article 1 and the following provisions of this Order as it applies to a Measure of the Northern Ireland Assembly.

(2)　In this Order –

"conveyance" includes any writing, other than a will, consisting of or comprising a transfer, lease, assignment, assent, vesting declaration, disclaimer, release or other assurance of property or of an interest therein but does not include a mortgage;

"the court" means the High Court or, in relation to premises with respect to which the county court has jurisdiction in actions for the recovery of land, a county court;

"demise", means the grant of a tenancy; and "sub-demise" is to be construed accordingly;

"dwelling-house" means a building or part of a building (together with any yard, garden, outhouses and appurtenances belonging to it or usually enjoyed with it) let for use wholly or mainly as a private dwelling;

"landlord" in relation to a tenancy means the person entitled to the reversion;

"lease" means the agreement (written, oral or implied) by which a tenancy is created, and includes a sub-lease; and in relation to any tenancy "the lease" means the lease which created that tenancy;

"leasehold estate" means the estate created by a lease for a term –

(a)　of less than a year, or

(b)　of a year or years, or

(c)　of a year or years and a fraction of a year, or

(d)　from year to year or any other period,

irrespective of whether or not the estate –

(i)　takes effect in possession or future,

(ii)　is at a rent,

(iii)　is subject to another legal estate or a legal interest,

(iv)　is for a term which is certain or liable to determination by notice, re-entry or operation of law or by virtue of a provision for cesser on redemption or in any other event (save the dropping of a life or the determination of a determinable life interest);

but does not include any estate for a term determinable with life or lives or with the cesser of a determinable life interest;

"licence" means an oral licence or a written licence, and includes permission, consent or agreement;

"modifications" means additions, omissions, amendments, adaptations, applications, extensions, restrictions and substitutions;

"mortgage" includes any charge or lien on any property for securing money or money's worth;

"mortgagee" and "mortgagor" include any person deriving title under, respectively, the original mortgagee and the original mortgagor;

"obligation" includes an obligation not to do something (and any reference to the performance or breach of an obligation is to be construed accordingly);

"possession" includes the receipt of, or the right to receive, rents and profits, if any;

"the premises" means the land which is the subject of a tenancy and, in relation to a landlord or tenant, means the land of which the former is landlord or the latter is tenant;

"the Property Order" means the Property (Northern Ireland) Order 1989;

"provision" in relation to a lease or assignment (except in the expression "statutory provision") includes a covenant, promise, proviso, agreement, stipulation, condition or limitation;

"rent" includes any annual or periodic payment in money or money's worth, reserved or issuing out of or charged upon land including a royalty, but does not include interest;

"repair" in relation to the exterior of premises includes keeping paintwork or other protective treatment in reasonable order;

"the reversion" in relation to a tenancy means the estate which but for the tenancy would carry the right to immediate possession of the premises, disregarding any mortgage;

"statutory provision" has the meaning given by section 1(f) of the Interpretation Act (Northern Ireland) 1954;

"tenancy" means –

(a) the leasehold estate created by a lease together with all the benefits conferred on the tenant by or in consequence of the lease and all tenant's obligations; or

(b) a tenancy at will;

and in relation to a tenant, or to a landlord and a tenant, "the tenancy" means the tenancy held by that tenant or held from that landlord by that tenant;

"tenant" means a person entitled to a tenancy, whether beneficially or not, but does not include a tenant at sufferance or any person who is in possession of land otherwise than in accordance with a lease; and in relation to any landlord, tenancy or premises "the tenant" means the tenant of that landlord in respect of that tenancy or those premises.

(3)   For the purposes of this Order, a tenancy from year to year, or a periodic tenancy which is based on any period less than a year, is a tenancy for a period not exceeding one year.

(4)   In this Order any reference to an obligation under a tenancy is a reference to –

(a) an obligation arising under Part III;

(b) an obligation arising between landlord and tenant in relation to the tenancy under any statutory provision other than a provision of Part III;

1324

(c) an obligation arising at common law between landlord and tenant in relation to the tenancy;

(d) an obligation imported by a provision contained or implied in the lease (including any such provision as modified by any statutory provision);

and "tenant's obligation" and "landlord's obligation" mean such obligations falling on the tenant and the landlord respectively.

(5)   In this Order "obligation to repair" includes an obligation to keep the premises in repair during the currency of the tenancy and, in the case of a tenant's obligation, an obligation to leave or put them in repair at the termination of the tenancy; and any reference to an obligation to keep the premises in repair includes an obligation to put them in repair if they are not in repair at the beginning of the tenancy.

# EXPLANATORY NOTE

ARTICLE 2                                   Property Bill Cl. 1(1),
                                            160(1)(2)
                                            Deasy's Act s. 1

This Article provides for the interpretation of certain expressions used in the Order.

*Paragraph (1)* makes the Interpretation Act (Northern Ireland) 1954 applicable to the Order.

*Paragraph (2)* defines certain expressions which appear in the Order as follows –

| *Expression* | *Article* |
|---|---|
| "conveyance" | 8, 17, 40, 41, Sch. 2 |
| "the court" | passim |
| "demise" "sub-demise" | 4, 44, 56, 61 |
| "dwelling-house" | 20, 21, 22, 52, 64, 65, 66, 71, 72 |
| "landlord" | passim |
| "lease" | passim |
| "leasehold estate" | 2(2) ("tenancy"), 4(2), 56 |
| "licence" | 42, 44, 45, 57, 59, 68, Sch. 1 |
| "modifications" | 12(2) ("modified"), 44(3)(f) |
| "mortgage" | 2(2) ("conveyance"; "the reversion"), 37(5), 44(5), 61, Sch. 2 |
| "mortgagee" "mortgagor" | 8, 37(5), 44(5), 58, 61, Sch. 2 |
| "obligation" | 2(4) and passim |
| "possession" | 5(2), 10(4), 13, 62, 65, 66, 69 |
| "the premises" | passim |
| "the Property Order" | 10, 44, 56, 61, 78, Sch. 2 |
| "provision" | 2(4)(d), 12, 68, 72, 73 |
| "rent" | 2(2) ("possession") and passim |
| "repair" | 2(5), 20, 21, 22, 23, 24, 26, 27, 28, 30, 31, 48, 49 |
| "the reversion" | 2(2) ("landlord"), 8, 9, 10, 40, 41, 49, 56 |
| "statutory provision" | 2(4), 10, 14, 16, 32, 34, 36, 37, 50, 79, Sch.1 |
| "tenancy" | passim |
| ("tenancy at will") | 2(2) ("tenancy"), 3, 5, 7, 44, 50, 52 |
| "tenant" | .passim |

*Paragraph (3)* defines a tenancy for a period not exceeding a year as including a tenancy from year to year and a tenancy based on a period of

1326

less than a year (i.e. from week to week, month to month, and so on). (Articles 3, 44, 58(6)).

*Paragraph (4)* defines "obligation under a tenancy". It includes any obligation arising between the landlord and the tenant by virtue of statute or common law or their own agreement. An obligation binding the tenant is a "tenant's obligation", and one binding the landlord is a "landlord's obligation". (*Passim*). See also Schedule 2 paragraph 12.

*Paragraph (5)* defines "obligation to repair" as including an obligation to keep the premises in repair during the currency of the tenancy and, where it is a tenant's obligation, to leave or put them in repair at its termination. (Articles 48, 49). An obligation to keep the premises in repair includes an obligation to put them in repair if they are out of repair (Articles 20 to 24).

## PART II
### CREATION, ETC., OF TENANCY

**Creation of tenancy**

**3.**—(1) Subject to paragraph (2), a tenancy is capable of being created only by writing signed by the landlord.

(2)   Writing is not necessary for the creation of –

(a)   a tenancy for a period not exceeding one year;

(b)   a tenancy at will.

# EXPLANATORY NOTE

ARTICLE 3                                  Property Bill, Cl. 161
                                           Deasy's Act s. 4

This Article is concerned with the formalities for creating a tenancy.

*Paragraph (1)* requires writing for the creation of a tenancy. "Writing" is defined in section 46(1) of the Interpretation Act (Northern Ireland) 1954 to include words typewritten, printed or otherwise represented or reproduced. The writing must be signed by the landlord (but this does not affect the law of agency under which a person holding a power of attorney can sign his principal's name). The writing should also be signed by the tenant (see the Note on Article 5(4)), but this paragraph does not make that essential.

*Paragraph (2)* sets out two exceptions to paragraph (1). In these cases a tenancy may be created orally or by implication. The exceptions are for tenancies for not more than one year (which by virtue of Article 2(3) include a tenancy from year to year or any lesser periodic tenancy) and tenancies at will. Tenancies at will commonly arise on a temporary basis where a tenant whose lease has expired holds over with the landlord's permission without having yet paid rent on a periodic basis, where a tenant takes possession under a mere agreement for a lease and has not yet paid rent, and where a purchaser has been let into possession pending completion. There will also be a tenancy at will where possession is taken under a void lease. It is unusual for a tenancy at will to be created as a definitive tenancy; but if the parties are genuinely agreed to create a tenancy at will they would be better not to rely on this paragraph but to use clear writing, because where rent is paid periodically, the court will tend to find a periodic tenancy, and where no rent is paid it may be inferred that there is a licence giving rise to a constructive trust. In *Manfield & Sons Ltd. v. Botchin* [1970] 2 QB 612, where there was writing, the court accepted that the tenancy was at will, because it had been made clear that the letting was temporary pending obtaining planning permission for the site.

### Reversion on tenancy

**4.**—(1) The term of a tenancy must be a period less than that for which the landlord's estate is capable of subsisting.

(2) Accordingly, where the landlord's estate is a leasehold estate, a contract to sub-demise, or a purported sub-demise, for a term equal to the unexpired residue of the term of that estate takes effect as a contract for, or as, an assignment of the tenancy encompassing that estate and not as a contract for, or as, a sub-lease.

# EXPLANATORY NOTE

## ARTICLE 4

This Article reverses so much of section 3 of Deasy's Act as renders a reversion unnecessary to the relation of landlord and tenant, and restores the common law rule that there must be a reversion on a lease.

*Paragraph (1)* prohibits a tenancy from being created without a reversion in the landlord- that is, the term of the tenancy must be less than the term of the landlord's estate. Where a subsisting lease is to be immediately followed by a reversionary lease, see Article 5(3).

*Paragraph (2)* spells out the effect of this as preventing the grant by a lessee of a sub-lease for the full term of his lease. A purported sub-lease without a reversion takes effect as an assignment of the lease out of which the sub-lease was intended to be carved: this restores the effect of the House of Lords decision in *Pluck* v. *Digges* (1832) 5 Bligh (N.S.) 31, 5 ER 219.

A lease for ever purported to be made by a fee simple owner cannot create a tenancy (see the definition of "leasehold estate" in Article 2(2)). In the past such a purported lease has been held to be a fee farm grant where appropriate words of limitation were used: in the absence of such words it would appear to have been ineffective. Fee farm grants will be incapable of being made in the future.

Transitional provisions make it clear that existing reversionless leasehold estates or interests are not affected (Schedule 2, paragraph 2).

**Beginning of tenancy**

5.—(1) Without prejudice to paragraphs (2) and (3), a tenancy takes effect –

(a)  on the day fixed for the beginning of the term of the tenancy; or

(b)  if no day is fixed, on the making of the lease;

without actual entry.

(2)  A tenancy at will does not take effect unless or until the tenant has possession of the premises.

(3)  Notwithstanding Article 4(1) and paragraph (1)(a), where the term of a reversionary lease is fixed to begin immediately upon the termination of the term of an existing lease, the reversionary lease takes effect on its making to the extent necessary to support a sub-lease for a term falling partly within the term of the existing lease and partly within the term of the reversionary lease.

(4)  For the purposes of paragraph (1)(b) a lease in writing is made when the writing is signed by the landlord.

# EXPLANATORY NOTE

ARTICLE 5                              Property Bill Cl. 162
                                       Deasy's Act s. 3
                                       LPA 1925 s. 149

This Article renders it unnecessary for a tenant (except a tenant at will) to take possession of the premises as a condition of his tenancy beginning. At common law, a tenant acquired no estate in the land until he took possession: all he had was an "interesse termini" – a legal interest which carried a right of entry. The doctrine of interesse termini is commonly thought to have been abolished by Deasy's Act. Whether or not that was so, the Article makes it clear that entry is unnecessary.

*Paragraph (1)* causes a tenancy to take effect on the day fixed for the beginning of the term or, if no day is fixed, on the making of the lease. No entry is needed.

*Paragraph (2)* makes an exception for tenancies at will, which depend upon the tenant having actual possession of the land. The tenant may either be in possession when the tenancy starts (as where a tenant for years holds over with the landlord's consent) or, being out of possession, he may take up possession (as where a vendor allows the purchaser into occupation pending completion).

*Paragraph (3)* deals with the case where a reversionary lease has been granted to take effect immediately upon the termination of an existing lease and the lessee wishes to grant a sub-lease whose term will span the terms of the two leases. If paragraph (1) stood unqualified he could not do this, because at the time of the grant of the sub-lease he has no tenancy in the land extending beyond the date of expiry of the existing lease (his tenancy under the reversionary lease will not arise until the day fixed for the term of that lease to begin). This paragraph gives the reversionary lease sufficient immediate effect to support the sub-lease.

*Paragraph (4)* A written lease should be signed by both the landlord and the tenant (or the original signed by the landlord and a counterpart by the tenant) because the landlord must demise the land and the tenant must accept the demise. This paragraph makes signing by the landlord the definitive act (cf. Article 3(1)) in the making of the lease.

### Evidence of lease

**6.** In all proceedings, proof by or on behalf of the landlord of the execution of the counterpart of a lease is equivalent to proof of the execution of the original lease; and where it appears that no counterpart existed, or that the counterpart has been lost, destroyed or mislaid, proof of a copy of the original lease or counterpart, as the case may be, is sufficient evidence of the contents of the lease as against the tenant.

# EXPLANATORY NOTE

ARTICLE 6                                    Property Bill Cl. 163
                                             Deasy's Act s. 23

This allows proof of a lease against the tenant by production of its counterpart i.e. an engrossment of the lease, signed by the tenant and held by the landlord (the original lease, signed by the landlord, being held by the tenant). Article 3(1) requires a lease to be executed by the landlord, so it could be difficult for the landlord to prove due execution when he does not have possession of the instrument bearing his signature. If there is no counterpart (i.e. if the lease took the form of a single instrument signed by both parties), or if it can be shown that the counterpart has been lost, destroyed or mislaid, the lease may be proved by production of a copy of the lease or (in the case of a missing counterpart) a copy of the counterpart. If none of the methods of proof mentioned in the Article is available, the ordinary rule of evidence will apply of allowing secondary evidence, of whatever kind is available, to prove the contents of the lease.

**Assignment of tenancy**

**7.**—(1) A tenancy other than a tenancy at will is assignable only by writing signed by the tenant.

(2) Paragraph (1) does not affect the transmission of a tenancy by operation of law.

(3) A tenancy at will is not assignable.

# EXPLANATORY NOTE

ARTICLE 7                        Property Bill Cl. 173
                                            Deasy's Act s. 9

This Article permits an assignment of a leasehold estate to be made only by writing executed by the tenant (or executed in the tenant's name by his properly-authorised agent).

This does not affect the transmission of a tenancy by operation of law (as when the tenancy passes to the tenant's personal representative on his death or to his trustee in bankruptcy).

The Article applies to all tenancies, except tenancies at will, whether created orally or by implication or in writing (see Article 3).

### Conveyance of reversion and attornment by tenant

**8.**—(1) A conveyance of the reversion in the premises expectant on a tenancy is valid without any attornment of the tenant.

(2)   Nothing in paragraph (1) –

(a) affects the validity of any payment of rent by the tenant to the person making the conveyance before notice of the conveyance is served on the tenant by the person entitled under the conveyance; or

(b) renders the tenant liable for any breach of obligation to pay rent, on account of his failure to pay rent to the person entitled under the conveyance before such notice is served on the tenant.

(3)   An attornment by the tenant in respect of the premises, to a person ("the claimant") claiming to be the landlord, is void unless –

(a) the attornment is made with the consent of the person ("the previous landlord") who was landlord immediately before the claimant's claim arose; or

(b) the claimant rightfully derives title under the previous landlord; or

(c) the attornment is made pursuant to a judgment of a court of competent jurisdiction; or

(d) the attornment is made to a mortgagee by a tenant holding under a tenancy from the mortgagor, where the right of redemption is barred.

# EXPLANATORY NOTE

ARTICLE 8                                   Property Bill Cl. 164
                                            1707 ss. 9, 10
                                            1741 ss. 7, 8
                                            LPA 1925 s. 151

This Article is concerned with attornments. An attornment is a formal acknowledgement by a tenant of a new landlord.

*Paragraph (1)* renders attornment by the tenant unnecessary where there is a conveyance of the reversion expectant upon a lease.

*Paragraph (2)* protects a tenant who pays rent to his former landlord before he is notified by the new landlord of the change of landlord. The payment of rent is valid and the tenant is not held to be guilty of breach of his obligation to pay rent merely because the rent was paid to the wrong person.

*Paragraph (3)* renders a fraudulent attornment void. In order to be valid an attornment must be made –

(a)  with the consent of the former landlord, or

(b)  to a genuine successor in title of the former landlord's (and it is for the tenant to make sure that the successor's claim is genuine); or

(c)  under a court order; or

(d)  to a mortgagee who has ousted the landlord-mortgagor under the Limitation Order.

**Effect of extinguishment of reversion**

**9.** Where the reversion expectant on a tenancy is surrendered or merged, the estate or interest which, as against the tenant, confers the next vested right to the premises is to be deemed the reversion for the purpose of preserving the same benefits and obligations as would have affected the original reversion had there been no surrender or merger thereof.

# EXPLANATORY NOTE

ARTICLE 9
Property Bill Cl. 165
1845 s. 9
LPA 1925 s. 139

This Article is concerned with the position of a sub-tenant whose landlord's tenancy has been surrendered or estate merged in a superior estate. The sub-tenancy has effect for the future as though it had been carved out of the superior estate.

## Validation of leases

**10.**—(1) Where, in the intended exercise of any power of leasing, whether conferred by a statutory provision or an instrument, a lease ("the invalid lease") is granted, which by reason of any failure to comply with the terms of the power is invalid, then –

(a) as against the person entitled, after the determination of the interest of the grantor, to the reversion; or

(b) as against any other person who, subject to any lease properly granted under the power, would have been entitled to the land comprised in the invalid lease;

the invalid lease, if it was made in good faith, takes effect as a contract for the grant, at the request of the lessee, of a valid lease under the power, of like effect as the invalid lease, subject to such variations as may be necessary in order to comply with the terms of the power.

(2) The lessee under the invalid lease is not, by virtue of any such implied contract, entitled to obtain a variation of the lease if the other persons who would have been bound by the lease had it been valid are willing and able to confirm the lease without variation.

(3) Where a lease granted in the intended exercise of such a power is invalid by reason of the grantor not having power to grant the lease at the date thereof, but the grantor's interest in the land comprised therein continues after the time when he might, in the exercise of the power, have properly granted a lease in the like terms, the lease takes effect as a valid lease in like manner as if it had been granted at that time.

(4) Where, during the continuance of the possession taken under the invalid lease, the person for the time being entitled, subject to such possession, to the land comprised therein or to the rents and profits thereof, is able to confirm the lease without variation, the lessee is, at the request of the person so able to confirm the lease, bound to accept a confirmation thereof, and thereupon the lease has effect and is deemed to have had effect as a valid lease from the grant thereof.

(5) Confirmation under paragraph (4) may be by a memorandum in writing signed by or on behalf of the persons respectively confirming and accepting the confirmation of the lease.

(6) Where, upon or before acceptance of rent under the invalid lease, any receipt is signed or confirmation is given by or on behalf of the person accepting the rent, that acceptance is, as against that person, deemed to be a confirmation of the lease.

(7) The foregoing provisions of this Article do not affect prejudicially any right of action or other right or remedy to which, but for those provisions or any statutory provision replaced by those provisions, –

(a) the lessee named in an invalid lease would or might have been entitled under any obligation on the part of the grantor in respect of title or quiet enjoyment which is contained in or implied by the invalid lease or which applies by virtue of Part III;

1342

(b)   the grantor or other person for the time being entitled to the reversion expectant on the termination of the lease would or might have been entitled by reason of any breach of an obligation under the lease which would have been a tenant's obligation if the lease had been valid.

(8)   Where a valid power of leasing is vested in or may be exercised by a person who grants a lease which, by reason of the determination of the interest of the grantor or otherwise, cannot have effect and continuance according to the terms thereof independently of the power, the lease is for the purposes of this Article deemed to have been granted in the intended exercise of the power although the power is not referred to in the lease.

(9)   This Article takes effect without prejudice to Article 15 of the Property Order (leases to be granted in the name and on behalf of the owner of the legal estate affected).

(10)   In this Article "lessee" includes a sub-lessee and means the person purporting to be the lessee under the invalid lease or any person who would have been a successor in title of his had the invalid lease been valid.

# EXPLANATORY NOTE

ARTICLE 10

Property Bill Cl. 166
Leases Act 1849
Leases Act 1850
LPA 1925 s. 152

This Article makes valid certain leases which otherwise would be invalid because of the lessors' failure to comply with the terms of the powers under which the leases were granted. There must be a valid power of leasing. The leases validated are those which suffer from some fairly minor technical flaw: the Article has no operation where the leasing power is itself in doubt (e.g. where a lease purports to embrace land extending beyond that to which the power properly applies, or where there are two powers of leasing and the lease was granted in purported exercise of the wrong one).

*Paragraph (1)* makes the invalid lease take effect as a contract for a valid lease which will contain such variations as are necessary for compliance with the power. The invalid lease has this effect whether or not the intended lessee has entered into possession of the land.

*Paragraph (2)* negatives paragraph (1) so far as it refers to variation, where the parties to the invalid lease are willing and able to confirm the lease without variation.

*Paragraph (3)* is concerned with a lease prematurely granted: when the purported lessor becomes vested with the necessary powers, the lease takes effect as though granted at that time.

*Paragraph (4)* deals with a case where the lessee under an invalid lease has gone into possession of the land and the person entitled to the reversion is able to confirm the lease without variation. In such a case the lessee must accept a confirmation of the lease.

*Paragraph (5)* provides for a confirmation to be in writing signed by all parties (including the lessee).

*Paragraph (6)* makes acceptance of rent equivalent to confirmation so far as concerns the payee.

*Paragraph (7)* preserves a lessee's right to claim damages from the grantor of an invalid lease for breach of his covenant for title or quiet enjoyment, and a lessor's rights or remedies for the lessee's breach of his obligations.

*Paragraph (8)* is concerned with a lease granted by a lessor which cannot have effect in accordance with its terms independently of some power vested in the lessor. Such a lease is one granted "in the intended exercise" of the power (within the meaning of paragraph (1)) even though the power is not expressly referred to.

*Paragraph (9)* refers to Article 15 of the Property Order which requires the grant of a lease, when made by a person other than the owner of the legal estate affected, to be made in the name and on behalf of that owner.

*Paragraph (10)* defines "lessee" for the purposes of the Article.

# PART III

## OBLIGATIONS

*Preliminary*

**Scope of Part III**

**11.**—(1) An obligation arising under this Part applies only to tenancies created after the commencement of this Order and replaces any obligation of the same nature which would otherwise arise by implication at common law.

(2) Subject to the provisions of this Part, an obligation arising under this Part applies to every tenancy and has the same force and effect as if it were imposed expressly by the lease.

# EXPLANATORY NOTE

ARTICLE 11                                    Cf. Property Bill Cl. 170, Sch. 3
                                              Law Com. No. 67 Cl. 1(1)

This Article defines the scope of the statutory obligations imposed by Part III. The Part provides for the rights and duties conferred or imposed on parties to a tenancy created after the commencement of the Order. These are classified as "overriding" (taking effect regardless of any provision of the lease) or "variable" (taking effect save to the extent that they are excluded or supplanted by the lease, either expressly or by implication) (Article 12). "Tenancy" is defined by Article 2(2).

*Paragraph (1)* confines the operation of Part III to tenancies created after the commencement of the Order. But see paragraph 5 of Schedule 3.

*Paragraph (2)* gives obligations arising under Part III the same force and effect as if they were incorporated in the relevant lease.

## Overriding and variable obligations

**12.**—(1) An obligation referred to in this Part as an overriding obligation applies to a tenancy notwithstanding any provision of the lease.

(2)   An obligation referred to in this Part as a variable obligation applies to a tenancy, save to the extent that it is excluded or modified by express provision in the lease or by necessary implication from the terms of the lease.

(3)   In relation to any overriding obligation of a landlord or a tenant, any provision of a lease is void in so far as it purports –

(a)   to exclude or limit the obligation either expressly or by implication (whether by imposing a more limited obligation on the same party or by imposing an obligation on the other party or otherwise); or

(b)   to impose on any party any penalty or disability in the event of his enforcing or relying on the obligation or to impose a liability to reimburse all or any part of the cost of performing the obligation.

# EXPLANATORY NOTE

ARTICLE 12                                Law Com. No. 67 Cl. 2, 3

This Article defines "overriding obligation" and "variable obligation".

*Paragraph (1)* provides that an obligation which is referred to in this Part as an overriding obligation applies to any tenancy falling within the Part, despite anything to the contrary in the lease.

*Paragraph (2)* defines a variable obligation as one that applies to a tenancy unless excluded, or except to the extent that it is modified, by a provision of the lease, either expressly or by necessary implication. There would be an implication where, for example, the lease deals with the same subject in a different way.

*Paragraph (3)* amplifies paragraph (1) by rendering void any provision of a lease so far as it purports to exclude or limit an overriding obligation or to cause any penalty to be incurred by reason of a party's relying on such an obligation.

*Overriding obligations: all tenancies*

**Possession**

13.—(1) The landlord has an overriding obligation to give the tenant possession of the premises on the day on which the tenancy begins or such other day as is specified in the lease.

(2) Where a lease expresses its term to begin on a day before the date of the lease, for the purposes of this Article the tenancy is deemed to begin on the date of the lease.

# EXPLANATORY NOTE

ARTICLE 13  Law Com. No. 67 Cl. 4

This Article imposes on the landlord an overriding obligation to give the tenant possession of the demised premises either on the day when the tenancy begins or, if some other day is specified in the lease as the day for giving possession, on that other day. If the day specified is a past day, for the purposes of giving possession the relevant day is the date of the lease (but, as explained below, in most such cases – but not necessarily all – the tenant will already be in possession).

This restates existing law.

A lease may express its term to commence –

(a) on a specified day before the date of the lease;

(b) on the date of the lease;

(c) on a specified day after the date of the lease.

If no date for possession is specially fixed, in cases (a) and (b) the date for possession will be the date of the lease; in case(c) the date for possession will be the specified day. A term is likely to be expressed to begin on a past date only where the tenant has been in *de facto* possession from that date (as where he entered into possession on the strength of an agreement for a lease or where there is an interval between the falling of a lease and the grant of a reversionary lease and the tenant has been in possession throughout).

"Possession" is defined in Article 2(2) as including the receipt of, or the right to receive, rents and profits, if any. This definition would be relevant to the present Article in the case of a concurrent lease (i.e., a lease of the reversion on an already subsisting lease).

**Quiet enjoyment**

**14.**—(1) The landlord has an overriding obligation to ensure that the tenant peacefully holds and enjoys the premises for the purpose and during the term of the tenancy without interruption by the landlord or any person lawfully asserting or enforcing a title or right (whether derived from or superior to the title of the landlord) to or in respect of the premises.

(2) Paragraph (1) does not apply to interruption by –

(a) the landlord or any other person in the exercise of any right or the performance of any obligation conferred or imposed on him by the lease or under any statutory provision;

(b) any person other than the landlord in consequence of a defect in the title of the landlord of which the tenant had notice, or of which the landlord did not have notice, at the time of the grant of the tenancy.

(3) In this Article –

"defect in the title of the landlord" includes –

(a) lack of any title to the premises;

(b) lack of any estate or interest in the premises sufficient in duration (in any event) to support the tenancy for the whole of its term;

(c) lack of power to grant the tenancy, or any condition or restriction affecting the power to grant it;

(d) any liability to have the landlord's estate terminated by an order of the court by reason of a breach by the landlord of his obligations to a superior landlord, where the breach occurred before or was subsisting at the time of the grant of the tenancy;

(e) any restriction affecting the use of the premises for the purpose of the tenancy;

(f) any easement or right over or against the premises;

"interruption" includes dispossession and disturbance and also, in relation to the use of the premises for the purpose of the tenancy, the enforcement of any restriction affecting that use;

"notice" means actual or constructive notice;

"purpose of the tenancy" means any purpose specified as such in the lease or known to the landlord at the time of the grant as that for which the tenancy is taken by the tenant, and, where two or more purposes are so specified or known, includes any of them.

ARTICLE 14                                    Law Com. No. 67 Cl. 5

This Article establishes the tenant's right to quiet enjoyment of the demised premises following the *grant* of a tenancy. (Article 106 of the Property Order is concerned with covenants – including a covenant for quiet enjoyment – implied between assignor and assignee on the *assignment* of a tenancy.).

*Paragraph (1)* imposes on the landlord an overriding obligation to give the tenant peaceful enjoyment of the premises for the purposes of the tenancy during its term without interruption by the landlord or any person lawfully asserting a title derived from the landlord's title or a superior title. The paragraph supersedes section 41 of Deasy's Act, which implied a covenant for quiet enjoyment without interruption by the landlord or anyone else. That section had the defects that it applied only to leases in writing and, more seriously, that it was capable of being displaced by a provision in the lease: in practice it became usual for leases to supplant it with a covenant limited to interruptions by the landlord and those deriving title under him – in effect restoring the common law position. The paragraph improves the tenant's position by adding interruptions by persons with a title superior to the landlord's.

*Paragraph (2)* excludes interruptions –

*sub-paragraph (a)* by the landlord or another person in doing something required or permitted by the lease or by a statutory provision (for example, entry to carry out repairs or abate a nuisance or under a statutory right of entry); or

*sub-paragraph (b)* by another person in consequence of a defect in the landlord's title of which the tenant had notice, or of which the landlord did not know, when he granted the tenancy.

*Paragraph (3)* defines expressions used in the Article –

"defect in the title of the landlord" includes –

(a) lack of title, as where the landlord has no title at all, or is merely in process of acquiring one, but has not yet acquired it, under the statute of limitation;

(b) lack of sufficient supporting title, as where a landlord holding on a yearly tenancy grants a sub-lease for a term exceeding one year;

(c) lack of power to grant the tenancy, as where the landlord holds under a lease which prohibits sub-letting;

(d) liability to have the landlord's estate terminated (where it is a leasehold estate) by reason of a breach of his obligations to the superior landlord, where the breach occurred before or was subsisting at the time when the tenancy was granted;

(e) restrictions on use of the premises, as where the premises are let for use for the sale of intoxicating liquor and such a use is prohibited by a covenant binding the landlord;

(*f*) easements or other rights which would be interfered with by the use to which the tenant proposes to put the premises (for example, an easement of light which would be infringed by the erection of a building by the tenant for the purposes of his tenancy).

"interruption" includes dispossession or disturbance. Where a superior landlord is entitled to the benefit of a restriction on the use of the premises for a particular purpose, and that purpose is a purpose of the tenancy, it also includes the enforcement of the restriction;

"notice" means actual or constructive notice.

"purpose of the tenancy" means any purpose which is either specified in the lease or tenancy agreement or is known to the landlord at the time of the grant as the purpose for which the tenant wants to use the premises.

This Article subsumes the landlord's implied covenant that he has a right to grant the lease. The covenant not to derogate from the grant continues independently as something implied in all conveyances.

## Rent

**15.**—(1) The tenant has an overriding obligation to pay any rent or other sums due from him to the landlord under the lease.

(2) Subject to the provisions of the lease, any rent payable thereunder is due in arrear at the end of the period in respect of which it is payable.

(3) Where a tenancy determines at any time before the day on which the rent would become payable, the landlord is entitled to a proportion of the rent according to the time that has elapsed from the beginning of the tenancy, or the last day for payment of rent, to the day of determination.

## EXPLANATORY NOTE

ARTICLE 15

Law Com. No. 67 Cl. 6
Deasy's Act s. 50

This Article imposes an overriding obligation on the tenant to pay any rent or other sums that have been agreed upon.

*Paragraph (1)* imposes an overriding obligation to pay any rent or other sums that have been agreed upon. The paragraph applies only where there is an agreement for rent and does not prevent the grant of a rent-free lease.

*Paragraph (2)* makes rent payable in arrear. This is subject to any express provision in the lease under which rent is agreed to be paid in advance. At present in Northern Ireland rent is payable in arrear unless the contract expressly or by clear implication provides for payment in advance, and the Article continues this rule.

*Paragraph (3)* entitles the landlord to a proportion of the rent when the tenancy terminates during a rent period.

**Protection of premises**

**16.**—(1) The tenant has an overriding obligation –

(a) to take all reasonable steps to prevent encroachment on the premises;

(b) to serve notice on the landlord forthwith of any such encroachment, any adverse claim to the premises and any notice or proceeding known to him (whether addressed to or taken against him or not) which may affect the landlord's interest in the premises;

(c) not to contravene any restriction imposed by or under any statutory provision with respect to use of the premises;

(d) not to do or allow to be done on the premises anything which constitutes a nuisance;

(e) not to use the premises or cause or allow the premises to be used for any illegal purpose.

(2)   For the purposes of paragraph (1)(d) and (e), a person allows to be done anything which he has the right to prevent if he does not take reasonable steps to enforce that right.

# EXPLANATORY NOTE

ARTICLE 16                                   Law Com. No. 67 Cl. 7
                                             LPA 1925 s. 145

This Article imposes on the tenant certain overriding obligations to protect the premises.

*Paragraph (1)* The obligations are –

   (*a*)  to prevent encroachments by taking such reasonable steps as the circumstances require;

   (*b*)  to notify the landlord forthwith (i.e. within a reasonable time – cf. *Hillingdon Corporation v. Cutler* [1967] 2 All ER 361) of any encroachment, adverse claim or notice or proceeding known to him which may affect the landlord's interest in the premises;

   (*c*)  to comply with statutory requirements about the use of the premises;

   (*d*)  not to cause a nuisance or allow one to be caused;

   (*e*)  not to use the premises, or allow them to be used, for an illegal purpose.

*Paragraph (2)* makes it clear that a person allows something to be done within the meaning of paragraph (1)(d) or (e) if he has power to stop the thing being done and fails to exercise the power.

## Disclosure of landlord's identity

**17.**—(1) The landlord has an overriding obligation to serve on the tenant a notice of the landlord's name and address, and, if different, the name and address of the person to whom the rent is to be paid, within –

  (a) eight weeks after any conveyance of the reversion or on or before the next occasion on which rent is payable under the lease after such a conveyance, whichever is the later;

  (b) three weeks after the service on him of a notice containing a request for the information reasonably made by the tenant at any time.

(2)   Where a notice containing a request under paragraph (1)(b) for the landlord's name and address is served on a person such as is mentioned in Article 74(2)(a), (c) or (d) that person has an overriding obligation to serve on the tenant a notice of the landlord's name and address within three weeks after the service on him of the notice containing that request.

(3)   In any notice under paragraph (1)(a) trustees may be described collectively as such and their address may be given as that from which the affairs of the trust are conducted; but no such notice is required of a conveyance effected solely for the purpose or in consequence of a change in the trustees.

(4)   Where the premises consist of part only of a building or a set of buildings, a notice under paragraph (1)(a) is to be deemed to be duly served if it is displayed for a reasonable period at or within the building or set of buildings in a position likely to be seen by the tenant in the ordinary course of his use of the premises.

(5)   Where the landlord is a body corporate, the tenant may serve on the landlord a notice containing a request for the name and address of every director and of the secretary of the landlord and the landlord has an overriding obligation to serve on the tenant a notice containing the information requested, and to do so within three weeks after the service on him of the notice containing the tenant's request.

(6)   A landlord or other person who fails to comply with any obligation imposed by this Article is guilty of an offence and is liable on summary conviction to a fine not exceeding level 2 on the standard scale, unless, in the case of a person other than the landlord, he shows to the satisfaction of the court that he did not know, and could not with reasonable diligence have ascertained, such of the facts required by the notice to be disclosed as were not disclosed by him.

(7)   In this Article "address", in relation to a person, means the place where he lives or where he carries on his business or, in relation to a company, its registered office.

(8)   Article 12(3) applies to an overriding obligation of a person under paragraph (2) in the same way as it applies to an overriding obligation of a landlord or a tenant.

1359

ARTICLE 17                          Law Com. No. 67 Cl. 8
                                    Rent Order Art. 73(2)(3)
                                    cf. Landlord & Tenant Act
                                    1985 ss. 1, 2

This Article aims to ensure that a tenant can ascertain the identity of his current landlord.

*Paragraph (1)* imposes on the landlord an overriding obligation to give the tenant, on two occasions, notice of (1) the name and address of the landlord and (2) the name and address of his rent agent (if any).

*sub-paragraph (a)* The first occasion is on a conveyance of the reversion: the notice must be given within eight weeks after the conveyance or on or before the next occasion on which rent is due after the conveyance, whichever is the later.

*sub-paragraph (b)* The second occasion is when the tenant reasonably makes a written request for the information: three weeks are allowed for compliance. A request would not be reasonable if made so often as to amount to harassment.

*Paragraph (2)* deals with the case where a notice containing a tenant's request for the name and address of the landlord is, under Article 74(2)(a), (c) or (d), served on a person other than the landlord (e.g. a rent agent). The person to whom the request is made must give the tenant the landlord's name and address within three weeks. (He must also forward the notice to the landlord under Article 74(5)).

*Paragraph (3)* makes it sufficient, where trustees are the landlord, for them to be described, following a conveyance, as "the trustees of the X trust" (naming it). Their individual names need not be given, nor need there be any notification of a conveyance occasioned only by a change in the trustees.

*Paragraph (4)* renders it unnecessary for the landlord to give notice to each individual tenant of an assignment of the reversion where there are several tenants in the same building (or set of buildings). It is sufficient to display a notice at a place in the building (or set) where it is likely to be seen by the tenants.

*Paragraph (5)* applies where the landlord is a company. The tenant may serve a notice asking for the names and addresses of the directors and the secretary. The landlord has an overriding obligation to give this information within three weeks. If, under Article 74(2), the notice is served on the landlord by being served on an agent of his under Article 74(2)(a), (c) or (d), the agent must pass it on to the landlord (Article 74(5)).

*Paragraph (6)* makes it an offence for the landlord not to give a notice required by the Article. The maximum fine is that fixed for level 2 on the standard scale of fines in Article 5 of the Fines and Penalties (Northern Ireland) Order 1984 (at present £100 – Criminal Penalties etc. (Increase)

Order (Northern Ireland) 1984, SR1984 No.253). It is similarly an offence for an agent not to give his landlord's name and address when requested (so far as known or ascertained by him), or not to pass on to a corporate landlord a request for the names and addresses of the directors and secretary.

*Paragraph (7)* defines "address" as meaning either a residential address or a business address: in the case of a company it means the registered office.
"Conveyance" and "the reversion" are defined in Article 2(2).

*Paragraph (8)* applies Article 12(3) (overriding obligations cannot be excluded, etc.) to the overriding obligation imposed on an agent by paragraph (2).

General provisions about the service of notices are contained in Article 74.

**Disclosure of tenant's identity**

**18.**—(1) The tenant has an overriding obligation to serve on the landlord a notice of the name and address of the person in whom the tenancy is vested within –

(a) eight weeks after any assignment of the tenancy;

(b) three weeks after the service on him of a notice containing a request for the information reasonably made by the landlord at any time.

(2)   A tenant who without reasonable excuse fails to comply with the obligation imposed by this Article is guilty of an offence and is liable on summary conviction to a fine not exceeding level 2 on the standard scale.

(3)   The expression "address" has the same meaning in this Article as in Article 17.

(4)   Article 17(3) applies to notices under paragraph (1)(a) ("conveyance" being read as "assignment").

ARTICLE 18                                    Law Com. No. 67 Cl. 9

This Article aims to ensure that a landlord can ascertain the identity of his current tenant.

*Paragraph (1)* imposes on the tenant an overriding obligation to give the landlord, on two occasions, notice of the name and address of the tenant.

*Sub-paragraph (a)* The first occasion is an assignment of the tenancy. The notice must be given within eight weeks of the assignment.

*Sub-paragraph (b)* The second occasion is when the landlord reasonably makes a written request for the information. The notice must be given within three weeks after receipt of the request.

*Paragraph (2)* makes it an offence for a tenant to fail to comply with his obligations under the Article, unless he can show a reasonable excuse for not doing so. The maximum penalty is the same as under Article 17.

*Paragraph (3)* attracts, for the purposes of this Article, the definition of "address" in Article 17(7).

*Paragraph (4)* attracts Article 17(3) where the tenants are trustees.

General provisions about the service of notices are contained in Article 74.

*Obligations of care and repair*

**Tenant's obligation of care**

**19.**—(1) The tenant has variable obligations –

(a)  to take proper care of the premises as a good tenant;

(b)  to make good any damage to the premises wilfully or negligently done or caused to the premises by the tenant, any tenant of his or any other person lawfully living in or lawfully visiting the premises;

(c)  not to carry out any alterations or do any other thing of which the actual or probable result is to destroy or alter the character of the premises or any part of them to the detriment of the interest of the landlord therein.

(2)  Without prejudice to the generality of paragraph (1)(a), the tenant's obligation of care includes an obligation to clear any blockage in any gutters, pipes or drains within or forming part of the premises (other than pipes or drains passing through the premises for the benefit only of other premises) or in any trap within the premises for foul or surface water from a building which comprises, or forms part of, the premises.

# EXPLANATORY NOTE

ARTICLE 19

Law Com. No. 67 Cl. 12
Cf. Rent (NI) Order 1978
Arts.40, 42(a), (c), (e)
and tailpiece

This Article defines the extent of a tenant's obligation to take care of demised premises. The obligations imposed by the Article are capable of being varied by the lease. They are subject to the qualifications set out in Article 30(2).

The Article lists the obligations.

*sub-paragraph (a)* obliges the tenant to take proper care of the premises as a good tenant: this includes a duty to see that the premises do not take fire through his negligence (which, under present law, may amount to waste).

*sub-paragraph (b)* obliges the tenant to make good any damage to the premises wilfully or negligently done or caused by the tenant, a sub-tenant or anyone lawfully living in or visiting the premises. The tenant is not responsible for damage caused by a trespasser. If the trespasser can be identified, the landlord will have an independent cause of action against him.

*sub-paragraph (c)* prohibits the tenant from carrying out alterations which would change the character of the premises to such an extent as to be detrimental to the landlord's interest.

*Paragraph (2)* expatiates on the duty of care in one particular respect – blockages in gutters or pipes. The tenant must clear any blockage in gutters, pipes or drains within the land which is the subject of the tenancy or in any trap for surface water or foul water from the premises. The paragraph repeats the last two lines of Article 42 of the Rent Order with appropriate amendments. The tenant is not concerned with pipes and drains servicing other premises which merely pass through his premises. Their upkeep is a matter for the dominant owner.

### Landlord's repairing obligations in furnished letting of dwelling-house

**20.** Where the premises are a dwelling-house let with furniture, the landlord has –

(a) an overriding obligation to ensure that the premises are fit for human habitation at the beginning of the tenancy;

(b) a variable obligation to keep in repair the entirety of the premises.

# EXPLANATORY NOTE

ARTICLE 20                                 Cf. Law Com. No. 67 Cl. 13

This Article imports obligations on a landlord who makes a letting of a furnished dwelling-house.

*Paragraph (a)* imposes an overriding obligation to ensure that the premises are fit for human habitation at the beginning of the tenancy. This corresponds to the warranty at present implied at common law.

*Paragraph (b)* imposes a variable obligation to keep the whole of the premises in repair.

A landlord's obligation to effect repairs carries with it an obligation to make good any consequential damage to decorations: *McGreal v. Wake* (*The Times*) 9/2/1984); *Bradley v. Chorley BC* (The Times 6/3/1985); Article 28.

**Landlord's and tenant's repairing obligations in unfurnished letting of dwelling-house for a term not exceeding 21 years**

**21.**—(1) Where the premises are a dwelling-house let without furniture for a term not exceeding 21 years, the landlord has –

(a) a variable obligation to ensure that the premises are fit for human habitation at the beginning of the tenancy;

(b) variable obligations –

(i) to keep in repair the structure and exterior of the dwelling-house (including, without prejudice to Article 19(2), drains, gutters and external pipes);

(ii) subject to the tenant's obligations, to keep in repair the interior of the dwelling-house;

(iii) to keep in repair and in proper working order –

(aa) the installations in the dwelling-house for the supply of water, gas and electricity and for sanitation (including basins, sinks, baths and sanitary conveniences but not, except as mentioned in the preceding provision of this sub-head, fixtures, fittings or appliances for making use of the supply of water, gas or electricity); and

(bb) the installations in the dwelling-house for space heating or heating water.

(2) Where the premises are a dwelling-house let without furniture for a term not exceeding 21 years, the tenant has, without prejudice to his obligations under Article 19, variable obligations –

(a) to keep in repair –

(i) open fireplaces (including tiles) in the dwelling-house;

(ii) glass, whether external or internal, in the dwelling-house (including mirrors);

(iii) tap washers and similar seals for taps in the dwelling-house;

(iv) boundary walls of the dwelling-house constructed by him or any previous tenant from whom he derives title;

(b) to keep the interior of the dwelling-house in reasonable decorative order (and, if it is not in that order at the beginning of the tenancy, to put it in that order).

# EXPLANATORY NOTE

ARTICLE 21

Cf. Law Com. No. 67 Cl. 10, 14
Cf. Rent (NI) Order 1978 Arts.40,41

This Article imposes obligations on both landlord and tenant where there is an unfurnished letting of a dwelling-house for not more than 21 years.

*Paragraph (1)* imposes on the landlord –

*sub-paragraph (a)* a variable obligation to see that the premises are fit for human habitation at the beginning of the tenancy.

*sub-paragraph (b)* variable obligations –

    (*i*) to keep the structure and exterior of the house in repair: this includes keeping paintwork in reasonable order (see the definition of "repair" in Article 2(2)) and repairing drains, gutters and external pipes (but it is the tenant's duty under Article 19(1)(a) and (2) to keep them, as well as internal pipes, clear of obstructions);

    (*ii*) to keep the interior of the house in repair, except so far as the tenant is obliged to do so;

    (*iii*) to keep in repair and proper working order –

        (*aa*) installations for the supply off water, gas and electricity and for sanitation (including basins, sinks, baths and toilets, but not appliances for the use of water, gas and electricity);

        (*bb*) space-heating or water heating installations.

*Paragraph (2)* imposes on the tenant variable obligations –

*sub-paragraph (a)* to keep in repair –

    (*i*) fireplaces,

    (*ii*) glass,

    (*iii*) tap-washers,

    (*iv*) boundary walls erected by himself or his predecessor in title;

*sub-paragraph (b)* to keep the interior in reasonable decorative order.

**Landlord's and tenant's repairing obligations in letting of premises other than a dwelling-house for a term not exceeding 21 years**

**22.**   Where the premises, not being a dwelling-house, are let for a term not exceeding 21 years –

(a) the landlord has a variable obligation to keep in repair the structure and exterior of the premises (including drains, gutters and external pipes, but not including window glass or door glass);

(b) the tenant has a variable obligation to keep in repair all parts of the premises other than those which the landlord is obliged to keep in repair under paragraph (a).

# EXPLANATORY NOTE

ARTICLE 22                                    Cf. Law Com. No. 67 Cl. 14

This Article imposes variable obligations on both landlord and tenant where premises other than a dwelling-house are let for 21 years or less.

*Paragraph (a)* obliges the landlord to keep the structure and exterior of the premises in repair.

*Paragraph (b)* obliges the tenant to keep all other parts in repair.

**Tenant's repairing obligation in letting of premises for term exceeding 21 years**

**23.** Where the premises are let for a term exceeding 21 years, the tenant has a variable obligation to keep in repair the entirety of the premises.

# EXPLANATORY NOTE

ARTICLE 23                          Law Com. No. 67 Cl. 15

This Article applies to premises let for a term of more than 21 years.

The tenant has a variable obligation to keep the whole of the premises in repair.

## Tenancies of parts of buildings

**24.**—(1) Where the premises consist of part only of a building, the landlord has a variable obligation to keep in repair the structure and exterior of the building or to ensure that they are kept in repair.

(2) Where the tenant of such premises is entitled (whether with others or not) to the use for access or other purposes of other parts of the building or its curtilage in the possession or control of the landlord, or to any facilities to be provided by the landlord, the landlord has a variable obligation to –

(a) keep in good order and condition any part of the building or curtilage which the tenant is entitled to use as aforesaid;

(b) ensure that, according to its nature, any part of the building or curtilage which the tenant is entitled to use for access is adequately lit and safe to use;

(c) ensure, so far as is practicable, that any facilities to which the tenant is entitled as aforesaid are continued at the proper level and that any installations for the provision of those facilities are safe to use and adequately perform their function.

(3) In this Article –

(a) the extent of the obligation of the landlord under paragraph (2) is to be ascertained by reference to the order and condition of the relevant part of the building or curtilage, or, as the case may be, the level of the facilities provided, at the beginning of the tenancy;

(b) "facilities" includes lighting, heating, hot water, lifts, attendance and services.

# EXPLANATORY NOTE

ARTICLE 24
Law Com. No. 67 Cl. 16<br>Rent (NI) Order 1978 Art.43

This Article sets out the landlord's obligations where there is a tenancy of part of a building. "The premises" is defined in Article 2(2). See Article 30(5) for the case where there is a commonhold.

*Paragraph (1)* The landlord has a variable obligation to keep the structure and exterior of the building in repair or see that they are kept in repair.

*Paragraph (2)* Where the tenant is entitled to use other parts of the building or its grounds for access or for the enjoyment of some facility, the landlord has a variable obligation –

*sub-paragraph (a)* to keep those other parts in good order and condition. Those parts may be, e.g., forecourts, entrance halls, stairways,passages, lavatories, bathrooms, laundry rooms or carparking spaces;

*sub-paragraph (b)* to ensure that any part used for access is adequately lit and safe to use. This extends to forecourt, entrance hall, stairs and passages;

*sub-paragraph (c)* to keep facilities at the proper level (defined in paragraph (3)) and to ensure that relevant installations are safe to use and operate properly.

*Paragraph (3)* defines the level at which standards are to be kept as that prevailing at the beginning of the tenancy. It also defines "facilities" as including lighting, space heating, hot water, lifts, attendance or services. The facilities may serve only the common parts or they may extend also to demised parts of the building.

**Access**

25. Where under a lease or tenancy agreement the tenant is entitled to use for all or any of the purposes of the tenancy a route or means of access to the premises over land in the possession or control of the landlord, not being a means of access to which Article 24(2)(a) or (b) applies, the landlord has a variable obligation to keep that route or means of access safe and fit for use for those purposes.

# EXPLANATORY NOTE

ARTICLE 25                                   Law Com. No. 67 Cl. 17

This Article imports into every tenancy a variable obligation on the part of the landlord to keep in order any route or means of access to the demised premises over land in the possession or control of the landlord which the tenant is entitled to use for all or any of the purposes of the tenancy and which is outside the curtilage of the premises.

The curtilage of a building is the land held with and so closely connected with the use of the building that it will be carried by a conveyance of the building without added descriptive words.

**Support and shelter**

**26.**—(1) Where the premises are a building or part of a building which enjoys support or shelter –

(a) in the case of a part of a building, by any other part of that building;

(b) in any case, by any adjacent or neighbouring building,

the landlord has a variable obligation to maintain during the term of the tenancy the support or shelter enjoyed at the beginning of the tenancy or support or shelter substantially equivalent thereto.

(2) Paragraph (1) –

(a) applies only to support or shelter by a building in the possession or control of the landlord or by which he has the right to support or shelter for the benefit of the premises, and in the latter case applies only to the extent of that right;

(b) does not require the landlord to carry out any repairs or reinstatement to make good a loss of support or shelter occasioned by any act or default of the tenant or any sub-tenant of the premises.

# EXPLANATORY NOTE

This Article deals with a tenant's rights to support and shelter for the demised premises.

*Paragraph (1)* applies where demised premises enjoy support or shelter from another part of the same building or from a neighbouring building. The landlord has a variable obligation to maintain the original support or shelter, or its equivalent, throughout the term of the tenancy. "Building" is used in its widest sense: cf. Article 151 of the Property Order where, by implication from paragraph (2), it includes a structure or erection.

*Paragraph (2)* contains two limitations on the operation of paragraph (1):

*sub-paragraph (a)* The tenant's right to support or shelter is derivative, and so can extend no further than a corresponding right in thelandlord.

*sub-paragraph (b)* The landlord is not liable for any loss of support or shelter which is caused by an act of the tenant himself or a sub-tenant of his.

**Entry and inspection**

**27.**—(1) Where the landlord is authorised or obliged by or under the lease or this Order or otherwise to carry out works of repair, improvement or alteration of the premises, or of any building of which the premises form part, the tenant has a variable obligation to permit the landlord, and persons authorised by him for the purpose, to enter the premises at reasonable times and upon service of a notice a reasonable period beforehand in order to inspect them and carry out any such works.

(2) Where the tenant is obliged by or under the lease or this Order to carry out any repairs of the premises, the tenant has a variable obligation to permit the landlord, and persons authorised by him for the purpose, to enter the premises at reasonable times and upon service of a notice a reasonable period beforehand in order to inspect their state of repair.

# EXPLANATORY NOTE

ARTICLE 27

Law Com. No. 67 Cl. 19
Property Bill Cl. 178

This Article gives the landlord a right to enter demised premises in order to carry out repairs or view the state of repair.

*Paragraph (1)* applies where the landlord is subject to an obligation to repair. The tenant has a variable obligation to permit him and his agents to enter the demised premises in order to inspect them and carry out repairs. The entry must be made at a reasonable hour and after reasonable notice.

*Paragraph (2)* applies where the tenant is obliged to repair. He must permit the landlord and his agents to enter the premises in order to inspect the state of repair. Again, the entry must be at a reasonable hour and after reasonable notice.

**Making good**

28.    Where the landlord is authorised or obliged by or under the lease, this Order or otherwise to carry out works of repair, improvement or alteration of the premises, or of any building of which the premises form part, the landlord has a variable obligation to make good any damage to the premises or property therein which may be occasioned by or in the course of carrying out the works or inspecting the premises for the purpose.

# EXPLANATORY NOTE

ARTICLE 28                                    Law Com. No. 67 Cl. 20

This Article imposes on the landlord a variable obligation to make good any damage caused by him or his agents in carrying out works of repair or inspecting the state of repair.

*General provisions as to repair obligations*

## Ascertainment of term of tenancy

**29.** The following provisions apply for ascertaining the term of a tenancy for the purposes of Articles 21, 22 and 23, namely –

(a) if a tenancy is granted for a term part of which falls before the grant, that part is left out of account and the tenancy is treated as for a term commencing with the grant;

(b) if the landlord has a right to terminate the tenancy, it is assumed that that right will be exercised as soon as available;

(c) subject to paragraph (b), if the tenant has an option to renew the tenancy for any period, that period is added to the original term.

ARTICLE 29                          Law Com. No. 67 Cl. 22

This Article helps to determine whether a lease falls within Article 21 or 22 (as being for a term not exceeding 21 years) or Article 23 (as being for a term exceeding 21 years).

*Paragraph (a)* Any part of the term falling before the date on which the lease is granted is ignored.

*Paragraph (b)* If the landlord has a right to terminate the tenancy, it is to be assumed that he will exercise that right as soon as he can.

*Paragraph (c)* If the tenant has an option to renew the tenancy, the period for which he can renew it is to be added to the original term.

## Qualifications of care and repair obligations

**30.**—(1) The obligations of the landlord under Article 20, 21, 22 or 24 do not require him –

(a) to carry out works or repairs for which the tenant is liable under Article 19 or would be so liable apart from any exclusion or modification of his obligation under Article 19;

(b) to keep in repair or maintain anything –

  (i) which was not constructed or provided by the landlord or any person from whom he derives title; or

  (ii) which the tenant is entitled to remove from the premises;

(c) to rebuild or reinstate the premises in the case of destruction or damage by fire, or by tempest, flood or other inevitable accident.

(2) The obligations of the tenant under Article 19 do not require him to –

(a) carry out works or repairs which the landlord is obliged to carry out under Article 24 or would be so obliged apart from any exclusion or modification of his obligation under Article 24;

(b) keep in repair or maintain anything which the tenant is entitled to remove from the premises;

(c) rebuild or reinstate the premises in the case of destruction or damage by fire, or by tempest, flood or other inevitable accident.

(3) The obligations of a tenant under Article 23 do not require him to –

(a) keep in repair anything which the tenant is entitled to remove from the premises;

(b) rebuild or reinstate the premises in the case of destruction or damage by fire, or by tempest, flood or other inevitable accident.

(4) The qualifications imposed by paragraph (1)(c), or paragraphs (2)(c) and (3)(b), do not apply where the destruction or damage would not have occurred were it not for some breach of, respectively, a landlord's obligation or a tenant's obligation.

(5) Where a building to which Article 24(1) applies comprises or forms part of a commonhold within the meaning of the Commonhold (Northern Ireland) Order 1989, that Article does not prejudice any obligation of the commonhold association or render the landlord liable for any defect resulting from a breach of such an obligation; but the landlord has a variable obligation to take all reasonable steps to ensure that the commonhold association's obligations are complied with.

# EXPLANATORY NOTE

ARTICLE 30

Law Com. No. 67 Cl. 23
Rent (NI) Order 1978 Art. 44

This Article qualifies the repairing obligations of landlord or tenant.

*Paragraph (1)* places limits on a landlord's repairing obligations. He is not required –

*sub-paragraph (a)* to do anything that falls upon the tenant in consequence of the duty of care imposed by Article 19 (or would have fallen had not that duty been varied);

*sub-paragraph (b)* to repair anything not provided by the landlord or a predecessor of his or to repair any tenant's fixture;

*sub-paragraph (c)* to rebuild or reinstate the premises in case of destruction or damage by fire or by tempest, flood or other inevitable accident. An inevitable accident is one which could not possibly be prevented by the exercise of ordinary care, caution and skill.

*Paragraph (2)* places limits on the tenant's duty of care under Article 19. It does not require him to –

*sub-paragraph (a)* repair any means of access or facility which the landlord is liable to repair under Article 24 (or would have been liable to repair had not his obligation under that Article been varied);

*sub-paragraph (b)* keep in repair any tenant's fixture;

*sub-paragraph (c)* rebuild or reinstate the premises in case of destruction by fire or by tempest, flood or other inevitable accident.

*Paragraph (3)* limits a tenant's duty to repair the whole premises, where he has a lease for more than 21 years, so as not to require him to –

*sub-paragraph (a)* repair any tenant's fixture;

*sub-paragraph (b)* rebuild or reinstate the premises in case of destruction by fire or by tempest, flood or other inevitable accident.

*Paragraph (4)* prevents the landlord or, as the case may be, the tenant from being exonerated from liability for damage caused by fire, tempest, flood or other inevitable accident where a breach of obligation on his part was a contributory factor.

Article 54 allows the tenant to surrender his tenancy in certain circumstances where the premises have been destroyed or damaged by reason of fire or tempest, flood or other inevitable accident.

*Paragraph (5)* applies to a case where a building to which Article 24 applies is or forms part of a commonhold and the landlord is a unit-owner whose unit consists of, e.g., a floor or several floors of the building divided into separate offices or apartments. The landlord is responsible for passages, stairs or other common utilities within the unit, but the commonhold association will be responsible for parts of the building used in common for the benefit of two or more units and for maintaining the structure and exterior of the building. The paragraph prevents the landlord from being liable to his tenants for defaults of the commonhold association, but places him under a variable obligation to do his best to see that the association complies with its obligations.

See also Schedule 3 to the Property (Consequential Provisions) Order which negatives the application of Articles 19, 21, 24, 30 and 31 to new regulated tenancies and continues the application of Articles 40 to 45 of the Rent (Northern Ireland) Order 1978 instead.

## Standard of repair and notice of disrepair

**31.**—(1) In determining the standard of repair required in respect of the obligations arising under Articles 20(b), 21, 22, 23 and 24, regard is to be had to the age, character and prospective life of the premises and the locality in which they are situated.

(2) Any obligation of the landlord to carry out works under Article 20(b), 21(1) or 22(a) is conditional upon his having actual knowledge (whether because of notice given by the tenant or otherwise) of the need for those works.

# EXPLANATORY NOTE

ARTICLE 31

Law Com. No. 67 Cl. 24
Rent (NI) Order 1978 Art. 45

This Article provides for the standard of repair applicable where there is a repairing obligation: it also sets out the rule that a landlord's obligation to repair is not activated until he becomes aware of the need for repairs.

The Article substantially reproduces existing law.

*Paragraph (1)* adopts the test laid down in *Proudfoot* v. *Hart* (1890) 25 QBD 42 (per Ld Esher MR at p. 52 and Lopes LJ at p. 55) that the relevant repairs are those which, *"having regard to the age, character and locality of the house*, would make it reasonably fit for the occupation of a reasonably-minded tenant of the class who would be likely to take it". A reference to "prospective life" has been added.

*Paragraph (2)* sets out the general rule that a landlord's repairing obligation is conditional upon his knowing of the need for repairs. This does not apply to premises or parts of premises retained by the landlord in his own control, so there is no mention of Article 24, 25 or 26. The wording of the paragraph largely follows Article 45 of the Rent Order.

*Other obligations*

**Outgoings**

**32.**—(1) The tenant has a variable obligation to bear the regional rate, the district rate and any other outgoings falling on the premises in consequence of their use by the tenant for a particular purpose.

(2)  The landlord has a variable obligation to bear all other outgoings in respect of the premises.

(3)  In this Article "outgoings" includes taxes, duties, levies, assessments and charges (whether recurrent or not) imposed after the beginning of the tenancy under a statutory provision on or in respect of the premises, and the cost of carrying out on or for the purposes of the premises improvements or other works required after that beginning under any statutory provision.

(4)  This Article does not affect any statutory provision providing for –

(a)  the recovery of particular outgoings against occupiers or persons having specified interests in the premises; or

(b)  the apportionment of the burden of such outgoings as between such occupiers or persons.

# EXPLANATORY NOTE

ARTICLE 32                           Law Com. No. 67 Cl. 21

This Article allocates the respective obligations of landlord and tenant to pay outgoings in respect of the demised premises. The obligations set out in the Article can be varied by the lease.

*Paragraph (1)* makes the tenant liable for rates and for any other outgoing which relates to the tenant's use of the premises for a particular purpose.

*Paragraph (2)* makes the landlord subject to all other outgoings.

*Paragraph (3)* defines "outgoings" as including taxes, duties, levies, assessments, charges and the cost of improvement works.

*Paragraph (4)* is a saving for any statutory provision which –

(a) provides for the recovery of particular outgoings from specified persons (e.g. Articles 18 and 20 of the Rates (Northern Ireland) Order 1977) – although a particular outgoing will be levied in accordance with the relevant statute, its ultimate incidence as between the landlord and the tenant will depend upon this Article (unless that incidence is varied by agreement);

(b) provides for apportionment of a particular outgoing (e.g. section 230 of the Public Health (Ireland) Act 1878).

## Tenant's fixtures

**33.**—(1) Subject to the other provisions of this Article, the landlord has a variable obligation to permit the tenant to remove from the premises any tenant's fixture at any time during the tenancy or upon its determination, provided the removal causes no irreparable damage to the premises.

(2) Where a tenancy is determined by notice of the landlord and the tenant wishes to remove a fixture but the length of the period of notice is insufficient to allow the tenant a reasonable period of time within which to remove the fixture, while complying with paragraph (3)(b), before the expiration of the notice, the landlord's obligation under paragraph (1) continues for the period (or the residue of the period) of notice mentioned in paragraph (3)(b) and for such further period as is reasonably necessary for removal of the fixture.

(3) With respect to removal of fixtures the tenant has a variable obligation –

   (a) before the removal, to pay all rent owing and to perform all his other tenant's obligations;

   (b) not to remove any fixture without serving on the landlord at least four weeks' notice of his intention to remove it;

   (c) not to do any avoidable damage to the premises;

   (d) immediately after the removal, to make good all damage occasioned to the premises by the removal or to pay the landlord compensation for the damage.

(4) At any time before the expiration of the notice served by the tenant under paragraph (3)(b) ("the tenant's notice"), the landlord may, by notice served on the tenant, elect to purchase any fixture specified for removal in the tenant's notice, stating the purchase price offered or the procedure proposed by the landlord for determining that price.

(5) If the tenant, within two weeks after the service on him of notice that the landlord has made an election under paragraph (4), serves on the landlord notice –

   (a) that he refuses to accept the election, or

   (b) that he disputes the purchase price offered by the landlord for any fixture or the procedure proposed by the landlord for determining that price,

the matter may be referred to the Lands Tribunal for determination; and, where the reference relates to the tenant's refusal of the landlord's election, the Tribunal may by order confirm the landlord's election or uphold the tenant's refusal and make such further order as it considers appropriate.

(6) Any dispute about the amount of compensation to be paid by the tenant under paragraph (3)(d), or about whether any period is reasonable, shall be referred to and determined by the Lands Tribunal.

(7)   In this Article, "tenant's fixture" includes any chattel, machinery, fencing or similar property or any building erected on or affixed to the premises by or on behalf of the tenant at his sole expense for –

(a)   any purpose of trade, manufacture or agriculture;

(b)   ornament;

(c)   the domestic convenience of the tenant in the occupation of the premises;

but not so erected or affixed in pursuance of, or in violation of, any obligation under the tenancy.

(8)   Where any tenant's fixture has been affixed to the premises during a tenancy and upon the determination of the tenancy the tenant remains in possession of the premises by virtue of a new tenancy (express or implied), the reference in paragraph (1) to the tenancy or its determination includes a reference to the new tenancy or its determination (and similarly where there is a succession of new tenancies).

# EXPLANATORY NOTE

This Article is concerned with a tenant's right to remove tenants' fixtures from the demised premises before or upon the ending of his tenancy.

*Paragraph (1)* imposes on the landlord a variable obligation to permit the tenant to remove any tenant's fixtures at any time during the currency of the tenancy or upon its determination. But the tenant may not remove anything whose removal causes irreparable damage to the premises.

*Paragraph (2)* applies where the tenancy is terminated by notice given by the landlord. If the period of notice is insufficient to permit the tenant to give four weeks' notice of his intention to remove any fixture (as required by paragraph (3)(b)) and thereafter to carry out the work of removal, the landlord's obligation to permit the tenant to remove the fixture continues after the termination of the tenancy until the notice under paragraph (3)(b) has expired and, thereafter, a reasonable time elapses during which the fixture could be removed.

*Paragraph (3)* imposes on the tenant, as variable obligations, certain restrictions –

*sub-paragraph (a)* before he removes any fixture, he must pay all rent due and perform all his other obligations (e.g. as to repair);

*sub-paragraph (b)* before removing any fixture, he must serve on the landlord at least four weeks' notice of his intention to remove it;

*sub-paragraph (c)* in removing a fixture he must not do any avoidable damage to the premises;

*sub-paragraph (d)* where damage is caused by the removal of a fixture, he must at once make it good or else pay compensation.

*Paragraph (4)* gives the landlord, when he is notified under paragraph (3)(b) of the tenant's intention to remove some particular fixture, a right to elect to buy the fixture. Notice of the election must be served on the tenant before the expiration of the four weeks specified in the tenant's notice, and must state the price the landlord offers or the procedure proposed by the landlord for fixing a price (e.g. reference to an expert valuer).

*Paragraph (5)* applies where the tenant rejects the landlord's election to buy the fixture or the proposed price (or the proposed method of arriving at a price). Either party or both parties may refer the dispute to the Lands Tribunal for determination, and, where the tenant has challenged the landlord's election, the Tribunal may uphold either party and may make such consequential order as it thinks fit (e.g., if it upholds the tenant's objection, allowing him a further time within which to remove the fixture).

*Paragraph (6)* enables any dispute about the compensation to be paid by the tenant for damage caused to the premises by him in the course of removing a fixture to be determined by the Lands Tribunal. The Tribunal may also decide any dispute about whether a particular period is reasonable for the purposes of paragraph (2). (Other provisions conferring jurisdiction on the Lands Tribunal are Articles 41(4) and 45 and Schedule 1 para. 6(3).)

*Paragraph (7)* defines "tenant's fixture" as including any chattel, machinery, fencing or similar property or any building erected on or affixed to the premises by the tenant at his sole expense for purposes of trade, manufacture or agriculture, for ornament or for the domestic convenience of the tenant. But it does not include anything erected or affixed in pursuance of a tenant's obligation or in violation of a provision of the lease.

*Paragraph (8)* makes it clear that where, upon the termination of a lease, the tenant continues in uninterrupted possession under a new tenancy he retains, until the termination of the new lease, his right to remove tenants' fixtures installed during the term of the former tenancy. This states the effect of the decision of the Court of Appeal in *New Zealand Government Property Corporation v. HM & S Ltd.* [1982] 2 WLR 837. The paragraph applies not only where a tenancy expires by effluxion of time, but also where it is terminated in any other way (e.g. by surrender). As the landlord's obligation is a variable one, it is, of course, subject to any express provision about tenant's fixtures which may be included in an instrument of surrender.

**Mines, quarries, turbary and trees**

**34.**—(1) The tenant has variable obligations –

(a)  not to open any mine or quarry on, or remove any turf, gravel, sand, surface soil or subsoil from, the premises;

(b)  where there is an opened quarry on the premises at the beginning of the tenancy or where any obligation mentioned in sub-paragraph (a) is excluded or modified, not to use any produce of a quarry on, or any turf, gravel, sand, surface soil or subsoil from, the premises for any purpose other than the improvement of the premises or his better enjoyment of them (and, in particular, not for any purpose of trade or manufacture or for profit or sale);

(c)  where the lease confers on the tenant a right of common of turbary on land not included in the tenancy, not to use any turf cut on that land for any purpose other than the improvement of the premises or his better enjoyment of them (and, in particular, not for any purpose of trade or manufacture or for profit or sale);

(d)  subject to paragraph (4), not to cut any tree on the premises.

(2)  In this Article "remove" or "use" includes allowing another to remove or use, "tree" means a growing tree (whether timber or not) and "cut" includes fell, top, lop, root-prune and grub.

(3)  For the purposes of paragraph (2), a person allows to be removed or used anything which he has the right to prevent being removed or used if he does not take reasonable steps to enforce that right.

(4)  Paragraph (1)(d) does not apply to –

(a)  a tree of a girth not exceeding one metre at a height of one metre from the ground;

(b)  a fruit tree;

(c)  the cutting of a tree in the course of proper thinning or husbandry, for the prevention of danger or for the prevention or abatement of a nuisance;

(d)  the cutting of a tree in compliance with any obligation imposed by or under a statutory provision;

(e)  the cutting of a tree where the cutting is immediately required for the purpose of carrying out development for which planning permission is in force.

# EXPLANATORY NOTE

ARTICLE 34                                      Deasy's Act ss.26 to 29 and 31

This Article imposes on the tenant variable obligations affecting his use of the demised land.

*Paragraph (1)* obliges him –

*sub-paragraph (a):* not to open mines or quarries or remove any turf, gravel, sand or soil.

*sub-paragraph (b):* where there is already an opened quarry at the beginning of the tenancy, or where an obligation imposed by sub-paragraph (a) is excluded or modified, not to use any produce of the quarry or any turf, gravel, sand or soil for commercial purposes or for the benefit of any land other than the demised land.

*sub-paragraph (c):* where the demised land carried a right of common of turbary in other land, not to use turf cut on that other land otherwise than for the benefit of the demised land.

*sub-paragraph (d):* not to cut any tree – this is subject to the qualifications in paragraphs (2) and (4).

By section 1 of the Mineral Development Act (Northern Ireland) 1969 all minerals (save those excepted by sections 2 to 7) were vested in the Ministry of Commerce (now the Department of Economic Development). The exemptions were for stone, gravel, sand, clay and soil; minerals vested in the Crown; minerals the property of religious denominations or educational institutions; minerals of little or no value previously merged by the Ministry in the fee simple; and minerals held with mines in work on 18 December 1969 where the owner's right was registered with the Ministry under section 8 on an application made before 1 March 1970. It is therefore unlikely (although possible in very exceptional cases – where title has been derived since 1969 from the Crown or a church or school) that a tenant would be in a position to open a mine (defined in section 56(2) as including both underground and surface workings) other than a stone quarry, a sand pit or a gravel pit. If he does work a mine (as distinct from a quarry or sand or gravel pit), the Article imposes no restriction on the use of minerals won – this will be a matter for agreement by the parties. It is assumed that the lease will not permit him to open a mine unless it also provides for the working of it and the removal of minerals gotten.

*Paragraph (2)* defines –

"removal" and "use" – this includes not only removal or use by the tenant, but also removal or use by anyone else allowed by the tenant;

"tree" – means a growing (and not a dead or fallen) tree;

"cut" – includes fell, top, lop, root-prune and grub.

*Paragraph (3)* makes it clear that a tenant allows a thing to be removed or used if he has the right to prevent that removal or use and does not try to stop it (cf. Article 16(2)).

*Paragraph (4)* sets out qualifications of the prohibition on cutting trees. The prohibition does not apply to –

*sub-paragraph (a)* a tree of a girth not exceeding one metre at a height of one metre from the ground.

*sub-paragraph (b)* a fruit tree.

*sub-paragraph (c)* the thinning of woodlands, prevention of danger or avoidance of nuisance.

*sub-paragraph (d)* compliance with a statutory provision (e.g. Article 28, Roads (Northern Ireland) Order 1980).

*sub-paragraph (e)* a tree whose immediate removal is required to enable approved development to take place.

These exceptions (save that sub-paragraph (a) is less restrictive) correspond to those in section 4(2)(b), (c), (e), (f) to (h), (k) and (l) of the Forestry Act (Northern Ireland) 1953.

**Abolition of tort of waste by tenant**

**35.** · In relation to a tenancy created after the commencement of this Order, no act, series of acts, omission or series of omissions by the tenant renders him liable in tort for waste.

# EXPLANATORY NOTE

## ARTICLE 35

This Article excepts from liability for the tort of waste a tenant whose tenancy is created after the commencement of the Order. The liability for waste of tenants under existing tenancies is not affected.

Waste is a tort (i.e. civil wrong) committed by a tenant who permits the demised premises to decay or does some positive act to damage them or change their character without the landlord's consent (even though the change might seem to the tenant to be an improvement).

The acts which would formerly have been regarded as waste are, in future, to be regulated by Article 19 (tenants' obligation to take care of the premises). It would be inconsistent if obligations under that Article (which are variable) were to be varied by the parties in the tenant's favour and the tenant were still to be held liable under the alternative head of waste.

See Schedule 3 to the Property (Consequential Provisions) Order which negatives the application of this Article to new regulated tenancies.

# PART IV

## THE RUNNING AND EFFECT OF BENEFITS AND OBLIGATIONS

*Running of benefits and obligations*

### Running of landlord's benefits and tenant's obligations

**36.**—(1) The landlord for the time being is entitled to all the benefits conferred on the landlord by the lease.

(2) The landlord for the time being may enforce all tenant's obligations against the tenant for the time being.

(3) This Article applies in relation to a benefit, and to an obligation which is variable by the parties, only if and so far as a contrary intention is not expressed or implied –

(a) in the lease, or

(b) in writing by which the tenancy was assigned to the tenant or a predecessor in title of his and which was signed by the landlord or a predecessor in title of his.

(4) In paragraph (3) "an obligation which is variable by the parties" means –

(a) a variable obligation arising under Part III; or

(b) an obligation which arises under any statutory provision other than a provision contained in Part III and which is capable of being varied by the parties; or

(c) an obligation arising at common law; or

(d) an obligation such as is mentioned in Article 2(4)(d).

ARTICLE 36

Property Bill Cl. 171
Deasy's Act s. 12
CA 1881 s. 10
CA 1911 s. 2
LPA 1925 s. 141

This Article gives the current landlord all the benefits of the original landlord and empowers the current landlord to enforce all tenant's obligations against the current tenant.

*Paragraph (1)* gives the current landlord all the benefits conferred on the original landlord by the lease. (The words "for the time being" are included for emphasis and clarity – in fact the definition of "landlord" in Article 2(2) has the same effect.)

*Paragraph (2)* empowers the landlord for the time being to enforce all tenant's obligations (see Article 2(4)) against the tenant for the time being. This Article resolves, in favour of Deasy's Act, a conflict between section 12 of that Act on the one hand and the Conveyancing Acts of 1881 and 1911 on the other.

*Paragraph (3)* derogates from paragraphs (1) and (2) in relation to any benefit or variable obligation as to which a contrary intention is expressed or implied in the lease or in an assignment of the tenancy which is executed by the landlord.

*Paragraph (4)* lists the obligations which are treated as variable for the purposes of the Article. They are –

*sub-paragraph (a)* variable obligations under Part III;

*sub-paragraph (b)* other statutory obligations which are capable of being varied by the parties;

*sub-paragraph (c)* common law obligations;

*sub-paragraph (d)* obligations created by agreement between the parties.

### Running of tenant's benefits and landlord's obligations

**37.**—(1) The tenant for the time being is entitled to all benefits conferred on the tenant by the lease.

(2) The tenant for the time being may enforce all landlord's obligations against the landlord for the time being.

(3) This Article applies in relation to a benefit, and to an obligation which is variable by the parties, only if and so far as a contrary intention is not expressed or implied –

  (a) in the lease, or

  (b) in a conveyance by which the landlord's estate was conveyed to the landlord or a predecessor in title of his and which was signed by the tenant or a predecessor in title of his.

(4) In paragraph (3), "an obligation which is variable by the parties" means –

  (a) a variable obligation arising under Part III; or

  (b) an obligation which arises under any statutory provision other than a provision contained in Part III and which is capable of being varied by the parties; or

  (c) an obligation arising at common law; or

  (d) an obligation such as is mentioned in Article 2(4)(d).

(5) The reference in paragraph (2) to the tenant includes a mortgagee of the tenant's estate who, in right of the mortgage, has entered into and is in possession of the premises.

# EXPLANATORY NOTE

ARTICLE 37

Property Bill Cl. 172
Deasy's Act s. 13
CA 1881 s. 11
LPA 1925 s. 142

This Article gives the current tenant all the benefits of the original tenant and empowers the current tenant to enforce all landlord's obligations against the current landlord.

*Paragraph (1)* gives the current tenant all the benefits (e.g. an option to purchase the reversion) conferred on the original tenant by the lease. (The words "for the time being" are included for emphasis and clarity – in fact the definition of "tenant" in Article 2(2) has the same effect.)

*Paragraph (2)* empowers the tenant for the time being to enforce all landlord's obligations against the landlord for the time being. Section 13 of Deasy's Act limited the running of landlord's covenants to those "concerning the lands", whereas section12 imposed no such limitation on the running of tenant's covenants: for future tenancies this Article gives landlord's covenants the same scopee as Article 36 gives tenant's covenants.

*Paragraph (3)* derogates from paragraphs (1) and (2) in relation to any benefit or variable obligation as to which a contrary intention is expressed or implied in the lease or in a conveyance of the reversion to which the tenant is a party. See also *paragraph 3 of Schedule 2* which qualifies paragraph (2) in relation to tenancies assigned before the commencement of the Order by restricting its operation to obligations *concerning the premises,* in accordance with section 13 of Deasy's Act (see the definition of "the premises" in Article 2(2)).

*Paragraph (4)* defines "variable obligation" in a corresponding way to Article 36(4).

*Paragraph (5)* enables a mortgagee in possession to enforce landlord's obligations.

### Position of landlord and tenant after assignment of tenancy

**38.**—(1) Where a tenant assigns his tenancy –

(a) he remains liable to the landlord and the landlord's successors in title for any breach of a tenant's obligation committed by him during or in respect of the period when he was tenant and is so liable for any breach of a tenant's obligation committed by his assignee or his assignee's successors in title during the period between his ceasing to be tenant and the day mentioned in paragraph (2);

(b) whether he is the original tenant or not, if the assignment is consistent with his tenant's obligations, it operates to discharge him from all liability to the landlord or the landlord's successors in title in respect of any breach of those obligations committed on or after the day mentioned in paragraph (2).

(2) The day referred to in paragraph (1)(a) and (b) is –

(a) where the landlord signs the writing by which the assignment is made, the day of his signing; or

(b) the day on which a notice giving particulars of the assignment is served on the landlord;

whichever first occurs.

(3) This Article applies only if and so far as a contrary intention is not expressed or implied in the lease or, where the writing by which the assignment is made is signed by the landlord, in that writing.

(4) Subject to Article 39, where the tenant assigns his tenancy as respects part only of the premises, this Article applies to any breach of obligation so far as concerns that part.

# EXPLANATORY NOTE

ARTICLE 38                              Property Bill Cl. 174
                                        Deasy's Act ss. 14, 16

This Article operates as a gloss on Article 37 by listing the consequences of an assignment of a tenancy.

*Paragraph (1)* deals with three situations.

*sub-paragraph (a)* Despite the assignment, the tenant remains liable to
the landlord for the time being for any breach of a tenant's obligation
which the tenant or the assignee had committed before the landlord
signed the instrument of assignment or received notice of the assignment
(see paragraph (2)). The tenant also remains liable for any breach of
obligation committed by him *in respect of* the period when he was tenant.
This could arise where the increased rent on a rent review has been fixed
after the increase date so as to operate retrospectively – the outgoing
tenant is liable for the increased rent between the increase date and the
date when he becomes quit of his other obligations.

*sub-paragraph (b)* This applies to all assignments made by tenants
(including those made by the original tenant). The assignment discharges
the tenant from liability for any future breach of a tenant's obligation. But
this is so only if the assignment is consistent with the tenant's obligations
(e.g. not if the assignment is improperly made because the landlord's
consent is required and is reasonably withheld). At common law the
original tenant was liable for all breaches of obligation committed by his
successors throughout the term of the tenancy.

*Paragraph (2)* defines the day on which the assigning tenant's liability is
cut off as –

*sub-paragraph (a)* Where the landlord has signed the assignment (e.g. in
order to signify that some specified tenant's obligation will not bind the
assignee (see Article 36(3)(b)), the date of the landlord's signing.

*sub-paragraph (b)* In any other case, the date on which notice of the
assignment is served on the landlord.

This paragraph supersedes section 15 of Deasy's Act which rendered
an assignee tenant who assigned to a further assignee between two gale
days liable on his obligations up to the gale day next following service on
the landlord of notice of the assignment.

*Paragraph (3)* allows the Article to be derogated from by a provision in
the lease or, if the landlord concurs, a provision of the assignment.

*Paragraph (4)* applies the Article to an assignment of part of the premises.

### Assignment of part of premises: equitable apportionment etc. of rent and obligations between assignor and assignee

**39.**—(1) Where in an assignment of a tenancy for valuable consideration as respects part only of the premises the rent reserved by the lease is, without the consent of the landlord signified as mentioned in paragraph (4), expressed to be –

(a) charged exclusively on the land assigned or any part of it in exoneration of the land retained by the assignor or other land; or

(b) charged exclusively on the land retained by the assignor or any part of it in exoneration of the land assigned or other land; or

(c) apportioned between the land assigned or any part of it and the land retained by the assignor or any part of it;

then, without prejudice to the rights of the landlord, the charge or apportionment is binding between the assignor and the assignee and their respective successors in title.

(2) Where in an assignment of a tenancy for valuable consideration as respects part only of the premises the rent reserved by the lease is not expressed to be charged or apportioned as mentioned in paragraph (1), then, without prejudice to the rights of the landlord, the rent is, as between the assignor and the assignee and their successors in title, deemed to be apportioned between the land retained and the land assigned according to the respective areas of those lands.

(3) Where –

(a) any default is made in payment of the whole or part of a rent by the person ("the defaulter") who, by reason of such charge or apportionment as aforesaid, is liable to pay the same; or

(b) any breach occurs of any of the tenant's obligations (other than, in the case of an apportionment, the obligation to pay the entire rent), so far as they relate to the land retained or assigned as the case may be;

the tenant for the time being of any other land comprised in the lease, in whom, as respects that land, the residue of the estate created by the lease is vested, who –

(i) pays or is required to pay the whole or part of the rent which ought to have been paid by the defaulter; or

(ii) incurs any costs, damages or expenses by reason of the breach of obligation;

may apply to the court for relief, and the court may make such an order as appears to it to be appropriate in the circumstances and, on a further application, may vary, suspend, revive or revoke any order made under this paragraph.

(4) The remedies conferred by this Article –

(a) take effect only so far as they might have been conferred by the assignment whereby the rent is expressed to be exclusively charged or apportioned as aforesaid;

1408

(b) do not apply to an assignment whereby the rent is expressed to be charged or apportioned with the consent of the landlord and which is signed by the landlord.

(5)  This Article applies only if and so far as a contrary intention is not expressed in the assignment whereby the rent is expressed to be charged or apportioned, and takes effect subject to the provisions of that assignment.

(6)  In this Article –

(a) references to the land conveyed or the land retained include any part thereof, and any reference to rent includes any part thereof;

(b) valuable consideration does not include a nominal consideration in money.

# EXPLANATORY NOTE

ARTICLE 39            Periodic Rents Bill, cl. 1
                                         LPA 1925 s. 190(3)-(7)

This Article is concerned with the effect of an equitable apportionment or charge of rent or of tenant's obligations on an assignment of part of a tenancy (i.e. an apportionment or charge which does not have effect at law because the landlord is not a party to it, but has effect only in equity between the parties to the assignment).

*Paragraph (1)* deals with three sets of circumstances –

*sub-paragraph (a)* The rent is charged on the land assigned in exoneration of the land retained;

*sub-paragraph (b)* The rent is charged on the land retained in exoneration of the land assigned;

*sub-paragraph (c)* The rent is apportioned between the land assigned and the land retained.

These circumstances are extended to cases where rent on other land is also involved or where the agreement relates only to part of the rent.

In these circumstances the charge or apportionment is enforceable between the parties to the assignment and their successors, but does not affect the landlord.

*Paragraph (2)* deals with the case where leasehold land is divided by an assignment of part of it, but there is no agreement to which paragraph (1) can apply. The rent is deemed to be divided between the assigned and retained parts of the land in proportion to their areas.

*Paragraph (3)* applies where there has been a division of leasehold land to which either paragraph (1) or paragraph (2) applies and subsequently, following a default by an assignee who is liable to pay the rent or part of the rent, the other party to the equitable arrangement has to pay the defaulter's dues or is held liable for a breach of some other obligation for which the defaulter is responsible. The aggrieved party may apply to the court for relief, and the court may make such an order as it considers appropriate. This could be an order giving the applicant possession of the defaulter's part of the land or the right to receive the income produced by it. The court has power to vary its order, or to suspend it (to give the defaulter a last chance to honour his obligations voluntarily), revive it (if he does not take that chance) or revoke it (if he does). Where the original order was made by a county court, any subsequent order may be made by a court held for the same division (Article 77(1)).

*Paragraph (4)* limits the application of the Article in two ways –

*sub-paragraph (a)* It does not extend the power of the parties to an assignment to make an agreement, but simply operates on an agreement made within their existing capacity.

*sub-paragraph (b)* It does not apply where the landlord signifies his consent by signing the assignment. In this case there is a legal charge or

1410

apportionment which is binding between the parties (including the landlord) at law.

*Paragraph (5)* enables the terms of the assignment to exclude the operation of the Article or to modify its terms.

*Paragraph (6)* makes it clear that references to the land conveyed, the land retained or the rent include parts of those. The Article applies only where there is an assignment for valuable consideration (paragraph (1)), but it is made clear here that this does not include a nominal sum.

**Position of landlord and tenant after conveyance of reversion**

**40.**—(1) Where a landlord conveys his reversion –

(a) he remains liable to the tenant and the tenant's successors in title for any breach of a landlord's obligation committed by him;

(b) the conveyance operates to discharge him from all liability to the tenant or the tenant's successors in title in respect of any breach of a landlord's obligation committed on or after the day when he ceased to be landlord;

(c) a successor in title of his may enforce tenant's obligations in respect of breaches committed before the successor became landlord.

(2)   This Article applies only if and so far as a contrary intention is not expressed or implied in the lease or, where the writing by which the conveyance is made is signed by the tenant, in that writing.

ARTICLE 40                                    Property Bill Cl. 174

This Article lists the consequences of a conveyance of the reversion. This could be a conveyance *inter vivos* or an assent following death. On the death of a landlord his reversion passes to his personal representative by operation of law – with effect from the time of death where an executor has been appointed and obtains probate or with effect from the date of the grant of letters of administration in other cases (the title in the meantime reposing in the Probate judge): an assent made by a personal representative to a beneficiary is a conveyance and the personal representative is the landlord for this (and other) purposes (see the definitions in Article 2(2)).

*Paragraph (1)* states three consequences of a conveyance.

*sub-paragraph (a)* The outgoing landlord continues liable to the tenant and the tenant's successors for breaches of obligation already committed by him.

*sub-paragraph (b)* The outgoing landlord is not liable for future breaches of obligation committed by his successors.

*sub-paragraph (c)* A successor of the outgoing landlord's may enforce tenant's obligations in respect of breaches committed by the tenant against the outgoing landlord or one of his predecessors (cf. *In re King decd.* [1963] 1 Ch. 459).

*Paragraph (2)* allows the Article to be derogated from by a provision in the lease or tenancy agreement or, if the tenant concurs, a provision of the conveyance.

**Apportionment of obligations on severance**

**41.**—(1) This Article applies where there is –

(a) severance by conveyance, surrender or otherwise of the reversion expectant on a tenancy; or

(b) avoidance or cesser in any manner of a tenancy as to part only of the land comprised therein.

(2) Where there is severance, –

(a) the tenant's benefits under the tenancy continue to subsist as they did before the severance took place;

(b) an obligation to pay rent or other sums becomes, in respect of rent or sums accruing due on or after the date of severance, an obligation to pay to each owner of a severed part of the reversion so much of the rent or sums as is apportionable to that part; and

(c) every other obligation under the tenancy –

    (i) is apportioned between, and remains annexed to, the several severed parts of the reversion, or, where a particular obligation is applicable only to a particular part or parts, remains annexed to that part or is apportioned between, and remains annexed to, those parts; and

    (ii) so far as it is so annexed, continues and is in force with respect to the tenancy, and may be enforced, as if the part of the premises on which each respective severed part of the reversion is reversionary had alone originally been comprised in the lease.

(3) Where there is avoidance or cesser, –

(a) the tenancy continues to subsist with respect to the part of the land as to which it has not been avoided or has not otherwise ceased ("the surviving part"); and

(b) an obligation to pay rent or other sums becomes, in respect of rent or sums accruing due on or after the date of avoidance or cesser, an obligation to pay so much of the rent or sums as is apportionable to the surviving part; and

(c) every other obligation under the tenancy continues and is in force with respect to the surviving part so far as it is applicable thereto.

(4) Any question arising under this Article about the applicability or apportionment of any obligation may be referred to, and shall be determined by, the Lands Tribunal.

# EXPLANATORY NOTE

ARTICLE 41

Property Bill Cl. 169, 171(2)
LPAA 1859 s. 3
CA 1881 s. 12
LPA 1925 s. 140(1)(3), 141(1)

Under this Article, where the reversion expectant on the determination of a tenancy is severed or part of the land demised ceases to be included in the tenancy, all relevant obligations under the tenancy continue to attach to the severed interests.

*Paragraph (1)* identifies two cases –

*sub-paragraph (a)* where the reversion is severed by conveyance, surrender or otherwise;

*sub-paragraph (b)* where a tenancy ceases to apply to part of the land demised.

*Paragraph (2)* In the case of severance –

*sub-paragraph (a)* The tenant's benefits are not affected by the severance: *Jelley* v. *Buckman* [1974] QB 488, *Neville Long* v. *Firmenich* [1984] 4CL160C. His obligations are affected to the extent provided in the following sub-paragraphs and Article 52(7).

*sub-paragraph (b)* An obligation to pay rent or other sums is apportioned between the owners of the severed parts.

*sub-paragraph (c)* Other obligations are apportioned between the severed parts, as appropriate. A development from this principle is Article 52(7), which allows a landlord of a severed part to serve a notice to determine the tenancy in respect of that part.

*Paragraph (3)* In the case of avoidance or cesser –

*sub-paragraph (a)* The tenancy continues with respect to the remainder of the land.

*sub-paragraph (b)* Rent is apportioned between the part of the land now excluded from, and that retained in, the tenancy.

*sub-paragraph (c)* Other obligations continue to apply to the remainder of the land so far as applicable.

*Paragraph (4)* Disputes about the applicability or apportionment of obligations are determinable by the Lands Tribunal.

*Paragraph 5 of Schedule 2* contains a transitional provision which partly reproduces the effect of section 12(2) of the Conveyancing Act 1881 (which prevented section 12 from applying to leases made before the commencement of that Act). Where a lease was made before 1 January 1882, the Article does not apply to a severance effected before the commencement of the Order: but it does apply to one made after that commencement.

1415

*Modification of obligations*

## Licence dispensing from tenant's obligation

**42.**—(1) A licence granted by a landlord to a tenant permitting any act which in the absence of the licence would be a breach of a tenant's obligation –

(a) operates as a complete dispensation from that obligation for the residue of the term of the tenancy only if it is contained in writing signed by the landlord which shows an intention that it should so operate;

(b) where it does not so operate, extends only to the particular act permitted (and accordingly, notwithstanding the licence, all rights to which the landlord is entitled by virtue of the tenant's obligations remain in full force, and may be enforced in the event of any subsequent breach of those obligations not specifically permitted, in the same manner as if no licence had been granted).

(2) In this Article references to acts include omissions.

# EXPLANATORY NOTE

ARTICLE 42

Property Bill Cl. 167, 168(2)
LPAA 1859 ss. 1, 2
Deasy's Act ss. 22, 43
LPA 1925 s. 143

This Article is concerned with a licence by a landlord authorising his tenant to do some future act which, in the absence of the licence would be a breach of a tenant's obligation.

*Paragraph (1)* makes it clear that a licence granted by the landlord dispensing the tenant from some obligation relates only to the particular occasion and is not a total dispensation, unless the intention that it be total is made clear. *Sub-paragraph(a)* deals with total dispensations. There must be writing signed by the landlord which shows an intention that the obligation should be completely done away with. *Sub-paragraph (b)* reproduces the effect of section 1 of the Law of Property Amendment Act 1859 which abrogated the rule in *Dumpor's Case* (1603) 4 Co. Rep. 119b that a licence to assign or sub-let operated as a total dispensation from a condition against assignment or sub-letting. Unless the licence makes it clear that the dispensation is to be total, the licence is to be taken to authorise only the particular breach of obligation in prospect.

*Paragraph (2)* makes it clear that references in the Article to acts include omissions.

### Waiver of sanction for breach of tenant's obligation

**43.**—(1) Where a tenant's obligation has been breached, a waiver by the landlord of any sanction for the breach –

(a) operates as a general waiver in respect of all past breaches of the obligation only if it is contained in writing signed by the landlord which shows an intention that it should so operate;

(b) where it does not operate as a general waiver, extends only to the particular instance, and the particular breach of a tenant's obligation, to which it is proved specially to relate.

(2) Without prejudice to any other form of implied waiver, waiver of any sanction for any breach of a tenant's obligation of which the landlord has actual knowledge is implied by a demand for rent received by the tenant or acceptance of rent; but –

(a) where, in a demand or receipt for rent, the landlord specifies with particularity any breach of obligation, other than the obligation to pay that rent, as not being waived, that breach is excluded from any waiver; and

(b) where rent is payable in advance, a demand for or acceptance of rent operates in relation to breaches of obligation continuing during the period for which the rent is paid or any part of that period as a waiver only of breaches known to the landlord, at the time when he demanded or accepted the rent, to be then continuing and to be likely to continue for the whole or that part of that period.

(3) For the purposes of paragraph (2)(a) a breach is specified with particularity if particulars sufficient to inform the tenant of any action required to remedy the breach are contained in the demand or receipt or in writing served on the tenant before or at the time of the delivery to him of the demand or receipt and referred to in the demand or receipt.

(4) In paragraph (2) "rent" means rent falling due after the breach.

# EXPLANATORY NOTE

ARTICLE 43

Property Bill Cl. 168
LPAA 1860 s. 6
Deasy's Act s. 43
LPA 1925 s. 148

This Article deals with the waiver by the landlord of the benefit of a breach of a tenant's obligation. Article 42 is concerned with advance authorisations which render lawful an act or omission by the tenant which would otherwise be a breach of some obligation of his: this Article is concerned with the case where the tenant has already breached his obligation without the landlord's prior permission and the landlord is prepared to waive the sanction for the breach (i.e. his right to redress by, e.g., claiming damages or applying for termination of the tenancy). A waiver may be express or implied.

*Paragraph (1)* provides that an express waiver –

*sub-paragraph (a)* operates as a general waiver of all past breaches of tenant's obligations only if it is contained in writing which shows that intention and is signed by the landlord;
*sub-paragraph (b)* otherwise extends only to the particular instance and the particular breach of obligation to which it is proved to relate.

*Paragraph (2)* deals with implied waiver. The most common occasion of implied waiver is the acceptance of rent. At present, a landlord accepting rent cannot reserve his right to take action for the breach *(Segal Securities Ltd. v. Thoseby* [1963] 1 QB 887 at pp. 897 *et seq.*), so it is useless for him to mark the receipt "without prejudice". The paragraph will permit him, in future, to reserve his rights in respect of particular breaches of obligation which are sufficiently identified in the receipt. If the rent is payable in advance, acceptance of the rent waives any continuing breaches of obligation which are known to the landlord to be in continuance at the time when he accepted the rent: the waiver extends through so much of the period for which the rent is paid as the landlord can foresee as the likely period of continuance of the breach. Rent is normally payable in arrear unless the lease requires it to be paid in advance (Article 15(2)).

*Paragraph (3)* explains what is sufficient identification of breaches of obligation for which the landlord wishes to reserve his rights when he accepts rent. Particulars which will adequately acquaint the tenant with the action required from him must be given in the demand or receipt for rent or in a separate paper which is referred to in the demand or receipt.

*Paragraph (4)* defines "rent" for the purposes of paragraph (2) as rent falling due after the breach. Demanding or accepting arrears of rent does not give rise to waiver: *Northern Ireland Housing Executive* v. *Duffin* 1985 NIJB No. 8 at pp. 71, 72.

## Obligations affecting alienation, change of user or improvements

**44.**—(1) A tenant's obligation not to do any of the following things, namely, –

(a) alienate the premises;

(b) alienate any part of the premises;

(c) alter the user of the premises;

(d) make any improvement on the premises;

(e) where the premises or part of them are sub-demised, grant a licence for a sub-tenant to do any of the aforementioned things,

is (if not so expressed) an obligation not to do that thing without the landlord's licence ("a licence").

(2) An obligation not to do any thing mentioned in paragraph (1) without a licence (whether of the landlord or of some other person), and an obligation on a landlord not to grant a licence for the doing of any such thing without the licence of a superior landlord or some other person, is subject to the qualification that a licence must not be unreasonably withheld (whether or not it is also subject to any other qualification).

(3) Schedule 1 has effect for the purposes of this Article.

(4) This Article does not apply –

(a) to a tenancy for a period not exceeding one year;

(b) to a tenancy expressed to be granted for or made dependent on the continuance of the tenant in any office, employment or appointment;

(c) to a tenancy expressed to be created for the temporary convenience of the landlord or the tenant;

(d) to a tenancy at will;

(e) so far as it relates to alteration of user, to a parcel of land within a development scheme under Part IX of the Property Order where there is a development obligation restrictive of user which would exclude the user proposed by the tenant;

(f) to a unit in a commonhold under the Commonhold (Northern Ireland) Order 1989 to the extent that the provision of paragraph 3(f) or (g) of Schedule 2 to that Order (stated purpose of commonhold; no sub-division of units) applies (with or without modification).

(5) In this Article and Schedule 1 –

"alienate" includes assign, sub-demise, charge and part with possession and also includes an assent by a personal representative;

"improvement" means making any addition to or alteration of a building or structure or erecting any ancillary or subsidiary building or structure (but not effecting any alteration or reconstruction of a building or structure such as to make it lose its original identity);

"tenant", where the tenancy is affected by a mortgage and the mortgagee proposes to exercise his statutory or express power of sale, includes the mortgagee.

1420

# EXPLANATORY NOTE

ARTICLE 44

Property Bill Cl. 175
C&LPA 1892 s. 3
L & TA 1927 s. 19
L & T (A) A 1980 (No. 10)
(Rep. of Ire.) Pt. V
L & TA 1988
Cf. Housing (NI) Order 1983
(NI 15) Arts.30-36

This Article qualifies obligations in leases restrictive of alienation, alteration of user or making improvements.

*Paragraph (1)* qualifies an absolute covenant against alienation of the premises (or any part of them), alteration of the use to which the tenant puts the premises, making improvements on the premises or granting consent to any of those actions by a sub-tenant, so that the covenant becomes one not to do the forbidden thing without the landlord's licence.

*Paragraph (2)* provides that a licence (whether required by para. (1) or by the lease) must not be unreasonably withheld. The question of reasonableness will normally be decided having regard to the landlord's own interests; but it is unreasonable for a landlord not to consider the detriment which would be suffered by the tenant in the absence of consent if that detriment would be extreme and disproportionate in relation to the benefit gained by the landlord (as where the value of the reversion is illusory): *International Drillings Fluids Ltd.* v. *Louisville Investments* [1986] 1 All ER 321. It will be for the landlord to show that it was reasonable for him to withhold a licence (Schedule 1, paragraph 1(5)).

*Paragraph (3)* attracts the provisions of Schedule 1.

*Paragraph (4)* excludes the Article from applying to certain short or temporary tenancies or where there is a fundamental restriction on change of user or sub-division.

*Paragraph (5)* contains definitions.

See also Article 130(4) and (5) of the Property Order (on assignment by mortgagee, landlord's licence not to be unreasonably withheld; on vesting in mortgagee under the Limitation Order, any need for landlord's licence to be ignored).

### Licence of landlord who cannot be found

**45.** Where –

(a) a tenant is under an obligation not to do any particular thing without the licence of the landlord, and

(b) the rent reserved by the lease has not been paid for five or more years, and

(c) the landlord is not known to, and cannot be found by, the tenant,

the Lands Tribunal, on the application of the tenant and after the publication of such (if any) advertisements as the Lands Tribunal directs, may authorise the tenant, subject to such (if any) conditions as the Lands Tribunal thinks fit to impose, to do the particular thing; and thereupon it is lawful for the tenant to do that thing, without the licence of the landlord, in accordance with the conditions (if any) imposed.

# EXPLANATORY NOTE

ARTICLE 45                 L & T (A) A 1980 (No. 10)
                                            (Rep. of Ire.) s. 69

This Article empowers the Lands Tribunal to dispense with a landlord's licence where the landlord cannot be traced.

Where a tenant is under an obligation not to do a particular thing without the landlord's licence (as under Article 44), no rent has been paid for at least 5 years and the landlord cannot be traced, the Lands Tribunal may authorise the tenant to do the prohibited thing without any licence. The Tribunal may require preliminary advertisements to be published and may impose conditions.

**Position of parties after sub-letting**

**46.**—(1) Where a tenant who has sub-let fails to pay to his landlord any rent payable in respect of the premises –

(a) the landlord, after the rent has remained unpaid for four weeks, may serve a notice on the sub-tenant requiring him to pay to the landlord or his agent specified in the notice so much of the rent payable by the sub-tenant to the tenant as is sufficient to discharge the rent unpaid by the tenant; and thereupon the sub-tenant is under an obligation to pay to the landlord all rent payable under the sub-lease or so much of it as is sufficient to discharge rent payable by the tenant which may accrue after service of the notice, until such time as the landlord serves on the sub-tenant a notice to cease such payment, and the landlord has all the rights and remedies of the tenant for enforcing payment of the sub-tenant's rent;

(b) the sub-tenant may, before any action for breach of his obligation to pay rent is brought by the tenant against the sub-tenant, pay to the landlord so much of the rent payable by the sub-tenant to the tenant as is sufficient to discharge the rent remaining unpaid by the tenant.

(2) The receipt of the landlord or his agent is a full discharge to the sub-tenant as against the tenant in respect of all rent paid under paragraph (1).

(3) Where there is a sub-letting which is not a breach of a tenant's obligation, the receipt of the tenant for rent paid to him by the sub-tenant before service of a notice under paragraph (1)(a) is a full discharge to the sub-tenant as against the landlord in respect of all rent issuing out of and theretofore due from the premises, except so much rent (if any) as remains due from the sub-tenant.

(4) This Article does not prejudice the rights and remedies of the landlord with respect to the balance of his rent as against the tenant or, where only part of the premises has been sub-let, the remainder of the premises.

# EXPLANATORY NOTE

ARTICLE 46                      Property Bill Cl. 176
                                          Deasy's Act ss. 19-21

This Article allows rent to be paid direct from a sub-tenant to the head landlord where the intermediate tenant has defaulted in paying his rent.

*Paragraph (1)* applies where a tenant who has sub-let fails to pay his own rent –

*sub-paragraph (a)* allows the landlord to serve on the sub-tenant a notice requiring him to pay his rent (or so much of it as equals the tenant's rent) to the landlord (instead of to the tenant). The notice remains in effect until it is revoked by a subsequent notice, and while it remains in effect the landlord has all the powers to enforce payment of the rent which the tenant would normally have.

*sub-paragraph (b)* allows the notice procedure to be by-passed by the sub-tenant voluntarily paying his rent to the landlord, but this can be done only before an action for payment of the rent is brought against the sub-tenant by the tenant.

*Paragraph (2)* makes the landlord's receipt for rent a full discharge to the sub-tenant as against the tenant.

*Paragraph (3)* prevents the landlord from seeking to obtain from the sub-tenant any rent he had already paid the tenant before he received a notice under paragraph (1)(a).

*Paragraph (4)* prevents the Article from affecting the landlord's rights against the tenant in respect of so much of the rent as is not satisfied by payments made by the sub-tenant.

*Enforcement of obligations*

## Powers of courts for enforcement of obligations

**47.**—(1) Without prejudice to any other power of the court, where one party to a lease is in breach of an obligation under the tenancy, the court may, in an action by the other party, –

(a) where the breach consists of failure to pay any rent or any other sum payable under the tenancy, order payment of the amount of that rent or that other sum;

(b) in the case of any other breach of obligation, award damages.

(2) Where during the existence of a tenancy either party to the lease is in breach of an obligation under the tenancy and the other party brings an action in the court in respect of that breach, if the action is contested the process by which it was begun shall be treated as an application under Article 57 or Article 59, as the case may be.

(3) Rules of court or county court rules may specify circumstances in which an action is to be treated as contested for the purposes of paragraph (2).

(4) Where in any proceedings under Article 62(1) of the Magistrates' Courts Order in respect of rent the defendant raises a defence or counterclaim, the proceedings shall be transferred under Article 75 of that Order to the county court which shall treat them as proceedings on an application under Article 57.

(5) A court of summary jurisdiction which transfers proceedings as mentioned in paragraph (4) may require the defendant to enter into a recognizance conditioned to pursue his defence or counterclaim and, if he does not do so, to pay any costs incurred by the plaintiff in consequence of the transfer; and where the defendant fails to comply with any condition of the recognizance a court of summary jurisdiction acting for the same petty sessions district as the court which made the transfer may, subject to Article 138(3) of the Magistrates' Courts Order (notice to party in default), estreat the recognizance, whereupon Article 138(4) of that Order (distress or committal) applies.

(6) In this Article any reference to a party to a lease is a reference to the landlord or the tenant (as the case may be) and, subject to Articles 38 and 40, any such reference in paragraph (1) includes a former landlord or a former tenant; and any reference in this Article to the Magistrates' Courts Order is a reference to the Magistrates' Courts (Northern Ireland) Order 1981.

(7) After the commencement of this Order no proceedings for ejectment for non-payment of rent shall be begun.

# EXPLANATORY NOTE

ARTICLE 47

Property Bill Cl. 182
Deasy's Act ss. 45, 50

This Article sets out the main powers of the court for the enforcement of obligations under a tenancy.

*Paragraph (1)* empowers the court –

*sub-paragraph (a):* to order payment of the amount of any rent in arrear or other sum due between the parties;

*sub-paragraph (b):* to award damages.

The paragraph does not affect any other power of the court – e.g. to order specific performance (Article 48; *Francis* v. *Cowcliff Ltd* (1976) 120 Sol. Jo. 353 – obligation to provide and maintain a lift) or to grant an injunction (County Courts (Northern Ireland) Order 1980 Art. 13).

*Paragraph (2)* prevents an action from proceeding under the ordinary jurisdiction of the court where the action is contested. It is converted into an application to the court to resolve the dispute between the parties under Article 57 or Article 59.

*Paragraph (3)* enables rules of court or county court rules to provide for circumstances in which an action is to be treated as contested. This particularly applies to proceedings by default civil bill or summary civil bill in the county court. It is envisaged that if the defendant disputes liability or alleges a counterclaim, future proceedings in the action will be under Article 57; but, if he does not do so, the action may proceed to judgment and enforcement.

*Paragraph (4)* applies a similar rule to proceedings in a court of summary jurisdiction. Upon a defence or counterclaim being raised, the action must be transferred to the county court.

*Paragraph (5)* requires the defendant in the summary court to enter into a recognizance to pursue his defence or counterclaim where the proceedings are transferred under paragraph (4), and provides for the recovery of the sum in which the recognizance is conditioned.

*Paragraph (6)* applies paragraph (1) to former landlords and former tenants, either after the assignment or conveyance of the interest of either (Articles 38, 40) or after the termination of the tenancy (Article 60).

*Paragraph (7)* abolishes the action for ejectment for non-payment of rent. Actions commenced before the commencement of the Order are not affected. This paragraph forms a foundation for the repeal of section 52 of Deasy's Act by the Consequential Provisions Order. As to ejectment on the title, see Article 51.

**Specific performance of landlord's obligation to repair**

**48.**—(1) In any proceedings in which a tenant alleges a breach on the part of his landlord of an obligation to repair any part of a building comprising or forming part of the premises or in which the premises are wholly or partly contained, the court may in its discretion order specific performance of that obligation, whether or not the breach relates to a part of the building let to the tenant and notwithstanding any equitable rule restricting the scope of that remedy.

(2)  In this Article –

"landlord", in relation to a tenant, includes any person against whom the tenant has a right to enforce an obligation to repair (whether the obligation arises under that tenant's tenancy or otherwise);

"obligation to repair" includes an obligation to construct or re-construct any building or structure;

"tenant" includes a statutory tenant under the Rent (Northern Ireland) Order 1978, and in relation to a statutory tenant "the premises" means the premises of which he is the statutory tenant.

# EXPLANATORY NOTE

ARTICLE 48
cf. HA 1974 s. 125<br>L&T A 1985 s. 17

This Article provides for the remedy of specific performance between tenant and landlord.

*Paragraph (1)* makes it clear that a court has jurisdiction to order specific performance of a landlord's obligation to repair on the application of the tenant, not only, where the demised premises form only part of a building, of the premises themselves but also of any other part of the building: for example, if the tenant occupies a flat or office he may obtain specific performance of the landlord's obligation to repair the roof, exterior walls, passages, staircases, etc. The decision whether or not to order specific performance in any particular case is entirely at the discretion of the court.

*Paragraph (2)* extends the reference in the Article to the landlord to include anyone else (for example, the tenant of another flat or office in the building) whose breach of an obligation to repair affects the tenant making the application. It also extends the meaning of "obligation to repair" to include construction and re-construction and applies the Article to a statutory tenant.

**Damages for breach of tenant's obligation to repair**

**49.**—(1) Where there is a breach of a tenant's obligation to repair the premises, the measure of damages for the breach is the amount (if any) by which the value of the reversion in the premises is diminished owing to the breach.

(2) Consequently, where the circumstances are such that repairs cannot be carried out in accordance with the obligation or, if carried out, would be of no effective value (for example, because the premises have been or are to be demolished, or have been or are to be altered to such an extent as to render the repairs impossible or valueless, or because the repairs, if carried out, would not render the premises capable of being profitably used) no damages are recoverable.

(3) Paragraph (2) does not apply where circumstances such as are mentioned in that paragraph would not have arisen were it not for the tenant's breach of his obligation to repair.

# EXPLANATORY NOTE

ARTICLE 49

L&TA 1927 s. 18
L&T(A) A 1980 (No. 10)
(Rep. of Ire.) s. 65

This Article applies a uniform rule to the measuring of damages for breach of a tenant's repairing obligation. At present the measure of damages varies, depending upon whether the breach occurs during the currency of the tenancy or at its termination: in the former case it is the amount of the diminution in the value of the landlord's reversion and in the latter it is the actual cost of the repairs.

*Paragraph (1)* lays down the uniform rule that in all cases the measure of damages is the amount of diminution in the value of the reversion owing to the breach. "The reversion" is defined in Article 2(2).

*Paragraph ((2)* contains the corollary that, if in a particular case repairs would be impossible or ineffective, there is no diminution "owing to the breach", and consequently no damages are recoverable.

*Paragraph (3)* makes an exception to paragraph (2) where demolition is necessitated by the tenant's failure to repair. This incorporates the decision in *Hibernian Property Co. Ltd.* v. *Liverpool Corporation* [1973] 1 WLR 751.

## PART V

## TERMINATION, ETC., OF TENANCY

*Methods of termination*

**Ways in which tenancies may be terminated**

**50.**—(1) A tenancy can terminate in one of the following ways, whichever first occurs, and in no other –

(a) where it was created for a term specified in the lease, on the expiration of that term;

(b) where it is subject to a provision of the lease by virtue of which it would, apart from Article 51, terminate or become terminable on the happening of a specified event, in accordance with that Article;

(c) where it is terminable by a notice served by the landlord on the tenant or the tenant on the landlord, on the expiration of such a notice duly served and, in particular, in the case of a notice to determine a periodic tenancy, served in accordance with Article 52 (but subject to paragraph (8) of that Article);

(d) by surrender by express or implied agreement between the landlord and the tenant in accordance with Article 53;

(e) by surrender under Article 54 following the destruction of, or damage to, the premises or by an order of the court under that Article;

(f) where the landlord believes the premises to have been abandoned, as mentioned in Article 55;

(g) where it is a long-term tenancy to which Article 56 applies, by enlargement into a fee simple in accordance with that Article;

(h) where there has been a breach of a tenant's obligation or a landlord's obligation, or where Article 51(3) applies, by an order of the court under Article 57 or Article 59;

(i) in accordance with the law of merger;

(j) without prejudice to sub-paragraph (i), on the enlargement of the tenancy into a fee simple under the Leasehold (Enlargement and Extension) Act (Northern Ireland) 1971 or the Ground Rents (Northern Ireland) Order1989;

(k) by disclaimer in accordance with the law relating to bankruptcy, arrangements, the winding-up of companies or the rights of minors;

(l) by frustration of the lease;

(m) in accordance with any statutory provision providing for its termination.

(2) From the commencement of this Order, any rule of law under which a lease can be forfeited or a periodic tenancy can be treated as

1432

terminated by reason of the tenant's denial of his landlord's title is abolished.

(3)  This Article does not apply to the termination of a tenancy at will.

ARTICLE 50                    Property Bill Cl. 183,191

This Article sets out the ways in which a tenancy may be terminated.

*Paragraph (1)* lists 13 methods of termination –

(a) by expiry of the term of the tenancy;

(b) by the operation of a limitation, condition or other provision bringing the tenancy, or allowing it to be brought, to a premature end, on the expiration of four weeks from the date of service on the tenant by the landlord of notice of the happening of that event (that is, where Article 51(4) applies) but not where the event is a breach of a tenant's obligation or something treated as a tenant's obligation (when termination can only be under paragraph(h));

(c) where the tenancy is terminable by notice, by the due service of a notice (Article 52);

(d) by surrender by express or implied agreement between the landlord and the tenant under Article 53;

(e) by surrender following the destruction of, or damage to, the premises (Article 54);

(f) where the premises are reasonably believed to have been abandoned (Article 55);

(g) by enlargement of a long-term tenancy into a fee simple (Article 56);

(h) by an order of the court made in consequence of a breach of a tenant's obligation or a landlord's obligation (Articles 57, 59), or where the Order makes Article 57 applicable (Article 51(3));

(i) in accordance with the law of merger (as where the tenant buys the immediately superior estate and his tenancy merges with that estate – see Property Order, Article 245);

(j) on the enlargement of the tenancy into a fee simple, e.g., following the redemption by the tenant of his ground rent (and all superior rents) under the Ground Rents (Northern Ireland) Order 1989;

(k) by disclaimer of the tenancy by the tenant's trustee in bankruptcy, by a liquidator (where the tenant is a company), or by the tenant (if he took the tenancy as a minor) upon attaining his majority. Articles 153 and 156 of the Insolvency (Northern Ireland) Order 1989 apply to the disclaimer of leaseholds by the liquidator of a company: Articles 290 and 294 apply to disclaimers by a trustee in bankruptcy. Under Articles 152(3)(a) and 288(3)(a) of that Order, a disclaimer operates to determine the rights, interests and liabilities of the company or bankrupt in or in respect of the property disclaimed. It seems that the landlord's reversion is accelerated (Ing "Bona Vacantia" p. 140). The grant or assignment of a lease to a minor can give him no more than an equitable interest, the legal estate being held on trust for him as on a settlement: he may disclaim his interest within a reasonable time of attaining his majority (unless it is a lease of a house which is a necessary of life to him);

(*l*) by frustration of the lease which created the tenancy (see the definition of "lease" in Article 2(2));

(*m*) in accordance with any statutory provision, e.g. Criminal Law Amendment Act 1912 s. 5(1) – cf. Schedule 2, paragraph 10(b)(iii).

*Paragraph (2)* abolishes the common law rule that a lease can be forfeited, and a tenancy agreement can be treated as terminated, where the tenant denies his landlord's title. It has been argued that that rule ceased to apply in Ireland on the coming into operation of section 3 of Deasy's Act. This paragraph puts the abolition of the rule beyond doubt (especially in view of the repeal of section 3).

*Paragraph (3)* prevents the Article from applying to a tenancy at will. A tenancy at will is terminable by either party at any time. In particular, the common law rule about the consequences of denying the landlord's title continues to apply to a tenancy at will. The words of Evershed MR in *Wisbeach St. Mary Parish Council* v. *Lilley* [1956] 1 WLR 121 at 125 (although spoken with reference to periodic tenancies) are apposite "... evidence of a disclaimer of the landlord's title by the tenant is evidence of the determination of the will of both parties . . .".

**Termination on or in consequence of the operation of a provision of a lease**

**51.**—(1) This Article applies where a tenancy is subject to –

(a) a provision by virtue of which the tenancy will (apart from this Article) terminate before the expiration of its term on the happening of a specified event; or

(b) a provision which (apart from this Article) makes the tenancy terminable by forfeiture by the landlord, or any other action by the landlord or the tenant, on the happening of a specified event.

(2) The provision is ineffective to terminate the tenancy or to make the tenancy terminable by the landlord or (as the case may be) the tenant, except to the extent and in the manner provided in this Article.

(3) Where the event is –

(a) a breach of an obligation under the tenancy; or

(b) an event against which a landlord or tenant would normally protect himself (if he protected himself at all) by means of an obligation under the tenancy; or

(c) an insolvency event affecting the tenant;

the party aggrieved may, on the happening of the event, make an application to the court under Article 57 or Article 59 (whichever is applicable), and may do so in a case such as is mentioned in sub-paragraph (b) or (c) as if the event were a breach of an obligation.

(4) In any other case, without prejudice to Article 65, the tenancy is terminable by four weeks notice of the happening of the event served by the party aggrieved on the other party within 26 weeks from the date of the happening (or the first happening) of the event.

(5) In this Article –

"insolvency event affecting the tenant" means –

(a) bankruptcy of a tenant or surety who is an individual;

(b) entering into liquidation, compulsory or voluntary, by any tenant or surety which is a body corporate, or having a receiver appointed in respect of any of its assets;

(c) a tenant or surety becoming an arranging debtor (that is, a person by, for or in respect of whose affairs there has been made a deed of arrangement to which Chapter I of Part VIII of the Insolvency (Northern Ireland) Order 1989 applies), or an application being made to the High Court by or in respect of him for an interim order under Chapter II of Part VIII of the Insolvency (Northern Ireland) Order 1989;

(d) a tenant suffering an order charging the tenancy to be made by the Enforcement of Judgments Office, or a tenant or surety suffering an order of seizure of property such as is mentioned in Article 32 of the Judgments Enforcement (Northern Ireland) Order 1981 to be made by that Office;

"party aggrieved" means whichever of the landlord or the tenant is aggrieved by the provision's being ineffective to terminate the lease or make the tenancy terminable in accordance with its terms;

"provision" means a provision of the lease;

"specified" means specified in the lease.

# EXPLANATORY NOTE

## ARTICLE 51

This Article alters the effect of a provision of a lease which is designed to terminate the tenancy, or render it terminable, on the happening of a given event before the full term has run.

*Paragraph (1)* defines the scope of the Article. It applies where there is a provision (normally a limitation) which expresses the tenancy to terminate automatically on the happening of a specified event, or a provision (normally a condition or proviso) which allows either party to take some action to terminate the tenancy on the happening of such an event.

*Paragraph (2)* renders any such provision ineffective to operate in the manner intended.

*Paragraph (3)* Where the event in question is (a) a breach of obligation under the tenancy or (b) something which would normally be a breach of obligation (if the lease or tenancy agreement had been drafted in accordance with the usual precedents) or (c) an insolvency event affecting the tenant (defined in paragraph (5)), the party aggrieved by the failure of the event to have the effect intended may apply to the court under Article 57 or 59 for an order terminating the tenancy or such other order as the court considers appropriate. The party aggrieved will normally be the landlord, but could be the tenant in a case where (e.g.) a particular limitation has been included in the lease at the tenant's request.

*Paragraph (4)* In any other case, the tenancy is terminable by four weeks notice of the event served by the party aggrieved on the other party. The notice must be served within 26 weeks of the event.

*Paragraph (5)* defines expressions used in the Article.

"insolvency event" means the bankruptcy or the liquidation of the tenant or a surety, or his becoming an arranging debtor or seeking the protection of the court under Part VIII of the Insolvency Order. It also includes a tenancy being charged for the enforcement of a judgment or the property of a tenant or surety being seized for enforcement purposes.

"provision" means a provision of the lease which created the tenancy. Typically, a provision of the kind mentioned in paragraph(1)(a) would be a limitation and that in paragraph (1)(b) would be a condition or a proviso to an agreement or covenant. But the language of paragraph (1) is kept wide in order to prevent attempted evasions by changes in form.

As to entry by the landlord, as distinct from re-entry, see Article 8 of the Property Order (which applies to both leases and fee farm grants).

**Termination by notice**

**52.**—(1) A periodic tenancy is terminable by a notice to determine the tenancy ("a notice to determine") served by the landlord on the tenant or the tenant on the landlord.

(2) Without prejudice to paragraphs (6) and (7), a notice to determine a tenancy from year to year –

(a) must be expressed to expire at the end of a yearly period (and for this purpose unless the contrary is proved a yearly period is to be taken to commence on the day next following the last day for payment of rent in any calendar year); and

(b) must be served at least two quarters (where the tenancy is fixed in relation to quarter days) or 26 weeks (in other cases) before the date on which it is expressed to expire.

(3) Without prejudice to paragraphs (4) to (7), a notice to determine a periodic tenancy which is based on a period less than a year –

(a) must be expressed to expire at the end of a relevant period; and

(b) must be served at least one period before the date on which it is expressed to expire;

and, for the purposes of this paragraph, unless the contrary is proved the period on which such a tenancy is based is to be taken to be the same as the period by reference to which rent is payable.

(4) Notwithstanding paragraph (3), a notice to determine a tenancy to which this paragraph applies of a dwelling-house must be served not less than four weeks before the date on which it is expressed to expire.

(5) Subject to Article 82(2), paragraph (4) applies to any tenancy except a tenancy the purpose of which is to confer on the tenant the right to occupy a dwelling-house for a holiday or a tenancy under which the estate of the landlord belongs to the Northern Ireland Housing Executive or a housing association registered under Part VII of the Housing (Northern Ireland) Order 1981.

(6) Where the period of notice given by a notice to determine is less than that required by paragraph (1)(b) or, as the case may be, paragraph (2)(b), the notice to determine, if otherwise valid, operates to terminate the tenancy on the expiration of the requisite minimum period of notice for the tenancy in question which next occurs after the date of service of the notice to determine.

(7) A notice to determine may be served by a person entitled to a severed part of the reversion on a tenancy which is subject to termination by notice, but, where such a notice to determine extends to part only of the premises, the tenant may, within four weeks from the date on which the notice to determine was served on him, terminate the tenancy in regard to the rest of the premises by serving on the owner or owners of the reversion in the rest a notice or notices to determine expressed to expire at the same time as the first-mentioned notice.

(8)  This Article –

(a)  applies only if and so far as a contrary intention is not expressed in the lease, and has effect subject to the provisions of the lease;

(b)  except paragraphs (4), and (5), does not apply to tenancies at will.

# EXPLANATORY NOTE

ARTICLE 52

Property Bill Cl. 194
Deasy's Act s. 6
LPA 1925 s.140(2)
Rent Order Arts. 2, 62
Housing (NI) Order 1981 Art.26A
Housing (NI) Order 1983 Sch.10

This Article is concerned with the formalities for terminating a tenancy by notice. Such a notice is referred to in the Article as a "notice to determine". It may be a notice served on the tenant by the landlord (a notice to quit) or one served on the landlord by the tenant.

*Paragraph (1)* provides that a periodic tenancy can be terminated by a notice served by either the landlord on the tenant or the tenant on the landlord.

*Paragraph (2)* applies to a yearly tenancy. A notice to determine must be expressed to expire at the end of a yearly period and must be served at least two quarters (where rent is payable quarterly) or 26 weeks (in other cases) before the date on which it is to expire. If there is doubt about when a yearly period begins or ends for the purpose of the tenancy, it is to be assumed to begin on the day following the last day for payment of rent in any calendar year. But evidence may be brought to show that a year for the purposes of the tenancy commences on some other day.

*Paragraph (3)* applies to other tenancies – weekly, fortnightly, monthly or quarterly. The notice must be expressed to expire at the end of a relevant period and must be served at least one period before it is due to expire; for this purpose it is to be assumed (unless proved otherwise) that the relevant period corresponds to the period for payment of rent (eg, if rent is paid weekly, the tenancy is presumed to be a weekly one, and so on). In the case of tenancies for periods of less than a month the paragraph must be read subject to paragraph (4).

*Paragraph (4)* requires at least 4 weeks' notice to terminate a tenancy of a dwelling-house. It applies whether the notice is served by the landlord or the tenant. The paragraph is subject to the qualifications in paragraph (5) (holiday homes) and Article 82 (Crown property).

*Paragraph (5)* prevents paragraph (4) from applying to a letting of a holiday home. Apart from that, it applies to any private tenancy, including a tenancy at will (but not to a Housing Executive or housing association tenancy, to which the similar provision in Article 26A of the Order of 1981 applies (see Housing (Northern Ireland) Order 1983, Sch. 10).

*Paragraph (6)* provides for the case where a notice to determine is served too late for the recipient to have the full period of notice he is entitled to under paragraph (2) or (3). This may be due to some mistake in the part of the person serving the notice or to extraneous causes (eg a delay in the post). The notice is ineffective to terminate the tenancy on the day on which it is expressed to expire, but is valid to terminate it on the next-following day which might properly have been so expressed.

*Paragraph (7)* covers the case where the reversion on a tenancy has been split and one of the reversioners serves a notice to quit. The tenant may serve on the others who have reversions in the premises a notice terminating his tenancy in relation to them on the same day as that expressed in the first reversioner's notice.

*Paragraph (8)* contains qualifications and exceptions.

*sub-paragraph (a)* the Article yields to any contrary provision in the lease or tenancy agreement.

*sub-paragraph (b)* excepts tenancies at will. The essence of such tenancies is that they are terminable forthwith by either party at any time. However, this exception does not extend to paragraph (4): where there is a tenancy at will of a dwelling-house, 4 weeks notice must be given.

**Termination by surrender**

53.—(1) A tenancy may be terminated by surrender –

(a) by writing signed by both the landlord and the tenant; or

(b) by such unequivocal conduct of both the landlord and the tenant as is inconsistent with the continuance of the lease.

(2)  The surrender of the tenancy of part of the premises does not in any way prejudice or affect the rights of the landlord with respect to the rest of the premises.

(3)  Where a tenancy is surrendered for the purpose of obtaining a new tenancy in its place –

(a) there is no need for a surrender of any sub-tenancy derived out of it;

(b) the tenant under the new lease is entitled to the same rights in respect of any breach of his sub-tenant's obligations as if the original tenancy had not been surrendered but were still vested in him;

(c) each sub-tenant is entitled to the premises comprised in his sub-tenancy (subject to performance of his obligations) as if the tenancy out of which the sub-tenancy was derived had not been surrendered.

# EXPLANATORY NOTE

ARTICLE 53

Property Bill Cl. 192
Deasy's Act ss. 7,8,44
LPA 1925 s.150

This Article provides for the termination of a tenancy by surrender.

*Paragraph (1)* provides that termination by surrender occurs –

*sub-paragraph (a)* – when both parties execute an instrument of surrender.

*sub-paragraph (b)* – when the parties by their unequivocal conduct show that they both regard the tenancy as no longer continuing.

*Paragraph (2)* allows part of the demised premises to be surrendered without the landlord's rights in respect of the rest (and, in particular, his right to recover the amount of rent properly apportionable to the rest) being affected.

*Paragraph (3)* deals with the consequences where a tenancy out of which a sub-tenancy has been carved is surrendered in order that a new tenancy may be granted in its place.

*sub-paragraph (a)* – there is no need for the sub-tenancy to be surrendered before the head-tenancy is surrendered.

*sub-paragraph (b)* – the tenant under the new head-tenancy has the same power to enforce his sub-tenant's obligations as if there had been no surrender.

*sub-paragraph (c)* – the rights of the sub-tenant continue as if there has been no surrender.

The Article contains no provision about the effects of the surrender of a lease out of which a sub-tenancy has been carved where no new lease is granted, because this is dealt with in Article 9. It is dealt with separately in this way because Article 9 refers to merger as well as surrender.

**Surrender of tenancy by tenant on destruction of, or damage to, premises**

**54.**—(1) Where the premises have been rendered incapable of being reasonably used for the purposes of the tenancy because of the destruction of or damage to them, or any part of them, by reason of fire or of tempest, flood or other inevitable accident, the tenant may serve –

(a) on the landlord, and

(b) on every other person ("the third party") who to his knowledge or belief has or may have an estate or interest in or derived out of the tenancy,

a notice of his intention to surrender the tenancy.

(2) If no notice of objection to the surrender is served on the tenant by the landlord or the third party within the period of four weeks from the date of service of the tenant's notice under paragraph (1), the tenancy terminates upon the expiration of that period.

(3) If within the period mentioned in paragraph (2) the landlord or the third party serves on the tenant notice of objection to the termination of the tenancy, the tenancy does not terminate; but the tenant may by action against the landlord, joining the third party (if any) as a defendant, apply to the court for an order terminating the tenancy.

(4) On an application under paragraph (3), the court may either dismiss the application or terminate the tenancy or vary the terms of, and obligations under, the tenancy (either for a limited period or permanently), and may make such further order as it considers appropriate.

(5) In this Article "the purpose of the tenancy" means the purpose for which the premises were being used by the tenant immediately before the destruction or damage mentioned in paragraph (1), or, if they were not then being used by him, the purpose for which he last used them or any other purpose for which he might reasonably be expected to use them if they had not been destroyed or damaged.

# EXPLANATORY NOTE

ARTICLE 54 Deasy's Act s. 40

This Article permits the tenant to surrender his tenancy where the premises have been destroyed or substantially damaged by fire or by tempest, flood or other inevitable accident. It follows from Article 30, which excepts damage caused by these events from the scope of the obligation to repair. Article 30 applies only to tenancies created after the commencement of the Order. In relation to pre-Order tenancies, section 40 of Deasy's Act applied only where the lease did not contain a tenant's express covenant to repair: the Article applies whether there is such a covenant or not, but see Schedule 2, paragraph 7.

*Paragraph (1)* applies where, in consequence of fire or some inevitable accident the premises are destroyed or are damaged to an extent which renders them incapable of being reasonably used for the purpose of the tenancy (defined in paragraph (5)). The tenant may serve on his landlord, and on his mortgagee or sub-tenant if he has one, notice of his intention to surrender the tenancy.

*Paragraph (2)* gives the landlord and the third party 4 weeks in which to object. If an objection is duly served, the tenant can ask the court to terminate the tenancy under paragraphs (4) and (5); if there is no objection the tenancy terminates on the expiration of 4 weeks.

*Paragraph (3)* applies where the landlord or a mortgagee or sub-tenant objects to the surrender of the tenancy. The tenant may apply to the court for an order terminating the tenancy. On such an application the court, under paragraph (4), may dismiss the application, or terminate the tenancy or vary the terms and obligations of the tenancy and may make such consequential order (e.g. an order about the matters mentioned in Article 60) as it thinks fit.

*Paragraph (4)* gives the court wide powers to deal with an application.

*Paragraph (5)* defines "the purpose of the tenancy" for paragraph (1) as the purpose for which the premises were being used by the tenant immediately before they were damaged or destroyed, or, if he was not then using them, the purpose for which he had last used them or any other purpose for which he might reasonably be expected to use them. Thus, the tenant might argue that he had intended to adapt the (vacant) premises for the storage of a particular kind of goods and that the damage rendered this impracticable.

**Protection of premises, or termination of tenancy, where premises believed to be abandoned**

**55.**—(1) Where –

(a) the landlord believes on reasonable grounds that the premises have been abandoned by the tenant; and

(b) some rent has been unpaid for four weeks, whether the rent was formally demanded or not,

paragraphs (2) to (5) apply.

(2) The landlord may take such reasonable action as he considers necessary to prevent deterioration of, or damage to, the premises or entry by trespassers, using such force as is necessary (but no more), and is not answerable for doing so except to the extent (if any) that his action, or any subsequent act or omission of his, prevents or hinders the tenant from entering and enjoying the premises.

(3) The landlord may serve on the tenant, and on every other person ("the third party") who to his knowledge or belief has or may have an estate or interest in or derived out of the tenancy, or is in occupation of the premises, a notice stating –

(a) that the landlord believes the premises to have been abandoned; and

(b) that the landlord is exercising his power under this Article to terminate the tenancy; and

(c) that, accordingly, the tenancy will terminate on the expiration of the period of eight weeks from the date of service of the notice, unless a notice of objection is received within that period.

(4) If no notice of objection to the termination of the tenancy is served on the landlord by the tenant or the third party (if any) within the period mentioned in paragraph (3)(c), the tenancy terminates upon the expiration of that period.

(5) If within the period mentioned in paragraph (3)(c) the tenant or the third party serves on the landlord a notice of objection to the termination of the tenancy, the tenancy does not terminate; but this provision does not preclude the landlord from making an application to the court under Article 57.

(6) This Article does not prejudice any provision of Part II of the Family Law (Miscellaneous Provisions) (Northern Ireland) Order 1984.

# EXPLANATORY NOTE

ARTICLE 55                                    cf. Housing (NI) O. 1983 Art.
                                              41

This Article allows the landlord to terminate a tenancy where the premises appear to have been abandoned by the tenant and no objection is made to him.

*Paragraph (1)* makes the Article applicable where –

*sub-paragraph (a):* the landlord believes in reasonable grounds that the premises have been abandoned; and

*sub-paragraph (b):* some rent has been unpaid for 4 weeks.

*Paragraph (2)* gives the landlord power to protect the premises from damage caused by, e.g., the entry of rain, or from intruders. The action he takes for this purpose must be reasonable and he must use no more force than is necessary. If he observes these conditions he is not answerable to the tenant (should the tenant turn up again) for his action, except where that action (e.g. changing the lock) or any subsequent act (e.g. refusing the tenant a key for the new lock) stops the tenant having full enjoyment of the premises.

*Paragraph (3)* gives the landlord a qualified right to terminate the tenancy. In order to exercise the right he must serve on the tenant and on everyone else whom he knows or believes to have a derivative interest in the premises (e.g. a mortgagee or sub-tenant) or to be an occupier a notice reciting the fact that he believes the premises to have been abandoned and stating that the tenancy will terminate in 8 weeks' time unless an objection is received in the meantime.

*Paragraph (4)* provides for the termination of the tenancy if no objection is received. The landlord must be sure that no-one is lawfully residing in the premises (Article 65).

*Paragraph (5)* sets out the consequences of an objection to termination being received. The tenancy cannot be terminated under this Article, but that does not preclude the landlord from having recourse to the court under Article 57.

*Paragraph (6)* is a saving for Part II of the Family Law (Miscellaneous Provisions (Northern Ireland) Order 1984 which is concerned with the rights of a spouse in the matrimonial home.

**Termination of long-term tenancy by enlargement into fee simple**

**56.**—(1) This Article applies to a tenancy where –

(a) the unexpired residue of the term is not less than 50 years; and

(b) there is no trust or right of redemption in favour of the landlord; and

(c) there is incident to the reversion –

    (i) no rent (whether by reason of there being no rent originally reserved or because a rent has since been released or barred by lapse of time or ceased in any other way to be payable), or

    (ii) only a nominal rent (and for the purposes of this Article any rent of a yearly sum of less than £1, or a peppercorn or other rent having no money value, is a nominal rent).

(2) Whether or not a tenancy to which this Article applies is subject to an incumbrance, the tenant may by deed declare to the effect that the tenancy is enlarged into an estate in fee simple absolute in possession ("the fee simple estate") and may make application to the Registrar of Titles for registration of his title to the fee simple estate.

(3) On an application under paragraph (2) –

(a) if the tenancy is in respect of a registered leasehold estate, section 27 of the Land Registration Act (Northern Ireland) 1970 applies (the references in that section to the leasehold estate's being converted or having not been converted being read as references to that estate's being or having not been the subject of a deed of declaration under paragraph (2));

(b) if the tenancy is not in respect of a registered leasehold estate and the application is made in such manner and subject to such conditions as may be prescribed by Land Registry Rules, the Registrar of Titles ("the Registrar") may register the tenant's title to the fee simple estate in accordance with the tenant's deed of declaration with such class of title as, after due examination of the title of the premises, appears to the Registrar to be appropriate (and, until the tenant's title to the fee simple estate is so registered, the deed under paragraph (2) has no effect).

(4) Upon registration of the title to the fee simple estate –

(a) that estate of the class shown in the register becomes vested in the tenant; and

(b) the reversion expectant upon the tenancy, and the reversion expectant upon any superior leasehold estate in the premises, is extinguished (without prejudice to any rights of the reversioner in respect of land other than the premises).

(5) Except where the Registrar is satisfied that the premises were subject to no superior rent (other than a rent such as is mentioned in paragraph (1)(c)(ii)) on the date of the execution of the deed under paragraph (2), the Registrar shall enter a note to the effect that the fee simple estate is subject to a rentcharge of so much (if any) of any superior

rent as would have been redeemed by virtue of Article 17(1) of the Ground Rents (Northern Ireland) Order 1989 ("the Ground Rents Order") if a ground rent to which the premises were subject had been redeemed under that Order on that date: such a note may be discharged in accordance with Land Registry Rules.

(6) The fee simple estate is subject to all the same trusts, powers, interests, rights and equities, and to all the same obligations, as it would have been subject to if the tenancy had yielded a monetary rent (other than a nominal rent) which had been redeemed (and the tenancy consequently enlarged into a fee simple) under the Ground Rents Order, and those obligations may be enforced by the same persons and in the same manner as if that Order applied.

(7) Where before the commencement of the Property Order land held for a leasehold estate was mortgaged by sub-demise or an assignment of the lease and, whether before or after that commencement, the right of redemption has become barred, the mortgagee may exercise the right of a tenant under this Article, if the requirements of this Article are otherwise satisfied, instead of exercising the right conferred on him by Article 130(5) of the Property Order to declare the leasehold estate to be vested in him discharged from the mortgage.

# EXPLANATORY NOTE

ARTICLE 56

Property Bill Cl. 193
CA 1881 s.65
CA 1882 s.11
LPA 1925 s.153

This Article allows a long leasehold to be enlarged into a fee simple if it is subject to no rent or only a nominal rent.

*Paragraph (1)* describes the leases to which the Article does or does not apply. For the Article to apply –

*sub-paragraph (a)* – The unexpired residue of the term must be not less than 50 years.

*sub-paragraph (b)* – There must be no trust or right of redemption (as where the lease was essentially a mortgage) in favour of the reversioner to the lease. (See also paragraph (7)).

*sub-paragraph (c)* – The lease must be either subject to no rent or subject only to a nominal rent (ie a rent of less than £1 a year). A lease is subject to no rent if it was originally granted without a rent or if (although a rent was originally payable) the landlord's right to recover it has been lost (e.g. because he has released it or because it has become statute-barred under Article 73(1)). If the rent is not a monetary one (e.g. it is a peppercorn), it is treated as nominal.

*Paragraph (2)* empowers the tenant of a leasehold estate to which the Article applies to execute a deed declaring that his estate is enlarged into a fee simple and to apply to the Registrar of Titles for registration of his freehold title.

*Paragraph (3)* provides for registration of the new title in the Land Registry –

*sub-paragraph (a)* – If title is already registered, section 27 of the Land Registration Act (Northern Ireland) 1970 applies (this directs the Registrar of Titles to cancel the entry in the register of leaseholders and register the new title in – for this type of transaction – the register of freeholders). But as the section is directed to the situation where the deed is expressed by statute to itself effect the elevation of title, and as this Article postpones the elevation until registration has been completed, some minor modification is made in the wording of the section.

*sub-paragraph (b)* – If the title is not already registered, then, if the application complies with Land Registry Rules, the Registrar may register the new fee simple estate with such class of title as he thinks appropriate.

*Paragraph (4)* – sets out the effects of registration –

*sub-paragraph (a)* – The fee simple estate becomes vested in the tenant; and

*sub-paragraph (b)* – The reversion on the leasehold estate and, where there are one or more superior leasehold estates, the reversion on it or

1451

each of them is extinguished. This settles the doubt raised by Challis's Law of Real Property (3rd Ed.) pages 333 and 334.

*Paragraph (5)* It may be clear to the Registrar that there is no superior rent payable out of the premises (except a nominal or non-monetary rent). If it is not clear, he must enter a note on the folio safeguarding so much of any superior rents as is referable to the premises.

*Paragraph (6)* makes the fee simple estate subject to the same obligations as if the tenancy had been subject to a substantial money rent redeemed under the Ground Rents (Northern Ireland) Order 1989. That Order makes a fee simple estate acquired under it a graft on the former leasehold estate, thus carrying forward all equitable obligations; easements, profits and some covenants are also expressly carried forward.

*Paragraph (7)* extends the benefit of the Article to a mortgagee where the mortgage was created before the commencement of the Property Order by sub-demise or assignment of a lease and the right of redemption is barred under Article 35 of the Limitation (Northern Ireland) Order 1989. Article 130(5) allows such a mortgagee to take over the leasehold title of the mortgagor; this paragraph allows him, instead, to claim the fee simple.

## Power of court to deal with breaches of obligation

**57.**—(1) Where, during the continuance of a tenancy, the tenant or landlord ("the defendant") is in breach of an obligation under the tenancy, the landlord or tenant ("the plaintiff") may make an application to the court under this Article ("the application").

(2)  It is not necessary for the application to request the court to make any particular order under this Article, and where it does make such a request the discretion of the court to make any other order is not affected.

(3)  In the proceedings on the application, the court shall consider whether, having regard to the evidence brought before it (including any evidence disclosing a breach of obligation on the part of the plaintiff) the relation of landlord and tenant ought or ought not to continue (that is to say, whether the tenant is so unsatisfactory a tenant that he ought not, in all the circumstances, to remain tenant of the premises, or the landlord is so unsatisfactory a landlord that the tenant ought not, in all the circumstances, to remain bound by the tenancy), and –

(a)  if the court considers that the relation ought to continue, the court may make such orders as it considers appropriate for remedying any breach of obligation by either the defendant or the plaintiff proved before it, including –

    (i)  an order for the payment of all or part of any arrears of rent, or all or part of any other sums payable under the lease;

    (ii)  an order for the payment of damages by either party to the other;

    (iii)  an order for the discontinuance of continuing breaches of obligation;

    (iv)  an order for specific performance of a landlord's obligation or a tenant's obligation;

    (v)  orders for the giving of security or the finding of sureties by the tenant for his good behaviour and for his future observance of his obligations;

(b)  if the court considers –

    (i)  that the relation ought not to continue because of an insolvency event affecting the tenant (within the meaning of Article 51), but

    (ii)  that the tenancy should continue in favour of a person who is willing to accept an assignment on reasonable terms (if such a person can be found) and in relation to whom it would be unreasonable for the landlord to withhold a licence (if the landlord's licence for an assignment of the tenancy is necessary),

the court may make an order for the assignment of the tenancy;

(c)  if the court considers that the relation ought not to continue and that the tenancy should be terminated, the court may make an order terminating the tenancy and may also make such other orders as it considers appropriate, including –

    (i) an order for recovery of the premises by the landlord;

    (ii) an order for the payment of all or part of any arrears or apportionment of rent, or all or part of any other sums payable under the lease;

    (iii) an order for the payment of damages by either party to the other;

    (iv) an order for the payment of compensation by the landlord to the tenant for the loss by the tenant of the benefit of the tenancy;

    (v) an order for the payment by either party to the other of compensation for any other loss suffered or expense incurred by that other in consequence of the termination of the tenancy.

(4) The compensation awarded by an order under paragraph (3)(c)(iv) or (v) may be assessed as if the lease were a contract which could be terminated through a repudiatory breach on the part of the party to whom the order is directed, and as if it were so terminated at the date on which the order under paragraph (3)(c) terminates the tenancy.

(5) In considering whether to make an order under paragraph (3)(a), (b) or (c), the court shall have regard to all the circumstances, including –

    (a) whether the plaintiff acted reasonably in making the application;

    (b) whether the party against whom a breach of obligation is proved had knowledge of the breach, and, if the breach is remediable, had a reasonable opportunity, or has taken reasonable steps, to remedy it;

    (c) whether and to what extent the tenant and the landlord have continued, during the currency of the proceedings consequent on the application, to observe their respective obligations;

and, in considering whether the relation of landlord and tenant ought or ought not to continue, the court may have regard to the course of behaviour of both parties throughout the tenancy and in particular to any past breaches of obligations, including breaches which have been the subject of implied or express waiver, other breaches which, apart from this provision, either party would be precluded from pleading and breaches which have been remedied either with or without recourse to the court.

(6) Pending final determination of the application, the court may make such interim orders as it considers appropriate, including –

    (a) orders for the remedying of any breach of a tenant's or landlord's obligation;

    (b) orders (which may be conditional) for the suspension or variation of the performance of all or any of the obligations of the tenant or the landlord, either as between themselves or in relation to third parties who have become parties to the action;

(c) orders for the giving of security or the finding of sureties by the tenant while he remains in possession of the premises for his good behaviour and for his future observance of his obligations;

and may vary or revoke any such order by a further order under this paragraph.

(7)   An order under paragraph (6)(b) suspending the performance of a tenant's obligation may, in particular, permit the tenant to withhold from the landlord payment of the rent or any other sums payable under the lease (or any part of the rent or such sums), subject to any conditions specified in the order, until –

(a)   the order is revoked; or

(b)   the landlord makes good any breach of a landlord's obligation specified in the order; or

(c)   an order is made under paragraph (3)(a), (b) or (c).

(8)   While an order under paragraph (6)(b) permitting the withholding of rent or other sums is in force, the tenant is not in breach of any tenant's obligation by reason only of his not paying to the landlord any rent or other sums to which the order applies; but this paragraph has effect only where all the conditions (if any) of the order are complied with.

(9)   Where, in an order under paragraph (3)(a)(i) or (c)(ii), the court orders payment of only part of any arrears of rent or part of any other sum, the balance of those arrears or that sum is irrecoverable.

(10)   Where the court makes an order terminating the tenancy it may suspend the order subject to such conditions as it thinks fit with or without leave for either party to relist the application if any specified condition is complied with; and where the application is relisted and comes before the court again, the court may revoke the order to terminate and vary or revoke any order made in conjunction with it.

(11)   Without prejudice to paragraph (3)(b) or Article 51(3), in this Article and Article 58 any reference to a breach of obligation includes a reference to an event such as is mentioned in Article 51(3)(b) or (c).

(12)   This Article does not prejudice the power of the court to give effect to any set-off.

# EXPLANATORY NOTE

ARTICLE 57 Property Bill Cls. 197, 200

This Article sets out the powers exercisable by the court where, during the continuance of a tenancy, the landlord alleges a breach of a tenant's obligation or the tenant alleges a breach of a landlord's obligation.

*Paragraph (1)* provides for an application to the court (defined in Article 2(2)) by the aggrieved party. In terms the paragraph applies to the case where there is a breach of obligation, but paragraph (11) and Article 51(3) extend it also to cases where the landlord has sought to protect himself by a limitation or condition (instead of the more usual covenant or agreement) or where there is an insolvency event (defined in Article 51(5)) affecting the tenant.

*Paragraph (2)* renders it unnecessary for the application to ask the court to make any particular order. The court will review the situation under paragraphs (3), (4) and (5) and make such order or orders as seem to it appropriate. This paragraph does not enable either party to take the other by surprise, because Article 58(3)(a) requires the applicant to specify the breaches he will rely upon with particularity.

*Paragraph (3)* requires the court, in the light of the evidence brought before it, to decide whether or not the relation of landlord and tenant has broken down.

*sub-paragraph (a)* if the court thinks the relation has not broken down, it may make such orders as it chooses for remedying the breach, including orders for the payment of arrears of rent or damages, for the discontinuance of continuing breaches, for specific performance, and for the giving by the tenant of security, or the finding by the tenant of sureties, for his future conduct.

*sub-paragraph (b)* if the court thinks the relation has broken down because of insolvency of the tenant or his surety, but that the tenancy can be sold to a suitable assignee (thus preserving at least part of its value for the benefit of the tenant or his creditors), the court may direct a sale of the tenancy.

*sub-paragraph (c)* if the court thinks the relation has broken down and the tenancy should be terminated it may make an order terminating the tenancy. It may also make such ancillary orders as it thinks appropriate, including an order for payment of arrears of rent or damages and, where the breakdown was the landlord's fault, an order for the payment by the landlord to the tenant of compensation for the tenant's loss of his tenancy.

*Paragraph (4)* allows compensation for loss of the benefit of a tenancy or consequential loss to be awarded in the same way as for a contract terminated by repudiatory (i.e. anticipatory) breach. This enables the tenant to claim recompense for the value of the tenancy of which he is deprived and consequential losses as though he had been evicted from the whole premises. These losses could include removal expenses, the cost of setting up in new premises (but not the cost of the premises themselves) and, in the case of a business tenant, loss of profits or goodwill. Cf. McGregor on Damages, 14th Ed, 770, 771.

*Paragraph (5)* requires the court to take account of all the circumstances before it decides to make any or what order. In particular, it should consider –

*sub-paragraph (a)* did the applicant act reasonably in bringing proceedings? Or is the damage caused by the breach trivial?

*sub-paragraph (b)* did the applicant give the other party a reasonable opportunity to remedy the breach (if it is capable of remedy), e.g. by giving him notice of the breach and time to put it right? And has the other party taken reasonable steps to remedy it?

*sub-paragraph (c)* have the parties observed their obligations since the application was made?

In order to help the court decide whether the relation has broken down, the court may look at the whole course of behaviour of the parties throughout the tenancy. Past breaches of obligations will be relevant for this survey even though they would no longer be capable of founding an application under paragraph (1) because, e.g., the breaches were ultimately corrected or they were waived.

*Paragraph (6)* empowers the court to make interim orders during the course of the proceedings. These may include –

*sub-paragraph (a)* orders for remedying any breach of an obligation. The court, although tempted to treat the landlord-tenant relation as having broken down, may be inclined to give the defaulter a last chance and so defer the making of a termination order until he has had further opportunity to take remedial action. Thus, the court may make an interim order for specific performance of a repairing obligation.

*sub-paragraph (b)* orders suspending or varying the performance of the obligations of either party pending the result of the proceedings – e.g., suspending the payment of rent until some obligation of the landlord's has been complied with (paragraph (7)). Such an order in favour of the tenant may be appropriate where the landlord's breach of obligation has deprived the tenant of possession of the premises.

*sub-paragraph (c)* orders requiring the tenant to give security for his acting as a good tenant while he retains possession of the premises.

*Paragraph (7)* specifically allows an interim order to suspend the tenant's obligation to pay rent or other sums until the landlord makes good some breach of obligation (or until the interim order is revoked or a final order is made).

*Paragraph (8)* excuses the tenant from his obligation to pay the rent or other sums to which an interim order applies, so long as the order is in force and any conditions imposed by it are complied with. On the revocation of the order, the landlord's right to the money withheld revives.

1457

*Paragraph (9)* provides that where, in a final order, only part of rent in arrear or other sums is ordered to be paid, the balance is irrecoverable.

*Paragraph (10)* empowers the court to suspend the operation of a termination order subject to conditions. The conditions may or may not affect the termination. For example, the court may wish to give the tenant an opportunity to settle his affairs or find new accommodation before the termination takes effect; or it may hope that, being now faced with the reality of termination, the tenant will at last observe his obligations – in this event, permission may be given to re-list the case and, upon its coming up again, the court may revoke the termination order. As to the county court, see Article 77(1).

*Paragraph (11)* completes the adaptation of the Article (and also adapts Article 58) for the purposes of an event to which Article 51(3)(b) applies (that is, an event which normally would be, but in a particular case is not, framed as constituting a breach of obligation) or for the purposes of an insolvency event affecting the tenant (Article 51(3)(c)).

*Paragraph (12)* makes it clear that any right of set-off is not affected (cf. section 48 of Deasy's Act).

## Proceedings under Article 57

**58.**—(1) In this Article, "the application" means an application under Article 57.

(2) Where the application is founded upon a breach of the tenant's obligation to pay rent, it may be made whether the rent was formally demanded or not, but shall not be made until some rent has been unpaid for four weeks.

(3) No prior notice of intention to make the application is necessary, but the plaintiff shall –

(a) specify in the application with particularity the breach upon which he intends to rely;

(b) serve notice of the application –

   (i) where he is not himself in occupation of the premises, on any person in occupation of them other than the defendant or a member of the defendant's household;

   (ii) on every other person who to his knowledge or belief has or may have an estate or interest in or derived out of the tenancy likely to be affected by an order made in the proceedings on the application;

   (iii) on any other person specified by the court;

(c) serve on the defendant notice of the persons on whom he has so served notice, whereupon the defendant may require notice to be served on any other person, as having an estate or interest in or derived out of the tenancy;

and a person on whom notice of the application is served under this paragraph is entitled to appear and be heard on the hearing of the application, and may be made a party to the proceedings.

(4) Paragraph (3) does not preclude the court from having regard under Article 57(5)(b) to whether the defendant had knowledge of the breach and, if the breach is remediable, had a reasonable opportunity to remedy it; and in deciding whether or not to make any particular order, or the terms of an order, (including an order for costs) the court, if satisfied that the defendant would have taken appropriate action to remedy the breach had the plaintiff given him time to do so, may take account of that.

(5) The defendant may apply for a stay of the proceedings on the application on the ground that continuance for the time being of the proceedings would be oppressive because he has taken or is taking steps to remedy the breach.

(6) In proceedings on the application where it relates to a tenancy for a period exceeding one year, if no notice has been served on a mortgagee under paragraph (3) the court shall inquire whether there is a mortgagee and, if there is, shall, if necessary, adjourn the proceedings in order to enable notice to be served on him; and where such proceedings are taken only for a breach of a tenant's obligation which is capable of being fulfilled

by a mortgagee and the mortgagee gives an undertaking to the court to fulfil it on behalf of the tenant, the court may dismiss the application.

(7)   Where the court would be minded to make an order under Article 57(3)(a) except that it is not satisfied that the party against whom the order would be directed is willing, and is likely to be able, to comply with the order, the court may conclude that the relation of landlord and tenant ought not to continue; and, in considering this, account may be taken of the fact (if it is the case) that the party in question has already been given adequate time to remedy any relevant breach of obligation and has not done so.

(8)   Where two or more persons are entitled to the tenancy as joint tenants and some one or more of them wish to have the tenancy terminated and the other or others do not, the court may, on the application of that other or of those others, vest the tenancy solely in him or them and make orders under Article 57(3)(a), if satisfied that its doing so would not unjustifiably prejudice the landlord.

(9)   Where there are joint landlords, an order may be made under Article 57(3)(a) for the remedying of a breach of a landlord's obligation only if they all agree to obey it; and if the court is minded to make a particular order and the landlords do not all agree, the court may conclude that the relation of landlord and tenant ought not to continue.

(10)   Where, pending the determination of the application, the landlord disposes of his estate in the premises, the court may set the disposition aside if satisfied that it is calculated to defeat the course of justice.

(11)   Where the application is grounded upon a breach of a tenant's obligation, the court may order the tenant to reimburse the landlord any reasonable costs properly incurred by the landlord –

(a)   in ascertaining the existence and nature of the breach and in deciding upon his course of action;

(b)   in the preparation and service on the tenant of any notice of the breach;

(c)   in the preparation and service of any notice required to be served under this Article.

(12)   An order under Article 57 terminating a tenancy is binding on the following persons in addition to those who are or are represented by parties to the proceedings, have notice of the proceedings or (by reason of having a like estate or interest as any party) are to be treated as privy to the proceedings, that is to say, all persons, whether ascertained or of full capacity or not, then entitled to the benefits or bound by the obligations of the tenancy or thereafter capable of becoming entitled to enforce those benefits or bound by those obligations.

# EXPLANATORY NOTE

ARTICLE 58 Property Bill Cl. 198

This Article contains provisions about the procedure under Article 57. It must be read subject to Article 57(11) which extends references to breaches of obligations to include, in appropriate contexts, references to events such as are referred to in Article 51(3)(b) or (c).

*Paragraph (1)* defines "the application" as an application under Article 57.

*Paragraph (2)* Where the relevant breach of obligation is a failure to pay rent, this paragraph dispenses with the need for a formal demand for rent; but some rent must be in arrear for four weeks before an application can be made under Article 57(1).

*Paragraph (3)* dispenses with any need for a formal notice of breach of an obligation to be served before an application is made to the court under Article 57(1) (but, because of Article 57(5)(b) and paragraph (4) of this Article, prior notice will usually be a practical necessity).
The applicant must –

*sub-paragraph (a)* give, in the application, particulars of the breaches of obligation he relies on;

*sub-paragraph (b)* serve notice of the application on –

    (i) the occupier of the premises (if he is not himself the occupier);

    (ii) anyone else who has an interest in the tenancy;

    (iii) anyone else specified by the court;

*sub-paragraph (c)* notify the defendant of the persons served with notice under sub-paragraph (b). The defendant may require some additional person to be also notified.
A third party notified under this paragraph may appear and be heard. As to sub-tenants and mortgagees, see Article 61.

*Paragraph (4)* empowers the court, in deciding what order (if any) it will make, to take account of the likelihood of the defendant's having remedied a breach of obligation had he been given an opportunity to do so.

*Paragraph (5)* empowers the defendant to ask the court for a stay of the proceedings to give him time to remedy the breach of obligation complained of.

*Paragraph (6)* applies where an application is made under Article 57(1) in the case of a tenancy for a period exceeding one year (see Article 2(3)). If no notice of the application has been served on a mortgagee, the court must inquire whether there is a mortgagee, and, if there is, must, if necessary, adjourn the proceedings to enable notice to be served on him. If the mortgagee appears and undertakes to discharge the obligation in respect of which the tenant is in default, the court may dismiss the application.

1461

*Paragraph (7)* makes the willingness and ability of a party against whom the court is inclined to make a remedial order a relevant factor. If it seems uncertain that the order will be obeyed (and past conduct is a consideration here), the court may conclude that the tenancy should be terminated.

*Paragraph (8)* deals with the case where joint tenants are in dispute as to whether the tenancy should be terminated. The court may vest the tenancy solely in those tenants who are willing to have the tenancy continue.

*Paragraph (9)* applies the contrary rule to joint landlords. If they do not all agree to a remedial order, the tenancy should be terminated.

*Paragraph (10)* is concerned with the case where, after an application has been made to the court, the landlord seeks to avoid some liability (for example, the liability to have a remedial or compensation order made against him) by conveying his estate in the premises to, say, an assetless company. The court is empowered to set the conveyance aside.

*Paragraph (11)* empowers the court to award to the landlord his costs (defined in section 46(2) of the Interpretation Act (Northern Ireland) 1954 as including expenses and other disbursements) incurred in taking technical or legal advice and issuing notices.

*Paragraph (12)* makes it clear that an order terminating a tenancy operates *in rem*. Cf. Article 182(5) of the Property Order. In particular, the order binds a squatter who is a statutory assignee of the tenancy under Article 240(1) of the Property Order.

### Powers of court following improper assignment

**59.**—(1) Where a tenant ("the assignor") has made an assignment of his tenancy to another person ("the assignee") in relation to all or part of the premises notwithstanding that –

(a) the lease imposed on him an obligation (with or without qualification by Article 44) not to assign the tenancy without the landlord's licence, and

(b) no such licence had been obtained, and

(c) where an application for a licence had been made and refused, it was not unreasonable for the landlord to have withheld a licence, or, where no such application had been made, it would not have been unreasonable for the landlord to have withheld a licence if an application had been made,

the landlord may make an application to the court under this Article ("the application").

(2) Both the assignor and the assignee shall be joined as defendants in the proceedings on the application.

(3) On the application, the court may make an order –

(a) directing the assignee to re-assign the tenancy to the assignor, where the assignor is willing to accept a re-assignment; or

(b) directing the assignee to assign the tenancy to some other person, where a person willing to accept an assignment on reasonable terms can be found and it would be unreasonable for the landlord to withhold a licence in relation to him; or

(c) terminating the tenancy.

(4) In the proceedings on the application, evidence may be given of any other breach of an obligation under the tenancy on the part of the assignor and of any breach of such an obligation on the part of the assignee or the landlord, and the court may make such orders as it considers appropriate in relation to any such breach, and may, in particular, make any order such as is mentioned in Article 57(3)(a)(i) to (v) or (c)(i) to (iii) and (v) as the case requires.

(5) Paragraphs (3), (6) and (11) of Article 58, so far as applicable, apply for the purposes of this Article, subject to any necessary modifications.

# EXPLANATORY NOTE

## ARTICLE 59

Article 57 is concerned with the position where the tenant who committed the breach of obligation is still the tenant at the time of the application to the court. This Article deals with the case where, because the breach of obligation was an improper assignment of the tenancy, the person who committed the breach is no longer tenant.

*Paragraph (1)* sets out the circumstances in which the Article applies, that is, where an assignment of the tenancy has been made in breach of an express obligation imposed by the lease, without the landlord's licence, and the facts are such as to justify the landlord in withholding a licence. In these circumstances the landlord may make an application to the court.

*Paragraph (2)* Both the assignor and the assignee should be cited as defendants.

*Paragraph (3)* The court may, as in its judgment seems best, either –

*sub-paragraph (a):* direct a re-assignment; or

*sub-paragraph (b):* direct an assignment to a third person, if a suitable assignee can be found; or

*sub-paragraph (c):* terminate the tenancy.

*Paragraph (4)* empowers the court to make ancillary orders for the remedying of other breaches of obligation proved before it. Such orders may be made against the landlord, the assignor or the assignee. Article 57(3)(a) is applied for this purpose, and, where the court terminates the tenancy, Article 57(3)(c) applies (except sub-paragraph (iv) relating to compensation to the tenant for loss of his tenancy, which is not appropriate because the tenant, having taken the assignment in breach of a clear provision of the lease, has only himself to blame for his loss).

*Paragraph (5)* applies Article 58(3), (6) and (11) for the purposes of this Article (identification of mortgagees and other holders of derivative interests; reimbursement of landlord's expenses).

*Consequences of termination*

**Position of parties after termination of tenancy**

**60.**—(1)  On the termination of a tenancy otherwise than by an order of the court under Article 57 or Article 59, –

(a)  the tenant remains liable to the landlord for any breach of a tenant's obligation committed by him during or in respect of the period when he was tenant; and

(b)  the landlord remains liable to the tenant for any breach of a landlord's obligation committed by him during the period when he was landlord;

but, where a tenancy is terminated under Article 54(2) or (4) because of destruction of or damage to the premises, or any part of them, by reason of fire or of tempest, flood or other inevitable accident, the tenant's liability to pay damages for a breach of an obligation to repair the premises does not extend to a breach where the circumstances are such as are mentioned in Article 49(2), except where the destruction or damage would not have occurred were it not for the breach.

(2)  In this Article "the tenant" and "the landlord" mean the persons who were, respectively, the tenant and the landlord immediately before the termination of the tenancy.

(3)  This Article does not prejudice the continuation after the termination of a tenancy of any liability of a former tenant or a former landlord which had previously continued under Article 38 or Article 40.

# EXPLANATORY NOTE

## ARTICLE 60

This Article provides for the continuing liability of the former tenant or landlord for breaches of obligation committed before the termination of a tenancy. It parallels Articles 38 and 40 which provide for a limited continuation of liability after the assignment of a tenancy or the conveyance of the reversion.

*Paragraph (1)* provides that –

*sub-paragraph (a):* the former tenant remains liable for breaches committed by him while he was tenant;

*sub-paragraph (b):* the former landlord remains liable for breaches committed while he was landlord.

The paragraph does not apply where the tenancy is terminated under Article 57 or Article 59, because in those cases the court is intended to resolve all disputes between the parties (see also Article 61). Where the tenancy is terminated under Article 54 because of damage or destruction caused by fire or inevitable accident, the tenant's continuing liability for breaches of obligation does not extend to a breach of an obligation to repair the premises where repairs are impossible or would be of no effective value, unless the breach was the ultimate cause of the destruction or damage.

*Paragraph (2)* defines who is "the tenant" or "the landlord" for the purposes of the Article – that is, those who held that position immediately before the termination.

*Paragraph (3)* makes it clear that the Article does not affect the position of an earlier tenant or landlord – that is, one who had assigned his tenancy to the pre-termination tenant or a predecessor in title of his, or who had conveyed his reversion to the pre-termination landlord or a predecessor in title of his.

## Position of third parties

**61.**—(1) Subject to the provisions of this Article, where the court makes an order under Article 57 or 59 terminating a tenancy (a "termination order") all estates and interests in or derived out of the tenancy and all rights and obligations conferred or imposed by or by virtue of the lease cease to exist; and for the purposes of this Article an order suspended under Article 57(10) is made when it ceases to be suspended.

(2)   Except where a vesting order is to be made under paragraph (3) or (5), the court shall not make a termination order unless it is satisfied –

   (a)  where there is a sub-tenant, either –

   (i) that he will be compensated for any loss flowing from the termination and that any objections he may have made are not sufficient to outweigh the desirability of termination taking place, or

   (ii) that he has consented to termination;

   (b)  where there is a mortgagee, –

   (i) that he will receive the amount of his debt or the value of his security, whichever is the less, or

   (ii) that he has consented to termination;

and where any other person who has an estate or interest in or derived out of the tenancy will suffer loss in consequence of the termination, the court may order the payment of compensation to him by the tenant.

(3)   Where the court makes a termination order, it may also, on the application of a sub-tenant of the premises or any part of them, make an order (a "vesting order") vesting the whole or part of the premises in the sub-tenant for the whole term of the sub-tenancy or any shorter term; but the court shall not vest the whole of the premises in a sub-tenant of part, if the landlord has offered the sub-tenant a lease for that part on the same terms as those on which he previously held as sub-tenant.

(4)   In making a vesting order, the court may impose such terms and conditions with respect to the tenancy as it thinks fit, and, in the case of an order in respect of part of the premises, may vest in the sub-tenant any ancillary rights or privileges previously enjoyed by the sub-tenant which it considers necessary for the reasonable use and enjoyment of that part.

(5)   The court may make a vesting order in favour of a mortgagee of the tenancy, whether or not the mortgage was effected by sub-demise, and, if it does so, paragraphs (3) and (4) apply with any necessary modifications and in particular, where the mortgage was effected otherwise than by sub-demise, as if the mortgagee were a sub-tenant for a term equivalent to the term of the tenancy less one day or such lesser term as the court thinks fit.

(6)   When a vesting order is made in favour of a mortgagee, it vests in the mortgagee a tenancy ("the vested tenancy") free from any right in the mortgagor to redeem, but the following provisions apply –

1467

(a) the mortgagor may bring an action for sale as if he were entitled to redeem;

(b) Article 117 of the Property Order applies to such an action as it applies to an action for sale alone, except that the court may not allow any time for redemption or for the payment of any mortgage money; and the mortgagor is a plaintiff to whom Article 117(3) (security for costs) applies; and for the purposes of Article 117, the "mortgaged property" is the vested tenancy;

(c) if the mortgagee assigns the vested tenancy, at law or in equity, Article 127 of the Property Order (duties in connection with sale) applies to the assignment as if it were an exercise of the mortgagee's statutory power of sale, and Article 132 applies to the proceeds thereof;

(d) if the mortgagee sub-lets, at law or in equity, all or part of premises comprised in the vested tenancy, Article 142 of the Property Order applies as if the mortgagee were exercising the leasing powers of a mortgagee in possession;

(e) where, by reason of any wilful default on the part of the mortgagee, the proceeds of a sale or assignment are, or the amount of any rent or fine reserved or taken on a sub-letting is, less than they or it would have been in the absence of such default, the mortgagee is liable to account to the mortgagor for the difference; and

(f) any mortgages which –

　(i) affected the tenancy ("the former tenancy") immediately before the making of the termination order, and

　(ii) then ranked in priority after the mortgage of the mortgagee in whose favour the vesting order is made;

affect the vested tenancy to the same extent and in the same order as they affected the former tenancy.

(7) Paragraphs (3) to (6) apply only to persons whose estates or interests were created before the commencement of proceedings under Article 57 or Article 59.

# EXPLANATORY NOTE

ARTICLE 61                                      Property Bill Cl. 199
                                                 C&LPA 1892 s. 4

This Article contains provisions for the protection of third parties where the court makes an order under Article 57 or Article 59 terminating a tenancy.

*Paragraph (1)* sets out the primary result of a tenancy's being terminated. All estates and interests derived out of it cease to exist. Paragraphs (2) to (5) contain consequential provisions for the protection of sub-tenants or mortgagees.

*Paragraph (2)* makes it clear that, where the tenant seeks and obtains a termination order, it is his responsibility to compensate all the holders of derivative interests who are adversely affected. The court, too, is under an obligation to satisfy itself that sub-tenants and mortgagees who have not consented to the termination are adequately safeguarded.

*Paragraph (3)* empowers the court, on the application of a sub-tenant, to elevate the sub-tenancy into a tenancy. This is a new tenancy, not a transfer of the tenancy that has been terminated: *Chelsea Estates Investment Trust Co. Ltd.* v. *Marche* [1955] Ch. 328; *Hammersmith London BC* v. *Toy Shop Centres Ltd.* [1989] 2 All ER 655. Where the sub-tenancy extends to only part of the premises the new tenancy may extend to that part or, if the court thinks fit, it may extend to the whole of the premises: but it cannot be extended to the whole of the premises if the landlord has offered the sub-tenant a letting of the part he previously occupied on the same terms as before. The power to elevate a sub-tenancy of part into a tenancy of the whole could save the landlord from being left with partly occupied premises on his hands in a case where it might be difficult to find a tenant for the remainder: any consequential changes in the terms of the tenancy which are needed can be ordered by the court under paragraph (4).

*Paragraph (4)* empowers a court making a vesting order under paragraph (3) to impose such terms and conditions on the tenancy created by the order as it thinks fit. In particular, where a sub-tenant of part of the premises enjoyed any ancillary rights over other parts of the premises (e.g. a right of way), the court may confirm him in those rights in his new capacity as tenant. As to the operation of vesting orders, see Article 15(3) of the Property Order.

*Paragraph (5)* empowers the court to make a vesting order under paragraph (3) for the benefit of a mortgagee, not only where the mortgage is by sub-demise (and therefore the mortgagee is in law a sub-tenant) but also where the mortgage was effected by assignment of the tenancy or by a registered charge (in the case of registered land) or where it is a charge by way of legal mortgage under Article 114 of the Property Order (cf. *Grand Junction Canal Co.* v. *Bates* [1954] 2 QB 160). In the latter case the mortgagee is treated as though he were a sub-tenant for a term of a day less than the term of the lease (*Chelsea Estates*

*Investment Trust Co. Ltd.* v. *Marche* at p. 335) or such lesser term as the court thinks fit.

*Paragraph (6)* sets out special rules for a case where a tenancy is vested in a mortgagee. Although the mortgagor's right to redeem the premises is lost (because otherwise a landlord who had instituted proceedings under Article 57 or Article 59 may, following redemption, find himself again saddled with the same unsatisfactory tenant), the mortgagor retains his interest in proceeds of sale or sub-letting.

*sub-paragraph (a)* the mortgagor may bring an action for sale of the premises as if he were still entitled to redeem.

*sub-paragraph (b)* the proceedings are the same as if the mortgagor still had an equity of redemption in the premises; the mortgagor may be required to give security for costs; but, as the mortgagor now has no right to redeem, there is no question of the court allowing him time to do so.

*sub-paragraph (c)* an assignment of the new tenancy by the mortgagee is treated as the exercise of his statutory power of sale, and money received for the assignment is treated as proceeds of sale so that any surplus proceeds (after paying costs and discharging the mortgage debt and any mortgages of lower rank) are paid to the mortgagor.

*sub-paragraph (d)* on a sub-letting by the mortgagee any fine is dealt with in the same way as proceeds of sale.

*sub-paragraph (e)* the mortgagee is liable on the basis of "wilful default" where a sale of the tenancy by him produces a smaller fine or rent than it should have done if he had conducted the sale properly.

*sub-paragraph (f)* mortgages of lower rank than that of the mortgagee who has become the new tenant affect the new tenancy in the same way as they affected the terminated tenancy.

*Paragraph (7)* makes it clear that the power of the court to make an order vesting a tenancy in a sub-tenant or mortgagee applies only where the creation of the sub-tenancy or mortgage preceded the institution of proceedings under Article 57 or 59.

**Ejectment for overholding**

**62.** Where a former tenant ("the tenant") after a lawful determination of his tenancy, does not give up possession of the premises to his landlord, the landlord may bring an action in the court for recovery of the premises from the tenant or any other person in occupation of them.

# EXPLANATORY NOTE

ARTICLE 62                                Property Bill Cl.188(1),(2),(4)
                                          Deasy's Act ss. 72, 75, 76

This Article facilitates a landlord in obtaining possession of the premises after a tenancy has ended. It empowers a landlord who has not been given by the former tenant possession of the demised premises after the termination of the tenancy to take an action in the court against the tenant or anyone else in occupation for recovery of the premises. By virtue of Article 12(1)(a) of the County Courts (Northern Ireland) Order1980, an action under this paragraph may be brought in the county court where the annual value of the land does not exceed £500. Reference is made in the paragraph to "a former tenant" because the definition of "tenant" in Article 2(2) excludes a tenant at sufferance.

A limited jurisdiction in ejectment for overholding is also conferred on a court of summary jurisdiction by Articles 67 to 71 of the Magistrates' Courts (Northern Ireland) Order 1981.

**Payments by tenant or occupier overholding**

**63.**—(1) A former tenant or an occupier of any premises who over-holds the premises after the tenancy or occupation has been lawfully determined is liable to pay to the landlord or owner in respect of the period during which he so overholds an amount equal to the rent or other sum, if any, which would have accrued due for that period if the tenancy or occupation had not been determined.

(2) The amount payable under paragraph (1) is a debt recoverable summarily.

(3) Where in any proceedings the court orders recovery of the premises by the landlord or owner for breach of a tenant's obligation or for overholding, it may, in addition to ordering the payment of any rent or other sums or mesne profits claimed in the proceedings, order the payment of such further sums or mesne profits as may have accrued from the day on which the rent claimed fell due or the day to which the sums or mesne profits claimed were calculated to the day of the trial or such earlier day as the court may specify.

(4) In this Article "owner" means a person who has an estate or interest in the premises entitling him to possession of them.

# EXPLANATORY NOTE

ARTICLE 63

Property Bill Cls. 188(5),(6), 189
Deasy's Act s. 77
Magistrates' Courts (NI) Order 1981 Art. 69

This Article provides for the recovery of sums equivalent to rent in respect of any period following the termination of a tenancy during which the former tenant remains in occupation of the demised land. It makes a corresponding provision in respect of sums payable by an occupier (e.g. a licensee).

*Paragraph (1)* renders the tenant or occupier liable to pay to the landlord or owner, for any period during which he unlawfully remains in occupation after the tenancy or lawful occupation has ended, sums equivalent to the rent under the tenancy or other agreed sums.

*Paragraph (2)* makes amounts payable under paragraph (1) recoverable summarily as a debt. Proceedings may be taken in a magistrates' court irrespective of the amount of the debt (Magistrates' Courts (Northern Ireland) Order 1981 Art. 62(2)), or in the county court if the debt does not exceed £5,000 (County Courts (Northern Ireland) Order 1980 Art. 10(1)).

*Paragraph (3)* empowers the court to extend the period for which sums under paragraph(1) or mesne profits are payable up to the date of trial. "Mesne profits" are strictly damages for trespass: this Article is concerned only with the case where the occupation of the person from whom the profits are claimed had a lawful origin (see Article 69 for other cases).

*Paragraph (4)* defines "owner".

## PART VI

## PROTECTION AGAINST HARASSMENT AND EVICTION WITHOUT DUE PROCESS OF LAW

### Unlawful eviction or harassment of occupier

**64.**—(1) If any person unlawfully deprives the tenant of a dwelling-house of his occupation of the dwelling-house or any part of it, he is guilty of an offence unless he proves that he believed, and had reasonable cause to believe, that the tenant had ceased to reside in the dwelling-house.

(2) If any person with intent to cause the tenant of a dwelling-house –

(a) to give up the occupation of the dwelling-house or any part of it; or

(b) to refrain from exercising any right or pursuing any remedy in respect of the dwelling-house or any part of it;

does acts likely to interfere with the peace or comfort of the tenant or members of his household or persistently withdraws or withholds services reasonably required for the occupation of the dwelling-house as a residence, he is guilty of an offence.

(3) A person guilty of an offence under this Article is liable –

(a) on summary conviction, to a fine not exceeding level 5 on the standard scale;

(b) on conviction on indictment, to a fine or to imprisonment for a term not exceeding two years or to both.

1475

ARTICLE 64                              Rent Order Arts. 2(2), 54

This Article protects the tenant of a dwelling-house from unlawful eviction or harassment.

*Paragraph (1)* renders it an offence for any person unlawfully to deprive a tenant of his dwelling-house. A landlord taking possession under Article 55 because he believed the premises to have been abandoned by the tenant would not be acting unlawfully. He could take action under that Article only if his belief were based on reasonable grounds. Similarly this Article gives relief to any other person dispossessing the tenant if he proves that he believed, and had reasonable cause to believe, that the tenant had ceased to reside in the dwelling-house. The words "or attempts to do so" which appear in Article 54(1) of the Rent Order are omitted from this Article, because attempts are now provided for in Articles 3 and 5 of the Criminal Attempts and Conspiracy (Northern Ireland) Order 1983 (NI 13).

*Paragraph (2)* penalises harassment, that is, interference with the tenant's (or his household's) enjoyment of the premises or non-provision of services, where these things are done with the intention of causing the tenant to leave the house or not to enforce his rights.

*Paragraph (3)* sets the maximum penalties which may be imposed on conviction of an offence under the Article. These are –

*sub-paragraph (a)*: on summary conviction a fine not exceeding the amount on level 5 of the standard scale. The standard scale is that set out in Article 5 of the Fines and Penalties (Northern Ireland) Order 1984 (NI 3): the present amount for level 5 is £2,000 (Criminal Penalties etc. (Increase) Order (Northern Ireland) 1984 SR 1984 No. 253 Art. 2(4) Sch. 4).

*sub-paragraph (b)*: on conviction on indictment, either a fine (the amount of which is entirely at the discretion of the court) or imprisonment for up to 2 years or both.

*Paragraph (4)* of Article 54 of the Rent Order (conviction under the Article not to prejudice any civil liability or remedy) is omitted from this Article in reliance on section 20(4) of the Interpretation Act ("An enactment creating criminal liability for an act or omission which, apart from that enactment, would give rise to civil liability shall not operate to prejudice the civil liability").

**Prohibition of taking possession of dwelling-house lawfully occupied, without due process of law**

65.　Where the premises are let as a dwelling-house and any person is lawfully residing in them or any part of them, it is not lawful for the landlord or any other person to take possession of them otherwise than in pursuance of proceedings in a court.

# EXPLANATORY NOTE

ARTICLE 65                    Rent Order Art. 55

This Article requires a landlord or any other person (e.g. an assignor to whom Article 68 applies) to have recourse to court proceedings if he wishes to take possession of a dwelling-house in which (or in part of which) some person (not necessarily the tenant) is lawfully residing.

## Prohibition of eviction without due process of law

**66.**—(1) Where any premises have been let as a dwelling-house under a tenancy and –

   (a)  the tenancy ("the former tenancy") has come to an end, but

   (b)  the occupier continues to reside in the premises or part of them,

it is not lawful for the owner to enforce against the occupier, otherwise than in pursuance of proceedings in a court, his right to recover possession of the premises.

(2)  Paragraph (1), with the necessary modifications, applies where the owner's right to recover possession arises on the death of the tenant under a statutory tenancy.

(3)  In this Article –

"the occupier" means any person lawfully residing in the dwelling-house at the termination of the former tenancy;

"the owner" means the person who, as against the occupier, is entitled to possession of the premises.

ARTICLE 66                                    Rent Order Art. 56

This Article prohibits eviction from a dwelling-house, after termination of a tenancy, without due process of law.

*Paragraph (1)* makes it unlawful for a landlord to recover (except under a court order) possession of the premises, after a tenancy has terminated, so long as a person who was formerly lawfully residing in the premises is continuing to reside there.

*Paragraph (2)* applies the Article in the situation arising from the death of a statutory tenant.

*Paragraph (3)* defines "the occupier" as any person lawfully residing in the premises at the termination of the former tenancy.

Article 62 provides for ejectment for overholding.

## Interpretation of Part VI

**67.**—(1) In this Part –

"the tenancy" includes a statutory tenancy;

"tenant" includes a statutory tenant;

"statutory tenancy" and "statutory tenant" have the same meanings as
in the Rent (Northern Ireland) Order 1978.

(2)   For the purposes of this Part a person who, under the terms of his
employment, had exclusive possession of a dwelling-house otherwise
than as a tenant is deemed to have been a tenant, and "let" and "tenancy"
are to be construed accordingly.

ARTICLE 67                              Rent Order Arts. 2(2), 58

This Article contains definitions for Part VI.

*Paragraph (1)* The definitions of "the tenancy" and "tenant" are from Article 2(2) of the Rent Order.

*Paragraph (2)* applies the Part to tied cottages and other dwelling-houses of which an employee has, as such, exclusive possession.

There are savings for Part VI in Schedule 2, paragraph 10.

## PART VII

## MISCELLANEOUS

**Termination by assignor of assignee's interest in tenancy**

**68.**—(1) This Article applies where an assignment of a tenancy is subject to a provision which (apart from this Article) makes the interest of the assignee in the tenancy terminable by re-entry by the assignor, or any other action by the assignor, on the happening of a specified event.

(2) The provision is ineffective to make the interest terminable by the assignor, except to the extent and in the manner provided in this Article.

(3) Where the event is –

(a) a breach of a covenant, condition, proviso or agreement in the writing by which the assignment was made; or

(b) an insolvency event affecting the assignee;

the assignor may, on the happening of the event, make an application to the court for an order terminating the assignee's interest in the tenancy and re-vesting the tenancy in the assignor.

(4) In any other case, without prejudice to Article 65, the assignee's interest in the tenancy is terminable by four weeks' notice of the happening of the event served by the assignor on the assignee within 26 weeks from the date of the event.

(5) On an application under paragraph (3) the court, whether or not it makes the order applied for, may make such orders as it considers appropriate for remedying any default by the assignee (and, in particular, any relevant order corresponding to an order mentioned in Article 57(3)(a) or (c), references in Article 57(3) to the landlord or the tenant being read as references to the assignor or the assignee and references to the relation of landlord and tenant continuing being read as references to the assignee continuing to have the benefit of the assignment) or, where paragraph (3)(b) applies, may make an order for an assignment of the tenancy, where a person willing to accept an assignment on reasonable terms can be found and it would be unreasonable for the landlord to withhold a licence in relation to him (if the landlord's licence for an assignment of the tenancy is necessary).

(6) In this Article –

"assignor" and "assignee" include their respective successors in title;
"insolvency event affecting the assignee" has a corresponding meaning to "insolvency event affecting the tenant" in Article 51;
"specified" means specified in the writing by which the assignment was made.

# EXPLANATORY NOTE

ARTICLE 68                                    Report para. 4.6.36

This Article imposes restrictions on the exercise by the assignor of a tenancy of a right of entry to the detriment of the assignee.

*Paragraph (1)* makes the Article applicable where an assignment of a tenancy is subject to the right of the assignor, in a particular event, to terminate the effect of the assignment and re-vest the tenancy in himself (as in *Shiloh Spinners* v. *Harding* [1973] 2 WLR 28, where a right of re-entry formed the sanction for the assignee's covenants to the assignor for fencing and the support of buildings).

*Paragraph (2)* makes such a right effective only in accordance with the Article.

*Paragraph (3)* gives the court power, on application being made to it, to make an order terminating the assignee's interest in the tenancy, where the relevant event is a breach of a covenant, condition, proviso or agreement or where the event is the insolvency of the assignee or his surety.

*Paragraph (4)* In any other event (that is, where the event is something extraneous to the assignee), the assignee's interest in the tenancy is terminable by four weeks' notice, but only if the notice is served within 26 weeks from the date of the event.

*Paragraph (5)* gives the court, where it does not make a termination order under paragraph (3), power to make orders, or, where it makes an order under paragraph (3), power to make additional orders, for remedying any default by the assignee (cf. Article 57(3)(a)(ii) to (v) and (c)(i), (iii) and (v) – orders for damages, discontinuance of continuing breaches, specific performance, giving of security or finding sureties, recovery of premises, compensation). Where the relevant event is an insolvency, the court may order an assignment of the tenancy, if that is practicable, so that the value of the tenancy may rank as an asset in the bankruptcy or liquidation.

*Paragraph (6)* contains definitions.

"assignor" and "assignee" include successors in title;
"insolvency event" is defined by reference to Article 51 where it includes bankruptcy, liquidation (compulsory or voluntary), receivership, voluntary arrangement or certain enforcement orders affecting the tenant (i.e. the assignee) or (in most cases) his surety;
"specified" relates to the writing by which the assignment was made.

**Action for use and occupation**

**69.**—(1) Paragraph (2) applies where a person who has no estate or interest in land –

   (a)  is in occupation of the land, otherwise than by overholding as is mentioned in Article 63, without the consent of the owner, or

   (b)  is in occupation of the land with the consent of the owner under an agreement which does not –

      (i)  specify the amounts of payments to be made by him to the owner in respect of his use and occupation of the land or the manner in which those amounts are to be determined, or

     (ii)  provide that the occupation is to be free of any such payments.

(2)   Without prejudice to any other right of action, the owner of the land may recover from the person in occupation, by action in the court, a reasonable sum for the use and occupation of the land by that person.

(3)   In this Article "owner" means a person who has an estate or interest in the land entitling him to possession of it.

ARTICLE 69                                   Property Bill Cl. 182(2)
                                             Deasy's Act s. 46

This Article applies where a trespasser is in occupation of land or a landowner, by agreement, suffers another to occupy his land. The owner of the land may recover from the person in occupation a reasonable sum for the use and occupation of the land.

The Article does not apply –

(a) where there is an agreement fixing sums equivalent to rent or the way in which such sums are to be determined, or

(b) where there is an agreement that the land is to be occupied free of rent.

"Owner" is defined as a person whose estate or interest entitles him to possession of the land. "Possession" is defined in Article 2(2).

For the position after an occupation has been lawfully determined, see Article 63.

**Evidence of payment of rent**

**70.** Where a receipt for a sum paid for or on account of rent does not specify the period for which the sum was paid and accepted, –

(a) the sum is to be treated as having been paid and accepted for or on account of the rent which became due on the date for payment of rent which was or immediately preceded the date on which the sum was paid, and

(b) the receipt is evidence that all rent which became due before the first-mentioned date has been satisfied.

ARTICLE 70                              Property Bill Cl. 182(3)
                                        Deasy's Act s. 47

This Article creates two presumptions in a case where a receipt for rent does not specify the rental period to which the payment relates.

*Paragraph (a)*: The payment is presumed to relate to the rental period which ended on, or last ended before, the date of payment.

*Paragraph (b)*: The receipt is evidence that all earlier instalments of rent have been satisfied. The words "prima facie" have been omitted from before "evidence", because all evidence is rebuttable if it is not expressly stated to be conclusive.

**Rent books for private tenancies**

**71.**—(1) The landlord of a dwelling-house held under a private tenancy ("the landlord") shall provide the tenant with a rent book for use in respect of the dwelling-house.

(2) A rent book provided in pursuance of paragraph (1) shall contain such particulars and information relating to the tenancy as may be prescribed.

(3) If the landlord fails to provide under paragraph (1) a rent book which complies with paragraph (2), he and, subject to paragraph (6), any person who on his behalf demands or receives rent in respect of the dwelling-house held under that tenancy while the failure continues is guilty of an offence.

(4) Any person guilty of an offence under paragraph (3) is liable on summary conviction to a fine not exceeding level 4 on the standard scale.

(5) If any default in respect of which the landlord is convicted of an offence under paragraph (3) continues for more than fourteen days after that conviction, the landlord shall be deemed to have committed a further offence under that paragraph in respect of that default.

(6) If any person other than the landlord is charged with an offence under paragraph (3), it is a defence for him to prove that he neither knew nor had reasonable cause to believe that paragraph (1) or (2) had not been complied with.

(7) In this Article –

"prescribed" means prescribed by regulations made by the Department of the Environment subject to negative resolution;
"private tenancy" means any tenancy except –

(a) a tenancy under which the estate of the landlord belongs to –

   (i) the Crown (whether in right of Her Majesty's Government in the United Kingdom or in Northern Ireland);
  (ii) a government department;
 (iii) the Northern Ireland Housing Executive;
 (iv) a housing association registered under Part VII of the Housing (Northern Ireland) Order 1981;

   or is held in trust for Her Majesty for the purposes of a government department;

(b) a tenancy the purpose of which is to confer on the tenant the right to occupy a dwelling-house for a holiday;

(c) a tenancy granted for a term certain exceeding 99 years, unless that tenancy is, or may become, terminable before the end of that term by notice given to the tenant.

# EXPLANATORY NOTE

ARTICLE 71

Rent (NI) Order 1978 Arts.
2(2), 38, 39, 74
Housing (NI) Order 1983 Sch.
9 Pt. II para. 6

This Article requires the landlord of a dwelling-house held under a private tenancy to provide the tenant with a rent book.

*Paragraph (1)* requires a rent book to be provided.

*Paragraph (2)* requires the rent book to be in the prescribed form (see paragraph(7)).

*Paragraph (3)* makes it an offence for a landlord not to provide a rent book in the proper form. Any person who collects rent while there is no rent book is also guilty of an offence.

*Paragraph (4)* fixes the maximum fine on summary conviction for an offence under paragraph (3) at level 4 on the standard scale (at present £1,000 – see Criminal Penalties, etc. (Increase) Order (Northern Ireland) 1984, SR 1984 No. 253, Sch.4).

*Paragraph (5)* makes it a further offence for a default to be continued by the landlord after conviction.

*Paragraph (6)* gives a special defence to a rent collector who is charged with an offence under paragraph (3). It is sufficient for him to prove that he did not know, and had no reason to believe, that a proper rent book had not been supplied.

*Paragraph (7)* contains definitions.

## Choice of insurer

**72.**—(1) Where a lease of a dwelling-house contains a provision requiring the house to be insured with an insurer specified in the lease or with such insurer as the landlord specifies, that provision is to be treated as imposing on the landlord an obligation to serve on the tenant, before the placing of the insurance, a notice listing no fewer than three insurers with any one of whom, chosen by the tenant, the house may be insured.

(2) Where, before the commencement of this Order, insurance was effected in accordance with such a provision as is mentioned in paragraph (1) and the tenant was not given a choice such as is described in that paragraph, the provision is to be treated as requiring the landlord, if so requested by the tenant, to serve on the tenant a notice specifying no fewer than three insurers with any of whom, chosen by the tenant, the house may be insured when the existing insurance falls due for renewal.

(3) Where the tenant chooses an insurer listed in the notice, the insurer so chosen is to be deemed to be a specified insurer for the purposes of any provision such as is mentioned in paragraph (1).

(4) Any agreement is void to the extent that it imposes on the tenant a duty to pay money to the landlord, or otherwise places him under a disadvantage, by reason of the tenant's choosing any insurer on the list in preference to some other.

(5) The reference in paragraph (1) to the placing of the insurance is a reference to the original placing or a re-placing when a change of insurer is proposed.

(6) Where the premises are subject to a mortgage to which Article 122 of the Property Order applies, any insurer specified in a notice served by the mortgagee under that Article is deemed to be included in a notice served by the landlord under this Article, and any insurer included in the latter notice is deemed to be included in the former.

1491

# EXPLANATORY NOTE

ARTICLE 72                                    cf. Property Order Art. 122

This Article gives a tenant some choice of insurer where the right to specify an insurer lies with the landlord.

*Paragraph (1)* provides that where a lease requires a dwelling-house to be insured with an insurer specified in the lease or specified by the landlord, the landlord must serve on the tenant a list of the names of three insurers from which the tenant may choose one to be the insurer of the property. The notice must be served before the placing of the insurance (see paragraph (5)).

*Paragraph (2)* allows a tenant who was not previously given that choice to have it before the first renewal of the insurance following the commencement of the Order.

*Paragraph (3)* allows the tenant to choose an insurer on the list (who then becomes the specified insurer).

*Paragraph (4)* prohibits any charge from being imposed on the tenant simply because he chooses an insurer which is not the first choice of the landlord.

*Paragraph (5)* explains what is meant by the placing of an insurance. "Placing" refers to the first placing or to re-placing when a change of insurer is proposed.

*Paragraph (6)* Article 122 of the Property Order contains a similar provision about mortgages. Any insurer on the mortgagee's list is deemed to be on the landlord's list, and *vice versa*.

**Adverse possession**

**73.**—(1) Where no payment in respect of a conventional rent has been made for a period equal to the limitation period –

(a) no action shall be brought to recover that rent, except arrears which are not within Article 30 of the Limitation (Northern Ireland) Order 1989 ("the Order of 1989"); and

(b) upon the expiration of that period any provision of the lease under which the rent was payable which relates to the rent ceases to have effect.

(2) In this Article –

"conventional rent" has the same meaning as in the Order of 1989;
"the limitation period", in relation to any person, means the period fixed by Article 21 of the Order of 1989 for that person to bring an action to recover land;

and for the purposes of paragraph (1)(b) a provision of a lease relates to rent if it provides for the amount of the rent or its payment or recovery or is otherwise concerned (directly or indirectly) with safeguarding the rent.

# EXPLANATORY NOTE

ARTICLE 73

This Article provides for the case where a tenant has not paid any rent for a period equal to the limitation period.

*Paragraph (1)* states the consequences of a conventional rent's having remained unpaid for a period equal to the limitation period. A conventional rent is defined by Article 2(2) of the Limitation (Northern Ireland) Order 1989 as a rent payable under a lease or other contract of tenancy (whether in writing or not and whether express or implied) or a rent payable by a tenant within the meaning of the Rent Order (a protected or statutory tenant), but not a fee farm rent payable under a grant which creates the relation of landlord and tenant. The paragraph refers to a period "equal to" the limitation period so as to attract the references in Article 21 of the Order of 1989 to specific periods (30 years, generally, for the Crown; 12 years for subjects) without involving the linking of those periods by the Article with the date on which a right of action accrued – a separate right of action accrues for each payment of rent falling due and the period within which each such payment must be enforced is 6 years.

*sub-paragraph (a)* prevents any recovery of rent after the expiry of the limitation period (except the previous 6 years arrears);

*sub-paragraph (b)* causes any provision of the lease relating to the rent to cease to have effect upon the expiration of the period in question (see paragraph (2)).

*Paragraph (2)* contains definitions of "conventional rent" and "the limitation period" (see under paragraph (1) above), and explains what is meant by a provision of the lease relating to rent.

**Notices**

**74.**—(1) Any notice to be served shall be in writing.

(2) Without prejudice to paragraph (4), any notice to be served on a landlord by a tenant may be served –

(a) on any agent of the landlord named as such in a rent book provided under Article 71; or, if service cannot be effected on such an agent,

(b) on the person notice of whose name and address was last served on the tenant under Article 17 as the name and address of the landlord; or, if no such notice under Article 17 has been served or service cannot be effected in that name and at that address,

(c) on the person notice of whose name and address was last served on the tenant under Article 17 as the name and address of the person to whom the rent is to be paid; or if no such notice under Article 17 has been served or service cannot be effected in that name and at that address,

(d) on the person who last demanded or received rent under the tenancy or on any other person for the time being acting as agent for the landlord in relation to the tenancy.

(3) Without prejudice to paragraph (4), any notice to be served on a tenant by a landlord may be served –

(a) on the person notice of whose name and address was last served on the landlord under Article 18 as the name and address of the person in whom the tenancy is vested; or, if no such notice under Article 18 has been served or service cannot be effected in that name and at that address,

(b) on the person who last paid rent under the tenancy or any other person for the time being acting as agent for the tenant in relation to the tenancy; or, if the person who last paid the rent cannot be traced and has no agent,

(c) on any person whom the landlord believes to be in occupation of the land.

(4) Where the estate of the landlord or the tenant is subject to a mortgage and either the mortgagee is in possession or a receiver is in receipt of the rents and profits, any notice to be served on the landlord or the tenant may be served on the mortgagee or the receiver, as the case may be.

(5) Without prejudice to Article 17(2), where a notice to be served on the landlord or the tenant is served on an agent of his, the agent shall forthwith forward it to the landlord or the tenant (as the case may be); and if he fails without reasonable excuse to do so he is guilty of an offence and is liable on summary conviction to a fine not exceeding level 2 on the standard scale.

(6) In the application of section 24(2)(c) of the Interpretation Act (Northern Ireland) 1954 to any notice to be served, the words "with some person apparently over the age of sixteen" are omitted.

(7)   In this Article "notice to be served" means a notice required or authorised by this Order to be served.

# EXPLANATORY NOTE

ARTICLE 74

Property Bill Cl. 271(1), (2)
1881 c. 41 s. 67(3) (part)
Rent Order Art. 73

This Article contains general provisions about the service of notices. For the manner of service, see section 24 of the Interpretation Act. Notices are mentioned in Articles 16, 17, 18, 27, 33, 38, 46, 50, 51, 52, 54, 55, 58, 68, 72 and Schedule1.

*Paragraph (1)* requires any notice that is to be served to be in writing. In a sense this states the obvious, because "serve" seems inappropriate for an oral notice; but it has the "advantage of statement".

*Paragraph (2)* indicates upon whom may be served a notice which is to be served on the landlord by the tenant.

*sub-paragraph (a)* first the agent named in a rent book provided under Article 71;

*sub-paragraph (b)*: failing that, the person whose name and address have been notified to the tenant under Article 17 as being the landlord;

*sub-paragraph (c)*: failing that, the rent agent whose name and address have been notified under Article 17;

*sub-paragraph (d)*: failing that, the person who last demanded or received rent, or any other person acting as agent for the landlord.

*Paragraph (3)* indicates upon whom may be served a notice which is to be served on the tenant by the landlord.

*sub-paragraph (a)*: first, the person whose name and address have been notified to the landlord under Article 18 as being the tenant;

*sub-paragraph (b)*: failing that, the person who last paid rent under the tenancy or any other person acting as agent for the tenant.

*Paragraphs (2) and (3)* are permissive. Obviously, where the tenant is in no doubt about the identity of his landlord, and vice-versa, service will be effected on the person concerned.

*Paragraph (4)* applies where a mortgagee is in possession of the premises or a receiver has been appointed in respect of either the landlord's or the tenant's interest. Notices may be served on the mortgagee or receiver, as the case requires.

*Paragraph (5)* deals with the case where a notice is served on an agent. The agent must forward it to his principal, and if he fails to do so without reasonable excuse he is liable to a fine at level 2 on the standard scale (at present a maximum of £100). The paragraph does not prejudice Article 17(2), which places on the agent a direct duty to give the information requested by the tenant's notice where that information is the landlord's name and address.

*Paragraph (6)* makes a modification in section 24 of the Interpretation Act, which sets out various methods by which service of notices can be effected –

(a) personal service;

(b) by post (registered or recorded delivery);

(c) by leaving the notice at the usual or last-known place of abode or business of the person to be served, with some person apparently over the age of 16;

(d) in the case of a body or association (corporate or unincorporate) by delivering it to the secretary or clerk at the registered or principal office;

(e) if the notice concerns premises and the name or address of the owner, lessee or occupier is unknown, by addressing the notice by that description and leaving it at or affixing it to the premises.

The paragraph provides that a notice left at premises need not be left with a person apparently over 16—e.g. it can be slipped under the door or put in a letter-box. This continues the effect of this first part of section 67(3) of the Conveyancing Act 1881.

*Paragraph (7)* makes it clear that a "notice to be served" means one required or authorised by the Order to be served.

## Obligations binding two or more persons

**75.**—(1) Where, because of this Order, two or more persons are bound by the same obligation under a tenancy, they are so bound jointly and severally.

(2)   For the purpose of providing for contribution between persons who, under this Order, are bound jointly and severally by an obligation, the Civil Liability (Contribution) Act 1978 has effect as if –

(a) liability to a person under an obligation were liability in respect of damage suffered by that person; and

(b) section 7(2) of that Act did not apply in respect of such liability.

# EXPLANATORY NOTE

ARTICLE 75                                          cf. Law. Com. No. 174

This Article deals with the liabilities of persons who are bound by the same obligations under a tenancy (see Article 2(4)).

*Paragraph (1)* applies where two or more persons become bound by the same obligation – say the repairing obligation of an outgoing landlord and an incoming landlord, and similarly as to tenants (Articles 36-40). In such cases their liability will be joint and several.

*Paragraph (2)* has the effect of enabling a person to recover contribution under the Civil Liability (Contribution) Act 1978 from another person who is jointly and severally liable with him for breach of the same obligation. Under the 1978 Act, the court can order such contribution as is just and equitable, and it has power to exempt any party from liability to make contribution.

*sub-paragraph (a)* makes the contribution provisions of the 1978 Act available to regulate the rights of those liable for the same obligation. At present the 1978 Act regulates only the mutual rights to contribution of persons liable for the same damage.

*sub-paragraph (b)* excludes section 7(2) of the 1978 Act which provides that the Act does not apply in respect of an obligation assumed before 1 January 1979. For the purposes of the Order, the 1978 Act will apply irrespective of when the lease was granted or when the obligation was assumed.

## Agreements cannot limit Order

**76.** Without prejudice to Article 12(3), save as permitted by this Order any provision of an agreement is void to the extent that it purports –

(a) to preclude the operation or effect of this Order;

(b) to impose on any person any penalty or disability in the event of the operation of this Order.

# EXPLANATORY NOTE

## ARTICLE 76

This Article prevents the operation of the Order from being excluded or modified by an agreement, except so far as permitted by the Order (e.g. as to variable obligations – Part III, or as in Articles 36, 37, 38, 39 or 40).

See also Article 72(4).

**The county court**

77.—(1) Where any provision of this Order empowers the court to vary, suspend, revive or revoke an order made by a county court or to deal with a relisted application, "the court" includes a county court held for the same division as the court which made the order.

(2) Without prejudice to any provision of Part VI of the County Courts (Northern Ireland) Order 1980, any party to the proceedings who is dissatisfied with a decision of a county court under this Order may appeal from that decision as if the decision had been made in exercise of the jurisdiction conferred by Part III of that Order and the appeal were brought under Article 60 of that Order.

# EXPLANATORY NOTE

ARTICLE 77

This Article contains general provisions about county courts.

*Paragraph (1)* applies where a provision of this Order (Articles 39(3); 57(6), (10)) empowers a court to vary, suspend, revive or revoke an order previously made by it or to deal with a relisted application (Article 57(10)). Unlike the High Court (Judicature (Northern Ireland) Act 1978, s. 57(1)), a county court is not a continuing court. The paragraph empowers the order for variation, etc., to be made by a court held for the same county court division as the court which made the original order.

*Paragraph (2)* gives a right of appeal to the High Court from a decision of a county court under the Order. The power to state a case on a point of law is not affected.

## Fee farm grants

**78.**—(1) The following provisions of this Order, namely, Article 2, Part IV, Articles 54, 59 to 63, Part VI and Articles 70, 74 to 76, 80 and Schedules1 and 2 apply, so far as applicable, to fee farm grants and their grantors and grantees with the necessary modifications and, in particular, with the substitution for references to the lease, the tenancy, the landlord or the tenant of references to the grant, the estate or interest of the grantee, or the grantor or the grantee (or their respective successors in title) and with the omission of any reference to Part III.

(2) Paragraph (1) does not prejudice Article 81 and Schedule 3, paragraph 9 of Schedule 2 or Article 8 or 9 of the Property Order (rights of entry or re-entry).

(3) In this Article, "fee farm grant" means a grant of a fee simple reserving or charging a perpetual rent (whether or not the relation of landlord and tenant subsists between the person entitled to receive the rent and the person liable to pay it) and includes a sub-fee farm grant.

# EXPLANATORY NOTE

## ARTICLE 78

This Article applies certain provisions of the Order to fee farm grants.

*Paragraph (1)* sets out the applied provisions. These are –

| | | |
|---|---|---|
| Article 2 | – | interpretation |
| Part IV, Sch. 1 | – | the running and effect of benefits and obligations |
| Article 54 | – | surrender of tenancy by tenant on destruction of, or damage to, premises |
| Article 59 | – | powers of court following improper assignment |
| Article 60 | – | position of parties after termination of tenancy |
| Article 61 | – | position of third parties |
| Article 62 | – | ejectment for overholding |
| Article 63 | – | payments by tenant or occupier overholding |
| Part VI | – | protection against harassment, etc. |
| Article 70 | – | evidence of payment of rent |
| Article 74 | – | notices |
| Article 75 | – | obligations binding two or more persons |
| Article 76 | – | agreements cannot limit order |
| Article 80, Sch. 2 | – | transitional provisions. |

Some of these provisions will, from their nature, have a limited application – e.g. Articles 44 and 59 (restrictions on alienation) may be relevant to a fee farm conversion grant under the Renewable Leasehold Conversion Act 1849, but will not be relevant to any other fee farm grant.

*Paragraph (2)* is a saving for paragraph 9 of Schedule 2, which continues the relation of landlord and tenant where created by a fee farm grant made under Deasy's Act. The paragraph also draws attention to Articles 8 and 9 of the Property Order which restrict the exercise of powers of entry or re-entry. And it contains a saving for Article 81 and Schedule 3, which continue certain provisions of Deasy's Act for fee farm grants, as well as for existing leases.

*Paragraph (3)* defines "fee farm grant".

## Repeal of statutory provisions relating to agricultural tenancies

**79.**—(1) The statutory provisions relating to agricultural tenancies cease to have effect, except in relation to tenancies to which they applied immediately before the commencement of this Order.

(2) In this Article "the statutory provisions relating to agricultural tenancies" means –

the Landlord and Tenant (Ireland) Act 1870;

the Landlord and Tenant (Ireland) Act 1871;

the Landlord and Tenant (Ireland) Act 1872;

the Notices to Quit (Ireland) Act 1876;

the Land Law (Ireland) Act 1881;

the Land Law (Ireland) Act 1887, Part I, section 26, Part III and, in Part IV, section 33(2), in section 34 the definitions of "ejectment", "judgment" and "landlord", and the Schedule;

the Land Law (Ireland) Act 1896 (except Part II so far as relating to the Land Purchase Acts, Part III and, in Part VI, in section 48(1) the definitions of "Land Purchase Acts", "prescribed" and "Receiver Judge", section 48(3), section 50(4) and (5) and section 51); and

the Irish Land Act 1903, Part III, and, in Part V, in section 98(1) the definitions of "the Land Law Acts" and "the Act of 1887" and section 100(3).

# EXPLANATORY NOTE

## ARTICLE 79

This Article lays a foundation for the repeal of the enactments relating to agricultural tenancies.

*Paragraph (1)* provides that the statutory provisions relating to agricultural tenancies shall cease to have effect. This does not affect existing tenancies.

*Paragraph (2)* defines the statutory provisions relating to agricultural tenancies. They are –

### Landlord and Tenant (Ireland) Act 1870

This Act declared the Ulster tenant-right custom to be legal, and provided for compensation to tenants where that custom did not apply. Part II provided for the sale to tenants of their holdings by agreement.

### Landlord and Tenant (Ireland) Act 1871

This Act safeguarded the tenants' rights under the 1870 Act in the case of a sale by the Landed Estates Court.

### Landlord and Tenant (Ireland) Act 1872

This was concerned with purchases of their holdings by tenants under Part II of the 1870 Act.

### Notices to Quit (Ireland) Act 1876

This generally required a year's notice to quit for new tenancies from year to year and six months' notice for then existing tenancies.

### Land Law (Ireland) Act 1881

This gave tenants a right to sell their holdings and amended the law about compensation for disturbance or improvements.

### Land Law (Ireland) Act 1887

Part I modifies the meanings of the expressions "bona fide occupation" and "town parks" in the Act of 1881. Section 26 operates on sections 44 and 45 of the Act of 1870, which have already been repealed. Part III and the Schedule are concerned with protection of the tenant in an action in ejectment for non-payment of rent. The other provisions mentioned in the Article are supplementary.

### Land Law (Ireland) Act 1896

This provided for the fixing of fair rents. The excepted provisions form part of the Land Purchase Acts.

Part III provides for appeals under the Land Law Acts. The other provisions mentioned are supplemental.

**Transitional provisions and savings**

80.   The transitional provisions and savings in Schedule 2 have effect.

# EXPLANATORY NOTE

## ARTICLE 80

This Article activates the transitional provisions and savings in Schedule 2.

**Provisions applying where the relation of landlord and tenant already exists**

**81.**—(1) The provisions of Schedule 3 apply where the relation of landlord and tenant was created between 31 December 1860 and the commencement of this Order and subsists at that commencement.

(2) For the purposes of this Article the relation of landlord and tenant is deemed to subsist in all cases in which there is an agreement by one party to hold land from or under another in consideration of any rent, whether or not there is a reversion.

(3) Without prejudice to Article 56, the fact (if it is the case) that the rent under a lease or tenancy agreement ceases to be payable after the commencement of this Order, by reason of the operation of the statute of limitation or for any other reason, does not affect the continued application of Schedule 3 (so far as applicable) where it applied before the cesser.

(4) For the purposes of this Article –

"agreement" includes every covenant, contract or condition expressed or implied in any lease;

"lease" means any instrument in writing, whether under seal or not, containing a contract of tenancy in respect of any land, in consideration of a rent or return;

"rent" includes any sum or return in the nature of rent, payable or given by way of compensation for the holding of any land;

"tenancy" and "tenant" are not limited by the definitions in Article 2(2).

# EXPLANATORY NOTE

ARTICLE 81                            Property Bill cl. 162(2)
                                      Deasy's Act ss. 1, 3

This Article and Schedule 3 continue certain existing statutory provisions for cases in which the relation of landlord and tenant already exists. Those provisions are the provisions of Deasy's Act which, for future leases, will be superseded by Part III of the Order.

*Paragraph (1)* applies Schedule 3 to cases where the relation of landlord and tenant, having come into existence between the commencement of Deasy's Act (immediately after midnight on 31 December 1860) and the commencement of the Order, continues to subsist at the commencement of the Order.

*Paragraph (2)* Those cases may involve either leases or fee farm grants.

*Paragraph (3)* The cesser of rent does not affect the continued application of the Schedule, in the case of a lease or an oral tenancy agreement (but not in the case of a fee farm grant). This does not prejudice Article 56, which enables a tenant holding free from rent to enlarge his estate into a fee simple by executing a deed poll and registering his new title in the Land Registry.

*Paragraph (4)* contains definitions, mostly taken from section 1 of Deasy's Act.

## Application to the Crown

**82.**—(1) Subject to paragraphs (2) to (4) and without prejudice to any provision which is expressed to apply only to a private tenancy, this Order binds the Crown.

(2) Article 52(4) does not apply to a tenancy in relation to which the estate of the landlord is a Crown estate, that is to say an estate which belongs to –

(a) the Crown in right of Her Majesty's Government either in the United Kingdom or in Northern Ireland; or

(b) a government department;

or which is held in trust for Her Majesty for the purposes of a government department ("government department" for the purposes of this paragraph including a department of the Government of the United Kingdom).

(3) Paragraph 4 of Schedule 1 does not bind the Crown further than the Crown is made liable in tort by the Crown Proceedings Act 1947.

(4) Without prejudice to paragraph (3), this Article has effect subject to the Crown Proceedings Act 1947.

# EXPLANATORY NOTE

ARTICLE 82                                        Rent Order Arts. 2(2), 62, 75

This Article provides for the application of the Order to the Crown.

*Paragraph (1)* generally makes the Order bind the Crown. This is inapplicable where a provision is expressed to apply only to a private tenancy – see Article 71 (rent books).

*Paragraph (2)* excepts the Crown from the requirement in Article 52(4) to give at least four weeks notice to quit a dwelling-house.

*Paragraph (3)* confines the Crown's liability in tort under paragraph 4 of Schedule 1 (liability in damages for unreasonable failure to grant licence, etc.) within the terms of the Crown Proceedings Act 1947.

*Paragraph (4)* is a reminder that the Crown Proceedings Act 1947 (as extended to Northern Ireland by the Crown Proceedings (Northern Ireland) Order 1981, S.I. 1981 No.233) contains provisions about proceedings affecting the Crown – e.g. section 17 (parties to proceedings) and section 21 which prevents an injunction, an order for specific performance or an order for recovery of land being made against the Crown but, instead, empowers the court to make a declaratory order (cf. Articles 48, 57(3) and 62).

# SCHEDULE 1

## LICENCES TO ALIENATE, CHANGE USER OR MAKE IMPROVEMENTS

### *Qualified duty to grant licence*

1.—(1) This paragraph applies in any case where there is a tenant's obligation not to do any thing mentioned in Article 44(1) without a licence of the landlord or some other person.

(2)  In this paragraph and paragraph 2 –

(a)  references to a proposed transaction are to the doing of any thing to which the tenant's obligation relates, and

(b)  references to the person who may grant a licence for a proposed transaction are to the landlord or the other person (if any) who may grant such a licence to the tenant.

(3)  Where there is served on the person who may grant a licence for a proposed transaction a written application by the tenant for such a licence, he owes a duty to the tenant within a reasonable time –

(a)  to grant a licence, except in a case where it is reasonable not to grant a licence,

(b)  to serve on the tenant written notice of his decision whether or not to grant a licence specifying in addition –

(i)  if the licence is granted subject to conditions, the conditions,

(ii)  if a licence is withheld, the reasons for withholding it.

(4)  Granting a licence subject to any condition that is not a reasonable condition does not satisfy the duty under sub-paragraph (3)(a).

(5)  It is for the person who owed any duty under sub-paragraph (3) –

(a)  if he granted a licence and the question arises whether he granted it within a reasonable time, to show that he did,

(b)  if he granted a licence subject to any condition and the question arises whether the condition was a reasonable condition, to show that it was,

(c)  if he did not grant a licence and the question arises whether it was reasonable for him not to do so, to show that it was reasonable,

and, if the question arises whether he served notice under that sub-paragraph within a reasonable time, to show that he did.

### *Duty to pass on applications*

2.—(1) If, in a case where paragraph 1 applies, any person receives a written application by the tenant for a licence for a proposed transaction and that person –

(a)  is a person who may grant a licence for the transaction or (though not such a person) is the landlord, and

(b) believes that another person, other than a person who he believes has received the application or a copy of it, is a person who may grant a licence for the transaction,

he owes a duty to the tenant (whether or not he owes him any duty under paragraph 1) to take such steps as are reasonable to secure the receipt within a reasonable time by the other person of a copy of the application.

(2) The reference in paragraph 1(3) to the service of an application on a person who may grant a licence for a proposed transaction includes a reference to the receipt by him of an application or a copy of an application (whether it is for his licence or that of another).

### *Qualified duty to approve grant of licence by another*

3.—(1) This paragraph applies in any case where a tenancy includes an obligation on the part of the tenant not without the licence of the landlord (his "approval") to grant a licence for the sub-tenant to do any thing mentioned in Article 44(1) in relation to the premises comprised in the sub-tenancy or any part of them.

(2) Where there is served on the landlord a written application by the tenant for approval or a copy of a written application to the tenant by the sub-tenant for a licence for a transaction to which the obligation relates the landlord owes a duty to the sub-tenant within a reasonable time –

(a) to give approval, except in a case where it is reasonable not to give approval,

(b) to serve on the tenant and the sub-tenant written notice of his decision whether or not to give approval specifying in addition –

(i) if approval is given subject to conditions, the conditions,

(ii) if approval is withheld, the reasons for withholding it.

(3) Giving approval subject to any condition that is not a reasonable condition does not satisfy the duty under sub-paragraph (2)(a).

(4) For the purposes of this paragraph it is reasonable for the landlord not to give approval only in a case where, if he withheld approval and the tenant granted a licence, the tenant would be in breach of a tenant's obligation.

(5) It is for a landlord who owed any duty under sub-paragraph (2) –

(a) if he gave approval and the question arises whether he gave it within a reasonable time, to show that he did,

(b) if he gave approval subject to any condition and the question arises whether the condition was a reasonable condition, to show that it was,

(c) if he did not give approval and the question arises whether it was reasonable for him not to do so, to show that it was reasonable,

and, if the question arises whether he served notice under that sub-paragraph within a reasonable time, to show that he did.

## Breach of duty

4. A claim that a person has broken any duty under this Schedule may be made the subject of civil proceedings in like manner as any other claim in tort for breach of statutory duty.

## Unreasonable or reasonable withholding or conditions

5. For the purposes of this Schedule it is reasonable for a person not to grant a licence for a proposed transaction only in a case where, if he withheld a licence and the tenant completed the proposed transaction (as defined by paragraph 1(2)(a)), the tenant would be in breach of a tenant's obligation.

6.—(1) Without prejudice to any ground on which it would be unreasonable or reasonable to withhold a licence, a licence is unreasonably withheld if its grant is conditional on or gives rise to the payment of a fine or increase of rent (and any such fine or increase of rent actually paid is recoverable from the landlord by the tenant as a debt); but this paragraph does not preclude the landlord –

(a) from requiring payment of a reasonable sum in respect of legal or other expenses incurred by him in connection with a licence; or

(b) from charging a reasonable fine or a reasonable increase of rent where a licence permits an alteration of the user of premises held under a lease originally granted for a term not exceeding 21 years;

(c) from reasonably requiring the payment of, or the giving of security for payment of, compensation for any loss or damage which a change of user or an improvement will or may cause to him and which is such that he would, apart from this paragraph, be entitled to require as a condition of giving his consent.

(2) In this paragraph "fine" includes any payment, consideration or benefit in money or money's worth.

(3) Any question arising as to whether any fine or increase of rent is reasonable for the purposes of sub-paragraph (1)(b) or as to whether any requirement about compensation is reasonable for the purposes of sub-paragraph (1)(c) shall, unless it arises in proceedings before the court, be referred to and determined by the Lands Tribunal.

7. A condition attached to a licence is not unreasonable only because it requires a prospective assignee to find a surety for his observance of tenant's obligations under the tenancy.

## Increase of rent following improvements

8.—(1) Where a tenant has made an improvement for which the landlord has or is taken to have granted a licence, in determining at any time whether or to what extent to increase the rent of the premises or to charge a fine in respect of them, the landlord shall, notwithstanding anything in the lease, treat the improvement as justifying only such part of any increase of rent, or of any fine, which would otherwise be attributable to the improvement as corresponds to the part of the cost of the improvement which neither has been borne by the tenant nor would have been borne by him if a grant in respect of the improvement had not been made by a government department or public body (and accordingly as not justifying any increase of rent, or any fine, if the whole of the cost has or would have been so borne).

(2)   In this paragraph "public body" means a body established by or under a statutory provision.

# EXPLANATORY NOTE

## SCHEDULE 1

This Schedule contains provisions about landlords' licences to alienate, change user or make improvements.

*Paragraph 1* imposes a qualified duty to grant a licence for the doing of anything to which Article 44(1) applies. The tenant must serve a written application for a licence and thereupon the person upon whom the application is served must, within a reasonable time, grant a licence (unless it would be reasonable not to do so) and must serve notice on the tenant of his decision (whether his decision is to grant a licence or not to grant one) specifying, where the licence is granted subject to conditions, those conditions, or where a licence is withheld, the reasons for withholding it. A licence purporting to be granted subject to unreasonable conditions is treated as withheld. Where the lease itself specifies what is or is not a good reason for withholding a licence, only a refusal coming within such grounds will be treated as reasonable: a licence cannot be withheld for extraneous reasons. The burden of proving reasonableness in all cases falls on the landlord or other person whose licence is required.

*Paragraph 2* applies where an application for a licence is served on the landlord who believes that the consent of some other person (particularly a superior landlord) is required, in addition to or instead of his own licence. The landlord must pass on the application.

*Paragraph 3* imposes obligations similar to those in paragraph 1 in a case where, before a landlord can grant a licence, he needs to get the approval of a superior landlord.

*Paragraph 4* renders a breach of duty under paragraphs 1 to 3 subject to an action for damages.

*Paragraph 5* prevents a licence from being withheld for extraneous reasons, if the lease itself specifies the only ground on which a licence can be refused. E.g. if the lease says a licence will be granted for assignment to a respectable person, and the proposed assignee is respectable, the licence cannot be refused on any other ground even though, in the absence of the express provision, that other ground would have been a good one.

*Paragraph 6* makes it clear that it would be unreasonable for the landlord to refuse his licence unless money is paid: but he may require the tenant to pay the reasonable expenses of the licence and he may charge a reasonable fine or increase of rent on a change of user of premises leased for 21 years or less or require compensation for any loss or damage a change of user or an improvement may cause to him.

*Paragraph 7* makes it clear that a condition requiring a prospective assignee to find sureties is not in itself unreasonable.

*Paragraph 8* prevents a landlord from charging a fine or increase of rent for an improvement approved (or treated as approved) by him so far as

1520

the value of the improvement represents expenditure defrayed by the tenant or out of public funds; but this does not apply to an improvement which the tenant has assumed an obligation to make, because in that case no licence would be required.

## SCHEDULE 2

## TRANSITIONAL PROVISIONS AND SAVINGS

*Transitional provisions*

1.   Except as otherwise expressly provided, this Order applies to all tenancies, whenever created.

2.   Article 4 (reversion on tenancy) does not affect any tenancy which was in existence immediately before the commencement of this Order, nor (without prejudice to any provision of the Grounds Rents (Northern Ireland) Order 1989) does it prejudice any agreement made before that commencement.

3.   Article 37 has effect in relation to a tenancy of which an assignment was first made before the commencement of this Order as if, after the words "obligations" in paragraph (2), there were inserted the words "concerning the premises".

4.   Article 38 or 40 does not apply to an assignment of a tenancy or a conveyance of a reversion made (in either case) by way of mortgage before the commencement of Article 114 of the Property Order.

5.   Article 41 applies whether the severance of the reversion or the partial avoidance or cesser of the tenancy was effected before or after the commencement of this Order; but where a tenancy was created before 1 January 1882, nothing in that Article affects the operation of a severance of the reversion thereon, or a partial avoidance or cesser of the tenancy, which was effected before the commencement of this Order.

6.   Article 44 applies only to applications for licences served after its commencement.

7.   Article 54 does not apply where the lease was granted before the commencement of that Article and contains an express covenant by the tenant to repair the premises.

*Savings*

8.   Except as expressly provided in the Property (Consequential Provisions) (Northern Ireland) Order 1989 ("the Consequential Provisions Order") nothing in this Order affects –

   (a)   section 7 of the Northern Ireland Land Act 1929 (determination of tenancies of holdings excluded from vesting in the Land Purchase Commission, Northern Ireland on account of building value);

   (b)   the Business Tenancies Act (Northern Ireland) 1964;

   (c)   the Rent (Northern Ireland) Order 1978;

   (d)   the Housing (Northern Ireland) Order 1981;

   (e)   the Housing (Northern Ireland) Order 1983;

(f) the Housing (Northern Ireland) Order 1986;

(g) the Housing (Northern Ireland) Order 1988.

9. Without prejudice to any provision of the Ground Rents (Northern Ireland) Order 1989 or the Property Order or to Article 78 or 81, nothing in this Order or the Consequential Provisions Order prevents the relation of landlord and tenant, where it subsisted immediately before the commencement of the Order otherwise than in relation to a tenancy, continuing to subsist as heretofore.

10. Nothing in Part VI affects –

(a) the jurisdiction of the High Court to enforce a mortgagee's right of possession in a case where the former tenancy (within the meaning of Article 66) was not binding on the mortgagee; or

(b) the operation of –

   (i) section 19 of the Defence Act 1842;

   (ii) section 91 of the Lands Clauses Consolidation Act 1845;

   (iii) section 5(1) of the Criminal Law Amendment Act 1912.

11. Nothing in this Order prevents –

(a) a landlord or tenant releasing a person from an obligation under the tenancy;

(b) the operation of any law relating to the release of guarantors.

12. Without prejudice to Article 11 or 12, where there is any conflict between an obligation such as is mentioned in Article 2(4)(b) or (d) and an obligation such as is mentioned in Article 2(4)(c), the former is to prevail.

# EXPLANATORY NOTE

## SCHEDULE 2

This Schedule contains transitional provisions and savings.

*Paragraph 1* applies the Order to all tenancies, whenever created. This is subject to Article 11(1), which confines the operation of Part III to tenancies created after the commencement of the Order (see Article 1(3)), and to the other provisions of the Order (e.g. paragraph 2).

*Paragraph 2* preserves existing reversionless leases and those already contracted for.

*Paragraph 3* preserves the effect of section 13 of Deasy's Act in relation to tenancies assigned before the commencement of the Order (see the explanatory note on Article 37(3)).

*Paragraph 4* prevents Articles 38 and 40 (position of parties after assignment of tenancy or conveyance of reversion) from applying to an assignment or conveyance made by way of mortgage before the coming into force of Article 114 of the Property Order (which substitutes for those forms of mortgage a charge by way of legal mortgage).

*Paragraph 5* applies to the severance of a reversion or the partial avoidance or cesser of a tenancy. Its background is explained in the explanatory note on Article 41.

*Paragraph 6* restricts the application of Article 44 to licence applications made after the Article comes into operation.

*Paragraph 7* restricts the application of Article 54 to leases granted after the commencement of the Article or those granted before then which did not contain a tenant's express covenant to repair.

*Paragraph 8* prevents the Order effecting any of the listed enactments, except so far as provision to the contrary is expressly made by the Consequential Provisions Order (which contains savings for some repeals or amendments made by it). Section 7 of the Northern Ireland Land Act 1929 has a limited application (it applies only to certain holdings excluded from vesting under the land purchase scheme). The main exceptions are for the Business Tenancies Act, the Rent Order and the Housing Orders. Some of the provisions of the Rent Order which are of general application are carried into this Order (see Part VI and Articles 52(4)(5) and 71) and repealed by the Consequential Provisions Order. Articles 41 to 45 of the Rent Order, although corresponding to Articles 19, 21, 24 and 30 of this Order are not repealed, because (subject to any express contrary provision in the contract of tenancy) they apply to regulated tenancies which came into existence before the commencement of this Order, whereas Part III of this Order applies only to tenancies created after that commencement. The paragraph prevents Article 44 from applying to secure tenancies under the Housing Order of 1983 (cf. Articles 30 and 32 of that Order).

*Paragraph 9* continues the existing relation of landlord and tenant in connection with fee farm grants which had been created under Deasy's Act.

*Paragraph 10* contains, in relation to Part VI, specific savings for –

*sub-paragraph (a)* the High Court's jurisdiction to enforce a mortgagee's right of possession where the former tenancy did not bind him;

*sub-paragraph (b)* the operation of –

  (i) Defence Act 1842 (c. 94) s. 19 (power of 2 justices to put HM Officers in possession of lands required for defence purposes);

  (ii) Lands Clauses Consolidation Act 1845 (c. 18) s. 91 (promoters of undertaking may obtain possession of lands through Enforcement of Judgments Office);

  (iii) Criminal Law Amendment Act 1912 (c. 20) s. 5(1) (court convicting, where premises used as a brothel, may make summary order for delivery of possession to landlord).

The paragraph reproduces Article 57 of the Rent Order.

*Paragraph 11* makes it clear that provisions about the variation of obligations on the occasion of the assignment of a tenancy or the conveyance of the reversion (Articles 36, 37) do not prevent a release being effected at other times.

*Paragraph 12* gives statutory or contractual obligations in a lease primacy over common law obligations.

# PROVISIONS APPLYING WHERE THE RELATION OF LANDLORD AND TENANT ALREADY EXISTS

### Agreements implied on behalf of landlord

1.   Unless otherwise expressly provided by the lease, a lease implies an agreement on the part of the landlord, his heirs, executors, administrators, and assigns, with the tenant that the landlord has good title to make the lease, and that the tenant shall have the quiet and peaceable enjoyment of the land comprised in the tenancy without the interruption of the landlord or any person whomsoever during the term contracted for, so long as the tenant pays the rent and performs the agreements contained in the lease to be observed on the part of the tenant.

### Agreements implied on behalf of tenant

2.   Unless otherwise expressly provided by the lease, a lease implies the following agreements on the part of the tenant, his heirs, executors, administrators, and assigns, with the landlord; that is to say,

   (a)   that the tenant shall pay, when due, the rent reserved and all taxes and impositions payable by the tenant, and shall keep the premises in good and substantial repair and condition:

   (b)   That the tenant shall give peaceable possession of the demised premises, in good and substantial repair and condition, on the determination of the lease (accidents by fire without the tenant's default excepted), subject, however, to any right of removal (or of compensation for improvements) that may have lawfully arisen in respect of them, and to any right of surrender under Article 54 in case of the destruction of the subject matter of the lease.

### Tenant, in lieu of emblements, to continue to hold until last gale day of current year

3.   Where the lease or tenancy of any farm or lands (held at rackrent) determines by the happening of any event without the act or default of the tenant, the tenant in occupation, in lieu of the right of emblements (where such right exists) shall, if he think proper so to do, continue to hold and occupy the farm or lands until the last gale day of the current year in which the tenancy determines, and shall then quit upon the terms of his lease or holding, in the same manner as if the lease or tenancy were then determined by effluxion of time or other lawful means, during the continuance of his landlord's estate; and the landlord or succeeding landlord or owner shall be entitled to recover rent from the tenant in the same manner as if the tenant's interest had only determined on such gale day; and the landlord, or the succeeding landlord or owner, and the tenant respectively, shall, as between themselves and as against each other, be entitled to all the benefits and advantages, and be subject to all the terms, conditions, and restrictions, to which the landlord or preceding landlord or lessor and such tenant respectively would have been entitled

1526

and subject in case the lease or tenancy had determined in manner aforesaid at the expiration of such current year: Provided always, that no notice to quit shall be necessary or required by or from either party to determine any such holding and occupation as aforesaid.

### Payment of proportion of rent in certain cases

4. In every case not coming within the provisions of paragraph 3, when the tenancy determines, otherwise than by the act of the landlord, at any time before the day on which the rent would become payable, the landlord at the time of such determination (unless it is otherwise agreed) is entitled to a reasonable proportion of the rent according to the time that has elapsed from the commencement of the tenancy, or the last gale day, to the day of the determination of the tenancy, including that day.

### Tenant's fixtures

5. Notwithstanding Article 11, Article 33, with the substitution of "an obligation" for "a variable obligation", applies except so far as is otherwise specially provided by the contract of tenancy.

### Tenant in fee farm not impeachable of waste

6.—(1) Subject to sub-paragraph (2), no tenant of land for a perpetual interest is impeachable of any waste.

(2) Sub-paragraph (1) does not apply –

(a) to fraudulent or malicious waste;

(b) to the extent that the tenant is, by any agreement in his lease or grant, prohibited from doing or permitting any act;

(c) in the case of a fee farm grant made under the Renewable Leasehold Conversion Act;

(d) in the case of the renewal of a lease made before 28 August 1860 where the renewal was granted after 1 January 1861 in pursuance of an agreement for renewal.

### Waste by other tenants

7. Paragraphs 8 to 13 apply to a tenant other than one to whom paragraph 6 applies.

8. The tenant shall not without the previous consent in writing of the landlord, being a person competent to grant such licence, or of his agent duly authorized to act on his behalf, open, dig for any unopened mines, minerals, or quarries, or (except as herein-after provided) remove the soil or surface or subsoil of the land comprised in the tenancy, or permit or commit any other manner of waste thereon, unless the land has been, in express terms, leased for the purpose or with the permission of being so used and enjoyed.

9. Where a mine had already been opened at the time when the tenancy was created, the tenant may enter upon and work the mine, and

follow and dig for minerals, whether or not a right to do so was granted in the lease, unless the lease otherwise provides.

10.   Where a quarry or pit for working stone, sand, gravel or soil had already been opened at the time when the tenancy was created, the tenant may, unless the lease otherwise provides, work the quarry or pit and follow and dig for those substances and use them; but he may do so only so far as may be necessary or useful for the purposes of agriculture and good husbandry or the lawful erection or repair of any necessary building on the land, but not for any purpose of trade or manufacture, or for profit or sale, unless the right so to use and enjoy the same has been expressly granted in writing by the landlord, being competent so to grant.

11.   Where –
(a)  the land comprised in the tenancy contains turf bog, unreclaimed and unprofitable for agriculture, or
(b)  the lease gives a right of turbary on the land, or
(c)  the lease confers a right of common of turbary on land not included in the lease,

the tenant may (unless the lease specially provides to the contrary) cut, use and enjoy turf so far as is necessary for its bona fide use on the demised land of the tenant and his lawful sub-tenants, but not for any purpose of trade or manufacture, or for profit or sale, unless the right so to use and enjoy the same has been expressly granted in writing by the landlord, being competent so to grant.

12.—(1)  The tenant shall not burn or permit to be burned the soil or surface of the land comprised in the tenancy or any part of it, unless the right to do so has been expressly granted in writing by the landlord, being competent so to grant.

(2)  A tenant contravening sub-paragraph (1) is liable to a penalty not exceeding £20 for each acre or part of an acre on which such burning has taken place, recoverable by the immediate landlord by civil bill.

13.—(1)  The tenant shall not cut down, top, lop or grub any tree or wood growing on the land comprised in the tenancy, unless –
(a)  he is authorized to do so by an agreement in the lease, or
(b)  the right to do so has been expressly granted in writing by the landlord, being competent so to grant, or
(c)  he has been lawfully required to do so.

(2)  A tenant contravening sub-paragraph (1) is liable to a penalty not exceeding £5 for each tree cut down, topped, lopped or grubbed, recoverable by the immediate landlord by civil bill.

### Landlord's right of entry to inspect waste

14.   The landlord of any premises upon which any waste, misuser, or destruction has been comitted or suffered, and his agent lawfully

authorized, may at any reasonable time enter upon the premises so wasted, or misused, and inspect, and, if necessary, survey the same for the purpose of ascertaining the nature and extent of any waste or injury done, or the quantity of land burned contrary to the provisions of this Schedule; and if any person hinders or obstructs such landlord or agent in making such an entry, inspection, or survey, he shall forfeit to the said landlord a sum not exceeding £10, to be recovered by civil bill action.

### Rights of landlord, where mines reserved

15.   Where land has been granted or leased for any estate or interest, excepting thereout the mines and minerals upon the demised premises, the person entitled to the rent thereof may open, dig for, and work all mines and minerals found in or upon the land, and carry away the ore thereof, or may lease the same to any person or persons for any term within the leasing power of such person in respect of mines and minerals; and such owner or his lessee shall have full liberty to enter on the said land, and to build and make all houses, railways, tramways, and conveniences necessary for the purpose of mining, and to employ all streams on the land not previously occupied, making to the tenant of the land such yearly or other compensation or allowance for the damage sustained by reason of such digging of the ore, or building the said houses, or otherwise using of the said lands or streams, as is agreed upon between the said parties, or, in case they do not agree, then such compensation or allowance as shall be ascertained by the county court upon a civil bill action brought for that purpose: Provided, however, that no person shall search for, open, or work any mine or minerals, by virtue of this paragraph, on any spot of ground on which any church or other place of worship, graveyard, cemetery, or public school is situate, nor within thirty yards thereof, nor upon any spot of ground on which any house, outhouse, garden, orchard, or avenue is situate, without the consent of the tenant in possession thereof first had and obtained.

### Cottier tenancies

16.—(1) Where any landlord has by any agreement or memorandum in writing let a tenement, wherever situate, consisting of a dwelling-house or cottage without land, or with any portion of land not exceeding half an acre, at a rent not exceeding the rate of £5 by the year, for one month, or from month to month, or in like manner for any lesser period of time, and has thereby undertaken to keep and maintain the said dwelling-house or cottage in tenantable condition and repair, that tenancy shall constitute and be deemed to be a cottier tenancy within the meaning of this Schedule, and shall be subject to the provisions of this paragraph.

(2)   In case any such tenancy shall be determined by notice to quit, served by the landlord, the landlord shall pay to the tenant a fair compensation for any crops which may be growing on the land belonging to the tenement, or any benefit accruing from the manuring of the land, to be recovered by civil bill.

1529

(3)  The landlord of such a cottier tenement is bound to keep and maintain the dwelling-house in tenantable condition and repair; and where it is proved that the said dwelling-house was, by the landlord's default, unfit for occupation by reason of the want of such repairs, no rent or compensation for the occupation of the tenement during the time it continues in such state and condition is recoverable.

## Ordinary remedies preserved

17.  Nothing in this Schedule deprives any landlord or owner of lands of any other remedy, either at law or in equity, which he might previously have had or pursued against any person for any loss or damage sustained by that landlord or other person, or for preventing such loss or damage.

# EXPLANATORY NOTE

## SCHEDULE 3

This Schedule, with Article 81, contains provisions derived from Deasy's Act which apply where the relation of landlord and tenant was created under that Act.

The paragraphs of the Schedule correspond to provisions of the Act as follows –

| Paragraph of Schedule | Section of Deasy's Act |
|:---:|:---:|
| 1 | 41 |
| 2 | 42 |
| 3 | 34 |
| 4 | 50 |
| 5 | cf. 17 |
| 6 | 25 |
| 7 | — |
| 8 | 26 |
| 9 | 27 |
| 10 | 28 |
| 11 | 29 |
| 12 | 30 |
| 13 | 31 |
| 14 | 38 |
| 15 | 32 |
| 16 | 81-83 |
| 17 | 39 |

RECOMMENDED DRAFT ORDER IN COUNCIL UNDER
PARAGRAPH 1 OF SCHEDULE 1 TO THE NORTHERN
IRELAND ACT 1974

DRAFT STATUTORY INSTRUMENTS

**1989 No.      (N.I.    )**

**NORTHERN IRELAND**

**Succession (Northern Ireland) Order 1989**

*Laid before Parliament in draft*

*Made*

*Coming into operation in accordance with Article 1(2)*

ARRANGEMENT OF ARTICLES

PART I

INTRODUCTORY

1534

At the Court at                    , the          day of                    1989

Present,

The Queen's Most Excellent Majesty in Council

Whereas a draft of this Order has been approved by a resolution of each House of Parliament:

Now, therefore, Her Majesty, in exercise of the powers conferred by paragraph 1 of Schedule 1 to the Northern Ireland Act 1974, and of all other powers enabling Her in that behalf, is pleased, by and with the advice of Her Privy Council, to order, and it is hereby ordered, as follows:-

## PART I

## INTRODUCTORY

**Title and commencement**

1.—(1)   This Order may be cited as the Succession (Northern Ireland) Order 1989.

(2)   This Order comes into operation on such day or days as the Head of the Department of Finance and Personnel may by order appoint.

(3)   If different days are appointed for the coming into operation of different provisions of this Order, any reference in a provision to the commencement of the Order is a reference to the commencement of that provision.

# EXPLANATORY NOTE

## ARTICLE 1

This Article gives the title of the Order and provides for its provisions to come into operation on an appointed day or days.

**Interpretation**

**2.**—(1)  The Interpretation Act (Northern Ireland) 1954 applies to Article 1 and the following provisions of this Order as it applies to a Measure of the Northern Ireland Assembly.

(2)  In this Order –

"personal representatives" means the executors or executor, original or by representation, or the administrators or administrator for the time being of a deceased person;

"property" includes any legal estate, legal interest or equitable interest in land, any chattels, any thing in action, and any rights which are treated commercially as property;

"the Property Order" means the Property (Northern Ireland) Order 1989;

"witness", in relation to a will, means a witness who attests the testator's signature or acknowledgment of his signature and signs the will in the presence of the testator or a witness who, having signed the will before the testator, acknowledges his signature in the presence of the testator.

(3)  In this Order, any reference to a person's "estate" is a reference to all property to which he is beneficially entitled for an estate or interest not ceasing on his death.

# EXPLANATORY NOTE

## ARTICLE 2

This Article provides for the interpretation of the Order.

*Paragraph (1)* attracts the Interpretation Act (Northern Ireland) 1954. Section 46(1) of that Act defines "will" as including codicil.

*Paragraph (2)* defines certain expressions which appear in the Order as follows –

| *Expression* | *Article* |
| --- | --- |
| "personal representatives" | 12(2); 29(3); 31 |
| "property" | 2(3); 12(2); 17; 19; 20; 21; 23; 31 |
| "the Property Order" | 26(e)(iv), (f)(i) |
| "witness" | 5; 7; 8; 9; 10; 11 |

*Paragraph (3)* explains what is meant by a person's "estate": see Articles 3; 29(3)(4).

# PART II
## WILLS

*Scope of, and power to make, will*

**Power to dispose of estate by will**

3.  Subject to this Part, a person may dispose of all his estate by a will.

## EXPLANATORY NOTE

ARTICLE 3                                 Property Bill Cl. 222(1)
                                          WA 1837 s. 3

This Article sets out the power of any person to dispose of his estate by will. "Estate" is defined in Article 2(3) as all property to which a person is entitled for an estate or interest not ceasing at his death. "Property" is defined in Article 2(2) as including any legal estate or legal or equitable interest in land, any chattels, any thing in action and any rights which are treated commercially as property. A will is normally positive (that is, it identifies the beneficiaries); but it may be wholly negative – the express wish that "all I possess is not given to my husband" deprives the husband of his intestate succession rights and by implication gives his share to others entitled on intestacy; *In re Wynn* [1984] 1 WLR 237.

The Article reproduces the substance of existing law.

**Minority**

4.—(1)  No will made by a person under the age of 18 years is valid, unless he is or has been married.

(2)  No will made before 1 January 1970 by a person under the age of 21 years is valid.

(3)  No will made before the commencement of this Order by a person who, at the date of the will, had not attained the age of 18 years is valid, even though he then was or had been married.

# EXPLANATORY NOTE

ARTICLE 4

Property Bill Cl. 223
WA 1837 s. 7
Age of Majority Act
(NI) 1969 s. 2
SR & O (NI) 1969 No.327

This Article renders a person competent to make a will if he has attained the requisite age or status.

If the will was made before 1 January 1970, the testator must have been aged at least 21 years when the will was made.

If the will was made between 31 December 1969 and the commencement of the Order, the testator must have been aged at least 18 years when the will was made.

If the will is made after the commencement of the Order it is sufficient that, when the will was made, the testator either had reached his eighteenth birthday or, if he was under 18, he was then married or had been married (that is, his spouse had died or there had been a divorce or a decree of nullity of a voidable marriage – see Matrimonial Causes (Northern Ireland) Order 1978 Article 18).

So much of paragraph (1) as permits a minor to make a will if he is or has been married is new.

*Execution of will*

## Formalities for execution

5.—(1) No will is valid unless it is in writing and is executed in accordance with the following requirements, that is to say, –

(a) it is signed by the testator, or by some other person in his presence and by his direction; and

(b) it appears from the will or is shown that the testator intended by his signature to give effect to the will; and

(c) the signature is made or acknowledged by the testator in the presence of two or more witnesses present at the same time; and

(d) each witness, in the presence of the testator (but not necessarily in the presence of any other witness), either –

(i) attests the testator's signature or acknowledgment of his signature and signs the will; or

(ii) acknowledges his signature.

(2) No form of attestation or acknowledgment is necessary.

# EXPLANATORY NOTE

ARTICLE 5

Property Bill Cl. 224
WA 1837 ss. 9, 13
Wills Act Amendment
Act 1852
AJA 1982 ss. 17,73(6)(a)

This Article, which supersedes section 9 of the Wills Act 1837 and the Wills Act Amendment Act 1852, corresponds to the section substituted for section 9 by section17 of the Administration of Justice Act 1982.

*Paragraph (1)(a)* requires the will to be in writing and to be signed by the testator or by some other person in his presence and by his direction. This repeats the former law.

*Paragraph (1)(b)* makes it sufficient that it should appear that the testator intended by his signature to give effect to the will. The former law was more strict, because it required the signature to be at the foot or end of the will (1837 s. 9) or, at least, at, after, following, under, beside or opposite the end (the 1852 Act).

*Paragraph (1)(c)* requires the signature to be made or acknowledged by the testator in the presence of two or more witnesses present at the same time. This repeats the former law.

*Paragraph (1)(d)* requires each witness either to attest and sign the will or to acknowledge his signature in the presence of the testator (but not necessarily in the presence of the other witness or witnesses). This repeats the former law, except that the provision about acknowledgement is new. To attest a will is to certify on it that it has been signed by the proper person as testator: attestation is required only from a witness who signs the will after the testator, and not from one who signs beforehand and acknowledges his signature after the testator has signed.

*Paragraph (2)* renders it unnecessary to have any particular form of attestation. This re-enacts the final passage of section 9 of the Act of 1837. Although no form of attestation is necessary, it is desirable that the circumstances of attestation be recited in a usual form – otherwise the Probate and Matrimonial Office will call for an affidavit of due execution (RSC Order 97 Rule 9). In a case where attestation is not necessary (i.e. where a witness acknowledges a signature he had made beforehand) the will may seem incomplete on the face of it, and the Probate and Matrimonial Office may be expected to ask for an affidavit of acknowledgement. If this is not forthcoming (e.g. because the witnesses have died), affidavits of handwriting of the testator and the witnesses may be asked for. If all this fails, it will be for the court to decide whether to admit the will to probate, applying the maxim *omnia praesumunter rite esse acta* *(Re Denning* [1958] 1 WLR 462). This Article is subject to the transitional provisions in paragraph 2 of the Schedule.

## Testamentary execution of power

**6.**—(1) No appointment made by will, in exercise of any power, is valid unless the will is executed in accordance with Article 5.

(2) Paragraph (1) applies notwithstanding anything to the contrary in the instrument creating the power.

(3) A will executed in accordance with Article 5 is, so far as respects the execution thereof, a valid execution of a power of appointment by will, notwithstanding that the instrument creating the power expressly requires that a will made in exercise of such power should be executed with some additional or other form of execution or formality.

# EXPLANATORY NOTE

ARTICLE 6
Property Bill Cl. 225
WA 1837 s. 10
WA 1963 s. 2(2)

This Article makes it clear that no exercise by a will of a power of appointment is valid unless the will is properly executed in accordance with Article 5; but if the will is so executed any additional formalities prescribed by the document creating the power to be observed on an exercise of the power may be ignored. A similar provision is made in Article 188 of the Property Order for instruments inter vivos.

The Article is applied by paragraph 17(2) of the Schedule to wills which do not comply with Article 5 but do comply with the rules governing the conflict of laws or with international law.

The Article is subject to the transitional provision in paragraph 3 of the Schedule.

## Incompetency of witness

**7.** If a witness to a will is at the time of its execution or becomes at any time afterwards incompetent as a witness to prove its execution, the will is not invalid on that account.

ARTICLE 7                                    Property Bill Cl. 227
                                             WA 1837 s. 14
                                             cf. Property Order Art. 83(5)

This Article prevents a will from being treated as invalid on the ground that a witness to it is incompetent to be sworn as a witness in legal proceedings to prove the execution of the will. At the present time the provision has very limited effect, because the only witness to a will who would be incompetent in a court would be a person of unsound mind. In 1837 the rules of incompetency were more widely drawn and would have affected a party to the court proceedings or his spouse or any person who had an interest in the result of the litigation.

The Article reproduces existing law.

### Gift to witness

**8.**—(1) Subject to paragraph (3), if a witness to a will is a person to whom, or to whose spouse, any estate or interest in property is given by the will (whether by way of gift or by way of exercise of a power of appointment, but other than by way of a charge or direction for the payment of debts), the gift or appointment is void so far as concerns that witness or his spouse or any person claiming under the witness or spouse.

(2)  Notwithstanding that property is given by will as mentioned in paragraph (1), the witness is competent as a witness to prove –

(a)  the execution of the will;

(b)  the validity or invalidity of the will.

(3)  Witnessing by a person to whom, or to whose spouse, property is given as mentioned in paragraph (1) is to be disregarded if the will is duly executed without his signature and without that of any other such person.

# EXPLANATORY NOTE

ARTICLE 8
Property Bill Cl. 228<br>WA 1837 s. 15<br>WA 1968 s. 1(1)

This Article makes a gift in a will void if the beneficiary, or his or her spouse, witnesses the will.

*Paragraph (1)* makes a gift to a witness or the spouse of a witness void. It is immaterial whether the gift is of the testator's own property or whether it relates to other property over which the testator had a power of appointment. In the former case the subject of the gift will fall into residue (Article 19) or, if the gift is one of residue, pass as on an intestacy; in the latter it will pass as in default of appointment. The paragraph does not apply to a charge or direction for the payment of debts.

*Paragraph (2)* makes it clear that although the gift is void the act of witnessing is valid. Paragraph (1) is concerned with the essential validity of the will and not with its form.

*Paragraph (3)* prevents paragraph (1) applying to a supernumerary witness (e.g. if there are three witnesses only one of whom is affected by the paragraph).

Paragraph (3) applies only to deaths occuring after the commencement of the Order: it does not matter when the will was executed (Schedule, paragraph 4).

**Witnessing by creditor**

**9.** Where a will charges any property with a debt, any creditor whose debt is so charged or the spouse of any such creditor, is not incompetent, on account only of the charge, –

(a) to act as a witness to the will; or

(b) as a witness to prove –

(i) the execution of the will; or

(ii) the validity or invalidity of the will.

# EXPLANATORY NOTE

ARTICLE 9                          Property Bill Cl. 229
                                   WA 1837 s. 16

This Article applies to a will which contains a clause charging property with a debt. Where the creditor entitled to the debt, or his spouse, witnesses the will, he or she is not disqualified, by reason of the charge, for acting as a witness in court proceedings to prove the will. Article 8(1) provides that such a creditor is not disqualified for taking the benefit of the charge.

The Article reproduces existing law.

**Witnessing by executor**

**10.** An executor of a will is not incompetent, on account only of his being an executor, –

(a) to act as a witness to the will; or

(b) as a witness to prove –

  (i) the execution of the will; or

  (ii) the validity or invalidity of the will.

# EXPLANATORY NOTE

ARTICLE 10                          Property Bill Cl. 230
                                    WA 1837 s. 17

This Article permits an executor to witness a will and to give evidence as a witness in probate proceedings.

The Article reproduces existing law.

**Alteration of will after execution**

   **11.**   No obliteration, interlineation or other alteration made in any will, after its execution, is valid, or has any effect except so far as the words or effect of the will before the alteration are not apparent, unless the alteration is executed in the manner in which a will is required to be executed; but the will, with the alteration as part of it, is duly executed if the signature of the testator and the subscription of the witnesses are made in the margin, or on some other part of the will opposite or near the alteration, or at the foot or end of or opposite a memorandum referring to the alteration and written at the end or some other part of the will.

# EXPLANATORY NOTE

ARTICLE 11                                     Property Bill Cl. 234
                                               WA 1837 s. 21

This Article prevents alterations in a will from being effective unless executed in the same way as a will. But where an obliteration is effective to destroy the original wording, so that it is not apparent, the obliteration achieves its object, even though not properly executed. For this purpose "apparent" means apparent on inspection of the document: extraordinary steps such as the use of infra-red rays cannot be had recourse to unless the obliteration was intended by the testator to be effective only on condition that some alternative provision (which fails for lack of proper execution) should be effective ("dependent relative revocation").

The Article reproduces existing law.

*Effect of marriage, divorce, etc.*

**Effect of marriage**

**12.**—(1) Subject to paragraphs (2) to (4), a will is revoked by the testator's marriage.

(2)  A disposition in a will in exercise of a power of appointment takes effect notwithstanding the testator's subsequent marriage unless the property so appointed would in default of appointment pass to his personal representatives.

(3)  Where it appears from a will that at the time it was made the testator was expecting to be married to a particular person and that he intended that the will should not be revoked by the marriage, the will is not revoked by his marriage to that person.

(4)  Where it appears from a will that at the time it was made the testator was expecting to be married to a particular person and that he intended that a disposition in the will should not be revoked by his marriage to that person, –

(a) that disposition takes effect notwithstanding the marriage; and

(b) any other disposition in the will takes effect also, unless it appears from the will that the testator intended the disposition to be revoked by the marriage.

# EXPLANATORY NOTE

ARTICLE 12

Property Bill Cl. 231
WA 1837 s. 18
Wills (Amendment) Act
(NI) 1954
AJA 1982 ss. 18(1),73(7)

This Article explains the effect of a testator's marriage on his will.

*Paragraph (1)* contains the general provision that a will is revoked by the testator's marriage.

*Paragraph (2)* is concerned with the exercise of a power of appointment by will. If the property which is the subject of the power would pass to the testator's personal representatives in default of appointment, the general revocation of the will extends to the appointment: if it would not so pass, the appointment is not affected by the revocation.

*Paragraph (3)* prevents a will being revoked by a marriage if it appears from the will that when it was made the testator expected to be married to a particular person and that he intended the will not to be revoked by the marriage.

*Paragraph (4)* is concerned with a particular disposition in a will (whereas paragraph (3) is concerned with the whole will). If it appears from the will that when it was made the testator expected to be married to a particular person and that he intended the disposition not to be revoked by the marriage, that disposition is not affected by the marriage and the rest of the will is also unaffected unless it appears from the will that the testator intended the rest to be revoked by the marriage.

Paragraph 5 of the Schedule prevents paragraph (4) applying to a will made before the commencement of the Order.

**Effect of dissolution or annulment of marriage or judicial separation**

**13.**—(1) Where, after a testator has made a will, a decree of a court dissolves or annuls his marriage or declares it void, or a decree of judicial separation is granted and is in force and the separation is continuing at the time of his death, then, except in so far as a contrary intention appears from the will, –

(a)  the will takes effect as if –

(i)  any appointment of his spouse as an executor or as the executor and trustee of the will were omitted (and where the will appoints a substitute executor or executor and trustee in the event of the spouse's death, as if the spouse had predeceased the testator), and

(ii)  any appointment of the spouse as being an object of a power of appointment exercisable by the will or any mention of the spouse as a beneficiary or potential beneficiary under any trust or power of appointment created by the will or having a power of appointment under the will were omitted; and

(b)  any devise or bequest to the spouse lapses.

(2)  Where a devise or bequest lapses by virtue of paragraph (1) and the will (or a codicil) contains a devise or bequest to some other person in the event of the spouse's death (whether expressed in terms of the spouse failing to survive the testator at all or for a specified period or otherwise), the spouse is to be deemed to have predeceased the testator.

(3)  Where a devise or bequest which lapses by virtue of paragraph (1) is one of a share of residue, the will takes effect as if the devise or bequest of the residue were to the other person or persons entitled thereto, to the exclusion of the spouse.

(4)  Paragraph (1)(b) is without prejudice to any right of the spouse to apply for financial provision under the Inheritance (Provision for Family and Dependants) (Northern Ireland) Order 1979.

(5)  Where –

(a)  by the terms of a will an interest in remainder is subject to a life interest; and

(b)  the life interest lapses by virtue of paragraph (1)(b),

the interest in remainder is to be treated as if it had not been subject to the life interest and, if it was contingent upon the termination of the life interest, as if it had not been so contingent.

(6)  In this Article "spouse" includes a former spouse and a putative spouse, and any reference to the event of a spouse's death includes any reference in the will to that death whether expressed in terms of the spouse failing to survive the testator at all or for a specified period.

# EXPLANATORY NOTE

ARTICLE 13                             cf. Mat. Causes (NI) O 1978
Art.20(2)
AJA 1982 ss. 18(2),73(6)(b)

This Article provides for the effect upon a will of the dissolution or annulment of marriage or judicial separation. A marriage may be dissolved on divorce or on a presumption of death under Article 21 of the Matrimonial Causes (Northern Ireland) Order 1978. A decree of nullity can be granted under Article 15 of that Order. A declaration of the invalidity of a marriage can be made under section 1 of the Legitimacy Declaration Act (Ireland) 1868 (to be replaced by Article 31(1) of the Matrimonial and Family Proceedings (Northern Ireland) Order 1989).

*Paragraph (1)* applies where (1) a marriage is dissolved, or (2) a marriage is annulled or (3) a marriage is declared void, or (4) the parties to a marriage are judicially separated and the separation is continuing. Where a testator who was (or is) a party to such a marriage has, by an existing will, appointed his former spouse (or spouse) as executor, or executor and trustee, the appointment is ineffective, and if the will makes any gift to the spouse the gift lapses. Where the will names a substitute executor (or trustee) whose appointment is expressed to take effect in the event of the spouse's death, the spouse is deemed (for that purpose) to have predeceased the testator. The paragraph also prevents the spouse from being the object of a power of appointment exercisable by the will or a beneficiary or potential beneficiary of a trust or a power of appointment created by the will or from being able to exercise a power of appointment created by the will (in which event the rights of persons entitled in default of appointment will not be affected – Theobald on Wills, 13th Ed. para. 2027). "Potential beneficiary" would include a person capable of benefiting under a discretionary trust. All this is subject to any contrary intention appearing from the will. In sub-paragraph (b) "lapse" has its ordinary meaning of "fail" *(In re Sinclair* [1985] 2 WLR 795).

*Paragraph (2)* applies where there is a substitute gift in the will dependent upon the spouse failing to survive the testator or failing to survive him for a particular period (say, one month). The substitute gift has effect as if the spouse had predeceased the testator.

*Paragraph (3)* applies where the lapsed gift is one of a share of residue. Ordinarily the lapsed share would devolve as on an intestacy, but the paragraph causes it to go to the other residuary legatee or legatees.

*Paragraph (4)* preserves the right of the former spouse (or spouse) to apply to the court for financial provision for his or her reasonable maintenance under the Inheritance (Provision for Family and Dependants) (Northern Ireland) Order 1979.

*Paragraph (5)* deals with the situation where the will confers an interest in remainder subject to a life interest in the former spouse and the life interest lapses under paragraph (1). The life interest is to be ignored and the remainder will be accelerated (and, if it is contingent upon the termination of the life interest, the contingency will be ignored).

*Paragraph (6)* contains definitions.

Paragraph 6 of the Schedule confines the operation of the Article to the wills of testators dying after the commencement of the Order.

**Revocation**

**14.**—(1) No will, or any part thereof, is revocable otherwise than –

(a)  in accordance with Article 12 (marriage); or

(b)  by another will; or

(c)  by some writing, declaring an intention to revoke the will, executed in the manner in which a will is required to be executed; or

(d)  by the testator, or some person in his presence and by his direction, burning, tearing or otherwise destroying the will, with the intention of revoking it.

(2)   No will is revoked by any presumption of an intention on the ground of an alteration in circumstances.

# EXPLANATORY NOTE

ARTICLE 14                          Property Bill Cl. 232, 233
                                    WA 1837 ss. 19, 20

This Article is concerned with revocation of a will.

*Paragraph (1)* lists the only ways in which a will can be revoked –

  (*a*)  by marriage in accordance with Article 12;

  (*b*)  by another will;

  (c)  by a document declaring an intention to revoke the will and executed in the same way as a will;

  (*d*)  by destruction of the will with the intent to revoke it: when the act of destruction is done by another at the testator's direction, it must be done in the testator's presence.

*Paragraph (2)* prevents a presumption of a testator's intention to revoke his will from arising because of some change in circumstances. For example, the fact that a testator by deed removed the greater part of a fund from the operation of his will did not prevent the will from operating on the residue of the fund: *Re Wells' Trusts*(1889) 42 Ch. D. 646.

The Article reproduces existing law.

**Revival of revoked will**

15.—(1) No will, or any part thereof, which has been revoked, is revived otherwise than by –

(a) re-execution of the revoked will; or

(b) a codicil showing an intention to revive the revoked will.

(2) When any will which has been, first, partly revoked, and later wholly revoked, is revived, the revival does not extend to the part revoked before the revocation of the whole will unless an intention to revive that part is shown.

# EXPLANATORY NOTE

ARTICLE 15                                    Property Bill Cl. 235
                                              WA 1837 s. 22

This Article is concerned with the revival of a revoked will.

*Paragraph (1)* permits revival only by re-execution of the revoked will or by a codicil showing an intention to revive the revoked will. Where a testator's will was revoked by his marriage, it was revived by his writing on the envelope containing the will "the herein named [executrix and sole beneficiary] is now my lawful wedded wife", the writing being duly signed and attested: *In the Estate of Davis* [1952] 2 All ER 509.

*Paragraph (2)* deals with a will which has been subject to partial revocation and which is later completely revoked. Revival of the will negatives only the final revocation: the parts of the will earlier revoked still stand revoked unless an intention to revive them is shown.

The Article reproduces existing law.

**Effect of re-execution or codicil**

16. For the purposes of this Order –

(a) every will which is re-executed is made at the time of the re-execution;

(b) every will which is confirmed or revived by a codicil is made at the time of the execution of the codicil.

ARTICLE 16                          Property Bill Cl. 246(2)
                                    WA 1837 s. 34

This Article treats a will which is re-executed as made on the date of re-execution and a will which is confirmed or revived by a codicil as made at the date of the codicil.

The effect of confirming a will by codicil is that the dispositions of the will have effect in the same way as if the words of the will had been contained in the codicil.

Paragraph 14 of the Schedule prevents paragraph (b) of the Article from applying to Article 27 (illegitimate children): the former rule continues to apply (that a reference in a will to "children" prima facie excludes illegitimate children) for a will made before midnight on 31 December 1977, even though the will is re-executed or is confirmed by codicil thereafter.

With the substitution of "confirmed" for "republished" the Article reproduces existing law. Publication of a will was formerly equivalent to delivery of a deed, but was made unnecessary by section 13 of the Wills Act 1837. Article 5, which sets out the formalities requisite to the execution of a will, has no requirement for publication.

*Dispositions*

**Will speaks from death**

**17.**—(1) Every will is to be construed, with reference to the property referred to in it, to speak and take effect as if it had been executed immediately before the death of the testator, unless a contrary intention appears from the will.

(2) No conveyance or other act, made or done subsequently to the execution of a will, of or relating to any property referred to in the will, prevents the operation of the will with respect to the estate or interest in that property of which the testator has power to dispose by will at the time of his death.

(3) The reference in paragraph (2) to an act does not include an act which revokes the will.

# EXPLANATORY NOTE

ARTICLE 17            Property Bill Cl. 236, 237
                                      WA 1837 ss. 23, 24

This Article is concerned with the property on which a will operates.

*Paragraph (1)* encapsulates the rule that a will is ambulatory and applies to property acquired by the testator between the date of the will and his death as well as to property held by him at the date of the will. This was always the rule for personal property, but before 1838 a contrary rule applied to realty.

*Paragraph (2)* prevents a gift of property from being revoked by reason of some alteration in the nature of the testator's interest in the property between the date of the will and the date of death. If the testator held a leasehold estate in land at the time when he made his will but had acquired the freehold before his death, a devise of the land by the will is not affected: *Saxton v. Saxton* (1879) 13 Ch. D. 359.

*Paragraph (3)* prevents paragraph (2) from applying to an act which revokes the will. The corresponding words seem to have been included in section 23 of the Wills Act 1837 out of caution, because a revoking act is doubtfully "an act ... relating to any property". Revoking acts are marriage (Article 12) and the acts listed in Article 14.

The Article reproduces existing law.

**Words of limitation unnecessary**

**18.**—(1) A devise of land passes the fee simple absolute in possession or other the whole estate or interest that the testator had power to dispose of by will.

(2) A devise creating an interest of any kind in land passes the largest interest of that kind which the testator had power to create in the land.

(3) This Article applies whether the devisee takes beneficially or on trust and is subject to any contrary intention which appears from the will.

ARTICLE 18                         Property Bill Cl. 242
                                         WA 1837 ss. 28, 30, 31

This Article renders words of limitation unnecessary in a devise of land.

*Paragraph (1)* causes a devise to carry the fullest interest in the land that the testator had power to dispose of.

*Paragraph (2)* applies a similar rule to the creation of a new interest (e.g. an easement).

*Paragraph (3)* makes it clear that the Article applies whether the devisee takes beneficially or on trust, but makes the Article subject to any contrary intention appearing from the will.

This Article reproduces existing law except so far as it refers to the creation of an estate or interest (as to which see Schedule, paragraph 7).

**Residuary dispositions to carry property comprised in lapsed and void dispositions**

**19.** Unless a contrary intention appears from the will, if a disposition in a will fails or is void by reason of the death of the intended beneficiary in the lifetime of the testator, by reason of being contrary to law, or otherwise, any property comprised or intended to be comprised in that disposition is included in the residuary devise or bequest (if any) contained in the will.

# EXPLANATORY NOTE

ARTICLE 19                          Property Bill Cl. 238
                                    WA 1837 s. 25

This Article contains the rule that, if a specific devise in a will fails to take effect, the property comprised in the devise falls into residue, unless the will indicates otherwise. If a gift of residue fails, the property passes as on an intestacy (Administration of Estates Act (Northern Ireland) 1955 s. 18).

The Article applies to all property a rule corresponding to that which, before 1838, had always applied to personalty.

The Article reproduces existing law.

## Implied execution of general power of appointment

**20.** A general or residuary disposition of property of any description (however expressed) is to be construed to include any property, to which the description extends, which the testator has power to appoint in any manner he thinks proper and operates as an execution of the power, unless a contrary intention appears from the will.

# EXPLANATORY NOTE

ARTICLE 20                          Property Bill Cl. 241
                                        WA 1837 s. 27

This Article causes a general or residuary devise or bequest to carry property over which the testator had a general power of appointment at the time of his death (whether or not he had such a power at the time of making the will). The Article does not apply to a power of revocation and re-appointment.

The Article reproduces existing law.

### Contingent and future testamentary gifts carry the intermediate income

**21.** A contingent or future specific devise or bequest of property, a contingent residuary devise of land and a specific or residuary devise of land to trustees upon trust for persons whose interests are contingent or executory all carry the intermediate income of that property or land from the death of the testator, except so far as that income, or any part of it, is otherwise expressly disposed of.

# EXPLANATORY NOTE

ARTICLE 21                           Property Bill Cl. 240
                                                LPA 1925 s. 175

This Article deals with the question of when contingent or other future gifts carry intermediate income. Generally, the determination of whether a gift carries intermediate income depends upon the testator's intention as shown by the will; but rules have been developed to cover cases where the intention is uncertain (i.e. where the income is not otherwise disposed of either expressly or by implication).

1. At present, the basic rule is that a contingent or future gift does not carry income.

2. A present specific devise or a present specific bequest, if vested, carries income from the death of the testator. The Article extends this to a contingent or future specific devise or bequest.

3. A contingent residuary bequest of personal estate carries the income and so does a gift of realty and personalty given together. The Article extends to realty the rule applicable to personalty and mixed residues, and causes a contingent residuary devise of land to carry the intermediate income.

4. Where there is a contingent residuary bequest of personalty, the income must be accumulated until the happening of the contingency. The Article extends this to devises of land to trustees for persons with contingent or future interests.

The provisions of the Article mentioned in paragraphs 2 and 3 above apply to contingent or future gifts where there is no intermediate interest – e.g. a gift to such members of a class of persons as attain 21. The Article also applies similar rules to such gifts which are preceded by some interest in another person – in this case there is a settlement and the property will be vested in the trustees of the settlement who will pay to that person the "income ... expressly disposed of" to him and will hold the balance for the person entitled in remainder.

The Article does not affect the practice of the Chancery Division under which a minor who is entitled under the will of his parent or of a person *in loco parentis* to a legacy contingently on his attaining his majority is entitled to maintenance during his minority out of the income of the legacy. See also sections 32 and 53 of the Trustee Act (Northern Ireland) 1958.

Paragraph 8 of the Schedule confines the operation of the Article to the wills of testators dying after the commencement of the Order.

**Gifts to children etc. who predecease testator**

**22.**—(1) Where –

(a) a will contains a devise or bequest to a child or remoter descendant of the testator; and

(b) the intended beneficiary dies before the testator, leaving issue; and

(c) issue of the intended beneficiary are living at the testator's death,

then, unless a contrary intention appears from the will, the devise or bequest takes effect as a devise or bequest to the issue living at the testator's death.

(2) Where –

(a) a will contains a devise or bequest to a class of persons consisting of children or remoter descendants of the testator; and

(b) a member of the class dies before the testator, leaving issue; and

(c) issue of that member are living at the testator's death,

then, unless a contrary intention appears from the will, the devise or bequest takes effect as if the class included the issue of its deceased member living at the testator's death.

(3) Issue take under this Article through all degrees, according to their stock, in equal shares if more than one, any gift or share which their parent would have taken and so that no issue take whose parent is living at the testator's death and so capable of taking.

(4) For the purposes of this Article –

(a) the illegitimacy of any person is to be disregarded; and

(b) a person conceived before the testator's death and born living thereafter is to be taken to have been living at the testator's death.

# EXPLANATORY NOTE

ARTICLE 22

Property Bill Cl. 243
WA 1837 s. 33
Family Law Reform (NI)
Order 1977 Art. 5
AJA 1982 ss. 19,73(6)(c),(d)

This Article preserves a testamentary gift to issue of a testator who predecease him but leave issue of their own who survive him.

*Paragraph (1)* provides that where a will makes a gift to a child or remoter descendant of the testator and the intended beneficiary predeceases the testator but leaves issue who survive him, the gift takes effect as one to the issue, unless a contrary intention appears from the will.

*Paragraph (2)* makes a similar provision for class gifts – the intended beneficiary's issue become members of the class in his place.

*Paragraph (3)* provides for the substituted issue to take by their stock (*per stirpes*) and not on an individual count (*per capita*). For a similar provision which operates on an intestacy, see the Administration of Estates Act (Northern Ireland) 1955 s.15.

*Paragraph (4)* provides for two special cases –

   (a)  The illegitimacy of any person is to be disregarded. This includes the illegitimacy of any person who takes as beneficiary and that of any person through whom he is traced. (See Article 31 for the protection of executors or trustees who distribute in ignorance of the existence of an illegitimate child).

   (b)  A child in his mother's womb at the time of the testator's death is to be treated as living at that time if he is subsequently born alive.

*Paragraph 9* of the Schedule confines the operation of the Article to the wills of testators dying after the commencement of the Order. Savings in the Property (Consequential Provisions) Order for section 33 of the Wills Act 1837 and Article 5 of the Family Law Reform (Northern Ireland) Order 1977 ensure that they continue to apply to the wills of testators dying before then.

**Presumption as to effect of gifts to spouses**

**23.** Except where a contrary intention is shown it is to be presumed that if a testator devises or bequeaths property to his spouse in terms which in themselves would give an absolute interest to the spouse, but by the same instrument purports to give his issue an interest in the same property, the gift to the spouse is absolute notwithstanding the purported gift to the issue.

## EXPLANATORY NOTE

ARTICLE 23                    AJA 1982 ss. 22,73(6)(c)

This Article is concerned with a will which makes an absolute gift of property to the testator's spouse but also purports to give his issue an interest in the same property. The Article renders the gift to the spouse absolute, unless a contrary intention is shown. Extrinsic evidence of intention is admissible.

The Article applies only to the will of a testator dying after the commencement of the Order – Schedule paragraph 10.

**Land subject to an option**

    **24.**   The exercise after a testator's death of an option to purchase land contained in or comprising his estate does not adeem a devise of the land or effect a conversion of the land with effect from any time other than that at which the option is exercised.

# EXPLANATORY NOTE

ARTICLE 24

This Article is concerned with one aspect of the equitable doctrine of conversion under which, for purposes of the devolution of property on death, land which is directed to be converted into money (as on a trust for sale) or has been contracted to be sold is treated as money, and money which is directed to be laid out in the purchase of land is treated as land. The aspect in question relates to the exercise of an option to buy land from a testator. Under present law, if the land is the subject of a specific gift and the will was made after the option was granted, the donee takes the land (or the proceeds of sale if the option is exercised after the testator's death); but if the option was created after the date of the will, its exercise after his death adeems the gift, and similarly if the devise is a residuary one the exercise of the option after the testator's death converts the land with effect retrospective to the death so that it passes as residuary personalty and not as residuary realty – this is so even though the option did not arise until after the testator's death.

The Article eliminates this element of retrospection where an option is exercised, by providing that there is no conversion with effect from any other time. Nor is a devise of the land adeemed (although the devisee will be bound by the option).

The Article applies only to the will of a testator dying after the commencement of the Order – Schedule paragraph 11.

**Extrinsic evidence**

**25.**—(1) This Article applies to a will –

(a) in so far as any part of it is meaningless;

(b) in so far as the language used in any part of it is ambiguous on the face of it;

(c) in so far as evidence, other than evidence of the testator's intention, shows that the language used in any part of it is ambiguous in the light of surrounding circumstances.

(2) In so far as this Article applies to a will extrinsic evidence, including evidence of the testator's intention, may be admitted to assist in its application.

# EXPLANATORY NOTE

ARTICLE 25                              AJA 1982 s. 21

Normally, the construction of a will is a matter of finding the testator's intention as conveyed by the language he has used. This Article allows extrinsic evidence to be admitted in order to assist in understanding a will, in certain limited circumstances.

*Paragraph (1)* sets out those circumstances –

- (*a*) where part of the will is meaningless;
- (*b*) where there is a patent ambiguity;
- (*c*) where there is a latent ambiguity shown up by evidence (but not evidence of the testator's intention).

*Paragraph (2)* allows the introduction of extrinsic evidence in those circumstances in order to assist the interpretation of the will. That evidence may include evidence of the testator's intention (that is, although evidence of his intention may not be admitted to uncover a latent ambiguity, once such an ambiguity is found by other means the probate court may then admit evidence of his intention to show what that intention really was).

As the extrinsic evidence is admissible only as an aid to interpretation, it is of no assistance unless the doubtful word or phrase, *read in its context*, is capable of bearing the meaning indicated by the evidence: *Re Williams (decd.)* [1985] 1 All ER 964 (home-made will merely listing 25 names in three groups – letter to solicitors indicating different amounts of legacy to those in each group – although admissible, the letter would be of no assistance unless the court were to re-write the will: the 25 named persons took equally).

Paragraph 12 of the Schedule confines the operation of the Article to the wills of testators dying before the commencement of the Order.

Other provisions of the Order permit extrinsic evidence, namely, those which allow something to be "shown" – see Articles 15(2) and 23 (and compare Articles12(3), (4), 13(1), 18(3), 19, 20, 22(1), (2), 26 and 27 which allow evidence only so far as it "appears from the will").

**Construction of certain expressions**

**26.** Unless a contrary intention appears from the will, in a will –

(a) "month" means calendar month;

(b) "person" includes a corporation;

(c) words in the singular include the plural, and words in the plural include the singular;

(d) words importing the masculine gender include the feminine, and words importing the feminine gender include the masculine;

(e) "land" includes –

    (i) buildings and other structures,

    (ii) land covered by water;

    (iii) any legal estate, legal interest or equitable interest in land;

    (iv) any beneficial interest, of which the testator could dispose by will, in capital money arising under the statutory trusts (within the meaning of the Property Order) of land;

    (v) if the testator dies owning no other property passing under a disposition of land, any beneficial interest, of which the testator could dispose by will, in proceeds of sale under a trust for sale of land;

(f) "realty" or any cognate expression includes –

    (i) any beneficial interest, of which the testator could dispose by will, in capital money arising under the statutory trusts (within the meaning of the Property Order) of a fee simple;

    (ii) if the testator dies owning no other property passing under a disposition of realty, any beneficial interest, of which the testator could dispose by will, in proceeds of sale under a trust for sale of a fee simple.

# EXPLANATORY NOTE

ARTICLE 26                                    Property Bill Cl. 77
                                              LPA 1925 s. 61
                                              cf. Property Order Art. 89
                                              WA 1837 s. 26

This Article lays down rules of construction for wills which, so far as the first three and part of the fourth and fifth are concerned, generally correspond to the rules applicable to the interpretation of Northern Ireland enactments. The rules apply only so far as a contrary intention does not appear from the will.

(a) "month" means calendar month (Interpretation Act s. 39(6)(c)): at common law "month" meant a lunar month *(Vone Securities Ltd.* v. *Cooke* [1979] IR59).

(b) "person" includes a corporation (Interpretation Act s. 37(1)).

(c) the singular includes the plural, and *vice versa* (Interpretation Act s.37(2)).

(d) the masculine includes the feminine, and *vice versa*: the first limb of this rule appears in s. 37(1) Interpretation Act, but there is no equivalent there of the second limb (that the feminine includes the masculine) – however, the second limb does appear in s. 61(d) Law of Property Act 1925 and s.6(b) Interpretation Act 1978 (which applies to United Kingdom enactments).

(e) "land" includes buildings and other structures, land covered by water and any legal estate, legal interest or equitable interest in land. This definition is briefer than those in s. 205(1)(ix) Law of Property Act 1925, s.45(1)(a) Interpretation Act (Northern Ireland) and Clause 1(1) Property Bill, and is close to that in Interpretation Act 1978 Sch. 1. Despite the verbal differences, the substance of all these provisions is the same – e.g. the Interpretation Act (Northern Ireland) s. 45(1)(a)(i) refers to messuages, tenements and hereditaments of any tenure: a messuage was simply a dwelling-house with the land that goes with it (cf. French "maison"), a tenement was property subject to tenure and a hereditament was property descending at common law to the heir – the first of these is covered by the reference to buildings and the other two by the references to estates or interests. The definition also brings in a reference to capital money representing settled land held on the statutory trusts (defined in Article 3 of the Property Order). Where the testator owns no land properly so called, but purports to dispose of land, the disposition will be capable of carrying his interest in the proceeds of land held on trust for sale (which, strictly, is personalty).

(f) "realty": this largely obsolete expression, if used, will be capable of covering capital money representing freehold land or, in the last resort, proceeds of freehold land held on trust for sale. The

1587

definition extends to cognate expressions, e.g. "real property" and "real estate".

The Article does not affect a will made before the commencement of the Order – Schedule paragraph 13.

## Construction of references to children or other relatives

**27.** (1) Unless a contrary intention appears from the will, in a disposition by will –

    (a) any reference (whether express or implied) to the child or children of any person is or includes a reference to any illegitimate child of that person; and

    (b) any reference (whether express or implied) to a person or persons related in some other manner to any person is or includes a reference to anyone who would be so related if he, or some other person through whom the relationship is deduced, had been born legitimate.

    (2) Paragraph (1) applies only where the reference in question is –

    (a) to a person who is to benefit or to be capable of benefiting under the disposition; or

    (b) for the purpose of designating such a person as is mentioned in sub-paragraph (a), to someone else to or through whom that person is related.

    (3) Paragraph (1) does not affect the construction of the word "heir" or "heirs".

    (4) In this Article, references to an illegitimate child include references to a child born illegitimate who is or becomes a legitimated person within the meaning of the Legitimacy Act (Northern Ireland) 1928 or a person recognised by virtue of that Act or at common law as having been legitimated.

    (5) Where under any disposition any property is limited (whether subject to any preceding limitation or charge or not) in such a way that it would, apart from this Article, devolve (as nearly as the law permits) along with a dignity or title of honour, then, whether or not the disposition contains an express reference to the dignity or title of honour, and whether or not the property or some interest in the property may in some event become severed therefrom, nothing in this Article operates to sever the property or any interest therein from the dignity or title, but the property or interest devolves in all respects as if this Article had not been enacted.

    (6) This Article is without prejudice to Articles 42, 43 and 46 of the Adoption (Northern Ireland) Order 1987 (which relate to the construction of dispositions in cases of adoption).

# EXPLANATORY NOTE

ARTICLE 27                          Family Law Reform (NI)
                                    Order 1977 Art. 4
                                    SR 1977 No. 343

For the purpose of identifying beneficiaries under a will, this Article treats illegitimate children equally with legitimate children. The Article applies only where no contrary intention appears from the will.

*Paragraph (1)* makes any reference to a child of any person include an illegitimate child, and any reference to a person related in some manner to another include a relationship traced through an illegitimate link.

*Paragraph (2)* confines the application of paragraph (1) to the identification of beneficiaries.

*Paragraph (3)* prevents the Article from applying to a reference to "heir" or "heirs" (for the meaning of these words see Administration of Estates Act (Northern Ireland)1955 s. 5 and Property Order Article 211(2)).

*Paragraph (4)* applies the Article to legitimated children as well as to those who have continued to be illegitimate. Generally, a legitimated person acquires property rights under a disposition only from the date of his legitimization.

*Paragraph (5)* prevents the Article applying to property which is limited to devolve with a dignity or title of honour.

*Paragraph (6)* preserves the rules about the property rights of adopted children. Trustees or personal represetnatives are protected under Article 31.

The Article reproduces existing law.

## Operative meaning to be preferred

**28.** If the purport of a devise or bequest admits of more than one interpretation, then, in case of doubt, the interpretation according to which the devise or bequest will be operative is to be preferred.

## EXPLANATORY NOTE

ARTICLE 28                                    Succession Act 1965
                                              (Rep. of Ireland) s. 99

Where two or more alternative meanings are capable of being applied to a provision of a will, this Article requires a meaning which gives rise to a valid gift to be preferred to a meaning that results in invalidity. The Article enunciates the rule of construction *ut res magis valeat quam pereat*.

*Rectification*

## Rectification of wills

**29.**—(1) If a court is satisfied that a will is so expressed that it fails to carry out the testator's intentions, in consequence –

(a) of a clerical error; or

(b) of a failure to understand his instructions,

it may order that the will shall be rectified so as to carry out his intentions.

(2)   An application for an order under this Article shall not, except with the permission of the court, be made after the end of the period of six months from the date on which representation with respect to the estate of the deceased is first taken out.

(3)   The provisions of this Article do not render the personal representatives of a deceased person liable for having distributed any part of the estate of the deceased, after the end of the period of six months from the date on which representation with respect to the estate of the deceased is first taken out, on the ground that they ought to have taken into account the possibility that the court might permit the making of an application for an order under this Article after the end of that period; but this paragraph does not prejudice any power to recover, by reason of the making of an order under this Article, any part of the estate so distributed.

(4)   In considering for the purposes of this Article when representation with respect to the estate of a deceased person was first taken out, a grant limited to settled land or to trust property is to be left out of account, and a grant limited to real estate or to personal estate is to be left out of account unless a grant limited to the remainder of the estate has previously been made or is made at the same time.

## EXPLANATORY NOTE

ARTICLE 29                                        AJA 1982 s. 20

This Article empowers a court to rectify a will so as to bring it into accord with the testator's intentions.

*Paragraph (1)* allows rectification on two grounds –

(*a*)  where there is a clerical error in the will, or

(*b*)  where the draftsman of the will failed to understand the testator's instructions.

*Paragraph (2)* requires an application for rectification to be made within six months of the grant of probate or administration. The court may extend this period.

*Paragraph (3)* deals with a case where the court permits an application for rectification to be made more than six months after the grant and allows the application. The personal representatives are not to be held liable because they distributed any of the estate to beneficiaries between the expiration of the six months and the making of the court order, but the assets they have distributed may be recovered from the beneficiaries, if necessary.

*Paragraph (4)* explains that references to the time when a grant was taken out are to a general or residuary grant, and a limited grant is to be ignored.

The Article applies only to the wills of testators dying after the commencement of the Order – Schedule paragraph 15.

## Substitute executors: uncertainty about order of deaths

**30.** Where a will contains a provision for a substitute executor operative if an executor designated in the will –

(a) dies before the testator, or

(b) dies at the same time as the testator,

and the executor so designated dies in circumstnces rendering it uncertain which of them survived the other, then, for the purpose of probate, the case for which the will provides is deemed to have occurred.

# EXPLANATORY NOTE

## ARTICLE 30

This Article deals with the case where a testator appoints A as his executor or, if A dies before or with the testator, then B. If both the testator and A die in circumstances which render it uncertain which died first (or whether they died simultaneously), the appointment of B as executor will take effect. See paragraph 2.14.6 of the Report.

**Protection of personal representatives and trustees**

**31.**—(1) Notwithstanding anything in the foregoing provisions of this Part, personal representatives or trustees may convey or distribute any property to or among the persons entitled thereto without having ascertained that there is not any person who is or may be entitled to any interest therein by virtue of Article 22(4)(a) or Article 27, and are not liable to any such person of whose claim they have not had notice at the time of the conveyance or distribution.

(2) Nothing in this Article prejudices the right of any such person to follow the property, or any property representing it, into the hands of any person, other than a purchaser, who may have received it.

(3) In paragraph (2) "purchaser" means a purchaser in good faith for valuable consideration and includes a lessee, mortgagee or other person who, for valuable consideration, acquires an interest in property.

# EXPLANATORY NOTE

ARTICLE 31            Family Law Reform (NI)
                                          Order 1977 Art. 6

Because of the difficulty which may be involved in tracing illegitimate children or their issue and the difficulty of proving a negative (i.e. that the testator left no illegitimate children), this Article permits personal representatives or trustees to distribute an estate without having ascertained that there are no such children. If an illegitimate child subsequently turns up, the personal representatives or trustees are not liable for distributing the estate, but the claimant can follow the assets (or property representing the assets) except where they or such property have been bought by a purchaser in good faith for valuable consideration.

The Article reproduces existing law.

# PART III

## MISCELLANEOUS

**Executors de son tort**

**32.** In Article 39 of the Administration of Estates (Northern Ireland) Order1979 (liability of person wrongfully obtaining or retaining estate of deceased), at the end of paragraph (3) (saving), there shall be inserted the words "or the Limitation (Northern Ireland) Order 1989".

# EXPLANATORY NOTE

## ARTICLE 32

This Article makes it clear that an executor de son tort (i.e. someone who intermeddles in an estate without lawful authority) can take advantage of the Limitation Order.

## Transitional provisions and savings

**33.** The foregoing provisions of this Order have effect subject to the transitional and saving provisions in the Schedule.

# EXPLANATORY NOTE

ARTICLE 33                                    Cf. Property Bill Cl. 226, 247-
                                              251

This Article activates the transitional and saving provisions in the Schedule to the Order.

# SCHEDULE

## TRANSITIONAL PROVISIONS AND SAVINGS

### *Transitional provisions*

1.  Except where otherwise expressly provided, the provisions of Part II apply to wills made before or after the commencement of this Order ("the commencement") whether the testator died before or after the commencement.

2.  In the application of Article 5 to the will of a testator who died before the commencement –

(a)  paragraph (1)(b) does not apply, but instead the will must be signed by the testator at the foot or end thereof as required by section 9 of the Wills Act 1837 (as explained by the Wills Act Amendment Act 1852);

(b)  paragraph (1)(d)(ii) and the reference to acknowledgment in paragraph (2) do not apply.

3.  In the application of Article 6 to the will of a testator who died before the commencement, the references to Article 5 are to that Article as it applies by virtue of paragraph 2.

4.  Article 8(3) applies only to the will of a person dying after the commencement, but in relation to such a person it applies whether the will was executed before or after the commencement.

5.  Article 12(3) does not apply to a will made before 22 June 1954, and Article12(4) does not apply to a will made before the commencement.

6.  Article 13 does not affect the will of a testator who died before the commencement.

7.  Article 18(2) does not affect the will of a testator who died before the commencement.

8.  Article 21 does not affect the will of a testator who died before the commencement.

9.  Article 22 does not affect the will of a testator who died before the commencement.

10.  Article 23 does not affect the will of a testator who died before the commencement.

11.  Article 24 does not affect the will of a testator who died before the commencement.

12.  Article 25 does not affect the will of a testator who died before the commencement.

13. Article 26 does not apply to a will made before the commencement, but in such a will "land" includes a leasehold estate (legal or equitable).

14. Article 27 does not apply to a will made before 1 January 1978; and, notwithstanding Article 16 or any rule of law, a disposition made by a will executed before that date is not to be treated for the purposes of Article 27 as made on or after that date by reason only that the will is confirmed by a codicil executed on or after that date.

15. Article 29 does not affect the will of a testator who died before the commencement.

*Savings*

16. Nothing in Part II prejudices section 11 of the Wills Act 1837 or the Wills (Soldiers and Sailors) Act 1918 (wills made by soldiers, sailors or airmen in certain circumstances).

17.—(1) Nothing in Part II prejudices the Wills Act 1963 (conflict of laws relating to the form of testamentary dispositions) or sections 27 and 28 of, and Schedule 2 to, the Administration of Justice Act 1982 (international wills).

(2) A will executed in accordance with the enactments mentioned in sub-paragraph (1) is, for the purposes of Article 6, as valid as a will executed in accordance with Article 5.

# EXPLANATORY NOTE

SCHEDULE

Property Bill Cl. 246(1) (and cf. Cl. 226, 247-251)
A of J Act 1982 s. 73(6)(7)

The Schedule contains transitional provisions (paragraphs 1-15) and savings (paragraphs 16, 17).

*Paragraph 1* applies the provisions of Part II to all wills, whenever the will was made and whenever the testator died, except where a particular provision is expressed to the contrary (see paragraphs 2-15). The paragraph also defines the expression "the commencement" (which recurs in the following paragraphs as meaning the commencement of the Order (see Article 1(3)).

*Paragraph 2* prevents the changes of law made by Article 5 from applying to the wills of testators who died before the commencement of the Order. Those changes are (1) paragraph (1)(b) which renders it sufficient that an intention appears that the testator's signature (wherever placed) should give effect to his will (instead, the former rule will apply, that the signature must be at the foot or end of the will), and (2) paragraph (1)(d)(ii) which allows a witness to acknowledge his signature already affixed to the will instead of attesting and signing the will in the testator's presence.

*Paragraph 3* makes it clear that when Article 6 (testamentary execution of power) refers to a will being executed in accordance with Article 5, in the case of the will of a testator who died before the commencement the reference to Article 5 is to it as modified by paragraph 2.

*Paragraph 4* refers to paragraph (3) of Article 8 which preserves a gift made by a will to the spouse of the testator, even though the spouse witnessed the will, provided that there were at least two other proper witnesses to the will. Paragraph (3) applies only if the testator died after the commencement of the Order; if he died after then it is irrelevant whether the will was executed before the commencement or after it.

*Paragraph 5* restricts the application of Article 12(3) (which prevents a will expressed to be made in contemplation of a particular marriage from being revoked by that marriage) to wills made after 21 June 1954 – this preserves the effect of the Wills (Amendment) Act (Northern Ireland) 1954 (c. 20). The paragraph also prevents Article 12(4) (which relates to particular dispositions to an intended spouse) from applying to wills made before the commencement of the Order.

*Paragraphs 6 to 12* prevent the following provisions from applying to a will made before the commencement of the Order –

Article 13   –  effect of dissolution or annulment of marriage or judicial separation;

Article 18(2)  –  a devise creating an interest in land passes the largest interest the testator is capable of creating;

| Article 21 | – | contingent and future testamentary gifts carry the intermediate income; |
|---|---|---|
| Article 22 | – | gifts to children, grandchildren, etc., of testator who predecease him to go to their issue; |
| Article 23 | – | contradictory gifts to spouse and issue to be treated as gift to spouse; |
| Article 24 | – | exercise after testator's death of an option to purchase land from him does not operate retrospectively to adeem a testamentary gift of the land or to treat the land as converted into the purchase money; |
| Article 25 | – | admission of extrinsic evidence to aid construction of will. |

*Paragraph 13* prevents the interpretation rules set out in Article 26 from applying to a will made before the commencement of the Order, except the definition of "land" as including a leasehold estate (Wills Act 1837 s. 26).

*Paragraph 14* restricts the application of Article 27 ("child" includes an illegitimate child, and similarly as to other relatives) to wills made on or after 1 January 1978 (when Article 4 of the Family Law Reform (Northern Ireland) Order 1977 (NI 17) came into operation). If the will was made before that date the Article does not apply even though the will has been confirmed by a subsequent codicil; but it does apply if the will is re-executed.

*Paragraph 15* prevents Article 29 (rectification of wills) from applying to the will of a testator who died before the commencement of the Order.

*Paragraph 16* contains a saving for the statutory provisions which preserve and extend the common law rules allowing soldiers and sailors, in certain circumstances, to make valid wills even though the requirements of this Part about the making of wills are not complied with. The provisions in question are –

Wills Act 1837 s. 11

Wills (Soldiers and Sailors) Act 1918.

These were amended by the Age of Majority Act (Northern Ireland) 1969 s. 2.

*Paragraph 17* contains a saving for two groups of enactments which are concerned with the private international law of wills. The Wills Act 1963 makes a will valid, notwithstanding that it does not comply with Article 5, if it is executed either in accordance with the law of the place where it is executed or in accordance with the law of the testator's place of domicile or habitual residence or the law of the state of his nationality. Sections 27 and 28 of the Administration of Justice Act 1982 adopt international rules for wills. An international will must be attested by an authorized person (a notary public or solicitor), and the dispensation in Article 5 permitting a witness to acknowledge his signature does not apply.

*sub-paragraph (1)* contains the savings.

*sub-paragraph (2)* makes wills complying with the Act of 1963 or the Act of 1982 effective for the purpose of executing powers of appointment.

RECOMMENDED DRAFT ORDER IN COUNCIL UNDER
PARAGRAPH 1 OF SCHEDULE 1 TO THE NORTHERN
IRELAND ACT 1974

## DRAFT STATUTORY INSTRUMENTS

**1989 No.    (N.I.   )**

**NORTHERN IRELAND**

**Property (Consequential Provisions) (Northern Ireland) Order 1989**

*To be laid before Parliament in draft*

*Made*

*Coming into operation in accordance with Article 1(2)*

## ARRANGEMENT OF ORDER

Article

At the Court at       , the       day of        1989

Present,

The Queen's Most Excellent Majesty in Council

Whereas a draft of this Order has been approved by a resolution of each House of Parliament:

Now, therefore, Her Majesty, in exercise of the powers conferred by paragraph 1 of Schedule 1 to the Northern Ireland Act 1974 and of all other powers enabling Her in that behalf, is pleased, by and with the advice of Her Privy Council, to order, and it is hereby ordered, as follows:-

**Title and commencement**

**1.**—(1) This Order may be cited as the Property (Consequential Provisions) (Northern Ireland) Order 1989.

(2) This Order shall come into operation on such day or days as the Head of the Department of Finance and Personnel may by order appoint.

**Interpretation**

**2.**—(1) The Interpretation Act (Northern Ireland) 1954 applies to Article 1 and the following provisions of this Order as it applies to a Measure of the Northern Ireland Assembly.

(2) Section 29 of the Interpretation Act (Northern Ireland) 1954 (effect of substituting provisions) has effect in relation to any statutory provision repealed by this Order and re-enacted or substituted for in any of the Orders as if the repeal were made by that Order and not by this Order.

(3) In this Order –

"the Ground Rents Order" means the Ground Rents (Northern Ireland) Order 1989;

"the Property Order" means the Property (Northern Ireland) Order 1989;

"the Landlord and Tenant Order" means the Landlord and Tenant (Northern Ireland) Order 1989;

"the Succession Order" means the Succession (Northern Ireland) Order 1989;

"the Orders" means the Ground Rents Order, the Property Order, the Landlord and Tenant Order and the Succession Order;

"statutory provision" has the meaning given by section 1(f) of the Interpretation Act (Northern Ireland) 1954.

**Repeals, amendments, etc., of statutory provisions**

**3.**—(1) In consequence of and in connection with the Orders, the following provisions of this Article have effect.

(2)   The statutory provisions specified in Schedule 1 are repealed to the extent specified in the third column of that Schedule.

(3)   The statutory provisions specified in Schedule 2 have effect subject to the amendments there specified.

(4)   The provisions of Schedule 3 for general modifications in statutory provisions, savings or other transitional purposes have effect.

**Power to make further provisions**

**4.**   Without prejudice to paragraph 25 of Schedule 10 to the Property Order, the Department of Finance and Personnel may by order made subject to negative resolution make such further repeals or amendments of statutory pprovisions, and such consequential, transitional, temporary or incidental provisions as appear to the Department to be necessary for the purposes of the Orders.

# SCHEDULES

## SCHEDULE 1

## REPEALS

Article 3(2).

| Chapter or Number | Short Title or Title | Extent of Repeal |
|---|---|---|
| *Acts of the Parliament of Ireland* | | |
| 10 Chas 1 sess. 2 c. 1. | Statute of Uses (Ireland) 1634. | The whole Act. |
| 10 Chas. 1 sess. 2 c. 3. | Conveyancing Act (Ireland) 1634. | The whole Act. |
| 7 Will. 3 c. 8. | Life Estates Act (Ireland) 1695. | The whole Act. |
| 7 Will. 3 c. 12. | Statute of Frauds (Ireland) 1695. | In section 2 the words from "or upon any contract" to "concerning them", and sections 4 to 6. |
| 9 Will. 3 c. 11. | Clandestine Mortgages Act (Ireland) 1697. | The whole Act. |
| 6 Anne c. 10. | Administration of Justice Act (Ireland) 1707. | Sections 9, 10 and 19. |
| 9 Geo. 2 c. 7. | Land Improvement Act (Ireland) 1735. | The whole Act. |
| 15 Geo. 2 c. 8. | Landlord and Tenant Act (Ireland) 1741. | The whole Act. |
| 17 & 18 Geo. 3 c. 49. | Leases for Lives Act (Ireland) 1777. | The whole Act. |
| 19 & 20 Geo. 3 c. 30. | Tenantry Act (Ireland) 1779. | The whole Act. |
| *Statutes of the Parliament of England* | | |
| 13 Edw. 1 c. 1. | Statute of Westminster the Second 1285. | The whole statute. |
| 18 Edw. 1 cc. 1, 2, 3. | Statutes of Westminster the Third 1289-1290. | The whole of the chapters. |
| *Acts of the Parliament of the United Kingdom* | | |
| 1830 c. 46. | Illusory Appointments Act 1830. | The whole Act. |
| 1830 c. 65. | Infants' Property Act 1830. | Sections 12 to 15, 17, 18, 20 and 21. |
| 1832 c. 71. | Prescription Act 1832. | The whole Act. |
| 1833 c. 74. | Fines and Recoveries Act 1833. | The whole Act. |
| 1834 c. 92. | Fines and Recoveries (Ireland) Act 1834. | The whole Act. |
| 1837 c. 26. | Wills Act 1837. | The whole Act except section 1 so far as it defines "personal estate" or relates to gender and section 11. |
| 1838 c. 62. | Renewal of Leases (Ireland) Act 1838. | The whole Act. |

| Chapter or Number | Short Title or Title | Extent of Repeal |
|---|---|---|
| | *Acts of the Parliament of the United Kingdom* (continued) | |
| 1845 c. 106. | Real Property Act 1845. | The whole Act. |
| 1845 c. 112. | Satisfied Terms Act 1845. | The whole Act. |
| 1847 c. 46. | Settled Land (Ireland) Act 1847. | The whole Act. |
| 1849 c. 26. | Leases Act 1849. | The whole Act. |
| 1850 c. 17. | Leases Act 1850. | The whole Act. |
| 1851 c. 20. | Fee-Farm Rents (Ireland) Act 1851. | The whole Act. |
| 1852 c. 24. | Wills Act Amendment Act 1852. | The whole Act. |
| 1855 c. 39. | Leasing Powers Act for Religious Worship in Ireland 1855. | The whole Act. |
| 1858 c. 42. | Prescription (Ireland) Act 1858. | The whole Act. |
| 1858 c. 72. | Landed Estates Court (Ireland) Act 1858. | The whole Act. |
| 1859 c. 35. | Law of Property Amendment Act 1859. | The whole Act. |
| 1860 c. 38. | Law of Property Amendment Act 1860. | The whole Act. |
| 1860 c. 154. | Landlord and Tenant Law Amendment Act, Ireland, 1860. | The whole Act. |
| 1864 c. 38. | Chief Rents Redemption (Ireland) Act 1864. | The whole Act. |
| 1867 c. 48. | Sale of Land by Auction Act 1867. | The whole Act. |
| 1867 c. 4 (31&32 Vict.). | Sale of Reversions Act 1867. | The whole Act. |
| 1868 c. 40. | Partition Act 1868. | The whole Act. |
| 1870 c. 46. | Landlord and Tenant (Ireland) Act 1870. | The whole Act. |
| 1871 c. 92. | Landlord and Tenant (Ireland) Act 1871. | The whole Act. |
| 1872 c. 32. | Landlord and Tenant (Ireland) Act 1872. | The whole Act. |
| 1874 c. 37. | Powers of Appointment Act 1874. | The whole Act. |
| 1874 c. 78. | Vendor and Purchaser Act 1874. | The whole Act. |
| 1875 c. 11. | Leasing Powers Amendment Act for Religious Purposes in Ireland 1875. | The whole Act. |
| 1876 c. 17. | Partition Act 1876. | The whole Act. |
| 1876 c. 63. | Notices to Quit (Ireland) Act 1876. | The whole Act. |

| Chapter or Number | Short Title or Title | Extent of Repeal |
|---|---|---|
| | *Acts of the Parliament of the United Kingdom* (continued) | |
| 1877 c. 18. | Settled Estates Act 1877. | The whole Act. |
| 1877 c. 33. | Contingent Remainders Act 1877. | The whole Act. |
| 1877 c. 59. | Colonial Stock Act 1877. | In section 4(1) the words from "thereunto" onwards. |
| | | In section 6 the words from "if given" to "attested". |
| 1881 c. 41. | Conveyancing Act 1881. | The whole Act, except sections1(1) and 48. |
| 1881 c. 49. | Land Law (Ireland) Act 1881. | The whole Act. |
| 1881 c. 65. | Leases for Schools (Ireland) Act 1881. | The whole Act. |
| 1882 c. 38. | Settled Land Act 1882. | The whole Act. |
| 1882 c. 39. | Conveyancing Act 1882. | The whole Act. |
| 1882 c. 75. | Married Women's Property Act 1882. | The whole Act. |
| 1884 c. 18. | Settled Land Act 1884. | The whole Act. |
| 1887 c. 30. | Settled Land Acts (Amendment) Act 1887. | The whole Act. |
| 1887 c. 33. | Land Law (Ireland) Act 1887. | Parts I and III. |
| | | Section 26. |
| | | In section 34 the definitions of "ejectment", "judgment" and "landlord". |
| | | The Schedule. |
| 1889 c. 36. | Settled Land Act 1889. | The whole Act. |
| 1890 c. 69. | Settled Land Act 1890. | The whole Act. |
| 1890 c. 70. | Housing of the Working Classes Act 1890. | Section 74(1). |
| 1892 c. 13. | Conveyancing and Law of Property Act 1892. | The whole Act. |
| 1892 c. 58. | Accumulations Act 1892. | The whole Act. |
| 1893 c. 21. | Voluntary Conveyances Act 1893. | The whole Act. |
| 1895 c. 25. | Mortgagees Legal Costs Act 1895. | The whole Act. |
| 1896 c. 47. | Land Law (Ireland) Act 1896. | The whole Act, except – |
| | | Part II so far as relating to the Land Purchase Acts, |
| | | Part III, |
| | | in Part VI, in section 48(1), the definitions of "Land Purchase Acts", "prescribed" and "Receiver Judge", section 48(3), section 50(4) and (5) and section 51. |

| Chapter or Number | Short Title or Title | Extent of Repeal |
|---|---|---|

*Acts of the Parliament of the United Kingdom* (continued)

| Chapter or Number | Short Title or Title | Extent of Repeal |
|---|---|---|
| 1899 c. 20. | Bodies Corporation (Joint Tenancy) Act 1899. | The whole Act. |
| 1899 c. 44. | Small Dwellings Acquisition Act 1899. | Section 14(2). |
| 1903 c. 37. | Irish Land Act 1903. | Part III. |
| | | In Part V, in section 98(1) the definitions of "the Land Law Acts" and "the Act of 1887" and section 100(3). |
| 1907 c. 18. | Married Women's Property Act 1907. | The whole Act. |
| 1911 c. 37. | Conveyancing Act 1911. | The whole Act. |
| 1919 c. 45. | Housing (Ireland) Act 1919. | Sections 26 and 33. |
| 1946 c. 73. | Hill Farming Act 1946. | Section 40(5). |
| 1964 c. 55. | Perpetuities and Accumulations Act 1964. | Section 15(8). |
| 1970 c. 31. | Administration of Justice Act 1970. | Sections 36, 38A and 39. |
| | | In section 54(6)(c), the references to those sections. |
| 1973 c. 15. | Administration of Justice Act 1973. | Section 8. |
| | | In section 21(2)(b) the reference to that section. |
| 1974 c. 39. | Consumer Credit Act 1974. | In Schedule 4, paragraphs 30 and 31. |
| 1978 c. 23. | Judicature (Northern Ireland) Act 1978. | Sections 87 to 90, 93 and 94. |
| | | In Schedule 5, Part II, the amendments of the Landed Estates Court (Ireland) Act 1858, the Settled Estates Act 1877, the Settled Land Act 1882. |
| 1986 c. 53. | Building Societies Act 1986. | In Schedule 4, paragraph 2(7)(a). |
| | | In Schedule 18, paragraph 24. |

*Acts of the Parliament of Northern Ireland and Orders in Council*

| Chapter or Number | Short Title or Title | Extent of Repeal |
|---|---|---|
| 1928 c. 8 (N.I.). | School Sites Act (Northern Ireland) 1928. | The whole Act. |
| 1939 c. 15 (N.I.). | Civil Defence Act (Northern Ireland) 1939. | Section 53(2). |
| 1941 c. 9 (N.I.). | Landlord and Tenant (War Damage) Act (Northern Ireland) 1941. | Section 3(2). |
| 1954 c. 20 (N.I.). | Wills (Amendment) Act (Northern Ireland) 1954. | The whole Act. |
| 1955 c. 24 (N.I.). | Administration of Estates Act (Northern Ireland) 1955. | In section 1(3) the words from "except" onwards. |

*Acts of the Parliament of Northern Ireland and Orders in Council* (continued)

| Chapter or Number | Short Title or Title | Extent of Repeal |
|---|---|---|
| | | In section 38, in subsection (3) the words "for the purposes aforesaid", subsection (4) and in subsection (5) the words from the beginning to "forty-three". |
| | | In section 40(5) the words from "but" onwards. |
| | | In section 44(c) the words from the beginning to "but" and the words "further or other". |
| | | In Schedule 2 the entries relating to the Landlord and Tenant (Ireland) Act 1870 and the Land Law (Ireland) Act 1881. |
| 1956 c. 17 (N.I.). | Administrative and Financial Provisions Act (Northern Ireland) 1956. | In section 1, paragraphs (a) to (d). |
| 1958 c. 23 (N.I.). | Trustee Act (Northern Ireland) 1958. | Section 12. |
| | | Section 13(4). |
| | | In section 14(1), paragraph (b) and the word "or" preceding it. |
| | | In section 16(2) the words from "or to trustees" onwards. |
| | | In section 20, in subsection (1) the words "or by a tenant for life impeachable for waste,", and subsection (3)(b). |
| | | In section 21(1) the words "for lives or years". |
| | | In section 26, subsection (3) and in subsection (8) the words from ", a tenant for life" to "1882" (where first occurring) and paragraphs (b) and (c). |
| | | In section 32(3)(a)(ii) the words ", or for an entailed estate or interest". |
| | | Section 56(4). |
| 1961 c. 18 (N.I.). | Rights of Light Act (Northern Ireland) 1961. | The whole Act. |
| 1964 c. 23 (N.I.). | Law Reform (Husband and Wife) Act (Northern Ireland) 1964. | Section 3. |
| 1964 c. 36 (N.I.). | Business Tenancies Act (Northern Ireland) 1964. | Section 2(1)(c). |
| | | Section 4(4). |

| Chapter or Number | Short Title or Title | Extent of Repeal |
|---|---|---|

| Chapter or Number | Short Title or Title | Extent of Repeal |
|---|---|---|
| | | In section 6(1) the words "or forfeiture, or by the forfeiture of a superior tenancy," and "or by lawful ejectment for non-payment of rent". |
| | | Section 17(5). |
| | | Section 27. |
| | | In section 31(1)(b) the words from "or, if" onwards. |
| | | In section 49, in subsection (1)(a) the words ", as for an improvement authorised by the said Acts," and in subsection (3) the words "a tenant for life or". |
| 1965 c. 23 (N.I.). | Land Development Values (Compensation) Act (Northern Ireland) 1965. | In section 19(3) the words "or in the beneficiaries under a settlement" and "or beneficiaries". |
| | | Section 22(2)(b). |
| | | In section 43(1) in the definition of "estate" the words "a legal or equitable fee tail" and the words "fee tail" where secondly occurring. |
| 1966 c. 2 (N.I.). | Perpetuities Act (Northern Ireland) 1966. | The whole Act. |
| 1967 c. 18 (N.I.). | Criminal Law Act (Northern Ireland) 1967. | In Schedule 1, paragraph 9. |
| 1968 c. 4 (N.I.). | Business Tenancies (Amendment) Act (Northern Ireland) 1968. | The whole Act. |
| 1968 c. 21 (N.I.). | Development Loans (Agriculture and Fisheries) Act (Northern Ireland) 1968. | In section 2(2)(a) the words from "compensation" to "borrower". |
| 1969 c. 28 (N.I.). | Age of Majority Act (Northern Ireland) 1969. | Section 2(1)(a). |
| | | In Schedule 1 Part I the entries relating to sections 12 and 17 of the Infants Property Act 1830, the Conveyancing Act 1881, the Settled Land Act 1882 and the Conveyancing Act 1882. |
| | | In Schedule 3, paragraph 7. |
| 1969 c. 30 (N.I.). | Judgments (Enforcement) Act (Northern Ireland) 1969. | In Schedule 4 Part II the entries relating to the Landlord and Tenant Law Amendment Act, Ireland, 1860. |

| Chapter or Number | Short Title or Title | Extent of Repeal |
|---|---|---|

*Acts of the Parliament of Northern Ireland and Orders in Council* (continued)

| Chapter or Number | Short Title or Title | Extent of Repeal |
|---|---|---|
| 1970 c. 18 (N.I.). | Land Registration Act (Northern Ireland) 1970. | In section 10(a)(ii) the words from "is for" to "where it". |
| | | In section 12 the words from the beginning to "minors"; in paragraph (a) and paragraph (c), in each case, the word "full"; paragraph (b); the word "or" following paragraph (c); and paragraph (d). |
| | | Section 14(1)(b). |
| | | In section 15, in subsection (1) the word "full"; subsection (2); and in subsection (3) the words from the beginning to "(2)". |
| | | In section 16, in subsection (1) and subsection (2), the words "full or limited". |
| | | In section 17, in subsection (1) the words "full or limited" and "full or, as the case may be, limited", and in subsection (2) the words "full or limited" and the words in brackets. |
| | | In section 18, in subsection (1) and subsection (2), the words "full or limited". |
| | | In section 19, in subsection (1)(a), the words from "or a person" to "life". |
| | | In section 20, in subsection (1) the word "full", subsection (2) and in subsection (3) the words from the beginning to "(2)". |
| | | In section 21, in subsection (1) the words "full or limited" and "full or, as the case may be, limited"; and in subsection (2) the words "full or limited". |
| | | In section 22, in subsection (1) the words "full or limited" and "full or, as the case may be, limited"; and in subsection (2) the words "full or limited" and the words in brackets. |
| | | In section 23, in subsection (1) and subsection (2), the words "full or limited". |
| | | In section 30(1) the words "or any trustee for him". |

| Chapter or Number | Short Title or Title | Extent of Repeal |
|---|---|---|

In section 32(2), paragraph (b) and the word "and" preceding it.

In section 34, in subsection (1) the words from "and subject" to "Acts"; in subsection (4) the word "full"; and subsection (6).

Section 35.

In section 36(2), in paragraph (a) the words "if he is full owner, "and in paragraph (b) the words "if he is not full owner,".

In section 37 the word "full" and the words from "and on" to the end.

In section 41, in subsection (2) the words "or by will"; subsection (3); in subsection (5) the word "full" and the words "and registered limited owners of land"; and subsection (6).

Section 43.

In section 55, subsection (1); in subsection (2) the words from "unless" to the end; and subsection (4).

Section 56(1).

Section 57.

Section 60.

Section 67(3).

In section 72(1) the words from ", and, if" to "ownership,".

Section 74.

In section 94, the definitions of "Conveyancing Acts", "full owner", "limited owner", "Settled Land Acts" and "settlement" and other expressions defined by reference to the Settled Land Acts.

In Schedule 4, in paragraph 1(1) the word "full"; in paragraph 4 the words "full owner or limited" and ", as the case may be"; and paragraph 6.

| Chapter or Number | Short Title or Title | Extent of Repeal |
|---|---|---|

*Acts of the Parliament of Northern Ireland and Orders in Council* (continued)

| Chapter or Number | Short Title or Title | Extent of Repeal |
|---|---|---|
| | | In Schedule 5 Part I, paragraph 4. |
| | | In Schedule 6, Part I, in entry 6, paragraph (a). |
| | | In Schedule 7, Part I, in paragraph 1 the words from ", not being" to "mortgage,", paragraph 5 and paragraph 9; and Part II. |
| | | In Schedule 8, Part I. |
| | | In Schedule 9, paragraph 8. |
| 1971 c. 7 (N.I.). | Leasehold (Enlargement and Extension) Act (Northern Ireland) 1971. | In section 5 and section 11, in each case, in subsection (1) the words "or a limited estate" and in subsection (2) the words "a minor or". |
| 1971 c. 33 (N.I.). | Powers of Attorney Act (Northern Ireland) 1971. | The whole Act except sections 2(2), 9, 11(1) and (3) and 12(1).<br>In section 9(1) the repeals made above in section 26 of the Trustee Act (Northern Ireland) 1958. |
| 1976 NI 21. | Financial Provisions (Northern Ireland) Order 1976. | Article 17. |
| 1977 NI 17. | Family Law Reform (Northern Ireland) Order 1977. | Article 3(5).<br>In Article 4, paragraphs (1) to (3), in paragraph (5) the words from "; and in section 3" onwards, paragraph (6) and paragraph (8).<br>Article 5.<br>In Article 6(1)(b) the words "or 5". |
| 1978 NI 4. | Property (Northern Ireland) Order 1978. | Articles 1(2), 3 to 13 and 16(2).<br>In Schedule 1, paragraphs 1 to 3.<br>Schedule 2. |
| 1978 NI 15. | Matrimonial Causes (Northern Ireland) Order 1978. | Article 55. |
| 1978 NI 20. | Rent (Northern Ireland) Order 1978. | In Article 2(2) the definition of "private tenancy".<br>Articles 38 and 39.<br>Part IX.<br>Articles 62 and 66.<br>In Article 69(2) the words "(except Part IX)".<br>In Article 70 the words "subject to Article 54(3)". |

| Chapter or Number | Short Title or Title | Extent of Repeal |
|---|---|---|

*Acts of the Parliament of Northern Ireland and Orders in Council* (continued)

| Chapter or Number | Short Title or Title | Extent of Repeal |
|---|---|---|
| 1979 NI 3. | Judgments Enforcement and Debts Recovery (Northern Ireland) Order 1979. | In Schedule 4 Part II the paragraph relating to the Landlord and Tenant Law Amendment Act, Ireland, 1860. |
| 1980 NI 3. | County Courts (Northern Ireland) Order 1980. | Article 10(3)(b). Article 12(2). In Schedule 1 Part I the paragraph relating to the Landlord and Tenant Law Amendment Act, Ireland, 1860. |
| 1981 NI 3. | Housing (Northern Ireland) Order 1981. | Article 31(6)(b). |
| 1981 NI 6. | Judgments Enforcement (Northern Ireland) Order 1981. | In Schedule 2 paragraph 5. |
| 1981 NI 26. | Magistrates' Courts (Northern Ireland) Order 1981. | Article 69. |
| 1983 NI 9. | Property (Discharge of Mortgage by Receipt) (Northern Ireland) Order 1983. | The whole Order. |
| 1983 NI 15. | Housing (Northern Ireland) Order 1983. | Article 10(6)(b). |
| 1984 NI 14. | Family Law (Miscellaneous Provisions) (Northern Ireland) Order 1984. | Article 16(2). |
| 1985 NI 12. | Credit Unions (Northern Ireland) Order 1985. | In Schedule 5, paragraph 4. |
| 1986 NI 4. | Mental Health (Northern Ireland) Order 1986. | In Schedule 5 Part II the entries relating to the Prescription Act 1832, the Fines and Recoveries (Ireland) Act 1834 and the Conveyancing Act 1881. |
| 1986 NI 5. | Commission on Disposals of Land (Northern Ireland) Order 1986. | The whole Order. |
| 1987 NI 16. | Enduring Powers of Attorney (Northern Ireland) Order 1987. | The whole Order. |
| 1989 NI 11. | Limitation (Northern Ireland) Order 1989. | Article 2(7)(b). Article 23. Article 69(3). |
| 1989 NI 19. | Insolvency (Northern Ireland) Order 1989. | In Schedule 3 paragraph 14. |

# SCHEDULE 2

## AMENDMENTS

## PART I

## AMENDMENTS OF ACTS OF THE PARLIAMENT OF THE UNITED KINGDOM

*Companies Clauses Consolidation Act 1845 (c. 16)*

1.  In section 97 for "under seal" substitute "executed as a deed".

2.  In Schedule (B) for "As witness our hands and seals" substitute "Executed as a deed by us".

3.  In Schedule (E) for "hereunto set my hand and seal" substitute "executed this instrument as a deed".

*Lands Clauses Consolidation Act 1845 (c. 18)*

4.  In section 75 and section 77, in each case, for the words from "it shall be lawful" to "any two of them" substitute "then, if the promoters of the undertaking think fit, it shall be lawful for the promoters to execute a deed poll under their common seal if they be a corporation, or, if they be not a corporation, for the promoters or any two of them to execute a deed poll".

5.  In section 85 for "under the hands and seals of" substitute "executed by".

6.  In Schedule (A) and Schedule (B), in each case, for "hereunto set my hand and seal" substitute "executed this instrument as a deed".

*Commissioners Clauses Act 1847 (c. 16)*

7.  In section 56 for "under seal" substitute "executed as a deed" and for "under the hands and seals" substitute "executed as a deed by them".

8.  In Schedule (B) for "hereunto set our hands and seals" substitute "executed this instrument as a deed".

9.  In Schedule (C) for "hereunto set my hand and seal" substitute "executed this instrument as a deed".

*Cemeteries Clauses Act 1847 (c. 65)*

10.  In the Schedules for "Given under our common seal, [*or* under our hands and seals, *as the case may be,*] substitute "Executed as a deed", and for "Witness my hand and seal" substitute "Executed as a deed".

*Literary and Scientific Institutions Act 1854 (c. 112)*

11.   In section 13 –

(a)  for "hereunto set their hands and seals [*or seals* only, as the case may be,]" substitute "executed this instrument as a deed"; and

(b)  for "Signed, sealed and delivered" substitute "Signed and delivered as a deed".

*Open Spaces Act 1906 (c. 25)*

12.   In section 2(3) for "under the hands and seals of" substitute "executed as a deed by".

*Small Dwellings Acquisition Act 1899 (c. 44)*

13.   In section 5(5) for "sections one hundred and thirty-eight to one hundred and forty-five of the County Courts Act 1888" substitute "Article 62 of the Landlord and Tenant (Northern Ireland) Order 1989".

*Hill Farming Act 1946 (c. 73)*

14.   For section 11 substitute –

"11.   Any operation which is to be treated as an improvement for the purposes of this Act, and which is of a kind prescribed by regulations made by the Minister of Agriculture, Fisheries and Food as being of a permanent character, is an improvement for the purposes of Article 55(1)(d) of the Property (Northern Ireland) Order 1989.".

*Transport Act 1962 (c. 46)*

15.   In Schedule 11, Part II, paragraph 9 for "section 9 of the Conveyancing Act 1881" substitute "Article 96 of the Property (Northern Ireland) Order 1989".

*Transport Act 1968 (c. 73)*

16.   In Schedule 17, Part II, paragraph 7 for "section 9 of the Conveyancing Act 1881" substitute "Article 96 of the Property (Northern Ireland) Order 1989".

*Consumer Credit Act 1974 (c. 39)*

17.   In section 177(6)(b) for "section 21 of the Conveyancing and Law of Property Act 1881 and section 5 of the Conveyancing Act 1911" substitute "Article 129 of the Property (Northern Ireland) Order 1989".

*Judicature (Northern Ireland) Act 1978 (c. 23)*

18.   In section 31(7)(b) for "section 17 of the Married Women's Property Act 1882" substitute "Article 235 of the Property (Northern Ireland) Order 1989".

*British Telecommunications Act 1981 (c. 38)*

19.   In Schedule 2, paragraph 4(b), for "section 9 of the Conveyancing Act 1881" substitute "Article 96 of the Property (Northern Ireland) Order 1989".

*Civil Aviation Act 1982 (c. 16)*

20.   In Schedule 3, paragraph 5(1), for "section 9 of the Conveyancing Act 1881" substitute "Article 96 of the Property (Northern Ireland) Order 1989" and for "section 9" (where secondly occurring) substitute "Article 96".

*Building Societies Act 1986 (c. 53)*

21.   In section 69(17), in paragraph (a) of the definition of "conveyancing services" for the words from "in the case of" to "that section" substitute "creating a tenancy to which Article 3(2) of the Landlord and Tenant (Northern Ireland) Order 1989 applies".

22.   In Schedule 4, for paragraph 2(7)(b), substitute –

"(b) in sub-paragraph (2) –

    (i)   for the words from "or incumbrance" to "Property Act 1925" there shall be substituted the words "on registered land, the receipt shall operate in accordance with Article 146(1), (7) and (9) of the Property (Northern Ireland) Order 1989"; and

    (ii)   for the words "subsection (1) of that section" there shall be substituted the words "paragraph (1) of that Article";".

## PART II

## AMENDMENTS OF ACTS OF THE PARLIAMENT OF NORTHERN IRELAND AND ORDERS IN COUNCIL

*Legitimacy Act (Northern Ireland) 1928 (c. 5)*

23.   In section 3, at the end, insert –

"(5)   Where there is a disposition to which Article 90 of the Property (Northern Ireland) Order 1989 or Article 27 of the Succession (Northern Ireland) Order 1989 (construction of references to children and other relatives) applies –

(a)   subsection (1)(b) does not apply to the disposition except as respects any interest in relation to which the disposition refers only to persons who are, or whose relationship is deduced through, legitimate persons; and

(b)   subsection (2) does not apply in relation to any right conferred by the disposition, unless the terms of the disposition are such that the children whose relative seniority is in question cannot include any illegitimate children who are not either –

    (i)   legitimated persons within the meaning of this Act; or

    (ii)   persons recognised by virtue of this Act as having been legitimated.".

*Stormont Regulation and Government Property Act (Northern Ireland) 1933 (c. 6)*

24.   In section 5(3) after "rights" insert ", neighbour obligations".

*Civil Defence Act (Northern Ireland) 1939 (c. 15)*

25.   In section 53(1) for the words from "the Settled Land Act" onwards substitute "Article 55(1)(d) of the Property (Northern Ireland) Order 1989".

*Landlord and Tenant (War Damage) Act (Northern Ireland) 1941 (c. 9)*

26.   In section 3(1) for the words from "the Settled Land Act" onwards substitute "Article 55(1)(d) of the Property (Northern Ireland) Order 1989".

27.   In section 32 for "Section 40 of the Landlord and Tenant Law Amendment Act (Ireland), 1860" substitute "Article 54 of the Landlord and Tenant (Northern Ireland) Order 1989".

*Charitable Trusts (Validation) Act (Northern Ireland) 1954 (c. 27)*

28.   In section 1(4) for "under seal" substitute "executed as a deed".

*Interpretation Act (Northern Ireland) 1954 (c. 33)*

29.   In section 45 –

(a)   in subsection (2) after "easement" insert "land obligation";

(b)   in subsection (3)(f) after "profit" insert "land obligation";

(c)   at the end insert –

> "(4)   In an enactment "land obligation", "neighbour obligation", "development obligation" and "development scheme" have the same meaning as in the Property (Northern Ireland) Order 1989.".

*Administration of Estates Act (Northern Ireland) 1955 (c. 24)*

30.   In section 38(3) for the words from "by reason of" to "acquired and" substitute "by virtue of Article 31(a) of the Property (Northern Ireland) Order1989 a settlement on the statutory trusts arises".

31.   In section 40(1), at the beginning of paragraph (c), insert "without prejudice to Article 29 or 31 of the Ground Rents (Northern Ireland) Order 1989,".

*Trustee Act (Northern Ireland) 1958 (c. 23)*

32.   In section 14 –

(a)   in subsection (1)(ii) for "arising under the Settled Land Acts, 1882 to 1890" substitute "within the meaning of the Property (Northern Ireland) Order 1989";

1623

(b) for subsection (2) substitute –

> "(2) This section does not apply to a sole personal representative selling or transferring land in exercise of a power conferred on him by the Administration of Estates Act (Northern Ireland) 1955.".

33. In section 20 –

(a) in subsection (1) for "Settled Land Acts, 1882 to 1890" substitute "Property (Northern Ireland) Order 1989";

(b) in subsection (3)(a) and subsection (4), in each case, for "Settled Land Acts, 1882 to 1890" substitute "Property (Northern Ireland) Order 1989" and for "those Acts" substitute "that Order".

34. In section 26(1) after "attorney" insert "created in accordance with Article 190 of the Property (Northern Ireland) Order 1989".

35. In section 32(3)(b) after "settled land" insert "held on the statutory trusts within the meaning of the Property (Northern Ireland) Order 1989".

36. In section 33(2)(a) for "Settled Land Acts, 1882 to 1890" substitute "Property (Northern Ireland) Order 1989".

37. In section 35(6) after "an additional trustee or" insert "(without prejudice to Article 42 of the Property (Northern Ireland) Order 1989)".

38. In section 46(b) after "land" insert "or for the discharge of the mortgage".

39. In section 64 –

(a) in subsection (1) for the words from "Settled" to "1881" substitute "Property (Northern Ireland) Order 1989";

(b) in subsection (2) for the words from "Settled" to "1890" substitute "Property (Northern Ireland) Order 1989", and for "the said Acts" (wherever occurring) substitute "that Order";

(c) in subsection (3) for "the said Acts" substitute "that Order".

40. In section 67, for the definitions of "tenant for life" and other expressions defined in the Settled Land Act 1882 substitute –

' "settlement" has the same meaning as in the Property (Northern Ireland) Order 1989, and "settled land" means land which is the subject of a settlement;'.

*Business Tenancies Act (Northern Ireland) 1964 (c. 36)*

41. In section 4(4) at the end insert "and paragraph 2 of Schedule 4 to the Ground Rents (Northern Ireland) Order 1989 (termination by at least one month's notice after the fall of the life or the happening of the event) does not apply".

42. In section 6 –

(a) in subsection (1) at the end insert "or by termination under Article 57 or 59 of the Landlord and Tenant (Northern Ireland) Order 1989, nor shall it prevent the termination of an assignee's interest in a tenancy under Article 68 of that Order";

(b) in subsection (4) at the end insert "and paragraph 2 of Schedule 4 to the Ground Rents (Northern Ireland) Order 1989 does not apply".

43. In section 17(4) for "section 18 of the Conveyancing Act 1881" substitute "Article 142 of the Property (Northern Ireland) Order 1989" and for "subsection (13) of that section" substitute "paragraph (11) of that Article".

44. In section 31(1)(b) for "forfeiture or re-entry" substitute "order of a court".

45. In section 48(2) at the end insert "or to serve a notice under Article 55(2) of the Landlord and Tenant (Northern Ireland) Order 1989".

46. In section 49 –

(a) in subsection (1) for "Settled Land Acts 1882 and 1890" substitute "Part V of the Property (Northern Ireland) Order 1989";

(b) in subsection (2) for the words from "a tenant" onwards substitute "capital money may be applied under Article 55 of the Property (Northern Ireland) Order 1989";

(c) in subsection (4) after "held on" insert "any settlement, including a settlement".

47. In section 55 at the end insert –

"(3) References in this Act to a tenancy dependent on the fall of a life or other uncertain event are to the tenancy into which such a tenancy is converted by Article 28(4) of, and Schedule 4 to, the Ground Rents (Northern Ireland) Order 1989".

*Land Development Values (Compensation) Act (Northern Ireland) 1965 (c. 23)*

48. In section 43(1) in the definition of "settlement" for the words from "the Settled Land Acts" onwards substitute "the Property (Northern Ireland) Order 1989".

*Industrial and Provident Societies Act (Northern Ireland) 1969 (c. 24)*

49. In section 13(1) for "subscribed his name and affixed his seal thereto" substitute "executed them as a deed".

50. In section 28(1) in paragraph (a) for "under seal" substitute "executed as a deed", and in paragraph (c) for "under seal", in the first two places where those words occur, substitute "executed as a deed".

51.   In Schedule 4, in form A for "Sealed with our seals" substitute "Executed by us as a deed" and for "Sealed and delivered" substitute "Signed and delivered as a deed"; and in form B for "sealed with my seal" substitute "executed by me as a deed", for "sealed with our seals" substitute "executed by us as a deed" and for "Sealed and delivered" substitute "Signed and delivered as a deed".

*Land Registration Act (Northern Ireland) 1970 (c. 18)*

52.   In section 27(1)(b) for "under" substitute "as mentioned in".

53.   In section 34, in paragraph (4) for "Conveyancing Acts" substitute "Property Order", and at the beginning of paragraph (5) insert "Without prejudice to Article 23 of the Property Order".

54.   In section 36(2) at the end of paragraph (a) insert "or".

55.   In section 38, in subsection (1) for the words from "without prejudice" to "1978 and" substitute "without prejudice to Article 183(1)(a) of the Property Order and"; and in subsection (2) and in section 39(2), in each case, for the words from "Without prejudice" to "1978" substitute "Without prejudice to Article 183(1)(a) of the Property Order".

56.   In section 41(2) after "deed" insert "(as a charge by way of legal mortgage)".

57.   In section 47 for the words from the beginning to "any such right" substitute "Registration of any right such as is mentioned in Article 33(3) or (4) of the Property Order".

58.   After section 48 insert –

"Manner of giving effect to court orders as to land obligations, etc.

48A.   Where a court refuses to grant some relief available under Article 171 of, or paragraph 7 of Part III of Schedule 4 to, the Property Order or Article 15 of the Commonhold Order for enforcing a land obligation, a maker's or manager's obligation under a development scheme or a commonhold association's obligation under Schedule 4 to the Commonhold Order, the Registrar shall, if the court so directs and an office copy of the order is lodged with him by or by the direction of the court, take such action on the register (whether by cancellation of an entry, the entry of a notice, the making of a reference or otherwise) as the court directs and cause the copy of the order to be filed in the registry.".

59. In section 51, after "privilege" (twice) insert "neighbour obligation".

60. In section 53, for subsection (2) substitute –

"(2) Where registered land is adversely possessed by a person ("the possessor") in circumstances such that, if the land had been unregistered, the title of the owner would be extinguished by operation of that Order, the title of the registered owner shall not be extinguished but, instead, the land shall be deemed to be held by the registered owner in trust for the possessor (but without prejudice to the estate or interest of any other person whose estate or interest is not extinguished).

(2A) The possessor, or a successor of his, ("the applicant") may apply in the prescribed manner to be registered as owner of the land.",

and at the end of subsection (4) for "Statute" substitute "Order".

61. In section 59 (as substituted by the Insolvency (Northern Ireland) Order 1989, Schedule 9, paragraph 71), in subsection (1) for "tenant in common" substitute "joint tenant".

62. At the beginning of section 61 (as substituted by the Mental Health (Northern Ireland) Order 1986, Schedule 5) insert "Without prejudice to the powers of a person appointed attorney under an enduring power which has taken effect".

63. In section 85(3)(h) after "easement" insert ", land obligation," and after "land" insert "or the effect of a development scheme or a commonhold declaration".

64. In section 94, insert the following definitions at the appropriate places in alphabetical order –

"fee simple" means a fee simple absolute in possession;
"Commonhold Order" means the Commonhold (Northern Ireland) Order 1989;
"Property Order" means the Property (Northern Ireland) Order 1989;
and for the definition of "leasehold estate" substitute –
"leasehold estate" has the same meaning as in the Property Order.

65. In Schedule 4, in paragraph 7 and in the heading of that paragraph, for "6" substitute "5".

66. In Schedule 5, in Part I, at the end of entry 15 insert –

"; or

(c) the right is an equitable interest to which Article 23 of the Property Order applies.";

and after that entry insert –

"16. Any covenant (within the meaning of the Ground Rents (Northern Ireland) Order 1989) which continues to burden land by virtue of Article 24(2) of that Order.".

67. In Schedule 6, Part I, in entry 11, after "easement" insert "land obligation" and after "reservation" insert "or by a development scheme"; in entry 12, after "condition" where it first occurs, insert "or any land obligation"; for entry 14 substitute –

"14. Any right such as is mentioned in Article 33(3) or (4) of the Property Order".

after entry 14A (inserted by the Family Law (Miscellaneous Provisions) (Northern Ireland) Order 1984, Schedule 2 Part I paragraph 1) insert –

"14B. Any equitable interest (within the meaning of Article 23 of the Property Order) in the land, whether acquired before or after the first registration of the land.";

and in entry 15 for "14A" substitute "14B";

and in Part II, in paragraph 4(a), for "10 or 14A" substitute "10, 14A or 14B".

68. In Schedule 11, in entry 16 for "section 1 of the Rights of Light Act (Northern Ireland) 1961" substitute "Article 159 of the Property Order".

*Registration of Deeds Act (Northern Ireland) 1970 (c. 25)*

69. At the end of section 2(1) insert "or by one witness who subscribes his name, address and occupation, where that one witness is a solicitor".

70. At the end of section 2(3A) and section 4(4A) (added by the Family Law (Miscellaneous Provisions) (Northern Ireland) Order 1984, Schedule 2, Part I) insert (in each case) –

"or any document prescribed in regulations made under Article 23(6) of the Property (Northern Ireland) Order 1989".

*Friendly Societies Act (Northern Ireland) 1970 (c. 31)*

71. In section 15(1) for "subscribed his name and annexed his seal thereto" substitute "executed them as a deed".

72. In Schedule 3 for "Sealed with our seals" substitute "Executed by us as a deed" and for "Sealed and delivered" substitute "Signed and delivered as a deed".

*Leasehold (Enlargement and Extension) Act (Northern Ireland) 1971 (c. 7)*

73. For section 5(4) substitute –

"(4) Without prejudice to the powers of a person appointed attorney under an enduring power of attorney which has taken effect, where a person who is required by this Act to convey or join in conveying the fee simple in the land is incapable, by reason of mental disorder within the meaning of the Mental Health (Northern Ireland) Order 1986, of managing and administering his property and affairs, his controller or (if no controller is acting for him) any person authorised in that behalf may, under an order of the High Court, represent him for all or any of the purposes of this Act.".

74.   For section 11(4) substitute the subsection substituted above for section 5(4) with the substitution for the words "to convey or join in conveying the fee simple in the land" of the words "to join in the apportionment of a rent".

75.   In section 21(2) for the words from "a tenant for life" onwards substitute "money may be applied under Article 55 of the Property (Northern Ireland) Order 1989".

*Powers of Attorney Act (Northern Ireland) 1971 (c. 33)*

76.   In section 9 the amendment in section 26 of the Trustee Act (Northern Ireland) 1958 specified above.

*Local Government Act (Northern Ireland) 1972 (c. 9)*

77.   In section 100(1) for "under seal" substitute "by deed".

*Planning (Northern Ireland) Order 1972 (NI 17)*

78.   In Article 46(8) for "sections 19, 21 and 22 of the Conveyancing Act 1881" substitute "Articles 123, 124, 128, 129, 131 and 132 of the Property (Northern Ireland) Order 1989".

*Social Security Pensions (Northern Ireland) Order 1975 (NI 15)*

79.   In Article 65(6)(a) for "section 3(1) of the Perpetuities Act (Northern Ireland) 1966" substitute "Article 230(1) of the Property (Northern Ireland) Order 1989".

*Rent (Northern Ireland) Order 1978 (NI 20)*

80.   In Schedule 4, Part V, paragraph 2(e)(i) for "section 19 of the Conveyancing Act 1881" substitute "Article 123 of the Property (Northern Ireland) Order 1989".

*Administration of Estates (Northern Ireland) Order 1979 (NI 14)*

81.   In Article 17(2)(a) for "under seal" substitute "executed as a deed".

*County Courts (Northern Ireland) Order 1980 (NI 3)*

82.   In Article 14 –

(a)   in paragraph (i) for "under the Settled Land Acts 1882 to 1890" substitute "in relation to land which is the subject of a settlement within the meaning of the Property (Northern Ireland) Order 1989";

(b) in paragraph (j) for "section 17 of the Married Women's Property Act 1882" substitute "Article 235 of the Property (Northern Ireland) Order 1989".

### Private Streets (Northern Ireland) Order 1980 (NI 12)

83.   In Article 15(11) for "sections 19, 21 and 22 of the Conveyancing Act 1881" substitute "Articles 123, 124, 128, 129, 131 and 132 of the Property (Northern Ireland) Order 1989".

### Housing (Northern Ireland) Order 1981 (NI 3)

84.   In Articles 42(6) and 111(5), in each case, for "sections 19, 21 and 22 of the Conveyancing Act 1881" substitute "Articles 123, 124, 128, 129, 131 and 132 of the Property (Northern Ireland) Order 1989".

### Clean Air (Northern Ireland) Order 1981 (NI 4)

85.   In Article 33(7) for "sections 19, 21 and 22 of the Conveyancing Act 1881" substitute "Articles 123, 124, 128, 129, 131 and 132 of the Property (Northern Ireland) Order 1989".

### Judgments Enforcement (Northern Ireland) Order 1981 (NI 6)

86.   In Article 52(1) for "mortgage by deed, within the meaning of the Conveyancing Acts 1881 to 1911" substitute "charge by way of legal mortgage, within the meaning of the Property (Northern Ireland) Order 1989" and for the words from "section 21(2)" to "1911" substitute "Article 129 of the Property (Northern Ireland) Order 1989".

### Magistrates' Courts (Northern Ireland) Order 1981 (NI 26)

87.   In Article 70(1) for "Article 69(1)" substitute "Article 63 of the Landlord and Tenant (Northern Ireland) Order 1989".

### Land Compensation (Northern Ireland) Order 1982 (NI 9)

88.   In Article 19(7) for the words from "settled land for" to "1890" substitute "subject to a settlement within the meaning of the Property (Northern Ireland) Order 1989" and for "those Acts" substitute "that Order".

### Housing (Northern Ireland) Order 1983 (NI 15)

89.   In Article 8(4)(a) at the beginning insert "subject to Article 31 of the Ground Rents (Northern Ireland) Order 1989".

90.   In Article 10(4)(a) for "Conveyancing Acts 1881 to 1892" substitute "Property (Northern Ireland) Order 1989".

91.   In Article 17(12) for "section 9 of the Real Property Act 1845" substitute "Article 9 of the Landlord and Tenant (Northern Ireland) Order 1989".

92.   In Article 92(1)(a) for the words from "except" onwards substitute –

"and cannot be brought to an end at the instance of the landlord before that expiry except by an order of a court".

93.   In Schedule 9 the amendment in Part V of Schedule 4 to the Rent (Northern Ireland) Order 1978 specified above.

*Family Law (Miscellaneous Provisions) (Northern Ireland) Order 1984 (NI 14)*

94.   In Article 12(2)(b) for "section 36 of the Administration of Justice Act 1970" substitute "Article 134 of the Property (Northern Ireland) Order 1989".

*Mental Health (Northern Ireland) Order 1986 (NI 4)*

95.   In Article 100, in paragraphs (2) and (3), in each case, for "Wills Act 1837" substitute "Succession (Northern Ireland) Order 1989", and in paragraph (2) –

(a)   for "section 9" substitute "Article 5"; and

(b)   for "that Act", wherever occurring, substitute "that Order".

*Companies (Northern Ireland) Order 1986 (NI 6)*

96.   In Article 46(1)(a) for "under seal" substitute "executed as a deed".

97.   In Article 48(2) for the words from "signed" to "his seal" substitute "executed by such an attorney on behalf of the company".

*Housing (Northern Ireland) Order 1986 (NI 13)*

98.   In Article 18, in paragraph (1)(a) for "section 19 of the Conveyancing Act 1881" substitute "Article 123 of the Property (Northern Ireland) Order 1989", and in paragraph (5) for "Conveyancing Act 1881" substitute "Property (Northern Ireland) Order 1989".

99.   In Article 33(11) for "section 9 of the Real Property Act 1845" substitute "Article 9 of the Landlord and Tenant (Northern Ireland) Order 1989".

*Agriculture and Fisheries (Financial Assistance) (Northern Ireland) Order 1987 (NI 1)*

100.   For Article 16(9) substitute –

"(9)   Such of the matters in respect of which expenditure may be approved for grant under a scheme made under this Article as may be specified in regulations made by the Department with the approval of the Department of Finance and Personnel shall be improvements to which Article 55(1)(d) of the Property (Northern Ireland) Order 1989 applies.".

### Adoption (Northern Ireland) Order 1987 (NI 22)

101.　In Article 43(1) for "Part II of the Family Law Reform (Northern Ireland) Order 1977" substitute "Article 90 of the Property (Northern Ireland) Order 1989 or Article 22 or 27 of the Succession (Northern Ireland) Order 1989".

### Limitation (Northern Ireland) Order 1989 (NI 11)

102.　In Article 15 for "an instrument under seal" (twice) substitute "a deed", and in paragraph (b) for "under seal" substitute "a deed".

103.　After Article 15 insert –

*"Time limit: actions for breach of a land obligation, etc.*

15A.　An action in respect of a contravention of a land obligation or any other obligation imposed by a development scheme may not be brought after the expiration of six years from the date of the contravention.".

104.　In Schedule 1 –

(a) in paragraph 7, for "forfeiture or breach of condition" in the heading and where that expression first occurs in sub-paragraph (1) and sub-paragraph (2)(a), in each case, substitute "breach of obligation"; for "forfeiture was incurred or the condition broken" in sub-paragraph (1) substitute "breach occurred"; and for "forfeiture or breach" in sub-paragraph (2)(b) and "forfeiture or breach of condition" in the concluding words of the paragraph substitute (in each case) "breach";

(b) in paragraph 9 for sub-paragraphs (a) and (b) substitute "any land which is subject to a settlement within the meaning of the Property (Northern Ireland) Order 1989".

### Insolvency (Northern Ireland) Order 1989 (NI 19)

105.　In Article 209(1) for "under seal" substitute "executed as a deed".

106.　In Article 309(3) for "Partition Act 1868" substitute "Property (Northern Ireland) Order 1989".

107.　In Schedule 2, paragraph 7 and Schedule 3, paragraph 10, in each case, insert at the beginning of the paragraph "Without prejudice to Article 29 or 31 of the Ground Rents (Northern Ireland) Order 1989".

108.　In Schedule 9, paragraph 71, the amendment of section 59(1) of the Land Registration Act (Northern Ireland) 1970 specified above.

1632

## GENERAL MODIFICATIONS, SAVINGS, ETC.

### PART I

### GENERAL MODIFICATIONS

1.  Where an instrument under seal that constitutes a deed is required for the purposes of a statutory provision passed or made before the commencement of Article 81 of the Property Order, that Article has effect as to the execution of the instrumenttby an individual (other than a corporation sole) in place of any such provision about signing, sealing or delivery.

2.  References in any statutory provision to waste, in connection with the relation of landlord and tenant, are to be construed, in relation to a tenancy created after the commencement of Part III of the Landlord and Tenant Order, as references to a breach of obligation under Article 19 of that Order, but subject to paragraph 19 of Part II.

3.  References in any statutory provision to ejectment on the title (however expressed) are to be construed as references to an application under Article 57 of the Landlord and Tenant Order.

4.  Any reference in a provision of any of the Orders to another provision of the same Order includes a reference to any statutory provision repealed by this Order which is replaced by that other provision.

5.  Any reference in a statutory provision to a mortgage includes a charge by way of legal mortgage.

### PART II

### SAVINGS, ETC.

1.  Nothing in the Orders affects any statutory provision conferring special facilities or prescribing special modes for disposing of or acquiring land, or providing for the vesting of land in trustees or any person or the holder of an office or a corporation aggregate or sole (including the Crown).

2.  Nothing in the Orders prejudices the creation or enforcement of any right arising under a statutory provision or any matter protected by registration in the Statutory Charges Register.

3.  Nothing in the Orders affects prejudically the right or interest of any person arising out of or consequent on the possession by him of any documents relating to a legal estate in land, nor any question arising out of or consequent upon any omission to obtain or any other absence of possession by any person of any documents relating to a legal estate in land.

4. The repeal of provisions of the Statute of Frauds (Ireland) 1695 does not affect their application to contracts made before the commencement of Article 67 of the Property Order.

5. The repeal of the Prescription Act 1832 and the Prescription (Ireland) Act 1858 does not affect the acquisition of an easement or profit à prendre by prescription under those Acts by reason of the completion, after the commencement of those repeals, of a period which had begun to run before that commencement.

6.—(1) The repeal of section 9 or 33 of the Wills Act 1837 does not affect the will of a testator who died before the repeal took effect.

(2) The repeal of section 26 of the Wills Act 1837 does not affect a will made before the commencement of Article 26 of the Succession Order.

7. The repeal of the Wills Amendment Act 1852 does not affect the will of a testator who died before the repeal took effect.

8.—(1) The repeal of section 5 of the Landlord and Tenant Law Amendment, Ireland, Act 1860 does not affect a new holding within the meaning of that section which had been deemed to be constituted before the repeal took effect.

(2) Article 38 of the Landlord and Tenant Order does not prejudice any liability of the assignor of a tenancy created before the commencement of that Article.

(3) The repeal of sections 52 to 69 of the said Act of 1860 does not affect ejectment proceedings begun before the commencement of that repeal.

9. The repeal of the statutory provisions relating to agricultural tenancies (within the meaning of Article 79 of the Landlord and Tenant Order) is subject to the exception in paragraph (1) of that Article.

10.—(1) The repeal of section 7 of the Conveyancing Act 1881 (covenants for title) does not affect the applicability of the covenants implied under that section in cases arising before the commencement of Article 106 of the Property Order.

(2) The repeal of section 58 of that Act (covenants to bind heirs, etc.) does not affect the operation of the section in relation to covenants entered into before the commencement of the repeal, or in relation to covenants entered into after that commencement in pursuance of an agreement made before then.

(3) The repeal of section 64 of that Act does not affect the construction of covenants implied in a deed by virtue of that Act.

11. The repeal of the Wills (Amendment) Act (Northern Ireland) 1954 does not affect a will made before the commencement of Article 12 of the Succession Order.

12.    The repeal of words in section 1(3) and section 44(c) of the Administration of Estates Act (Northern Ireland) 1955 does not affect the descent of an entailed estate or interest or, subject to Article 6 of the Property Order, the nature of the estate or interest of a deceased person in an estate tail where the person in question died before the commencement of that Article 6.

13.    The repeal of section 12 of the Trustee Act (Northern Ireland) 1958 does not affect the power to sell by fee farm grant or by a lease with a nominal reversion in a case where Article 29(3) or 31(5) of the Ground Rents Order applies.

14.    Except as expressly provided in the Orders and this Order, nothing in the Orders affects the Land Registration Act (Northern Ireland) 1970 or the Registration of Deeds Act (Northern Ireland) 1970.

15.—(1) The following provisions of this paragraph apply in relation to the Land Registration Act (Northern Ireland) 1970 ("the Act").

(2)    Any registration of a person as full owner of land is to be treated as registration as owner.

(3)    Where a person is registered as limited owner of land –

(a)    where he is a tenant in tail, the Registrar of Titles may alter the registration so as to show him as owner of the land (and may do so without any application);

(b)    in any other case, pending the registration as owners (on an application under section 36(1) of the Act) of the persons entitled to be registered as such, his registration is not affected by the repeal of references in the Act to limited owners, but he is incapable of exercising any power of an owner under the Act.

(4)    Subject to sub-paragraph (3)(b), no charge created by a limited owner and no equitable mortgage by deposit of a land certificate by him is affected by the repeal of references in the Act to limited owners.

(5)    The repeal in section 41 of the Act of words in subsection (2) and of subsection (3) does not affect any charge by will already registered before the commencement of the repeal.

(6)    The repeal of paragraphs 2 and 5 of Part I of Schedule 8 to the Act does not affect any entry under paragraph 2 or the power to make an entry under paragraph 5 pending the registration of the trustees as owners under section 36 of the Act.

16.    The repeal of Article 5 of the Family Law Reform (Northern Ireland) Order1977 (construction of section 33 of the Wills Act 1837) does not affect the will of a testator who died before the repeal took effect.

17.—(1) The repeal of section 93 of the Judicature (Northern Ireland) Act 1978 (suits for possession of land by mortgagors) does not affect its application to a mortgagor to whom it applied before the repeal took effect.

(2) The repeal of section 94 of that Act (relief from ejectment) does not affect the powers of any court under that section in connection with a judgment or decree given or made before the commencement of the repeal or after then in consequence of paragraph 8(3).

18. The repeal of section 13 of the Property (Northern Ireland) Order 1978 (disposition of property to husband and wife) does not imply that in any circumstances spouses are to be treated as one.

19. In relation to a dwelling house let under a regulated tenancy after the commencement of Part III of the Landlord and Tenant Order, the provisions of Articles 40 to 45 of the Rent (Northern Ireland) Order 1978 apply instead of the provisions of Articles 19, 21, 24, 30 and 31 of the Landlord and Tenant Order and Article 35 of the Landlord and Tenant Order does not apply.

# DRAFT PROPERTY (CONSEQUENTIAL PROVISIONS) (NORTHERN IRELAND) ORDER 1989

## EXPLANATORY NOTE

1.  This Order contains provisions which are consequential on the main Orders. These repeal superseded enactments, amend (either expressly or by way of general modifications) continuing legislation which is incidentally affected and, in some cases, set out temporary exceptions to the repeals or amendments by way of savings.

2.  See also sections 28 (effect of repeal) and 29 (effect of substituting provisions) of the Interpretation Act (Northern Ireland) 1954. These affect "transferred provisions" rather than "statutory provisions", but it is not thought necessary to substitute the latter provision for the former in the sections.

3.  There are transitional provisions in Schedule 10 to the Property Order, Schedule 2 to the Landlord and Tenant Order and the Schedule to the Succession Order, and the second and third of these also contain savings.

4.  The following paragraphs deal only with those matters arising out of the Property (Consequential Provisions) Order which seem to call for special comment.

5.  We have considered whether it would be possible to repeal section VIII of the Tenures Abolition Act (Ireland) 1662 which provided that future grants of land could be made only in free and common socage. The wording of the section (which falls in the middle of a group of provisions relating to the guardianship of minors) shows that its main purpose was to abolish the payments which could formerly be imposed by a feudal lord upon his tenants on the occasion of succession to a tenant on death, the wardship or marriage of the successor where he was an infant, the knighting of the lord's son or the marriage of the lord's daughter. The expression "socage" has no significance in modern law – indeed its origin and precise meaning are uncertain, and it seems to have been referred to in 1662 only because it had the negative virtue of involving no feudal incidents. Article 4 of the Property Order provides that the only estates in land capable of subsisting at law are a fee simple absolute in possession and a leasehold estate: any other interest in land can take effect only in equity. The Survey, in paragraph 38, hesitated to recommend the section for repeal, without putting anything in its place, for fear that there could be allegations that old tenures had been revived or, at best, that there might be uncertainty. It might be argued that section 28(2)(a) of the Interpretation Act (Northern Ireland) 1954 (which prevents the repeal of a repealing provision from reviving the former law) is sufficient authority for the repeal; but in the end we have concluded that if tenure is not to be totally abolished (as the Survey had proposed) it is necessary to preserve socage as the universal tenure, so, with some reluctance, we have

excluded section VIII from repeal, even though, at the present day, new grants of land are not, in practice, made by the Monarch.

6. The Statute of Marlborough (1267) prohibited waste by "fermors" or, possibly, "termors" – see note 11 on Chapter 4.3 of the Report. The latter expression would include both tenants under leases and tenants at will and also life tenants of settled land. As to waste by the former group, see paragraph 4.3.14: as to the latter, the ownership and management of trust land will, in the future, be confided to the trustees of the settlement, not (as in the past) the tenant for life; and even where management powers are delegated to the tenant for life the trustees will have a supervisory role. Nevertheless, there will still be scope for the commission of waste by existing tenants, and there will be some (although reduced) scope for waste by a beneficiary under a future settlement. In view of this, it seems best to leave the Statute unrepealed.

7. The third Statute of Westminster (1289-90), also known as Quia Emptores, prevented sub-infeudation – a conveyance of freehold land was not to put the grantor into the position of feudal lord in relation to his grantee. This was derogated from in some seventeenth century grants of Irish lands giving rise to a system of fee farm grants. The future making of fee farm grants will be prohibited by Article 29 of the Ground Rents Order (subject to transitional exceptions). Future conveyances of a fee simple will give the grantee the same estate as had been held by his grantor: the question of sub-infeudation will not arise. Where title to land is acquired by adverse possession, a common opinion is that the possessor acquires a fee simple which is not that of the disentitled owner but a new one of his own: but even in this case the proposal made by the Survey and recommended in this Report is that the possessor should acquire the disentitled owner's fee. Schedule 1 lists the Statute for repeal.

8. The Survey proposed the repeal of the British Subjects Act 1751. We agree that, for the most part, this Act is ripe for repeal. It is concerned with the tracing of heirs through aliens, and heirship was abolished by the Administration of Estates Act (Northern Irelane) 1955. But we have just one doubt. Section 2 (although not section 1) of the Act refers to honours, and dignities and titles of honour are excepted matters under the Northern Ireland Constitution Act 1973. In view of this, we have omitted the Act from our repeal Schedule. We suggest that its suitability for repeal might be considered as a matter of statute law revision.

9. The Partition Act 1868 and the Partition Act 1876 operated upon an existing jurisdiction ("in a suit for partition where, if this Act had not been passed, a decree for partition might have been made ..."). That jurisdiction seems to have been an equitable one, because the legal jurisdiction, which had been created by the Irish statute "An Act for Jointenants" (33 Hen. 8 c. 10), disappeared with the abolition of the Writ of Partition (de participatione facienda) by section 36 of the Real Property Limitation Act 1833 (c. 27). The statute of Henry VIII was formally repealed by the Statute Law Revision Act 1950 (c. 6) Schedule 2.

1638

In future, partition will be dealt with under Articles 25, 45(1)(a) and 62 of the Property Order: the trustees may sell the land, or partition it with the consent of the beneficiaries, and refusal to exercise their powers, or any withholding of consent, may be referred to the court.

10.    The repeals of the Landlord and Tenant (Ireland) Acts of 1870, 1871 and 1872 and of the other statutory provisions listed in Article 79(2) of the Landlord and Tenant Order are consequential on that Article. See chapter 4.9 of the report.

11.    Section 3 of the Legitimacy Act (Northern Ireland) 1928 contains provisions about the rights of legitimated persons to take interests in property. The scope of the section was restricted by paragraph (5) of Article 4 of the Family Law Reform (Northern Ireland) Order 1977 (which created a presumption that in dispositions of property references to children and other relatives include references to, and to persons related through, illegitimate children). The substance of Article 4 is proposed for re-enactment in Article 90 of the Property Order and Article 27 of the Succession Order: paragraph (5) is now reproduced in the form of a direct textual amendment of the Act of 1928, namely, the addition to section 3 of a new subsection numbered (5). In the new subsection –

*sub-paragraph (a)* narrows down section 3(1)(b) in consequence of Articles 90 and 27. Before 1 January 1978 section 3(1)(b) gave a legitimated person, his family and descendants the right to take property under a disposition coming into force after the date of legitimation. Most of the area covered by that provision is now covered by the Articles, i.e. where the disposition refers simply to, say, "children", the Article will apply. But if the disposition refers to "legitimate children" the Article will not apply, so section 3(1)(b) is kept in force in a modified form in order to confer the property rights of legitimate children on legitimated children.

*sub-paragraph (b)* modifies section 3(2), which determines seniority as between children by making a legitimated person rank as if he had been born on the date of his legitimation. This is not generally applicable for the purposes of the Articles, under which the seniority of legitimated children, as of legitimate or illegitimate children, will depend on their dates of birth. But it does continue to apply where a disposition benefits only legitimate or legitimated children, but not illegitimate children (as in the example given above where the disposition refers to "legitimate children"). The reference in head (ii) to persons recognised by virtue of the 1928 Act as having been legitimated is to the child of a father who was at the date of his marriage domiciled in a country which recognised legitimation *per subsequens matrimonium* but had not been so domiciled at the date of the child's birth. If the father had been domiciled in that country on both occasions, the legitimacy of the child would have been recognised at common law: in the particular circumstances section 8 of the Act of 1928 treated the child as legitimated at the commencement of the Act or the date of the marriage, whichever last happened.

12. Part I of the Law Reform (Miscellaneous Provisions) Act (Northern Ireland) 1937 abolished former restrictions on the capacity of married women to hold property, and in other respects. In paragraph 2.13.1 of the Report we have expressed the view that the repeal of the property provisions of Part I would not revive the former law under which, on marriage, a husband obtained paramount rights over his wife's property. Nevertheless, we have not listed Part I for repeal. The Part deals with other matters as well as property rights, e.g., liability in tort or contract, capacity to be sued and insolvency. Rather than tinker with the Part by partial repeals, we prefer to leave it as it stands until the whole of it can be repealed together. This might best be done under the heading of family law. The same may apply to the Married Women (Restraint Upon Anticipation) Act (Northern Ireland)1952 and to some provisions of the Law Reform (Husband and Wife) Act (Northern Ireland) 1964.

13. Section 5(1)(c) of the Business Tenancies Act (Northern Ireland) 1964 permits a tenant to make a request for a new tenancy where his current tenancy is one granted for a period dependent on the fall of a life or other uncertain event which is continued by section 3 of the Act. Such a current tenancy is converted by Article 28 of and Schedule 4 to the Ground Rents Order into a tenancy for a fixed term certain, subject to termination by notice on the occurrence of the event in question. It might seem that, in view of this, paragraph (c) could be repealed. However, paragraphs (a) and (b) both refer to a tenancy "granted" for a term certain and so do not seem apt to cover a tenancy originally granted for a life and subsequently converted into a tenancy for a term certain. We think it best to leave paragraph (c) undisturbed. We propose the addition of a new subsection to section 55 of the Act (interpretation) clarifying this.

14. The changes made in the general law by the Property Order give rise to far-reaching alterations in the Land Registration Act (Northern Ireland) 1970. These two pieces of legislation need to be dovetailed (see the remarks of Lord Oliver in *City of London Building Society* v. *Flegg* [1987] 2 WLR 1266 at 1282-4), but they cannot be fully integrated (e.g. "purchaser" in the Property Order generally means a purchaser in good faith for valuable consideration, but there is no mention of good faith in the Land Registration Act, except in section 67A(6) which was inserted by paragraph 72 of Part II of Schedule 9 to the Insolvency (Northern Ireland) Order1989). The main changes to be made are that (1) the vesting of the legal estate in settled land in the trustees of the settlement, rather than in the tenant for life, means that the concept of "limited owner" disappears, and there is no need to refer ( by way of distinction) to a "full" owner; (2) the disappearance for the future of mortgages by demise or conveyance, and their replacement by charges by way of legal mortgage, mean that there will no longer be a difference between the form of a charge on registered land and a mortgage of unregistered land (Property Order Article114; Act, section 41); (3) a charge created by will (see section 41(2) and (3)) ceases to have effect at law and operates only in equity unless and until the personal representatives give it legal effect by creating a charge by deed; (4) the law of tacking is now to be the same

for both kinds of land (Article 140; section 43); (5) rights of residence are treated in the same way (Article 33; section 47); (6) so are reservations (Article 97; section 74); (7) a minor can no longer be a registered owner (Articles 10, 31; section 60); (8) provision has to be made for land obligations (e.g. neighbour obligations (Article 162), development obligations (Part IX) and the obligations attaching to a unit in a commonhold). Where, in consequence of the Property Order, title passes – e.g. from a life tenant or minor to trustees or from co-owners some of whom are not of full capacity to those of full capacity – the effect can be registered under Article 36(1)(f). In the case of a settlement, the names of the trustees will already be recorded in the Land Registry under Schedule 8 and it might seem that they could be substituted in the folio by the Registrar of his own motion as registered owners. But this does not seem satisfactory, because the particulars may be out of date and, in any event, a fee should be paid to remunerate the Registrar for time spent in regularizing the title (see the Law Commission's Working Paper No.94) (Trusts of Land) paragraph 11.2) – otherwise the work would, in effect, be done at the expense of other persons using the services of the Land Registry. Provisions about the Land Registry are also contained in the Ground Rents Order, the Property Order and the Commonhold Order.

15.—(1) Articles 19, 21, 24, 30 and 31 of the Landlord and Tenant Order (contained in Part III of that Order, which applies only to future tenancies, i.e. those beginning after the commencement date) substantially reproduce Articles 40 to 45 of the Rent (Northern Ireland) Order 1978. Generally the Rent Order applies only to existing tenancies (Article 3 as amended by Article 96 of the Housing (Northern Ireland) Order 1983), but in limited circumstances it can apply to new tenancies, where the new tenancy is substituted for an existing protected or statutory tenancy (Article 5). In these cases the Rent Order provisions will continue to apply.

(2) In Part I of Schedule 4 to the Rent Order, Case 3 refers to waste. For future tenancies the tort of waste by tenants is abolished by Article 35 of the Landlord and Tenant Order, but this does not apply to the substituted tenancies referred to in sub-paragraph (1). Of course, Case 3 continues to apply to existing tenancies, as do other statutory references to waste (as in Article 14(h) of the County Courts (Northern Ireland) Order 1980).

16. Article 33 of the Limitation (Northern Ireland) Order 1989 provides that at the expiration of the time limit for a mortgagee to bring an action claiming sale of the mortgaged land, the title of the mortgagee to the land is extinguished. We have proposed no amendment of this Article on the ground that "title of the mortgagee to the land" is capable of covering the bundle of rights possessed by a mortgagee under a charge by way of legal mortgage as well as the legal title which a mortgagee by conveyance, assignment or sub-demise obtains under present practice.

17. As to paragraph 10(2) of Part II of Schedule 3, see paragraph 2.5.41.

18. As to paragraph 13 of Part II of Schedule 3, see paragraph 2.4.17.

1641

RECOMMENDED DRAFT ORDER IN COUNCIL UNDER
SECTION 38(2) OF THE NORTHERN IRELAND
CONSTITUTION ACT 1973

---

## DRAFT STATUTORY INSTRUMENTS

---

### 1989 No.

### NORTHERN IRELAND

**The Enduring Powers of Attorney (Northern Ireland Consequential Amendment) Order 1989**

*To be laid before Parliament in draft*

*Made*

*Coming into Operation in accordance with Article 1(b)*

At the Court at          , the          day of          1989

Present,

The Queen's Most Excellent Majesty in Council

Whereas a draft of this Order has been approved by resolution of each House of Parliament:

Now, therefore, Her Majesty, in exercise of the powers conferred by section 38(2) of the Northern Ireland Constitution Act 1973(**a**) as extended by paragraph 1(7) of Schedule 1 to the Northern Ireland Act 1974(**b**), and of all other powers enabling Her in that behalf, is pleased, by and with the advice of Her Privy Council, to order, and it is hereby ordered as follows:–

---

(a) 1973 c. 36; section 38 was amended by paragraph 6 of Schedule 2 to the Northern Ireland Act 1982 (c. 38).
(b) 1974 c. 28.

**Title, commencement and extent**

**1.** This Order –

(a) may be cited as the Enduring Powers of Attorney (Northern Ireland Consequential Amendment) Order 1989;

(b) shall come into force on the day appointed for the coming into operation of Chapter II of Part XII of the Property (Northern Ireland) Order1989(**a**); and

(c) extends to the whole of the United Kingdom.

**Amendment of Enduring Powers of Attorney Act 1985**

**2.** In section 7(3) of the Enduring Powers of Attorney Act 1985(**b**), for the words "or under the Enduring Powers of Attorney (Northern Ireland) Order 1987"(**c**) there shall be substituted the words "or under Chapter II of Part XII of the Property (Northern Ireland) Order 1989".

**Revocation**

**3.** The Enduring Powers of Attorney (Northern Ireland Consequential Amendment) Order 1987 is hereby revoked.

Clerk of the Privy Council

---

(a) S.I. 1989/      (N.I.    ).
(b) 1985 c. 29.
(c) Inserted by the Enduring Powers of Attorney (Northern Ireland Consequential Amendment) Order 1987 (S.I. 1987 No. 1628).

Section 7(3) of the Enduring Powers of Attorney Act 1985 provides that an office copy of an instrument registered under that Act is to be evidence in any part of the United Kingdom of the contents of the instrument and of the fact that it has been registered.

This Order, which is made in consequence of the re-enactment of the Enduring Powers of Attorney (Northern Ireland) Order 1987 in the Property (Northern Ireland) Order1989, substitutes for a reference to the Order of 1987 a reference to the Order of 1989.

## TABLES OF COMPARISON

*Notes –*

(1)  In these Tables –

GR  =  the Grounds Rents Order
P  =  the Property Order
L&T  =  the Landlord and Tenant Order
S  =  the Succession Order
P(CP)  =  the Property (Consequential Provisions) Order

(2)  The association in these Tables of any Article with any clause, section or Article does not necessarily indicate that they are identical: in some cases they simply deal with the same general subject-matter.

(3)  Unqualified references in the "Remarks" column to paragraphs, chapters, or Parts are to paragraphs, chapters or Parts of the Report.

## TABLE 1

### TABLE OF COMPARISON OF THE PROPERTY BILL AND THE PERIODIC RENTS BILL APPENDED TO THE SURVEY WITH THE DRAFT ORDERS IN COUNCIL

| Clause or Schedule of Bill | Subject-matter | Article or Schedule of draft Order | Remarks |
|---|---|---|---|
| | PROPERTY BILL | | |
| | PART I | | |
| | GENERAL DEFINITIONS | | |
| 1 | General definitions. | P2(2), L&T2 | |
| | PART II | | |
| | GENERAL PRINCIPLES AS TO LEGAL ESTATES, TENURE, EQUITABLE INTERESTS AND POWERS | | |
| 2 | Definition of legal estates, equitable interests and powers. | | paras. 2.1.12-2.1.20 |
| (1) | | P4(1) | |
| (2) | | P4(2) | |
| (3) | | P11(1) | |
| (4) | | P4(3) | Except as to "estate owner" |
| (5) | | P4(4) | |

| Clause or Schedule of Bill | Subject-matter | Article or Schedule of draft Order | Remarks |
|---|---|---|---|
| (6) | | P4(5),10(1) | paras. 2.2.1-2.2.7 |
| (7) | | P12 | |
| (8) | | P11(1),12 | |
| (9) | | P13 | |
| 3 | Definition of fee simple absolute, and exercise of power to dispose of or create a legal estate. | | paras. 2.1.2-2.1.11 |
| (1) | | P5(1)(a),(b)(i),2(a) | cf. P5(2)(d) |
| (2) | | P(CP) | |
| (3) | | P15(1) | |
| 4 | Prohibition of future fee farm grants and rent charges. | GR29,30 | paras. 1.6.1-5 |
| 5 | Abolition of feudal tenure. | — | para. 2.1.26 |
| 6 | Abolition of fee tail estate. | P6 | para. 2.1.28 |
| 7 | Conversion of certain perpetually renewable leases into terms of years. | GR27,Sch.3 | paras. 1.6.6-1.6.12 |
| 8 | Position of parties after conversion. | GR Sch.3 | |
| 9 | Financial adjustments after conversion. | GR Sch.3 | |
| 10 | Determination of disputes on conversion. | GR39 | |
| 11 | Conversion of leases for lives. | GR28,Sch.4 | |
| 12 | Overreaching of certain equitable interests and powers by conveyance of a legal estate. | | cf. paras. 2.2.38-41 |
| (1) | | P17 | |
| (2) | | — | |
| (3) | | — | Unnecessary |
| 13 | Discharge of certain incumbrances on sale or exchange. | | |
| (1)-(3) | | — | Omitted in absence of provision for a Public Trustee |
| (4)-(10) | | P76 | |

| Clause or Schedule of Bill | Subject-matter | Article or Schedule of draft Order | Remarks |
|---|---|---|---|
| 14 | Manner of giving effect to equitable interests and powers. | P16 | |
| 15 | Creation and disposition of equitable interests, and of certain legal interests. | | |
| (1) | | P11(2)(3) | |
| (2) | | P14(1)(2) | |
| (3) | | — | cf. P8,9,14 |
| 16 | Merger of satisfied terms in the reversion expectant thereon. | P Sch.10 p.5 | paras. 2.1.29-2.1.32 |
| 17 | Certain legal powers to grant leases. | P15(2) | |
| 18 | Operation of vesting orders and dispositions of legal estates as conveyances by an estate owner. | P15(3)-(5) | |
| 19 | Title to be shown to a legal estate, and liability of solicitor. | | |
| (1) | | P18 | |
| (2) | | P243(6) | |
| 20 | Saving as to law of limitation of actions, land obligations, rights of persons in possession of documents and interests of persons in possession of land. | | |
| (1) | | — | Unnecessary |
| (2) | | P(CP) | |
| (3) | | — | para. 2.2.37 |
| 21 | Presumption that parties to a conveyance are of full age. | P10(2) | |

PART III

SETTLEMENTS

| Clause or Schedule of Bill | Subject-matter | Article or Schedule of draft Order | Remarks |
|---|---|---|---|
| 22 | What constitutes a settlement upon the statutory trusts. | | Chapter 2.3 |
| (1) | | P30(1) | |
| (2) | | P31(a) | |

| Clause or Schedule of Bill | Subject-matter | Article or Schedule of draft Order | Remarks |
|---|---|---|---|
| (3) | | P30(3) | para. 2.1.28 |
| (4) | | — | |
| (5) | | P33 | |
| (6) | | P Sch.10 p.12 | |
| (7) | | P30(4) | |
| 23 | Effect of a purported conveyance of a legal estate to an infant. | P31(b),(c) | As to a gift by will to two or more infants see P21(3),(4) |
| 24 | Definition of "the statutory trusts". | | |
| (1) | | P3 | |
| (2) | | P55(2) | |
| 25 | Overreaching effect of conveyances of trust land, etc. | P54(1)(a), (c),(d) | |
| 26 | Construction of certain settlements. | | |
| (1) | | P34 | |
| (2) | | P46 | |
| 27 | Consents to the execution of a trust for sale. | | para. 2.4.5 |
| (1) | | P47(1)(c), (2)(a) | |
| (2) | | P47(1)(d), (2)(b) | |
| (3) | | P47(3) | |
| (4) | | P47(4) | |
| 28 | Consultation by trustees with beneficiaries. | P44 | paras. 2.4.6-2.4.8 |
| 29 | Purchasers not to be concerned with the trusts of capital money or proceeds of sale. | P54(5) | |
| 30 | Actual and deemed delegation of powers of management by trustees. | | para. 2.4.16 |
| (1) | | P48(1) | |
| (2) | | P48(3) | |
| (3) | | P48(2) | |
| (4) | | P48(4) | |
| (5) | | P48(3) | |
| (6) | | P48(5) | |

| Clause or Schedule of Bill | Subject-matter | Article or Schedule of draft Order | Remarks |
|---|---|---|---|
| 31 | Notice to trustees to exercise power of sale and powers of court when trustees refuse to exercise their powers, etc. | | |
| (1) | | — | paras. 2.4.9, 2.4.10 |
| (2) | | P62(1)(2) (4)(d) | paras. 2.4.24-2.4.27 |
| 32 | Trusts of mortgaged property where right of redemption is barred. | P57 | |
| 33 | Land to be held on trust for sale where capital money has been invested therein by trustees of personal property. | P39 | |
| 34 | Settled land to be held by trustees upon the statutory trusts. | P Sch.10 p.6,13 | |
| 35 | Vesting of land previously settled in trustees. | P Sch.10 p.13 | |
| 36 | Who are trustees for the purposes of the Act. | | para. 2.3.6 |
| (1)(2) | | P35(1), (2)(a)-(e), (g) | |
| (3)-(5) | | P35(4)-(6) | |
| 37 | As to trustees of referential settlements. | P36 | |
| 38 | General powers of trustees upon the statutory trusts | P45(1)(a) (b),(2) (opening words) | para. 2.4.17 |
| 39 | Conveyances to be for the best consideration. | P50(1)(2) | |
| 40 | Leasing powers of trustees. | P51 | para. 2.4.18 |
| 41 | Regulations concerning leases. | | |
| (1) | | P52(1)(a)(b) | para. 2.4.19 |

| Clause or Schedule of Bill | Subject-matter | Article or Schedule of draft Order | Remarks |
|---|---|---|---|
| (2) | | P52(1)(c) | |
| (3) | | — | |
| (4),(5) | | P52(4)(5) | |
| (6) | | P51(4) | |
| (7) | | P52(6) | |
| 42 | Leasing powers for special objects. | P51(2)(a)(b) | |
| 43 | Mortgages of trust land. | P53 | |
| 44 | Modes of investment or application. | P55(1)(2) | paras. 2.4.20, 2.4.21 |
| 45 | Limitation of the number of trustees. | P42 | |
| 46 | To whom capital moneys or proceeds of sale are payable. | P43 | |
| 47 | Power of trustees to reimburse themselves. | P58(1) | |
| 48 | Prohibition or limitation against exercise of powers void, and provision against forfeiture. | P59 | See also P47(1) (a)(b) |
| 49 | Saving for and exercise of other powers. | | |
| (1) | | P60(1) | cf. P41(2) |
| (2) | | P60(2)(3) | |
| (3) | | P61 | |
| 50 | Saving for additional or larger powers under settlement. | P60(1)(2) | |
| 51 | Protection of purchasers. | P54(4) | |
| 52 | Payment of costs out of trust property. | P58(2) | |
| 53 | Cutting and selling timber, and capitalisation of part of proceeds. | — | See P45(1)(e), (2)(a),(3) paras. 2.4.11-13 |
| 54 | Termination of settlements and trusts | | paras. 2.4.28-2.4.32 |
| (1) | | P63 | cf. P64(1) |
| (2) | | P54(2) | |

1652

| Clause or Schedule of Bill | Subject-matter | Article or Schedule of draft Order | Remarks |
|---|---|---|---|
| | | PART IV | |
| | CO-OWNERSHIP | | |
| 55 | Effect of dispositions to co-owners. | | |
| (1) | | P19(1) | Chapter 2.2 |
| (2) | | P21(1)(2) | cf. P20 |
| (3) | | P21(7) | |
| (4) | | P21(4) | |
| (5) | | P21(5) | |
| 56 | Severance of joint tenancies in equity. | P24 | |
| 57 | Protection of purchaser on sale of land by survivor of joint tenants. | P26 | |
| 58 | Partition of land held by co-owners. | P25 | |
| 59 | Husband and wife to be treated as two persons. | — | para. 2.13.1 |
| 60 | Body corporate as joint tenant. | P27 | |
| 61 | Severance of party structures. | P28 | |
| | | PART V | |
| | CONTRACTS, CONVEYANCES AND OTHER INSTRUMENTS | | |
| 62 | Contracts for sale or other dispositions of land to be in writing. | P67 | paras. 2.5.1-2.5.10 |
| 63 | Stipulations as to time or otherwise not of the essence of a contract. | P69 | |
| 64 | Right of purchaser to insist upon obtaining the legal estate, and avoidance of certain stipulations in contracts relating to land. | | |
| (1) | | P70(1) | |
| (2)(-(4) | | P70(3)-(5) | As to P70(2) see cl.104 |

1653

| Clause or Schedule of Bill | Subject-matter | Article or Schedule of draft Order | Remarks |
|---|---|---|---|
| 65 | Fifteen years substituted for forty years as statutory length of title, and other provisions as to root of title. | | para. 2.5.14 |
| (1) | | P71(1) | The Article makes the words following the semi-colon more specific. |
| (2) | | P71(2) | para. 2.5.16 |
| (3) | | P71(3) | |
| (4)(5) | | — | P71(4),(5) substituted. |
| (6) | | P71(6) | |
| (7)-(10) | | P71(7)-(10) | |
| 66 | Other statutory conditions of sale. | | |
| (1)-(4) | | P73(1)-(4) | As to P73(5) see cl. 105 |
| (5)(11) | | P73(6)-(13) | |
| 67 | Application of insurance money on completion of a sale or exchange. | — | para. 2.5.17 |
| 68 | Stipulations preventing a purchaser or lessee from employing his own solicitor to be void. | — | cf. Solicitors (NI) Order 1976 Art.70 |
| 69 | Applications to the court by vendor and purchaser. | | |
| (1)(3) | | P74 | |
| (2) | | P75 | |
| 70 | Lands lie in grant only. | P78 | |
| 71 | Conveyances to be by deed. | P79 | |
| 72 | Instruments required to be in writing. | | |
| (1) | | — | |
| (2)-(4) | | P80 | |
| 73 | Persons taking who are not parties to a deed. | P88 | |
| 74 | Provisions as to supplemental instruments. | P91 | |

| Clause or Schedule of Bill | Subject-matter | Article or Schedule of draft Order | Remarks |
|---|---|---|---|
| 75 | Conditions and certain covenants not implied. | P105 | |
| 76 | Words of limitation not required to convey or transfer fee simple, and no resulting trust in voluntary conveyance. | | paras. 2.5.28-2.5.30 |
| (1)(2) | | P92(1)(2) | |
| (3) | | P93(1) | |
| (4) | | P92(4), 93(2) | |
| 77 | Construction of certain expressions used in deeds and other instruments. | P89 S 26 | |
| 78 | Conveyance of land to include all rights belonging to or enjoyed with the land. | P95(1)(2) (5) | |
| 79 | All estate clause implied. | P94 | |
| 80 | Production and safe custody of documents. | P96 | para. 2.5.31 |
| 81 | Reservation of legal estates. | P97 | para. 2.5.32 |
| 82 | Confirmation of past transactions. | P98 | |
| 83 | Certain documents to be deeds even though not under seal. | | |
| (1)(2) | | P81(1)(2) | cf. P83(2) |
| (3) | | P83(2)(4) | The witness must add address and description wherever he lives |
| (4) | | P81(3) | |
| 84 | Description of deeds. | P81(2)(a) | |
| 85 | Execution of deeds by an individual | P82 | paras. 2.5.33-2.5.35 The reference to placing his mark is omitted (Interpretation Act ss.35,46(11)) |

| Clause or Schedule of Bill | Subject-matter | Article or Schedule of draft Order | Remarks |
|---|---|---|---|
| 86 | Execution of instruments by or on behalf of corporations. | P84 | see also para. 2.5.36 |
| 87 | Rights of purchaser as to execution. | P87 | |
| 88 | Deed between parties to have same effect as indenture. | P81(4) | |
| 89 | Receipt in deed sufficient. | P99 | |
| 90 | Receipt in deed or endorsed sufficient evidence. | P100 | para. 2.5.38 |
| 91 | Receipt in deed or endorsed authority for payment to solicitor. | P101 | para. 2.5.39 |
| 92 | Release of part of land affected from a judgment. | P103 | |
| 93 | Conveyance by a person to himself and others. | P104 | As to P104(4) see Property (NI) Order 1978 Art.10(4) |
| 94<br>(1)-(6)<br>(7) | Covenants for title. | P106<br>P113 | paras. 2.5.45-2.5.50 |
| 95 | Implied covenants on assignment of a term of years. | P107 | |
| 96 | Benefit of covenants relating to land. | P(CP) | paras. 2.5.40-2.5.42 and see P.111 |
| 97 | Burden of covenants relating to land. | — | |
| 98 | Effect of covenant with two or more jointly. | P109 | |
| 99 | Covenants or agreements entered into by a person with himself and another or others. | P110 | |
| 100 | Covenants with two or more person. | P108 | |

| Clause or Schedule of Bill | Subject-matter | Article or Schedule of draft Order | Remarks |
|---|---|---|---|
| | | PART VI | |
| | | FEES AND COMMISSIONS | |
| 101 | Meaning of "lease" in this Part. | — | |
| 102 | Stipulation that party to sale or demise pay another party's costs to be void. | — | See Solicitors (NI) Order 1976 Art.70(1) |
| 103 | Stipulations preventing dealings in land except through lessor's solicitor and at purchaser's expense, or restricting purchaser's right to choose his solicitor, to be void. | — | See *ibid*. Art.70(2)(3) |
| 104 | Stipulation that purchaser shall contribute to costs of appointment of trustees, obtaining vesting order, etc., to be void. | P70(2) | |
| 105 | Expenses incurred by vendor at purchaser's request to be borne by purchaser. | P73(5) | |
| 106 | Stipulation that purchaser pay vendor's agent to be void. | P112(1) | |
| 107 | Costs of solicitor as mortgagee recoverable from mortgagor. | P149 | |
| 108 | Costs of solicitor as mortgagee charged upon the mortgaged property. | P150 | |
| | | PART VII | |
| | | MORTGAGES | |
| 109 (1) | Form of mortgage. | P114(1) | paras. 2.6.1-2.6.3 |

| Clause or Schedule of Bill | Subject-matter | Article or Schedule of draft Order | Remarks |
|---|---|---|---|
| (2) | | P116(2) | |
| (3)-(6) | | P114(2)-(5) | |
| 110 | Position of mortgagee, and registration. | | |
| (1) | | P116(1) | |
| (2) | | P133(1), 134(1) | para. 2.6.15 |
| (3) | | — | cf. P134(2)-(7), paras. 2.6.4-2.6.15 |
| (4) | | P114(6) | |
| 111 | Conveyance by mortgagee. | P130 | |
| 112 | Realisation of equitable mortgages. | P147 | paras. 2.6.22, 2.6.23 |
| 113 | Sale in redemption action. | P117 | |
| 114 | Mines and minerals | P126 | |
| 115 | Consolidation | | |
| (1) | | P139 | |
| (2) | | P118, 139(2) | |
| (3) | | P119 | |
| 116 | Tacking. | P140 | para. 2.6.24, 2.6.25 |
| 117 | Transfer in lieu of discharge. | P120 | |
| 118 | Inspection, production and delivery of documents, and priorities. | | |
| (1)(2) | | P121 | |
| (3) | | P141 | |
| 119 | Action for possession by mortgagor. | — | Unnecessary cf s. 93 Judicature (NI) Act 1978 |
| 120 | Leasing powers of mortgagor and mortgagee in possession. | | |
| (1)(2) | | P142(1)(2) | |
| (3) | | — | Omitted in view of Art.31 Ground Rents Order |
| (4) | | — | Unnecessary: Interpretation Act s.28(2)(c) |
| (5) | | — | Unnecessary: Interpretation Act. s.17(3) |

| Clause or Schedule of Bill | Subject-matter | Article or Schedule of draft Order | Remarks |
|---|---|---|---|
| (6) | | P142(3)(a) | cf P52 |
| (7) | | P142(3)(b) (c),(5) | |
| (8) | | — | |
| (9) | | P142(8) | |
| (10) | | — | |
| (11) | | P142(6) | |
| (12)-(14) | | P142(9)-(11) | |
| (15) | | P142(12) | |
| (16)-(18) | | — | |
| (19)(20) | | P142(13)(14) | |
| 121 | Powers of mortgagor and mortgagee in possession to accept surrenders of leases. | P143 | |
| 122 | Powers incident to interest of mortgagee. | P123 | paras. 2.6.26-2.6.28 |
| 123 | Undivided shares in land. | P Sch.10 p.20 | |
| 124 | Regulation of exercise of power of sale. | P125 | para. 2.6.30 |
| 125 | Conveyance on sale. | | |
| (1)(3) | | P128 | |
| (2) | | P129 | |
| 126 | Duty of mortgagee to obtain best price reasonably obtainable. | | para. 2.6.33 |
| (1)-(7) | | P127 | |
| (8) | | — | Unnecessary (see P127(3)(a)-(g)) |
| 127 | Application of proceeds of sale. | P132 | |
| 128 | Provisions as to exercise of power of sale. | P124 | |
| 129 | Mortgagee's receipts, discharges, etc. | P131 | |
| 130 | Amount and application of insurance money. | | |
| (1)(2) | | P136(1)(2) | |
| (3)(4) | | P136(4) | |
| 131 | Appointment, powers, remuneration and duties of receiver. | P137 | |

1659

| Clause or Schedule of Bill | Subject-matter | Article or Schedule of draft Order | Remarks |
|---|---|---|---|
| 132 | Effect of bankruptcy of the mortgagor on the power to sell or appoint a receiver. | P138 | |
| 133 | Effect of advance on joint account. | P144 | |
| 134 | Notice of trusts on transfer of mortgage. | P Sch.10 p.22 | |
| 135 | Notice of trusts affecting mortgage debts. | P148 | |
| 136<br>(1)(2)<br>(3)<br>(4)<br>(5) | Transfer of mortgages | <br>P145(1)(2)<br>—<br>P145(3)<br>— | |
| 137 | Discharge of mortgage by endorsed or annexed receipt. | P146 | para. 2.6.34 |
| 138 | Right of limited owner to prevent discharge on redemption. | — | Unnecessary – P146 does not permit a receipt to operate as a transfer |
| 139 | Form of charge by way of legal mortgage. | — | |
| 140 | Forms of statutory transfer of charge by way of legal mortgage. | — | |
| 141 | Implied covenants, joint and several. | — | |

PART VIII

POWERS GENERALLY

| Clause or Schedule of Bill | Subject-matter | Article or Schedule of draft Order | Remarks |
|---|---|---|---|
| 142 | Release of power. | P184 | |
| 143 | Disclaimer of power. | P185 | |
| 144 | Protection of purchaser in good faith claiming under fraudulent appointment. | P186 | |
| 145 | Validation of appointment where object is excluded or takes illusory share. | P187 | |

| Clause or Schedule of Bill | Subject-matter | Article or Schedule of draft Order | Remarks |
|---|---|---|---|
| 146 | Execution of non-testamentary power. | P188 | |
| 147 | Application of Part VIII. | P189 | |

### PART IX

### POWERS OF ATTORNEY

| | | | |
|---|---|---|---|
| 148 | Definitions. | — | These clauses have been superseded by the Powers of Attorney Act (NI) 1971 – see Table 2 under that Act and chapter 2.10 |
| 149 | Payments, etc., by attorney under power without notice of death, etc. | — | |
| 150 | Execution under power of attorney. | — | |
| 151 | Certified copies of powers. | — | |
| 152 | Effect of irrevocable power by way of security. | — | |
| 153 | Devolution of a power of attorney given to a purchaser. | — | |

### PART X

### EQUITABLE INTERESTS

| | | | |
|---|---|---|---|
| 154 | Abolition of the rule in Shelley's case, and as to heirs taking by purchase. | P211 | |
| 155 | Construction and effect of references to failure of issue. | P212 | |
| 156 | Equitable waste. | P213 | |
| 157 | Extension of the rule in *Dearle* v. *Hall* | P214 | chapter 2.11 |
| 158 | Power to nominate a trust corporation to receive notices | P215 | |

| Clause or Schedule of Bill | Subject-matter | Article or Schedule of draft Order | Remarks |
|---|---|---|---|
| 159 | Notice to one of several trustees of dealing with equitable interest. | P216 | |

PART XI

LANDLORD AND TENANT

| Clause or Schedule of Bill | Subject-matter | Article or Schedule of draft Order | Remarks |
|---|---|---|---|
| 160 | Relationship of landlord and tenant. | | |
| (1) | When relationship subsists. | — | chapter 4.2 |
| (2) | Meaning of "term of years". | P7, L&T2 | |
| (3) | Saving for existing relationship. | L&T Sch.2 p.9 | para. 2.1.12 |
| 161 | Creation of relationship. | L&T 3 | |
| 162 | Doctrine of interesse termini, and reversionary leases. | | |
| (1) | | L&T 5(1) | |
| (2) | | L&T 81 | chapter 4.10 |
| 163 | Evidence relating to leases. | L&T 6 | |
| 164 | Attornments by tenants. | L&T 8 | |
| 165 | Effect of extinguishment of reversion. | L&T 9 | |
| 166 | Leases invalidated by reason of non-compliance with terms of powers under which they are granted. | L&T 10 | |
| 167 (1)(2) | Licences granted to lessees. | L&T 42 | |
| (3)(4) | Rights of re-entry. | — | Unnecessary. Rights of re-entry are no longer exercisable as such (L&T 51) |
| 168 | Waiver of covenants. | L&T 43 | paras. 4.4.10-4.4.15 |
| 169 | Apportionment of conditions on severance. | L&T 41 | The Article applies the provision to obligations: its application to conditions and rights of re-entry is no longer relevant (L&T 51) |

| Clause or Schedule of Bill | Subject-matter | Article or Schedule of draft Order | Remarks |
|---|---|---|---|
| 170 | Implied covenants. | L&T Pt. III | The limited provisions of Cl.170 and Sch.3 are superseded by Pt.III for future tenancies. Ss.41 and 42 of Deasy's Act (on which Cl.170 was based) continue to apply to existing tenancies – L&T Sch. 3 p. 1, 2) |
| 171 (1)(3) | Running of tenant's covenants. | L&T 36, Sch.2 p.1 | chapter 4.3 |
| (2) | Effect of severance of reversion. | L&T 41 | Subs.(2)(b) (condition of re-entry or forfeiture) not now relevant |
| 172 | Running of landlord's covenants. | L&T 37 | paras. 4.4.1-4.4.7 |
| 173 | Assignment of term of years. | L&T 7 | |
| 174 | Position of parties after assignment. | L&T 38, 40 | |
| 175 | Restrictions against assignment, subletting, etc. | L&T 44 | paras. 4.4.16-4.4.24 |
| 176 | Position of parties after subletting. | L&T 46 | |
| 177 | Waste. | — | para. 4.3.14. Deasy's Act to continue in force for existing tenancies (L&T Sch.3 p. 7-13). |
| 178 | Rights of landlord. | — | cf. L&T 27 |
| 179 | Precept to restrain waste. | — | para. 4.10.9 |
| 180 | Tenant's fixtures. | L&T 33 | para. 4.10.4 |
| 181 | Insurance of demised premises. | — | para. 4.3.27 |
| 182 | Actions for rent. | | |
| (1) | Action for recovery of rent. | L&T 47(1)(a) | para. 4.5.1 |
| (2) | Action for use and occupation. | L&T 69 | |
| (3) | Payment of rent presumed to be for most recent gale. | L&T 70 | |
| 183 | Termination of tenancies. | L&T 50 | chapter 4.6 |

| Clause or Schedule of Bill | Subject-matter | Article or Schedule of draft Order | Remarks |
|---|---|---|---|
| 184 | Ejectment for non-payment of rent. | — | Ejectment for non-payment of rent abolished (L&T 47(7)) |
| 185 | High Court proceedings under section 184. | — | |
| 186 | County court proceedings under section 184. | — | |
| 187 | Relief from ejectment for non-payment of rent. | — | |
| 188 | Ejectment for overholding. | L&T 62 | |
| 189 | Recovery of mesne profits. | L&T 63 | para. 4.6.34 |
| 190 | Recovery of abandoned or deserted premises. | L&T 55 | paras. 4.6.8, 4.6.9 |
| 191 | Termination in accordance with agreement | L&T 50(1) (a),(c) | |
| 192 | Termination by surrender. | L&T 53 | |
| 193 | Enlargement of long terms. | L&T 56 | paras. 4.6.10-4.6.12 |
| 194 | Termination by notice. | L&T 52 | paras. 4.6.2-4.6.5 |
| 195 | Termination for frustration. | — | paras. 4.2.5-4.2.7 |
| 196 | Proceedings under section 195 | — | |
| 197 | Termination for breach of the tenant's obligations, etc. | L&T 57 | paras. 4.6.16-4.6.29 |
| 198 | Proceedings under section 197. | L&T 58 | para. 4.6.30 |
| 199 | Position of third parties. | L&T 61 | |
| 200 | Termination, and other remedies, for breach of landlord's obligations. | L&T 57 | paras. 4.6.16-4.6.29 |

1664

| Clause or Schedule of Bill | Subject-matter | Article or Schedule of draft Order | Remarks |
|---|---|---|---|
| | | PART XII | |
| | | PERPETUITIES | |
| 201 | Power to specify perpetuity period. | P219 | chapter 2.12 |
| 202 | Presumption and evidence as to future parenthood. | P66, 229 | |
| 203 | Uncertainty as to remoteness. | P221, 230 | |
| 204 | Reduction of age and exclusion of class members to avoid remoteness. | P231 | |
| 205 | Condition relating to death of surviving spouse. | P232 | |
| 206 | Saving and acceleration of expectant interests. | P233 | |
| 207 | Powers of appointment. | P234 | |
| 208 | Administrative powers of trustees. | P228 | |
| 209 | Other restrictions on the perpetuity rule. | P224 | |
| 210 | Options relating to land. | | |
| (1)(2) | | P226 | |
| (3) | | P220 | |
| 211 | Avoidance of contractual and other rights in cases of remoteness. | P223 | |
| 212 | Rights for enforcement of rentcharges. | P227 | |
| 213 | Conditions subsequent, possibilities of reverter, etc. | P222 | |
| 214 | Abrogation of the rule in *Whitby* v. *Mitchell*. | — | para. 2.12.14 |
| 215 | Interpretation, etc. | | |
| (1) | | P2(4), 218(1) | |
| (2) | | P218(2) | |

| Clause or Schedule of Bill | Subject-matter | Article or Schedule of draft Order | Remarks |
|---|---|---|---|
| (3) | | P217(3) | |
| (4) | | P217(1) | |
| (5) | | P217(2) | |

PART XIII

## HUSBAND AND WIFE

| | | | |
|---|---|---|---|
| 216 | General position of married women. | — | paras. 2.13.1-2.13.4 |
| 217 | Questions between husband and wife. | P235 | |
| 218 | Saving of special position of spouses, and extension of presumption of advancement. | — | paras. 2.13.5-2.13.9 |

PART XIV

## VOIDABLE DISPOSITIONS

| | | | |
|---|---|---|---|
| 219 | Voluntary conveyances to defraud creditors. | — | para. 2.14.2 |
| 220 | Voluntary disposition of land in relation to subsequent purchaser. | P237 | |
| 221 | Sales of reversions. | P238 | |

PART XV

## WILLS

| | | | |
|---|---|---|---|
| 222 | All property may be disposed of by will. | S3 | para. 5.2.5, 5.2.6 |
| 223 | Infancy. | S4 | para. 5.2.7 |
| 224 | Formalities for execution of wills. | S5 | paras. 5.2.8-5.2.11 |
| 225 | Testamentary execution of power. | S6 | |
| 226 | Soldiers, seamen and airmen. | — | para. 5.2.12 |
| 227 | Incompetency of attesting witness. | S7 | |
| 228 | Gift to witness. | S8 | para. 5.2.13 |
| 229 | Attestation by creditor. | S9 | |
| 230 | Attestation by executor. | S10 | |

| Clause or Schedule of Bill | Subject-matter | Article or Schedule of draft Order | Remarks |
|---|---|---|---|
| 231 | Revocation of will by marriage. | S12 | para. 5.2.15 |
| 232 | No revocation by alteration in circumstances. | S14(2) | |
| 233 | Revocation generally. | S14(1) | |
| 234 | Alteration of will after execution. | S11 | |
| 235 | Revival of revoked will. | S15 | |
| 236 | Subsequent acts not revocation. | S17(2) | |
| 237 | Wills speak from death. | S17(1) | |
| 238 | Residuary devises to carry property comprised in lapsed and void devises. | S19 | |
| 239 | Interpretation of "realty", "personalty" and "land". | S26(e)(f) | |
| 240 | Contingent and future testamentary gifts to carry the intermediate income. | S21 | |
| 241 | Implied execution of power of appointment. | S20 | |
| 242 | Words of limitation unnecessary. | S18 | |
| 243 | Restriction of lapsing of gifts to issue. | S22 | para. 5.2.20 |
| 244 | Secret trusts. | — | paras. 5.2.21-5.2.24 |
| 245 | Abolition of equitable doctrine of conversion. | — | paras. 5.2.25-.5.2.28: cf S24 |
| 246 | Application of this Part. | | |
| (1) | | S Sch. p.1 | |
| (2) | | S16 | |
| 247 | General rule as to formal validity. | — | paras. 5.2.37-5.2.39 |

| Clause or Schedule of Bill | Subject-matter | Article or Schedule of draft Order | Remarks |
|---|---|---|---|
| 248 | Additional rules. | — | |
| 249 | Certain requirements to be treated as formal. | — | |
| 250 | Construction of wills. | — | |
| 251 | Interpretation and application of sections 248-251. | — | |

PART XVI

LAND OBLIGATIONS

| Clause or Schedule of Bill | Subject-matter | Article or Schedule of draft Order | Remarks |
|---|---|---|---|
| 252 | Definitions and general. | — | The Survey's scheme of land obligations is not recommended by the Report. Generally, see Parts VIII and IX of the Property Order (chapters 2.7 and 2.8) |
| 253 | Statutory land obligations. | — | cf. P151 (para. 2.7.8) |
| 254 | Statutory land obligations where building divided into units or where building part of a scheme. | — | cf. P152 (paras. 2.7.9—2.7.26) and Common-hold Order (Part 3) |
| 255 | Classes of land obligations. | — | paras. 2.7.2-2.7.5 |
| 256 | Creation of land obligations by deed. | — | cf. P162; see also chapter 2.8 |
| 257 | Land obligations arising by implication of law on a division of land. | P152 | paras. 2.7.23-2.7.26 |
| 258 | Imposition of land obligations by long user. | — | cf. P154, 155, paras. 2.7.32-2.7.42 |
| 259 | Land obligations imposed by Lands Tribunal | — | paras. 2.9:11-2.9.13 |
| 260 | Enforcement, duration and determination of land obligations. | — | cf. P Sch.4 Pt. III paras. 4-6, 10 and P169(3)(4),170,174 |

| Clause or Schedule of Bill | Subject-matter | Article or Schedule of draft Order | Remarks |
|---|---|---|---|
| 261 | Power to discharge or modify land obligations and other restrictions affecting land. | P180 | chapter 2.9 |
| 262 | Powers of the court. | P181 | |
| 263 | Remedies. | | |
| (1) | | P158 | para. 2.7.43 |
| (2) | | — | cf P Sch.4 Pt.II p.3 and P Sch.5 Pt.II p.3 |

PART XVII

MISCELLANEOUS

| | | | |
|---|---|---|---|
| 264 | Provisions as to corporations. | P242 | |
| 265 | Protection of solicitor and trustees adopting Act. | P243 | |
| 266 | Fraudulent concealment of documents and falsification of pedigrees. | P244 | |
| 267 | Presumption of survivorship in regard to claims to property. | — | See P239, S30, paras. 2.14.3-2.14.6 |
| 268 | Merger. | P245 | |
| 269 | Release of rights of pre-emption. | P14(3) | |
| 270 | Power to direct division of chattels. | P246 | |
| 271 | Regulations respecting notices. | P247 L&T74 | |
| 272 | Restrictions on constructive notice. | P248 | |
| 273 | Notice of land obligations. | — | cf P163 |

PART XVIII

JURISDICTION AND GENERAL PROVISIONS

| | | | |
|---|---|---|---|
| 274 | Payment into court, jurisdiction and procedure. | | |
| (1) | | P250 | para. 2.14.23 |

| Clause or Schedule of Bill | Subject-matter | Article or Schedule of draft Order | Remarks |
|---|---|---|---|
| (2) | | P249 | |
| (3),(4) | | — | Unnecessary (Judicature (NI) Act 1978 ss.17, 59; County Courts (NI) Order 1980 Arts.34, 48; Lands Tribunal and Compensation Act(NI) 1964 s.8(7)) |
| 275 | Orders of court conclusive. | P251 | |
| 276 | Repeals and amendments. | — | See P(CP) |
| 277 | Adaptions of references in documents. | — | See P(CP) |
| 278 | Application to the Crown. | P253 L&T 82 | paras. 2.14.24-25: chapter 4.11 |
| 279 | Transitional provisions. | P252, Sch.10 | |
| 280 | Short title. | P1(1) | |
| Sch. 1 | Covenants implied in conveyances. | P Sch.1 | paras. 2.5.45-2.5.50 |
| Sch. 2 | Mortgage forms. | — | No provision is recommended about statutory forms of mortgage |
| Sch. 3 | Covenants implied in leases. | — | See L&T Pt.III |
| Sch. 4 | Land obligations procedure. | — | paras. 2.7.12-2.7.22 |
| Sch. 5 | Enactments repealed | P(CP) | |
| Sch. 6 | Amendment of enactments. | P(CP) | as to S.28, Statute of Limitations (NI) 1958, see P.240, paras. 2.14.7 et seq. |

PERIODIC RENTS BILL

| | | | |
|---|---|---|---|
| 1 | Equitable apportionment of leasehold rents. | L&T39 | See Part 1 – generally, the recommendations differ substantially from the Survey's Bill. |
| 2 | Remedies for recovery of annual sums charged on land. | — | cf P8 and paras. 2.1.21-2.1.23 |

| Clause or Schedule of Bill | Subject-matter | Article or Schedule of draft Order | Remarks |
|---|---|---|---|
| 3 | Partial release of security from a rentcharge. | P102 | |
| 4 | Overreaching on sale or exchange of land subject to a rentcharge. | — | cf GR4,8,13,14, Sch.2 |
| 5 | Overreaching on sale or exchange of part of land subject to a rentcharge. | — | cf GR5, Sch.1 |
| 6 | Rentcharges to which this Act applies. | — | cf GR3, 26 |
| 7 | Overreaching on sale or exchange of land held under a fee farm grant | — | |
| 8 | Procedure for overreaching fee farm rents. | — | cf GR4,8,13,14, Sch.2 |
| 9 | Overreaching on sale or exchange of part only of land held under a fee farm grant. | — | cf GR5, Sch.1 |
| 10 | Other interests in land held under a fee farm grant. | — | cf GR22-25 |
| 11 | Discharge apart from a sale or exchange of land held under a fee farm grant. | GR4 | |
| 12 | Covenants affecting land held under a fee farm grant. | — | Unnecessary |
| 13 | Certain contracts to be void. | GR33 | |
| 14 | Regulations. | — | cf GR38(4) |
| 15 | Definitions. | GR2(2) | paras. 1.5.3-7 |
| 16 | Application to the Crown. | GR40 | |
| 17 | Short title. | GR1(1) | |

# TABLE 2

## TABLE OF COMPARISON OF STATUTORY PROVISIONS IN FORCE IN NORTHERN IRELAND WITH THE DRAFT ORDERS IN COUNCIL

| Section or Schedule of Act or Article of Order | Subject-matter | Article or Schedule of draft Order | Remarks |
|---|---|---|---|
| | *Acts of the Parliament of Ireland* | | |
| | **STATUTE OF USES (IRELAND) 1634**<br>(sess. 2 c. 1) | | |
| 1 | Execution of Uses. | — | cf. P 13, 14(4) |
| 2 | Joint interests. | — | |
| 3 | Saving of former rights. | — | |
| 4 | Cestui que use to be adjudged in possession. | — | |
| 9 | Saving of other Acts, etc. | — | |
| 11 | Fines for alienation, etc. | — | Rep. by effect of 1662 c.19 (I) ss. 1, 5; 1698 c. 7 (I) s. 5. |
| 17, 18 | Inrollment of bargain and sale. | — | cf. P. 78(1). |
| | **CONVEYANCING ACT (IRELAND) 1634**<br>(sess. 2 c. 3) | | |
| 1-5, 11 | Fraudulent conveyances to deceive purchasers void. | — | Superseded by Registration of Deeds Acts. See also P237. |
| 10, 14 | Voluntary conveyances to defeat creditors. | — | Para. 2.14.1, 2.14.2 s.10 repealed Insolvency (N.I.) Order 1989 Sch.10. |
| | **TENURES ABOLITION ACT (IRELAND) 1662**<br>(sess. 4 c. 19) | | |
| VIII | Future grants to be in socage. | — | See Explanatory Note on Consequential Provisions Order. |

| Section or Schedule of Act or Article of Order | Subject-matter | Article or Schedule of draft Order | Remarks |
|---|---|---|---|
| | **LIFE ESTATES ACT (IRELAND) 1695 (c. 8)** | | |
| 1-3 | Presumption after 7 years of death of persons for whose lives leases are held. | — | Leases for lives or for years determinable upon lives abolished GR28. |
| | **STATUTE OF FRAUDS (IRELAND) 1695 (c. 12)** | | |
| 2 | Defendant not to be charged upon (inter alia) contract or sale of land unless in writing and signed. | P 67 | 2.5.1 s. 2 is not affected so far as it relates to a promise to answer for the debt of another. |
| 4 | Declaration of trust of land to be in writing. | P 80(1) | |
| 5 | Exception for implied or testamentary trusts. | P 80(3) | |
| 6 | Assignment of trusts. | P 80(2) | |
| | **CLANDESTINE MORTGAGES ACT (IRELAND) 1697 (c. 11)** | | |
| 1 | Mortgagor not giving notice in writing to mortgagee of prior incumbrances not to have equity of redemption. | — | Superseded by Registration of Deeds Acts. |
| 2 | Subsequent mortgagees without notice also hold free of equity of redemption. | — | |
| 3 | Subsequent mortgagees may redeem the former. | — | |
| | **ADMINISTRATION OF JUSTICE ACT (IRELAND) 1707 (c. 10)** | | |
| 9 | Conveyances good without attornment. | L&T 8(1) | |
| 10 | Tenant not prejudiced by payment of rent before notice. | L&T 8(2) | |
| 19 | Warranties by life tenant void against remainderman. | — | Cannot arise in future as life tenant will have only an equitable interest (cf. P48). |

| Section or Schedule of Act or Article of Order | Subject-matter | Article or Schedule of draft Order | Remarks |
|---|---|---|---|
| | **LAND IMPROVEMENT ACT (IRELAND) 1735**<br>(c. 7) | | |
| 1 | Personal representative of life tenant planting timber to be entitled to a moiety. | — | para. 2.4.14.<br>cf. P 45(2)(a), 48(7). |
| | Exception for ornamental, etc., trees. | — | cf. P. 45(4). |
| 2, 3 | Provisos. | — | |
| | **LANDLORD AND TENANT ACT (IRELAND) 1741**<br>(c. 8) | | |
| 7 | Fraudulent attornments. | L&T 8(3) | |
| 8 | Exceptions. | L&T 8(3) | |
| | **LEASES FOR LIVES ACT (IRELAND) 1777**<br>(c. 49) | | |
| 11 | Power in settlement to lease for life includes power to lease for years determinable on life. | — | cf. GR 28. |
| | **TENANCY ACT (IRELAND) 1779**<br>(c. 30) | | |
| 1 | Relief from failure to pay fines under leases for lives renewable for ever. | — | cf. GR 27 |
| 2 | Manner of notice where tenant cannot be discovered. | — | |

*Statutes of the Parliaments of England and Great Britain*

| | | | |
|---|---|---|---|
| | **STATUTE OF MARLBOROUGH 1267**<br>(52 Hen. 3 c. 23) | | |
| 23 | Farmers shall do no waste. | — | cf. L&T 35<br>paras. 4.3.14-15 |
| | **STATUTE OF WESTMINSTER THE SECOND 1285**<br>(DE DONIS CONDITIONALIBUS)<br>(13 Edw. 1 c. 1) | | |
| 1 | Entails. | — | P 6: para. 2.1.28 |

| Section or Schedule of Act or Article of Order | Subject-matter | Article or Schedule of draft Order | Remarks |
|---|---|---|---|
| | **STATUTE OF WESTMINSTER THE THIRD 1289-90 (QUIA EMPTORES) (18 Edw. 1 cc. 1, 2, 3)** | | |
| 1 | Freeholders may sell their lands; so that the feoffee do hold of chief lord. | P 14 | cf. GR 29: see Explanatory Note on Consequential Provisions Order. |
| 2 | Sale of part. | — | |
| 3 | Extent. | — | |
| | **BRITISH SUBJECTS ACT 1751 (c. 39)** | | |
| 1 | Heir traced through alien. | — | Heirship (save as to entails), primogeniture and co-parcenery abolished 1955 c. 24 NI s.1(3). |
| 2 | Daughter displaced by later-born son; daughters taking as co-parceners. | — | See Explanatory Note on Consequential Provisions Order. |
| | *Acts of the Parliament of the United Kingdom* | | |
| | **ILLUSORY APPOINTMENTS ACT 1830 (c. 46)** | | |
| 1 | Appointment not impeachable as illusory. | P 187(1) | |
| 2 | Saving for instrument declaring minimum share of object of power. | P 187(2) | |
| 3 | Act not to give any other force to an appointment than if a substantial share had been appointed. | — | |
| | **INFANTS' PROPERTY ACT 1830 (c. 65)** | | |
| 12 | Surrender, etc. of leases for lives or leases for terms of years, either absolute or determinable on death. | — | Except as to terms of years absolute, see GR28: as to such terms, see P45(1)(a), (c). |

| Section or Schedule of Act or Article of Order | Subject-matter | Article or Schedule of draft Order | Remarks |
|---|---|---|---|
| 14 | Charges attending renewal to be charged on infant's estates. | — | P58(1) |
| 15 | New leases to be to the same uses as the leases surrendered. | — | cf. P3, 55 |
| 17 | Court may authorize leases. | — | P45(1)(a), 62 |
| 18 | Appointment of person to act for person bound to renew. | — | |
| 20 | Fines to be paid before renewal and counterparts executed. | — | |
| 21 | Fines, how to be applied. | — | |

PRESCRIPTION ACT 1832
(c. 71)

| | | | |
|---|---|---|---|
| — | — | — | para. 2.7.32. The Act is superseded by P154-158; see also P Sch. 10 p. 23 and P(CP). |

FINES AND RECOVERIES ACT 1833
(c. 74)

| | | | |
|---|---|---|---|
| — | — | — | The Act is concerned with the bankruptcy of tenants in tail: see P6. |

FINES AND RECOVERIES (IRELAND) ACT 1834
(c. 92)

| | | | |
|---|---|---|---|
| — | — | — | The Act is concerned with the barring of entails and the bankruptcy of tenants in tail: see P6. |

WILLS ACT 1837
(c. 26)

| | | | |
|---|---|---|---|
| 1 | Interpretation: | | |
| | "Will" | — | Unnecessary. |
| | "Real estate" | — | These expressions are not used in S. |
| | "Personal estate" | — | |
| | Number | — | Interpretation Act s.37(2). |
| | Gender | — | Ibid s. 37(1). |

| Section or Schedule of Act or Article of Order | Subject-matter | Article or Schedule of draft Order | Remarks |
|---|---|---|---|
| 3 | All property may be disposed of by will. | S3 | para. 5.2.5. |
| 7 | No will of a person under age valid. | S4 | para. 5.2.7. |
| 9 | Formalities for execution. | S5 | para. 5.2.8. |
| 10 | Appointments. | S6 | |
| 11 | Saving as to wills of soldiers and mariners. | — | para. 5.2.12. |
| 13 | Publication not requisite. | — | See Note on S16. |
| 14 | Incompetency of witness. | S7 | |
| 15 | Gift to witness. | S8 | para. 5.2.13. |
| 16 | Creditor as witness. | S9 | |
| 17 | Executor as witness. | S10 | |
| 18 | Effect of marriage. | S12 | para. 5.2.15. |
| 19 | No revocation by alteration in circumstances. | S14(2) | |
| 20 | Modes of revocation. | S14(1) | |
| 21 | Alteration after execution. | S11 | |
| 22 | Revival of revoked will. | S15 | |
| 23 | Subsequent acts not revocation. | S17(2)(3) | |
| 24 | Wills speak from death. | S17(1) | |
| 25 | Residuary devises include property in lapsed and void devises. | S19 | |
| 26 | General devise of land includes leaseholds as well as freeholds. | S26 | |

| Section or Schedule of Act or Article of Order | Subject-matter | Article or Schedule of draft Order | Remarks |
|---|---|---|---|
| 27 | General gift of realty or personalty includes property subject to general power of appointment. | S20 | |
| 28 | Words of limitation unnecessary. | S18(1) | |
| 29 | Meaning of "die without issue" etc. | P212 | |
| 30 | Devise of realty to trustees, etc. | S18(3) | |
| 31 | Trustees for more than a life to take the fee. | S18(2) | |
| 32 | Devises of estates tail not to lapse where inheritable issue survives. | — | Estate tail abolished P6. |
| 33 | Gifts to children leaving issue. | S22 | Mod. 1977 (N.I. 17) Art.5; para. 5.2.20. |
| 34 | Extent of Act: effect of re-execution. | S16 | |

### RENEWAL OF LEASES (IRELAND) ACT 1838
#### (c. 62)

| | | | |
|---|---|---|---|
| 1 | Masters of the Court of Chancery may grant renewals of leases for lives or years, where the persons to do so are out of the jurisdiction. | — | See GR 27, 28. |

### REAL PROPERTY ACT 1845
#### (c. 106)

| | | | |
|---|---|---|---|
| 2 | Corporeal tenements to lie in grant as well as in livery. | — | cf P78. |
| 3 | Feoffments, etc., to be by deed. | P79 | |
| 4 | Abolition of tortious feoffment. | — | |
| | Exchange or partition not to imply any condition in law. | P105(1) | |

| Section or Schedule of Act or Article of Order | Subject-matter | Article or Schedule of draft Order | Remarks |
|---|---|---|---|
| | Words "give" and "grant" not to imply covenant. | P105(2) | |
| 5 | Strangers may take immediately under an indenture. | P88 | |
| | A deed purporting to be an indenture shall take effect as such. | P81(4) | |
| 6 | Contingent and other like interests shall be alienable by deed, saving estates tail. | P14(1)(a) | See P6 as to estates tail. |
| 8 | Contingent remainders protected against the premature failure of a preceding estate. | — | See P5(2)(a), 11(1). |
| 9 | When the reversion on a lease is gone the next estate to be deemed to be the reversion. | L&T 9 | |

### SATISFIED TERMS ACT 1845
### (c. 112)

| | | | |
|---|---|---|---|
| 1 | Satisfied terms of years attendant on inheritance etc. of land on 31 December 1845 to cease, but to afford the same protection as if still subsisting but not assigned or dealt with. | — | para. 2.1.29. |
| 2 | Terms becoming satisfied, and attendant upon inheritance etc. of lands after 31 Dec. 1845 to cease. | P Sch.10 p.5 | |
| 3 | Interpretation of terms. | — | |

| Section or Schedule of Act or Article of Order | Subject-matter | Article or Schedule of draft Order | Remarks |
|---|---|---|---|
| | **SETTLED LAND (IRELAND) ACT 1847** (c. 46) | | |
| 1 | Trustees etc. of settled estates may petition the High Court for permission to lay out monies arising from sale or exchange of settled lands, in the improvement of lands already settled. | — | See P55(1)(d). |
| 2 | Court may refer petition to a master, and obtain his report. | — | |
| 3 | Report of master and order of court thereon. | — | |
| 4 | Reference to and report of master as to expenditure. | — | |
| 5 | If master report that advances ought to be repaid, such advances to be charged on lands improved. | — | |
| 6 | Tenants for life etc. bound to pay charges and maintain works. | — | |
| 7 | Further applications; costs; rules and orders. | — | |
| | **LEASES ACT 1849** (c. 26) | | |
| 1 | Interpretation (Number, gender, "person") | — | Unnecessary. |
| 2 | Leases granted under intended exercise of powers, but invalid owing to deviation from the terms of the powers, to be in certain cases valid as contracts. | L&T 10(1), (2) | |

1681

| Section or Schedule of Act or Article of Order | Subject-matter | Article or Schedule of draft Order | Remarks |
|---|---|---|---|
| 4 | Leases invalid by reason that the grantor could not lawfully grant them, in certain cases to become valid. | L&T 10(3) | |
| 5 | Where grantor of lease has a valid power of leasing it shall be deemed to be granted in exercise of power. | L&T 10(8) | |
| 6 | Saving of rights of lessees under covenants, and lessors' rights of re-entry. | L&T 10(7) | |
| 7 | This Act not to extend to certain leases. | — | Survey para. 298. |

RENEWABLE LEASEHOLD CONVERSION ACT 1849
(c. 105)

| | | | |
|---|---|---|---|
| 1-40 | Conversion of renewable leases into fee farm grants. | — | para. 1.6.8. Rep. GR 42; s.37 saved GR27(7). |

LEASES ACT 1850
(c. 17)

| | | | |
|---|---|---|---|
| 2 | In certain cases acceptance of rent under invalid lease to be deemed a confirmation of lease. | L&T 10(6) | |
| 3 | Where during possession under invalid lease reversioner is able and willing to confirm such lease without variation, lessee shall accept such confirmation on request. | L&T 10(4) | |

FEE-FARM RENTS (IRELAND) ACT 1851
(c. 20)

| | | | |
|---|---|---|---|
| 1 | Ss. 20, 21 of 1849 c. 105 to extend to all fee-farm rents, etc. | L&T 47, 78 | |

| Section or Schedule of Act or Article of Order | Subject-matter | Article or Schedule of draft Order | Remarks |
|---|---|---|---|
| | **WILLS ACT AMENDMENT ACT 1852**<br>(c. 24) | | |
| 1 | Position of testator's signature. | — | para. 5.2.8.<br>S5(1)(b) |
| 2 | Act to extend to certain wills already made. | — | Spent. |
| 3 | Interpretation of "will". | — | |
| | **LEASING POWERS ACT FOR RELIGIOUS WORSHIP IN IRELAND 1855**<br>(c. 39) | | |
| 1-13 | Power of mortgagors, tenants in tail, tenants for life, etc., to grant leases for places of worship. | — | P45, 51, 142. |
| | **PRESCRIPTION (IRELAND) ACT 1858**<br>(c. 42) | | |
| 1 | 1832 c. 71 extended to Ireland. | — | See under 1832 c.71. |
| | **LANDED ESTATES COURT (IRELAND) ACT 1858**<br>(c. 72) | | |
| | Power of court to sell estates. | — | cf. GR 26; P Pt. V. |
| | **LAW OF PROPERTY AMENDMENT ACT 1859**<br>(c. 35) | | |
| 1 | Restriction on effect of licence to do a specified act. | L&T 42 | |
| 2 | Restricted operation of partial licences. | L&T 42 | |
| 3 | Apportionment of conditions of re-entry in certain cases. | L&T 41 | |
| 10 | Release of part of land charged not to be an extinguishment of the rentcharge. | P102 | |
| 11 | Release of part of land charged not to affect judgment. | P103 | |

| Section or Schedule of Act or Article of Order | Subject-matter | Article or Schedule of draft Order | Remarks |
|---|---|---|---|
| 12 | Mode of execution of powers. | P188 | |
| 13 | Sale under power not to be avoided by reason of mistaken payment to tenant for life etc. | — | |
| 14 | Devisee in trust may raise money charged on land by sale or mortgage, notwithstanding want of express power in the will. | — | cf. 1955 (c. 24) NI ss.31, 32, 40. |
| 15 | Powers given by last section shall extend to survivors, etc. | — | |
| 16 | Executors to have power of raising money charged on land, where there is no sufficient devise. | — | |
| 17 | Purchasers etc. not bound to inquire as to due execution of powers. | — | cf. P54. |
| 18 | Ss. 14-16 not to affect certain sales etc. nor to extend to devises in fee or in tail. | — | |
| 24 | Punishment of vendor etc. for fraudulently concealing deeds etc. or falsifying pedigree. | P244 | |
| 25 | Interpretation. | — | |

LAW OF PROPERTY AMENDMENT ACT 1860
(c. 38)

| | | | |
|---|---|---|---|
| 6 | Restriction of effect of waiver. | L&T 43 | para. 4.4.10. |
| 7 | Future and contingent uses to take effect by force of the original estate, etc. | — | |

| Section or Schedule of Act or Article of Order | Subject-matter | Article or Schedule of draft Order | Remarks |
|---|---|---|---|
| 8 | Amendment of 1859 c. 35 s. 24. | P244 | |
| 15 | Extent of Act. | — | |

### LANDLORD AND TENANT LAW AMENDMENT ACT, IRELAND, 1860
(c. 154)

| | | | |
|---|---|---|---|
| 1 | Interpretation of terms. | L&T 81(4) | As to "perpetual interest" see GR27. |
| 2 | Short title. | — | |
| 3 | Relation to rest on contract of parties, etc. | — | Para. 4.2.19. |
| 4 | Contract for definite periods to be by deed or note in writing. | L&T 3 | |
| 5 | Continuance of possession after expiration of contract may be deemed a new holding. | — | cf. L&T 63. |
| 6 | Presumed commencement of tenancy from year to year. | — | cf. L&T 52. |
| 7 | Surrenders to be by deed or note in writing or by operation of law. | L&T 53(1) | |
| 8 | Lease may be renewed without surrender of under-tenancies, etc. | L&T 53(3) | |
| 9 | Modes of assignment of estate and interest of tenant. | L&T 7 | |
| 10 | Restriction on assignment contrary to agreement. | — | cf. L&T 44. |
| 11 | Assignee subject to condition against assignment or subletting. | — | cf. L&T 36 |

| Section or Schedule of Act or Article of Order | Subject-matter | Article or Schedule of draft Order | Remarks |
|---|---|---|---|
| 12 | Benefit of agreements to enure against assignee, etc. of the tenant and in favour of heir or assignee of the landlord. | L&T 36 | para. 4.4.1 |
| 13 | Benefit of agreements to enure against assignee of the landlord, and in favour of heir, etc. or assignee of the tenant. | L&T 37 | |
| 14 | Benefit and liability of assignee to cease after assignment over. | L&T 38 | |
| | Notice of assignment to landlord. | — | cf. L&T 7, 18(1)(a), 38 |
| 15 | Assignee liable till next gale day. | — | cf. L&T 15(3), 38(1)(b), Sch.3 p.4. |
| 16 | Discharge of tenant from agreements, on assignment with consent of landlord. | L&T 38 | |
| 17 | Fixtures of trade or agriculture, etc. erected by the tenant may be removed. | L&T 33, Sch. 3 p. 5 | para. 4.10.4. |
| 18 | Subletting contrary to the agreement to be void. | — | para. 4.4.16. cf. L&T 44. |
| 19 | In cases of subletting with consent, payment to tenant shall free sub-tenant from liability to landlord. | L&T 46(3) | |
| 20 | Landlord may give notice to sub-tenant to pay rent to him. | L&T 46(1)(a) | |
| 21 | Sub-tenant may voluntarily pay rent to landlord. | L&T 46(1)(b) | |
| 22 | Subletting with consent not a general waiver. | — | cf. L&T 42. |

| Section or Schedule of Act or Article of Order | Subject-matter | Article or Schedule of draft Order | Remarks |
|---|---|---|---|
| 23 | Proof of contents of lease by counterpart or copy. | L&T 6 | |
| 24 | Proof of landlord's title, when derivative. | — | Survey para. 295. |
| 25 | Tenant in fee not impeachable of waste. | L&T Sch. 3 p. 6 | para. 4.10.5. |
| 26 | Tenant of lesser interest not to open mines or quarries or to commit other waste. | L&T Sch. 3 p. 8 | cf. L&T 34. |
| 27 | Tenant may work mines already opened. | L&T Sch. 3 p. 9 | para. 4.3.15 |
| 28 | Tenant may work quarries already open, but not for profit or sale. | L&T Sch. 3 p. 10 | |
| 29 | Tenant may cut turf, but not for profit or sale. | L&T Sch. 3 p. 11 | |
| 30 | Tenant shall not burn land. | L&T Sch. 3 p. 12 | paras. 4.10.5,6 |
| 31 | Tenant shall not cut or lop trees. | L&T Sch. 3 p. 13 | paras. 4.3.15, 4.10.6,7 |
| 32 | Where mines are reserved, landlord may work or lease the mines. | L&T Sch. 3 p. 15 | |
| 33 | Compensation to be ascertained by civil bill action. | — | As now in force, this section adds nothing to s.32. |
| 34 | Tenant, in lieu of emblements, shall continue to hold until last gale day of current year. | L&T Sch. 3 p. 3 | para. 4.10.8. |
| 35 | Justice's precept to restrain waste. | — | para. 4.10.9. |
| 36 | Punishment of disobedience of precept. | — | |

1687

| Section or Schedule of Act or Article of Order | Subject-matter | Article or Schedule of draft Order | Remarks |
|---|---|---|---|
| 37 | Annulling of precept, etc. | — | |
| 38 | Landlord may enter to inspect waste. | L&T Sch. 3 p. 14 | |
| 39 | Ordinary civil remedies preserved. | L&T Sch. 3 p. 17 | |
| 40 | On destruction of subject of the lease, tenant may surrender the lease. | L&T 54 | paras. 4.2.8-10; 4.10.10. |
| 41 | Agreements implied on behalf of landlord. | L&T Sch. 3 p. 1 | paras. 4.3.1, 4.10.11. |
| 42 | Agreements implied on behalf of tenant. | L&T Sch. 3 p. 2 | |
| 43 | Waiver and dispensation of covenants. | L&T 43 | para. 4.4.10 |
| 44 | Surrender of portion of premises not to prejudice rights of landlord. | L&T 53(2) | |
| 45 | Action for rent in arrear. | L&T 47(1)(a) | cf. County Courts (NI) Order1980 Art. 10. |
| 46 | Action for use and occupation. | L&T 69 | |
| 47 | Receipts to specify gale, and, if not, to be deemed to apply to last gale. | L&T 70 | |
| 48 | Set-off against rent. | — | para. 4.10.12. |
| 50 | Provision for cases not coming within the provisions of clause 34. | L&T Sch. 3 p. 4 | para. 4.10.13. cf. L&T 15(3), 47 |
| 52 | Ejectment for year's rent unpaid. | — | P9, L&T 47(7). |
| 53 | Proof of demand, etc., and of legal reversion unnecessary. | — | |
| 58 | Judgment by default. | — | |
| 63 | Tender before civil bill decree executed. | — | |

| Section or Schedule of Act or Article of Order | Subject-matter | Article or Schedule of draft Order | Remarks |
|---|---|---|---|
| 64 | Tender before order for delivery of possession executed. | — | |
| 65 | Amount of rent to be stated in order for delivery of possession; stay of enforcement. | — | |
| 66 | Remedy for rent not to be prejudiced by recovery of possession. | — | |
| 68 | Appeal from civil bill decree. | — | |
| 69 | Appeal not to stay execution unless rent lodged. | — | |
| 72 | Civil bill ejectment in case of overholding of tenements whose annual value does not exceed £75. | L&T 62 | |
| 75 | Security from overholding tenant in civil bill ejectment. | — | |
| 76 | Payment of double rent for overholding. | — | para. 4.10.14. cf. Magistrates' Courts (NI) Order 1981 Art. 69(2) and L&T 63. |
| 77 | Premises and mesne profits to the day of trial may be recovered in ejectment. | L&T 63(3) | cf. para. 4.6.34 |
| 79 | Justices may view premises and give certificate of desertion. | — | L&T 55. |
| 81 | What to be deemed cottier tenancies under this Act. | L&T Sch. 3 p. 16(1) | para. 4.10.15. |
| 82 | When cottier tenancy is determined by landlord, compensation to be made for crop, etc. | L&T Sch. 3 p. 16(2) | |

| Section or Schedule of Act or Article of Order | Subject-matter | Article or Schedule of draft Order | Remarks |
|---|---|---|---|
| 83 | Cottier tenements to be repaired by landlord. | L&T Sch. 3 p. 16(3) | |
| 100 | No action against justice for granting warrant. | — | para. 4.10.9. |
| 101 | Title to lands not to be drawn in question. | — | para. 4.10.16. |
| 103 | Schedules to be part of the Act. | — | |
| 104 | Repeal of Acts and parts of Acts in Sch. (B). | — | |
| 105 | Commencement of Act. | — | |
| Sch. A | Form of precept to restrain waste. | — | |
| Sch. B | Acts and parts of Acts repealed. | — | |

## CHIEF RENTS REDEMPTION (IRELAND) ACT 1864
### (c. 38)

| | | | |
|---|---|---|---|
| — | — | — | The Act provided for the redemption of ground rents by agreement. See now GR 4. |

## SALE OF LAND BY AUCTION ACT 1867
### (c. 48)

| | | | |
|---|---|---|---|
| 1 | Short title. | — | |
| 3 | Interpretation. | — | |
| 4 | Sales of land invalid in law from employment of puffer to be also invalid in equity. | — | |
| 5 | Rules respecting sale without reserve, etc. | P68 | para. 2.5.13 |
| 6 | Rule respecting sale subject to right of seller to bid. | P68(4) | |

| Section or Schedule of Act or Article of Order | Subject-matter | Article or Schedule of draft Order | Remarks |
|---|---|---|---|
| 7 | Discontinuance of practice of opening biddings, on sale of land by order of Court of Chancery. | — | |
| 8 | Saving. | — | |

**SALES OF REVERSIONS ACT 1867**
(c. 4 – 31 & 32 V.)

| | | | |
|---|---|---|---|
| 1 | Undervalue alone not to invalidate sale of reversionary interests. | P238 | |
| 2 | Interpretation. | — | |

**PARTITION ACT 1868**
(c. 40)

| | | | |
|---|---|---|---|
| 1 | Short title. | — | See Explanatory Note on Consequential Provisions Order. |
| 2 | As to the term "the Court". | — | cf. P249. |
| 3 | Power to Court to order sale instead of division in suit for partition. | — | cf. P25. As to trustees' power of sale, see P45. As to powers of court, see P62. |
| 4 | Sale instead of division on application of certain proportion of parties. | — | |
| 5 | On application of one party Court may direct sale unless the other parties undertake to purchase his share. | — | |
| 6 | On sale, Court may allow parties interested to bid. | — | |
| 8 | Application of 1856 c. 120 ss. 23-25 to money received on sale. | — | |
| 9 | Parties to petition suits. | — | |

| Section or Schedule of Act or Article of Order | Subject-matter | Article or Schedule of draft Order | Remarks |
|---|---|---|---|
| | **LANDLORD AND TENANT (IRELAND) ACT 1870** (c. 46) | | |
| Part I | Claim to compensation. | — | See Ch. 4.9 and L&T79. |
| Part II | Sale of land to tenants. | — | |
| Part IV | Supplemental provisions. | — | |
| Part V | Miscellaneous. | — | |
| | **LANDLORD AND TENANT (IRELAND) ACT 1871** (c.92) | | |
| 1 | Saving certain rights of tenants. | — | |
| | **LANDLORD AND TENANT (IRELAND) ACT 1872** (c.32) | | |
| 1 | Regulations with respect to purchase of their holdings by tenants. | — | |
| 2 | In certain cases where advances made for purchase of a holding notwith-standing forfeiture, Board may proceed to a sale. | — | |
| 3 | Short title and construction. | — | |
| | **POWERS OF APPOINTMENT ACT 1874** (c.37) | | |
| 1 | Appointments to be valid notwithstanding one or more objects excluded. | P187(1)(b) | |
| 2 | Proviso. | P187(2) | |
| | **VENDOR AND PURCHASER ACT 1874** (c.78) | | |
| 1 | Forty years substituted for sixty years as the root of title. | — | para. 2.5.14. cf. P71(1) |
| 2 | Rules regulating obligations and rights of vendor and purchaser. | P71(2)(5), 73(7)-(10) | para. 2.5.16 |

| Section or Schedule of Act or Article of Order | Subject-matter | Article or Schedule of draft Order | Remarks |
|---|---|---|---|
| 9 | Vendor or purchaser may obtain decision of judge of High Court as to requisitions or objections, or compensation, etc. | P74 | |
| 10 | Short title. | — | |

### LEASING POWERS AMENDMENT ACT FOR RELIGIOUS PURPOSES IN IRELAND 1875
#### (c. 11)

| | | | |
|---|---|---|---|
| 1-5 | Extension of benefit of 1855 c.39 to Church of Ireland; power to surrender lease and grant new one. | — | See under 1855 c.39. |

### PARTITION ACT 1876
#### (c.17)

| | | | |
|---|---|---|---|
| 1-7 | Amendment of 1868 c. 40. | — | See under 1868 c.40. |

### NOTICES TO QUIT (IRELAND) ACT 1876
#### (c. 63)

| | | | |
|---|---|---|---|
| 1-8 | Length, etc., of notice to quit. | — | Ch. 4.9 and L&T79. |

### SETTLED ESTATES ACT 1877
#### (c. 18)

| | | | |
|---|---|---|---|
| 1-59 | Power of court to authorise leases or sales of settled land, sales of timber, making of streets or other works. | — | cf. P45, 49, 51, 52, 55, 62. |

### CONTINGENT REMAINDERS ACT 1877
#### (c. 33)

| | | | |
|---|---|---|---|
| 1 | Cases in which contingent remainders capable of taking effect. | — | cf. P11. |

### CONVEYANCING ACT 1881
#### (c. 41)

| | | | |
|---|---|---|---|
| 1 | Short title, commencement. | — | |

| Section or Schedule of Act or Article of Order | Subject-matter | Article or Schedule of draft Order | Remarks |
|---|---|---|---|
| 2 | Interpretation. | — | cf. P2(2). |
| 3 | Application of stated conditions of sale to all purchasers. | P71(5), 73 | |
| 4 | Completion of contract after death. | — | Unnecessary following abolition of heirship |
| 5 | Provision by Court for incumbrances, and sale freed therefrom. | P76 | |
| 6 | General words in conveyances of land, buildings, or manor. | P95 | |
| 7 | Covenants for title to be implied. | P106, 107 Sch. 1 | para. 2.5.45. |
| 8 | Rights of purchaser as to execution. | P87 | |
| 9 | Acknowledgment of right to production, and undertaking for safe custody of documents. | P96 | |
| 10 | Rent and benefit of lessees covenants to run with reversion. | L&T 36 | para. 4.4.3 |
| 11 | Obligation of lessors covenants to run with reversion. | L&T 37 | |
| 12 | Apportionment of conditions on severance, etc. | L&T 41 | |
| 13 | On sub-demise, title to leasehold reversion not to be required. | P71(4) | |
| 14 | Restrictions on and relief against forfeiture of leases. | — | cf. L&T 57. |
| 15 | Obligation on mortgagee to transfer instead of reconveying. | P120 | |
| 16 | Power for mortgagor to inspect title deeds. | P121 | |
| 17 | Restriction on consolidation of mortgages. | P119 | |

1694

| Section or Schedule of Act or Article of Order | Subject-matter | Article or Schedule of draft Order | Remarks |
|---|---|---|---|
| 18 | Leasing powers of mortgagor and of mortgagee in possession. | P142 | |
| 19 | Powers incident to estate or interest of mortgagee. | P123 | |
| 20 | Regulation of exercise of power of sale. | P125 | |
| 21 | Conveyancing, receipt, etc., on sale. | | |
| (1) | | P128 | |
| (2) | | P129 | |
| (3) | | P132 | |
| (4) | | P124(1) | |
| (5) | | — | No provision is made about foreclosure. |
| (6)(7) | | P124(2)(3) | |
| 22 | Mortgagees' receipts, discharge, etc. | P131 | |
| 23 | Amount and application of insurance money. | P136 | |
| 24 | Appointment, powers, remuneration and duties of receiver. | P137 | |
| 26-29 | Statutory mortgage. | — | |
| 41 | Sales and leases on behalf of infant owner. | P31 | cf. P10. |
| 42 | Management of land and receipt and application of income during minority. | — | See P Pt. V. |
| 43 | Application by trustees of income of property of infant for maintenance, etc. | — | See Trustee Act (NI) 1958 s. 32. |
| 44 | Remedies for recovery of annual sums charged on land. | — | cf. P8,9 |
| 48 | File kept of deposited powers of attorney: office copies. | — | Not to be repealed. |

1695

| Section or Schedule of Act or Article of Order | Subject-matter | Article or Schedule of draft Order | Remarks |
|---|---|---|---|
| 49 | Use of word grant unnecessary. | P78(2) | |
| 51 | Words of limitation in fee or in tail. | P92(3) | As to fees tail, see P6. |
| 52 | Powers simply collateral. | P184 | |
| 53 | Construction of supplemental or annexed deed. | P91 | |
| 54 | Receipt in deed sufficient. | P99 | |
| 55 | Receipt in deed or indorsed, evidence for subsequent purchaser. | P100 | para. 2.5.38. |
| 56 | Receipt in deed or indorsed, authority for payment to solicitor. | P101 | para. 2.5.39. |
| 57 | Sufficiency of forms in Fourth Schedule. | — | |
| 58 | Covenants to bind heirs, etc. | — | paras. 2.5.40, 2.5.41. P(CP) Sch. 3. |
| 59 | Covenants to extend to heirs, etc. | — | |
| 60 | Effect of covenant with two or more jointly. | P109 | |
| 61 | Effect of advance on joint account, etc. | P144 | |
| 62 | Grants of easements, etc., by way of use. | — | cf. P97. |
| 63 | Provision for all the estate, etc. | P94 | |
| 64 | Construction of implied covenants. | — | cf. P89. P(CP) Sch. 3. |
| 65 | Enlargement of residue of long term into fee simple. | L&T 56 | para. 4.6.10. |
| 66 | Protection of solicitor and trustees adopting Act. | P243 | |

| Section or Schedule of Act or Article of Order | Subject-matter | Article or Schedule of draft Order | Remarks |
|---|---|---|---|
| 67 | Regulations respecting notice. | | |
| (1)(2) | | P247 | |
| (3)(4) | | — | cf. Interpretation Act (NI) 1954, S.24, L&T 74(6). |
| (5) | | — | |
| 69 | Regulations respecting payments into court and applications. | | |
| (1) | | | para. 2.14.23. |
| (2) | | P250 | |
| (4)-(6) | | — | These are matters for rules of court. |
| 70 | Orders of Court conclusive. | P251 | |
| 73 | (Repeal of 1874 c. 78 s. 5) | — | |
| Sch. 3 | Statutory mortgage. | — | |
| Sch. 4 | Short forms of deeds. | — | |

LAND LAW (IRELAND) ACT 1881<br>(c. 49)

| | | | |
|---|---|---|---|
| Part I | Ordinary conditions of tenancies. | — | Ch. 4.9 and L&T 79. |
| Part II | Intervention of court. | — | |
| Part III | Exclusion of Act by agreement. | — | |
| Part IV | Provisions supplemental to preceding Parts. | — | |
| Part V | Acquisition of land by tenants, etc. | — | |
| Part VI | Court and Land Commission. | — | |
| Part VII | Definitions, etc. | — | |

LEASES FOR SCHOOLS (IRELAND) ACT 1881<br>(c. 65)

| | | | |
|---|---|---|---|
| 1 | Interpretation of terms. | — | cf. P45(1)(a), 51, 52. |

| Section or Schedule of Act or Article of Order | Subject-matter | Article or Schedule of draft Order | Remarks |
|---|---|---|---|
| 2 | Power of making lease. | — | |
| 3 | Provision in case of disability. | — | |
| 4 | Limitation of lease. | — | |
| 5 | Covenants implied. | — | |
| 6 | Form of lease. | — | |
| 7 | Effect of lease. | — | |
| 8 | Short title. | — | |

SETTLED LAND ACT 1882
(c. 38)

| Section or Schedule of Act or Article of Order | Subject-matter | Article or Schedule of draft Order | Remarks |
|---|---|---|---|
| 1 | Short title, etc. | — | |
| 2 | Definitions. | | |
| (1) | | P2(2), 30(1)(a) | |
| (2) | | P30(3) | |
| (3)-(7) | | — | |
| (8) | | P35(2)(a)-(c) | |
| (9) | | — | cf. P2(2). |
| (10) | | P2(2) | See also Interpretation Act ss. 45(1), 46(1). |
| (11) | | — | cf. P249. |
| 3 | Powers of tenant for life to sell, etc. | — | cf. P45 as to trustees para. 2.4.9. |
| 4 | Regulations respecting sale. | P49 | |
| 5 | Transfer of incumbrances on land sold. | P49(4) | |
| 6 | Power to lease. | P51(1) | para. 2.4.18 |
| 7 | Regulations respecting leases generally. | P52 | para. 2.4.19 |
| 8 | Regulations respecting building leases. | | |
| (1) | | — | |
| (2) | | P52(3) | |

| Section or Schedule of Act or Article of Order | Subject-matter | Article or Schedule of draft Order | Remarks |
|---|---|---|---|
| (3) | | — | |
| 9 | Regulations respecting mining leases | — | para. 2.4.15. |
| 10 | Variation of building or mining lease according to circumstances of district. | — | |
| 11 | Part of mining rent to be set aside. | — | cf. P45(3), 51(4). |
| 12 | Leasing powers for special objects. | P51(2)(a),(b) | |
| 13 | Surrender and grant of leases. | P45(1)(c) | |
| 16 | Dedication of streets, open spaces, etc. | — | cf. P50(2). |
| 17 | Separate dealing with surface and minerals. | — | cf. P49(2). |
| 18 | Mortgage for equality money. | — | cf. P45(1)(a), 53, 56(2)(a). |
| 19 | Concurrence in exercise of powers as to undivided shares. | — | |
| 20 | Completion of sale, lease, etc., by conveyance. | — | |
| 21 | Capital money. | P55 | |
| 22 | Regulations respecting investment, devolution, and income of securities, etc. | | |
| (1)-(4) | | — | |
| (5)(6) | | P55(2) | |
| (7) | | — | |
| 23 | Settlement of land purchased, taken in exchange, etc. | — | |
| 25 | Description of improvements authorized by Act. | — | cf. P45(1)(d), 55(1)(d). |

| Section or Schedule of Act or Article of Order | Subject-matter | Article or Schedule of draft Order | Remarks |
|---|---|---|---|
| 26 | Approval by Commissioners of Public Works in Ireland of scheme for improvement and payment thereon. | — | |
| 27 | Concurrence in improvements. | — | |
| 28 | Obligation on tenant for life and successors to maintain, insure, etc. | — | cf. P3, 46(b): see TA (NI) 1958 s.19 as to insurance. |
| 29 | Protection as regards waste in execution and repair of improvements. | — | |
| 31 | Power for tenant for life to enter into contracts. | — | |
| 32 | Application of money in Court under Lands Clauses and other Acts. | — | |
| 33 | Application of money in hands of trustees under powers of settlement. | P55(4) | |
| 34 | Application of money paid for lease or reversion. | — | |
| 35 | Cutting and sale of timber, and part of proceeds to be set aside. | — | cf. P45(1)(e), (2)(a), (3). paras. 2.4.11-13 |
| 36 | Proceedings for protection or recovery of land settled or claimed as settled. | — | |
| 37 | Heirlooms. | — | |
| 38 | Appointment of trustees by Court. | — | cf. Trustee Act (NI) 1958 s.40. |
| 39 | Number of trustees to act. | P43 | |

| Section or Schedule of Act or Article of Order | Subject-matter | Article or Schedule of draft Order | Remarks |
|---|---|---|---|
| 40 | Trustees receipts. | — | cf. Trustee Act (NI) 1958 s.14. |
| 41 | Protection of each trustee individually. | — | |
| 42 | Protection of trustees generally. | — | |
| 43 | Trustees reimbursement. | P58(1) | |
| 44 | Reference of differences to Court. | — | cf. P61, 62. paras. 2.4.24-27 |
| 45 | Notice to trustees. | — | |
| 46 | Regulations respecting payments into Court, applications, etc. | | |
| (2) | | P250 | |
| (3)-(6) | | — | These are matters for court rules. |
| (10) | | — | cf. P249(2) |
| 47 | Payment of costs out of settled property. | P58(2)(3) | |
| 48 | Powers of Commissioners of Public Works in Ireland. | — | |
| 49 | Filing of certificates, etc., of Commissioners. | — | |
| 50 | Powers not assignable: contract not to exercise powers void. | — | |
| 51 | Prohibition or limitation against exercise of powers void. | — | |
| 52 | Provision against forfeiture. | — | |
| 53 | Tenant for life trustee for all parties interested. | — | |
| 54 | General protection of purchasers, etc. | P54(4) | |
| 55 | Exercise of powers: limitation of provisions, etc. | | |

| Section or Schedule of Act or Article of Order | Subject-matter | Article or Schedule of draft Order | Remarks |
|---|---|---|---|
| (1) | | — | Interpretation Act s.17(1). |
| (2) | | — | Ibid. s. 17(3). |
| (3) | | — | |
| 56 | Saving for other powers. | P60(1)(3), 61 | cf. P41(2) |
| 57 | Additional or larger powers by settlement. | P60(2) | |
| 58 | Enumeration of other limited owners, to have powers of tenant for life. | | |
| 59 | Infant absolutely entitled to be as tenant for life. | — | |
| 60 | Tenant for life, infant. | — | |
| 62 | Tenant for life, lunatic. | — | |
| 63 | Provision for case of trust to sell. | — | cf. P48(4). |
| 65 | Modifications respecting Ireland. | — | |

CONVEYANCING ACT 1882
(c. 39)

| | | | |
|---|---|---|---|
| 1 | Short titles; commencement; extent; interpretation. | | |
| (1)(2) | | — | |
| (3) | (Definitions; "property"; "purchaser"). | P2(2) | |
| 3 | Restriction on constructive notice. | P248 | |
| 4 | Contract for lease not part of title to lease. | P71(8) | |
| 6 | Disclaimer of power by trustees. | P185 | |
| 10 | Restriction on executory limitations. | P212(3)(5) | |
| 11 | Amendment of enactment respecting long terms. | — | cf. L&T 56. |

| Section or Schedule of Act or Article of Order | Subject-matter | Article or Schedule of draft Order | Remarks |
|---|---|---|---|
| 12 | Reconveyance on mortgage. | P120(2) | |

**MARRIED WOMEN'S PROPERTY ACT 1882**
(c. 75)

| Section or Schedule of Act or Article of Order | Subject-matter | Article or Schedule of draft Order | Remarks |
|---|---|---|---|
| 17 | Questions between husband and wife as to property to be decided in a summary way. | P235 | Ch. 2.13. |
| 23 | Legal representative of married woman. | P235(13) | |
| 24 | Interpretation ("property"). | P2(2) | |
| 25 | Commencement. | — | |
| 26 | Short title. | — | |

**SETTLED LAND ACT 1884**
(c. 18)

| Section or Schedule of Act or Article of Order | Subject-matter | Article or Schedule of draft Order | Remarks |
|---|---|---|---|
| 1 | Short title. | — | |
| 2 | Interpretation. | — | |
| 3 | Construction. | — | |
| 4 | Fine on a lease to be capital money. | P51(4) | |
| 5 | Notice under 1882 c. 38 s. 45 may be general. | — | |
| 6 | As to consents of tenants for life. | — | cf. P47. |
| 7 | Powers given by s. 63 to be exercised only with leave of the Court. | — | cf. P48(4). |

**SETTLED LAND ACTS (AMENDMENT) ACT 1887**
(c. 30)

| Section or Schedule of Act or Article of Order | Subject-matter | Article or Schedule of draft Order | Remarks |
|---|---|---|---|
| 1 | Amendment of s. 21 of the Settled Land Act 1882. | — | |
| 2 | S. 28 of Settled Land Act 1882, to apply to improvements within preceding section. | — | |

1703

| Section or Schedule of Act or Article of Order | Subject-matter | Article or Schedule of draft Order | Remarks |
|---|---|---|---|
| 3 | Short title. | — | |

LAND LAW (IRELAND) ACT 1887<br>(c. 33)

| Section or Schedule of Act or Article of Order | Subject-matter | Article or Schedule of draft Order | Remarks |
|---|---|---|---|
| Part I | Amendments of Land Law (Ireland) Act 1881. | — | See L&T 79. |
| Part III | Equitable provisions. | — | See L&T 47(7) and 79. |
| Part VI | Miscellaneous. | — | See L&T 79. |
| Schedule | Form of notice after judgment in ejectment. | — | See L&T 47(7) and 79. |

SETTLED LAND ACT 1889<br>(c. 36)

| Section or Schedule of Act or Article of Order | Subject-matter | Article or Schedule of draft Order | Remarks |
|---|---|---|---|
| 1 | Construction and short title. | — | |
| 2 | Option of purchase in building lease. | — | |
| 3 | Price to be capital money. | — | |

SETTLED LAND ACT 1890<br>(c. 69)

| Section or Schedule of Act or Article of Order | Subject-matter | Article or Schedule of draft Order | Remarks |
|---|---|---|---|
| 1 | Short title. | — | |
| 2 | Acts to be construed together. | — | |
| 3 | Interpretation. | — | |
| 4 | Instrument in consideration of marriage, etc., to be part of the settlement. | — | |
| 5 | Creation of easements on exchange or partition. | — | cf. P45(2) (introductory words). |
| 6 | Power to complete predecessor's contract. | — | |
| 7 | Provision as to leases for 21 years. | — | |
| 8 | Provision as to mining leases. | — | cf. P2(2) ("rent"). |

| Section or Schedule of Act or Article of Order | Subject-matter | Article or Schedule of draft Order | Remarks |
|---|---|---|---|
| 9 | Power to reserve a rentcharge on a grant in fee simple. | — | cf. GR 29, 30. |
| 10 | Restriction on sale of mansion. | — | |
| 11 | Power to raise money by mortgage. | — | cf. P53(2), 55(1)(d). |
| 12 | Provision enabling dealings with tenant for life. | — | |
| 13 | Application of capital money. | — | |
| 14 | Capital money in Court may be paid out to trustees. | — | |
| 15 | Court may order payment for improvements executed. | — | |
| 16 | Trustees for the purposes of the Act. | P35(2)(d)(e) | |
| 19 | Power to vacate registration of writ. | | |

### CONVEYANCING AND LAW OF PROPERTY ACT 1892
### (c. 13)

| Section or Schedule of Act or Article of Order | Subject-matter | Article or Schedule of draft Order | Remarks |
|---|---|---|---|
| 1 | Short title and extent. | — | |
| 2 | Costs of waiver, and forfeiture in case of bankruptcy or execution. | | |
| (1) | | — | cf. L&T 58(11). |
| (2) | | — | cf. L&T 57(3)(b). |
| 3 | No fine to be exacted for licence to assign. | L&T Sch. 1 p. 6 | para. 4.4.24(2) note 42. |
| 4 | Power of court to protect under-lessees on forfeiture of superior leases. | L&T 61 | |
| 5 | Definitions. | — | |

| Section or Schedule of Act or Article of Order | Subject-matter | Article or Schedule of draft Order | Remarks |
|---|---|---|---|
| | **ACCUMULATIONS ACT 1892**<br>(c. 58) | | |
| 1 | No accumulation beyond minority. | — | para. 2.12.18. |
| 2 | Short title. | — | |
| | **VOLUNTARY CONVEYANCES ACT 1893**<br>(c. 21) | | |
| 1 | Short title. | — | |
| 2 | Voluntary conveyances if bona fide not to be avoided under 1634 c. 3 (I) (10 Chas. 1 sess. 2). | P237(2) | |
| 3 | Saving transactions completed before passing of Act. | — | |
| 4 | Definition of conveyance. | — | cf. P2(2). |
| | **MORTGAGEES LEGAL COSTS ACT 1895**<br>(c. 25) | | |
| 1 | Short title. | | |
| 2 | Charges, etc., where mortgage is made with solicitor. | P149 | |
| 3 | Right of solicitor with whom mortgage is made to recover costs, etc. | P150 | |
| 4 | Definition of mortgage. | P2(2) | |
| | **LAND LAW (IRELAND) ACT 1896**<br>(c. 47) | | |
| Part I | Land law – fair rents and procedure. | — | See L&T 79. |
| Part II | Land Commission and Land Judge. | — | |
| Part III | Land purchase. | — | Outside scope of the Orders. |
| Part IV | Congested districts board. | — | Not applicable to N.I. |

1706

| Section or Schedule of Act or Article of Order | Subject-matter | Article or Schedule of draft Order | Remarks |
|---|---|---|---|
| Part V | Evicted tenants. | — | Rep. SLR 1950. |
| Part VI | Supplemental. | — | See L&T 79. |

### BODIES CORPORATE (JOINT TENANCY) ACT 1899
(c. 20)

| | | | |
|---|---|---|---|
| 1 | Power for corporations to hold property as joint tenants. | P27 | |
| 2 | Short title. | — | |

### IRISH LAND ACT 1903
(c. 37)

| | | | |
|---|---|---|---|
| Part I | Land purchase. | — | |
| Part III | Land law. | — | See L&T 79. |
| Part IV | Supplemental. | — | See L&T 79. |

### MARRIED WOMEN'S PROPERTY ACT 1907
(c. 18)

| | | | |
|---|---|---|---|
| 3 | Married woman entitled to prior estate to be protector of settlement alone. | — | See P6. |
| 4 | Short title: construction. | — | |

### CONVEYANCING ACT 1911
(c. 37)

| | | | |
|---|---|---|---|
| 1 | Discharge of incumbrances by the court. | P76 | |
| 2 | Benefit of condition already broken to run with reversion. | — | cf. L&T 36, 40(1)(c). |
| 3 | Powers (with a view to the grant of an authorised lease) for the mortgagor and mortgagee in possession to accept surrenders of leases. | P142(13), 143 | |
| 4 | Powers incident to estate or interest of mortgagees. | P123 | |

| Section or Schedule of Act or Article of Order | Subject-matter | Article or Schedule of draft Order | Remarks |
|---|---|---|---|
| 5 | Amendments of section 21 of the Act of 1881. | | |
| (1) | | P129 | |
| (2) | | P124(2) | |
| 6 | Remedies for recovery of annual sums charged on land. | — | cf. P8 |
| 9 | Provisions respecting mortgaged property where the right of redemption is barred. | — | cf. P57. |
| 10 | As to dispositions on trust for sale. | | |
| (1)(2) | | P39 | |
| (3) | | P54(2) | |
| (4) | | — | |
| 11 | Notice of restrictive covenants. | P163 | |
| 13 | Notice of trusts on transfer of mortgage. | P Sch. 10 p. 22 | |
| 16 | Short title, commencement and construction. | — | |

WILLS ACT 1963
(c. 44)

| | | | |
|---|---|---|---|
| 2(2) | (Exercise of power of appointment). | — | cf. S 6(3): paras. 5.2.37-39 |

ADMINISTRATION OF JUSTICE ACT 1970
(c. 31)

| | | | |
|---|---|---|---|
| 36 | Additional powers of court in action by mortgagee for possession of dwelling-house. | P134(2)-(5) | para. 2.6.4. |
| 38A | Exclusion of Pt. IV in case of regulated agreement within the meaning of the Consumer Credit Act 1974. | P134(9) | |
| 39 | Interpretation of Part IV. | P2(2), 134(8) | |

| Section or Schedule of Act or Article of Order | Subject-matter | Article or Schedule of draft Order | Remarks |
|---|---|---|---|
| | ADMINISTRATION OF JUSTICE ACT 1973 (c. 15) | | |
| 8 | Extension of powers of court in action by mortgagee of dwelling-house. | P134(6)(7)(8) | |
| | *Acts of the Parliament of Northern Ireland and Orders in Council* | | |
| | SCHOOL SITES ACT (NORTHERN IRELAND) 1928 (c. 8) | | |
| 1 | Amendment of 1881 c. 65 as to leases for schools. | — | cf. P45(1)(a), 51, 52. |
| 3 | Short title and interpretation. | — | |
| | WILLS (AMENDMENT) ACT (NORTHERN IRELAND) 1954 (c. 20) | | |
| 1 | Wills in contemplation of marriage. | S12(3) | para. 5.2.15 |
| 2 | Short title. | — | |
| | ADMINISTRATION OF ESTATES ACT (NORTHERN IRELAND) 1955 (c. 24) | | |
| 38 | Power to appoint trustees of infant's property. | P31(c) | |
| 40 | Power to deal with estate, etc. | | |
| (5) | (Personal representatives to be trustees of settlement.) | P35(5) | |
| 44 | Meaning of "real estate", etc. | | |
| (c) | (Estates tail, etc.) | — | cf. P6 |
| | TRUSTEE ACT (NORTHERN IRELAND) 1958 (c. 23) | | |
| 12 | Power of trustees to sell by auction, etc. | | |
| (1) | | P49(1) | |
| (2) | | — | cf. GR29. |

| Section or Schedule of Act or Article of Order | Subject-matter | Article or Schedule of draft Order | Remarks |
|---|---|---|---|
| (3) | | — | |
| (4) | | P54(3) | |
| (5) | | P49(2) | |
| (6) | | — | cf. P47. |
| 13 | Power to sell subject to depreciatory conditions and under 1874 c. 78. | | |
| (4) | (Application of 1874 c. 78 s. 2.) | — | cf. P243. |
| 14 | Power of trustees to give receipts. | | |
| (1)(b) | (Receipt of capital money by sole trustee.) | — | cf. P43. |
| 16 | Power to raise money by sale, mortgage, etc. | — | cf. P45. |
| (2) | (Exception for settled land trustees.) | — | |
| 21 | Power of trustees of renewable leaseholds to renew and raise money for the purpose. | — | cf. GR 27. |
| 33 | Power of advancement. | | |
| (2) | (Exception of settled land, etc.) | — | |
| 56 | Power of court to authorise transactions relating to trust property. | | |
| (4) | (Application to settled land.) | — | |
| 64 | Application of Act to Settled Land Act Trustees. | — | |

RIGHTS OF LIGHT ACT (NORTHERN IRELAND) 1961
(c. 18)

| | | | |
|---|---|---|---|
| 1 | Registration of notice in lieu of obstruction of access to light. | P159(1)-(5) | para. 2.7.44. |

| Section or Schedule of Act or Article of Order | Subject-matter | Article or Schedule of draft Order | Remarks |
|---|---|---|---|
| 2 | Effect of registration of notice. | P159(6)-(8) | |
| 4 | Application to Crown land. | P253 | |
| 5 | Interpretation. | — | |
| 6 | Short title. | — | |

TRUSTEE (AMENDMENT) ACT (NORTHERN IRELAND) 1962
(c. 10)

| | | | |
|---|---|---|---|
| 5 | Extension of 1958 c. 23 s. 57 (power to vary trusts) to settlements. | — | |

LAW REFORM (HUSBAND AND WIFE) ACT (NORTHERN IRELAND) 1964
(c. 23)

| | | | |
|---|---|---|---|
| 3 | Extension of s. 17 of Married Women's Property Act 1882 (c. 75). | P235(8)-(12) | |
| 5 | Contract for benefit of spouse and children. | — | cf. P88 |

BUSINESS TENANCIES ACT (NORTHERN IRELAND) 1964
(c. 36)

| | | | |
|---|---|---|---|
| 17 | Carrying out of order for new tenancy. | | |
| (4)(5) | (Application of 1881 c. 41 s. 18 and 1911 c. 37 s. 3.) | — | |

PERPETUITIES ACT (NORTHERN IRELAND) 1966
(c. 2)

| | | | |
|---|---|---|---|
| 1 | Power to specify perpetuity period. | P219 | chapter 2.12 |
| 2 | Presumption and evidence as to future parenthood. | | |
| (1)-(4) | | P229 | |
| (5) | | P66 | |
| 3 | Uncertainty as to remoteness. | | |
| (1)-(3) | | P230 | |
| (4)-(5) | | P221 | Survey para. 341. |

| Section or Schedule of Act or Article of Order | Subject-matter | Article or Schedule of draft Order | Remarks |
|---|---|---|---|
| 4 | Reduction of age and exclusion of class members to avoid remoteness. | P231 | |
| 5 | Condition relating to death of surviving spouse. | P232 | |
| 6 | Saving and acceleration of expectant interests. | P233 | |
| 7 | Powers of appointment. | P234 | |
| 8 | Administrative powers of trustees. | P228 | |
| 9 | Other restrictions on the perpetuity rule. | P224 | |
| 10 | Options relating to land. | | |
| (1)(2) | | P226 | |
| (3) | | P220 | |
| 11 | Avoidance of contractual and other rights in cases of remoteness. | P223 | |
| 12 | Rights for enforcement of rent-charges. | P227 | The Article takes account of the repeal of CA 1881 s. 44 and 1911 s. 6 by P(CP). |
| 13(1),(3)-(5) | Conditions subsequent, possibilities of reverter, etc. | P222 | |
| (2) | | — | cf. P227. |
| 14 | Contingent remainders. | — | Unnecessary when all future interests are equitable. |
| 15 | Abolition of double possibility rule. | — | Spent – para. 2.12.14. |
| 16 | Short title and interpretation. | | |
| (1) | | — | |
| (2) | | P218(1) | As to wills, see P2(4) and Interpretation Act s. 46(1) |

| Section or Schedule of Act or Article of Order | Subject-matter | Article or Schedule of draft Order | Remarks |
|---|---|---|---|
| (3) | | P218(2) | |
| (4) | | P217(3) | |
| (5) | | P217(1) | |
| (6) | | P217(2) | |

### AGE OF MAJORITY ACT (NORTHERN IRELAND) 1969
### (c. 28)

| Section or Schedule of Act or Article of Order | Subject-matter | Article or Schedule of draft Order | Remarks |
|---|---|---|---|
| 1(3) | | — | cf. P212 |
| 2 | Provisions relating to wills. | | |
| (1)(a) | (Amendment of 1837 c. 26 s. 27.) | S4 | |

### LAND REGISTRATION ACT (NORTHERN IRELAND) 1970
### (c. 18)

| Section or Schedule of Act or Article of Order | Subject-matter | Article or Schedule of draft Order | Remarks |
|---|---|---|---|
| 41 | Creation and effect of charges on registered land. | — | cf. P114. See Explanatory Note on Consequential Provisions Order. |
| 43 | Priority of registered charge for future advances. | — | cf. P140. |
| 47 | Right of residence on registered land. | — | cf. P33(3)(4). |
| 74 | Execution of documents containing reservations. | — | cf. P97. |
| Sch. 7 | Provisions relating to charges on registered land. | — | |

### LEASEHOLD (ENLARGEMENT AND EXTENSION) ACT
### (NORTHERN IRELAND) 1971
### (c. 7)

| Section or Schedule of Act or Article of Order | Subject-matter | Article or Schedule of draft Order | Remarks |
|---|---|---|---|
| 21 | Application of capital money under Settled Land Acts. | — | |
| 26 | (Mortgage by sub-demise.) | | |
| (2) | | — | |

### POWERS OF ATTORNEY ACT (NORTHERN IRELAND) 1971
### (c. 33)

| Section or Schedule of Act or Article of Order | Subject-matter | Article or Schedule of draft Order | Remarks |
|---|---|---|---|
| 1 | Execution of powers of attorney. | — | para. 2.10.4. cf. P190. |

| Section or Schedule of Act or Article of Order | Subject-matter | Article or Schedule of draft Order | Remarks |
|---|---|---|---|
| 2 | Abolition of deposit or filing of instruments creating powers of attorney. | — | The section remains in force to preserve rights of searching, inspecting, etc. |
| 3 | Powers of attorney given as security. | P191 | |
| 4 | Protection of donee and third persons where power of attorney is revoked. | P192 | |
| 5 | Additional protection for transferees under stock exchange regulations. | P193 | |
| 6 | Statutory declaration in the case of a company. | P194 | |
| 7 | Execution of instruments, etc., by donee of power of attorney. | P195 | |
| 8 | Delivery of power of attorney relating to unregistered land to purchaser. | P196 | |
| 9 | Power to delegate trusts, etc., by power of attorney. | — | See Trustee Act (NI) 1958 s. 26. |
| 10 | Effect of general power of attorney in specified form. | P197 | |
| 11 | Amendments, repeals and savings. | — | |
| 12 | Short title and commencement. | — | |
| Sch. 1 | Form of General Power of Attorney for purposes of section 10. | P Sch. 6 | |

| Section or Schedule of Act or Article of Order | Subject-matter | Article or Schedule of draft Order | Remarks |
|---|---|---|---|

FAMILY LAW REFORM (NORTHERN IRELAND) ORDER 1977
(N.I. 17)

| Section or Schedule of Act or Article of Order | Subject-matter | Article or Schedule of draft Order | Remarks |
|---|---|---|---|
| 4 | Presumption that in dispositions of property references to children and other relatives include references to, and to persons related through, illegitimate children. | P90 S27 P(CP) | Para. (4), the introductory words of para. (5) and paras. (7) and (9) apply to the Trustee Act (NI) 1958. See Explanatory Note on P(CP) |
| 5 | Meaning of "child" and "issue" in section 33 of Wills Act 1837. | S22(4)(a) | para. 5.2.20 |
| 6 | Protection of trustees and personal representatives. | P90(8) S31 | The Article also applies for purposes of Article 3 of the 1977 Order and the Trustee Act. |

PROPERTY (NORTHERN IRELAND) ORDER 1978
(N.I. 4)

| Section or Schedule of Act or Article of Order | Subject-matter | Article or Schedule of draft Order | Remarks |
|---|---|---|---|
| 1 | Title and commencement. | — | chapter 2.9 |
| 2 | Interpretation. | — | |
| 3 | Application and interpretation of Pt. II. | P178 | |
| 4 | Power of Lands Tribunal to define scope, etc., of impediments. | P179 | |
| 5 | Power of Lands Tribunal to modify or extinguish impediments. | P180, 182(1)-(3) | |
| 6 | Powers of court. | P181 | |
| 7 | Supplementary provisions. | P182(4)(5) | |
| 8 | Registration of orders. | P183 | |
| 9 | Interpretation of Pt. III. | P2(2) | |
| 10 | Conveyance by a person to himself and others. | P104 | |

| Section or Schedule of Act or Article of Order | Subject-matter | Article or Schedule of draft Order | Remarks |
|---|---|---|---|
| 11 | Convenants or agreements entered into by a person with himself and another or others | P110 | |
| 12 | Covenants with two or more persons. | P108 | |
| 13 | Disposition of property to husband and wife. | — | Para. 2.13.1. |
| 14 | Costs in Land Registry cases. | — | |
| 15 | Application to Crown. | P253 | |

### MATRIMONIAL CAUSES (NORTHERN IRELAND) ORDER 1978 (N.I. 15)

| | | | |
|---|---|---|---|
| 55 | Extension of section 17 of Married Women's Property Act 1882. | P236(1) | |

### RENT (NORTHERN IRELAND) ORDER 1978 (N.I. 20)

| | | | |
|---|---|---|---|
| 2(2) | Interpretation "private tenancy" "tenancy" "tenant" | chapter 4.3 L&T 71(7) L&T 67(1) L&T 67(1) | Cf. L&T 52(5), 82, 4.11.3. |
| 38 | Rent books for private tenancies. | L&T 71(1), (2), (7) | |
| 39 | Offences under Article 38. | L&T 71(3)-(6) | |
| 40 | Provisions applied to regulated tenancies. | — | cf. L&T 12(2). See Explanatory Note on Consequential Provisions Order. |
| 41 | Landlord's duties to repair, etc. | — | cf. L&T 21(1)(b), 2(2) ("repair"). |
| 42 | Care of premises by tenant. | — | cf. L&T 19. |
| 43 | Landlord's obligations under regulated tenancy of parts of building. | — | cf. L&T 24. |
| 44 | General qualifications on landlord's duties. | — | cf. L&T 30(1) |
| 45 | Standard of repair and knowledge of disrepair. | — | cf. L&T 31. |
| 54 | Unlawful eviction and harassment of occupier. | L&T 64 | para. 4.7.3. |

| Section or Schedule of Act or Article of Order | Subject-matter | Article or Schedule of draft Order | Remarks |
|---|---|---|---|
| 55 | Restriction on re-entry without due process of law. | L&T 65 | |
| 56 | Prohibition of eviction without due process of law. | L&T 66 | |
| 57 | Savings. | L&T Sch. 2 p. 10 | |
| 58 | Interpretation of Part IX. | L&T 2(2), 66(3), 67 | |
| 62 | Length of notice to quit under tenancies of dwelling-houses. | L&T 52(4),(5) | |
| 73 | Service of notices on landlord's agents. | L&T 17(2)(6), 74(2) (a) (d), (5) | |
| 74 | Regulations. | L&T 71(7) ("pres-cribed") | |
| 75 | Application to Crown property. | L&T 82 | chapter 4.11 |

MAGISTRATES' COURTS (NORTHERN IRELAND) ORDER 1981
(N.I. 26)

| | | | |
|---|---|---|---|
| 69 | Liability of overholding tenant or occupier. | L&T 63 | para. 4.6.34 |

PROPERTY (DISCHARGE OF MORTGAGE BY RECEIPT)
(NORTHERN IRELAND) ORDER 1983
(N.I. 9)

| | | | |
|---|---|---|---|
| 1 | Title and commencement. | — | |
| 2 | Interpretation. | — | |
| 3 | Discharge of mortgage by endorsed or annexed receipt. | P146 | See also P2(2). |
| Schedule | Form of receipt on discharge of mortgage. | P Sch. 2 | |

| Section or Schedule of Act or Article of Order | Subject-matter | Article or Schedule of draft Order | Remarks |
|---|---|---|---|
| | | | |

FAMILY LAW (MISCELLANEOUS PROVISIONS) (NORTHERN IRELAND) ORDER 1984
(N.I. 14)

| Section or Schedule of Act or Article of Order | Subject-matter | Article or Schedule of draft Order | Remarks |
|---|---|---|---|
| 16 | Property of engaged couples. | | |
| (2) | (Application of Married Women's Property Act 1882, section 17.) | P236(2) | |

COMMISSION ON DISPOSALS OF LAND (NORTHERN IRELAND) ORDER 1986
(N.I. 5)

| | | | |
|---|---|---|---|
| 1 | Title and commencement. | — | |
| 2 | Interpretation. | — | |
| 3 | Certain stipulations concerning disposals of land and revision of rents to be void. | P112, Sch. 10 p. 17 | |

ENDURING POWERS OF ATTORNEY (NORTHERN IRELAND) ORDER 1987
(N.I. 16)

| | | | |
|---|---|---|---|
| 1 | Title and commencement. | — | |
| 2 | Interpretation. | P198 | See also P2(2). |
| 3 | Enduring power of attorney to survive mental incapacity of donor. | P199 | |
| 4 | Characteristics of an enduring power. | P200 | |
| 5 | Scope of authority etc. of attorney under enduring power. | P201 | paras. 2.10.6, 2.10.11 |
| 6 | Duties of attorney in event of actual or impending incapacity of donor. | P202 | |
| 7 | Functions of court prior to registration. | P203 | |
| 8 | Functions of court on application for registration. | P204 | |

| Section or Schedule of Act or Article of Order | Subject-matter | Article or Schedule of draft Order | Remarks |
|---|---|---|---|
| 9 | Effect and proof of registration, etc. | P205 | |
| 10 | Functions of court with respect to registered power. | P206 | |
| 11 | Protection of attorney and third persons where power invalid or revoked. | P207 | |
| 12 | Application of Mental Health Order provisions. | P208 | |
| 13 | Application to joint and joint and several attorneys. | P209 | |
| 14 | Power to modify pre-registration requirements in certain cases. | P210 | |
| Sch. 1 | Notification prior to registration. | P Sch. 7 | |
| Sch. 2 | Further protection of attorney and third persons. | P Sch. 8 | |
| Sch. 3 | Joint and joint and several attorneys. | P Sch. 9 | |

# TABLE 3

## TABLE OF COMPARISON OF STATUTORY PROVISIONS NOT IN FORCE IN NORTHERN IRELAND AND OF LAW COMMISSION DRAFT BILLS WITH THE DRAFT ORDERS IN COUNCIL

| Section or Schedule of Act or Clause of Draft Bill | Subject-matter | Article or Schedule of draft Order | Remarks |
|---|---|---|---|
| | | *Acts* | |
| | **LAW OF PROPERTY ACT 1922** (c. 16) | | |
| 145 | Conversion of perpetually renewable leaseholds. | GR27 | |
| Sch. 15 | Provisions relating to perpetually renewable leases and underleases. | | |
| pp. 1-6 7(1), 10-15, 17 | | — | cf GR 27, Sch. 3 |
| p. 7(3) | | GR28, Sch. 4 | |
| p. 8 | | — | cf GR33(3), (5)(a) |
| | **SETTLED LAND ACT 1925** (c. 18) | | |
| 1 | What constitutes a settlement. | P30 | |
| 7 | Procedure on change of ownership. | P63 | |
| (5) | (Person becoming absolutely entitled to settled land.) | | |
| 30 | Who are trustees for purposes of Act. | P35 | 2.3.6 |
| 32 | As to trustees of referential settlement | P36 | |
| 39 | Regulations respecting sales. | | |
| (1) | (Sale to be for best consideration) | P50(1) | See P2(2) ("conveyance") |
| 40 | Regulations respecting exchanges. | | |
| (1) | (Exchange to be for best consideration) | P50(1) | |

| Section or Schedule of Act or Clause of Draft Bill | Subject-matter | Article or Schedule of draft Order | Remarks |
|---|---|---|---|
| 41 | Power to lease for ordinary or building or mining or forestry purposes. | — | cf. P51(1) 2.4.16, 18 |
| 42 | Regulations respecting leases generally. | P52 | |
| 43 | Leasing powers for special objects. | P51(2) | |
| 52 | Surrenders and regrants. | — | cf P45(1)(c) |
| 55 | Power to grant land for public and charitable purposes. | P50(2) | |
| 66 | Cutting and sale of timber. | P45(1)(e) (2)(a), (3), (4) | See P48(7) 2.4.11 |
| 71 | Power to raise money by mortgage. | — | cf P53 |
| 72 | Completion of transactions by conveyance | | |
| (2) | (Effect of conveyance.) | P54 | |
| 73 | Modes of investment or application. | P55(1) | |
| 75 | Regulations respecting investment, devolution, etc. | | |
| (5) | (Devolution of capital) | P55(2) | |
| 77 | Application of money in hands of trustees under powers of settlement. | P55(4) | para. 2.4.20 |
| 94 | Number of trustees to act. | P43 | |
| 100 | Trustees' reimbursements. | P58(1) | |
| 106 | Prohibition or limitation against exercise of powers void. | P59 | |
| 108 | Saving for and exercise of other powers. | | |
| (1)(2) | (Additional powers.) | P41(4), 60 | |

| Section or Schedule of Act or Clause of Draft Bill | Subject-matter | Article or Schedule of draft Order | Remarks |
|---|---|---|---|
| (3) | (Doubts about extent of trustees' powers.) | P61 | |
| 109 | Saving for additional or larger powers under settlement. | P60 | |
| 110 | Protection of purchasers, etc. | | |
| (1) | (Purchaser to be taken to have given best price.) | P54(4) | |
| 114 | Payment of costs out of settled property. | P58(2) | |

**LAW OF PROPERTY ACT 1925**
(c. 20)

| Section or Schedule of Act or Clause of Draft Bill | Subject-matter | Article or Schedule of draft Order | Remarks |
|---|---|---|---|
| 1 | Legal estates and equitable interests | | |
| (1)(2) | | P4(1)(2) | ch. 2.1 |
| (3)(8) | | P11(1), 12 | |
| (4)(5) | | P4(3)(4) | |
| (6) | | P10(1), 19 | |
| (7) | | P12 | |
| (9) | | P13 | |
| (10) | | — | cf. Interpretation Act s. 28(2)(b) |
| 2 | Conveyances overreaching certain equitable interests and powers. | P17 | |
| 3 | Manner of giving effect to equitable interests and powers. | P16 | |
| 4 | Creation and disposition of equitable interests. | | |
| (1) | | P11 | |
| (2)(3) | | P14 | |
| 5 | Satisfied terms. | — | cf. P Sch. 10 p. 5, para. 2.1.29 |
| 7 | Saving of certain legal estates and statutory powers. | | |
| (1) | | P5 | |
| (2)(3) | | — | |
| (4) | | P15(1) | |

| Section or Schedule of Act or Clause of Draft Bill | Subject-matter | Article or Schedule of draft Order | Remarks |
|---|---|---|---|
| 8 | Saving of certain legal powers to lease. | | |
| (1) | | P15(2) | |
| (2) | | — | |
| 9 | Vesting orders and dispositions of legal estates operating as conveyances by an estate owner. | P15(3)-(5) | |
| 10 | Title to be shown to legal estates. | | |
| (1) | | P18 | |
| (2) | | P243(6) | |
| 14 | Interests of persons in possession. | — | para. 2.2.37 |
| 15 | Presumption that parties are of full age. | P10(2) | |
| 19 | Effect of conveyances of legal estates to infants. | — | cf. P21, 31 |
| 23 | Duration of trusts for sale. | P54(2) | |
| 25 | Power to postpone sale. | | |
| (1)-(3) | | P46 | |
| (4) | | P34 | |
| 26 | Consents to the execution of a trust for sale. | P47 | para. 2.4.5 |
| (3) | | P44 | para. 2.4.6 |
| 27 | Purchaser not to be concerned with the trusts of the proceeds of sale which are to be paid to two or more trustees or a trust corporation. | | |
| (1) | | P54(5) | |
| (2) | | P43 | |
| 28 | Powers of management, etc, conferred on trustees for sale. | | |
| (1) | | P46 | |

1724

| Section or Schedule of Act or Clause of Draft Bill | Subject-matter | Article or Schedule of draft Order | Remarks |
|---|---|---|---|
| (2) | | — | |
| (3)(4) | | P25 | |
| 29 | Delegation of powers of management by trustees for sale. | P48 | |
| 30 | Powers of court where trustees for sale refuse to exercise powers. | P62 | para. 2.4.24 |
| 31 | Trust for sale of mortgaged property where right of redemption is barred. | P57 | |
| 32 | Implied trust for sale in personalty settlement. | P39 | |
| 34 | Effect of future dispositions to tenants in common. | P21 | ch. 2.2 |
| 35 | Meaning of the statutory trusts. | — | Contrast P3 |
| 36 | Joint tenancies. | | |
| (1) | | — | cf. P20 |
| (2) | | P24 | cf. 1926 c.11, P26 |
| (3) | | — | |
| 38 | Party structures. | P28 | |
| 39 | Transitional provisions. | PSch. 10 | |
| 40 | Contracts for sale, etc., of land to be in writing. | P67 | See 1989 c. 34 s.2, para. 2.5.1 |
| 41 | Stipulations not of the essence of a contract. | P69 | |
| 42 | Provisions as to contracts. | P70 | |
| 44 | Statutory commencements of title. | P71 | paras. 2.5.14, 16 |
| 45 | Other statutory conditions of sale. | P73 | |
| 47 | Application of insurance money on completion of a sale or exchange. | — | para. 2.5.17 |

| Section or Schedule of Act or Clause of Draft Bill | Subject-matter | Article or Schedule of draft Order | Remarks |
|---|---|---|---|
| 49 | Applications to the court by vendor and purchaser. | — | |
| (1)(3) | | P74 | |
| (2) | | P75 | |
| 50 | Discharge of incumbrances by the court on sales or exchanges. | P76 | |
| 51 | Lands lie in grant only. | P78 | |
| 52 | Conveyances to be by deed. | P79 | |
| 53 | Instruments required to be in writing. | P80 | |
| 56 | Persons taking who are not parties and as to indentures. | | |
| (1) | | P88 | |
| (2) | | P81(4) | |
| 57 | Description of deeds. | P81(2)(a) | |
| 58 | Provisions as to supplemental instruments. | P91 | |
| 59 | Conditions and certain covenants not implied. | P105 | |
| 60 | Abolition of technicalities in regard to conveyances and deeds. | | |
| (1)(2) | | P92(1)(2) | para. 2.5.28 |
| (3)(4) | | P92(4) 93 | |
| Proviso (a) | | P92(3) | |
| 61 | Construction of expressions used in deeds and other instruments. | P89 S26 | |
| 62 | General words implied in conveyances. | P95 | |
| 63 | All estate clause implied. | P94 | |
| 64 | Production and safe custody of documents. | P96 | para. 2.5.31 |

| Section or Schedule of Act or Clause of Draft Bill | Subject-matter | Article or Schedule of draft Order | Remarks |
| --- | --- | --- | --- |
| 65 | Reservation of legal estates. | P97 | para. 2.5.32 |
| 66 | Confirmation of past transactions. | P98 | |
| 67 | Receipt in deed sufficient. | P99 | para. 2.5.38 |
| 68 | Receipt in deed or indorsed evidence. | P100 | |
| 69 | Receipt in deed or indorsed authority for payment to solicitor. | P101 | para. 2.5.39 |
| 70 | Partial release of security from rentcharge. | P102 | |
| 71 | Release of part of land affected from a judgment | P103 | |
| 72 | Conveyances by a person to himself, etc. | P104 | |
| 73 | Execution of deeds by an individual. | P82 | para. 2.5.33 |
| 74 | Execution of instruments by or on behalf of corporations. | P84 | |
| 75 | Rights of purchaser as to execution. | P87 | |
| 76 | Covenants for title. | P106 | para. 2.5.45 |
| 77 | Implied covenants in conveyance subject to rents. | P107 | |
| 78 | Benefit of covenants relating to land. | — | para. 2.5.40 |
| 79 | Burden of covenants relating to land. | — | para. 2.5.40 |
| 80 | Covenants binding land. | — | cf. 1881 c. 41 s. 59 |
| 81 | Effect of covenant with two or more jointly. | P108, 109 | |

| Section or Schedule of Act or Clause of Draft Bill | Subject-matter | Article or Schedule of draft Order | Remarks |
|---|---|---|---|
| 82 | Covenants and agreements entered into by a person with himself and another or others. | P110 | |
| 83 | Construction of implied covenants. | — | cf. 1881 c. 41 s. 64 |
| 84 | Power to discharge or modify restrictive covenants affecting land. | P180 | ch. 2.9 |
| 85 | Mode of mortgaging freeholds. | P114 | para. 2.6.1 |
| (1) | | P116 | |
| 86 | Mode of mortgaging leaseholds. | P114 | |
| 87 | Charges by way of legal mortgage. | | |
| (1) | | P116 | |
| 88 | Realisation of freehold mortgages. | P130 | |
| 89 | Realisation of leasehold mortgages. | P130 | |
| 90 | Realisation of equitable charges by the court. | P147 | para. 2.6.22 |
| 91 | Sale of mortgaged property in action for redemption or foreclosure. | P117 | |
| 92 | Power to authorise land and minerals to be dealt with separately. | P126 | |
| 93 | Restriction on consolidation of mortgages. | P118 | |
| 94 | Tacking and further advances. | P140 | para. 2.6.24 |
| 95 | Obligation to transfer instead of reconveying, and as to right to take possession. | P120 | para. 2.6.15 |

| Section or Schedule of Act or Clause of Draft Bill | Subject-matter | Article or Schedule of draft Order | Remarks |
|---|---|---|---|
| 96 | Regulations respecting inspection, production and delivery of documents, and priorities. | | |
| (1) | | P121 | |
| (2) | | P141 | |
| 98 | Actions for possession by mortgagors. | — | |
| 99 | Leasing powers of mortgagor and mortgagee in possession. | P142 | |
| 100 | Power of mortgagor and mortgagee in possession to accept surrenders of leases. | P143 | |
| 101 | Powers incident to estate or interest of mortgagee. | P123 | para. 2.6.26 |
| 103 | Regulation of exercise of power of sale. | P125 | |
| 104 | Conveyance on sale. | | |
| (1)(3) | | P128 | |
| (2) | | P129 | |
| 105 | Application of proceeds of sale. | P132 | |
| 106 | Provisions as to exercise of power of sale. | | |
| (1)(3)(4) | | P124 | |
| 107 | Mortgagee's receipts, discharges, etc. | P131 | |
| 108 | Amount and application of insurance money. | P136 | para. 2.6.27 |
| 109 | Appointment, powers, remuneration and duties of receiver. | P137 | |
| 110 | Effect of bankruptcy of the mortgagor on the power to sell or appoint a receiver. | P138 | |

| Section or Schedule of Act or Clause of Draft Bill | Subject-matter | Article or Schedule of draft Order | Remarks |
|---|---|---|---|
| 111 | Effect of advance on joint account. | P144 | |
| 112 | Notice of trusts on transfer of mortgage. | — | cf. P Sch. 10 p. 22 |
| 113 | Notice of trusts affecting mortgage debts. | P148 | |
| 114 | Transfers of mortgages. | P145 | |
| 115 | Reconveyances of mortgages by endorsed receipts. | — | cf. P146: as to ss. (2) see para. 2.6.34 |
| 121 | Remedies for the recovery of annual sums charged on land. | — | cf. P8 |
| 130 | Creation of entailed interests in real and personal property. | — | cf. P6 |
| 131 | Abolition of the rule in Shelley's case. | P211 | |
| 132 | As to heirs taking by purchase. | — | cf. P211(2) |
| 134 | Restriction on executory limitations. | P212 | |
| 135 | Equitable waste. | — | cf. P45(4) |
| 136 | Legal assignments of things in action. | P241 | |
| 137 | Dealings with life interests, reversions and other equitable interests. | P214 | ch. 2.11 |
| 138 | Power to nominate a trust corporation to receive notices. | P215 | |
| 139 | Effect of extinguishment of reversion. | L&T 9 | |
| 140 | Apportionment of conditions on severance. | | |
| (1)-(3) | | L&T 41 | |
| (2) | | L&T 52(7) | para. 4.6.3 |

| Section or Schedule of Act or Clause of Draft Bill | Subject-matter | Article or Schedule of draft Order | Remarks |
|---|---|---|---|
| 141 | Rent and benefit of lessee's covenants to run with the reversion. | L&T 41 L&T 36 | ch. 4.4 |
| 142 | Obligations of lessor's covenants to run with reversion. | L&T 37 | |
| 143 | Effect of licences granted to lessees. | L&T 42 | |
| 144 | No fine to be exacted for licence to assign. | L&T Sch. 1 p.6 | |
| 145 | Lessee to give notice of ejectment to lessor | L&T 16 | |
| 146 | Restrictions on and relief against forfeiture of leases and underleases. | | |
| (2) | | L&T 61(3) | See LP(A) A1929 s. 1 |
| 148 | Waiver of a covenant in a lease. | L&T 43 | para. 4.4.10. |
| 149 | Abolition of interesse termini, and as to reversionary leases and leases for lives. | L&T 5 | |
| 150 | Surrender of a lease, without prejudice to underleases with a view to the grant of a new lease. | L&T 53 | |
| 151 | Provision as to attornments by tenants. | L&T 8 | |
| 152 | Leases invalidated by reason of non-compliance with terms of powers under which they are granted. | L&T 10 | |
| 153 | Enlargement of residue of long terms into fee simple estates. | L&T 56 | para. 4.6.10 |
| 155 | Release of powers simply collateral. | P184 | |
| 156 | Disclaimer of power. | P185 | |

| Section or Schedule of Act or Clause of Draft Bill | Subject-matter | Article or Schedule of draft Order | Remarks |
|---|---|---|---|
| 157 | Protection of purchasers claiming under certain void appointments. | P186 | |
| 158 | Validation of appointments where objects are excluded or take illusory shares. | P187 | |
| 159 | Execution of powers not testamentary. | P188 | |
| 161 | Abolition of double possibility rule. | — | para. 2.12.14 |
| 173 | Voluntary disposition of land how far voidable as against purchasers. | P237 | |
| 174 | Acquisitions of reversions at an under value. | P238 | |
| 175 | Contingent and future testamentary gifts to carry the intermediate income. | S21 | |
| 180 | Provisions as to corporations. | P242 | |
| 182 | Protection of solicitor and trustees adopting Act. | P243 | |
| 183 | Fraudulent concealment of documents and falsification of pedigrees. | P244 | |
| 184 | Presumption of survivorship in regard to claims to property. | — | cf. P239, para. 2.14.3 |
| 185 | Merger. | P245 | |
| 186 | Rights of pre-emption capable of release. | P14 | |
| 187 | Legal easements. | — | |
| 188 | Power to direct division of chattels. | P246 | |

| Section or Schedule of Act or Clause of Draft Bill | Subject-matter | Article or Schedule of draft Order | Remarks |
|---|---|---|---|
| 190 | Equitable apportionment of rents and remedies for non-payment or breach of covenant. | | |
| (3)-(7) | | L&T 39 | |
| 196 | Regulations respecting notices. | P247 | cf. L&T 74 |
| 199 | Restrictions on constructive notice. | P248 | |
| 200 | Notice of restrictive covenants and easements. | P163 | |
| 203 | Payment into court, jurisdiction and procedure. | | para. 2.14.23 |
| (1) | | P250 | |
| 204 | Orders of court conclusive. | P251 | |
| 205 | General definitions. | P2(2), 7 | para. 2.3.5 |
| Sch. 1 | Transitional provisions. | — | cf. P Sch. 10 |
| Sch. 2 | Implied covenants. | P Sch. 1 | |

LANDLORD AND TENANT ACT 1927
(c. 36)

| Section or Schedule of Act or Clause of Draft Bill | Subject-matter | Article or Schedule of draft Order | Remarks |
|---|---|---|---|
| 18 | Provisions as to covenants to repair. | | |
| (1) | (Measure of damages) | L&T 49 | paras. 4.5.5-9 |
| 19 | Provisions as to covenants not to assign, etc., without licence or consent. | — | cf. L&T 44: para. 4.4.17 |

LAW OF PROPERTY (JOINT TENANTS) ACT 1964
(c. 63)

| Section or Schedule of Act or Clause of Draft Bill | Subject-matter | Article or Schedule of draft Order | Remarks |
|---|---|---|---|
| 1 | Assumptions on sale of land by survivor of joint tenants. | P26 | |
| 2 | Retrospective and transitional provisions. | — | |
| 3 | Exclusion of registered land. | P26(1) | |

| Section or Schedule of Act or Clause of Draft Bill | Subject-matter | Article or Schedule of draft Order | Remarks |
|---|---|---|---|
| | **WILLS ACT 1968**<br>**(c. 28)** | | |
| 1 | Restriction of operation of Wills Act 1837 s.15. | — | cf. S 8(3) |
| | **LAW OF PROPERTY ACT 1969**<br>**(c. 59)** | | |
| 23 | Reduction of statutory period of title. | P71 | para. 2.5.14 |
| 25 | Compensation in certain cases for loss due to undisclosed land charges. | P72 | para. 2.5.15 |
| 28 | Powers of Lands Tribunal and court in relation to restrictive covenants affecting land. | P180 | ch. 2.9 |
| Sch. 3 | LPA 1925 s. 84, as amended. | P180 | |
| | **ADMINISTRATION OF JUSTICE ACT 1982**<br>**(c. 53)** | | |
| 17 | Relaxation of formal requirements for making wills: | S 5 | paras. 5.2.9-11 |
| 18 | Effect of marriage or its termination on wills. | | |
| (1) | | S 12 | para. 5.2.15 |
| (2) | | S 13 | paras. 5.2.17, 18 |
| 19 | Gifts to children etc. who predecease testator. | S 22 | para. 5.2.20 |
| 20 | Rectification. | S 29 | para. 5.2.31 |
| 21 | Interpretation of wills – general rules as to evidence. | S 25 | paras. 5.2.32-35 |
| 22 | Presumption as to effect of gifts to spouses. | S 23 | para. 5.2.29 |

| Section or Schedule of Act or Clause of Draft Bill | Subject-matter | Article or Schedule of draft Order | Remarks |
|---|---|---|---|
| 73 (6)(7) | Transitional provisions and savings. | S Sch. p. 2, 5, 6, 9, 10, 12, 15 | |

### LANDLORD AND TENANT ACT 1985
#### (c. 70)

| | | | |
|---|---|---|---|
| 1 | Disclosure of landlord's identity. | L&T 17 (1)(b), (6) | |
| 2 | Disclosure of directors, etc., of corporate landlord. | L&T 17(5) | |
| 3 | Duty to inform tenant of assignment of landlord's interest. | L&T 17(1) (a) | |
| 4-7 | Provision of rent books. | — | cf. L&T 71 |
| 8, 10 | Implied terms as to fitness for human habitation. | — | paras. 4.3.22, 23 |
| 11-14 | Repairing obligations in short leases. | — | cf. L&T 21, para. 4.3.19 |
| 17 | Specific performance of landlord's repairing obligations. | L&T 48 | paras. 4.5.2-4 |

### LANDLORD AND TENANT ACT 1988
#### (c. 26)

| | | | |
|---|---|---|---|
| 1 | Qualified duty to consent to assigning, underletting etc. of premises. | L&T 44 Sch. 1 p. 1 | paras. 4.4.16-24 |
| 2 | Duty to pass on applications. | L&T Sch. 1 p. 2 | |
| 3 | Qualified duty to approve consent by another. | L&T Sch. 1 p. 3 | |
| 4 | Breach of duty. | L&T Sch. 1 p. 4 | |
| 5 | Interpretation. | — | |
| 6 | Application to Crown. | L&T 82 | |
| 7 | Short title etc. | — | |

| Section or Schedule of Act or Clause of Draft Bill | Subject-matter | Article or Schedule of draft Order | Remarks |
|---|---|---|---|
| | **HOUSING ACT 1988**<br>(c. 50) | | |
| 29 | Offences of harassment. | L&T 64(2) | para. 4.7.3 |
| | **LAW OF PROPERTY (MISCELLANEOUS PROVISONS) ACT 1989**<br>(c. 34) | | |
| 1 | Deeds and their execution. | P81, 82, 83, 86 | paras. 2.5.33-35 |
| 2 | Contracts for sale etc. of land to be made by signed writing. | P67 | para. 2.5.9 |
| 3 | Abolition of rule in Bain v. Fothergill. | P77 | paras. 2.5.19-27 |
| | *Law Commission Draft Bills* | | |
| | **DRAFT LANDLORD AND TENANT (IMPLIED COVENANTS) BILL**<br>(Law Com. No. 67) | | |
| 1 | Application, interpretation and extent. | | Chapter 4.3 |
| (1) | | L&T 11(1) | |
| (2) | | L&T 21(1) (b)(i), 22(a) | para. 4.3.34 |
| (3) | | — | |
| 2 | Overriding covenants. | L&T 12(1)(3) | |
| 3 | Variable covenants. | L&T 12(2) | |
| 4 | Possesion. | L&T 2(2), 13(1) | |
| 5 | Quiet enjoyment | | para. 4.3.5 |
| (1)(2) | | L&T 14 (1)(2) | |
| (3)(4) | | L&T 14(3) | |
| 6 | Rent | | |
| (1) | | L&T 15(1) | |
| (2) | | — | cf. L&T 15(2) |
| 7 | Protection of premises. | L&T 16 | |
| 8 | Disclosure of landlord's identity. | L&T 2(2), 17 | L&T 17(2)(5), (6) are new |
| 9 | Disclosure of tenant's identity. | L&T 18, 74 (2)(c) | L&T 18(2) is new |

| Section or Schedule of Act or Clause of Draft Bill | Subject-matter | Article or Schedule of draft Order | Remarks |
|---|---|---|---|
| 10 | Repairs under short tenancy of dwelling-house. | — | cf. L&T 21 |
| 11 | Application of section 10 and supplementary provisions. | — | |
| 12 | Care of premises by tenant. | L&T 19(1) | paras. 4.3.8-4.3.13 |
| 13 | Landlord's repairs: furnished lettings up to 20 years. | — | cf. L&T 20: paras. 4.3.6 4.3.22 |
| 14 | Landlord's and tenant's repairs: lettings up to 20 years. | — | cf. L&T 21, 22 |
| 15 | Tenant's repairs: lettings over 20 years. | — | cf. L&T 23 As to repairs generally, see paras. 4.3.18-4.3.25 |
| 16 | Landlord's obligations: tenancies of parts of buildings. | L&T 24 | para. 4.3.26 |
| 17 | Maintenance by landlord of means of access. | L&T 25 | |
| 18 | Maintenance by landlord of support and shelter. | L&T 26 | |
| 19 | Entry and inspection. | L&T 27 | |
| 20 | Making good | L&T 28 | |
| 21 | Outgoings. | L&T 32 | para. 4.3.35 |
| 22 | Ascertainment of term of tenancy. | L&T 29 | |
| 23 | General qualifications. | L&T 30 | |
| 24 | Standard of repair and notice of disrepair. | L&T 31 | |
| 25 | Exclusion of agricultural holdings. | — | |
| 26 | Repeals | — | |
| 27 | Short title and commencement. | — | |

| Section or Schedule of Act or Clause of Draft Bill | Subject-matter | Article or Schedule of draft Order | Remarks |
|---|---|---|---|
| | DRAFT LAND OBLIGATIONS BILL (Law Com. No. 127) | | |
| 1(1) | Land obligations. | P162(1), 166(2) | para. 2.7.55, Ch. 2.8 |
| (2)(a)(c) | | P162(1) | |
| (2)(b) | | P166(2) | |
| (3)(4) | | P162(2), 166(3) | |
| 2(1) | Development schemes. | — | cf. P165(1) |
| (2) | | P167(1) | |
| (3)(4) | | P165(3) | ss. (4) is varied |
| (5) | | P165(2) | |
| 3(1) | Provisions of development schemes, etc. | P168(1), (2) | |
| (2) | | P166(4)(c) | |
| (3)(a) | | P166(4)(a)(b) | |
| (b) | | P176 | |
| (c) | | — | cf. P175 |
| (d) | | P175(6) | |
| (4) | | P175(1(2) | |
| (5) | | — | cf. P169(1) |
| (6) | | P176(2) | |
| (7) | | P168(4) | |
| (8) | | — | Unnecessary – the manager will not be named in the scheme (P168(1)) |
| 4(1) | Manner and effect of creating land obligations. | P Sch. 4 Pt. III para. 1(1) | cf. P165(1) |
| (2)(3) | | P Sch. 4 Pt. III para. 1(2) | cf. P165(2(3) |
| (4) | | — | Unnecessary |
| (5)(6) | | P Sch. 4 Pt. III para. 1(3) (4) | Inapplicable to development obligations |
| (7) | | P225 | |
| (8)(9) | | P172(5)(6) P Sch. 4 Pt. III para. 1(5)(6) | |
| 5 | Registration of land obligations. | cf. P, Sch. 4 Pt. III para. 2 | |
| 6(1) | Persons entitled to enforce land obligations. | P Sch. 4 Pt. III para. 3 | |

| Section or Schedule of Act or Clause of Draft Bill | Subject-matter | Article or Schedule of draft Order | Remarks |
|---|---|---|---|
| (2) (3)-(7) | | P169 — | |
| 7(1)-(3) (4) | Persons bound by land obligations. | P, Sch. 4 Pt. III para. 4 — | cf. P169(1)(3)(4) |
| 8 | Extent of enforceability of land obligations. | 170, Sch. 4 Pt. III para. 5 | |
| 9 | Restriction of enforceability of liability. | P167(2), 168(3), Sch. 4 Pt. III para. 6 | |
| 10(1) (2) (3)(4) (5) (6)-(9) | Remedies for enforcing land obligations, etc. | P171(1), Sch. 4 Pt. III para. 7(1) P171(1) P171(2)(3), Sch. 4 Pt. III para. 7(2)(3) P171(4) P171(5)-(8), Sch. 4 Pt. III para. 7(4)-(7) | |
| 11 | Enforcement by charge on servient land. | — | cf. P172, Sch. 4 Pt. III para. 8 |
| 12(1)-(3) | Duty to give information as to servient interests. | P173, Sch. 4 Pt. III para. 9 | Subs. (4)-(6) omitted: cf. s. 24 Interpretation Act. New (4)(5) – cf. L&T 17(6)(7) |
| 13 (1) (2)(3) (4)(5)(6) | Additional powers of the court. | — — P168(5)(6) — | cf. P178(1)(c) cf. P181(1)(a), (2)(a) |
| 14(1) (2) (3) | Provisions supplemental to s. 13 | — — — | cf. P182(5) cf. P183(1)(a) cf. P182(4) |
| 15 | Merger | P174, 181(1), Sch. 4 Pt. III para. 10 | |

1739

| Section or Schedule of Act or Clause of Draft Bill | Subject-matter | Article or Schedule of draft Order | Remarks |
|---|---|---|---|
| 16 | Equitable variations, releases and apportionments. | P Sch. 4 Pt. III para. 11 | As a development scheme must be registered, variations can be made only by an entry in the register (cf. P175(3)-(5) |
| 17 | Power of Lands Tribunal to modify or extinguish land obligations and development schemes. | — | cf. P180 as to neighbour obligations. |
| 18 | Provisions supplemental to s. 17. | — | |
| 19 | Restrictions on future covenants and rent charges. | P111 | |
| 20 | Power to convert existing freehold flat schemes. | — | Unnecessary |
| 21 | Consequential amendment of the law. | — | See P(CP) |
| 22 | Model forms, etc. | — | |
| 23(1) | Interpretation, etc. | P2(2), 164, Sch. 4 Pt. IV | |
| (2) | | — | Unnecessary |
| (3) | | — | |
| 24 | Application to the Crown. | P253 | |
| 25 | Short title, commencement and extent. | — | |
| Sch. 1 | The scope of land obligations. | | |
| Pt. I | Obligations capable of subsisting as neighbour obligations. | P Sch. 4 Pt. I, | |
| Pt. II | Obligations capable of subsisting as development obligations. | P Sch. 5 Pt. I | |

1740

| Section or Schedule of Act or Clause of Draft Bill | Subject-matter | Article or Schedule of draft Order | Remarks |
|---|---|---|---|
| Pt. III | Supplementary provisions. | P Sch. 4 Pt. II, Sch. 5 Pt. II | |
| Sch. 2 | The exercise of the power of the Lands Tribunal under section 17. | — | |
| Sch. 3 | Consequential amendments. | — | See P(CP) |

### DRAFT ACCESS TO NEIGHBOURING LAND BILL
(Law Com. No. 151)

| Section or Schedule of Act or Clause of Draft Bill | Subject-matter | Article or Schedule of draft Order | Remarks |
|---|---|---|---|
| 1 | Access orders. | | paras. 2.7.49-54 |
| (1) | | P161(1) | |
| (2)(3) | | P161(2) | |
| (4) | | P Sch. 3 p. 1 | |
| (5) | | P161(4) | |
| 2 | Power of court to impose terms and conditions. | | |
| (1) | P Sch. 3 p. 2 | | |
| (2)-(6) | | P Sch. 3 p. 3 | |
| 3 | Effect of access order. | P Sch. 3 p. 4 | |
| 4 | Enforcement. | P Sch. 3 p. 5 | |
| 5 | Discharge and variation of access orders. | P Sch. 3 p. 6 | cf. P249(3) |
| 6 | Jurisdiction and transfer of proceedings. | P161(7)-(11) | |
| 7 | Supplementary provisions. | P161(5), (6) | |
| 8 | Short title, interpretation, etc. | P161(1), (9), (12) | |

Printed in the United Kingdom for HMSO
Dd. 0286519   C.3   12/90   55-8923